# COURAGE TO DISSENT

# COURAGE TO DISSENT

*Atlanta and the Long History of the Civil Rights Movement*

TOMIKO BROWN-NAGIN

OXFORD
UNIVERSITY PRESS
2011

# OXFORD
## UNIVERSITY PRESS

Oxford University Press, Inc., publishes works that further
Oxford University's objective of excellence
in research, scholarship, and education.

Oxford    New York
Auckland    Cape Town    Dar es Salaam    Hong Kong    Karachi
Kuala Lumpur    Madrid    Melbourne    Mexico City    Nairobi
New Delhi    Shanghai    Taipei    Toronto

With offices in
Argentina    Austria    Brazil    Chile    Czech Republic    France Greece
Guatemala    Hungary    Italy    Japan    Poland    Portugal    Singapore
South Korea    Switzerland    Thailand    Turkey    Ukraine    Vietnam

Copyright © 2011 by Tomiko Brown-Nagin

Published by Oxford University Press, Inc.
198 Madison Avenue, New York, New York 10016

www.oup.com

Oxford is a registered trademark of Oxford University Press

Library of Congress Cataloging-in-Publication Data
Brown-Nagin, Tomiko, 1970–
Courage to dissent : Atlanta and the long history of the
civil rights movement / Tomiko Brown-Nagin.
p. cm.
Includes bibliographical references and index.
ISBN-13: 978-0-19-538659-2 (hardcover : alk. paper)
ISBN-10: 0-19-538659-0 (hardcover : alk. paper)
1. Segregation—Law and legislation—Georgia—Atlanta—History.   2. Segregation—
Law and legislation—United States—History.   3. Segregation—Georgia—
Atlanta—History.   4. Civil rights movements—Georgia—
Atlanta—History—20th century.   I. Title.
KF4757.B76 2010
342.7308'5—dc22        2010010825

1 3 5 7 9 8 6 4 2

Printed in the United States of America
on acid-free paper

*To my parents,*
*Willie J. and Lillie C. Brown*

# CONTENTS

# ABBREVIATIONS KEY

*Organizations*

| | |
|---|---|
| ACLU | American Civil Liberties Union |
| ANVL | Atlanta Negro Voters League |
| APSTA | Atlanta Public School Teachers Association |
| ASLC | Atlanta Summit Leadership Conference |
| AU | Atlanta University |
| CLAS | Committee for Legal Assistance to the South |
| COAHR | Committee on Appeal for Human Rights |
| CORE | Congress of Racial Equality |
| FDC | Fulton-Dekalb Interracial Committee |
| GBA | Gate City Bar Association |
| HEW | United States Department of Health, Education, and Welfare |
| ILD | International Labor Defense |
| GTEA | Georgia Teachers and Education Association |
| LDF | NAACP Legal Defense Fund |
| MPC | Metropolitan Planning Commission |
| NAACP | National Association for the Advancement of Colored People |
| NBA | National Bar Association |
| NLG | National Lawyers Guild |

| NWRO | National Welfare Rights Organization |
| SALC | Student-Adult Liaison Committee |
| SCLC | Southern Christian Leadership Conference |
| SNCC | Student Non-Violent Coordinating Committee |
| SRC | Southern Regional Council |
| WSMDC | Westside Mutual Development Committee |

*Newspaper and Periodicals*

| AC | Atlanta Constitution |
| ADW | Atlanta Daily World |
| AI | Atlanta Inquirer |
| AJ | Atlanta Journal |
| AJC | Atlanta Journal-Constitution |
| AW | Atlanta World |
| NYT | New York Times |
| SSN | Southern School News |
| USN&WR | U.S. News & World Report |
| WP | Washington Post |
| WSJ | Wall Street Journal |

*Archives*

| APSA | Atlanta Public School Archives |
| CAU | Clark-Atlanta University |
| NARA | National Archives and Records Administration |
| AHC | Atlanta History Center Library and Archives |
| MARBL | Manuscript, Archives, and Rare Book Library, Emory University |
| MLK CNTR | Martin Luther King Jr. Center for Non-Violent Social Change |

*Archival Documents*

| | |
|---|---|
| TD | typed document |
| TL | typed letter |
| TLS | typed letter signed |
| TM | typed manuscript |
| ND | Undated |

# Introduction

Austin Thomas ("A.T.") Walden, the son of illiterate former slaves, graduated with honors from the University of Michigan Law School in 1911. Walden established a law practice in Georgia in 1912, while Thurgood Marshall, who one day would be known nationwide as the man who slew Jim Crow, was still in high school. Walden—one of the South's first African-American attorneys—charted Atlanta's path toward racial equality in the years before and after *Brown v. Board of Education*. He fought for black advancement through activism in civic, social, church, and political organizations, as well as through his work at the bar.[1]

Walden, the president of the Atlanta branch of the NAACP for many years, became Thurgood Marshall's "man" in Atlanta once Marshall took the helm of the NAACP's legal committee. In public, at annual conferences and at meetings of the legal committee, Walden dutifully pledged allegiance to Marshall's strategy. Walden's alliance with the NAACP and his activism on behalf of African Americans landed him on the hit list of the Ku Klux Klan. Walden was "living on borrowed time," declared a Klansman who confronted him on the street one day during the 1940s. In the Klansman's view, Walden, an ally of the NAACP, unquestionably threatened the racial status quo.[2]

In practice, the story was more complicated. Rather than obediently follow the NAACP's strategy, Walden and other leaders in Atlanta, the thriving metropolis of black education and culture, exercised considerable agency and independence. Reflecting the perspectives of the band of middle-class blacks that W. E. B. Du Bois had called the "Talented Tenth," Walden added his own designs to Marshall's blueprint for achieving equality through law. He fashioned a brand of socially conscious lawyering that fit local circumstances, and deviated in crucial ways from the model of legal activism of the NAACP Legal Defense Fund (LDF). Walden did not oppose elements of the NAACP's strategy because he and his clients lacked an affirmative vision of racial justice. Rather, black Atlanta's leadership deviated from the NAACP's course for what it saw as compelling reasons. Most tellingly, leaders sought to preserve the economic self-sufficiency that black elites had achieved under Jim Crow, expand black political influence, and preserve personal autonomy.[3]

This book terms this approach pragmatic civil rights. Pragmatism privileged politics over litigation, placed a high value on economic security, and rejected the idea that integration (or even desegregation) and equality were one and the same. Pragmatism counseled skepticism about the NAACP's court-centered approaches to racial progress. When civil rights litigation was undertaken, pragmatism sometimes dictated different targets from those chosen by the NAACP and its legal arm, the NAACP LDF. Walden and other black leaders in the pragmatic tradition enthusiastically supported the NAACP's voting rights campaign. They joined the association's campaign for equal teacher salaries and increased expenditures for black schools. But in other areas, the pragmatists sought reform within the confines of Jim Crow, or sought to strip away Jim Crow more slowly than the NAACP. In many circumstances, Walden sought to remedy racial injustice through negotiation and without resort to litigation. Perhaps most important, he and other black elites in Atlanta never fully embraced school desegregation.[4]

During the 1960s, Walden and like-minded leaders greeted calls for direct action with great skepticism. His approach to civil rights activism, now expressed in tepid support for civil disobedience, cost him many admirers. Some among a new generation of dissenters from the racial status quo now called Walden—a man whom the Klan had wanted dead because of his work for the cause of racial equality—an "Uncle Tom."[5]

\*\*\*

Walden's skepticism could not hold back the new wave of dissenters. They forever changed the politics of racial pragmatism in Atlanta in 1960. At precisely 11:30 A.M. on March 15 of that year, two hundred African-American students from the city's historically black colleges fanned out across the city. The well-trained students, dressed in their best Sunday clothes under their winter coats, were on a mission. They planned to break the law.

Morehouse College undergraduates Lonnie King and Julian Bond had carefully planned every detail of the day. The pair directed their peers to divide themselves into small groups, and in perfectly ordered processions, to enter eating facilities at ten locations. With the simple act of requesting service at local eateries, the students committed illegal acts. Despite their fancy dress and good manners, Jim Crow forbade the students from entering these facilities.[6]

The Atlanta police department responded swiftly and decisively. Officers arrested seventy-seven protesters, charging them under state laws banning trespassing and unlawful assembly. Policemen placed the students—the pride of the black middle class—in handcuffs, led them to police wagons, and drove them to the city jail. As the patrol cars rolled away, a leader of the student group declared that the collegians were "striving for the freedom that should be ours under the Constitution." The sit-in movement, which already had reached fifty cities, had come to Atlanta.[7]

In Atlanta and elsewhere, the sit-ins raised numerous questions—ranging from the practical to the legal. Would such efforts at civil disobedience succeed in helping to loosen Jim Crow's hold over public accommodations? Who would represent the students, now bound in jail, against the charges they faced? Did the Constitution truly confer upon the students a right to enter and use these properties? Could the students really hope to claim constitutional rights through social activism in the streets? How would traditional black civic leaders respond to this burgeoning social movement? How would local NAACP leaders respond? How would national NAACP leaders respond? How would the media cover the sit-ins? How would the white public respond? How would the black public respond? What role would the Student Non-violent Coordinating Committee (SNCC), the organizational vanguard of the new student movement, founded in April 1960, play in the struggle for civil rights and how would it relate to civil rights lawyers?[8]

Unsurprisingly, the advent of the sit-in movement and the emergence of SNCC caused alarm within Atlanta's white power structure. But it also inspired uneasiness among some prominent blacks. Soon after the sit-ins began, reports surfaced of a rift between sit-in leaders and civil rights lawyers, who already had done so much to weaken Jim Crow. The national media claimed that the sit-ins constituted a shift in the direction and the leadership of the civil rights movement. Just six years earlier, the LDF, the nation's premier civil rights law firm, had achieved its great legal victory in *Brown*, the landmark Supreme Court decision outlawing segregation in public schools. Now, the lawyers of the NAACP—the nation's oldest and largest civil rights organization—had apparently been toppled as leaders of the civil rights movement.[9]

Thurgood Marshall, director-counsel of LDF, only recently had resigned himself to sharing the stage with Dr. Martin Luther King, Jr. The young minister had gained fame as leader of the Montgomery bus boycott of 1955. The upstart threatened to overshadow Marshall just after LDF had won victory in *Brown*, the pinnacle of his career and a milestone in American history. Marshall regarded King as overrated, and he disapproved of the minister's extralegal tactics. Now, a new set of competitors had risen to challenge the civil rights lawyer's priorities—and King's tactics had inspired their insurrection.[10]

Aware of how jealously Thurgood Marshall and leaders of the NAACP guarded their leadership roles, Dr. King responded cautiously to reports that SNCC and the NAACP were at loggerheads. He denied that tension existed between leaders of the NAACP and student leaders who preferred direct action to litigation. King claimed instead that legal advocacy and direct activism could be perfectly compatible, even necessary to each other. "[D]irect action and legal action complement one another; when skillfully employed, each becomes more effective," he insisted.[11]

Marshall disagreed, at least initially. The famed lawyer doubted the value of African Americans waging battle against segregation themselves, in the streets, rather than through intermediaries at the bar and on the bench. In conversations with leaders of the burgeoning sit-in movement, Marshall insisted that the "way to change America" was "through the courts." In private, Marshall scoffed at the idea that a mass movement of people untrained in law could break Jim Crow. Martin Luther King had led the youth astray. Marshall counseled the sit-inners to end their nonsense or else risk "get[ting] people killed." On this, Marshall and Walden agreed.[12]

The leaders of SNCC spurned the advice of both men. Marshall's criticism of direct action left the students bitterly disappointed. "It was clear," said SNCC cofounder John Lewis, "that Thurgood Marshall, along with so many of his generation, did not understand the essence of what we...were doing." The students, including Julian Bond and Lonnie King, lived by Dr. King's dictum that "anyone can serve." But that perspective seemed mostly lost on Marshall. The students now viewed leaders of the NAACP and the LDF, as well as Walden and the Atlanta pragmatists, as "too conservative" and behind the times.[13]

\*\*\*

Then, the tables turned. During the early 1970s, new rebels emerged. A group of desperately poor  African Americans, mostly women, arose to challenge some of the same student leaders who had been such fierce critics of the NAACP, the LDF, and the Atlanta pragmatists. Ethel Mae Mathews, the president of the Atlanta chapter of the National Welfare Rights Organization, took center stage in this drama. Mathews had arrived penniless in Atlanta, with a sixth-grade education, in 1950, after toiling with her parents, Alabama sharecroppers, on "Mister Charlie's farm." Ten years later, Mathews still toiled for whites—now as a maid—but had found her political voice. A community organizer, she coordinated a push for school desegregation among fellow public housing residents.[14]

Mathews squared off against Lonnie King, the heroic sit-in activist who ten years earlier had led the student movement's assault on segregation. He now led an assault on LDF's interpretation of *Brown*. King, who had become president of the Atlanta NAACP branch, repudiated his long-held position that *Brown* required pupil integration. He cited job loss among black administrators and teachers during the student desegregation process as the justification for his about-face. The choice between jobs for black professionals and student integration was, King declared, an easy one. In lieu of pursuing a massive student busing plan to achieve school desegregation—which, King argued, would be quickly undermined by white flight—he proposed to settle Atlanta's school desegregation suit. The settlement would focus on administrators and teachers rather than students. It would cure "years of discrimination in hiring at the top levels" of the school system. Pursuant to King's plan, an African American would become Atlanta's school superintendent and blacks would gain other top posts in the city school system. Most African Americans, King proclaimed, agreed with his plan to prioritize black administrative control of the school system over student desegregation.[15]

Mathews and others in some of Atlanta's poorest neighborhoods did not, however. They vocally opposed King's plan. Life's circumstances—racism, poverty, oppression—had deprived them of the possibility of high-quality schooling and gainful employment. But, like other Americans, they longed for better opportunities for their children. The children of the black poor languished in the city's worst schools, apart from whites, and even apart from much of the black middle class. "[Y]ou don't know how it makes a mother feel," Mathews explained at a 1973 court hearing on King's proposed settlement, "when her child go all the way through twelve grades and come out, can't even spell her name." Unsure of what a racially mixed educational experience might hold for their children, community members such as Mathews nevertheless deemed it an option worth pursuing; it could hardly be worse than the racially separate regime. For them, it made sense to support school desegregation, whatever the potential costs to black professionals. After all, African Americans already taught in many of the schools touted in King's proposal; opponents of the settlement wanted their children to flee some of the same schools that King championed. "Now the principal, they sit back there, and the teacher too, and draw this big money," Bernice Collins exclaimed in court, while her third-grade son could not do simple math. "I know that teacher don't know what he is doing and the teacher don't care what he is doing," charged Collins, in her critique of King's settlement plan.[16]

Mathews and her comrades were fighting an uphill battle. Prominent blacks—who now held influential posts because of changes in the racial landscape wrought by landmark civil rights litigation—embraced Lonnie King's point of view. Dr. Benjamin Mays, a mentor of Dr. King and the first black chairman of the Atlanta Board of Education, headed the luminaries who backed

King and the proposed settlement. The two other black members of the school board supported, not to mention many black teachers and administrators. King also secured the backing of Maynard Jackson, who soon became Atlanta's first black mayor. Jackson would greatly expand the black middle class during his mayoralty through muscular affirmative action policies in municipal contracting; as a fellow champion of black prosperity and workplace equality, he naturally allied himself with King. Rev. Andrew Young, a former lieutenant to Dr. King who had become Georgia's first black U.S. congressman since Reconstruction, also vocally supported the local NAACP's effort to focus on faculty rather than pupil integration. Unleashed from the bonds of Jim Crow, all of these black leaders intended to secure economic and political power for themselves and their peers, and thus, they believed, for the black community as a whole. School desegregation, as LDF conceived of it, limited these prospects.[17]

Not every black leader was aligned with King. Some appreciated just how complex the school desegregation issue had become by the 1970s. Julian Bond, then a member of the Georgia legislature, found himself torn. Bond had campaigned on an antipoverty platform and sought to represent the interests of the poor through his work in the legislature and as founding president of the Southern Poverty Law Center. He favored school desegregation in principle and publicly supported Mathews and her comrades—his constituents. Nevertheless, in numerous addresses, Bond eloquently articulated a perspective that dovetailed, in important respects, with Lonnie King's concerns. Desegregation "has almost been more painful than the result has been beneficial," Bond said in one speech; the "burden of bringing justice to American education fell exclusively" on "the pocketbooks" of black teachers and principals, and on the "small shoulders of our children."[18]

With the passage of the Voting Rights Act, what John Lewis, now a Congressman, called the "finest hour" of the black freedom struggle, civil rights activists had assumed that black access to the political process would yield effective political representation. A cohesive black community, it was thought, could achieve its policy goals by voting for preferred candidates and by continuing to work through interest groups such as the NAACP. Civil rights litigation, the tool of social change that Thurgood Marshall had used to tear down Jim Crow and to begin opening up the political process, would continue to be vital, buttressing African Americans' political and social position. Yet, reality proved more complicated than imagined. The community did not always unite as hoped. Black leaders, elected and self-appointed, did not, and perhaps could not, represent the entire community. Interest groups did not easily rise to the challenges of the new racial order. Civil rights litigation could have unintended, negative consequences. Meanwhile, white domination still constrained the world in which all African Americans lived.[19]

Ethel Mae Mathews and Atlanta's black poor confronted this uncertain world. Many of the old student radicals and much of new black middle class, now a part of the establishment, had become a part of the problem, they believed. "Middle-class professional blacks have proven that they have about as much concern for poor black people as white people do," summed up one working-class critic of the Atlanta branch's school desegregation settlement. These activists lost faith in black representatives, spurned the local NAACP, and even LDF, whose lawyers proved unreliable sources of help. Ultimately, Mathews and others turned to the American Civil Liberties Union and an iconoclastic white woman lawyer, Margie Pitts Hames, for assistance. Hames represented the group of activists in a lawsuit that accused public and private actors in Atlanta of weaving a web of school and housing segregation that kept poor blacks in "ghetto schools." In court, Hames faced off against venerable members of the civil rights establishment who preferred neighborhood schools. The affair, featuring open warfare between opposing black factions, each armed with its own team of lawyers and spokespersons, starkly revealed the intersections of racial and class inequalities in majority black Atlanta. The episode reinforced how difficult it always had been for African Americans to represent multidimensional black interests—whether battles against racism occurred inside or outside of the courtroom.[20]

*\*\**

The disagreements between Walden and Marshall during the 1940s and 1950s, between Marshall, Walden, and sit-in leaders during the 1960s, and between Mathews and black officials during the 1970s were three of many important conversations within black communities about the goals, strategies, and tactics of the civil rights struggle. This book tells the story of these divisions, and the vibrant debates that accompanied them, in Atlanta—simultaneously home to many of the South's leading civil rights organizations, to its largest black middle class, and to black ghettos ravaged by poverty—from the postwar era through the 1970s.[21]

In telling these stories, I seek to answer the following question: What would the story of the mid-twentieth-century struggle for civil rights look like if legal historians de-centered the U.S. Supreme Court, the national NAACP, and the NAACP LDF and instead considered the movement from the bottom up? The answer, I contend, is this: a picture would emerge in which local black community members acted as agents of change—law shapers, law interpreters, and even law makers. Each contested and contingent step in the struggle for racial change comes into clearer focus. One can only see this picture by looking beyond the Court and the national NAACP and LDF, and examining developments in local communities before, during, and after lawyers launched civil rights litigation.

To these ends, this study uncovers the agency of local people in Atlanta—lesser-known lawyers and organizers, litigators and negotiators, elites and the grassroots, women and men—and visions of law and social change that sometimes were in conflict with that of the national NAACP and the NAACP LDF. In so doing, the perspectives of local client communities have been moved from the periphery to the center of the legal history of the civil rights era. These Atlantans and their stories show how struggles for social change involving the law and lawyers look in action on the ground. This local perspective is crucial. As important as national organizations and national leaders were, local actors helped to define equality, too—and did so in profound ways. Local actors worked to create the conditions necessary to achieve change. They played leading roles in everyday struggles to ameliorate inequalities in the social and political order. And they experienced the gap between civil rights and remedies once the movement achieved formal equality. [22]

By analyzing tensions and synergies between the national and local civil rights movements, this project seeks to understand more fully the interaction between civil rights lawyers and communities. I consider consensus and conflict between those who championed equality inside the courts and those who did so outside the courts. The complicated and changing relationships between leaders of the national and local NAACP, and between leaders of the national and local civil rights bars, are at the root of this narrative. In the story told here, members of the national bar and bench, considered the primary engines of racial change even in much recent scholarship, play important, but less commanding roles. They remain protagonists and catalysts of change, but I critically examine the national actors in relation to the local clients and communities on whose behalf they labored.

This bottom-up narrative makes intraracial conflict central to the legal history of the civil rights movement. Long before "black power" emerged and gave black dissent from the mainstream civil rights agenda a name, disagreement flourished between civil rights lawyers and civil rights activists, between civil rights organizations and their client communities, between gradualists and advocates of "Freedom Now!" and between proponents and skeptics of integration. Even in the shadow of Jim Crow, and against a backdrop of intense, frequently violent, white resistance, African Americans in Atlanta questioned the meaning of equality and the strategies necessary to obtain a share of the American dream. Blacks played out these disagreements in the courts, in the streets, and in the informal and formal arenas of politics. These disagreements revealed why some blacks supported the NAACP's definition of equality, its chosen strategies, and its view of the role that lawyers and courts would play in the struggle for social justice—and why others did not. Conflicts over the black struggle for freedom continued well into the 1970s, long after the movement often is said to have entered a period of decline. In this story, the movement evolved. Using the courtroom as an arena of struggle, elements of the black working class asserted a distinct, dual identity as civil rights plaintiffs—as the "black and poor"—and sought to claim the right to educational equality and school integration.[23]

In telling this kind of story, my aim is to bridge legal and social history, and national and local history. This book builds upon the work of social historians of the grassroots struggle for civil rights who have paid considerable attention to organizational and ideological cleavages within the movement. However, this prior scholarship, focused on unsung heroes and developments in local communities, seldom analyzed the intersection of the movement and the law. I add this missing legal dimension by focusing in depth on relationships among communities, lawyers, and courts in the long civil rights movement.[24]

I aim to answer, from a sociolegal perspective, historian Jacquelyn Dowd Hall's call for works that stress the depth and breadth of the struggle for civil rights. Hall made this plea in response to the oversimplified narrative about the civil rights struggle that she believed had taken hold. This narrative gained currency, Hall argued, because Americans were told to valorize a single phase of the movement: its classical period, which began with the NAACP's victory in *Brown v. Board of Education* and culminated with Congress's passage of the Civil Rights Act of 1964 and the Voting Rights Act of 1965. These beginning and ending points permitted the nation to understand racial oppression as a deviant strain within the body politic. In this morality tale about the movement, blacks sought and gained "simple justice." This "master narrative," as Hall called it, fails in several ways. The story obscures the long-standing white backlash against the movement, erases the movement's demands for economic justice, and minimizes the interrelationship of gender-, race- and class-based oppression. In sum, it "prevents one of the most remarkable mass movements in American history from speaking effectively to the challenges of our time."[25]

This effort to answer Hall's call for greater analytical depth also emphasizes how the movement was "continuously and ferociously contested," and it also seeks to defy morality tales. However, whereas Hall emphasized interracial conflict, I focus on conflict within black communities, as well. In addition, I seek to counter juricentric examinations of law and social change that do not consider the full implications of such a dynamic, in-the-trenches civil rights struggle. My work intervenes in two different genres of scholarship. One tradition emphasizes civil rights lawyers' starring roles in the past struggle for "integration," while the other bemoans the Supreme Court's inability to alter race relations substantially. Both traditions focus on the "liberal legal" vision of civil rights, which entailed federal court litigation to achieve desegregation in public institutions, a framework that legal histories of the era before *Brown* already have questioned.[26]

The latter school of thought, which criticizes the Court's role in social change, holds that U.S. courts can virtually "never be effective producers of significant social reform." The seminal work in this school argued that *Brown* failed, for example, and undermined the civil rights movement by "siphoning" resources and talent away from more promising political strategies for achieving change. A more recent and more nuanced iteration of this claim finds a perverse relationship between the Supreme Court's most famous decision and racial change. *Brown* only advanced racial change indirectly, through a perverse "backlash effect." Violent white resistance to the decision and black protests inspired passage of the Civil Rights Act, which actually desegregated society. In light of such skepticism of the Court, scholars who write in this tradition have cautioned proponents of social reform against overreliance on the Supreme Court and litigation. Some have conceded that civil rights litigation had the virtue of inspiring African Americans, but nevertheless concluded that, overall, the NAACP's litigation campaign undermined black agency. Civil rights litigation encouraged blacks to have faith in elite black lawyers and white judges instead of themselves.[27]

This work does not challenge the claim that the Supreme Court has followed rather than been in the vanguard of the struggle for racial change. In many ways, it substantiates this view. However, the Court's institutional capacity—what the Court can do for social movements—and movements' responses to courts, the law, and lawyers—are distinct matters. The leading works on law and social change mostly analyze the former set of questions, whereas this work mostly considers the latter. The difference in emphasis is significant. The orientation of the leading works is top-down: mostly focused on the Supreme Court and Congress, and to a much lesser extent, on LDF lawyers who litigated in the Court, and on the white resistance and its interaction with black protesters. By contrast, my orientation is mostly bottom-up: focused on activists as much as on the law and lawyers, and even then, on a fuller complement of lawyers than LDF, as well as on the Supreme Court and lower federal, state, and municipal courts. This is not to say that the bottom-up view is superior; rather, it is distinctive in important respects.

This book takes the view that the relationship between law and social change looks different when viewed from the bottom-up perspective. That is, the people, places, and events that scholars choose to examine alter our analysis of law and social change in the civil rights movement. When the Supreme Court and LDF's New York–based lawyers no longer are the only centers of analysis, the movement looks much more fluid, and a new picture emerges. One can see an array of movement actors who did not idealize the Supreme Court or who were skeptics of civil rights litigation. One is less prone to overestimate or underestimate lawyers' efficacy in struggles for social change. Social movement activists who engaged in political action instead of, or in addition to, court action and who were attentive to the economic and cultural dimensions of racial oppression come into focus. Clients who asserted values, opinions, and preferences distinct from both the national and local civil rights bars emerge. In short, this book features visionaries on the Left and the Right who sought something different from or more complicated than "integration" into the American "mainstream." Accordingly, these advocates participated in litigation both less frequently and more opportunistically than is often presumed. Hence, wins or losses in the Court, the question that captivates leading scholars of law and social change, is a less dominant inquiry here. At the same time, this work places into sharper relief a variety of factors upon which change is contingent—intraracial dynamics, economic developments, culture, lawyer-client relationships, local politics, even the biographies and personalities of change agents. Seeing civil rights history unfold in such granular detail makes the victories that the civil rights movement did achieve so much more remarkable. For me, those details spotlight how much agency citizens once had, and perhaps can have again, against fantastic odds—not how little.[28]

This book also challenges a tradition of legal historical writing very different from the revisionist literature on law and social change: scholarship that chronicles the work of the national NAACP and LDF without carefully weighing the perspective of those who dissented from these organizations' strategic choices. Early scholarship, and even many recent legal and social histories of the movement, recapitulated a central theme of the NAACP's postwar civil rights struggle. In an effort to unify African Americans around its work, the NAACP dismissed as unprincipled and cowardly those blacks who questioned its legal campaign against segregation. Leading accounts of the movement and the NAACP's role in it followed suit: these works embraced the organization and its vision of racial change and dismissed the association's critics. These accounts labeled those who did not embrace integration "accommodationists." The accommodationists opposed "any active efforts to alter" the racial status quo, it was said. The interests of blacks who opposed the NAACP's legal attack on Jim Crow in schools were even equated with those of segregationists—avowed white supremacists.[29]

The story of the long civil rights movement in Atlanta makes clear that skeptics of integration and the NAACP's worldview were not, of necessity, socially or politically inactive opponents of racial change. If men like A. T. Walden accommodated segregation, they also protested it when and how they saw fit. The conventional assumption that accommodationists opposed efforts to challenge inequality improperly uses loyalty to the NAACP as the sole criterion for assessing blacks' commitment to racial justice, and misunderstands how change occurred in the multifaceted postwar social movement against racial discrimination. And it underestimates both the enormous pressures that segregation imposed on blacks and the ingenuity and complexity of blacks' responses to racism.[30]

Certainly, it took tremendous courage to challenge Jim Crow. The assault on Jim Crow surely was radical from the perspective of most Americans. Many African Americans shrank from opposing the system out of fear. Others profited from the racial status quo. This account does not overlook any of these realities. To the contrary, much of this analysis turns on how class, race, and self-interest shaped the legal and political strategies of activists. At the same time, I aspire to understand the difficult choices that African Americans made in the face of white supremacy. Above all else, white domination framed and constrained the paths toward equality that each of this story's actors took.

This book's sensitivity to local perspectives and to instances of conflict is not intended, however, to diminish the NAACP's generative role in the struggle for civil rights. It is possible to both value the organization's long role in the black struggle and to recognize tensions between the national organization and local movements on the ground. After all, NAACP loyalists themselves recognized this friction. The lawyers knew that their strategies were controversial. Robert Carter, a lieutenant of Thurgood Marshall who helped to devise the *Brown* strategy, conceded that "there was no compelling demand" from local branches for a direct attack on school segregation. "[L]ocal units," he concluded, "would have been satisfied" with litigation that "upgrade[d]" black schools. But regarding themselves as community stewards, LDF lawyers pushed ahead. "[S]ometimes in major social movements," wrote Charles Hamilton Houston, the chief architect of the NAACP's legal strategy against Jim Crow, "it may be necessary to sacrifice the peace of a community in the greater interests of the whole."[31]

Far beyond the New York offices of the NAACP and LDF, however, the lawyers, the law, and its categories shaped, but did not necessarily determine, the course of African Americans' struggles for equality. The NAACP and its lawyers never constituted the exclusive voices in the struggle for equality in local African-American communities. The NAACP's prerogatives and the legal precedents that its lawyers won always remained subject to interpretation and debate, among whites and blacks alike. As important as the NAACP and its lawyers were, members of local black communities, in Atlanta and elsewhere, steered the movement's course on a day-to-day basis.

***

This book unfolds in three parts. The first five chapters make up Part I and explore the period before 1960. This part locates the roots of struggles in Atlanta between lawyers and direct activists, and between community representatives and constituencies, during the 1960s and 1970s, in this much earlier period. Tensions had long existed within local communities, and between local communities and the NAACP and LDF, over the national organizations' priorities about how, when, and even whether to challenge Jim Crow.[32]

Part I begins by introducing to readers A. T. Walden, a critical figure who mediated locals' relationships with the national NAACP and shaped civil rights. It then discusses the concept of pragmatic civil rights. The five chapters of Part I analyze pragmatism in theory and practice and explain that, from the locals' perspective, their pragmatism was principled. Chapter 1 describes the milieu in which Atlanta's pragmatic approach to civil rights developed. The next chapters examine how this pragmatic approach to civil rights played itself out in particular areas of black life. Chapter 2 discusses voting. Chapter 3 considers housing. Chapter 4 surveys education. And chapter 5 considers public recreation and transportation.

The book's next four chapters comprise Part II. Much of the book identifies points of conflict between the more pragmatic and the more orthodox approaches to civil rights, but much of this part chronicles how Walden and the Atlanta pragmatists shared Marshall's skepticism of direct action. Chapter 6 describes how the advent of the sit-ins initially frayed relations between the students and civil rights leaders on the national and local levels.

Two Atlanta-based student groups, SNCC and its local affiliate, the Committee on Appeal for Human Rights (COAHR), found allies in new generations of the black bar—Len Holt, Donald Hollowell, and Howard Moore, Jr. Chapters 7, 8, and 9 discuss the student activists' evolving views about legal advocacy and these lawyers' roles in the movement.

Chapter 7 focuses on SNCC's collaboration with Len Holt. Holt introduced the students to a style of civil rights lawyering compatible with direct action—"movement lawyering." Chapter 8 describes the relationships between student activists and Donald Hollowell. The courtly Donald Hollowell represented young activists in court when other lawyers would not.

Chapter 9 discusses passage of the Voting Rights Act of 1965 and chronicles pivotal turning points in the constellation of social movements that developed during the late 1960s, in all of which lawyer Howard Moore, SNCC's general counsel, had a hand. This chapter provides a window onto SNCC's work in the civil rights, antipoverty, and peace movements.[33]

The final three chapters, which make up Part III, address LDF's two-decade-long effort to implement *Brown v. Board of Education* in Atlanta. Chapter 10 discusses how LDF lawyer Constance Baker Motley litigated the Atlanta school desegregation, but without the support of a social movement united behind her pursuit of pupil integration. It shows how the black middle class's concerns about workplace discrimination overtook the school desegregation litigation, just as the U.S. Court of Appeals for the Fifth Circuit committed itself to desegregating the schools "root and branch."

Chapter 11 expands the pantheon of heroic figures in the struggle for racial justice far beyond civil rights lawyers and famed student activists. After students no longer were the leading edge of the civil rights movement, a new group of dissenters—the low-income community members that SNCC had viewed as its primary constituency—stepped into the void. Chapter 11 tells the story of the challenge that this third wave of community activists posed to Lonnie King and the local NAACP branch's stewardship of the school desegregation litigation in the 1970s.

Chapter 12 further explores the Atlanta NAACP's decision to abandon the goal of school desegregation and how that decision played out in court. The litigation exposed inter- and intraracial fault lines, further fractured by inequalities of class and gender. It vividly demonstrated the dimensions of disadvantage that still existed in now majority black Atlanta, despite Jim Crow's demise.

In the conclusion, I consider what lessons can be learned—about law and social change and the struggle for racial equality—from the long history of the civil rights movement in Atlanta.

# PART I

# A. T. Walden and Pragmatic Civil Rights Lawyering in the Postwar Era

CHAPTER 1

# "Aren't Going to Let a Nigger Practice in Our Courts"

## The Milieu of Civil Rights Pragmatism

I began alone; for a long, long time, I was the only Negro in Georgia engaged in the full time practice of law. (1963)

A. T. Walden

The struggle for civil rights was like guerrilla warfare...so Colonel Walden may have had one face at one time and another face at another time, but the efforts he took...could very well have cost him his life. (2010)

Howard Moore, Jr.

Austin Thomas (A. T.) Walden, one of the South's first African-American lawyers and later the first black judge in Georgia since Reconstruction, personified the legal realists' hope that lawyers would be social engineers.[1] For the first five decades of the twentieth century, Walden—a son of slaves who rose to prominence in law and politics—defined civil rights. Through his work at the bar and in politics, Walden had a hand in nearly every undertaking in Georgia that concerned the rights and well-being of African Americans. Many considered him the "elder statesman of the civil rights movement in the South."[2]

A man "gifted in the law," Walden not only used his own legal skills on behalf of black plaintiffs but also encouraged the few other black lawyers in the state at the time to do so.[3] In 1947, he founded a bar association for Atlanta's small cadre of black attorneys. Members of the Gate City Bar Association (GBA) dedicated themselves to fighting racial discrimination. The lawyers vowed to "uphold and extend the principles of justice in every phase of American life." In founding the association, Walden hoped to replicate the National Bar Association (NBA) on a local level. The black counterpart of the segregated American Bar Association, the NBA brought black attorneys together for professional and racial advancement.[4]

From his well-appointed office in Atlanta, Walden collaborated with the small network of NAACP lawyers, based in New York, who also were making civil rights law. As a member of the NBA's civil rights committee, Walden worked alongside Charles Hamilton Houston, chief architect of the NAACP's legal strategy to end Jim Crow. Walden, also a member of the NAACP's national legal committee, cocounseled with Thurgood Marshall, the man who executed Houston's legal plan, and other lawyers with the NAACP LDF. As president of the Atlanta branch of the NAACP for twelve years, and as chief counsel to the branch for decades, Walden maintained close ties with the national NAACP. Through his numerous relationships with the nation's premier civil rights organization and its litigating arm, Walden signified his support for an all-out push against discrimination and for integration. In public and on the national stage, he declared that Atlanta would be on the cutting edge of the fight for equality.[5]

But Walden's actions were not always consistent with his rhetoric. As daring as it was for a black man to take a stand in support of the NAACP and the principle of racial equality in the early twentieth-century South, in reality it was difficult to know exactly where one's commitment to that principle should lead. In everyday practice, Walden wrestled with what equality meant, with how far to push whites in pursuit of it, and with how a lawyer should square his professional role with his political goals and personal ambitions, not to mention those of the clients and communities whom he represented.

Walden resolved these dilemmas imperfectly, and often with no hint of the tension inherent in his many roles. He fashioned a brand of socially conscious lawyering that deviated in important respects from the NAACP and LDF's program, but never did so in open defiance of national leaders. A reserved and coolly rational personality, Walden was amiable and genteel, even as he was pragmatic and shrewd. Together with a small group of peers—a black elite— Walden customized his civil rights strategy and tactics to fit local circumstances. Rather than following the racial agenda of the national NAACP and LDF, Atlanta's postwar black leaders set their own agenda and priorities.

In practice, the pragmatic approach meant several things. It meant attacking Jim Crow at a slower pace and in a more targeted fashion than the national NAACP would dictate. It meant sometimes seeking better conditions under segregation instead of an immediate end to Jim Crow, and favoring interracial diplomacy over broad-ranging litigation as a means of achieving racial progress. Segregation permeated every sector of southern society; and it was an oppressive social, economic, and political system. To be sure, the local leaders found rank inequality intolerable. And they certainly did challenge Jim Crow. But Atlanta's black leaders did not experience and view racial separation in all the many and varied aspects of daily life touched by Jim Crow—parks, pools, playgrounds, libraries, public transit, housing, education, employment, and the electoral system—as having precisely the same effects. They distinguished greater from lesser evils and thus had preferences about which institutions and practices were priorities.

Critically, they championed the pursuit of political power and hoped to leverage it to press for reform in priority areas, rather than insist on integration in every area at once. They would initially seek better conditions in the social realm—*within* the Jim Crow systems of education, housing, and public accommodations—rather than devote all their energies to directly challenging the legal regime of segregation in all of its breadth and depth. At the same time, the pragmatists greatly valued black economic independence and reacted skeptically to litigation, particularly in the areas of housing and education, that might undermine the economic position of the black middle class. In sum, they privileged political rights, deemphasized social rights, and sought to advance the economic position and cultural cohesiveness of blacks, particularly the middle class.[6]

The occasions on which Walden did and did not turn to litigation in the years surrounding *Brown* reflected these priorities. Walden enthusiastically supported LDF's voting rights campaign. But rather than follow LDF's push for residential desegregation in court, Atlanta's blacks used their political leverage to push for black residential development within the system of segregated housing. Similarly, they sought a new black hospital rather than join LDF's campaign for hospital desegregation. And they successfully fought rate increases on city buses rather than insist on desegregation of public transportation. Put together, these decisions spoke volumes about how local visions of civil rights complemented and deviated from the national NAACP's agenda for racial advancement.

Meanwhile, Walden did initiate litigation that sought to protect the economic fortunes of African Americans. In 1955, he filed a lawsuit that challenged discrimination against black railroad workers. Walden sued to prevent the Brotherhood of Locomotive Firemen and Enginemen from implementing an agreement with two railroad companies that reduced the work hours of black firemen. Walden alleged that the all-white union had failed to represent his clients fairly, as required by federal labor law. The issues raised in Walden's suit never reached trial. However, that Walden, the consummate negotiator and proponent of targeted civil rights litigation, was prepared to attack workplace discrimination in court suggests the importance of context to understanding the choices that black Atlantans made in pursuing advancement.[7]

The Atlanta pragmatists supported the national NAACP and LDF's goals, but aspired to use their political power and social and economic capital to make choices that often differed from those the NAACP lawyers might have made for them. They pursued desegregation in a less hurried and more tar-geted fashion than the NAACP and LDF, yet no less earnestly than the national groups. Their conception of equality overlapped in significant ways with that of W. E. B. Du Bois, the NAACP cofounder who advocated political equality but embraced "voluntary segregation" in institutions such as black schools, churches, and colleges—a position that in 1935 had led to Du Bois's expulsion from his own organization.[8]

One can therefore begin to understand why Walden received criticism for his comparatively moderate goals and tactics. As LDF's wide-ranging legal strategy to end segregation gained acceptance within the NAACP, the few, like Du Bois, who questioned it increasingly fell out of favor. The LDF's worldview dominated contemporary observers' conceptions of appropriate racial struggle. Indeed, LDF's strategy came to define civil rights activism. Racial protest and an all-out push in the courts against Jim Crow were seen as one and the same, and a lawyer demonstrated his commitment and ingenuity by litigating on behalf of courageous black southerners in the courts. If alternative or supple-mentary strategies gained notice, they seldom struck prominent commentators as legitimate or effective. The hero or villain trope framed discussions, leaving pragmatists and others vulnerable to the charge that they valued expediency over principle. This tendency became even more pronounced when the NAACP's legalistic approach to advocacy lost ground to the direct action mode of protest against Jim Crow during the 1960s. Moderates had looked conserva-tive in relation to the NAACP's legalism. Compared to demonstrators, they looked positively retrograde. Before long, moderates found themselves com-pared to the caricature of Booker T. Washington, the maligned "Great Accom-modator" of segregation.[9]

Walden's reputation reflected his complicated relationship with the integra-tionist philosophy, LDF's heroic tradition of aggressive civil rights litigation, and direct action. While many have praised his achievements as a race man, others have damned him. Charles Hamilton Houston acknowledged Walden as one of a small group of socially conscious southern black lawyers who were "pioneer[s]," "trying cases in many instances at the risk of their personal safety." Horace Ward, who later became a federal judge, and who set out in 1950 to desegregate the University of Georgia (UGA) School of Law, credited Walden with piquing his interest in "practicing law as a means of taking on social responsibility." And Vernon Jordan, the prominent lawyer who ranks among the most influential African Americans, has called Walden his inspiration, his "hero." Walden fired the young boy's interest in law and politics. "Mr. Walden was so impressive....He was so moving, so articulate," Jordan explained. "I wanted to be a lawyer like A. T. Walden. I wanted to walk like him and talk like him and hang out my shingle on Auburn Avenue just like Walden." Walden taught scores how to use the law as a tool for "social change" and worked tirelessly in the courts to kill that "old rascal," segregation, as Walden sometimes called Jim Crow, according to Jordan.[10]

But prominent figures who manned the front lines of the battle against Jim Crow during the 1950s and 1960s found Walden less praiseworthy. LDF lawyer Constance Baker Motley described Walden as a skilled and highly respected lawyer, but a "typical upper-class Southern[er]." By her account, Walden's style was "soft-spoken, nonaggressive, and exceedingly polite" and ineffective for "pierc[ing] the wall of segregation." Motley could turn to developments in what might have been a landmark higher education test case to underscore her point. At one time, Walden served as chief counsel in Horace Ward's potentially pathbreaking suit against UGA. Filed in 1952, the UGA case was one of the first to name a flagship Deep South institution as a defendant in a NAACP higher education case. By 1956, Walden had lost favor with the local NAACP, the sponsor of the litigation: observers were convinced that he was too beholden to the white power structure to attack Jim Crow. The branch asked Walden to step aside. Motley and a younger, local lawyer, Donald Hollowell—judged a more "aggressive" litigator—replaced Walden as lead counsel. The saga did not end happily for Ward. Due to repeated delays and other difficulties, Ward never broke the racial barrier at UGA Law School. For years after his unsuccessful suit, black applicants continued to trek out of state to earn law degrees. It fell to Motley and Hollowell to litigate the case that finally brought down Jim Crow at UGA; the duo attacked segregation at the undergraduate level, resulting in desegregation there in 1961, eleven years after Ward had begun the fight.[11]

The complaint that Walden did too little, too late to challenge segregation had been heard well before the lawyer's involvement in the UGA case, and would be heard again well after it. The charge had been hurled by national and state NAACP activists during the 1930s, the 1940s, and the 1950s. Critics—including competitors for influence—complained to Thurgood Marshall that Walden made unilateral decisions, refused to provide aid to communities in need, or took inadequate or untimely action. On the Left, the International Labor Defense attacked Walden for allegedly allowing his representation of black criminal defendants to be compromised by his relationships with white city fathers. By the 1960s, the accusations against Walden had reached a crescendo. During the sit-in movement, students called Walden—no proponent of street protests—an "Uncle Tom." Student leaders Julian Bond and Lonnie King faulted his deliberate, biracial process of decision making and his criticism of direct action. The students lionized Hollowell, Howard Moore, Jr., and others as uncompromising advocates of racial justice, while Walden, by his own admission, viewed compromise as endemic to mature racial leadership. "Mature leadership often finds it necessary to take the middle of the road approach to problems," he once said. The legacy of Walden—a man who shaped civil rights in Georgia for half a century—is tarnished because of the ways he deviated from the priorities and methods of, first, LDF and, later, the students.[12]

The pragmatists' preference for gradualism and interracial diplomacy, and their skepticism of no-holds-barred civil rights litigation, can certainly be viewed as having accommodated segregation, at least when compared to the alternatives. But that would be a simplistic conclusion. A different picture emerges when we consider Walden and other pragmatists in full and in context—on their own terms and in view of their own times. By that light, pragmatists such as A. T. Walden appear to have embraced a sophisticated, if ultimately limited, form of sociopolitical activism. Their approach featured several key elements: a concern about intraracial interests and local autonomy; a belief in elite, expert, top-down leadership; an awareness that multiple layers of racial inequality pervaded society; and a skepticism that courts and legalism could alone, or could effectively, bring about positive racial change. Even as Marshall and many other liberals proclaimed the judiciary's role in protecting minority rights, pragmatists such as Walden appeared keenly aware that rights could be illusory in the absence of a strong socioeconomic structure within black communities, black self-help, and political support within white communities. It was this insight that made the pragmatists' role so important in the struggle for civil rights. The pragmatic approach sometimes complemented, and at other times undercut, LDF's court-based protest strategy and direct activists' political theater. Ultimately, the pragmatists' commitment to building social, political, and economic capital within black communities taught an apt lesson: the distance between racial change as declared by the courts and sociopolitical change on the ground with traction in the communities and neighborhoods whose residents were the intended beneficiaries of efforts to reform the law.

By uncovering the rich history of civil rights lawyering at the local level and the world of practitioners like Walden, we can expand our understanding of who civil rights lawyers were—beyond Charles Hamilton Houston, Thurgood Marshall, and loyal lieutenants such as LDF's Constance Baker Motley—and how they shaped the course of the long civil rights movement. The messy groundwork laid by lawyer Walden—engaged in backroom deals, politicking, or litigation, under pressure from the forces of white resistance on the Right, and black activists on the Left, behaving selfishly at times and gallantly at others—demystifies the work of change agents. The fraught interactions humanize these historical actors, adding a dimension to the more familiar narratives of civil rights lawyers' heroic struggles to slay Jim Crow.[13]

Before taking up how the pragmatic localism of Atlanta elites translated into policy and practice, we must first consider an antecedent question: why would the goals and tactics of Atlanta's black leadership have been different in kind or degree from the all-out, full-speed-ahead battle against Jim Crow that the NAACP LDF waged in the courts and promoted in the postwar era? To answer that question, we need to look in several places: Walden's background and personal qualities; the elitist and paternalistic racial uplift ideology common to pioneering blacks in early twentieth-century Atlanta; and the viciousness of local white racism, which was unremitting despite the "New South" rhetoric of white elites.

## SOCIALLY CONSCIOUS LAWYERING: THE VIEW FROM THE GROUND

The story of how Charles Hamilton Houston, the Howard University School of Law vice dean and NAACP special counsel, inspired a generation of lawyers to work in the courts for social justice is well known. Houston extolled the virtues of leadership by members of the bar: attorneys were to be "mouthpiece[s] of the weak" and "sentinel[s] guarding against wrong." Beginning in the 1930s, Howard's army of social engineers attacked discrimination in the many areas of American society plagued by racial bias—schools, transportation, voting, the criminal justice system, and the labor market, among them. Houston hoped the Supreme Court would embrace his view that racial discrimination violated the U.S. Constitution. After Houston's untimely death in 1950, the task of executing his legal strategy fell to his protégé, Thurgood Marshall, and Marshall's lieutenants in the national office, Robert Carter, Jack Greenberg, and Constance Baker Motley.[14]

Although their advocacy has seldom received serious study, A. T. Walden and other local NAACP counsel shared in the work of seeing Houston's plan through to completion. By unearthing the story of how Walden and Atlanta's black elite pursued equality in the years following World War II, we can observe how Houston's ideas and Marshall's efforts to execute them found expression within local communities. Moreover, we can see Walden—a lawyer who was ten years older than Houston and who had been a member of the bar for fourteen years before Marshall would finish high school—chart a course of racial justice in his own right. Walden's leadership of the civil rights struggle highlights how social, political, and economic context, as well as personal style and background, influenced the character of social engineering in practice.[15]

Walden shared Houston's commitment to socially conscious lawyering. He took a special interest in the black bar, and exhorted its members to service. Walden sought to increase the number of African-American lawyers practicing in his state by fighting the discrimination that prevented blacks from being admitted to the Georgia bar. The bar exam, the "graveyard for the aspirations of many blacks," was notorious for the extraordinarily high rate at which blacks failed it, no matter how well prepared. "The motto of the white bar might well be," some said, "'Blacks shall not pass!'"[16]

Walden also fought the racial hostility that black attorneys confronted even after admission to practice. Black attorneys in Georgia and throughout the South—Walden included—could never be sure of fair and dignified treatment in the courts. Bar associations accepted whites only. Judges, juries, and fellow attorneys, steeped in the norms of Jim Crow, regularly treated black attorneys with disdain. African-American lawyers could not count on "even the most elementary courtesies"; instead, they found themselves ridiculed and even physically abused as they went about their work. Blacks appealed for privileges at public law libraries, while whites used the facilities as a matter of course. In short, they endured humiliating discrimination. Unsurprisingly, black lawyers found it difficult to obtain clients. White clients were usually out of the question. But black attorneys even had trouble enlisting clients within their own communities. African Americans, like whites, questioned their ability to compete in a virtually all-white profession. White counsel who boasted to prospective black clients of their personal relationships with judges and others of influence—relationships that black lawyers could not cultivate in a segregated society—helped to engender the distrust.[17]

These handicaps generated a feeling among African Americans that "the law was not his field," Walden explained at a 1937 NBA conference. African Americans "did not even allow [themselves] to dream of a career in the law" because of the "tentacles of the subservient and defeatist...psychology created by 250 years of chattel slavery" and a "dominant race which magnified and deified everything white, while minimizing [and] depreciating...everything black." Given these stereotypes, often "openly and brazenly supported by the law," the "future" was "cloudy, even ominous," for black lawyers, Walden concluded.[18]

These professional challenges inspired Walden and nine other lawyers to found the Gate City Bar Association. Walden called the group together in 1948 and suggested that the small band of attorneys form a bar association. Those who gathered in Walden's office eagerly accepted his proposal. The black lawyers of Atlanta did not benefit from the conferences and seminars that the city's white attorneys typically attended to keep abreast of legal developments. Nor were they privy to social events where they could develop friendships and networks that could boost careers. Atlanta's black lawyers banded together in the Gate City Bar Association "out of necessity." They joined forces to help each other professionally; at the same time, they hoped to help black citizens "get justice."[19]

The association's charter emphasized its altruistic aims. The founders established the organization, they decreed:

> to create in our community a practical appreciation for the legal profession; to encourage persons of outstanding promise, to attend first rate law schools and to return to the communities which...show need [for] their services most, to be alert to oppose arbitrary and capricious laws in our state with all the force and fiber of which we are capable as an organization, to uphold and extend the principles of justice in every phase of American life to the end that no man shall be discriminated against by reason of his color, race, religious belief, or national origin.[20]

Walden, the first president of the Gate City Bar Association, had set out to develop his own cadre of social engineers. Henceforth, the lawyers met to thrash out troublesome cases on each counsel's docket. They also "discussed very freely" the "everyday bread-and-butter" matters they faced such as how to obtain, keep, and do an "excellent job representing your clients." The lawyers socialized together. And they reached out to the few other black lawyers in the nation for support.[21]

Indeed, within months of the local bar association's birth, it made its professional debut on the national stage when it hosted the annual convention of the NBA. Walden and his colleagues planned for months to make the NBA's meeting in the Gate City the "biggest and best ever." Once the meeting got under way in September, 1948, Walden mixed with more than 350 members of the national black bar. The Gate City Bar Association hosted sessions on "Problems of the Negro Lawyer," "Reciprocal Obligations of Negro Communities and Their Lawyers," and "Current Constitutional Law Problems." Thurgood Marshall headlined a session in which he provided a "Civil Rights Summary." By the convention's end, Walden had raised his national profile; the gathering had been a success.[22]

Walden confronted and shaped the contours of the very same problems that participants discussed at the NBA's convention in Atlanta time and again in the years ahead, as he handled dozens of cases on race and the law. Yet, "cause lawyering" was then in its infancy. Thus, as Walden pursued racial reform through law and politics, he upset long-standing professional norms. He had cast aside the idea that a lawyer should be a neutral expert for a client. He engaged the fight for racial justice as an expert, but also a partisan. His identity and that of his client merged. He was both a lawyer for African Americans and, as an

African American, a member of the client community whom he represented. Walden's personal values and the norms of his community mediated one another, and powerfully influenced his legal work.[23]


# PERSONAL STRIVING


Walden's biography provides important clues about why his approach to social engineering varied in some respects from that of the national NAACP. Charles Hamilton Houston's vision of lawyering derived from theories developed in relatively elite intellectual and social spaces. Houston hailed from the unparalleled black aristocracy of Washington, D.C. His father was a lawyer and his mother a teacher. Family traditions and expectations deeply influenced his path in life. "Who he was and how he met life and handled its changing fortunes were, in part, givens," explained Houston's biographer. Houston was expected to study law and join his father's successful law firm after graduation; in fact, he was constantly reminded of the dream of "Houston and Houston, attorneys at law." Houston also became interested in a career in law as a means of combating the racial injustices visited upon blacks during and after World War I. A first-rate intellect, Houston attended Harvard Law School; although one of just a few blacks, he excelled. He became the first African-American member of the *Harvard Law Review*. He found a mentor in Professor Felix Frankfurter, the future Supreme Court justice, who touted an early iteration of legal realism, or antiformalism. Houston's brilliant legal strategy and courtroom advocacy methodically applied to the race problem the sociological jurisprudence that Frankfurter taught. Thurgood Marshall inherited and applied Houston's realist orientation toward law and politics.[24]

Less lofty surroundings rooted Walden's orientation toward life and social engineering. Walden's understanding of life's challenges and opportunities, and his pragmatic approach to the race question, developed in the context of late nineteenth-century rural Georgia. He climbed into the ranks of trailblazing lawyers from abject poverty. Walden entered life in the rural town of Fort Valley, Georgia, on April 12, 1885, twenty years after the Civil War ended. He grew up in slavery's shadow: his parents had been held in bondage. By the time of Walden's birth, his mother and father had moved up in the world: now, they were sharecroppers. Walden grew up destitute, the third of seven children. As a youngster, he labored in the cotton fields alongside his parents and siblings, the usual fate of black children in rural Georgia at the time.[25]

There, in the dusty cotton patches, he became acquainted with white men's power over blacks and began to develop a strategy of resistance. Whites' power derived from economic control of blacks. He could observe that reality in the relationship between his parents and the men from whom they rented the land and implements for farming. Walden himself "worked for some of the meanest white men in Houston County, but... got along with them." He learned to avoid trouble and show deference, just as his father taught him. "[W]hen a man hires you," Walden's father said, "he doesn't buy you. But he buys your time and he's entitled to all of your time. If you don't give him all of your time, you're robbing and stealing from him." The young Walden followed the advice of his pious father, and avoided the violence and harassment visited upon so many African Americans. "Never once—at any time—did one of them abuse me or say a harsh word to me." Walden did what he was paid to do "how they wanted me to do it" and reaped the dividends of hard work and a good reputation among powerful whites. He had learned one way to negotiate oppression.[26]

Walden attained a secondary school education by a fluke of nature: frail in health, Walden was found unfit to continue working in the fields. His parents sent him to school instead. Walden demonstrated strong intellectual abilities in the segregated schools of his small Georgia town. School "fascinated" him from day one. And he was "soon acknowledged to be the brightest boy in Fort Valley, black or white." Walden developed a burning desire to succeed. In fact, the lad determined that he wanted to be a lawyer by age fifteen, before he even attended college.[27]

The legal profession was a peculiar aspiration for him—an impoverished black boy in rural Georgia, before the dawn of the twentieth century. "Everybody" thought Walden's dream of a career in law was "crazy." It also posed a threat. White men in the town learned of Walden's desire and tried to stamp out his ambition. They told his father that Walden's plan to pursue a law degree was a "great mistake." "He can't do anything with law," his father's "white friends" cautioned. For, although they were "sorry to say it," "white folks aren't going to let a nigger practice law in our courts."[28]

The ways of white folks in the South—what they would and would not permit blacks to do—had provoked Walden's interest in law. More precisely, what whites could *do* to blacks caused the teenager to seek a career in law. During Walden's youth, a white mob had lynched Banjo Peters, a black man. The whites "put him [Peters] on an express wagon and exhibited him." Peter's dead body lay on the wagon, displayed in the town square to all onlookers, for two days. Walden "naturally" grew to "resent them," the whites who had so barbarously murdered this black man. "Somebody had to do something about" whites' disregard for the "Negro's rights." A. T. Walden determined that he would take on that burden: "I felt my people needed me." He vowed to study law and wield it as a weapon against lawlessness.[29]

First, however, he completed college. Walden's ambition and intellect took him to AU. He attended college on scholarship and worked to support himself throughout his time as an undergraduate. He excelled at debate. He studied under W. E. B. Du Bois, a teacher he called a "prophet and a seer." Many of Walden's instructors noticed his "native brilliance" and predicted that he would go far in life. Walden graduated from AU in 1907.[30]

Then, pursuing his dream, Walden did the unthinkable. He entered law school at the University of Michigan. The school accepted Walden for admission after a period of professionalization and expansion. It had toughened admissions standards and adopted the case method of teaching, as well as written exams to measure student progress. The faculty taught law as a science. Many of the law school's more than eight hundred students flunked out of Michigan during their first year of study. But Walden—a son of illiterate former slaves who earned tuition by waiting tables at a white fraternity house and hotel—distinguished himself. He won several prestigious oratorical prizes and performed extraordinarily well in the classroom. Walden finished among the top dozen students in the class of 1911. The eloquent and hardworking graduate was on his way to becoming a first-rate advocate.[31]

Walden built a law practice from the ground up. He began his career in the small town of Macon, Georgia, in 1912. World War I interrupted his work. After attending the segregated training school for black officers at Des Moines, Iowa, he served in the army with distinction during a tour of duty in France. Walden rose to the rank of captain of the 365th Infantry, commanding Company I; he also served as trial judge advocate of the Ninety-Second Division.[32]

After the war, Walden moved his practice to Atlanta. There, he toiled for many years, handling small matters. Eventually, he became a prosperous and well-respected lawyer, and clients and community members came to call him "Colonel." Once he became established, Walden's practice consisted largely of trusts and estates work for individuals and contractual work on behalf of small businesses and a few large corporations. Most notably, he worked as legal counsel to the Atlanta Life Insurance Company and the Citizens Trust Company, the city's largest black-owned businesses, both with millions in assets. Walden did race work, as well. His work in race cases dominates his legacy. But the deal-making, negotiation, and problem-solving skills that Walden honed as a corporate lawyer shaped his approach to civil rights practice.[33]

Given the time and place in which Walden lived and worked, he could hardly have avoided being approached about race cases. Walden was one of a handful of black lawyers in early twentieth-century Georgia. He remembered: "I began alone; for a long, long time, I was the only Negro in Georgia engaged in the full time practice of law...." For decades, the number of black lawyers in the state hovered in the single digits, and did not increase appreciably until 1970, when the state still could only boast fifty-eight African-American lawyers.[34]

The dearth of black lawyers, juxtaposed to the great need for legal services within the African-American community, placed Walden in high demand. One contemporary noted that "Like most black attorneys,...[Walden] carried a heavy burden....It was often necessary for...[him] to travel throughout the South to handle cases that other lawyers could not, or would not, handle." Walden rarely received adequate compensation for the work he did for African Americans, often criminal defendants in far-flung areas of the state and region.[35]

These cases could be lucrative for young, inexperienced attorneys in another way, however, as Walden well knew: A lawyer could make a name for himself in these cases. As president of the Gate City Bar Association, Walden offered this practical advice to black attorneys. In a letter soliciting African-American lawyers to serve as counsel for indigent clients, Walden noted that such representation afforded "excellent practice as well as a means for becoming known to the great body of our people who frequent our criminal courts." Walden tended to focus on practicalities—the practical and personal costs and benefits of various courses of action—rather than dwell on the ideals and principles involved in the struggle for racial justice. This tendency—unabashed in Walden—would define his leadership of the civil rights struggle.[36]

So did his circumspect personality. Walden was no firebrand. Unlike Charles Hamilton Houston, whose sense of mission for racial justice struck most everyone he met, or Thurgood Marshall, whose colorful personality and blunt manner of speech were key factors in his success, or Dr. King, whose moral convictions about social justice inspired thousands of followers, Walden came across to those he encountered as "Buddha-like." He made public utterances as "direct as a legal brief," and rarely displayed passion. No showman, he did not impress through charisma or bravado. Walden's sometimes cocounsel, Donald Hollowell, summed up his colleague's attributes and personality: Walden was "reserved, bright" and a "hard-working fellow," but not "demonstrative." Yet Walden was "strong if the occasion demanded it" and "played the political game close" and as he "wanted it played." Over the course of a career that featured epic battles against the Ku Klux Klan, hostile judges, and courtroom opponents, Walden personified calm and civility. He cultivated cordial relationships with powerful whites and valued consensus, even as he pushed his agenda forward. As a child in Fort Valley, Georgia, he had learned to abide his enemies in order to survive and advance, and he never forgot that lesson. Walden tackled life, law, and the struggle for racial equality as a masterly counselor and negotiator.[37]

The fight for racial justice in Atlanta reflected Walden's personal journey and qualities. His modest start and steady climb toward success due to high intelligence, shrewdness, and hard work went hand in hand with his determined yet patient and relatively moderate actions as a race man. A statement he made in 1961 summed up that approach. "Things have to be accomplished step by step," Walden remarked, "and not by violent changes."[38]

## THE EXTERNAL WORLD

The social, political, and legal milieu in which Walden lived naturally shaped him and how he negotiated his professional and political roles in the community. This context motivated his fight against racial injustice, but also made him wary of the most militant forms of social engineering.

The milieu in which Walden found himself differed—*not* in kind, but in *degree*—in two important respects from the stage on which Houston and Marshall operated. As counsel to the NAACP and LDF, Houston and Marshall operated on a national stage. To be sure, the pair traveled extensively throughout the South, investigating segregation and then rallying local communities around their cause. However, the lawyers remained in offices apart from local clients in the South. They were final arbiters of their organizational agendas; indeed, they approached local communities with their plan to end Jim Crow firmly in mind. Houston and Marshall also answered to a constituency: financial backers of the NAACP and LDF. This constituency, which included many liberal whites unaffected directly by Jim Crow, fully supported the NAACP's legal strategy. Indeed, by the postwar era, the legal strategy's most prominent critic—Du Bois—had long been ostracized, and other naysayers marginalized. Moreover, the emerging dynamics of the Cold War soon helped make a direct attack on segregation even more likely. All of these factors gave the lawyers in the national office and their plan credibility, and made them less accountable to local communities than they otherwise might have been.[39]

Walden answered to the hometown crowd to a degree that these national figures did not. He answered to clients and constituents, African Americans in local communities, or at least, a slice of them. Walden operated within the confines of the black elite's deeply entrenched values and norms—a cultural context that differed from the liberal ethos that pushed Houston and Marshall toward an all-out attack on Jim Crow. Beyond that, he also answered to local whites—those who controlled the levers of power within Atlanta's political, economic, and legal orders. These local actors—black and white—pushed and pulled Walden and his peers on a pragmatic course of civil rights.[40]

## The World of the Black Elite

The worldview of Atlanta's pioneering black elite, who managed to build a functioning, even thriving, society out of the ashes of the Civil War and the crucible of Jim Crow, shaped A. T. Walden's own sense of the world. Made up of both male and female lawyers, educators, intellectuals, doctors, ministers, and entrepreneurs, this elite group clustered along "Sweet" Auburn Avenue, christened the "richest Negro street in the world" by *Fortune* magazine. African Americans could find a collection of businesses to serve their needs on the avenue—grocers, tailors, florists, restaurants, barbershops, shoeshine stands, pharmacies, cleaners, insurers, banks. These black-owned businesses, large and small, also provided employment to African Americans locked out of jobs in white establishments. Walden knew the Auburn Avenue elite intimately, as clients, neighbors, and friends. He shared their values—most important, a racial uplift ideology premised on autonomous black institutions, social respectability, the pursuit of education, and economic self-sufficiency, or a "sound racial economy." "Nothing," Walden said, was "more important" than black "self-help."[41]

Schools of higher education loomed especially large in shaping the elite's consciousness. Indeed, the city's distinction of being home to a flourishing black middle class soon after emancipation turned, in part, on Atlanta's position as the capital of African-American higher education. Atlanta had boasted the highest concentration of historically black institutions of higher education of any city in the nation since the late nineteenth century. The oldest of these institutions, Atlanta University (AU), established in 1865, was the intellectual home for many years of NAACP cofounder W. E. B. Du Bois. Atlanta was also home to Morehouse College, the alma mater of Dr. Martin Luther King, Jr.; Spelman College; Clark University; and Morris Brown College. The overwhelming majority of Atlanta's African-American leadership during the postwar years had attended one of the city's historically black colleges, worked at one of them, as faculty, staff, or administrator, or knew someone who had close ties to the colleges.[42]

These institutions all emphasized classical liberal education and "middle-class," Victorian values. Faculty inculcated high morals and religious devotion, chastity, conservatism in dress and behavior, refined cultural tastes, status-consciousness, the pursuit of wealth, and a concern for projecting an image that blacks were "decent" folks capable of existing freely in society, alongside whites. The cultivation of norms of "respectability" served the subversive political purpose of confounding stereotypes used to justify discrimination. But the norms also promoted a hierarchy in which the self-appointed leaders of the African American elite imposed bourgeois ways of viewing and negotiating the world upon workaday folks. It differentiated blacks with education and relative wealth (those who practiced "good" habits and conformed to societal expectations) from those who were uneducated and poor—the primary objects of the campaign for respectability. The paternalistic and elitist attitudes taught at the colleges, and encouraged by social and civic clubs, found their way into Walden's approach to racial activism.[43]

Anti-communism infused the black ethos. During the 1930s, Atlanta played host to high-profile trials of alleged Communist sympathizers. Middle-class leaders' experiences with the Community Party and its legal arm, the International Labor Defense (ILD), during those trials left them deeply disaffected. Blacks recoiled when the ILD publicly criticized A.T. Walden and Atlanta NAACP leaders for being insufficiently supportive of Red-baited African Americans. The ILD even claimed—wrongly—that Walden's mishandling of a case had been a factor in the state's execution of an innocent black man whom an all-white jury had convicted of the rape of a white woman. In fact, Walden had not handled the phase of the man's defense that had led to his execution. Relations deteriorated further when Red-baiting devolved into a full-scale Red Scare. The state's repression of party radicals alienated blacks, elites and working-class, from the Communist Party and the ILD. Thereafter, anti-communism and a pragmatic approach to racial reform intertwined.[44]

The philosophies of both Booker T. Washington and W. E. B. Du Bois, pillars of thought within the black colleges and elite black circles, shaped the pragmatic outlook, as well. Walden studied under Du Bois at AU. His teacher's caution about the "smokescreen of social equality" had profoundly impressed the young man. In writings he crafted during the era when Walden was his student, Du Bois extolled the social capital indigenous to African-American communities. He urged "the Talented Tenth," who had been trained in segregated common schools by teachers of "their own race and blood" who placed before "every Negro child an attainable ideal," and then, in black colleges that taught learning as well as "life," to "save" the rest of the race. These views grounded the scholar's skepticism about reforms that overvalued social integration, more fully developed as Walden crafted his approaches to civil rights. It is small wonder that his teacher's credo informed the lawyer's own beliefs about the relative importance of social, political, and economic rights in racial reform efforts.[45]

The Wizard of Tuskegee also influenced black thought. Washington and Du Bois are often discussed as if they existed on opposite sides of a great fault line in African-American intellectual and political history. But, in fact, the two men's philosophies converged at important points. Despite the caricature of Washington as an accommodator of segregation, many contemporaries, including Du Bois and others unquestionably committed to blacks' rights, believed that self-help and economic advancement could be viable paths to black betterment. Moreover, we now know that Washington did, in fact, support black political and civil rights. Secretly, Washington funded lawsuits attacking segregation on railroads, discrimination in voting, peonage, and exclusion of blacks from juries.[46]

Du Bois's views, too, were nuanced. As Walden, the student, would have known, Du Bois tempered his racial liberalism with a realistic appraisal of contemporary sociopolitical conditions. Theories of racial advancement "must start on the earth where we sit and not in the skies whither we aspire," he wrote. He encouraged blacks to develop self-sustaining institutions and a cooperative economy as antidotes to white supremacy. And in a controversial 1934 *Crisis* editorial, Du Bois advocated that the NAACP turn away from its singular focus on attacking segregation to a program focused on black association and cooperation. He decried rights-consciousness unmoored from an appreciation of the community-building value of black institutions.[47]

Du Bois's ambivalence about an equality strategy focused on integration and the courts, coupled with his appreciation of racially separate social spaces, show that his and Washington's approaches ought to be viewed as interrelated rather than antagonistic. The points of convergence, as well as the more publicized areas of conflict between the two men, illuminated the circuitous paths that Walden and Atlanta's black elite traversed in the fight for formal equality. Together, Du Bois and Washington created a dialectic about race that helped to set the terms and shape the course of Walden's racial leadership. He and other members of Atlanta's black middle-class leadership embraced accommodationism and rights-consciousness. They were both principled and practical. Atlanta's black leadership class pursued a centrist plan for racial progress, one that rejected the view that Bookerite and Du Boisian philosophies were incompatible.[48]

## A Culture of Lawlessness

Walden's civil rights practice hewed closely to the ground in another sense. He answered to whites. He frequently negotiated with Atlanta's white moderates, who were far less likely than the national NAACP's northern, white liberal constituents to support an attack on Jim Crow. Just as important, but less commented on and appreciated, he had to contend with intense white resistance.

Walden practiced amid violent white racial hatred and the threat of racial terror on a daily basis for most of his professional life.

Of course, white supremacy colored the professional lives of Houston, Marshall, and other NAACP counsel, as well. Houston and Thurgood Marshall's near misses as they traveled throughout the South investigating the conditions under which blacks lived in an effort to build support for test cases are legend. They also suffered indignities. Justice McReynolds turned his back on Houston as he argued *Missouri ex rel. Gaines v. Canada* in 1938. Shameful though it was, the McReynolds incident underscores the point that Walden dealt with racist attitudes, threats, and the reality of white violence—as well as judicial discourtesy—at every turn, and typically, not in such lofty places as the Supreme Court. The Georgia lawyer literally risked his life as he engaged in social engineering—a point that Houston once saw fit to make in a tribute to Walden.[49]

Georgia brimmed with barely controlled white hostility toward blacks during Walden's heyday. Yet, myth shrouds the extent of violence in the state, especially in Atlanta and other urban areas. A 1906 riot generally is considered a deviation from Georgia racially moderate history, as compared to other southern states. However, racial violence and intimidation  commonly occurred in the state during the early to middle twentieth century. Between 1882 and 1923, Georgia led the nation in the number of lynchings. There were 505 lynchings in Georgia during this period, and in most cases the lynch mobs took their victims from the custody of officers of the law. The rash of vigilante murders before 1923 included two in Atlanta or its environs: Floyd Carmichael, an African American, was lynched in 1906, and Leo Frank, a Jewish businessman, was murdered in 1915. Overall, during the almost one hundred years stretching from Reconstruction to the assassination of Martin Luther King, Jr., only Mississippi exceeded Georgia in the number of lynchings, 581 to 531.[50]

A. T. Walden experienced the way that mob violence and the threat of it hovered over the daily lives of African Americans, and he fought against the forces of terror during his career. As president of the local branch of the NAACP, Walden worked with the national NAACP for federal antilynching legislation. (Congress never enacted an antilynching law). Walden's antiterror work went even further than touting new laws, however. He became personally involved in the fight against a wave of terror perpetrated in Georgia by a fascist group known as the "Black Shirts." The Black Shirts violently opposed black competition in the labor market, as well as black civil and political rights. They harassed African Americans throughout the state, parading in full regalia in Atlanta. These displays culminated in the lynching of Dennis Hubert, an African-American student and driver for the Morehouse College president. Walden helped the Fulton County prosecutor obtain convictions of two of the men responsible for lynching Hubert. In doing so, Walden made history: he was the first African American in the history of Georgia ever to aid in the prosecution of a white man. His reputation within the black community swelled as a result of his heroic efforts against the Black Shirts. Meanwhile, white supremacist groups expressed outrage at Walden's audacity—and not for the last time.[51]

This prosecution proved an outlier: police brutality, harassment, intimidation, and neglect typically reigned, and they all facilitated mob rule of the state well into the mid-twentieth century. The Ku Klux Klan infiltrated the state's police and political system at all levels. Numerous members of the Atlanta Police Department joined the Ku Klux Klan after its post–World War I revival at Stone Mountain, Georgia. For a time the Klan's membership included police chief Herbert Jenkins, who headed the city's police department from 1947 to 1972. The Klan's influence extended far beyond the Police Department to include mayors, city council members, governors, congressmen, senators, and judges—members of the "Invisible Empire." In the U.S. Congress, senators Richard B. Russell, Thomas Watson, and William J. Harris and representative Willie Upshaw numbered among them.[52]

Even as Walden fought the pernicious entanglement of law enforcement, the apparatus of government, and organized terror groups, police harassment and brutality remained a persistent problem. Working-class and poor blacks experienced the worst abuses, but any African American who defied social convention could become ensnarled in the clutches of racist officers. A few examples show the range of problems that African Americans faced. One case involved the repeated arrest on "trumped-up" charges of one "Preacher" Sullivan. Mr. Sullivan's "crime" was operating a car wash that attracted customers whom the white owner of a nearby filling station desired. By claiming that the preacher had committed various offenses, the white man hoped to run Sullivan out of business. In another case, T. D. Smith, a white man, had been "deputized" by a local sheriff to work as a "watchman" at the John Hope Homes, a public housing project. A grand jury indicted Smith for assault with intent to murder Robert Taylor, a black man whom Smith claimed had committed assault and battery. Two witnesses, including a minister and a businessman, stated that Smith had beaten Taylor with a pistol and shot him several times. But when police arrived on the scene, they "arrested the Negro and was about to let the white man go" until several witnesses insisted that the watchman had been at fault. The incident left Taylor hospitalized, with a brain injury.[53]

Officials rarely took African Americans' complaints against police officers seriously. Commissioner Scott Candler of Dekalb rejected the claims of black witnesses that officers had acted negligently during an accident. A collision had occurred between a truck containing thirty blacks and a car containing four white boys. With black bodies strewn hurt on the street, a white ambulance driver came to the scene, "saw that the white people were already gone," and left. He later called "three Negro ambulances" to retrieve the blacks. Rather than insist that the white driver take the blacks to the hospital, an officer on the scene affirmed the decision. "I don't blame him, I wouldn't haul no damn nigger in my car if he was dying." Some of the injured blacks lay on the highway for as long as two hours, with no help. Four blacks lost their lives and ten sustained serious injuries in the crash. Yet, Commissioner Candler commended the officers who had watched as blacks lay helpless "for their proper conduct" during the accident.[54]

Despite persistent complaints by black citizens from all walks of life about incidents of unlawful arrest and police brutality, local judges invariably sided with white officers. A judge dismissed charges against G. S. Robertson, a police officer who beat a twenty-one-year-old black man, Earl Sands, with a black-jack and an iron link chain. The officer, who was cruising in his police car, claimed that Mr. Sands had disturbed the peace on his walk from one house to another—two doors down—at 2 A.M. on August 7, 1940. Robertson also alleged that Mr. Sands had resisted arrest; the young man proclaimed his innocence and begged to go home to his nearby wife and child. The officer denied ever hitting Sands, but admitted transporting the man to the hospital for treatment before taking him to jail. In dismissing the charges against the white officer, Judge Robert Carpenter commended him, saying, "being a police officer is no easy job." The judge offered that Sands was "lucky" if Officer Robertson had *not* struck him; he should have known not to disturb a neighborhood in the wee hours of the morning, and known not to resist when approached by an officer of the law.[55]

In view of problems of this sort, advocates turned to Atlanta's mayor, William Hartsfield, for assistance. They noted that police officers had an immense incentive to make arrests on specious charges—by statute, 25 percent of all fines collected from arrests went to the policemen's pension fund. The mayor rebuffed them. Hartsfield concluded that little could be done to "weed out unworthy officers" protected by civil service rules. The mayor also leveled charges of his own. The Police Department was bound to have "enemies among a class who will not hesitate to stoop to anything in order to try to discredit them in the eyes of the better element," he claimed. Hartsfield had a solemn duty to "back up" officers and "preserve the moral[e] of the department."[56]

Meanwhile, wartime stress, coupled with increasing black demands for redress, exacerbated white violence and intimidation. The *Southern Patriot*, the newsletter of the Southern Conference for Human Welfare, chronicled the wave of terror that spread through the South in the late 1930s and the 1940s. "The Ku

Klux Klan Rides Again," the *Patriot* announced, "in a desperate effort to halt labor's organizing drive on the one hand, and voting of Negroes in Democratic primaries, on the other." Georgia remained one of the most active staging grounds for the Klan. Sixty-five thousand Georgians, including twenty thousand Atlantans, joined the Klan between 1915 and 1944, placing the state second only to Texas in Klan membership. Atlanta still served as the Klan's national headquarters, as well as the home base of the Columbians, a terror group dominated by white veterans. The Klan flogged and terrorized sixty-three blacks in and around Atlanta, killing two of them. Rare convictions in 1940 of eight of the twenty men (including three sheriffs' deputies) involved in the floggings were wiped away when Georgia's governor, Eugene Talmadge, an outspoken white supremacist, pardoned them.[57]

Extremist groups felt a renewed license to kill after Talmadge's victory in the 1946 Democratic primary over a candidate who showed interest in black citizens. Whites murdered blacks throughout the state within a span of a few weeks. The deaths included the July 25, 1946, lynching of two couples in Monroe, Georgia, fifty miles outside of Atlanta. The Klan flogged a twenty-one-year-old black navy veteran near Atlanta's airport in February of 1945, and murdered a black taxicab driver in Atlanta in August of 1945. The group then gathered on Stone Mountain, Georgia, near Atlanta, in October 1945, where they burned a cross three hundred feet tall. The Atlanta Police Department, still a Klan haven, did nothing to apprehend the perpetrators of these crimes. In fact, during the same time that the Klan and other extremist groups reemerged, the problem of antiblack violence and intimidation by the police force continued unabated. During the period November 1945 through October 1946 alone, police officers and streetcar motormen exercising "police powers" shot and killed six blacks, including three veterans.[58]

In light of the ongoing white terror campaign and police abuse and neglect, Walden and other African-American leaders counted the hiring of black police officers among their highest priorities. After years of lobbying, the city finally hired eight black officers in 1948. By that time, over forty other southern cities already had black officers. Atlanta did relax the color bar in law enforcement, but with considerable limitations. It hired the black officers on a trial basis and under terms designed to ensure that they created no friction between the races. The black officers worked in a segregated precinct and patrolled on a segregated basis. They could not exercise police power over whites. The Georgia Supreme Court upheld the restrictions: the justices construed these conditions as personnel decisions and held them exempt from judicial review.[59]

The horrific violence and racial oppression directed at blacks in Georgia and Atlanta in the interwar and postwar years make plain an important fact: Walden operated in an unsafe world. It became less safe as his reputation as a race man grew. An encounter that Walden had on the street in 1943 demonstrated the point; a Klansman stopped the lawyer on the street and informed Walden that he "was living on borrowed time." Unlike his northern comrades in the civil rights movement, he could never return home to New York City or Washington, D.C., to find relative sanctuary from the vilest forms of white supremacy.[60]

## WHAT PATH SHALL WE TAKE?

The virulence of white racism in early twentieth-century Atlanta, juxtaposed to the highly functional socioeconomic order that pioneering blacks had created in response to it, guided A. T. Walden's approach to civil rights activism in the postwar years. Under the steady leadership of black professionals and the influence of Du Bois and Washington, the black middle class had created an impressive separate society. Pushed into a compact geographic space along Auburn Avenue, African Americans had developed a collection of businesses and a cohesive network of organizations and individuals committed to racial uplift and respectability. They treasured the world they had made.

All around them, they could see white power arrayed against them. White supremacy was more than an influential force in social relations and local politics. It was entrenched in the *legal* system, as well. White racism operated at the very highest levels of government—in the courtroom and the criminal justice system—and its omnipresence shaped African-American consciousness. Walden and his peers could see that judges and police officers belonged to the Klan or sympathized with its racial ideology; they witnessed the injustices perpetrated against African Americans by the police and in the courts on an ongoing, daily basis.

Long experience with such lawlessness informed Walden's choices as he considered how the law and the courts might be used to effect racial change. It shaped the pace and character of the change he sought. Martin Luther King, Sr., explained it best. "Walden had fought the Klan as a young man in rural Georgia." "Walden knew how hard-headed crackers could be, and how violent they could be on the subject of race," King claimed. "He knew how to fight on more than one level, toe-to-toe with enemies who forced him to that method, and also reasonably, with a knowledgeable use of the legal apparatus available to all Americans."[61]

And so he did. Walden faced enormous tasks in his career: reconciling lawlessness and law, prejudice and principle, reality with ideals, personal and professional identities. By the time he examined and scrutinized the national NAACP's legal strategy, he had been negotiating life under a white supremacist regime for decades. Given what Walden and other black decisionmakers had already witnessed and achieved, a militant, court-based strategy of racial justice might well have appeared foolhardy to them, even irresponsible. They had measured confidence, not blind faith, in the judicial process.

Nevertheless, the viability of alternative paths remained unclear. How could blacks move forward when their status under local laws and the pervasive climate of lawlessness so limited the social and political space in which they could operate? This conundrum had given rise to Charles Hamilton Houston's litigation strategy, in the first place. Walden and other leaders wrestled with this dilemma throughout the postwar years. The lawyer resolved to challenge Jim Crow, but with a keen sense of timing and perspective on which battles should be engaged frontally and urgently, and which should not. A "civic counselor"—as Walden called himself in the twilight of life—he believed he should use his expertise and experience to guide the community on a "practical" course of racial reform.[62]

CHAPTER 2

# The Roots of Pragmatism

*Voting Rights Activism inside and outside the Courts, 1944–1957*

The sole bulwark of protection for Negroes are courts of the law. There is no other way out. (1937)

E. Washington Rhodes, Esq.

The ballot is a cheaper method than the courts in procuring full citizenship rights. (1961)

A. T. Walden

In the run-up to Georgia's 1946 statewide primary election, A. T. Walden was a wanted man. The Klan planned to kill him.[1] Walden had led recent efforts to register African-American voters in the wake of the Supreme Court's 1944 *Smith v. Allwright* decision. In Smith, the Court, found unconstitutional the "white primary," which barred blacks from voting in primary elections.[2] With the justices who actually had rendered *Smith* out of reach, the Klan turned its attention to local targets, including Walden. The idea of assassinating Walden was raised at a meeting in May 1946, days after the Klan had announced its rebirth in Georgia by burning a cross at Stone Mountain. At the May gathering, a Klan leader who had headed the Georgia Bureau of Investigation just a few years earlier and had recently served in the Atlanta Police Department suggested that the group abduct and kill Walden. Walden's reputation as the city's black political boss was steadily increasing; his death would serve as an example of what lay in store for other African Americans who dared to defy Jim Crow.[3]

The Klan's plot was unknown to Walden. Had he known about it, the old soldier might have been afraid, but at the same time he would have been pleased. The threat would have confirmed that Walden was shaking things up, making the forces of white supremacy uncomfortable. And he wanted his voting rights activism to do nothing less.

For A. T. Walden and many other black leaders in Atlanta, the right to vote was the first among rights. The denial of the suffrage made African Americans citizens in name only. "To help build and create a Nation, to blend our blood freely as we have in all its great wars,... and then be denied by subterfuge and cunning the right to participate in government... is hell itself." These words, written in October 1944 by E. E. Martin, an executive of Atlanta Life Insurance Company, a leading black-owned business, eloquently expressed the centrality of the suffrage to citizenship and the struggle for racial equality.[4]

The Atlanta pragmatists made voting rights the top priority on their agenda for racial progress because they viewed the vote as the single best route to protect individual rights, ensure property rights, and secure patronage. In the absence of the right to vote, African Americans were limited in their ability to pursue their entrepreneurial ambitions and professional callings, and they were unable to protect the fruits of their labors. Without direct political influence, even the most successful blacks were forced to rely on client-patron relationships with whites to get ahead. These sorts of arrangements undermined the personal dignity of the black supplicant and interfered with the attainment of respectability, the prized attribute of both bootstrapping blacks and those who had already arrived in the middle class.

Black elites hoped that participation in the electoral system would end the client-patron dependency with individual whites and open the door to political coalition with moderate white elite voters and elected officials. Blacks' electoral votes would translate into political influence, as white candidates would no longer be able to disregard black interests. The white power structure would consider African-American interests when local government formulated policy, enacted laws, meted out civil service jobs, allocated municipal facilities—playgrounds, schools, housing, libraries—and services such as fire and police protection—or protection *from* the police. The ballot would be a "powerful force," Walden believed. Democracy would work for African Americans.[5]

The local black leadership's eminently reasonable plan to leverage the vote for concrete benefits had been successfully employed by many before them. Successive waves of European immigrants and black migrants had used the strategy to gain a foothold in urban America. After World War I, black migrants to the North, no longer disfranchised, had begun demanding patronage and policy reforms, including antidiscrimination laws, from political machines in Chicago, Detroit, New York, Philadelphia, and elsewhere. Northern blacks had witnessed their political leverage steadily increase in size and importance; soon, black officeholders peppered the region, and by 1936, African Americans in the North, who voted decisively for President Franklin D. Roosevelt, had coalesced into a decisive voting bloc and propelled civil rights onto the national agenda.

For northern blacks, the ballot had "without doubt been a means of protection in the hands of people peculiarly liable to oppression," explained W. E. B. Du Bois. "Public and private oppression had been lightened by the knowledge of the power of the black vote."[6]

Down South, A. T. Walden and other leaders planned to accumulate sufficient political capital to bargain for racial advances, as well—if only they could liberate black voters from systemic discrimination and intimidation. At the same time, they hoped that black electoral power would facilitate informal interracial diplomacy and enhance black influence within the white power structure. In personal meetings with white leaders and at election time, black leaders would wield the power of the black voting bloc—organized and race-conscious—as a threat to compel white decisionmakers to adopt racial reforms. A. T. Walden's political activism made him a visionary—and, in the Klan's view, a dangerous dissenter from the South's racial status quo.

The story of local and national relations in the voting context is largely a narrative of consensus. The leadership in Atlanta enthusiastically embraced the NAACP's and LDF's voting rights campaigns. Indeed, in their common emphasis on the crucial place of the black vote in the struggle for racial equality, local activists and the NAACP and LDF marched in lockstep.

But the locals' pursuit of political power diverged in a crucially important respect from the national program. For the NAACP and LDF, voting rights constituted just one element of a comprehensive fight against all forms of segregation and discrimination. The LDF attacked any and all types of discrimination in the courts on the assumption that political, social, and civil rights were indivisible. Meaningful political power reinforced and could not exist apart from other rights. And integration in the social sphere was a precondition to equality in every other area. Thus, LDF attacked racially restrictive covenants in housing and segregation in education, even as it sued to end racial discrimination in the exercise of the franchise.[7]

By contrast, the Atlanta pragmatists proceeded as if political and social rights could be pursued separately and at different paces, if not functionally severed. As late as 1964, Walden—citing the "credo" of his "teacher," W. E. B. Du Bois—spoke out against efforts to "equate demands for legal equality" with "demands for social intimacy and relationships" with whites. The vote was the linchpin of Walden's efforts to attain legal equality: it occupied an exalted position in the strategic arsenal of the pragmatists. By achieving voting rights, they hoped to facilitate local autonomy, advance intraracial interests—especially the interests of the middle class—and obviate the need for aggressive litigation of the type that LDF pursued in areas such as education and housing.[8]

## BEGINNINGS OF A POLITICAL APPROACH
## TO RACIAL ADVANCEMENT

The Supreme Court's 1944 decision in *Smith v. Allwright* was a precondition to the ultimate success of black Atlanta's political strategy for equality. But A. T. Walden and many others had campaigned for political power for years before the Supreme Court's ruling. Decades prior to *Smith*, black leaders had been trying to undermine a 1908 Georgia law that prevented most African Americans from participating in both general and primary elections by means of poll taxes and literacy, residency, character, and other requirements designed to block access to the ballot.[9]

The 1908 law had not, however, completely eradicated the black vote. Some African Americans still managed to vote in general elections, as well as special elections (for instance, bond, tax, and recall elections). A small number, ranging from a few hundred to two thousand, remained on the rolls in Atlanta prior to *Smith*. During the 1920s and 1930s, activists worked hard to increase the number of blacks eligible to vote despite the racially motivated restrictions in place.[10]

One of their first efforts to increase the black vote occurred after World War I. The war was a profoundly disillusioning time for African Americans who had followed Du Bois's advice to "Close Ranks" with whites to defeat the nation's enemies. Rather than laying the groundwork for citizenship rights, blacks' show of loyalty during the war reaped few positive gains; to the contrary, a wave of racial violence ensued.[11]

Even amid this tumult, Atlanta's black leaders gained some advantage. In July 1918 and March 1919, black voters helped to defeat school bond issues and a proposed property tax increase that ignored black schools. The vote to defeat the bond issue demonstrated blacks' ability and willingness to engage in the competitive world of local politics. Earlier bond measures had been passed with black political support after white leaders had assured African Americans that black schools would benefit. Those promises had not been kept. When the new bond was defeated with black votes, whites took notice; in 1921, after yet another bond measure was on the ballot, blacks voted in favor and were appropriately "rewarded." The city allotted monies for improving existing black schools and building new ones, including the Booker T. Washington High School, Atlanta's first high school for blacks, which opened in 1924.[12]

The saga of the bond measures set the stage for rising levels of black registration and voting during the 1930s. Voter registration campaigns increased substantially during the New Deal, when the expansion of the federal bureaucracy provided new opportunities for African-American professionals to participate in government. Graduates of the Atlanta School of Social Work gained positions in New Deal agencies as social workers and administrators of relief programs, and at wages equal to those paid to whites.[13]

Leaders sought to solidify the new-found socioeconomic status signified by the entry of African Americans into the federal bureaucracy. They did so by engaging in new forms of political activism. In 1933, A. T. Walden, then president of the Atlanta NAACP branch, and Lugenia Burns Hope, founder of the Neighborhood Union, a social welfare organization, organized "citizenship schools." The schools familiarized potential voters with registration procedures through mock elections and lessons in government. Walden wrote the primer used to teach the students about democracy, the U.S. Constitution, and concepts such as federalism and separation of powers.[14]

In 1935, the local NAACP and other groups seized upon an opportunity to demonstrate the electoral power of newly informed black voters. A large bond issue for sewer and school renovations provided the occasion. The NAACP branch led a registration drive and threatened to withhold support for the bond unless the city set aside an equitable share of funds for black schools. John Wesley Dobbs, leader of the Masons, a prominent black civic group, also trained his sights on bond issues as a means of acquiring access to political power. In 1936, Dobbs formed the Atlanta Civic and Political League with the intention of delivering a black bloc of ten thousand voters for the Republican Party. Dobbs, a charismatic and imposing figure, declared: "When 10,000 Negroes in Atlanta get registered, the Signal Light of Opportunity will automatically turn from red to green." On another occasion, he chided, "Here in Atlanta, Ga., we are asleep at the switch. If you give me 10,000 Registered Negroes...I'll show you how to walk into Jerusalem just like John." Dobbs and his league set their sights on a school bond measure set for a vote in 1938.[15]

But, in a foreboding sign for the election-centered strategy for achieving equality, neither Walden's nor Dobbs's efforts to create an effective black voting bloc saw much success. Very few students "graduated" from the citizenship schools, and few registered to vote for or against the 1935 or 1938 bond issues. It remained unclear whether the vote would be efficacious for attacking black Atlantans' Depression-era social and economic problems.[16]

Black leaders' inability to inspire the sort of collective racial identity needed to cultivate mass interest in voting rested on a number of factors. Two are worth noting. First, the vote appealed most to those who had assets and aspirations to protect using the apparatus of representative government. The ballot logically struck upper-strata figures such as A. T. Walden, Lugenia Burns Hope, and African Americans who were finding professional homes in the bureaucracies of the New Deal as a worthy goal. Voting constituted a conservative strategy, and a person of this milieu had much to conserve. By comparison, the difficulties inherent in trying to convince the Depression-era black poor and working classes that they had anything to conserve through voting were significant. These vestiges of political disenfranchisement—interpreted as "political apathy" by elites—would plague efforts to build a powerful black voting bloc for decades to come.[17]

Second, the legal barriers to voting, especially for a poor person with a rudimentary education, remained tremendous. Qualification tests and the poll tax were serious impediments to voter registration. These obstacles, coupled with the failure of black leaders to appreciate fully their impact on workaday people—Dobbs actually required payment of the poll tax as a prerequisite for membership in his league—limited the extent to which poor and working-class African Americans would become invested in voting as the predominant strategy for loosening the bonds of Jim Crow. This was especially true when the candidates for whom blacks were asked to vote were whites whose racial views conformed to the norms of Jim Crow. Nevertheless, the seeds that Walden, Dobbs, and others sowed in the 1930s were important precursors to the more successful voting rights activism of the 1940s.[18]

It took increased consciousness of racial oppression, occasioned by World War II, as well as a new legal order, to inspire significant numbers of blacks to attempt to register to vote and to find success when they sought to do so. The racial violence and discrimination that greeted black servicemen returning from the front, along with the segregation and discrimination they suffered within the armed forces, inspired outrage. Georgia's Ku Klux Klan, other white supremacist organizations, and vigilantes had regrouped, along with racist elements within law enforcement, and often turned their racial anxiety and hatred on black veterans.

These tensions reached their height in 1946, when whites lynched four African Americans, two men and two women, fifty miles east of Atlanta. One of the victims was a veteran who had just returned from the front, another a woman who was seven months pregnant. The *Atlanta Daily World* called the crime "history's worst lynching," and it made national headlines. The *World* reported that the bodies of the victims, Roger and Dorothy Malcom and George and Mae Dorsey, were riddled with shotgun slugs as well as rifle and pistol bullets, their flesh punctured and torn by literally hundreds of wounds. The "horrible sight" reminded one columnist of "similar incidents in Europe under Hitler." In fact, the writer noted, "Hitler at his worst could not have done a more mutilating job than was done here in Walton County Georgia, USA." The Georgia Committee on Interracial Cooperation went further, proclaiming that the "mob outdid Hitler or the devil himself." The murders made blacks and some white moderates demand that federal authorities address the issue of civil rights. At the behest of President Truman, the FBI joined the state's investigation of the murders, and the national NAACP offered a $10,000 reward for information leading to the conviction of the lynch mob. Yet, the crime remained unsolved. It is still unsolved to this day.[19]

Such racial violence in the United States, while blacks fought for the United States against fascism abroad, lit a fire under African-American leaders and advocacy organizations. On October 20, 1942, a group of prominent southern blacks convened a conference on race relations in Durham, North Carolina, and memorialized the connection between the two. The attendees included Atlanta's Benjamin Mays, president of Morehouse College, Rufus Clement, president of AU, and C. A. Scott, publisher of the *Atlanta Daily World*. The conferees issued a statement declaring that the "war has sharpened the issue of Negro-white relations in the United States, particularly in the South." The group called on whites to realize that blacks' "loyalty" and "full contribution to the war effort" were inextricably tied to "elementary" improvements in Negro status. "The effect of the war has been to make the Negro...the symbol and protagonist of every other minority in America and in the world at large." The conferees called for "simple efforts" to "correct obvious social and economic injustices" and thus preserve the legitimacy of American democracy. These inarguable inequities included security from random acts of violence, whether perpetrated by mobs or by officers of the law, and equal access to the ballot—the "safeguard of democracy." The conferees cited abolition of the white primary and poll tax as necessary first steps to ensure a fair electoral process. Within two years, a coalition of civil rights lawyers, stretching from Thurgood Marshall in New York to A. T. Walden in Atlanta, was able to meet the first of these two goals. They had helped to abolish the white primary and thus establish a more open system of representative government.[20]

## AN "EPOCHAL" LEGAL VICTORY

On April 3, 1944, the Supreme Court declared Texas's white primary unconstitutional. *Smith v. Allwright* constituted a significant step toward fairer elections in the South. It represented the culmination of a series of court challenges to Texas's discriminatory voting system. Texas's original white primary statute, enacted in 1923, was simple and effective. It stipulated that African Americans were not eligible to vote in Democratic Party primary elections, which in one-party states such as Texas determined the winner of general elections. The LDF quickly challenged the law, and it was declared unconstitutional in a 1927 case, *Nixon v. Herndon*. In that case, the Court held that color was not a legitimate basis upon which a state could regulate the right to vote.[21]

In a series of subsequent cases, the Court considered Texas's efforts to maintain the white primary without using overtly discriminatory statutory language. Each case featured a scheme through which Texas hoped to escape the reach of the Court's antidiscrimination jurisprudence. In 1932, in *Nixon v. Condon*, the Court struck down a Texas statute that omitted the racially discriminatory language of the 1923 law but produced the same effect by vesting authority over voter qualifications in the Democratic Party executive committee. Three years later, in *Grovey v. Townsend*, the Court faced the question of whether Texas's extensive regulation of political parties, combined with its oversight of discriminatory Democratic Party primary elections, gave rise to state action within the meaning of the Constitution. A Texas official had refused a ballot to a black man who wished to vote absentee in a primary election, in keeping with Democratic Party rules and state law. The man sued, lost in the district court, and on appeal, asked the justices to hold that the official's action violated the Fourteenth Amendment, which prohibits states from denying "equal protection" or "due process" of laws, and the Fifteenth Amendment, which prohibits racial bars on voting. The Supreme Court profoundly disappointed him. The Court refused to characterize the official's action as discriminatory state action on grounds that the Democratic Party had paid for the primary, furnished and counted the ballots used in it, and otherwise managed the process. As a private organization, the party could select any criteria for membership.[22]

Coming on the heels of *Townsend*, the NAACP's challenge to the white primary in *Smith* was viewed as a make-or-break moment. *United States v. Classic*, a 1941 decision in which the Court had upheld the conviction of a Louisiana man for falsifying primary elections, was the NAACP's best hope of broadening the Court's interpretation of state action. The *Classic* majority had made clear that primaries were an integral part of the electoral process. However, Texas persisted in its argument that the state Democratic Party, a private, voluntary association, was free to select its members on the basis of race.[23]

The Supreme Court's decision in *Smith* was a landmark. The justices held that the Texas Democratic Party, a state actor, had been complicit in discriminating against black voters in primary elections in violation of the Fifteenth Amendment. The decision would greatly facilitate the registration of black voters. Yet, *Smith* was not a complete victory. Some language in the decision was susceptible to the reading that if states removed themselves from the business of regulating political parties, those parties would not be considered state agents for purposes of establishing discrimination under the Constitution.[24]

Even with that limitation, black leaders in Texas—and in Georgia—greeted the *Smith* decision with jubilation. The *Atlanta Daily World* hailed the decision as "far-reaching and momentous for Negroes and for the South." It predicted that blacks in Atlanta would fully take advantage of the "long-awaited ruling." A. T. Walden called the decision "epochal—a landmark along the tedious road of constitutional democracy."[25]

Walden soon announced plans to back his words with action. He, along with C. A. Scott, publisher of the *Atlanta Daily World*, Forrester B. Washington, director of the AU School of Social Work, C. L. Harper, president of the Atlanta NAACP, and Rev. Martin Luther King, Sr., pastor of the Ebenezer Baptist Church, announced that they would test *Smith*'s effectiveness in Georgia by attempting to vote in the next statewide election.[26]

Local activists also formed new institutions to promote black participation in politics. In May 1944, Walden and Scott founded the Fulton County Citizens Democratic Club, with the goal of helping African Americans register to vote in the upcoming statewide primary election. And under the aegis of an umbrella organization, the Georgia Association of Democratic Clubs, Walden organized eleven satellite clubs throughout Georgia, again with the objective of supporting black voter registration. He achieved phenomenal success. Ten thousand black Georgians registered by the deadline for voting in the primary—a record for a registration campaign. The lawyers and activists had laid the foundation necessary to take advantage of the new Supreme Court precedent.[27]

## TESTING THE LAW

Registration was one thing; actually voting in the primary, quite another. The question then became: would Walden and company follow through with their plan to confront the forces of white supremacy and insist that the state comply with *Smith*? They did. As promised, on July 4, 1944, a group of Atlanta's Talented Tenth attempted to exercise the franchise in Georgia's traditionally all-white primary. The group of *Smith* testers had been selected from among the officers and members of the Fulton County Democratic Club. The testers included Clarence Bacote, AU professor of history, Eugene Martin, vice-president of the Atlanta Life Insurance Company, V. W. Hodges, assistant publisher of the *Daily World*, and Walden, the mainstay.[28]

The act of testing the law demanded tremendous bravery. When rumors spread that Walden and other blacks would attempt to vote in the July primary, white supremacists, including the former governor of Georgia, Eugene

Talmadge, threatened violence. Talmadge warned that "blood would run through the streets of Atlanta" if Walden and the others went through with their plans. The testers stood firm.

Media from across the state and nation watched as Walden, Bacote, Martin, and Hodges made their historic attempt to vote. Whites "lined up on the[ir] porches," in apparent disbelief, as the four black men strode to the polling place and dared to violate the racial order. Perhaps owing to the presence of the media, the men entered the precinct without incident. Since the poll tax would not be declared unconstitutional for two decades, Walden and his comrades were first obliged to present their poll tax receipts to the precinct manager. The manager then checked the voting rolls to confirm whether the men were duly registered voters. It was a foregone conclusion that, as "colored" men, and by virtue of local custom and state law, their names were not, in fact, listed. Accordingly, the precinct manager informed the men that they could not vote. Walden, Bacote, Martin, Hodges, and several other designated *Smith* testers were turned away.[29]

Georgia had spoken loudly: *Smith v. Allwright* did not apply to it. The state's defiance was soon the subject of a petition by Walden and others to the U.S. Department of Justice to enforce *Smith* in Georgia and other southern states. Later, Harry S. Strozier, a white liberal attorney from Macon, and Arthur D. Shores, a black lawyer from Birmingham, Alabama, with the help of LDF's Thurgood Marshall, filed a lawsuit challenging the Democratic Party's refusal to allow blacks to vote in the July 1944 primary. Rev. Primus E. King, a resident of Columbus, Georgia, headed the list of plaintiffs in this case, *Chapman v. King*. King, like Walden and the others in Atlanta, had been turned away by the precinct manager during the July primary despite being qualified to vote.[30]

The plaintiffs in *King* won a resounding victory in the federal district court. The judge found *Smith* controlling. The court then held that excluding Primus King from the Democratic Party primary constituted state action in violation of his rights under the Fourteenth, Fifteenth, and Seventeenth Amendments to the Constitution. As the case wound its way through the federal appellate courts, Walden sought to capitalize on the district court victory.[31]

## IMPLEMENTING THE LAW

Walden set out to realize *Smith*'s promise in a signal 1946 election. In January and February 1946, the congressman for the Fifth Congressional District of Georgia announced that he would vacate his seat in the middle of the term.

Eighteen candidates vied to win the seat in a February special election. Walden worked to demonstrate how instrumental blacks could now be by uniting African-American voters around a single candidate. The candidate of choice was Helen Douglas Mankin, a five-term Georgia state legislator and New Dealer. Mankin actively campaigned for the black vote, albeit out of the white public's eye, while her main opponent ignored the African-American community and its interests.[32]

Walden, playing party boss at the Wheat Street Baptist Church on the eve of the election, addressed a full house. His words to the assembled congregation were few, but clear and compelling. "Vote for the woman," he said. John Wesley Dobbs, Atlanta's most prominent black Republican, seconded Walden's endorsement. Word of the endorsement passed along the grapevine to the members of the black community who did not attend the meeting. On election day, African Americans voted in record numbers—a solid racial bloc. On election night, the votes in Precinct 3B, the largest black precinct in Atlanta, and the last to have its returns collected, determined the winner of the race. Walden was precinct manager, and his precinct secured "the woman's" victory. Newspaper and radio reporters covering the unfolding events reported that Mankin won 936 of the 1,038 votes cast in 3B.[33]

The nation took notice. African Americans had provided the margin of victory in the election of Georgia's first female member of Congress, and it was big news. "The Negro vote did it," said *Time*.[34]

Just two months after Walden helped to assure Mankin's victory, the Supreme Court inspired more hope in African-American leaders that the focus on voting rights would prove to be a winning strategy. On April 1, 1946, the Court let stand a decision by the U.S. Court of Appeals for the Fifth Circuit in the *King* case striking down Georgia's white primary. The Democratic Party operatives who had lost in the appellate court had asked the justices to consider their appeal. But the Court had declined to review the Fifth Circuit's unequivocal decision. The Fifth Circuit concluded that the state had, in effect, unconstitutionally excluded Primus King and other qualified black voters solely on account of their race.[35]

Following the victory in *Chapman v. King*, black leaders in Atlanta sought to reassure the white moderates with whom they hoped to form a coalition. But in doing so, their rhetoric sounded an elitist note. A. T. Walden declared that those African Americans who became registered voters would be the best blacks, folks intent on advancing the common good. "Georgia," he stated, "has absolutely nothing to fear from Negroes who are sufficiently interested in their state to qualify and vote. They are just as solicitous for the welfare of Georgia as are other citizens and they only desire the opportunity to make their contribution toward good government." Similarly, Rufus Clement noted that "qualified" blacks would only augment the ranks of the "intelligent electorate" who should participate in the affairs of state." These black elites were prepared to prove the race worthy of the vote.[36]

## THE PROMISE AND PERILS OF VICTORY

Seeking to build on the momentum created by *Smith* and *Chapman*, Walden, Dobbs, and others continued their drive to increase African-American participation in formal politics. Walden supported the formation of the All Citizens Registration Committee, a bipartisan group established in 1946, in cooperation with the Atlanta NAACP chapter. With the financial support of black businesses, including the Atlanta Life Insurance Company and Citizens Trust Bank, and the political backing of Walden and prominent ministers and other leaders, the All Citizens Registration Committee helped to dramatically increase registration in Fulton County (of which Atlanta is the county seat). A block-by-block registration effort by the committee yielded 21,244 registered voters in the months following the Fifth Circuit's decision in *Chapman*. Previously, there had been only 6,876 black voters in the same area.[37] (Table 2.1 in the appendix documents the dramatic increase in Atlanta's black electorate during this period.)

The increasing numbers of black registrants in Atlanta tracked a larger pattern across the South. These changes were tied to court decisions such as *Smith*, as well as to the demographic, economic, and social developments accompanying World War II. Only 3 percent of African Americans in the South were registered voters in 1940. By 1952, 20 percent of blacks had gained a place on the voter registration rolls.[38]

The surge in registered African-American voters in Atlanta after *Smith* and *Chapman* was impressive, but did not last. The dramatic success in recruiting new voters leveled off quickly after the initial rush of new registrants. Between 1946 and 1958, the number of black voters increased by a mere 6,188 registrants, from 21,244 to 27,432. New black registrants slowed to a trickle during the late fifties.

That black voter registration plateaued might seem strange at first blush. *Brown v. Board of Education*, the school desegregation case, was decided in 1954, and the Montgomery bus boycott, a defining moment in the burgeoning civil rights movement, began in 1955. These developments seemed likely to inspire further black political participation. Moreover, by the 1950s, the type of violence and intimidation that would keep blacks in the Mississippi Delta away from the polls into the mid-1960s did not seem to be the key factor in keeping blacks in Atlanta from registering to vote.[39]

What, then, explained the slowdown in black voter registration rates in Atlanta? A. T. Walden and national civil rights leaders repeatedly cited voter complacency as the major problem underlying the downturn. They decried the presumed lack of interest shown by southern blacks in exercising their hard-won right to vote. *Smith v. Allwright* had not "release[d] an avalanche" of black voting power, noted NAACP head Roy Wilkins. "[T]he Negro voter's fate is in his own hand," Wilkins chided.[40]

But "monumental" levels of apathy were to be found in the population as a whole, among whites and others who were eligible to vote but did not. If anything, blacks conformed to the norm.[41]

Moreover, black leaders had more work to do to energize voters. Despite their years of activism and the critical legal victories they had achieved, many African Americans simply had not embraced electoral politics as the weapon of choice in the battle against racial injustice. Voting rights activists in Atlanta assumed that the breakthrough decision in *Smith* would inspire interest in voting. They underestimated how much more work had to be done to cultivate mass black participation in politics. Walden already had done a great deal on the local level to promote black politics. Yet, his outreach efforts extended primarily to those whom he viewed as the "better class" of blacks.[42]

The relatively modest numbers of new registrants during this period are one measure of the effectiveness of the pragmatists' political strategy; what those who *did* register were able to accomplish with their political power is another. Between 1946 and 1958, blacks constituted about 25 percent of Atlanta's total voting population, a sizable figure, no doubt. Statewide, blacks made up 20 percent of voters in 1947 and 26 percent by 1958. But were these numbers enough, and were the voters sufficiently unified to constitute the voting bloc about which A. T. Walden and John Wesley Dobbs dreamed? At the state level, the answer to that question was clearly no. In Atlanta, the answer to the question was more complex.[43]

It was clear that African Americans were not yet a dominant electoral force in state politics in the fall of 1946. Helen Mankin lost her seat in Congress to James C. Davis, a former Klansman. Mankin went down to defeat, despite winning overwhelmingly among African Americans and in Fulton County. The county-unit system—which ensured rural domination of state elections— undermined Mankin and the coalition of blacks and moderate whites who supported her. Under this system, the overall number of popular votes won by a candidate did not necessarily determine the winner of statewide elections in Georgia, including campaigns for governor, the state legislature, U.S. senator, and U.S. congressperson (if the Democratic Party so stipulated). Instead, the Democratic Party awarded votes on a county-by-county basis. In effect, the county-unit system weighted votes so that the more rural and racially regressive areas had substantially more electoral power than urban ones. Political scientist V. O. Key called it the "rule of the rustics." The county-unit system impeded the ability of a statewide black voting bloc to exert much power.[44]

Two gubernatorial elections, in 1946 and 1948, also demonstrated that while the specter of black voting excited white supremacists, African-American electoral power remained minimal and racially repressive policies of every stripe remained in place. In 1946, Eugene Talmadge won the Democratic primary (and thus the election) by relying on the vilest racial demagoguery. Talmadge campaigned on a single-issue platform—keeping blacks in their place by denying them the vote. The 1946 election was marred by fraud committed by Talmadge's operatives, who purged black votes in numerous counties. Talmadge's victory was a grave defeat for the black leadership, which had been hopeful that the Supreme Court's decision in *Smith v. Allwright* would bring about change. After being declared the winner, Talmadge publicly declared that he "had to win for the good of the South and the nation" and vowed that "[n]o Negro will vote in Georgia for the next four years." The new Talmadge administration promised to beat back African-American progress. Morehouse College president Benjamin Mays, a minister and a theologian, made a plea. He called for the governor's inauguration day to be a "day of prayer" in which supplicants would ask God to soften Talmadge's hatred for blacks.[45]

The 1948 gubernatorial contest was a special election held because Eugene Talmadge died before he could take office in 1947, perhaps fortifying some African-Americans' belief in the power of prayer. Herman Talmadge, son of Eugene and heir to his father's racial ideology, sought to succeed his father in the governor's mansion and ran in the Democratic primary. His opponent was Melvin E. Thompson, a school superintendent. Herman Talmadge's campaign mirrored his father's. After the All Citizens Registration Committee's successful voter registration efforts and the *Chapman* decision, Talmadge whipped up white support by harping on A. T. Walden's supposed political influence with Thompson. Talmadge charged that Thompson had promised blacks that he would end the county-unit system, without which, he said, "that bloc voting crowd would meet in A. T. Walden's office on Auburn Avenue and pick you a governor in about five minutes."[46]

True enough, Walden was firmly opposed to Herman Talmadge's election, saying it was "vital" that "decent white voters along with Negroes rid Georgia politics of race-baiting." Under the auspices of the Georgia Association of Citizens Democratic Clubs and the Fulton County Democratic Club, Walden and Scott sponsored mass meetings throughout Georgia that featured information about candidates and the use of voting machines in a bid to defeat Talmadge. Walden admonished voters to "[l]et nothing except death keep you from the polls." But Talmadge's race-baiting carried the day. With African Americans voting one hundred to one for Thompson, Talmadge *lost* the overall popular vote. Yet he *won* the 1948 election in a landslide, measured in county-unit terms, on the strength of the vote in the rural counties.[47]

On the local level, meanwhile, black voter influence was much more significant. The organizational prowess of A. T. Walden and John Wesley Dobbs was key. In July 1949, Walden, a Democrat, and Dobbs, his Republican rival, cofounded the nonpartisan Atlanta Negro Voters League (ANVL). The members of ANVL were free to vote as they wished in national elections but were expected to unite around the candidate deemed best for the African-American community in local and state elections. After interviewing candidates, Dobbs and Walden announced ANVL's endorsements. In this way, Walden and Dobbs were said to be able to "deliver" twenty-five thousand votes to their preferred candidates.[48]

The best example of ANVL's power came just four months after ANVL's formation, when William Hartsfield sought reelection to a fourth term as mayor of Atlanta. Hartsfield, who earlier had told African Americans who lobbied for the hiring of black policemen and physical improvements to black neighborhoods to "come back to see me when you have 10,000 votes," now had to contend with ANVL and its twenty-five thousand votes. By election day in 1949, black voters constituted over 27 percent of Atlanta's total electorate. ANVL's demands to Hartsfield and his main opponent, Charlie Brown, the Fulton County commissioner, were clear. The league insisted on African-American firemen and policemen, more parks and playgrounds in black neighborhoods, public housing for low-income blacks, and tracts on which working- and middle-class black families could build homes. The two men vied for ANVL's endorsement. However, Hartsfield, in meetings with ANVL officials, emphasized that he had a proven track record of aiding Atlanta's black community; he promised to support ANVL's list of demands in the future if reelected. Ultimately, ANVL endorsed Hartsfield, helping to elect him to a fourth term as mayor.[49]

African Americans, together with upper-middle-class white voters—the same business and civic elites whom Walden hoped to influence in forming

ANVL—provided Hartsfield's slim margin of victory. Hartsfield acknowledged the importance of black voters to his win. In a statement to the *Atlanta Daily World*, Hartsfield "extend[ed] [his] thanks to the officers and members of the Atlanta Negro Voters' League and to all colored people who supported me in this campaign. I hope all of our citizens will now close ranks and march forward to a greater Atlanta." Overall, all but two of the candidates whom ANVL endorsed in the election prevailed.[50]

Walden was pleased not only with the outcome of the election but also with what he saw as its larger meaning for race relations in Atlanta. He thought that Hartsfield and Brown's open courting of the African-American vote represented a turning point. Walden expressed his views in a letter to Hartsfield. "Regardless of the outcome of the election, it is felt that this gesture of interest and good will has made a distinct contribution toward mutual understanding in the interest of better and more effective government," he wrote. Articles in the *Atlanta Daily World* recounted the "smiles of gratification and civic pride" of African Americans who had cast votes, unfettered by racial shackles, for the "first time in [the] modern history of Atlanta." Walden and other leaders believed that the 1949 election had launched a new "biracial coalition" whose members would work to resolve the race problem in Atlanta.[51]

In the years to come, African-American voters helped to secure other important electoral victories within the city of Atlanta. Rufus Clement's election in 1953 as the first black member of the Atlanta Board of Education was a landmark of African Americans' electoral influence. Clement's victory marked the first time that an African American had been elected to public office in Atlanta since 1870. Clement's margin of victory was large; he carried a supermajority of precincts and garnered 22,259 votes to 13,936 for his white opponent. Twelve thousand whites voted for Clement. In the very same election that put Dr. Clement on the school board, the voters elected A. T. Walden and Dr. Miles G. Amos to the City Democratic Executive Committee. In 1957 Clement was reelected to the Board of Education. Bill Hartsfield was reelected as mayor, again with African-American support. Clement, who prevailed against an opponent touting white supremacy, interpreted his victory as a statement that "race relations here [in Atlanta] remain good" and that "there is no tension between the two [racial] groups."[52]

In statewide races, however, African-American voters continued to face profound obstacles. Marvin Griffin, an avowed racist and opponent of school desegregation, was elected governor in 1954, despite overwhelming black support for his opponent. Herman Talmadge was elected to the U.S. Senate in 1956, joining Richard B. Russell, a former Klansman.[53]

## HOW DO THE VOICELESS ATTAIN POWER?

*Smith v. Allwright* traditionally has been seen as a critical moment in the early phase of the struggle for black political power in the South. A. T. Walden's struggle for political power in Atlanta certainly capitalized on *Smith*, but the Supreme Court victory over the white primary constituted just one element of a long and carefully planned strategy for citizenship. That strategy rested not primarily on court action, but on the personal resolve and imagination of local people. First and foremost, Walden and fellow activists had a clear vision of citizenship, one based on the expectation that political participation—including but not limited to exercise of the franchise—would yield specific advances for a mobilized and cohesive black community. It also involved community- and institution-building. Walden—one of the most effective organizers of black voting in modern times—founded (or cofounded) several state and local organizations during the course of this effort. With the Democratic Party closed to blacks, Walden formed these institutions out of necessity; the establishment of these autonomous institutions, where persuasion and deal-making could occur, went hand in hand with the effort to create a cohesive black power base and leverage it for advantage from white decisionmakers. Walden also led citizenship education groups whose purpose was to build and solidify a black political base. All of these efforts and initiatives occurred outside of the New York offices of LDF, but greatly complemented the attorneys' litigation campaign against the white primary. The national civil rights bar's campaign could not have begun to advance its goal of increasing black political power were it not for such on-the-ground ingenuity and vitality.

A. T. Walden's political activism, launched in concert with activists in black colleges and black civic and social groups, produced some impressive results. Even before the victory in *Smith v. Allwright*, blacks in Atlanta managed to bring pressure to bear on municipal government. A small group of black professionals, including Walden, the black college presidents, and a few entrepreneurs, wielded influence with the white power structure. Walden's magnificent show of bravery as a *Smith* tester marked him as a race rebel. His leadership ensured his place at the negotiating table, first among equals in the small group of blacks acceptable as interracial diplomats. Moreover, after the white primary's fall, the size of the black electorate expanded exponentially, and an African-American voting bloc developed that had significantly more influence in electoral politics than ever before.

But apportionment rules and other forms of white resistance kept black influence in statewide elections to a minimum. The major electoral victories for African Americans occurred in the realm of local politics and were limited to just a few posts in city government. Moreover, after an initial spike of participation after *Smith*, black voter participation in elections leveled off. The decline pointed to two weaknesses in political strategy.

First, politics did not uniformly appeal to community members, and the leadership class made no particular effort to galvanize the entire citizenry. Outreach to the working class was limited or nonexistent. From the viewpoint of Atlanta's black elite, many blacks were not yet ready to enter the respectable world of electoral participation.

Second and related, Walden's strategy did not account for vestiges of disfranchisement and discrimination. His conception of citizenship rested on an ideal of democracy, when, in fact, defects riddled the system. He and national NAACP officials complained about political "apathy" among people long told that voting was the prerogative of whites only. Even after *Smith v. Allwright*, Walden and other black elites still distinguished "worthy" from "unworthy" classes of black voters. Such elitism may well have dampened black enthusiasm for the political process and played a part in so-called voter apathy. Beyond that, numerous factors limited black voters' ability to attain meaningful representation and reforms consistent with their interests. Thus, favorable municipal election results said little about whether the black elites' strategy of focusing on voting rights succeeded as a substantive matter. That African Americans, as a bloc, could ensure Mayor Hartfield's reelection and send Clement to the school board was one thing. Whether the election of these representatives and the reality that blacks now had an electoral voice substantially furthered the agendas of African-American leaders in areas of public policy such as education, employment, housing, health care, public accommodations, and transportation requires deeper analysis.

I next turn my attention from the voting booth to the struggle for equality in the other substantive areas of public policy. I consider how the certitude of Walden and other leaders that the ballot was a "cheaper" route to full citizenship than the courts, coupled with their faith in interracial diplomacy, influenced their goals and tactics, and to what ends. In short, I examine how pragmatism looked and what it yielded in practice. Rufus Clement's optimistic view and John Wesley Dobbs's wishful thinking notwithstanding, the doors of opportunity did not necessarily open wide for blacks because of their newfound electoral prowess. For as Gunnar Myrdal, the Swedish sociologist, observed, "Negroes are grossly discriminated against in what they get from politics." Voting, participating meaningfully in the political process, and reaping significant benefits from such participation turned out to be three separate and distinct enterprises.[54]

CHAPTER 3

# Housing Markets, Black and White

*Negotiating the Postwar Housing Crisis, 1944–1959*

Whether or not an area is in the white market or Negro market is based on…the decision of property owners, buyers, sellers, exercising their constitutional rights. (1959)

Robert Stuart

[C]ertain agreements were made voluntarily, all on a high basis, nobody's feelings were hurt, in which the Negro citizen agreed to stay out of certain sections that were tension areas. (1959)

William B. Hartsfield

The presiding officer at a 1959 hearing in Atlanta convened by the U.S. Civil Rights Commission cited a grim statistic. African Americans made up more than a third of Atlanta's population, but were "compressed" into less than one-sixth of the city's developed residential areas.[1] Many blacks lived in overcrowded, dilapidated homes, amid squalid conditions.[2] Rundown black neighborhoods dotted the city's landscape, yet received little notice from the white power structure.[3]

Indeed, Atlanta's mayor, William Hartsfield—the reputed ally of the city's black leadership—extolled residential segregation. The city actively promoted racially separate living areas, he explained at the hearing, in order to preserve social harmony and goodwill. "[W]e must live with public opinion," Hartsfield said, and "that is the overwhelming public opinion in the South." Any move toward racially integrated neighborhoods would be counterproductive. Segregation, the glue that held the city together, must stand. The director of Atlanta's Metropolitan Planning Commission (MPC) claimed that separation not only furthered the public interest but also advanced the imperatives of the market. The market preferred the certainty of segregation to the uncertainty of "racial transition" in residential areas. "Race," he said, "has a way of confusing the housing market picture." It "hurts both Negroes and whites" to inject the specter of racial mixing into the market—a factor that caused white "panic."[4]

The president of the Atlanta Real Estate Board agreed that blacks "voluntarily" accepted residential segregation, just as whites did. Given the opposition to racial mixing, the city endorsed both public policies and private agreements that preserved the racial integrity of neighborhoods. Several African-American witnesses confirmed that they did not challenge residential segregation.[5]

But Atlanta's black leaders had not exactly "accepted" Jim Crow housing. They had resigned themselves to it. Black elites had worked to increase the amount of living space allotted to blacks through negotiation with the white power structure. From the perspective of local black leaders, pragmatism in the housing context made sense. It did not make sense, however, to leaders of the national NAACP and LDF. Years earlier, the national NAACP had resolved: "Enforced residential segregation and restriction of racial minorities are at the core of the whole racial segregation issue in all phases of American life." Lawyers at the LDF had litigated cases to tear down the wall of separation between the black and white markets for years. Local and national priorities were in stark conflict.[6]

## THE SOCIOLEGAL CONTEXT FOR PRAGMATISM

Residential segregation was the norm in Atlanta both before and after *Buchanan v. Warley*, the NAACP's earliest legal victory against discrimination in housing. In that 1917 case, the U.S. Supreme Court struck down a Louisville ordinance mandating neighborhood segregation under the Fourteenth Amendment.[7]

Prior to *Buchanan*, Atlanta had passed numerous ordinances establishing residential segregation. These laws included a 1913 provision that mandated racially separate neighborhoods. One section of the law stated that an occupant of a house in a mixed block could object to a person of another color moving in next door. Even during this period , when Southern judges scarcely looked favorably upon discrimination claims, the Georgia Supreme Court struck down such naked efforts to perpetuate residential segregation.[8]

*Buchanan* did not, however, deter Atlanta officials. The city disregarded the decision. Atlanta's 1924 code included ordinances establishing black-only and white-only residential districts and requiring building inspectors and zoning boards to enforce neighborhood segregation. Likewise, the city's first municipal zoning plan, developed in the early 1920s, defined residential districts by race. A state constitutional amendment that permitted segregated zoning passed in 1928.[9]

Spatial separation became an increasingly important element of white social control of African Americans beginning in the interwar period and continuing thereafter. Black migrants flowed into the city from rural areas. Atlanta's black population doubled during the period 1890–1920; it nearly doubled again between 1920 and 1950. Whites' insistence on regulating African-American movement within the city—whether through law, policy, custom, or more direct forms of coercion such as violence—increased with the growth of the black population.[10]

The areas designated for African-American living space were in the center of the city and in areas east and west of downtown. W. E. B. Du Bois memorably described black Atlantans' residential pattern: African Americans were "stretched like a great dumbbell across the city, with one great center in the east and a smaller one in the west, connected by a narrow belt." Poor and working-class blacks lived in overcrowded, dilapidated slums in undesirable places near cemeteries, industrial plants, floodplains, and railroad lines. Professional blacks, including doctors, businessmen, lawyers, dentists, and civil servants, lived in much higher quality housing, typically on the opposite side of town. The elite clustered east of downtown, near the black business district, in the city's fourth ward, which contained the fashionable addresses of the middle class, as well as some substandard dwellings for the poor. A few blacks lived in other sections of the metropolitan area. In some areas, residential segregation did not pervade every neighborhood; some streets had a "checkerboard appearance," while in others, vacant lots, cemeteries, parks, highways, or other barriers separated black and white homes. Segregation in the city only increased over time.[11]

The black housing shortage became a full-fledged crisis after World War II for a number of reasons. Slum clearance, urban renewal, and highway expansion efforts, commissioned by white business and civic leaders to provide space for new commercial developments and to revitalize the central business district, displaced thousands of African Americans.[12] In addition, thirty-eight thousand African Americans migrated to Atlanta between 1950 and 1960; with these additions, blacks now constituted more than 38 percent of the city's overall population. The living space allotted to blacks—19 of 110 census tracts, or about 10 percent of the city's land—was far too small to accommodate the combination of migrants, those displaced by economic development, returning veterans, and Atlanta's existing black population. In addition to being inadequate in number, the black housing stock tended to be old, rundown, and overpriced. Fifty-seven percent of black housing units, or 23,124 of 40,426 dwellings, lacked bathing facilities. Forty-three percent lacked toilets, and 28 percent needed major repairs.[13]

With nowhere else to go, African Americans sought to move into areas designated for whites or into vacant, undeveloped lands. These attempts were met by a united front of white resistance. The Klan and individual white terrorists used violence to warn blacks against moving into white areas. Urban planners used zoning policies, placement of highways and railroad tracks, and barriers such as cemeteries and parks to contain the black population. White homeowners relied on racially restrictive covenants to prevent the transfer of property in white areas to blacks seeking to buy or rent. And real estate agents and banks used discriminatory lending, block busting, and assorted other practices to prevent black expansion into neighborhoods not designated for black residential use.[14]

## THE RISE OF BIRACIAL NEGOTIATION IN THE HOUSING SPHERE

Black elites entered this volatile environment armed with their emergent political power in city politics and their skills as interracial diplomats. Collectively, they negotiated with the city fathers for housing tracts for blacks, including vacant lands for new construction, for existing housing that could be transitioned from white to black occupancy, and for the construction of low-income public housing projects.[15]

The elites' approach to the housing shortage was intriguingly limited. They pushed for black expansion into white or undeveloped areas in the city of Atlanta and Fulton County, but they worked within customary racial boundaries in doing so. In other words, they pressed for new black enclaves but not for racially integrated residential areas. In fact, they sought expansion of black housing opportunities in precisely those areas where white business and political leaders wanted blacks to be sequestered. The black elites persisted in using this limited approach to expanding the black housing stock even as the postwar racial climate became more favorable to black demands. They also persisted in relying on biracial negotiation strategies despite the national NAACP's legal campaign against housing segregation, which culminated in *Shelley v. Kraemer*, the 1948 Supreme Court decision barring judicial enforcement of racially restrictive covenants between private parties.[16]

The initial agreement among black leaders about how to address the housing crisis was reflected in a 1947 measure approved by an umbrella group called the Atlanta Housing Council. The council consisted of representatives of the Atlanta Urban League, the Atlanta Life Insurance Company, the Trust Company

Bank, the Empire Real Estate Board, an organization of black realtors, Blayton's Accounting Company, and other black commercial interests. The council endorsed not a challenge to segregated housing but the expansion of areas where segregated housing would be available to blacks. The council justified its desire to increase black housing opportunities in these areas through a report it distributed to white and black business and civic leaders. The council "recognized that the [proposed] areas cannot legally be designated as areas for expansion of Negro housing." But it reasoned that new housing in segregated areas "properly guided for accomplishment by private enterprise" should be endorsed as the best option for preserving social stability and avoiding economic and racial conflict.[17]

The council made its 1947 decision in response to emergency conditions. At the time, forty-five hundred dwellings were needed to meet blacks' immediate housing needs. The editorial page of the *Atlanta Daily World*, a prominent black daily newspaper, readily endorsed the decision. "For a very large number of our people the issue now is that of finding any place at all to live, with or without white neighbors." By 1949, six hundred new homes in four subdivisions, including Fair Haven, Bennett, Simpson Heights, and Port Drive-Leathers Circle, had been built under the council's auspices—satisfying a fraction of the postwar demand for black housing.[18]

Notwithstanding the severity of the black housing crisis during this period, white resistance thwarted numerous expansion efforts—even within the segregated framework. In 1949, for example, a group of black veterans seeking to develop land for black use followed the pattern established during the 1947 crisis. In a petition to the Fulton County Commissioners of Roads and Revenues, the veterans sought to "secure...a suitable tract to develop a subdivision providing homes for Negro Occupancy." The appropriateness of this particular parcel of land for designation as a subdivision, to be known as the Urban Villa, turned on the fact that it would not disturb the color line. "This tract is most suitable for development," the veterans wrote in their petition to the commissioners, "because it is surrounded on three boundaries by areas presently owned and/or occupied by Negroes." Thus, the space would "permit...a logical, practical, and economically sound development of the Metropolitan area."A. E. Fuller, the Fulton County manager, responded to the petition by noting official awareness of the need for "better housing conditions" for blacks and promising that the commission would consider the proposal carefully.[19]

White resistance soon put a hold on the project, however. In a follow-up letter to Fuller, S. S. Robinson, an attorney for Urban Villa Inc., beseeched the commissioners not to reject the petition on the basis of a backlash within the white community over the apparent existence of a restrictive covenant on the properties. The Grove Park Civic Club had sold the land to Fulton County with the "apparent condition that it never be sold to Colored People," and Robinson feared that "public consideration" of the project would be unfavorably influenced by the covenant. In arguing that the commissioners should continue to seriously entertain the project, Robinson appealed to the city's commitment to good government. Instead of deferring to segregationist fears of black encroachment, Robinson wrote, the commissioners should feel obligated to "consider…the interests of all parties before entering upon any community development." Thus far, African-American leaders had been shut out from the development process, he claimed, despite their large stake in attaining more living space for black citizens. "[N]o Negro or any friend of the Negro was privileged to sit at the conference planning table," Robinson argued, with the consequence that the "welfare of the Colored man was purposefully ignored." Robinson was quite literally asking for a seat at the table, for a chance to have a voice in the power structure.[20]

He then attempted to persuade the administrators that it was their professional obligation, not to mention in the interests of the white majority, to attend to the black urban crisis. Even as Robinson vowed that he did not mean to "condemn the board," his language was at its strongest and most accusatory on this point. He argued that it was "criminal" for planners to ignore the black plight, and continued,

> It is refreshing to see the dozens of new White communities but is pathetic and outrageous to see the squalor and ghettoes in which the great masses of Negroes must live and to add insult to misery by being chided that their interests are being cared for. Vast residential areas in which Negroes are living are being condemned to make parks and playgrounds for white people[,] while colored people are living in slums[,] and other communities are unfriendly to them. In still other vast[,] fashionable Negro residential areas[,] the Board of Commissioners, in the absence of consideration of the parties actually concerned, is considering…building multiple low cost rental housing and the creation of a business center in their midst. [T]he whole population of Negroes [is] aware of the one sided approach of the Board in solving the problems of the community.…[A] solid white group is totally incompetent to handle our welfare.

The exchange between Robinson and city planners over the Urban Villa project illustrated the combination of factors that black leaders faced in their efforts to address the housing crisis. As was true throughout this period, some white administrators expressed concern, but followed with decisions that maintained the status quo in the face of vocal white public opposition to black expansion.

Black leaders sought to address the housing crisis through mediation, interracial diplomacy, and the language of political inclusion. Litigation or the rhetoric of civil rights were not their tools of choice. Thus, even though Robinson's language was tough, he never referred to state and federal legal authorities that might have rendered the Urban Villa's restrictive covenant null and void. However, the attorney's indirect approach was not successful. Ultimately, the veterans lost the battle over the Urban Villa project.[21]

## Mutual Development Amid Crisis

African-American elites achieved their greatest housing successes when they collaborated with white business and civic leaders. In 1952 the West Side Mutual Development Committee (WSMDC), a biracial organization, was formed in order to locate "suitable" areas for black expansion. The WSMDC came into existence at the behest of Mayor Hartsfield, who for years had guided the Atlanta Housing Council's expansion efforts behind the scenes. Like the council, the WSMDC facilitated the development of areas for black expansion on a segregated basis. Robert Thompson of the Atlanta Urban League explained that the "committee met, made agreements, then the real estate interests, white and black... attempted to implement their agreement[s]." The committee members worked out agreements regarding where black/white boundary lines were to be drawn.[22]

In large part, the WSMDC was a community relations organization whose mission was to "put out fires." Part of its purpose was to assess citizen support for particular expansion plans and then manage public reactions to those plans and alternatives. For example, the WSMDC mailed surveys to residents of certain areas of the city "in order to determine upon a course of action that will establish your block as either a white or a Negro real estate market." The WSMDC then organized meetings during which residents could discuss projects under consideration or in development. On many occasions, the WSMDC's role was to persuade residents to accept developers' plans by convincing them, for example, that a partition such as a road or other barrier was sufficient to protect white areas from black encroachment. By acting as a sounding board for white resistance and a vehicle for channeling whites' fears in nonviolent directions, the WSMDC played a vital role in maintaining residential segregation as the city, with the blessing of black leaders, took halting steps to address the black housing shortage.[23]

The WSMDC was not the only organization set up as an acceptable conduit for mediating the black housing crisis. African-American collaboration with the

MPC also reflected the political and legal environment in which black elites operated and the costs and benefits of their consensus-based strategy. The Georgia General Assembly established the MPC, a nominally private group, in 1947; it was to be an advisory agency on issues of community development and planning. Like the WSMDC, the MPC was created to increase areas available for black occupancy, while sustaining social equanimity—that is, segregation.[24]

In 1952 the MPC announced its first major development plan, described in a report called *Up Ahead*. The report proposed several areas for black expansion. The city fathers hoped that the commission's planning process would keep white terrorist responses to the housing crisis in check. During the 1950s, whites burned, firebombed, and fired weapons into homes recently purchased by blacks in white areas or transitional neighborhoods. This kind of terroristic violence had its intended effect; many blacks decided to resell homes they had purchased in transitional areas to whites and others were scared away from seeking to encroach into "unsuitable" areas. In February of 1956, for instance, Jewell Stewart Jr., an African-American man who had moved into a white neighborhood on a Saturday morning, told an officer investigating an explosion in his front yard that he would sell his house and move "first thing Monday morning." The group of 500 to 700 "neighbors" who gathered at the scene to protest the sale of homes in the area to blacks no doubt facilitated Stewart's decision-making process. The next month, March 1956, an African-American family of five literally was "blown out of bed," but miraculously escaped injury, when a dynamite blast at four in the morning heavily damaged the home they had recently purchased in a white area. The house was knocked off its foundation. Again, white onlookers crowded around as the black family left the neighborhood.[25]

The white observers on the scenes of these crimes may have been members of organized efforts to beat back black residential expansion. A number of white "civic clubs" bent on halting black occupancy or construction in transitional areas formed during the 1950s. These groups often created corporations to repurchase homes already sold to blacks or to buy all available houses on the market in an area to keep blacks from arriving. Whites in the Grove Park–Center Hill area, which was adjacent to the largest black community in the city, organized a corporation that bought twenty-five to thirty houses near Hightower and Simpson Roads to block black development.[26]

Whites even filed lawsuits to prevent black expansion, notwithstanding the Supreme Court's pronouncements in *Buchanan v. Warley* and *Shelley v. Kraemer*. Whites in the Grove Park–Center Hill area sought an injunction to prevent the construction of an apartment project for blacks during the 1950s; they won in Atlanta Superior Court, only to have the injunction voided by the Georgia Supreme Court. City fathers hoped that the MPC's plan for controlled expansion and containment of black mobility would appease such white resistance, including those bent on using violence to thwart the movement of blacks into white neighborhoods.[27]

The MPC managed black expansion in part by coordinating efforts between and among white homeowners, developers, and real estate agents and African-American real estate agents, contractors, banks, insurance companies, and civic leaders. The commission coordinated the construction of new, private homes and apartments for blacks in six areas on the south and west sides of the city; the transition of existing housing in areas throughout the city from white to black occupancy; and the development of new low-income public housing projects for blacks. The activities of the MPC were supported by the "forces of private enterprise, the home builders, land developers, home improvement and home financing businesses, [and] the building material suppliers," as well as 'the official family' of city and county departments, and neighborhood civic groups."[28]

That the MPC was supported by "powerful community resources managed by experienced executives and backed by the financial strength of the community" was confirmed by a fifty-one-person roster of those involved in its "neighborhood improvement program." The list included Mayor Hartsfield, Ralph McGill, editor of the *Atlanta Constitution*, and M. B. Satterfield, executive director of the Atlanta Housing Authority, together with officers of local title and realty companies and banks.[29]

Blacks were not officially members of the MPC, but, critically, African-American leaders worked informally with the organization and acceded to its practice of allowing black expansion on a segregated basis. Blacks influenced the MPC indirectly and directly, through collaboration with the WSMDC. Those most obviously involved in the MPC's activities were black brokerages, real estate agencies, and banks associated with the Empire Real Estate Board. Members of the Atlanta Urban League, in particular Grace Hamilton, the league's executive director, and A. T. Walden, president of the league's board of directors, also advanced the MPC's objectives. Hamilton and Walden spearheaded the Urban League's decision to act as an agent of the city and the MPC throughout the 1950s in expansion, slum clearance, and urban renewal efforts. Black elites' advisory role with the MPC represented the fulfillment, at least partially, of an ambition that they had been pursuing for years—what S. S. Robinson had called a "seat at the conference planning table."[30]

Yet, the black elites who advised the MPC worked within a very limited framework, as they well knew. Whites' objectives continued to dominate the development agenda, while black residents, especially poor ones, were allocated far too few areas for expansion to meet their needs. Consider, for example, the MPC's enthusiasm for urban renewal. The practice had an overwhelmingly negative impact on blacks, especially the poor and the working class, leading to the displacement of thousands of citizens. In the process of "renewing" urban neighborhoods, planners destroyed black neighborhoods without providing adequate numbers of replacement dwellings. During a five-year period in the late 1950s, 3,406 African-American families lost shelter as a result of urban renewal. Because of its widely known negative impact on the black community, the urban renewal process came to be known informally as "Negro removal." As Robert Weaver, then a fair housing expert and soon a U.S. cabinet secretary for urban affairs, explained in a 1955 article, slum clearance was only good policy if coupled with a large construction program of low-cost and middle-income housing. Where both of these components were absent, urban renewal was an unmitigated loss for low-income communities.[31]

The Urban League tried to blunt the impact of the renewal process by accepting money from the city to relocate "back-alley" dwellers—Hamilton's term for those homeless to begin with and those left homeless due to the demolition of their housing. However, neither the Urban League nor any of the other black organizations that advised the MPC challenged the city to replace as much housing as it destroyed.[32]

Nor did black leaders resist the basic limitation of the MPC's planning process—its policy of maintaining and perpetuating residential segregation. Segregation was the root cause of the housing crisis because it confined African Americans to so small a percentage of the city's land mass in the first place. The MPC, with the tacit approval of its black supporters, repeatedly reinforced the existing system of housing segregation and scarcity. The MPC's decision during the 1950s to end Willis Mill Road five blocks south of Gordon Road (now Martin Luther King Drive) so that it would be impossible to drive from Gordon into Cascade Heights, a white neighborhood, illustrated the point. That decision left one hundred acres of land undeveloped.[33]

Each time the MPC left land undeveloped in this manner or approved the creation of artificial barriers to cordon blacks off from whites, it artificially limited the land area available for black expansion. True enough, these barriers had utility if they were parks or access roads, rather than dead-end streets, walls, or vacant lots; but, typically, only whites benefited from such buffer zones and, in any event, their primary purpose was to control black mobility. Robert Thompson, the Atlanta Urban League's housing secretary during much of the shortage, later recounted that the organization did take a small step to register its discomfort over such racially biased planning policies. The league "issu[ed] a letter over the signature of the late [A. T.] Walden, who was chairman of the board at the time, saying that these areas [designated for black expansion in the MPC's 1952 report] are flexible and should not be considered as permanent areas."[34]

## THE NAACP, LDF, AND HOUSING POLICY

Walden's letter notwithstanding, the policies and practices of the Atlanta Housing Council, the WSMDC, and the MPC conflicted with the national NAACP's and LDF's ongoing legal efforts to challenge residential segregation. In 1948, the Supreme Court's decision in *Shelley v. Kraemer* established that judicial enforcement of racially restrictive covenants violated the federal equal protection clause. The *Shelley* Court did not rule that covenants between private parties barring sales to African Americans were themselves unconstitutional; in fact, it had held just the opposite in a 1926 case, *Corrigan v. Buckley*. However, its 1917 decision, *Buchanan v. Warley*, stood; in that case, the Court had ruled that it was unlawful for a municipality to bar blacks from certain residential areas. Together, *Shelley* and *Buchanan* suggested that state actors should refrain from advancing policies that produced residential segregation; only purely private discrimination remained unregulated by the Constitution.[35]

Thurgood Marshall called *Shelley* the "greatest blow to date...against the pattern of segregation existing within the United States." The decision would give "thousands of prospective home buyers...new courage and hope in the American form of government." The *New York Times* reported that civil rights groups throughout the country hailed the ruling as a "blow" against discrimination in housing. Advocacy organizations planned to cite the precedent in renewed efforts to inspire individuals and communities to protest exclusionary policies in courts of law. In Atlanta, A. T. Walden, a member of the national NAACP legal committee, called the decision a "milestone" that gave "flesh and substance to the Constitutional guarantee of equality under law" and a decision that "increased [his] faith that our courts will declare the law." The *Atlanta Daily World* predicted that *Shelley* portended the "end of restricted communities and ghettos and slums."[36]

Federal officials recognized *Shelley* as a landmark, as well. After *Shelley*, the Truman administration issued new directives meant to convey the message that the federal government should no longer condone racial discrimination. The Federal Housing Authority (FHA) and the Veterans Administration (VA) announced that they would no longer guarantee mortgage loans on properties carrying racially restrictive covenants after February 15, 1950. In addition, the FHA announced that eligibility for federal assistance would no longer be based on the racial composition of neighborhoods; the agency would make loans for housing on a nondiscriminatory basis. To be sure, the local officials in the Atlanta Housing Authority, who were responsible for implementing federal policies, did not necessarily follow the nondiscrimination orders of their Washington superiors.[37]

Nor could local authorities have been expected to subvert community norms in the absence of pressure from African Americans and their lawyers. That pressure was nonexistent in Atlanta during the 1940s and 1950s, despite the availability of causes of action, despite favorable court precedents, and despite the fact that housing was segregated mainly by custom, policy, and biracial practice, rather than by juridical or statutory law.[38]

Indeed, federal law and national NAACP policy seem to have been all but ignored by Atlanta's black decision-makers as they tackled the postwar housing crunch. Other lawyers throughout the country, in step with the NAACP's campaign, filed test cases challenging discrimination by public housing authorities. Walden did defend against suits in which white plaintiffs attempted to enforce restrictive covenants against his clients. But he and others avoided systematic and affirmative efforts to impede or uproot discrimination in housing, whether through law or politics. In 1949, for instance, Atlanta's black elites held meetings with FHA officials, realtors, and city and state officials to draw up plans for "all Negro subdivisions" in transitional areas. W. H. Aiken, the realtor who served as spokesperson for African Americans during the meeting, justified the plan by pointing out that building "Negro housing developments not too far from important white residential areas would prove of great help" to white families who employed blacks, especially domestic servants. Maids "would have ready access to the homes where they work, effecting a great saving of time," Aiken said in his statement.[39]

The Atlanta leaders persisted in their pragmatic approach to housing even as the national NAACP's commitment to rooting out residential segregation and housing discrimination, especially in the public sector, gained new momentum. The NAACP's housing docket grew during the 1950s, and it defined housing discrimination as a primary cause of African-American disadvantage. At its annual convention in St. Louis in 1953, the national body passed a resolution stating,

> Enforced residential segregation and restriction of racial minorities are at the core of the whole racial segregation issue in all phases of American life. The eradication of every vestige of racial segregation or racial restriction in housing that receives any form of public aid or support must be our prime goal. No federal subsidies, funds, credits or powers should be used to aid any housing, whether public or private, unless there is an assurance against any type of racial or religious discrimination or segregation in such housing. This applies to all public or private housing, slum clearance, and urban redevelopment that benefit from federal aid, whether loans, grants, subsidies, credits, loan-insurance or guaranty or other federal powers.

In 1957, at the NAACP's southeastern regional conference held in Atlanta, the national association called on its local branches to support the attack on racial bias practiced by mortgage lenders, real estate brokers, and public housing authorities. The national NAACP's position on housing discrimination was crystal clear: it left no room for compromises. Yet, in Atlanta, compromise not only was routine; it was the rule.[40]

While black leaders rejected litigation as a tactic for challenging housing segregation in Atlanta, blacks in other parts of Georgia forged ahead with the national NAACP's preferred course. One such lawsuit challenged segregation in public housing in nearby Savannah. In fact, A. T. Walden collaborated with the national NAACP lawyers on the case.[41]

On May 20, 1954, three days after the Supreme Court announced its decision in *Brown v. Board of Education*, Thurgood Marshall and Constance Baker Motley of the NAACP, with Walden's help as local counsel, brought a lawsuit against housing authority officials in Savannah and the federal Public Housing Administration, including Arthur Hanson, its Atlanta field office director. Eighteen African-American plaintiffs claimed that the authorities practiced discrimination in the application process for public housing and segregation in the placement of blacks approved for public housing. As a consequence, African Americans were barred from all but three of the public housing projects in Savannah. By their actions, the plaintiffs alleged, the local housing officials had violated the federal equal protection and due process clauses and several federal statues, including the Civil Rights Acts of 1866 and 1870 and the Housing Act of 1937. As amended, the Housing Act, the enabling legislation for the federal public housing program, required "equitable provision" of housing to families of "all races" based on the "volume and urgency of their respective needs."[42]

Completely disregarding the Housing Act and several relevant precedents, the trial court in the Savannah case, *Heyward v. Public Housing Administration*, dismissed the NAACP's suit on grounds that the facilities available to blacks and whites were equal. "Separate but equal is still the law of the land and controls this case," the court held. The Fifth Circuit Court of Appeals reversed and reinstated the plaintiffs' civil rights act claims. On remand, the trial court again dismissed the suit: seventeen plaintiffs had withdrawn from the case, and the one remaining plaintiff could not show to the court's satisfaction that she had ever formally applied to the housing authority or was refused her preferred placement. In a June 1958 opinion, the Fifth Circuit affirmed, noting, in dicta, that "[n]either the Fifth nor the Fourteenth Amendment operates positively to command integration of the races but only negatively to forbid governmentally enforced segregation." The LDF had attempted, albeit unsuccessfully, to undermine Jim Crow housing in Savannah, despite threats that "riots and disorder" would ensue if the courts ordered the city's public housing projects desegregated.[43]

Walden's participation in *Heyward* makes the fact that he and other Atlanta decision-makers declined to challenge residential segregation in Atlanta especially intriguing. On one theory, the Savannah case might have been Walden's initial foray into housing discrimination litigation—the opening salvo for housing lawsuits in Atlanta. Yet no sources suggest that this was so. The Atlanta Housing Authority continued to openly practice segregation into the late 1960s, and the first reported housing discrimination cases in Atlanta were not filed until the 1970s. So the question remains why black elites refused to address the housing crisis in Atlanta by frontally attacking the combination of federal, state, local, and private party policies that limited African Americans—including the middle class—to small parcels of segregated land.[44]

## THE CASE FOR PRAGMATISM

To understand why black leaders chose such a pragmatic path in response to the housing crisis and segregation, one needs to appreciate the roles played by violent white resistance to black expansion, discrimination in the housing market, self-interest, practical concerns, and the limited success of LDF's housing desegregation litigation. Some of the same factors existed in other parts of the country, and could, and sometimes did, constrain the broad-based legal attack on residential segregation elsewhere.

Violence or the threat of violence was a formidable deterrent for African Americans who sought housing in the postwar years. Some thirty racist bombings occurred in Atlanta in the two decades after World War II—more than in Birmingham over the same period. By agreeing to the conditions that white elites placed on black efforts to expand, including the continuation of segregated housing tracts, the black leadership surely acted out of concern for the safety of African Americans. At the same time, in yielding to these threats, black elites followed the lead of white businessmen and politicians, including Mayor Hartsfield, who were intent on suppressing public awareness about white terrorists who attacked black homeowners and renters.[45]

Other kinds of white defiance, while less extreme, were still extremely embarrassing to a city "too busy to hate." In neighborhoods such as Southwest Kirkwood and Adair Park, for example, whites posted signs reading "This is a White Area." Black efforts to push back against residential segregation would have been followed by retribution from white supremacists, thus undermining

Atlanta's image and fracturing, if not destroying, the biracial political coalition in which black elites had invested so much over so many years. Black elites were aware of these stakes, and they decided that openly fighting residential segregation was too costly a proposition.[46]

Moreover, some African Americans reaped benefits from the existing system of segregation. Black real estate agencies had access to a small but captive black market under the segregated system, and there was a certain logic in maintaining this status quo. The black realtors board cooperated with the MPC on numerous occasions, agreeing not to accept listings from whites desperate to sell their homes in areas expected to "go black" before those neighborhoods were approved for transitional, or interracial, sales. During tension over the Adamsville transition area, for example, the members of the black Empire Real Estate Board refused listings in the area and notified the white civic club of "owners trying to sell to Negroes" until such time as the club and the city decided to "approve" the transition. Similarly, during the Mozley Park area transition, members agreed not to sell to blacks past a certain boundary—the north side of Westview Drive. Black realtors also wielded significant influence among whites seeking to exit transitional areas in the postwar years by selling to blacks before such transactions gained formal approval.[47]

Coveted business and professional opportunities were not confined to realtors, however. Black banks, builders, entrepreneurs, and managers also profited from segregated markets. In extolling the construction of the 452 rental Highpoint Apartments, the Atlanta Urban league noted, for example, that a "highly competent Negro managerial staff was in charge of the project." Securing jobs for blacks in the housing industry was a major part of the league's local and national agenda during the postwar shortage. In his testimony before the U.S. Civil Rights Commission on the housing crisis, the Atlanta Urban League's housing director, Robert Thompson, urged the hiring of "qualified Negro personnel" by federal housing agencies; these employees would "increase the ability of these agencies to deal more realistically" with housing problems. Ironically, Thompson urged the employment of black professionals "on an integrated basis in all regional offices" to continue segregated housing practices. Along with African-American civil servants, black social service and civic organizations, which played major roles in building segregated housing through land development corporations, gained stature and wielded power in the process of making deals, as well. With each new project completed, these groups increased their credibility within white circles of influence and tightened their hold over those African Americans who sought their services.[48]

Black homeowners who had previously lived in overcrowded, substandard dwellings also reaped certain benefits from the system. Thompson weighed the benefits of homeownership against the cost of expansion on a segregated basis as he decided whether to accept black expansion on a restricted basis. When a member of the U.S. Civil Rights Commission questioned the "judgment of Negro witnesses" in Atlanta who had decided against a push for housing desegregation, Thompson responded:

> Whenever an individual comes to us and says, "I want a house," and knowing that he is living in a substandard structure, I don't think I should assume the role of saying to him. "Don't improve your housing situation. You must wait for the millennium to come." That individual is interested in securing a decent, safe, and sanitary house at the moment and not when the millennium comes. So we have to work within the pattern of what we have here of segregation in Atlanta.[49]

Blacks gained the pride that accompanies living in comfortable housing, especially for the first time, among other African-American strivers. As a July 30, 1950, article in the *Atlanta Journal-Constitution* explained, "Negro efforts, white enterprise, and federal credit" had made the "American dream" available to hundreds of African Americans for the first time. Biracial deal-making had created and expanded a "Negro middle class with middle-class incomes living in modern, middle-class surroundings." The satisfaction that African Americans received from acquiring housing, even in a segregated context, cannot be gainsaid, particularly when new residential developments came with bonuses, such as badly needed shopping centers, parks, and schools. A "Negro country club" was even planned for one of the new black housing developments catering to higher income families.[50]

To many black Atlantans, the "separate but equal" solution to the postwar housing crisis was an achievement to be celebrated rather than a questionable deviation from principle. Far from doubting their accomplishments, black business and civic leaders congratulated themselves on working with whites in city government and the federal housing administration, among others, to "ease" the "negro housing bottleneck." As Grace Towns Hamilton of the Atlanta Urban League explained, "Honest co-operation of white persons and Negroes all along the line has made this new housing possible. The co-operation has proved its worth." Assessing the league's activities years later, Robert Thompson, Hamilton's colleague, explained that the board of the Urban League felt that practical considerations justified the undeniable fact that the league's policies and practices "contributed to segregation."[51]

> Our Board was inter-racial and we had to make certain crucial decisions on the very practical basis of how to . . . eliminate and minimize tension, on the one hand,

by providing decent housing…but from a theoretical or philosophical point of view, we recognized that what we did…did not coincide with the objectives of the Urban League, that is of…one society, not a black society or black community or white community, but a community.[52]

In fact, the Atlanta league's pragmatic position seriously breached the National Urban League's commitment to "ending racial discrimination…in every area of civic life," housing included. During the same time that the local league pursued policies that perpetuated segregation, the National Urban League vowed to "check the suicidal trend toward racial ghettos observed in the spread of restrictive property owners' covenants and the spawning of segregation in new areas by erecting separate public housing projects."[53]

Nevertheless, the black leadership in Atlanta was not alone in its willingness to deviate from the national NAACP and Urban League's position against residential segregation. In other urban areas, African Americans sought increased living space, but did not necessarily associate that goal with desegregation. The pursuit of desegregated housing mainly appealed to upwardly mobile, middle-class blacks who already had access to homes. Many blacks, confined to the worst housing stock in every section of the country, simply wanted decent housing—period. Logically, they considered the lack of housing the most blatant form of race-based discrimination.[54]

Such practical prerogatives had abundant appeal. Before World War II, Robert Weaver, the African American who became the first secretary of housing and urban development, had found himself, a racial liberal, making and justifying decisions that perpetuated segregation on precisely such grounds. Weaver had worked as an adviser to the federal housing agency during the 1930s. Amid a housing shortage, necessity dictated that federal officials bow to local norms favoring segregation, he had concluded. Thus, time and time again, Weaver set aside his own philosophical belief in integration and supported segregated public housing projects not only in Atlanta but also in Chicago, Detroit, Philadelphia, and New York City. Though Weaver had become a part of the NAACP coalition that opposed racially restrictive covenants by the postwar era, the implications of his earlier decisions lived on in neighborhoods in Atlanta and elsewhere, long after he left government and fully embraced the integrationist position. In the housing context, the logic of necessity to justify residential segregation could explain a great deal.[55]

Many other solid justifications supported existing arrangements. Local black politicians found a strategic reason not to disturb the status quo. They observed that growing black political power rested on geographic cohesiveness. Dispersal ran counter to the interests of blacks. Entrepreneurs coveted the ready-made clientele in all-black enclaves. Still others enjoyed freedom from the unwelcome scrutiny of whites and welcomed the company of those who shared bonds of kinship, culture, and community.[56]

## The Limits of Litigation

Finally and most important, although the national NAACP's litigation plan may well have been in African Americans' long-term best interests, ample evidence suggested that the political climate was not ripe for a broad-based attack on the web of discrimination in public and private housing. Residential segregation was entrenched across the nation during the 1940s; the concept of integrated housing was a radical idea. Two well-known cases from the North suggest why Atlanta's leaders might have thought it reasonable, under the circumstances, to strike Faustian bargains in the housing context in the South. The two dramas unfolded when private developers constructed massive new housing stores in Stuyvesant Town in New York City, while World War II raged on, and in Levittown, Pennsylvania, after the war had drawn to a close.

Stuyvesant Town revealed rank discrimination in New York City. The riverside development on the city's Lower East Side occupied eighteen city blocks, consisted of thirty-five buildings and 8,755 apartments, and housed about twenty-five thousand people. Twelve acres of land had been condemned and ten thousand low-income tenants had lost their homes to make way for the development. The Metropolitan Life Insurance Company, the owner of the Stuyvesant Town Corporation, made it clear that blacks need not apply for tenancy in the building. "Negroes will be excluded," explained the company's chairman, Frederick Ecker, in 1943, after he signed a contract to develop the project. Ecker cited public opinion to justify the private development's all-white policy. "Negroes and whites don't mix," he said of postwar American society. "A hundred years from now, maybe they will."[57]

In fact, a public outcry arose when the company's brazen opposition to integration came to light. Shocked by the company's open commitment to discrimination, hundreds of New Yorkers called on city officials—including Mayor Fiorello LaGuardia, reputedly a racial liberal—to demand open occupancy at Stuyvesant Town. But LaGuardia, intent on "slum clearance through private enterprise," would not intervene. Metropolitan Life's building plans continued unchecked; construction began in 1945 and was complete four years later. Harlem councilman Adam Clayton Powell, Jr., summed up the situation in an editorial: "Hitler won a victory in New York City." While A. T. Walden and his friends plotted their course in the face of the housing crisis in Atlanta, New York City—885 miles north—became a symbol of developers' power to discriminate with impunity and official acquiescence to discrimination.[58]

A few years later, the very same type of bias marked race relations in a starkly different setting, Levittown, Pennsylvania. An area in Bucks County, Pennsylvania, dotted with seventeen thousand suburban tract homes, Levittown had the makings of a postwar boomtown. Adjacent to highways and industry, the town promised employment and single-family homes (no matter that they were identical small, boxy units)—the American dream—for defense employees at the U.S. Steel Company. If the employee's skin was white, that is. Levitt, the developer, the grandson of a rabbi and the son of a real estate lawyer, refused to sell or rent to African Americans. Levitt pointed to white homeowners' preference for segregation, typically expressed by flight from, intimidation of, and violence against black interlopers, to explain his blanket exclusionary policy. He refused to make an exception to the ban on blacks in Bucks County, despite the fact that there were many African Americans in U.S. Steel's workforce. "We can solve a housing problem, or we can solve a racial problem," Levitt said. "But we cannot combine the two." "The Negroes in America are trying to do in 400 years what the Jews in the world have not wholly accomplished in 600 years." Even as Levitt claimed that he was helpless against the tide of social custom to open his development to blacks, a few white residents of Levittown opposed his all-white policy. They called the new neighborhood "Bigot Town" and organized against it. But the vast majority of white Levittowners accepted segregation, and hundreds actively and violently resisted integration when wayward neighbors sold to blacks. The confrontations made headlines worldwide. Levittown became synonymous with white intransigence and opposition to interracial neighborhoods.[59]

Civil rights organizations rose to the challenge posed by these events. Residential segregation had intensified in the North at a time when activists hoped the political environment would become *more* favorable to improvements in race relations. Thurgood Marshall and local lawyers turned to the courts to regain lost ground. In New York, the attorneys sued both developers and governmental officials. The lawyers claimed that the Metropolitan Life Company had received enough governmental aid to transform the nominally private company into an agent of the state for purposes of constitutional analysis. The company received a twenty-five-year tax exemption, numerous acres of land, street access, and other assistance from the city and state of New York. Yet, it had rejected the application of Marshall's model plaintiffs, black veterans.[60]

Similarly, in Pennsylvania, Marshall argued that the actions of the federal government and the Levitt Corporation were so entangled that the United

States could be held accountable for the company's discrimination. The FHA and the federal VA had provided Levitt with mortgage insurance and other assistance that enabled Levittown's development. The interrelationships of state and private actors in the construction of both developments made the sale and rental policies of Stuyvesant Town and Levittown federal constitutional matters. Undoubtedly, Marshall argued, the equal protection clause prohibited the racial discrimination evident in both communities.[61]

The civil rights lawyers' arguments, made in both state and federal courts, before and after *Shelley*, proved unpersuasive. Metropolitan Life prevailed after two different New York courts (in 1947 and 1949) rejected the claim that the benefits bestowed upon it by the city had transformed a private business to a quasi-public entity. The company, the courts held, remained a private entity. As such, Metropolitan Life could choose its tenants on any arbitrary basis, such as race. Cases such as *Smith v. Allwright*, in which the U.S. Supreme Court had held private actors' discriminatory conduct in the voting process unconstitutional, did not stand in the way of the courts' analysis. Context mattered, held a majority of the esteemed New York Court of Appeals. Metropolitan Life had not exercised a traditional governmental function.[62]

In 1955, the U.S. District Court followed a similar analysis in the Levittown case. The Levitt Corporation's acceptance of federal mortgage insurance had not converted it into the government of the United States, the court concluded; nor had the government, by aiding Levitt, converted into a builder or developer. Moreover, the government had no affirmative duty to prevent residential segregation. Despite how clear-cut Marshall's case appeared to some liberal observers, the jurists appeared confident in ruling that the U.S. Constitution did not proscribe the discriminatory policies in Levittown and in Stuyvesant Town.[63]

The lawsuits had backfired. The courts had affirmed that, unlike in other areas of LDF's civil rights litigation—schools, criminal law, voting—the Constitution had little application in the private housing market. No civil right to buy or rent private property existed. Nor were the judges prepared to create such a right. The courts' reluctance demonstrated the limited nature of the victory that the justices had delivered in *Shelley v. Kraemer*. The Court had issued an important but very narrow ruling: judicial enforcement of racially restrictive covenants violated the Constitution. The justices had not explored the implications of its landmark ruling, such as the questions raised in the Levittown and Stuyvesant Town cases about what other types of state involvement in residential discrimination perpetrated by private parties created a federal constitutional claim. Those thorny questions remained unsettled for many years. Walden—sophisticated, well-read, and well-connected to the national civil rights bar—was surely aware of the battle over segregation at Stuyvesant Town in New York and Levittown in Pennsylvania and their ignominious results.[64]

The challenges of housing desegregation litigation during the postwar era come into starker relief when one reconsiders *Heyward v. Public Housing Administration*, the Savannah litigation cocounseled by Marshall and Walden. Theoretically a much easier case than the Levittown and Stuyvesant Town litigation, *Heyward* failed just as resoundingly. Unlike the Levittown and Stuyvesant Town cases, *Heyward* involved allegations of discrimination by state actors, rather than entwined public and private conduct. Moreover, the federal courts could cite recent precedent, won by LDF lawyers and local counsel, favorable to the Savannah plaintiffs. In 1955, for example, NAACP lawyers had won a federal case in Detroit that involved a similarly straightforward scenario of officials allocating public housing on a racially discriminatory basis. The Sixth Circuit had affirmed the lower court's decision. State courts in California and New Jersey had issued comparable rulings. Still, *Heyward* got nowhere. The court did not even mention *Shelley* and disregarded *Brown* as well. Thurgood Marshall's plans notwithstanding, Walden must have concluded, the courts offered little hope of relief from the burdens of residential segregation.[65]

## HOUSING ACTIVISM IN THE MARKETPLACE

Atlanta's African-American leaders did not follow the national NAACP's blueprint for aggressive housing litigation, but this does not mean that they altogether failed to push back against Jim Crow. True, members of the Empire Real Estate Board were indispensable partners in the "separate but equal" solution to the housing crisis demanded by white elites. But black realtors sometimes challenged the color line—each time eliciting swift retaliation. Occasionally, the psychology of the transitional marketplace, led by panicked white sellers, got ahead of the MPC. In some instances, black realtors followed the momentum of the market, accepting listings from whites in unapproved areas, in the process meeting the demand from black buyers. J. H. Calhoun transgressed the established system in the postwar era by responding to whites who desired to sell their homes in the Mozley Park area to African Americans, the only interested buyers, even though the neighborhood had not been approved for interracial sales. His disobedience did not go unpunished. When the Georgia Real Estate Commission revoked Calhoun's license to sell real estate because of his failure to abide by the color line, the Empire Real Estate Board protested.[66]

The Empire Board underwrote a lawsuit against the commission challenging the revocation. Q. V. Williamson, president of the black realty board between 1951 and 1958, claimed that the board's suit, filed in Fulton County Superior Court, prompted an about-face on the part of the commission. Reconsidering its decision, the commission reinstated Calhoun's license, and the board dropped its suit. But whites continued to wage war over Mozley Park. "White banks" refused "point blank" to make loans in Mozley Park, thus preventing black realtors' efforts to sell in the neighborhood. Black economic power would ultimately carry the day, however. Black banks made the transition of the Mozley Park neighborhood possible by guaranteeing the first mortgages to African Americans in the area. After witnessing the brisk business that black lenders were doing in Mozley Park, white banks bowed to market imperatives and started making loans in the neighborhood as well. By 1954, the Mozley Park area had transitioned from a white to a black residential area.[67]

Still, these endeavors contrasted with the housing activism favored by integrationists. While Atlanta's leadership worked to open new areas to African-American residents, activists elsewhere, committed to racially mixed living, campaigned for antidiscrimination laws. Following the disappointing outcome of the Stuyvesant Town litigation, New York activists lobbied for and eventually won passage of the nation's first fair housing laws. Massachusetts, Illinois, Michigan, Connecticut, and other states in the North also enacted legislation that barred discrimination in public or publicly assisted housing during the 1950s. But such vanguard legislative campaigns—impractical in the Deep South—did not fundamentally change the makeup of America's neighborhoods. The statutes were not particularly effective. Enforcement generally fell to local agencies, and these authorities often did not vigorously investigate complaints or insist upon compliance with the new laws. Tellingly, the Stuyvesant Town development remained virtually all-white (99.2 percent) in 1960, long after passage of the New York's groundbreaking fair housing law. A mere forty-seven blacks lived among the housing complex's 22,405 tenants. After years of litigation and even legislation, Stuyvesant Town, New York, in 1960 did not look substantially different from Mozley Park, Atlanta, in 1954.[68]

## HOW WILL WE SHELTER OUR PEOPLE?

In the wake of the U.S. Supreme Court's 1948 decision in *Shelley v. Kraemer*, the *Pittsburgh Courier*, a leader of the black press, described the ruling in tragically overstated terms: "'Live Anywhere'! High Court Rules!" The Court's action, the paper continued, had "doom[ed]" a "vicious custom."[69]

The justices had done no such thing. The nightmarish tangle of policies and practices—discrimination in sales, rental, lending, zoning, and building, coupled with intimidation and violence—that confined the vast majority of African Americans to distinct neighborhoods and inferior homes persisted. Segregation would remain a fact of American residential life into the foreseeable future. The quest for equality in housing represented one of the most intractable terrains of postwar civil rights struggle.[70]

The national NAACP and LDF, committed to pursuing residential desegregation in the courts, achieved a few legal victories following *Shelley*. But litigation provided no surefire solution to the structural and interpersonal dynamics that kept blacks out of white areas. At best, the organizations' litigation record in the housing area post-*Shelley* was mixed. Defeats in cases involving the ever more common pattern of intermixed public and private discrimination stood out more than the spate of wins, mostly in public housing cases; and even in these theoretically easier cases, the NAACP did not always prevail.

In Atlanta, A. T. Walden both endorsed and departed from the national civil rights strategy. He hailed *Shelley*. And he joined Thurgood Marshall's unsuccessful effort to desegregate public housing in Savannah. But in the main, Walden and other pragmatic leaders in Atlanta chose an approach to housing reform that deemphasized litigation and desegregation. Interracial diplomacy certainly yielded some positive results in the housing area. The progress that African Americans made in attaining housing, especially in transitional areas, occurred largely because of the pioneering efforts of black financial institutions.[71]

But the process occurred slowly and produced limited solutions. The black population continued to far outstrip the available housing stock, despite the fact that nineteen thousand additional housing units had been made available to blacks by 1960, largely as a consequence of black elites' advocacy. The Atlanta Urban League was itself responsible for 8,795 new housing units, including 2,000 new public housing units, during the period from 1946 to 1957. Notwithstanding the additions, African Americans continued to live in overcrowded, dilapidated housing, just as they had before World War II. Whites felt little pressure to alter the situation. As late as 1959, a reporter for the *Atlanta Journal-*

*Constitution* could proclaim that "[i]ntegrated housing isn't the issue at present. It's a question of what segregated housing is going where."[72]

By this time, the housing crisis looked acute to increasing numbers of African Americans. Those not a part of the traditional decision-making class, along with a few who were, began to express frustration over the slow pace and scope of change in the housing context. The local NAACP chapter, along with some individuals who had initially supported the Atlanta Housing Council's endorsement of MPC policies, now voiced misgivings. In 1958, the Atlanta NAACP chapter requested that the U.S. Civil Rights Commission encourage federal agencies such as the Department of Housing and Urban Development to halt urban renewal efforts in the city. More housing was being demolished than was being rebuilt or repaired, and the concentration of public housing in confined spaces created concentrated socioeconomic problems. Black businessmen expressed concerns that the urban renewal process was destroying their client base. Finally, in 1965, the local NAACP, "pushed and supported" by the national and state NAACP, began to publicly complain about the "rigid" segregation of public housing. Still, the branch did not challenge housing discrimination in a court of law.[73]

All told, the decision of Atlanta's black leaders to address the postwar housing crisis within the racial parameters demanded by white elites, and through diplomacy rather than confrontation, had long-lasting consequences. The MPC's practices and policies—supported by the black pragmatists— helped to entrench segregation and create the central city ghettoes that the Atlanta NAACP branch decried beginning in 1965. For many African Americans, the long-term consequences of the expanding black ghettos, islands bereft of opportunity, increasingly set apart even from the black middle class, would be dire.[74]

## CHAPTER 4

# "Segregation Pure and Simple"

*School, Community, and the NAACP's Education Litigation, 1942–1958*

> We don't worry about the [black] minority who want to go the other way.
> We will try to convert them to our way of thinking. But we will walk over
> them if they get in our way. (1954)
>
> Thurgood Marshall
>
> We were, in our aggressive program to end segregation, out in front of
> many members of the black community. (1994)
>
> Jack Greenberg

The NAACP (LDF) made a controversial but winning argument about the meaning of separate schools in *Brown v. Board of Education.*[1] Even if segregated schools were equal in terms of resources and other tangible factors, they were "inherently unequal" in the eyes of the law, Chief Justice Earl Warren wrote, because the fact of separation is "usually interpreted as denoting the inferiority of the negro group." "[T]his sense of inferiority...has a tendency to [retard] the educational and mental development of Negro children."[2] Psychological and sociological studies collected by LDF supported the claim, but proved a shaky basis for the Court's landmark decree in the judgment of many constitutional scholars.[3]

Nevertheless, with its embrace of the stigma rationale for school desegregation, the U.S. Supreme Court had blessed LDF's litigation strategy and begun to cleanse constitutional law of the stain of Jim Crow. At Warren's urging, the *Brown* Court had spoken out, in one voice, against a form of racism that embarrassed the nation in the post-Nazi, Cold War era.[4]

Despite the legal and moral certitude of *Brown*'s rhetoric, complications abounded. Neither the Supreme Court's sweeping decision nor LDF's all-or-nothing legal strategy could acknowledge the thorny sociopolitical issues lurking in the shadows of the great constitutional case. The certainty of white resistance demanded that neither the Justices nor the lawyers concede ambiguity; any weakness might be leveraged for political advantage by the NAACP's (and the Court's) opponents. The imperatives of the civil rights class action compelled LDF to pose as spokespersons for the entire black community, united around a common cause.[5]

But the "united black community," such as it was, had been a strategic construct; it had been imagined for the purposes of litigation. The LDF had not represented, and the justices had not captured, the complex perspectives of African Americans on separate schools. Undeniably, Jim Crow was designed to ensure white supremacy and black oppression. Nevertheless, blacks did not view segregated *schools*—a particular, racially defined space—*exclusively* through the lens of deprivation. Indeed, some African Americans, including members of the "Talented Tenth," among them the distinguished intellectual and NAACP cofounder W. E. B. Du Bois, considered the central premise of the Court's landmark opinion debatable. Separate schools had economic and social functions within black communities, quite apart from the meaning that whites ascribed to them, and notwithstanding the discrimination to which they might be subject. Black schools provided employment and opportunities to black teachers, and offered socially and emotionally safe spaces for some black students. In other words, some within black communities could exercise agency within these schools, despite discrimination. Ultimately, questions about the viability of separate schools and doubts about the feasibility of school desegregation—matters that neither the Court nor LDF countenanced in 1954—demanded attention.[6]

To fully understand the social, economic, and political factors that shaped black communities' responses to LDF's educational campaign, one must look beyond the Supreme Court and the national civil rights bar. Upon engaging in a bottom-up historical analysis—featuring local lawyers, activists, clients, and organizations, alongside more traditional repositories of legal power—an incredibly complex picture emerges. In Atlanta, as elsewhere, African Americans negotiated inequality at a distance from courts, the national civil rights bar, and its institutional concerns. They did not reflexively endorse LDF's litigation strategy in the educational context, any more than they had fully accepted its housing strategy. Instead, political and educational identities, forged under segregation, powerfully influenced citizens' responses to LDF's all-out assault on Jim Crow in education. The city's pragmatic leadership, anchored by lawyer A. T. Walden, embraced some features of the national NAACP and LDF's plan, but took a more circumspect view about other aspects of it. The views of educators dominated decision-making. Students and parents of school-aged children had little role in agenda setting, although *Brown* turned on the idea that segregation posed peculiar harms to black students. Whatever the harms of Jim Crow, A. T. Walden and his clients never wholeheartedly embraced Thurgood

Marshall's desegregation plan. Slow to accept litigation at all, they viewed equalization lawsuits, which increased funding for black schools, as potentially more beneficial, and sought to leverage such suits to achieve a range of remedies for inequality, rather than seek desegregation alone.

The Supreme Court, following LDF's lead, had imagined a united class of constitutional victims clamoring for the inexorable decision that equality and separate schools were an impossibility. In reality, the perspectives of African Americans did not map easily onto the national bar's conceptions of harm and remedy and corresponding legal decisions. Law's categories—the choice in the Court's equal protection jurisprudence between "separate" and "unequal" versus "desegregated" and "equal" schools—did not translate very well for African Americans in Atlanta. Equality could encompass multiple dimensions, including pupil placement, student achievement, school administration, curriculum, and community building. Black Atlantans hoped for an educational campaign that could capture all of these dimensions of equality.

Yet, local representation did not, in and of itself, ensure a close fit between communities' interests and the goals of activism. In environments populated by citizens with tremendous need, limited skills, and few opportunities for political empowerment, the pragmatists—those best positioned under segregation—determined paths of racial progress consistent with their own interests and values. Their racial vision did not necessarily coincide with the diffuse interests of the larger community, any more than the prerogatives of the national civil rights bar necessarily overlapped with the goals of local people.[7]

## EDUCATION, DEMOCRACY, AND CITIZENSHIP

Black leaders considered education an engine of democracy and equality. In Atlanta, they sought educational opportunities with the same abandon that they championed the vote. Indeed, their commitments to better education and political power went hand in hand. Education increased the likelihood that blacks would participate in the political process. Academic achievement also enhanced black employment opportunities. In particular, it made African Americans better situated to become educators and entrepreneurs—prized pursuits. In short, the rise from slavery to freedom depended on increasing levels of literacy.

The high priority that leaders placed on learning went hand in hand with Atlanta's status as the capital of black higher education. The city has boasted the highest concentration of historically black institutions of higher education of any city in the nation since the late nineteenth century. The oldest of these institutions, AU, established in 1865, served as the intellectual home for many years of W. E. B. Du Bois. Atlanta also is home to Morehouse College, founded in 1867, the alma mater of the city's famous native son Dr. Martin Luther King, Jr. In addition, Spelman College, Clark University, and Morris Brown College, all established by 1885, are located in the city. These colleges constituted the center of academic, social, and political influence among blacks.[8]

Graduates of the black colleges pursued careers in law, medicine, social work, government, and science, but a career in education was second to none in the community's esteem. From their inceptions, AU and Spelman College made teacher education a central part of their educational programs. The emphasis arose, in part, from necessity. Teaching was one of the few professions open to African Americans, especially black women. By 1910, 45 percent of professional blacks were teachers; 76 percent of these teachers were women. By 1940, an overwhelming majority of black college graduates, sixty-three thousand, worked as educators (as compared to one thousand lawyers, thirty-five hundred doctors, and seventeen thousand ministers). Census figures for Georgia for the period 1920–1960 reveal similar trends.[9] During the decades leading up to and the years following *Brown*, teachers constituted the greatest share of Georgia's black middle class (figs. 4.1 and 4.2, appendix).

Influential by virtue of numbers alone, black teachers also gained status by playing a crucial role in the community's social mobility and overall vision of racial advancement. Educators taught academic skills, of course. In fact, they considered black literacy an act of emancipation. Statutes such as the 1829 Georgia law that criminalized teaching people of color to read and made it punishable by whipping were never far from these teachers' minds as they contemplated their classroom duties. Years later, the educational deprivation prescribed by the law of slavery persisted. Often, teachers' commitment to educating black students required them to establish schools from the bottom up. Free public education for whites had been established under Georgia's constitution in 1877, and the state developed a common school system for whites during the 1880s and 1890s. But Georgia did not fully develop even a rudimentary school system for blacks until the 1930s, and then only reluctantly. Meanwhile, the majority of the black elementary and secondary school students attended makeshift schools housed in the black colleges, where teachers struggled to provide the best education possible under the circumstances. As the teachers taught reading, writing, and arithmetic, they advanced the community's social, political, and economic status one student at a time. Just as important, black teachers promoted middle-class cultural and social norms and engendered a sense of duty to community among their students. The teachers also taught students to develop the mental toughness required to endure the daily challenges to one's humanity leveled by white supremacy.[10]

In short, Jim Crow–era black teachers served as ambassadors of racial uplift. They provided culturally relevant instruction that emphasized the relationship between school and community. At their best, black teachers personified the belief that same-race role models could lead by "precept and example." W. E. B. Du Bois captured this faith in his 1935 essay "Does the Negro Need Separate Schools?" Du Bois had the superlative teacher described here in mind when he urged that "the proper education of any people includes sympathetic touch between teacher and pupil, on the basis of social equality; knowledge on the part of the teacher, not simply of the individual taught, but of his surroundings and background, and the history of his class and his group."[11]

But not all teachers measured up. Academic preparation among black teachers was uneven. Prior to the 1920s, some of them were not graduates of academic colleges. Advocates of universal, quality black education lobbied for and obtained requirements raising the qualifications for teaching during the twenties. They did so over the objections of white southerners, whose tax and school authorities *preferred* undereducated black teachers to well-educated ones.[12]

Nevertheless, black teachers' qualifications steadily improved over time, particularly in urban areas. In fact, the credentials of black educators in Atlanta outpaced those of many educators elsewhere, especially in rural areas. Increasingly, these educators' credentials even matched or *exceeded* those of white teachers in Atlanta. Where segregated schools were populated by socially conscious, well-trained black teachers, they represented African Americans' best effort to develop a functioning society and live peaceably amid unrelenting white oppression.

## THE NAACP'S SALARY EQUALIZATION CAMPAIGN

The leaders of the NAACP's campaign against segregation, Charles Hamilton Houston and Thurgood Marshall, together with other early to mid-twentieth-century black NAACP officials, had all been educated in segregated schools and taught by black teachers at one time or another. Thus, they had firsthand knowledge of the enormous economic, social, and political influence that black teachers held in communities throughout the South. Indeed, the NAACP perceived African-American educators as being at once a core constituency of, and a political threat to, the association's agenda. Without the support of the teachers—a large segment of the NAACP's middle-class constituency—the NAACP could not be effective.

The NAACP conceived the teacher salary equalization campaign, in part, to shore up its support among educators. Few initiatives could be more appealing to teachers, it seemed, than a drive to end school districts' policy of paying black educators less than their white counterparts. The campaign was not only politically astute but also on strong legal ground. Given the dramatic differences between black and white teachers' salaries, lawyers could demonstrate discrimination without difficulty.[13]

Lawyers at the NAACP nevertheless encountered setbacks over the course of the campaign, and the teachers themselves constituted the main barriers to success. Black educators often doubted the utility of the teacher pay suits. Several factors animated their skepticism. Black teachers and principals depended on white authorities for their livelihoods and educational resources. They faced pressure from white officials to avoid lawsuits; whites threatened retribution if black teachers signed on as plaintiffs in salary equalization suits. Consequently, teachers did not readily line up to demand better salaries in open court, although, in theory, the suits advanced their economic interests. Some black educators attempted to capitalize on the NAACP's pay equity suits, while making an end run around the NAACP. They tried to negotiate pay raises with white administrators, rather than litigate the issue. Still others attempted to settle equalization cases behind the NAACP's back, when the lawsuits' pace proved slow. The teacher salary cases, straightforward in theory, showcased problems in the relationship among the NAACP, its lawyers, and client communities in practice.[14]

## The Fight for Parity in Atlanta

The NAACP's teacher salary equalization campaign in Atlanta moved forward relatively smoothly—once it got off the ground. It took some time, however, for teachers to decide to agitate publicly for higher salaries. For many years, the Georgia Teachers and Education Association (GTEA), the black teachers' organization, agreed to forego litigation in exchange for a promise from state officials of a gradual pay raise. Most of Atlanta's African-American teachers agreed that salary parity made sense, but they did not rush to the courthouse to make their claim. The teachers first relied on interracial diplomacy as a means of achieving better salaries. They only turned to litigation several years after the national NAACP's victories in equalization cases in Maryland and Virginia. By then it was clear that biracial negotiation was a futile approach to winning pay raises across the board in Atlanta.

During the period before they filed suit, Atlanta's African-American teachers brought the issue before the Board of Education. They also brought the matter before the white teachers' union, the Atlanta Public School Teachers' Association (APSTA), an American Federation of Labor (AFL) affiliate. In a letter to Ira Jarrell, president of the APSTA, C. L. Harper, president of the GTEA, also an AFL affiliate, made the black teachers' case for equity. In seeking salary equalization, the GTEA was trying to "make our State a working democracy in fact as well as in theory." Paying black teachers on the same scale as white ones was "only in keeping with the ideals of Democracy which we are preaching to the world today." Harper urged APSTA to support black teachers' effort to join the regular salary schedule out of a sense of civic duty. The GTEA "is working for a solution of this problem without legal procedure," he reminded the school superintendent. But Harper also raised the prospect of court-ordered relief. He noted that petitioners had won several decisions from federal courts, and "so it seems that the Negro teachers have all the law on their side." "These matters," Harper continued, "can be worked out without resorting to the courts if the school authorities will do their best to conform to the law." The problem, Harper suggested, could be resolved even short of full equalization: a substantial salary increase would satisfy black teachers.[15]

Harper's plea for cooperation from the white union and his desire for an out-of-court settlement did not bear fruit. Around the same time that Harper reached out to Ira Jarrell, she and the APSTA's executive board met with Jack Savage, the city attorney, to identify how they could avoid meaningful salary equalization. One white teacher suggested that the executive committee adopt a resolution favoring "eventual negro equalization," even as it maintained the discriminatory salary schedule. Higher salaries for black teachers "can only come out of the salaries of white teachers," the educator noted. Equalization would lead to the unacceptable result of higher salaries for black teachers in Atlanta than for most white teachers in other parts of the state. That would never do.[16]

## Litigating Pay Equity

African-American teachers turned to teacher salary litigation when, after numerous entreaties, it became clear that the school administration would never eliminate pay disparities on its own. When the GTEA finally decided to go forward with litigation, most of the city's large corps of African-American educators supported the suit. There were dissenters—black teachers who refused to back the effort to win better salaries and who even agreed to testify for the defense during trial. But, unlike in the housing context, where African-American leaders viewed biracial negotiation for segregated living spaces a necessary evil, they excoriated teachers whose support for the salary equalization campaign lagged. Such educators were guilty of "deceit" and "trickery" and "ought to be banished from our schools," an *Atlanta Daily World* editorial argued. A prominent minister, William Holmes Borders, appeared at a citywide teachers conference days before the start of the trial to keep educators on board. He called those who agreed to support the school board "sell-outs" lacking in "self-respect" and "not worthy of the confidence of his or her people."[17]

The salary cases did not, of course, challenge segregation, but demanded equal pay in separate facilities. Thus, it was not the dissenting teachers' failure to stand up for equality in the abstract, dignitary sense that so disturbed black leaders.

Rather, the issue of unequal pay was, at root, economic. The school board's discrimination deprived individual teachers, and the community, of coveted resources. The teachers' failure to demand equal pay offended the shared commitment among Atlanta's black elite leadership to economic self-sufficiency—no matter the social inequalities imposed by white society. The comments of a journalist covering the trial for the *World*, registered at the end of a devastating presentation by the plaintiffs' attorneys about racial disparities in pay, explained the core issue best. He wrote, "One could perhaps tolerate such disparity under other conditions. But not this—for there is no race discrimination when it comes to levying city, county and state taxes from which the money [to pay teachers] comes." From the perspective of hardworking middle-class leaders, unequal pay for equal workloads was economically unjust and thus unacceptable.[18]

A. T. Walden filed a pay equity suit in 1942—his first foray into civil rights litigation. He sued the Georgia Board of Education on behalf of William Reeves, an African-American school principal. The board responded to the suit by abolishing the dual salary schedules. The court then dismissed Reeves's case.[19]

But the fight for equal pay had only begun. The board replaced the explicitly racially separate scales challenged by Reeves with a "Track and Step System." The new scheme perpetuated racial discrimination under the guise of formal evenhandedness. African Americans continued to be concentrated in the lowest paying tracks and steps under the new system.[20]

Consequently, in 1943, A. T. Walden, together with LDF's Thurgood Marshall, filed a class action suit attacking the new, but still discriminatory, system. They filed suit on behalf of Samuel L. Davis and other African-American teachers and principals. The lawyers charged that black personnel continued to be paid less, despite qualifications and experience equal to those of whites.[21]

The trial in the case lasted six days and generated great interest in the community. On each of the six days of trial, black spectators packed the courtroom.

They were eager to witness the city's first public showdown over discrimination, argued by black attorneys.[22]

During the trial, Ira Jarrell, now superintendent of the Atlanta schools, was the school board's star witness. She had helped to create the track-step system, and she vigorously defended it. Jarrell categorically rejected the idea that discrimination explained the enduring differences in pay rates between African-American and white teachers. Under questioning about how administrators made salary determinations, Jarrell insisted:

> In building salary schedules, they must be made for human beings, not for academic degrees[,] nor years of teaching. No two teachers are alike.... Tracks are built to fit the individual. Assignment to tracks and steps are based upon tangible and intangible factors. The assignments depend upon the teacher.... The teacher places herself in the schedule.

Jarrell implied that blacks had all but chosen their inferior positions on the pay scale.[23]

But the plaintiffs' lawyers forced Jarrell and Ed Cook, president of the Board of Education, to make damning concessions. The school administrators could not deny the "close correspondence" between the teachers' previous salaries and their positions in the new schedules. Neither disputed that for decades prior to the litigation, black teachers' salaries had been systematically lower than whites' solely on account of race. Blacks' salaries had not been equalized prior to the implementation of the track-step system. Hence, past discrimination had been built into the "new" scale—bias formed the foundation of Atlanta's teacher pay system.[24]

Moreover, evidence adduced at trial showed that the district systematically underpaid black teachers even after it implemented the supposedly individuated track-step system. The disparity started at the point of hire—before experience or "intangibles" could account for their unfavorable treatment relative to whites. For example, a white elementary school teacher hired in 1944 received a beginning salary of $105 a month, while a black teacher received a salary of $85. In 1945, the same white teacher was hired at $110 a month, and the black teacher at $75 a month. For the 1946–47 academic year, the average monthly salary for all teachers and principals was $173 for whites, but only $125 for blacks. In one particularly damning example of inequity, the Board of Education had hired an African-American high school teacher with a doctorate in philosophy and thirteen years of teaching experience at the same pay rate as a white teacher with only a master's degree and four years of teaching experience. All told, the salary inequities were "gross," "systematic," and "apparently deliberate," according to an accountant who testified as an expert witness for the plaintiffs.[25]

When presented with such evidence, Jarrell continued to insist that only differences among individuals could explain the results. These were often "intangible" or subjective factors, Jarrell had to admit, given the impressive credentials of many of Atlanta's black teachers. Thus, she made the remarkable concession that a teacher's degrees and academic training were not the main factors determining salaries. Rather, "the teacher's mark on the child" accounted for salary differentials. Jarrell did not explain, however, the criteria by which administrators determined which teachers had made sufficient "marks" on their students to warrant higher pay. Despite the best efforts of A. T. Walden and his colleagues to pin the superintendent down, Jarrell's testimony was filled with general statements touting administrators' fairness and good intentions, rather than specific explanations for the depressed salaries of black teachers.[26]

In his summation, Walden retorted that only one factor could reasonably explain the "vast gulf" between black and white teachers' average salaries. "Race and race alone!" is the only plausible explanation for the disparity, Walden argued. He pounded his fist on the counsel's table for emphasis.[27]

During the final days of the trial, plaintiffs' attorneys augmented the mountain of documentary evidence regarding pay disparities with the live testimony of African-American elementary school principals. These administrators had decades of experience in the Atlanta public school system. The principals' testimony raised further questions about precisely how the superintendent determined teacher pay rates. Jarrell never consulted them about how effective their teachers were, although the principals had firsthand knowledge of, and daily contact with, all of the educators whom the superintendent rated. Moreover, they testified that black teachers had complained to the Board of Education about the salary disparities over the years, only to have their complaints fall on deaf ears. Cora Finley, principal of the Young Street School and treasurer of the Gate City Teachers Association, explained that numerous requests to the Board of Education to correct the salary discrimination had been ignored. "We were well received" and "no one ever told us we were wrong," Finley noted of the black delegations' conferences with board members. "But nothing was ever done."[28]

The district court ruled in favor of Atlanta's black teachers in *Davis v. Cook*, only to be reversed on appeal. In finding for the plaintiffs, the district court judge relied on the NAACP's initial victories in the salary equalization fight. The judge held salary differentials between Atlanta's African-American and white teachers patently unconstitutional under these precedents.[29]

But four years later, the Fifth Circuit reversed the judgment on procedural grounds. The appeals court conceded that the "minimum salary scale" was "materially lower for colored than white teachers each year." Yet it held that the black teachers had failed to pursue the complaint and appeal procedures put into place by the Atlanta Board of Education in 1944, along with the track-step salary system. Because the plaintiffs had not exhausted their administrative remedies before bringing suit, the Fifth Circuit threw out their case. The plaintiffs argued that the appeals process was "illusory"; the same administrators who had wronged them in the first place oversaw it. But the court disagreed, responding only that "[t]hese excuses are not good." After losing in the Fifth Circuit, the LDF appealed to the U.S. Supreme Court, but to no avail. The High Court let the circuit court's judgment stand.[30]

After years of litigating the issue, Atlanta's black teachers were left without a decree holding officials to the precedent set in the NAACP's earlier equalization cases. The *Atlanta Daily World* expressed the community's bitter disappointment with the outcome. The reversal was "incongruous and incoherent" given the evidence presented in the trial court, the paper editorialized. The decision "rest[ed] more on figment and fancy than on logic and fact."[31]

Despite the setback on appeal, the litigation had been successful in part. The Atlanta Board of Education had abolished facially discriminatory salary scales as a result of it. Many black teachers received pay increases, if not full equalization. The partial victory in Atlanta was not unusual. Most of the NAACP's teacher salary cases ended in similar outcomes. Overall, black teachers' salaries rose from 55 percent of white teachers' salaries to 65 percent of white teachers' salaries as a result of the equalization campaign. But the lawsuits did not touch the so-called intangibles, discrimination based on the subjective criteria that perpetuated the black-white pay gap.[32]

## The Ambiguous Impact of the Court-Based Fight for Equal Pay

The equalization litigation constituted the most unapologetic and uncompromising stand for equality that Atlanta's black leadership had taken thus far. The city's black teachers had not been the leading edge of the equalization litigation first begun by the NAACP in the Upper South in the mid-1930s. But when they moved forward, they acted decisively. The level of unity among teachers in Atlanta far surpassed that in many other communities.

Nevertheless, the limited success of the teacher salary case disappointed Atlanta's black leadership. The teachers' legal claims arguably reinforced rather than undermined Jim Crow education. Even so, Atlanta's white establishment had been unwilling to buttress the segregated educational system by equalizing the pay of black teachers. Instead, the Board of Education had devised a pay scale that perpetuated discrimination. And it had defended it by arguing that African-American teachers—even those with the same credentials as whites—lacked the "intangible" qualifications necessary to merit higher salaries. Black teachers had been hearing such insults and excuses for years before the litigation. Moreover, the track-step system, which had led to raises for some black teachers, had been implemented in anticipation of litigation, not as a consequence of the case itself. After six years of litigation, many African-American teachers remained in largely the same place as before—underpaid and overworked in overcrowded, segregated schools.

The outcome confirmed a prediction that a local Congress of Industrial Organizations (CIO) affiliate had made even before the litigation ended. The CIO warned blacks not to rely solely on lawsuits as the "complete solution" to their problem. "Even a favorable decision will not conclude this issue," the union had predicted. The Board of Education and school administration, which "have been so ingenious and persistent in maintaining the system of unequal salaries over the years, will not suddenly become transformed and repentant by any court order," it said. Events had proven the union correct.[33]

Yet, black educators' willingness to bring the litigation at all, and their victory in the district court, must have made an impression on Atlanta's white power structure. But the overarching lesson that white school board officials had learned did not bode well for the NAACP's litigation campaign. Whites had seen that discrimination could continue even if blacks managed to file a lawsuit and secure victory at trial.

Atlanta's black leadership had witnessed the weaknesses of a court-based strategy for forcing change. The leaders would not have forgotten the lessons about civil rights litigation that the teacher salary cases had taught them. When they set out to fight discrimination in other areas, the leaders must have been more circumspect than ever about the value of court cases to improve socioeconomic conditions for African Americans.

## THE SCHOOL FUNDING
## EQUALIZATION CAMPAIGN

One of the other areas that absorbed the energies of Atlanta's black leadership related closely to the teacher salary campaign: the condition of black schools themselves. Leaders relentlessly sought additional funding for black schools, and repeated the pattern and tactics used in the context of teacher salary disparities in their campaign for reform. For many years, the leaders attempted to ameliorate school funding inequities through interracial outreach and negotiation. Black leaders turned to litigation to equalize the schools in 1950, just as the NAACP transitioned from equalization litigation to a direct attack on Jim Crow education. Ultimately, many of Atlanta's black decision-makers objected to the strategic change, some vocally, some behind the scenes. Once lawyers filed suit, the pragmatists used the case as leverage *not* to seek desegregation, but to continue their fight for increased expenditures for black schools. The year 1950 marked the beginning of a battle over the wisdom of LDF's choice to define quality education and integrated education as one and the same.

## Negotiating Pupil Expenditures

Long before the national NAACP began its fight in the courts to improve the quality of black education, local leaders in Atlanta charted their own course toward better schools. African-American women activists associated with the Neighborhood Union finally prevailed in their effort to gain the first high school for blacks in Atlanta in 1924—years after Birmingham, Little Rock, Dallas, Nashville, Houston, and Knoxville already had established high schools for blacks. Next, black activists set out to address the constellation of problems besetting African-American schools at all levels. Inadequate facilities, supplies, and faculty were the most pressing ills. Students crammed into overcrowded and understaffed schools, with out-of-date books and meager supplies. Statistics amply demonstrate the extent of the crisis. During the 1934–35 school year, the students per teacher figure was 82.7 for black students, and 35.4 for white students. To accommodate the growing number of black students, administrators instituted double and even triple sessions, where students attended school for only part of a normal school day. The situation had improved considerably by the 1949–50 school year, with 36.2 pupils per teacher in black schools, and 22.6 students per teacher in white schools. Still, black schools continued to be overcrowded, the teachers overloaded, and the students undereducated.[34]

All of these problems could be ameliorated by additional resources. Groups such as the Atlanta Urban League, the Gate City Teachers' Association, the local NAACP branch, and the Atlanta Civic and Political League advocated for funding increases. They detailed evidence of the city's neglect of black schools and then lobbied the Board of Education to rectify the inequalities. The Atlanta Urban League, led by Grace Towns Hamilton, compiled sophisticated statistical reports documenting and publicizing fiscal inequality. In 1944, for example, the league commissioned a study that revealed the inadequacy of the Board of

Education's postwar budget plans. The Urban League's report showed that the $1 million allotted for the improvement of black schools would not even maintain the existing level of disparate school funding. In order to prevent the disparity from increasing, an additional $3 million must be allotted to black schools, the league recommended. The league's advocacy raised the community's consciousness about racial disparities in education and influenced the budget. In April 1946, the Board of Education announced a revised school plan that featured the allocation of $4 million of a $9 million bond issue for improvements to the city's black schools; voters subsequently approved the bond issue.[35]

The victory proved pyrrhic, however. In 1948, the Urban League issued a supplemental report on public school facilities for blacks (see table 4.1). This report found that although spending on black students had increased, the overall gap between spending on black and white students had also increased. Where the average per pupil expenditure for black students had been $44.11 in the school year 1943–44, by 1946–47 that figure was $59.88. Nevertheless, the 1946–47 figure for blacks remained far below the average per pupil expenditure for white students of $139.73. As a practical matter, these funding disparities translated into overcrowded classrooms, decrepit school buildings, inadequate numbers of textbooks, schools lacking libraries, cafeterias, and gymnasiums, high student-teacher ratios, and teachers and administrators who were underpaid compared to their white counterparts (despite the teacher salary litigation). Furthermore, double and triple sessions—perhaps the most destructive of all of the ills—persisted; 85 percent of all black elementary school students attended class for only half the day during the 1947–48 school year.[36]

## The Turn to Litigation

The post–World War II era thus found Atlanta's African-American leadership in a cruel education predicament. Black leaders considered education the single, best avenue to individual success and group advancement. But white administrators refused to allot sufficient funds to place a meaningful educational experience within the reach of black students. Jim Crow confined most black students to ramshackle schools.[37]

African Americans across the South shared black Atlanta's plight. A 1947 Howard University study, covered in a front-page article in the *Atlanta Daily World*, confirmed the scope of the educational crisis. Howard's survey of segregated school systems in seventeen states, including Georgia, showed that "[i]n no separate school system does the Negro receive equal to that of white students." The report continued, "At the present rate of progress, it would take 60 years before the buildings and equipment in Negro common schools would become substantially equal to those provided for white pupils in 1945, to say nothing of the future." In one of the few areas where blacks recently had made gains—teacher salaries—litigation or the threat of litigation had forced progress. It was "clear that segregation in education based upon race must be abolished," beginning with the graduate and professional schools, the survey concluded.[38]

The *World* agreed—up to a point. The editors had long expressed support for the NAACP's school funding campaign. During a 1946 national NAACP legal strategy session, hosted in Atlanta by A. T. Walden, lawyers authorized the filing of equalization suits in Georgia, Louisiana, Florida, Maryland, Virginia, and South Carolina. The *World* applauded the concept of lawsuits designed to gain "complete equalization" of schools. In fact, after the NAACP's victory in the Louisiana salary litigation in 1947, the *World* ran an editorial practically urging a suit. "The day is coming," the editors wrote, "when...Negro parents must go into the courts in order to halt equally serious discrimination against their children, in the matter of equal facilities [and] in the apportionment of school equipment and outlay." However, unlike the national NAACP, which viewed equalization suits as routes to school desegregation, the *World*'s support for such litigation hinged on the preservation of separate but equal schools. The paper's coverage of the NAACP's school funding suits in other states emphasized that school boards could avoid constitutional liability by complying with *Plessy*'s separate but equal rule. The newspaper did not offer any support for a legal attack on segregation itself.[39]

The propriety of desegregation, as opposed to equalization, remained an unsettled issue on September 19, 1950. On that date, A. T. Walden, together with LDF attorneys Thurgood Marshall and Robert L. Carter, filed a lawsuit challenging race-based inequities in Atlanta's public schools. The suit, *Aaron v. Cook*, a product of the NAACP's 1946 conference in Atlanta authorizing equalization cases, chronicled stark differences in the physical plants and academic offerings of the city's black and white schools. The lawyers argued that Atlanta's policy of denying black students schools on a par with those designated for whites violated the Constitution. The attorneys sought a permanent injunction opening the doors of white schools to black students, or requiring equalization of the separate schools. In demanding desegregation *or* equalization, the lawyers followed what had been standard LDF practice.[40]

But the lawyers filed *Aaron v. Cook* at a transitional moment. Just a few months earlier, the U.S. Supreme Court had announced its unanimous decision in *Sweatt v. Painter*. In this case, the Court ordered the University of Texas Law School to admit black applicant Heman Sweatt, rather than educate him in a separate facility. The law school that Texas had created for Sweatt and other blacks featured the same curriculum as the flagship white law school. The Court nevertheless held that Sweatt could not receive an equal education there. The segregated school lacked the "intangible" elements of a quality education, such as the reputation of the faculty, the experience of administrators, and the powerful alumni that "make for greatness in a law school," the justices held. The *Sweatt* decision suggested the Court's openness to a legal assault on segregation itself. The ruling compelled Thurgood Marshall's decision, approved by resolution of the NAACP board of directors in July of 1950, to frontally attack segregation in future cases. From that point forward, the NAACP would no longer represent plaintiffs merely seeking equal funding for black schools. The lawfulness of segregation itself rose to the top of the NAACP and LDF's agendas.[41]

*Aaron v. Cook* placed Atlanta at the forefront of the campaign against segregated schools. Given the city's stature in the New South, observers considered *Cook* a monumental test case. But few in the state welcomed the attention. Georgia officials stood united in opposition to the NAACP's audacious move and the "Northern-owned newspapers and left-wingers" said to back the suit. Governor Herman Talmadge's stance typified their response. He lambasted the idea of integrated schools, offered all of the state's resources to defend the status quo, and warned that court-ordered desegregation would precipitate violent resistance. Any attempt by Negroes to enter traditionally white public schools "would create more confusion, disorder, riots and bloodshed than anything since the War Between the States," Talmadge predicted. "There are not enough troops or police in the United States to enforce" a school segregation order, he declared.[42]

Other officials suggested that Atlanta's honor had been diminished and its good faith betrayed by the suit. Lieutenant governor Marvin Griffin claimed that "Negro school facilities in the big city of Atlanta are superior to white schools in many of Georgia's rural counties." Yet, white people in those counties were not "contemplating bringing a suit against the state." Similarly, Ralph McGill of the *Atlanta Constitution*, considered a racial moderate, called the suit unnecessary; the state already was taking steps to provide better educational opportunities for blacks, he explained. That NAACP lawyers had filed a "test case" in "progressive" Atlanta was "productive of resentment," McGill charged. An *Atlanta Constitution* editorial likewise concluded that "[b]y filing the suit...the Negroes have succeeded in alienating the support of a great many who have worked continuously through the years for equal schooling opportunities." Ed Cook, chairman of the Atlanta Board of Education, agreed: "I think this is a very unwise and uncalled for move. In the end, the Negro people will be the losers, regardless of who wins the suit."[43]

The case rocked the African-American community, as well. *Cook* stoked widespread disagreement among blacks about the proper course to chart in the struggle for civil rights. Several religious and civic groups quickly announced support for the suit. But other blacks questioned its timing and propriety. Many conveyed a lack of enthusiasm through silence.

C. A. Scott, the editor of the *Atlanta Daily World* and a leading force in black politics, topped the list of critics. He called equalization of segregated schools a "practically obtainable" and "just" goal. But *Cook* went well beyond the objective of putting black schools on par with white ones. The suit sought to desegregate the schools, and this imperative Scott could not support for philosophical and practical reasons. He rejected the idea that equality under segregation was impossible and distinguished secondary from collegiate education. Scott saw the logic of opening institutions of higher education to African Americans; consequently, he backed Horace Ward's initial application for admission to UGA, filed around the same time as the *Cook* case. But Scott believed that separate schools worked best in elementary and secondary education. "[W]e seriously doubt the desirability or necessity for our seeking entrance to white [common] schools," he wrote. Interracial lower school education represented a "most sensitive" and "difficult" proposition—arousing whites' fears of interracial intimacy. Forcing the issue would only exacerbate these fears "to the detriment of our community."[44]

Others expressed a lack of enthusiasm for the suit through uncharacteristic silence. Organizations that had been at the forefront of school equalization efforts—the Atlanta Urban League, the Gate City Teachers' Association, and the GTEA—offered no comment on *Cook*. The Atlanta Urban League's coyness about the suit held special significance. Before *Cook*, the league had been a thorn in the side of the Atlanta Board of Education. It had lobbied the board for school funding increases nonstop, compiling reports year after year that detailed the vast differences in expenditures for black and white schools. The NAACP relied on precisely this sort of data in its equalization cases. But in the months leading up to *Cook*, the league gave no indication that it even planned to challenge the board's funding policies in court, much less file a suit directly attacking Jim Crow. The league's head, Grace Towns Hamilton, did participate in a 1949 meeting in which black leaders discussed the possibility of filing an equalization suit. However, Hamilton limited her role to discussing the league's data on school inequality, and she only took this step, news reports stressed, at the behest of the Atlanta NAACP. Hamilton's presence at the meeting nevertheless lent the league's imprimatur to a school equalization suit.[45]

But after Walden filed *Cook*, the league distanced itself from the case. Flooded with requests for information comparing black and white schools, the league issued a press release denying any connection to the suit. The league "is not associated with the present court action in any way, and does not consider it its function to comment on the legal merits of the case," the statement read. Some viewed the league's disclaimer disingenuous and a consequence of its dependence on white financial support. A fuller explanation for the league's reticence must take its ideological proclivities into account, however; the organization declined to take a public stand against residential and hospital segregation long after the National Urban League, its parent organization, spurned Jim Crow and urged local leagues to follow suit. The Atlanta Urban League's response to *Cook* reflected continuity, not change, in its position.[46]

Black teachers also were noticeably silent in response to *Cook*. Typically, the *World* exhaustively covered the educators' activities and opinions on issues of the day. Just prior to *Cook*, teachers trained their sights on the Georgia legislature's inadequate teacher salary increases and on their own suit for salary parity. The teachers also showed avid interest in legislative efforts to improve per pupil expenditures in black schools. At its April 1950 annual meeting, the GTEA exhorted members to lobby local school boards for more funding. The GTEA also skirmished with the Atlanta Board of Education over its decision to close three of four black evening schools. These institutions constituted important community assets, the teachers argued. They provided the only conduit to self-improvement for "underprivileged," functionally illiterate adults, and a rich source of employment for black teachers, the GTEA explained. The organization renounced the board's move to close them as a naked "attempt to reduce the teaching personnel by almost one-half" and eliminate black administrators from the school system. In the face of the teachers' mobilization, the board soon reversed its decision.[47]

The NAACP's school desegregation effort portended an even greater threat to the fabric of the community and teachers' livelihoods. At the same time, NAACP litigation recently had brought pay increases for many black teachers. The educators thus found themselves in a bind, fearful of what *Cook* meant for them, but unable to bite the hand that fed them. Public silence resulted. Despite their high profile in every other education-related issue, the teachers expressed neither approval nor disapproval of *Aaron v. Cook*.[48]

Privately, fear and discontent about the suit soon grew so prevalent that two prominent African-American leaders felt it necessary to respond publicly to the criticisms. Charles L. Harper, president of the local NAACP branch and past president of the GTEA, wrote an open letter "to our teachers." He sought to dissuade educators from publicly breaking ranks with the NAACP. Harper beseeched the teachers to "keep silent" and be "noncommittal" if questioned by the press; they should claim "that they are not sufficiently informed as to the background and details of the case to form an intelligent opinion." He also attempted to reassure teachers who feared that the suit might provoke retaliation. "There will be no bloodshed," he wrote, and "teachers will not lose their positions on account of this suit." Harper closed with the prediction that "[o]ur problems will be worked out amicably on a local basis."[49]

Benjamin Mays, president of Morehouse College, addressed the rancor caused by *Cook* in an October 4, 1950, radio broadcast. Mays began his address with the acknowledgment that "some Negroes," along with "the Atlanta press," had condemned *Cook*. Mays sought to mollify critics by explaining the "motives that lie behind the suit and place it in its proper perspective." "To argue that the suit makes an attack on segregation because the initiators of the suit want Negro children to go to school with white children is to miss the point entirely," Mays claimed. "[M]ixed schools" are not "the heart of the suit." Rather, the lawyers hoped to obtain parity for black students. "The stress is not on mixed schools," he claimed, but on the inequality that results from the dual educational systems." Mays even emphasized that "our [Georgia] laws plainly say that there must be separation," notwithstanding his prediction that the Supreme Court would soon issue an order outlawing school segregation. Mays held out to doubters the possibility that the lawyers had challenged segregation as a matter of strategy, rather than principle.[50]

Mays's explanation lacked candor. Walden and *Cook*'s other backers surely understood that the suit could only be considered a principled assault on Jim Crow. After all, Walden had participated in a number of strategy sessions with Thurgood Marshall, including the 1950 conference at which LDF rejected equalization suits once and for all and adopted direct challenges to school segregation as its central strategy. Moreover, Marshall had been preparing clients for the strategic shift well before 1950, as he toured the country—including Atlanta—delivering speeches denouncing separate schools. The *Atlanta Daily World* regularly covered these speeches about LDF's shifting strategy. In a 1948 address in Texas, Marshall stated that the NAACP "opposes all forms of segregation." He noted that the association had passed a resolution at its annual convention stating that "complete equality of educational opportunities cannot be obtained in a dual system of education." Marshall lashed out in personal terms against critics of the NAACP's position on equalization suits. He questioned the integrity of blacks who supported equalization suits, calling them "Negroes...willing to sell [the] race down the river" for personal gain. Marshall's reaction to the Supreme Court's decision in *Sweatt v. Painter* also signaled the NAACP's hard line against Jim Crow. The "complete destruction of all enforced segregation is now in sight," Marshall declared in *Sweatt*'s wake. In this context, one could hardly doubt what motivated *Cook*'s filing, however much Mays attempted to obscure its purpose.[51]

But whatever LDF's intentions, the conversation that took place in Atlanta after *Cook* indicated a gap between Thurgood Marshall's rhetoric and local realities. A significant segment of the local client community responded with ambivalence to the direct attack on segregation.

This reaction could hardly have surprised the national NAACP and LDF. Signs of dissent abounded. At the association's 1951 annual convention, held in Atlanta, delegates debated whether NAACP lawyers could be made to honor the NAACP's "strict non-segregation policy." The NAACP's existing constitution and bylaws only bound the branches to national NAACP policy, it turned out. Officials at the NAACP also knew that skepticism of the direct assault ran deep among educators. In a 1951 *Journal of Negro Education* article, LDF's Jack Greenberg responded to black teachers' growing fears about their "fate" if the NAACP prevailed in its school cases. Greenberg's concession that "innocent persons" would suffer as a "price" of integration likely provided small consolation to teachers. His conclusion that "there is a great deal that can be done through the courts" to protect black teachers' jobs—without a promise that LDF would fight those necessary legal battles—likely rankled, as well.[52]

The *Crisis* provided further evidence of ambivalence about the NAACP's course of action. The magazine featured numerous essays on the topic. In 1951, Lester Granger, the National Urban League's executive director, published an article titled "Does the Negro Want Integration" in the *Crisis*. He offered no conclusive answer to the question. The answer depended on which blacks one queried, Granger said, since blacks had many different reactions to the economic and social pressures associated with segregation. Yet he was clear on one essential point. "If we are perfectly honest with ourselves," Granger stated, "we will admit that throughout the country there are literally millions of Negroes" who are "unready" and "unwilling" to undergo desegregation. "By no means [do] all of us (or even a majority of us) want integration," Granger surmised. He nevertheless endorsed the pursuit of integration, insisting that "progress and leadership has always been achieved by the foresight and leadership of a few." Granger's essay captured the complex relationship between lawyers' objectives and client communities' preferences as the campaign against segregation unfolded. Marshall and his staff barreled ahead with the direct assault, convinced of its rightness, working on the assumption that local people who might disagree would eventually bend to LDF's will.[53]

Meanwhile, Atlanta's black leaders expected that local prerogatives would shape *Cook's* impact, whatever its outcome in court. C. L. Harper's statement to teachers that "[o]ur problems will be worked out amicably on a local basis" reflected this view. Mays also implied the salience of local politics to the legal process in his October 1950 radio address; he suggested that the national organization's preference for desegregation could be reconciled with locals' preference for equalization. It was not unthinkable to Mays and others that a middle ground—acceptable to those who wanted de jure segregation wiped off the books and those who wanted to preserve racially separate but equally funded black lower schools—could be reached. After all, *Sweatt* only applied to higher education, as the *Atlanta Daily World*'s editorial emphasized. Moreover, Mays took pains to underscore that the *Sweatt* Court had "evaded" the question of whether segregation itself constituted discrimination. Mays explained:

> In the *Sweatt* case, the University of Texas was ordered to admit a Negro because the school at Houston is not as good as the law school at the University of Texas. The implication is that if the school at Houston were equal to the law school at the University of Texas then it would have been all right to have segregated Sweatt.... The U.S. Supreme Court has not ruled that segregation on the basis of color or race is discriminatory.[54]

Even if *Cook* resulted in a court order commanding school desegregation, Atlanta's black leadership would have choices about how to implement it. In a 1954 talk, Mays predicted that even if the Supreme Court itself ordered desegregation, the process "would be slow." "Some localities will move immediately toward desegregation as some states have done in the case of higher education, but others may have to be ordered to do so by the courts," Mays observed. He went on:

> Negro parents will move very cautiously in many parts of the South. There will be no run on the bank. Parents will not risk their children being embarrassed and for that reason they will not rush in just because the Supreme Court has voted against segregation.... Once Negroes have gained the right to attend non-segregated schools...the pressure for non-segregation will be removed. There will be a tendency for Negroes to relax.

Mays' prediction was based on his sense that "The very fact that the law says to Negroes 'You cannot' and 'You must not' makes them determined to get the law changed. Human nature is like that." The mere fact that the court removed the prohibition would not necessarily cause blacks to fill the breach.[55]

### The Specter of Desegregation as Leverage for Equalization

Above all else, *Cook* offered a mechanism to wrest from whites more funding for black schools. African Americans could reap long-awaited monetary rewards—a goal that no one protested—without actually pushing for or even aspiring to school desegregation. Mays' insistence that the Atlanta school desegregation case was not actually about "mixed schools" but a strategy for attaining parity articulated this perspective. In an address to a white audience, Mays tried to "allay white fears" by reiterating that *Cook* was not designed to obtain "mixed schools." Rather, the suit was a means to force white politicians to appropriate the $100 million that Mays estimated would be needed to bring Georgia's black schools "up to the white standard." "White politicians," he said, "would never agree to spend the money unless the courts forced them."[56]

Mays's prediction made sense. Like legislatures throughout the South, the Georgia General Assembly started pouring money into black education at the mere threat of litigation. In a sensational break with the state's past neglect of black schools, the legislature enacted a minimum foundation program in 1949. This program increased overall appropriations for education and mandated the allocation of state educational funds to local school districts on a nondiscriminatory basis; black schools benefited considerably from this change, as they did from a new school building program enacted in 1951.[57]

In the years after *Aaron v. Cook*, black leaders set about trying to capitalize on the litigation in precisely the manner that Mays described. Instead of pushing school desegregation, they stepped up efforts to obtain school equalization. Numerous civic groups, including the Atlanta NAACP and teachers' association, along with the *Atlanta Daily World*, lobbied the state legislature, the state and city boards of education, and politicos to bring facilities and resources in black schools up to the white standard. The GTEA's 1952 annual meeting, organized around the theme "Better Education for Youth," focused on implementation of the minimum foundation program. The *World* ran numerous editorials demanding that the legislature comply with the legal mandate of separate but equal. In one column the paper virtually shouted: "EQUALITY is what we are LEGALLY entitled to and EQUALITY is what we want."[58]

The legislature felt the pressure. In enacting a bill allocating $10 million for the school building fund, house speaker George Hand quipped, "This answers the segregation problem.... If we dilly-dally much longer, the courts are going to make us do it." Even so, the task of allocating state funds fell to local authorities who were not necessarily on board with the new imperative to equalize black schools. Hence, black groups worked to ensure that officials used the state money for its intended purposes. Three activist religious groups, the Atlanta Baptist Ministers' Alliance, the African Methodist Episcopal (AME) Ministers' Alliance, and the Interdenominational Ministers' Alliance, passed resolutions calling on the Georgia Board of Education to ensure disbursement of adequate funds for black schools under the new school building fund program.

As new black schools emerged, the Georgia and Atlanta boards of education trumpeted the progress toward eliminating racial disparities in education.

After announcing that 50 percent of the building funds had been allocated to black schools, Ira Jarell boasted: "We believe children of all races should have equal opportunity and they are going to get it straight down the line." Similarly, after announcing a building plan set to create twelve new black schools, Dr. Kenneth A. Williams, chairman of the Georgia Board of Education, declared, "we have a moral obligation to every youngster in Atlanta and we [will] discharge that obligation."[59]

In *Cook*'s wake, pragmatism had worked well for blacks who had long sought increased school funding. White policy-makers had developed a newfound, if self-serving, commitment to black education, spending more money on African-American education than ever before. But how would African Americans' ambivalence about desegregation be reconciled with LDF's ambition to attack segregation itself? The *Cook* litigation promised to be the battleground for resolving this profound dilemma.

But it would not be so. The district court never adjudicated the case. It removed *Aaron v. Cook* from its calendar, pending the outcome of similar cases filed in South Carolina, Kansas, Delaware, Virginia, and the District of Columbia. The plaintiffs agreed to delay prosecution of the case indefinitely. Atlanta would not be a theater in the new civil war after all.[60]


## A PRAGMATIC RESPONSE TO BROWN

While *Cook* idled, the U.S. Supreme Court consolidated the other cases, to be known the world over as *Brown v. Board of Education*, and issued its landmark opinion. The Court's 1954 decision struck down segregated public schools, declaring them inherently unequal. Even if black schools equaled white ones in resources, they fell short constitutionally. Separate schools stigmatized black students and retarded their "educational and mental development," the Court decreed, citing LDF's sociological evidence.[61]

Georgia's political leaders denounced the decision. Led by Governor Talmadge, officials condemned *Brown* as an affront to states' rights. Talmadge and others quickly proposed strategies to circumvent the ruling, including selling the public schools to a private entity, repealing the state's compulsory attendance law, and providing tuition grants to (white) students so they could avoid desegregated schools. Without offering specifics, Atlanta's Mayor Hartsfield, a putative ally of black elites, also promised to defend school segregation. A host of whites—ministers, teachers, school officials, editorial writers, businessmen—followed the politicians' lead, denouncing *Brown* as well.[62]

A few white groups broke ranks with the majority. The Christian Social Relations Department of United Church Women accepted *Brown* "with humility" as a step toward a "Christian Society in which the human spirit is no longer burdened by this [racial] problem." Similarly, the North Georgia Methodist Conference adopted a resolution urging church members to obey the Supreme Court's decision as a matter of Christian "duty." B'nai Brith, the Jewish service organization, endorsed *Brown*. Two interracial organizations, the Southern Regional Council and the Georgia League of Women Voters, also supported the decision.[63]

In the face of overwhelming white opposition to the Supreme Court's edict, the traditional African-American leadership stood firmly behind the landmark decision in their public pronouncements. Figures such as Morehouse president Benjamin Mays, AU president Rufus Clement, prominent ministers, and other leading blacks endorsed *Brown*. Clement's statement was characteristic of the themes they sounded. He noted that the decision "lived up to the high moral principles which are the foundation upon which this country has been built" and gave an "effective and a resounding reply to Communist criticism of our treatment of our minority group." The *Atlanta Daily World* published an editorial endorsing *Brown*, the "decision of the century," marking an about-face for editor C. A. Scott. The editorial noted that the Court had "liberalized with the trend of the times" and took a bow to international political dynamics, which counseled a decision barring segregation as a way of demonstrating the authenticity of American democracy.[64]

A. T. Walden announced that he believed "Georgia would obey the law," and said that plans would soon be made to implement *Brown* in Atlanta. At a two-day meeting of regional NAACP officials and lawyers held in Atlanta days after *Brown* was announced, Atlanta leaders joined in a statement issued by the national NAACP calling for an "immediate" halt to the practice of school segregation. The signatories to the "Atlanta Declaration" promised that there would be "no compromise" on the issue. They called on all NAACP branches in "every affected area to petition their local school boards to abolish segregation without delay." The Atlanta NAACP "heartily endorsed" the declaration in a resolution unanimously adopted by a special committee headed by A. T. Walden.[65]

Yet, echoing the controversy surrounding *Aaron v. Cook*, some black Atlantans responded to the decision with caution. The local Baptist ministers association endorsed *Brown*, but only after a "heated discussion" held two months after the Court announced its decision. Controversy even erupted over A. T. Walden's views about *Brown*. Walden vigorously denied reports that he "favored waiting until the courts clarified their ruling outlawing school segregation" before moving forward with plans to implement *Brown*. The lawyer claimed to have been "misquoted" and vowed his support for the national NAACP's plans for immediate integration. Benjamin Mays's public comments about the implementation of *Brown* raised questions as well. He repeatedly emphasized how long the transition to desegregated schools would take, implying to some that he supported gradualism. Mays and other black leaders, including black college presidents, also noted that residential segregation would limit the amount of school desegregation. Mays remarked, "Even in the North there are segregated schools due mainly to the fact that the people who live in the area are either Negroes or whites. This pattern will be followed in the South."[66]

Elementary and secondary level educators proved the greatest skeptics—of the decision itself, not merely its implementation. Both the Gate City Teachers Association and the GTEA refused to endorse *Brown*, despite pressure from the Atlanta NAACP to do so. Mays, on record as supporting the decision, chastised black teachers for "hanging back" and wanting to maintain segregation for "personal gain." True to Mays's claim, the teachers were reluctant to support *Brown* primarily because they feared losing their jobs. William Gordon, managing editor of the *World*, exposed the teachers' anxiety in a column published on August 8, 1954. Gordon recounted how he had received "desperate" phone calls from individuals who believed that black educators would suffer as a consequence of the ruling. The *World*, providing perhaps the best description of black educators' outlook in *Brown*'s aftermath, concluded that they had adopted a "wait-and-see" attitude. Torn over desegregation, the teachers hoped that their worst fears would not be realized.[67]

Indeed, some teachers' positions softened a bit in the coming months and years, when massive resistance to *Brown* made actual desegregation a distant prospect. The GTEA endorsed *Brown* in 1956, two years after the Supreme Court's pronouncement (though a small group within the organization held out even then, and still refused to endorse the decision). Encouraged by leaders like Mays, many black educators believed that school desegregation might be indefinitely delayed. One principal commented that "inasmuch as Negroes generally live in their own communities, the school situation would not be too greatly affected by abolishing segregation." Even if resistance abated, neighborhood segregation would preserve the status quo—separate schools for black students, taught by black teachers.[68]

The teachers' skepticism of *Brown* fit a pattern. "[L]ittle leadership came from the blacks best trained to supply it." The three dozen or so black public school teachers of Topeka "wanted no part in any drive to desegregate the schools." Individual black teachers and black teachers' associations in Mississippi, Texas, South Carolina, Oklahoma, and Little Rock, Arkansas, were on record as opposing school desegregation in the first few years following *Brown*.

Lewis L. Butler, principal of a black school in Bamberg, South Carolina, wrote a letter to his local paper opposing desegregation on grounds that "Negro children and Negro teachers in the South" would be "thrust into a most peculiar situation which will be beset with many perplexing problems and grave consequences." He predicted that "Negro children's educational opportunities will suffer." In Mississippi, a group of Negro educators vowed that they would accept voluntary segregation in exchange for "immediate and full equalization of their schools."[69]

Black teachers' skepticism about the NAACP's legal strategy grew dramatically during the mid-1950s, when a number of southern states, including Georgia, began an anti-NAACP witch hunt. The states threatened to fire teachers who refused to disavow membership in the NAACP, which had been branded a subversive organization. At the same time, the Georgia Board of Education adopted a rule to revoke the license of any teacher with an NAACP membership; the board repealed the rule after a public outcry. But Eugene Cook, Georgia's attorney general, pressed on with his intimidation agenda, which involved an investigation of the local NAACP branch's corporate records to determine whether it had properly paid taxes. The harassment took its toll. Many teachers quit the organization rather than face economic ruin. In South Carolina, a black school principal and pastor lashed out against the organization, saying that blacks suffered because of the NAACP, a "loud-speaking scheming minority." Notwithstanding the pressures that teachers faced, NAACP officials and other civil rights organizations expressed "disgust" with educators' lack of support.[70]

Critics chalked up educators' opposition to school desegregation to self-interest and fear. But concerns about the quality of education available to black students in desegregated schools also motivated some teachers. Many black parents and leaders shared educators' worries about how black students would fare when instructed by white teachers far removed from their communities. These skeptics placed a high value on black teachers' ability to relate interpersonally to black students, as well as to stimulate intellectual growth. Parents doubted that white teachers would care for their children in the manner to which they had grown accustomed.[71]

Whatever the concerns of educators who were ambivalent about *Brown*, Marshall found it difficult to countenance them. He had no patience for uncertainty about school desegregation. Marshall made his perspective clear in the days following the decision. At the Atlanta Declaration conference, Marshall bowed to teachers' anxieties by promising "to "protect any teacher who loses his or her job solely because of race." Yet, he also vowed, "We don't worry about the [black] minority who want to go the other way. We will try to convert them to our way of thinking. But we will walk over them if they get in our way." Marshall underestimated the impact that this putative minority could have on the unfolding of his strategy at the local level, however. Even as he uttered those words, local people in Atlanta shaped what meaning *Brown* would have.[72]

Despite Walden's assurances that he walked in step with LDF's plans to implement *Brown*, in reality he did little, at first, to pursue desegregation. Neither Walden nor anyone else associated with the Atlanta NAACP branch made any effort to restore *Aaron v. Cook* to the court's calendar or to bring a new suit to implement *Brown* in the months—indeed in the years—following the Supreme Court's May 1954 decree. The Atlanta Declaration had urged local officials to petition for desegregation without delay, but compromise and delay characterized the tack taken by Atlanta NAACP officials in *Brown*'s wake. Instead of urging speedy compliance with *Brown*, the Atlanta NAACP branch, on Walden's counsel, ordered an "exhaustive study" of how desegregation should proceed.

At first glance, Walden's choice to "study" the problem at hand was indeed strange given his avowed commitment to immediately implement *Brown*. The burden to move litigation forward fell on the plaintiffs, as he and other black leaders well knew. And Walden proceeded in this cautious fashion despite the fact that Eugene Cook had made it perfectly clear that he would vigorously litigate each and every request for desegregation. The Supreme Court immeasurably aided the attorney general's defiance. In 1955, it issued its remedial decree, *Brown II*, which did not set a date for *Brown* compliance but instead ordered a "prompt and reasonable" start toward desegregation "with all deliberate speed." Many took the Court's unclear language as indicative of a lack of resolve to enforce its 1954 school desegregation decree. According to Cook, *Brown II* paved the way for "generations or centuries of litigation." "Suits would have to be filed in each of our 159 counties and each suit adjudicated individually," he said.[73]

But upon further inspection, Walden's unhurried pace after *Brown I* and *II* was hardly surprising. It reflected the wishes of Atlanta's black middle-class leaders. Several of them openly applauded the *Brown II* Court's decision not to set a date certain for school desegregation. John Wesley Dobbs, the black political leader, welcomed the Court's decision as "a very wise one." *Brown II* would "have a tendency to forestall the extremists and hot heads on both sides of the controversy," Dobbs continued. C. A. Scott at the *Atlanta Daily World* called the justices' decision to avoid setting a firm deadline for desegregation a "cool and collected" choice. Gradualism perplexed none of these leaders; they welcomed deliberate speed, an approach to civil rights that they had long embraced.[74]

Accordingly, in the months and years after the *Brown* decisions, Walden and other local counsel followed a gradual course. Walden heeded Mays's suggestion that blacks delay litigation in favor of "first seek[ing] action through the various boards of education and directly with public school officials." More than a year after the Court's decree in *Brown* but just a few days after it announced *Brown II*, Walden initiated a series of out-of-court appeals to the Board of Education. On June 3, 1955, Walden and other members of the Gate City Bar Association filed petitions seeking the desegregation of Atlanta's public school system. The attorneys acted on behalf of nine black students and under the auspices of the Atlanta NAACP. The branch's outreach to the board was in keeping with the locals' desire to avoid litigation. But LDF also encouraged the step as a precursor to litigation. By giving the school board "an opportunity to act," plaintiffs would undermine any claim by the school board that plaintiffs had not exhausted administrative remedies prior to filing suit.[75]

The petitions struck a deferential tone. The attorneys pledged that "there would be no need for pressing for court action"—"if" the board was "in a position to move toward integration now." "Consequently," they continued, "it is hoped that you will give favorable consideration to these petitions." The Atlanta Board of Education did not respond to the petitioners. The board referred the requests to a special committee, where they languished.[76]

The Atlanta NAACP's entreaties to the Board of Education continued for years without success. Lawyers filed four different sets of petitions between 1955 and 1956 requesting compliance with *Brown I* and *Brown II*, only to have the requests referred to committee for study. Even so, Atlanta's African-American leaders persisted in relying on press releases and resolutions to seek *Brown's* implementation. They did so well after the deadline set by the Atlanta branch of the NAACP, in collaboration with the national NAACP, for instituting litigation should petitions fail to produce desegregation. Immediately after *Brown II*, NAACP delegates from sixteen southern states and the District of Columbia, meeting in a "Southwide Emergency Conference" in Atlanta, had passed a resolution stipulating that "in the absence of any affirmative action by the school boards in September 1955, our branches will take whatever action is necessary to initiate the process of desegregation."[77]

That date loomed large for LDF. The lawyers initially had asked the Supreme Court to order immediate desegregation, saying that calls for "gradual" desegregation and "opposition to immediate action" stemmed from "a desire that desegregation not be undertaken at all." But if the Court chose not to issue an immediate order of desegregation, LDF asked the justices to designate September 1955 as the date for compliance with *Brown*. Though the Court had resisted setting any date for compliance, LDF made it clear how branches should proceed. "If no plans are announced or no steps towards desegregation by the time school begins this fall, 1955, the time for a law suit has arrived," the national NAACP announced in a directive to branches issued after the emergency conference. Thurgood Marshall specifically stated that he "expected legal action" in Georgia and other states in the conference at this time.[78]

The fall of 1955 came and went with no move by the Atlanta Board of Education toward desegregation. To the contrary, on August 8, 1955, the board passed a resolution stating that "no sudden, radical, or revolutionary changes in the operations of the schools should be initiated under the circumstances without full preparation." The board also voted unanimously to "make a thorough study of the effects of integration before any action is taken." The issues to be studied included "differences" in "average educational training, intelligence quotients, standards of achievement" between black and white students, and "differences" in the "average teaching efficiency of Negro teachers, as compared to white teachers." Dr. Rufus Clement, president of AU, member of the board, and leading light of the black elite, supported the Board of Education's action in "good faith." On the same day that the board passed its resolution making no suggestion that it would comply with *Brown*, it announced that the Georgia Avenue School, which had been designated "white," would be opened as a black school in the fall of 1955 because the surrounding neighborhood had become "predominantly Negro" over time. Rather than moving toward integration, the board was perpetuating segregation.[79]

The Atlanta branch of the NAACP did not object to the school board's foot-dragging. In response to the board's August 8, 1955 resolution, the branch issued a conciliatory statement. It declared, "We wish to state that we fully appreciate the position of the Atlanta Board of Education that no sudden, radical, or revolutionary changes in the operations of the schools should be initiated under the circumstances without full preparation." The branch's response continued with a reference to the Supreme Court's controversial phrase in *Brown II* regarding an implementation timetable. "[W]e believe that all resources available to the Board should be used with deliberate speed in making full preparation [for compliance]." The branch also called on the board to issue a "firm statement of policy that the schools will be desegregated." No such declaration came. Even so, it was not until 1958, after four years of inaction by the Board of Education, that Walden finally filed suit to enforce *Brown* in Atlanta.[80]

## WHO SPEAKS FOR LOCAL PEOPLE?

In large swaths of the country, desegregation proceeded in step with the ideal envisioned by national NAACP officials and LDF lawyers. A number of localities, mostly in Border States, desegregated swiftly, often at the urging of activist

African-American communities. Just before or soon after the Supreme Court issued its May 1954 mandate, schools were desegregated—on a token basis, to be sure—in several cities in Missouri, including St. Louis, Kansas City, Columbia, and Cape Girardeau; in twelve counties in West Virginia; in Baltimore; in the District of Columbia; and in parts of Delaware, Arkansas, and Kansas.[81]

Thurgood Marshall and his comrades touted such speedy compliance with *Brown* at every turn. At the NAACP's annual convention in Atlantic City in 1955, Marshall declared, "The gradual approach to integration does more harm than good. We are opposed to any 'piecemeal plan' for desegregation." He expected the desegregation process to be completed by September 1956. He called school boards' claim that blacks did not want integration "poppycock."[82]

But many African Americans apparently disagreed with Marshall. As was true in Atlanta, many localities embraced a more gradual approach to implementing *Brown*, often at the behest of local African-American leaders. Blacks in Houston and Dallas; Charlotte and Catawba County, North Carolina; Nashville; Charleston, South Carolina; Henderson County and Lexington, Kentucky; Carter County, Oklahoma; Mound Bayou, Mississippi; and numerous localities in Missouri, among other places, went on record as desiring a gradual implementation process. Without a doubt, white resistance influenced blacks' "preference" for gradualism in many cases and many places, especially the rural areas.[83]

However, these African Americans' caution cannot simply be dismissed out of hand as a product of oppression, fear, greed, or an inadequate commitment to equality. In the minds of African Americans in Atlanta and elsewhere, *Brown II*'s flexible approach to desegregation, including its "mandate" of "all deliberate speed," made sense. School desegregation amounted to not merely a legal but also a political mandate. And politics was local. For all of the social, political, and economic changes wrought by World War II and Thurgood Marshall's tireless efforts to prepare the way for *Brown*, in Atlanta and in many other places, the sociopolitical milieu did not support an all-out push for school desegregation.

Atlanta's black leadership class viewed moderation as appropriate to their time and place. They had spent decades building a highly functional, separate society, complete with many well-trained black teachers. They showed no eagerness to tear their institutions down all at once for the promise of equality through desegregation. The leaders feared what might lie ahead. To them, the desegregated world imagined by NAACP lawyers might not be a categorical improvement over the socioeconomic order that black elites had fashioned under Jim Crow. The leaders believed that desegregation might have costs, both immediate and long-term. The mixed results of teacher salary equalization litigation and the NAACP's ambivalence about the fate of black teachers in desegregated schools did not reassure these skeptics.

Local decision-makers' preferences reflected the socioeconomic stratification, values, and norms of black Atlanta, mediated by postwar American culture. Elites dominated the decision-making process on the local level, just as national elites—the professionals and lawyers of the national NAACP—had presumed to set the civil rights agenda for local communities. Locals responded most favorably to the elements of the national litigation plan that advanced the economic and political interests of local black middle-class leaders. The aims of educators, united in a strong teachers' association, topped the agenda. The pragmatists constituted a distinct, highly politicized, and self-interested segment of society.

The pragmatists' circumspect view about school desegregation recalled the doubts of none other than NAACP cofounder W. E. B. Du Bois. Du Bois had lamented the NAACP's obsession with the mere fact of segregation and questioned the narrow pursuit of "mixed schools." "The thinking colored people of the United States must stop being stampeded by the word segregation," he wrote. "There should never be an opposition to segregation pure and simple," he argued, unless it "involve[s] discrimination."[84]

The initial battle in Atlanta over school desegregation did not resolve the question of whether racially separate schools could exist without discrimination. That issue forever dogged the NAACP's campaign to desegregate schools. As we shall see, the national and local NAACP eventually were torn apart by the decision of Atlanta's black leaders to repudiate LDF's canonical view that *Brown* required school integration.

## CHAPTER 5

# More Than "Polite Segregation"

## Brown *in Public Spaces, 1954–1959*

We are trying to be law-abiding and we don't want any friction; so we will
wait until the courts work it out. (1955)

Rev. Oliver W. Holmes

Do not be drawn into argument about segregation, desegregation, or integration; talk as little as possible and always in a quiet voice. (1959)

Rev. William Holmes Borders

In its 1954 annual report, the national NAACP touted yet another of its campaigns for change.[1] The organization announced its intention to end discrimination in recreation. What was more, it cited an Atlanta case as a shining
example of its effort to apply *Brown v. Board of Education* in this new arena. The
NAACP and Atlanta's black leadership may have disagreed about the wisdom of
school desegregation.[2] But they agreed that *Brown* could be utilized to achieve
change in an array of contexts other than schools.[3]

A. T. Walden and others in Atlanta leveraged *Brown* in the recreation and
public transit areas, but not precisely as the national NAACP and LDF might
have imagined. The pragmatists continued to chart their own path toward racial
progress. Desegregation did not dominate their agenda. To a significant extent,
they aimed for what the NAACP dismissed as more "polite segregation."

Atlanta's black elite pushed hardest and fastest to desegregate realms that
few blacks might have prioritized. The first lawsuit filed in Atlanta after *Brown*
challenged Jim Crow not in public schools but on public golf courses. The leadership gave lower priority to those recreational facilities—swimming pools,
parks, and playgrounds—most important to the vast majority of blacks. In
public transit, the black pragmatists initially protested the indignities of segregation through negotiation, administrative appeals, and tort suits, rather than
by filing a constitutional challenge to segregation itself. Later, leaders took steps
to desegregate the buses, but a resulting lawsuit unfolded slowly and crowded

out mass protest. In the end, the leaders chose a halting approach to implementing their victory in the public transit desegregation case.

Even so, the pragmatic politics and tactics of Atlanta's black leadership had changed. In *Brown*'s wake, Atlanta's black leaders had to confront new organizations and new forms of activism. Increasingly, blacks across the South protested discrimination in very public and vocal ways. The Montgomery bus boycott heralded the new face of black protest. The pragmatism of Atlanta's black decision-makers remained intact, but was transformed under the influence of nonviolent civil disobedience.

## RECREATIONAL FACILITIES

Atlanta's African-American leaders had long pursued the goal of increasing the number of golf courses, parks, pools, and playgrounds available to blacks. They were offended that the municipality used their tax dollars to provide numerous facilities for whites, while blacks were left with a few dilapidated and crowded sites. Using the tool of interracial diplomacy, community activists had pursued new recreational facilities under the rubric of separate but equal. After *Brown*, Atlanta's black leaders turned to litigation, with mixed results, to end discrimination in recreational facilities.[4]

### The Links

Jim Crow first came tumbling down in Atlanta at a site frequented by a small number of African Americans. The city opened its municipal golf courses to blacks by virtue of the U.S. Supreme Court's decision in *Holmes v. Atlanta*, issued in November 1955. In the months following *Brown*, the Court issued opinions in *Holmes* and several other cases in which it analogized the practices found unconstitutional in the school segregation cases to discrimination in other public facilities. In this way, the *Holmes* decision itself did not seem extraordinary. But the circumstances surrounding the initiation and implementation of *Holmes* are quite significant. They illustrate the continued commitment of A. T. Walden and others in Atlanta's black leadership to interracial diplomacy and the separate but equal principle—*even* in the post-*Brown* era. At the same time, the case shows the determination of others to directly challenge Jim Crow, even if in a context that held limited benefits for African Americans as a whole.[5]

The three plaintiffs who filed the suit hailed from a single, prominent family. H. M. Holmes, an African-American doctor, and his two sons, Alfred, the director of a funeral home, and Oliver, a minister, were avid golfers. Alfred was an amateur champion. All of the Holmeses held memberships at the New Lincoln Golf and Country Club, a privately operated golf club for African Americans. The club had 150 members. There was no municipal golf course for blacks in Atlanta.[6]

Whites, by contrast, could choose to play at several public courses. One of them, the Bobby Jones Golf Course, was considered one of the best in the region. In July 1951, the Holmeses requested permission from park officials to use the Bobby Jones Course. The request was denied. However, as a consequence of it, the city agreed to set aside funds for the construction of a course for use by African-American golfers. Unsurprisingly, the city moved slowly; years passed with no progress. The black golfers then determined to settle the matter through litigation. R. E. Thomas, one of the Gate City Bar Association's founding members, decided to "take a chance" on the suit after a furtive meeting with the Holmeses in the basement of a local café. Thomas listened as the golfers explained that "they wanted to play golf on the city-owned golf courses" because "they were taxpayers" just like whites.[7]

The first round of court action brought a victory for the plaintiffs, but on the grounds set forth in the Supreme Court's 1896 *Plessy v. Ferguson* decision. On July 9, 1954, almost two months after the Supreme Court had handed down *Brown*, the U.S. District Court for the Northern District of Georgia ruled that the city had violated the Constitution's equal protection clause by failing to provide facilities for the black golfers' use. The court determined that Atlanta could remedy the violation not by integrating the courses but by providing the plaintiffs with a segregated golfing facility. Moreover, the court postponed the implementation of the order until such time as the city could actually provide separate but equal courses for black golfers. *Brown* apparently held no sway in federal district court in Georgia.[8]

The district court had essentially left the plaintiffs where they had been prior to entering litigation—at the mercy of city officials—who continued to procrastinate in constructing the "separate but equal" links. The district court's order would have to be appealed, in a direct challenge to Jim Crow. Conflict surfaced. Many blacks did not want Thomas to go forward with the challenge; skeptics called a meeting at the Bethel AME Church to discuss the matter. Prominent figures—men so prominent that Thomas refused to name them decades later—asked Thomas to drop the suit. By inference, A. T. Walden must have opposed the suit. "No decision by any group in Atlanta after the 1940s was made without consulting A. T. Walden," according to Gate City Bar member

Howard Moore. Naysayers advised Thomas and the Holmeses that they were "making a huge mistake" in going forward with the suit. But Thomas "steadfastly refused" to back down. Dr. Holmes found enough support for his suit within the Atlanta chapter of the NAACP to move forward with the challenge to Jim Crow.[9]

The local NAACP chapter then turned to LDF for assistance. Attorneys Thurgood Marshall, Robert Carter, and Jack Greenberg argued the case on appeal. The lawyers failed in their efforts to gain a reversal of the lower court's order. The Fifth Circuit affirmed the district court order that had granted the plaintiffs a pyrrhic victory. The LDF next appealed the case to the High Court. More than a year later, in November 1955, the Supreme Court issued its per curiam opinion requiring the desegregation of Atlanta's golf courses under the principles enunciated in *Brown*.[10]

Only then did the city and state's white power structure have to confront in earnest the issues raised in *Holmes*. Georgia's leaders denounced the ruling. Governor Marvin Griffin vowed that integration would never be permitted at any state recreational facility. Along with the state's still influential former governor, Herman Talmadge, Griffin suggested closing the municipal links in order to avoid desegregating them. Georgia attorney general Eugene Cook went much further. The state's chief law enforcement officer trumpeted the view that the Court's ruling about golf courses would result in bloodshed.[11]

Atlanta officials handled the situation more deftly. William Hartsfield, the city's mayor and a defendant in *Holmes v. Atlanta*, suggested that passion remain in check because the Supreme Court's decision only applied to golf courses. The ruling did not threaten the racial integrity of any other municipally owned recreational facilities. He did not indicate whether the city would comply with the Court's order to end Jim Crow on the links. Nor did he side, however, with those state leaders who championed the closing of the courses in order to thwart the ruling. Hartsfield instead noted Atlanta's "good reputation" and said that he would "do the right thing" about the golf controversy after consulting a biracial group of citizens.[12]

A month later, in December 1955, when the *Holmes* plaintiffs announced that they would, in effect, test the segregationists' resolve by attempting to play golf at a municipal course, Hartsfield announced his decision to defer to the Court. Candidly, the mayor explained that the city's decision to comply with the court order had nothing to do with whether desegregating the links was the "right thing" to do. Rather, the decision reflected the city fathers' assessment that compliance with *Holmes* would entail few costs to whites, but yield great benefits. Hartsfield explained that closing the course would deprive nearly seventy thousand white players and nearly one hundred city employees of their jobs and their rights, all in an effort to deny just a few dozen Negro players the use of the golf links. The effort to close the course was neither worthwhile nor necessary, he said. "Golf by its very nature is a segregated game," and given the "uniformly very small" number of black players, it would remain segregated. "The future use of the courses by the majority of white players will determine whether Golf is continued as a Municipal project in the future," Hartsfield surmised. He also reiterated his belief that the court order applied to the municipal golf courses only. "Swimming pools and playgrounds are not affected and will continue to operate as before," he said. With this caveat, he reassured segregationists of Talmadge's stripe, who viewed the "intermingling" of African-American and white children in such "intimate settings" as swimming pools as the road to the holocaust of "intermarriage."[13]

Hartsfield's announcement that Atlanta would comply with the Court's edict was based on two considerations: the small number of African-American golfers and the slim chance that whites would interact with them on the courses. The 150 members of the New Lincoln Golf and Country Club—that is, the pool of African Americans who could potentially integrate the municipal courses—accounted for less than one-tenth of 1 percent of the city's black population. Moreover, only 3 of the 150 had expressed an interest in playing at the white courses. Even if all 150 black golfers wanted to use the links on an integrated basis, they could only do so with the cooperation of white golfers. That cooperation did not appear to be forthcoming. As late as 1959, black golfers reported encountering resistance from white golfers when they attempted to use the city's municipal courses. In light of these realities, Hartsfield knew that integration was unlikely to occur on the links, *Holmes* notwithstanding. Thus, governmental resistance to the Supreme Court's edict was unnecessary. Still, Hartsfield might have feigned resistance through rhetorical posturing; but that would have carried the unnecessary risk of tarnishing the city's moderate image and alienating the black voters who were a vital part of his electoral coalition. Hartsfield's decision to comply with the Supreme Court's order was a logical choice for the mayor personally, for the city, and for white elites.[14]

But what were the implications of Hartsfield's handling of the *Holmes* crisis for African Americans? The decision to comply with *Holmes* had a limited impact on the black community as a whole. True, Hartsfield's choice benefited the three golfers who filed the case and the 147 others who associated with the New Lincoln Club. But for the rest of the African-American community—the 99 percent who were not golfers—Hartsfield's compliance with the golf order, coupled with his refusal to recognize its applicability to other recreational facilities, made little difference. The vast majority of blacks remained relegated to a small number of segregated facilities that were in much greater demand than golf courses. These facilities—playgrounds, ball fields, pools—remained strictly segregated and allocated on a discriminatory basis after *Holmes*, as they had been for decades. R. E. Thomas's challenge to the status quo had been courageous, but it had not actually changed much in the daily existence of African Americans.

## Parks, Pools, Playgrounds

Even as Hartsfield limited the reach of *Holmes* and even though there had been modest improvements over the years, Jim Crow's hold on Atlanta's municipal recreation system was unmistakable. As of 1954, the city designated only 4 parks for black use, while whites enjoyed 128. Whites had twenty-one playgrounds at their disposal; blacks could only use three. African Americans were limited to three of eight pools, one of seven indoor gyms, three of twenty-two baseball fields, five of twenty-four basketball courts, five of twenty-three football fields, and eight of ninety-six tennis courts. The dearth of recreational facilities affected the entire African-American community, but it was particularly hard on school-aged children.[15]

African-American leaders had demanded more and better parks, playing fields, pools, and the like since the 1930s. Blacks on the Fulton-Dekalb Interracial Committee (FDC) expressed concern that the limited number of recreational facilities stunted the development of African-American children. These children "suffer[ed]" from a lack of facilities, space, and equipment, and were unable to "awaken to their opportunities" as a result. At the time, the Works Progress Administration, the New Deal agency, subsidized the development of new recreational facilities in the city. The FDC, which included Atlanta University president Rufus Clement and the dean of AU's school of social work, Forrester Washington, lobbied for the inclusion of African Americans in the expansion program.[16]

The unequal number and quality of recreational facilities topped the political agendas of black advocacy organizations. The Atlanta Urban League was out in front on the issue. The league documented racial disparities in facilities and used its reports to demand that the city allocate additional funds for adequate services. A. T. Walden's ANVL also lobbied for a more equitable distribution of facilities, especially parks. The league even relied on how candidates stood on the issue as a way of deciding whom to endorse. In fact, Hartsfield's proclaimed commitment to developing recreational areas for blacks had figured in ANVL's decision to back him during his bid for a fourth term as Atlanta's mayor.[17]

Despite pressure from black middle-class leaders, the city did little to remedy the racial disparities in recreational facilities. It allocated no additional funds for black parks, pools, playgrounds, gyms, or playing fields from a special tax levy conducted in 1951. In 1953, the city proposed to allocate 33 percent of tax income to the development of a golf course for African Americans; but it never followed through on the proposal. Nor did it earmark any resources for the facilities that most blacks in Atlanta used or wanted to use.[18]

White elites held up improvements in part because of the volatile housing situation. The MPC would only recommend sites for additional recreational facilities for blacks in approved areas. African Americans achieved one victory in March of 1954, when the Westside Mutual Development Committee (WSMDC)—the biracial committee charged with managing black expansion and migration—approved the transfer of Mozley Park from white use to black use. Even then, the city compensated whites for the loss of Mozley Park by constructing a new whites-only swimming pool in the summer of 1954.[19]

*Holmes v. Atlanta* should have proven a valuable asset to those interested in challenging the city's discriminatory recreational policies. But black leaders did not seek to use the precedent to force an end to the lopsided allocation of facilities. A. T. Walden remained conspicuously silent in public discussions of the golf course controversy, likely due to opposition to his colleague's decision to file the suit. We also can infer that his silence signaled acceptance of the course that Hartsfield steered. Walden almost certainly participated behind the scenes in Hartsfield's decision-making process. He had been the most prominent of the small number of blacks whom Hartsfield customarily consulted about racial problems. When Hartsfield's claim that his decision-making about the Supreme Court's order in *Holmes* had been influenced by consultation with a "biracial group of citizens," he signaled that black elites such as Walden supported his decision to nominally comply with *Holmes* while limiting its impact.

Yet, Hartsfield's assertion that *Holmes* did not apply to municipal recreational facilities as a whole was a questionable legal position, as Walden surely knew. The Supreme Court's order in *Holmes* vacated judgments from the federal district and appellate courts in the plaintiffs' favor on the grounds of the separate but equal doctrine. The justices ordered the district court to enter a decree in conformity with *Mayor & City Council of Baltimore v. Dawson*. In that case, the Supreme Court, reasoning by analogy to *Brown*, had affirmed an order by the Fourth Circuit that found racial segregation on public beaches and bathhouses unconstitutional. The Fourth Circuit's reasoning in *Dawson* confounded Hartsfield's position that *Holmes* only applied to golf courses. The appeals court's opinion had stated: "[I]t is obvious that racial segregation in recreational activities can no longer be sustained as a proper exercise of the police

power of the State; for if that power cannot be invoked to sustain racial segregation in the schools…it cannot be sustained with respect to public beach and
bathhouse facilities." There was no way to get around the Supreme Court's
directive to the district court presiding in *Holmes.* Hartsfield's interpretation of
the order's scope defied logic: *Holmes* required desegregation of all municipal
recreational facilities.[20]

Still, the city's foot-dragging—and black acquiescence to it—went on for
seven long years. Atlanta would not begin to desegregate its parks, pools, playgrounds, gymnasiums, and playing fields until the mid-1960s. It would take the
student protest movement to finally bring an end to Jim Crow's presence in
Atlanta's recreational facilities.[21]

## PUBLIC TRANSPORTATION

Change occurred in public transit context against the backdrop of civil disobedience in a sister city. On December 5, 1955, the Montgomery bus boycott
began. For 381 days Montgomery's African-American community—fifty thousand strong—sustained the protest. They demanded an end to segregated seating and discriminatory treatment by bus drivers. In 1956, the boycott yielded
an important U.S. Supreme Court precedent, *Gayle v. Browder.* The decision
affirmed a district court's holding that segregation on public transportation,
like that in public schools and recreational facilities, violated the Fourteenth
Amendment of the Constitution. Montgomery's bus system did, in fact, desegregate. The synergy of *Brown* and the social movement in Montgomery had
wrought real change.[22]

The postwar struggle for civil rights had reached a transition point. The
Montgomery bus boycott launched the direct action phase of the civil rights
movement. The boycott galvanized African Americans in other southern cities. In its wake, blacks in Mobile, Memphis, New Orleans, Tallahassee, Miami,
Albany, Georgia, and Rock Hill, South Carolina, among other cities, launched
their own boycotts of segregated transportation. These boycotts constituted a
sea change in race relations: blacks fought back, en masse, against segregation. They made claims to full citizenship in the streets and won equal rights
in the courts. To many Americans, the boycotts signaled the start of a social
revolution.[23]

In Atlanta, the boycott put tremendous pressure on the black leadership, long
committed to a moderate course. At first, black leaders wrestled with the question of how to respond to the events in Montgomery. There were months, even

years, of inaction. Ultimately, they decided that they could implement *Gayle*, but in a manner that allowed them to satisfy competing objectives: appeasing white resistance and mollifying blacks who were intent on pursuing desegregation. The path that black elites chose allowed Atlanta to avoid both the disorder of white resistance to change and the disorder of black protest against the status quo. The buses would be desegregated, but on a token basis and without any mass black protest action. The pace and terms of desegregation would be negotiated by the city's traditional white and black leadership. There would be no boycotts, no demonstrations, or any uncertainty that might threaten locals' control over the direction of the struggle for racial equality in Atlanta.

## More Polite Segregation

It is a fact of history often overlooked that the Montgomery boycotters' initial goal was better treatment on segregated buses, rather than integration, even though their boycott began well after *Brown*. The national NAACP refused to support the boycott in its early stages because of the boycotters' goals. The staff dismissed the locals' objective of better service as a request for little more than "polite segregation." The NAACP would consider no objective other than desegregation.[24]

In Atlanta, black elites fully embraced the goal of better service on segregated buses. For the national NAACP, this was a modest objective. To be sure, the goal of improved service on segregated buses could be viewed in those terms. But it also was a logical goal under the circumstances, as several episodes from Atlanta before and after *Brown* demonstrated. Blacks wanted to be treated with dignity; they wanted relief from the daily insults and hostility inflicted upon them by white drivers and passengers. African-American riders sought to end the humiliation that they routinely experienced as they negotiated the aisles, doorways, and race-specific seating patterns on overcrowded trains, streetcars, and buses.

Several cases filed by A. T. Walden illustrate the point. Walden's acclaim as a race man was premised on his representation of two prominent African-American citizens in a suit over their mistreatment on a city streetcar in 1930s Atlanta. Dr. C. A. Spence, a dentist, and his wife, a pharmacist, were beaten during an altercation between the streetcar conductor and another black passenger. White bystanders and employees of the company attacked the Spences for the "crime" of refusing to follow the conductor's command "[e]very damn nigger get off [the car]!" during the fight. Though the mob victimized the Spences, the city filed disorderly conduct charges against *the Spences*.[25]

Walden came to their defense. He represented the doctor and his wife against the city's charges, and he succeeded in obtaining an acquittal on all counts. Walden then brought a suit against the streetcar company for the injuries that the Spences had suffered in the brawl. In a triumph considered astounding for the time, Walden secured a judgment for $1,500 in damages from the company. The *Crisis* hailed Walden's victory. The magazine called it a sign that blacks could obtain justice in southern courts—albeit with "great difficulty"—and a harbinger that change was coming "with persistent determination, legal talent, and a just cause."[26]

Blacks continued to battle rough and disrespectful treatment on public transportation during the 1940s. After a series of racial disturbances on city buses and streetcars, leaders turned to negotiation with company officials to address persistent problems. Reminiscent of the Spence case and others from an earlier period, some of these incidents had led to the wrongful arrest of black citizens. In November 1942, a committee of the Georgia Interracial Commission met with officials of the Georgia Power Company in an effort to "ease interracial tension and prevent friction on Atlanta's street cars and buses." The committee urged company officials to impress upon drivers the need for "every courtesy" to "all riders" and "tolerance" in "every situation." In addition, the committee suggested that officials increase the number of inspectors on public transportation to spot check for problems. They also recommended an educational campaign to instruct citizens on the "etiquette of race relations" and remind them of the need for "obedience" of bus drivers and "respect" for other passengers, especially during wartime, when public transportation was overcrowded and overtaxed. Owners of buses and streetcars readily agreed to the committee's suggestions. They also promised to remove problematic drivers from routes that primarily served black customers.[27]

During the mid-1950s Walden represented blacks in a dispute with city officials and transit owners that highlighted a different dimension of the transportation service problem and demonstrated how social class colored African-Americans' priorities. Discourteous conduct retreated into the background as an issue when African Americans in the Dixie Hills neighborhood, one of the city's poorest areas, complained of high fares and inconvenient and inadequate service routes. To air these complaints, blacks elite formed the Committee for Improvement of Westside Transit Service. The committee hired A. T. Walden as its counsel. The residents' complaints about service coincided with the Dixie Hills Bus Lines' application for a fare increase with the Public Service Commission.[28]

In October 1953, Walden filed a complaint with the commission protesting the rate increase and challenging the bus line's class A certification. He made the petition on behalf of Ruby Blackburn, a black woman who was well known as a civic and political activist in the community, and Irene Sims Hendrix. Blackburn, a former maid who had organized other domestic workers, conducted membership drives for the NAACP branch, and founded the Georgia League of Negro Women Voters, led the protest. In sworn affidavits, Blackburn and Hendrix objected to the rate hike on the grounds that "service rendered is totally inadequate" and "because we now have to pay two fares in order to get down town from our homes." In fact, the two claimed that bus service in Dixie Hills was "substandard when measured against service provided by other public transportation facilities for the City of Atlanta." Under the circumstances, Walden argued, the bus company did not even deserve an operating license, let alone a rate increase.[29]

The same month, in a letter to the mayor and city council, Walden reiterated his complaints. He argued that the Dixie Hills Bus Service subjected riders in the area to "grossly unfair" hardships. "Poor Negro families have to pay four bus fares each day to and from work" and have to pay "six and eight fares" in instances where "domestics work further out" from the neighborhood. In addition, Walden complained that service routes were inadequate and unreliable: there were too few of them for the population served, and drivers did not keep to their schedules. Sometimes drivers never showed up at all due to repeated breakdowns of antiquated equipment. These problems, Walden said, constituted "outright discrimination against the poorest economic group in the City."[30]

The residents' protest struck a nerve with white elites, undoubtedly in part because the affected riders—wage laborers—were the backbone of the downtown and in-home service economy. Many of the transit company's customers were black women who worked as domestic servants in the homes of wealthy whites in the exclusive Buckhead area. The *Atlanta Journal-Constitution* came out against the proposed rate hike and in favor of service improvements on the Westside. And the Atlanta City Council unanimously passed a resolution calling on the Public Service Commission to cancel the bus line's permit if it did not offer better transportation in the Dixie Hills area. For his part, J. C. Steinmetz, the owner of Dixie Hills, professed his eagerness to "rectify any reasonable complaints." Against the backdrop of growing public complaints about its service in the area, Dixie Hills eventually withdrew its request for a fare increase, handing the residents a rare victory. By 1956, the protesters had achieved even more. The Atlanta Transit System created and implemented new and expanded bus routes for Westside patrons. Under the rubric of "better service," the residents of Dixie Hills had blocked a rate hike—a tremendously meaningful outcome for the black working poor—and made the daily experience of commuting to work and school more tolerable—all without mention of "desegregation."[31]

## The Implementation of *Gayle v. Browder*

Owing to the events in Montgomery, Atlanta did eventually confront the matter of segregated transportation. The city's circuitous path toward compliance with *Browder* unfolded over two years. The elites negotiated a plan to desegregate the city buses during the summer of 1957. The sessions were attended by the usual collection of biracial negotiators, including the two principals, Mayor Hartsfield and A. T. Walden. The group also included Robert Sommerville, the president of Atlanta Transit Company; aware that African Americans accounted for 53 percent of his bus line's passengers, Sommerville understood that the negotiations were a business imperative. Together these men devised a plan to comply with *Browder* that steered clear of the social unrest and economic peril that had accompanied events in Montgomery.[32]

This plan only came about because black and white elites were pressured to act. The plan was formulated in response to a not-so-veiled threat from William Holmes Borders, a well-known local minister, who suggested he would file a *Browder* test case in Atlanta. It was January 1957, more than a year after the Montgomery boycott had started, when Borders announced that he and other area ministers would bring the movement for desegregation of public transportation to Atlanta. In explaining his action, Borders noted that although the Supreme Court had ruled that segregation on local buses was unlawful, the "best legal opinion is . . . that this decision cannot be enforced in Atlanta . . . until there has been a specific decision to that effect." A. T. Walden had provided this legal advice to Borders.[33]

Borders's protest must be understood within the context of the pressure that he felt after Montgomery. Borders headed one of the city's largest congregations, and his membership included many college students the demographic that would be at the forefront of the direct action movement. Borders's congregation expected him to be the conscience of the community. He was under increasing pressure to push a civil rights agenda, thanks to the influence of the homegrown leader of the Montgomery bus boycott, Rev. Martin Luther King, Jr. In fact, two days prior to Borders's announcement that he would bring the boycott movement to Atlanta, he had met with Dr. King and ministers from other cities engaged in the movement to desegregate public transportation. Many of the ministers at this meeting would go on to form the Southern Christian Leadership Conference (SCLC). Borders's commitment to bringing Atlanta into the thick of the direct action movement grew out of his intermingling with clergy who had made the choice to move off of the sidelines and into the vanguard of the black protest movement. Yet, he remained within the moderate elites' circle of influence.[34]

Borders's act of protest took place in January 1957, under the auspices of the "Love, Law, and Liberation Movement," known as "Triple L." Whereas organizers of the Montgomery bus boycott kept their initial plans secret to thwart white attempts to intimidate would-be black protesters, Borders divulged the details of his protest well ahead of time. He made sure that fellow members of the biracial elite, whites and blacks, and all African Americans who rode city buses were aware of his plans to lead a group of blacks—a handpicked group of ministers—to sit in the "white" section of the city buses. Borders announced the protest during a meeting at his Wheat Street Baptist Church and in the *Atlanta Daily World*. At the appointed hour, 10 A.M. on January 9, 1957, in full view of the media, Borders and a group of twenty ministers violated the law and custom that required blacks to sit at the back of city buses.[35]

The ministers' action was low-key, and it produced no incidents of violence. They boarded a virtually empty bus, and the driver designated the route "special" as they boarded. As a result, only two whites remained on the bus for a few blocks after the ministers "desegregated" it. Moreover, once alerted to which bus the ministers were riding, the bus company provided a second bus, which "ran ahead of the test vehicle and took on all further passengers." As an *Atlanta Constitution* writer explained, "The trolley, in effect, ran segregated." The next day, the city's police chief issued warrants for the arrest of five of the ministers, including Borders, charging them with violating the state's segregation law. With A. T. Walden and R. E. Thomas acting as their attorneys, the ministers were released an hour later, each on a $1,000 bond; the prosecution did not proceed with the cases further. Having established the factual basis needed for a *Browder* test case, Borders announced that the courts would now determine whether Atlanta was bound by the Supreme Court's decree. The "movement" was over. Borders and other leaders now instructed blacks to behave—to continue to comply with the bus segregation rules—until such time as the courts ruled otherwise. Borders and Walden received loud criticism from some blacks for refusing to give them the "go-ahead" to ride desegregated on the buses until the courts resolved the legal case.[36]

It was not until January 1959 that the federal court in Atlanta ruled that *Gayle v. Browder* applied to the local bus desegregation case, *Williams v. Georgia Public Service Commission*. In response to the ruling, Mayor Hartsfield issued a statement asking white Atlantans to "take [the judge's ruling] in stride," because resistance was inimical to their economic interests. "Any violence or discord," he explained "would simply hurt the transit system and do great damage to downtown merchants and finally would cost white folks far more financial loss than any other group." As a practical matter, Hartsfield's warnings were unwarranted, because the *Williams* court did not issue an injunction ordering authorities to cease enforcing the segregation statute. Segregation remained the norm on the buses, and that fact did not seem to rankle elites, white or black.[37]

Rather than asking the court to reconsider its action, A. T. Walden and other attorneys issued a statement saying that they "felt that the court might well have issued the injunction prayed for, but there are many cases supporting the principle of abstention as regards injunctions in situations similar to this." Borders and others involved with the Triple L protest actively discouraged challenges to the traditional, segregated seating arrangements. After the *Williams* decision was announced, the Triple L group issued a statement indicating that they would "advise" the black community "as to how to proceed" at meetings to be held later in the week at the Wheat Street Baptist Church. Meanwhile, African-American bus riders were instructed to respond to any white hostility about the *Williams* ruling with "complete non-violence" and by "observing ordinary rules of courtesy and good behavior."[38]

At the meetings on the implementation of the bus ruling, Borders advised against a mass test of the ruling. Instead, he said, the actual desegregation of the buses should be left to "individual action" and "judgment." He warned, "don't sit down by any white woman." "You don't want to be drawn into any trap that might hurt all of us," "irritat[e] anybody," or "get involved in any incident that could bring shame on our race." Dr. Benjamin Mays and *Atlanta Daily World* editors chimed in, advising that the court's ruling itself made the buses integrated as a matter of law and therefore there was no need to address the issue on a mass basis. At Sunday services across the city, ministers throughout the city, including Martin Luther King, Sr., concurred. There were scattered reports of desegregated riding in the days and weeks after *Williams*, but no indication that black bus riders had strayed from the directives issued by their leaders.[39]

## WHAT COUNTS AS PROGRESS?

African Americans viewed interracial diplomacy as a means of demonstrating their political power, but white opponents of desegregation benefited from the practice, as well. Atlanta's white elites ceded very little ground in negotiations over racial problems, whatever the issue—even when Atlanta's black leadership wanted no more than separate but equal.

The *Holmes* litigation constituted steps forward for the black leadership, which had spent years avoiding litigation as an avenue for challenging racial injustice. At the same time, blacks' challenge of segregation on golf courses but not in other recreational facilities signaled continuity in their posture toward whites. Atlanta's compliance with the *Holmes* decree came at no cost to white elites and relatively little gain for most African Americans. With no pressure from Walden and others to apply *Holmes* to the recreational facilities generally, whites were encouraged to obstruct Supreme Court decisions by relitigating settled issues in the state and federal courts. Meanwhile, the more pressing needs of most blacks for improved access to parks, playgrounds, and swimming pools went overlooked by white and black elites alike.

In the realm of public transportation, Walden and other Atlanta activists did achieve measurable improvements for local people. It was erroneous to discount these changes as "polite segregation," merely because the modes of activism and goals did not conform to the national NAACP's desegregation imperative. Walden's complaint against the rate increase and substandard services, lodged on behalf of black women activists and the working class, stands out as particularly significant. The campaign constituted one of the few instances in which Atlanta's black elites forcefully attacked "outright discrimination against the poorest" blacks—and won. That was a praiseworthy initiative, if not one designed to integrate Americans' social lives.

The response of black leaders to the Montgomery bus boycott exposed a remarkable dynamic: the leaders' astute observation of the changing political terrain, coupled with their hesitance to seize opportunities to push for desegregation. Decision-makers superficially embraced direct action. Atlanta's bus "boycott" was a set piece—a single, carefully planned act of protest—not really a boycott at all. The plan was a strategic one. It mimicked the type of nonviolent direct action that Atlanta's native son, Dr. Martin Luther King, Jr., so famously and effectively used, thereby appeasing those in the national and local black community who were ready to attack segregation directly. But at the same time, the plan ensured that the nature and pace of change would occur as the biracial coalition wished, and without the involvement of anyone outside of this elite circle. Atlanta's approach to the desegregation of public transportation was, in effect, a plan to control the pace of change. It delayed by three years the implementation of the Supreme Court's unambiguous decree that segregation on city buses was unconstitutional.[40]

The Triple L movement forced decision-makers to confront *Browder* and led to a test case culminating in the *Williams* decision. Viewed in light of some black leaders' prior unease over litigating at all, *Williams* looked like a great stride toward a more aggressive pursuit of civil rights. Unlike the *Holmes* decision, which affected so few African Americans, *Williams* advanced the rights of all blacks who rode the city's buses every day. In these senses, the Montgomery boycott had, in fact, galvanized Atlanta, too.

At the same time, the test case initiated by Triple L set Atlanta apart from Montgomery. The circumstances surrounding the initiation and implementation of *Williams* diminished the possibility that a mass-based protest movement would develop in Atlanta. Borders had orchestrated a one-day bus protest designed to give white elites the power to determine the applicability of *Browder* to Atlanta. This set-piece boycott impeded any momentum for a Montgomery-style boycott in Atlanta. In effect the *Williams* litigation channeled and controlled dissent, checking the impulses of those who might have been interested in challenging Jim Crow outside of the parameters determined by white and black elites. Furthermore, black leaders' slowness to insist on implementation of the bus desegregation order led whites to expect that the racial status quo could be maintained, for a while at least, even if plaintiffs prevailed in court. The lessons that Atlanta's black leaders had learned about litigation were not the ones that the national NAACP and LDF wanted to teach.

A. T. Walden and like-minded black elites' approach to implementing *Gayle v. Browder* marked the beginning of the end of their hegemony over civil rights in Atlanta. Eventually, the leaders of Atlanta's African-American community did accept the goal of the national civil rights organizations and the direct action groups: desegregation. Some even embraced it. Still, the preference for interracial diplomacy influenced the manner in which these leaders went about interpreting and implementing new antidiscrimination norms. The traditional leadership attempted to ensure that the new generation of direct action leaders shared their worldviews, but their goals and tactics came under fire. With the dawn of direct action, the older generation's tight control over the reins of leadership was no longer secure. From that point forward, Walden and his comrades would face genuine challenges to their leadership. These challenges would come from a new generation of student activists who favored uncompromising goals and aggressive tactics. The students contested, reconceptualized, and ultimately rejected both the Atlanta elites' pragmatic racial politics and the LDF's legalism. The students called for a new brand of social and economic justice, and they found their imperatives incompatible with both pragmatism and legalism.

# PART II

# The Movement, Its Lawyers, and the Fight for Racial Justice during the 1960s

CHAPTER 6

# Seeking Redress in the Streets

*The Student Movement's Challenge to Racial Pragmatism
and Legal Liberalism, 1960–1961*

If it weren't for Negro lawyers, we wouldn't be where we are today. (1960)

A. T. Walden

The NAACP was the "alpha and omega" of civil rights...until 1960.
(1965)

Len Holt

The jeers that greeted A. T. Walden as he stood before the congregation of the normally staid Warren Memorial Methodist Church on March 10, 1961, were deafening. Looking out on the hostile crowd, Walden must have felt more like the accused standing before a crowd of vigilantes than a distinguished officer of the court standing before those who had benefited from his counsel. Walden had practiced law in Atlanta for fifty years; he was the national NAACP's and LDF's "man" in Georgia. Not long ago, he had been on the Ku Klux Klan's hit list because of his intrepid civil rights activism. Walden rightly viewed himself as a pioneering African-American attorney—one who had laid the ground-work for the historic changes in race relations that began to occur in 1960 under the auspices of the student-led sit-in movement. In the twilight of a life spent serving the cause of racial justice, Walden must have felt a sense of betrayal as he stood before the angry Warren Memorial congregation. The elder statesman of Atlanta's African-American community, Walden deserved respect and grati-tude, not scorn.[1]

But scorn nevertheless flowed from the lips of many of the students who had gathered at the church that evening: they believed A. T. Walden had proven himself an "Uncle Tom." The reason for the students' displeasure with Walden was clear. On the morning and afternoon of March 10, word had spread throughout the black community that Walden had brokered a "compromise" with white civic leaders to end demonstrations that AU students had been staging against segregated businesses since March 1960. The deal had been reached in a secret meeting with Atlanta's white business and civic leaders a few days earlier. Walden had been the chief negotiator of an agreement to desegregate the city's lunch counters to which the students had not given their prior approval. Not only were the students angry that Walden had failed to consult with them before reaching the agreement—they found the compromise plan itself objectionable.

The students criticized the agreement on several grounds. White leaders had not agreed to full desegregation; only a limited number of venues would be opened to blacks. The schedule was too gradual; desegregation of public accommodations was tied to desegregation of the schools, which was not to occur until months later, in September. Finally, the students' demands that Atlanta's businesses improve employment opportunities for black workers had not been included in the deal at all. The settlement brought the students' long battle for an "open city" to a bitterly disappointing conclusion. For the students, Walden and his counterparts—pragmatists committed to negotiation and litigation rather than direct action—moved too slowly and settled for too little—much less than the students' goal of "Freedom Now."

The volatile scene at Warren Memorial Methodist Church that night in March of 1961 tells us much about the changing dynamics of the civil rights movement in Atlanta and the nation. It reflected the tensions between a new generation of black activists and the traditional civil rights leadership, which had long been dominated by the black bar, the national NAACP, and the LDF. This chapter explores the complex connections between and among the sit-in movement, the NAACP, and LDF's litigation campaign, including *Brown v. Board of Education*. It discusses how the sit-in movement was propelled, at least in part, by dissatisfaction with the court-based strategies pursued by NAACP lawyers.[2]

The chapter holds a magnifying glass to the sit-in movement in Atlanta during its first year and finds enormous and perhaps surprising complexity in African Americans' conceptions of equality and the law. Civil rights litigation, most famously successful in *Brown*, may well have inspired black activists, as conventional wisdom holds. But during the initial phase of the sit-in movement, which began in February 1960, the NAACP's litigation campaign had a negative, rather than a positive or inspirational, relationship to the civil rights movement. By 1960 student leaders did not see the Supreme Court as a beacon of hope, but as a powerful manifestation of official indifference to the cause of racial equality. White resistance to school desegregation, and the Court's acquiescence to it, bred frustration with litigation and drove embittered student activists to seek redress in the streets rather than in the courts.[3]

Paradoxically, then, the Court's failure to enforce *Brown* and its subsequent civil rights decisions, and the failure of the NAACP's court victories to bring about tangible improvement in numerous areas of race relations, reaped bountiful fruits for the direct action movement. These failures helped redirect the energy of the civil rights movement toward the tactics of student protesters, which proved to be one of the factors crucial to Congress's passage of the Civil Rights Act in 1964. Frustration with the law was not the *only* precipitant of the student movement. Nor did the activists have a one-note response to the NAACP's court-centered challenges to Jim Crow. Rather, the students' attitudes toward litigation varied, from positive to negative and points in between, along with developments in the movement. The activists, clever and restless, modulated their attitudes toward civil rights lawyers and court-centered activism as circumstances dictated. By shaping politics, they helped to make civil rights law.

Scholars of law and social change who argue that Supreme Court litigation undermined political mobilization during the civil rights era have not fully engaged these points. Civil rights litigation siphoned resources from more fruitful political avenues for change, it is said. *Brown* is thought to have been a unique impediment to direct action. Only when Congress and the executive branch became involved in civil rights did any significant change occur. This understanding of how social change occurred, and this perspective on what counts as change, persuasively argues that the U.S. Supreme Court is not a driving force in social reform. Yet, it does not fully account for the agency of student activists and their supple interaction with courts and lawyers. The dynamics of activists on the ground—the "guerilla warfare" of movements for change—are hidden when scholars focus primarily on the work of the Court and the roles of national institutions. These dynamics also are overshadowed when sharp distinctions are not drawn, or points of commonality are not recognized, between student activists and legal activists, as appropriate. The work of the courts and lawyers naturally captivates the attention of legal scholars. Nevertheless, the activities of lay activists—improvised, yet capable of responding to the changing legal and political environments—laid the groundwork for the sweeping legislative and executive branch changes that the Court, as scholars rightly note, lacked the capacity and will to implement on its own.[4]

With the advent of the sit-in movement, students wrested exclusive control over the struggle for racial equality from civil rights lawyers. The locus of struggle now resided in a community-based social movement, rather than in the Court, Congress, or the executive branch. In local communities throughout the South, college students, operating primarily in the arena of politics, became the predominant agents of social and political change.

A national organization based in Atlanta, SNCC orchestrated the student movement; SNCC and its Atlanta affiliate, the Committee on Appeal for Human Rights (COAHR), strove mightily to democratize the civil rights movement. The students (almost all of them African Americans initially, joined here and there by a few whites) created a community-based strategy for change: racial justice could only be achieved by mobilizing citizens to pursue equality for themselves, they believed. Thinking that young leaders and ordinary citizens not beholden to structures of power could be more effective leaders than older and established members of the community, the students jealously guarded their independence. The students even distanced themselves from the SCLC and Dr. King, who had inspired and sponsored the student wing of the direct action movement. The sit-in movement set off fierce competition for power and influence between direct and legal activists. In Atlanta, A. T. Walden became the flashpoint for the students' disappointment with the law and lawyers—a critique that catapulted the movement into a spectacular new phase.

## "SITTING ON CONSTITUTIONAL RIGHTS"

The pursuit of legal rights, in particular the right to be free of state-imposed segregation in places of public accommodation, framed the struggle for racial advancement in Atlanta during the first half of the 1960s. Students untrained in formal law, rather than licensed lawyers, ignited the struggle for desegregation. Student leaders invoked the Constitution in pursuit of their rights, but their most potent weapon was not the kind of affirmative civil rights litigation that dominated the NAACP LDF's agenda. For the students, *Brown*'s aftermath had been a huge disappointment. The Court's 1955 remedial order, *Brown II*, suggested that the white South could proceed slowly in implementing *Brown*. Even *Cooper v. Aaron*, the Court's September 1958 decision asserting its supremacy in the face of the Little Rock, Arkansas, school desegregation crisis, provided short-lived inspiration for the students.[5]

On the heels of *Cooper*, in late 1958, about a year before the sit-ins began, the Supreme Court refused to strike down pupil placement laws designed to ensure only token compliance with *Brown*. Such laws required that black applicants to white schools undergo burdensome application procedures, including psychological and intelligence tests. One of these cases, *Shuttlesworth v. Birmingham Board of Education*, involved an attempt by Birmingham's nationally prominent civil rights activists, Rev. Fred and Mrs. Ruby Shuttlesworth, to enroll their daughters in all-white Phillips High School. When the Shuttlesworths presented their daughters for enrollment at the high school on September 9, 1957, a white mob beat the Reverend with baseball bats and bicycle chains and stabbed Mrs. Shuttlesworth. Alabama school officials were "jubilant" when the Supreme Court, on November 24, 1958, affirmed a decision upholding the law that had denied the Shuttlesworth daughters admission to Phillips. The decision vindicated *Brown*'s opponents, explained a *New York Times* commentator. "The affirmation…accepted by plain inference the prospect that, in many Southern areas, generations, not years, will elapse before Negro pupils in general can no longer constitutionally be excluded from white schools."[6]

*Shuttlesworth* and other post-*Brown* precedents demonstrated that litigation was an unreliable partner in the struggle for desegregation. Dr. King pointed to *Shuttlesworth* as the origin of a crisis in the civil rights movement over the use of litigation to undermine Jim Crow. According to King, the decision demonstrated "government default," segregationists' ability to defy legal decisions "boldly and brazenly," and consequently, it "precipitated" the student movement. The outcome in *Shuttlesworth* and other cases showed that civil rights litigation, which frequently dragged on for years, had not resolved the underlying inequities that it had been filed to combat.

Indeed, leaders of the student movement repeatedly cited disappointment with the aftermath of *Brown* and frustration with the NAACP-led litigation process in explaining the participatory democratic forms that their protests against Jim Crow took. John Lewis, a chairman of SNCC who later became a member of Congress, explained that after *Brown*, "[W]e thought we would be going to better schools, and it just didn't happen." "Nothing" in his life "had changed." Other student leaders echoed Lewis's disappointment with the pace of school desegregation. Lonnie King, leader of the Atlanta student movement, cited the failure to implement *Brown* as the reason for COAHR's demonstrations and its mistrust of elder black leaders who insisted that civil rights litigation was the proper tool to use against segregation. "We have left the Supreme Court decision to the courts, and in six years, barely one per cent of the school districts in the South have been integrated," he explained in the fall of 1960. Disillusioned with courts and lawyers, King, Lewis, and other students turned to the sit-in, a new iteration of the direct action tactics associated with the Montgomery bus boycott. The students viewed the boycott as the "beginning of the non-violent revolution in the South," primarily a political form of activism controlled by ordinary citizens. For Julian Bond, the sit-ins represented an exciting new extension of the involvement of people *without* legal expertise in the civil rights movement, a development inaugurated in Montgomery. Before the boycott and the sit-ins, the movement had been all about "filing a suit,"

Bond explained. The sit-ins, demonstrations, pickets, and rallies associated with the student movement afforded every citizen the opportunity to contribute to the struggle for equality. Black activists, rather than the courts, drove the momentum of the sit-in movement and conceived its strategies.[7]

The students wanted not only to remove the courts from their roles as mediators of the struggle for civil rights but also to eliminate the NAACP and LDF as the strategic and tactical leaders of the movement. The sit-ins would be an antidote to the NAACP and LDF. These organizations, the students charged, relied too heavily on the law and underutilized community members themselves as agents for change. James Lawson, a sit-in leader who trained one of the students involved in the Greensboro sit-in, dismissed the NAACP and LDF as "a fund-raising agency, a legal agency" that had "by and large neglected the major resource that we have—a disciplined, free people who would be able to work unanimously to implement" the "Constitution" and the "ideals of freedom and justice." For Lawson, the NAACP was "too conservative" and a "black bourgeois club." Julian Bond agreed that one objective of the sit-ins was to uproot the NAACP, which he claimed had "lost touch with the people." Like Lawson, Bond dismissed the NAACP as "too conservative," "too Uncle Tomish," and "too traditional." Dr. King, an early supporter of the student movement, called the sit-ins "an answer" to the problems posed by civil rights litigation. John Lewis explained it best. "[W]e were all about" a "mass movement, an irresistible movement of the *masses*. Not a handful of lawyers in a closed courtroom, but hundreds, thousands of everyday people... taking their cause and belief to the streets." A speech by Thurgood Marshall, in which the LDF director-counsel insisted that the students should leave the work of tearing down segregation to the lawyers, led to an epiphany. "Thurgood Marshall was a good man, a historic figure," Lewis conceded, "but watching him speak on that April evening in Nashville convinced me more than ever that our revolt was as much against this nation's traditional black leadership structure as it was against racial segregation and discrimination."[8]

The leaders of the NAACP and LDF knew that they might be casualties of the students' rebellion. In an article published in the *Crisis*, Thurgood Marshall conceded that direct action imperiled the dominance of the legalistic approach to ending Jim Crow. "These young people are just simply sick and tired of waiting patiently without protest for the rights they know to be theirs." Roy Wilkins, executive secretary of the NAACP, agreed, admitting that the students had "tired of the legal approach" and, more particularly, "the snail-like pace of [school] desegregation." Behind the scenes, Marshall and Wilkins fumed at the students. Wilkins protested the students' "open attacks" on the NAACP. Marshall questioned whether LDF should represent "crazy colored students" who had the temerity to trespass on whites' property in clear violation of the law. He was a "lawyer, not a missionary," he scoffed, and at his core, did not "believe in" civil disobedience. In any event, Marshall told his staff, "the law was clear that the students were trespassing on private property." Both men fretted over what competition from the students would mean for the NAACP and LDF.[9]

Wilkins and Marshall ultimately decided that their organizations had no choice but to come to the students' aid. Pressure from NAACP members, black churches, black newspapers, and others who insisted that the organizations help the students backed the NAACP into a corner. The NAACP and LDF could only remain relevant by supporting the sit-in movement, at least in public. But outside of public view, the NAACP used its influence, resources, and LDF's legal expertise in an effort to tame the wayward students. Len Holt, a young attorney who counseled student activists, later summed up the situation, "The NAACP was the 'alpha and omega' of civil rights . . . until 1960." It was in 1960 that the students jolted America and the civil rights establishment by taking the movement directly to the public.[10]

Using the streets as their courtroom, the public as their jury, and the liberal and alternative media as their judges, the students demanded an end to Jim Crow in every facet of life. Most urgently, they wanted an end to segregation in hotels, restaurants, department stores, theaters, and municipal facilities. The students' demonstrations against segregation were designed to dramatize the injustice of Jim Crow. Their objective was to show the "intelligence and decency" of black students and their white supporters, arrayed against the "ignorance and depravity" of white segregationists. The arrests that resulted from the demonstrations were a key element of this tactic: students literally were denied their liberty—confined in jail by openly racist southern policemen—as a consequence of their struggle for freedom. Initially, the students did not contemplate affirmative constitutional litigation against segregation. If their strategy and tactics worked, they would obviate the need for litigation.[11]

Students in Atlanta looked for inspiration and guidance to black collegians in Greensboro, North Carolina, who inaugurated the sit-in phase of the civil rights movement on February 1, 1960. On that date, four students from historically black North Carolina Agricultural and Technical College (A & T) sat down at a Woolworth's lunch counter and ordered cups of coffee. The students' request defied southern law, local custom, and company policy. Woolworth's personnel informed the four that they did not serve "Negroes." In the face of the rebuff, the students remained in their seats, rather than leave. On the following day, they returned with other students who joined their challenge to Woolworth's segregationist policy.

The Greensboro Four had chosen non-violent civil disobedience as their protest form, justifying their action on the ground that the laws and customs of segregation were unjust and thus undeserving of obedience.[12]

Within days of the A & T protest, students in several other North Carolina communities followed suit; within the month, the sit-in movement spread to other cities, including Nashville, Richmond, Baltimore, Montgomery, and Chattanooga. Within two months, the sit-in movement had spread to more than fifty cities. In all these places, students repeated the pattern of the Greensboro Four, staging acts of civil disobedience and typically refusing to respond to violent opposition with violence.[13]

The sit-ins not only showcased a tactical innovation but also spotlighted the emergence of new organizations. On the weekend of April 16–18, 1960, the sit-in movement entered a new phase when a group of students formed SNCC under the tutelage of Ella Baker, executive director of SCLC and a longtime civil rights organizer. The mission of SNCC was to coordinate protest activities, educate students in the principles of nonviolence, and develop rank-and-file, community-based leaders. The organization openly opposed the idea of top-down, professional and ministerial leadership of the civil rights movement. The students in SNCC vowed to maintain autonomy from organizations that embraced top-down leadership such as SCLC, the national NAACP, and LDF. The demands of SNCC for equality went beyond the formal legal equality sought by the NAACP and LDF. The leaders of SNCC demanded economic justice and the empowerment of everyday people to become involved in the political process. John Lewis, chairman of SNCC, described its earliest activities as the "birth pains of the body politic." Other commentators called the student group the "shock troops" of the civil rights movement, or the "new abolitionists." Over the next two years, SNCC became one of the most effective and prominent of all organizations dedicated to racial equality, outpacing the older, more established groups as the most dynamic, cutting-edge civil rights organization in the field.[14]

The Greensboro sit-ins and the advent of SNCC added a powerful new dimension to the direct action movement for civil rights that had seen its greatest achievement in 1955 with the Montgomery bus boycott. The sit-ins "sparked... [a] civil rights revolution" that "constituted a watershed in the history of America" and a "decisive break with the past." Legal action was displaced as the paramount strategy for achieving civil rights, replaced by direct action staged on a mass scale by thousands of young people who had previously been on the sidelines of the struggle for racial justice. Like nothing before, the sit-ins dramatized the evil of segregation and its incompatibility with the ideas of democracy and equality. The students' nonviolence made their demonstrations especially poignant. When whites, including members of the Ku Klux Klan, responded angrily and sometimes violently to the students' simple requests for service, the sit-inners refused to retaliate. They turned, instead, to prayer for consolation. The image beamed across America on nightly news programs was profound: doves were being attacked by wolves. Observers were moved and amazed by the personal sacrifice and dignity displayed by the students. Anthony Lewis of the *New York Times* called the sit-ins "an extraordinary moment, displaying as really nothing else had the suffering in the soul of the Negro. When young people... risked literally everything to demonstrate for equal treatment as human beings, it was impossible for the South to talk convincingly about 'outside agitators' or Northern politicians or the Supreme Court as the source of the 'trouble.'"[15]

The sit-ins had ignited the most daring challenge yet to segregation. Militant youths, weary of the slow pace of desegregation of schools and other public facilities, had taken over the movement for racial change, determined at last to wipe out Jim Crow with dispatch. The *Nation* called the sit-ins a "brilliant" tactical innovation led by a "New Negro" that "dramatized" the "absurdity of Jim Crow" and "herald[ed] a new day in race relations." A statement by the Southern Regional Council (SRC), an Atlanta-based interracial organization, crystallized the racial situation after this new breed of black leaders, supported by a small group of whites, had launched the sit-ins: "Those who hoped that token... school desegregation would dispose of the racial issue are on notice to the contrary. We may expect more, not less, protests of this kind against enforced segregation in public facilities and services of all types." In early 1960, America stood on a racial precipice, and it had been taken there by black collegians and their white allies, who had managed to devise a strategy for burying Jim Crow that put them, rather than the Supreme Court, NAACP lawyers, or southern politicos, in the driver's seat. Or so it seemed.[16]

## APPEALING FOR RIGHTS

Many commentators looked to Atlanta as the epicenter of the sit-in movement—the place where it would achieve its greatest victory or meet lasting defeat. "As Atlanta goes, so goes the South," explained *Look*. The city featured a potentially volatile mix of personalities, traditions, and organizations. At the dawn of the sit-in movement, pragmatism remained the dominant approach to racial advancement. Middle-class professionals, for whom life was "considerably less grim" than it was for blacks in other parts of the South, dominated the ranks of black leadership. These leaders were wary of public confrontations about race. The white power structure, on both the state and local levels, remained resistant to racial change. Governor Ernest Vandiver had won office in a landslide victory in 1958 by promising that "no, not one" white child would ever attend a racially mixed school in Georgia. Georgia's U.S. senators, Richard Russell and Herman Talmadge, both Democrats, had led the massive resistance movement against *Brown* and remained openly hostile to civil rights. More genteel in their defense of Jim Crow, Atlanta's white political and business leaders were no less committed than vocal opponents of desegregation to preserving the status quo. Yet, Atlanta clung to its image as a racially liberal southern city: it was good for business. The city fathers' desire to preserve this image could be leveraged in favor of the cause of civil rights. During the early 1960s, a small band of white moderates, most affiliated with the interracial Southern Regional Council, sought to use Atlanta's progressive reputation as a wedge to loosen Jim Crow's firm grip on the city.[17]

By far, however, the black protest groups constituted the biggest wild card in the tumult of early 1960s Atlanta. Both wings of the direct action movement, the student-dominated SNCC and the minister-controlled SCLC, had headquarters in Atlanta. In addition, thousands of college students—the very type of individuals who had led the sit-ins in other cities—attended Atlanta's historically black colleges and appeared likely converts to the civil rights cause. At the same time, A. T. Walden and Atlanta's black middle class traditionally molded the city's racial agenda. The influence of Walden and the black elders loomed especially large as tensions between student leaders who embraced direct action and national leaders in the NAACP and LDF who preferred litigation and lobbying elected representatives unfolded. This combination of actors and organizations, operating in a dynamic urban environment, ensured that Atlanta would be a nationally significant battleground as the struggle for civil rights moved forward.

Given the city's prominence and liberal reputation, King's association with it, and its army of black college students, many observers expected sit-ins to be launched in Atlanta immediately following the Greensboro movement. But, in fact, Atlanta experienced relative quiet in the immediate aftermath of the Greensboro protests. The city was not among the localities to which the sit-in tactic first spread, and the city's prominent black organizations and individuals (aside from SCLC head Dr. Martin Luther King, Jr.) did not rush to speak out in favor of the nascent student movement. The Atlanta sit-ins began a month and a half after the Greensboro protests, well after students in dozens of other cities, including Durham, Winston-Salem, Charlotte, Raleigh, Nashville, Chattanooga, Charleston, Rock Hill, Norfolk, Portsmouth, Richmond, and Montgomery, had already followed the example of the North Carolina A & T students.

The delay in the start of protests in Atlanta, which had by far the largest black college student population, held great significance.[18]

During February and early March 1960, Atlanta's traditional black leadership delayed the students' effort to instigate direct action, funneling their energies into a lawsuit and negotiation instead. The leadership quickly moved to head off trouble when they got word, just days after the Greensboro sit-ins had started, that students at Morehouse College and AU planned to launch sit-ins in Atlanta. In a series of February meetings, A. T. Walden and the presidents of the city's black colleges, led by Morehouse president Benjamin Mays, counseled against the idea. The problem was not the students' goal; the older leaders assured local college students that they supported the push to end segregation in public accommodations. It was the students' preferred tactic that bothered the established leaders; they objected to direct action as too confrontational and disruptive of the customary method of resolving racial controversies—biracial negotiation. Walden and Mays suggested that the students file a lawsuit challenging segregation in public accommodations, in collaboration with the NAACP.[19]

Rev. Martin Luther King, Sr., a member of the biracial decision-making elite that had long dominated Atlanta, confirmed that many black leaders felt apprehensive about direct action, never more so than at the beginning of the sit-in movement. "There were Negroes in Atlanta who were embarrassed by the thought of making a public display of any concern they had, no matter how deep," he wrote in his autobiography. King Sr. himself was torn. He supported the old, cooperative way but understood the appeal of direct action. "Many of us hoped it would not come to such a point. And many of us knew it had to." His and other pragmatists' misgivings about direct action sprang from three main sources. As cultural conservatives, the elites found direct action undignified. The sit-ins recalled the sit-down strikes used by organized labor during the 1930s; for blacks striving to attain or maintain middle-class status, it seemed inappropriate to borrow the tactics of the laboring classes. As participants and believers in a tradition of biracial negotiation, they feared that street protests would alienate white moderates and would likely fail to achieve desegregation in public accommodations. The possibility that desegregation actually would occur as a result of direct action exposed a problem of a different kind. Even as African Americans despised racial discrimination, many still had anxieties about desegregation; concerns about how the transition to the new racial regime would impact black life informed the pragmatists' skeptical reaction to direct action, a tactic meant to quickly and radically disrupt the racial status quo.[20]

For Atlanta's African-American and white leaders, Daddy King's son, Martin Luther King, Jr., personified the problem posed for Atlanta by direct action.

King, the famed leader of the Montgomery bus boycott, had returned to his hometown from Montgomery in January 1960 and made Atlanta the head-quarters of the SCLC. Many observers feared that the students interested in starting sit-ins in Atlanta would fall under his sway. It seemed natural that Atlanta's student leaders would seek his counsel, given news reports that had him predicting that sit-ins soon would come to Atlanta. Consequently, some in Atlanta's biracial leadership admonished SCLC's leader not to make trouble in Atlanta. Governor Vandiver publicly declared that King was not welcome in Georgia. "Where M. L. King, Jr., has been there has followed in his wake a wave of crimes including stabbing, bombings, and inciting of riots, barratry, destruc-tion of property and many others. For these reasons, he is not welcome in Georgia." The commentary of Ralph McGill, the *Atlanta Constitution* editor who had gained a reputation as a racial liberal, was more telling. "I must say, I feel like a citizen of a medieval walled city who has just gotten word that the plague is coming." Remarkably, Daddy King, acting as emissary for those fearful that his son might shake up race relations in the city, made his son promise not to lead demonstrations in Atlanta. The father also publicly announced that his son had not moved back to Atlanta to "cause trouble."[21]

While stalwart black leaders attempted to reassure whites, state officials turned to the law to head off the sit-ins before they could begin. On February 11, 1960, state representative Francis W. Allen introduced a bill designed to "elimi-nate such incidents as we are seeing in North Carolina" by providing businesses with "machinery" to keep their establishments open in the event that "undesir-able patrons" attempted sit-down strikes. The bill proposed to criminalize a per-son's failure to leave the premises of certain establishments when requested to do so by proprietors. Within a week, the Georgia Senate had unanimously passed a revised version of the proposed bill. The law made it unlawful "for any person, who is on the premises of another, to refuse and fail to leave said premises when requested to do so by the owner or any person in charge of said premises." Those convicted of violating the law could be imprisoned for a maximum of eighteen months and fined $1,000. With the passage of the law, legislators committed to "law and order" signaled their intent to use facially neutral laws to defeat direct action, just as they had undermined LDF's school desegregation strategy with pupil placement laws. Attorney General Cook promised that the law would be invoked against "gangs of Negroes" who demanded service from the state's white merchants. The sit-in movement would be bottled up in court, as its members were prosecuted for engaging in protest.[22]

By the end of February 1960, well before the Atlanta sit-ins even started, liti-gation of a different sort already had stalled the students' efforts to bring direct action to Atlanta. In addition to cautioning student leaders that demonstrations would undermine Atlanta's tradition of biracial negotiation and hurt the city's economy, the biracial elite argued that sit-ins would undermine LDF's effort to implement *Brown* in Atlanta. Direct action was unnecessary, Walden and other African-American leaders argued, because the school desegregation controversy was on the brink of a favorable resolution. Walden and LDF lawyer Constance Baker Motley had filed *Calhoun v. Latimer*, the Atlanta school desegregation case, in 1958. The plaintiffs had prevailed, and a federal court had ordered the Atlanta Board of Education to submit a plan of desegregation by December 1959. Since Georgia law forbade race mixing in the public schools, the federal court order had created a "constitutional crisis." State legislators had to decide whether to continue to massively resist school desegregation, or to amend state law to permit Atlanta to comply with the federal court's order. The matter of how Georgia officials would deal with *Brown* topped the state's political agenda, at the same time that the sit-ins got under way across the South.[23]

Pointing to the showdown over school desegregation, Walden and other black leaders asked Atlanta-area college students to cool their heels. Atlanta's white moderate political and business elites had witnessed events in Little Rock, Arkansas, where officials had closed the public schools rather than desegregate them, only to face the rebuke of the Supreme Court and a sharp economic downturn. The moderates had accepted the idea that desegregation was inevitable, Walden believed; some already were pressuring the state legislature to amend the segregation laws to permit compliance with the federal court's school desegregation order. Notwithstanding the heated rhetoric of the white resistance, the city and state were poised to enter a new era of race relations, Walden promised. This line of argument against direct action held appeal to the students. In Atlanta and elsewhere, students had turned to direct action partly out of exasperation with the slow pace of the school desegregation process; they did not want to jeopardize any effort to desegregate the schools, if that goal truly was within reach. Hence, the *Brown* argument worked. The students agreed to defer action.[24]

The reprieve was short-lived. The students had agreed to delay, not to forego, their protests. They burned to show solidarity with protesters in other cities. Morehouse College students Lonnie King and Julian Bond were poised to lead the sit-in movement in Atlanta. Soon after the Greensboro sit-ins started, Lonnie King approached Bond about staging similar demonstrations in Atlanta. King and Bond were both "Morehouse men," as students at the single-sex college were called, and they felt that it was imperative that their "brothers" and "sisters" at Morehouse and Atlanta's other storied black colleges join the protests against Jim Crow that were sweeping the country. Morehouse men were supposed to be "social and civic role models," an ideal personified by the college's most famous graduate, Martin Luther King, Jr. Morehouse president Benjamin Mays expounded on the theme, "The Morehouse man learned well that a man's reach should exceed his grasp"; the "sky was his goal, even though, all too often, his wings were clipped." King and Bond shared the Morehouse ethic, but in other respects they could not have been more different.[25]

Julian Bond was very well born. He hailed from the "black aristocracy"; he was the scion of a distinguished family of educators. His father, Horace Mann Bond, had been the first black president of Lincoln University. The elder Bond had published groundbreaking work on racial discrimination in education. The LDF litigators who prevailed in *Brown v. Board of Education* used the research of Horace Mann Bond to help make their case. And in an era when few white women, and even fewer black women, went to college, Bond's mother, Julia, had earned a master's degree and worked as an educator. Bond had attended integrated private schools in Pennsylvania before moving to Atlanta in 1957, at the age of seventeen. Once he arrived, Bond and his family lived in faculty housing on the campus of AU, where his father was dean of the School of Education. He lived among black elites, sheltered from "the harsh realities of southern life" and apart from most other blacks.[26]

Even so, Bond knew the American dilemma of race very well. Conversations with his parents and interactions with their guests tutored the young man in the realities of racial injustice. Bond's parents instilled in their son a fierce opposition to racism and a powerful sense of racial pride. Visits to the Bond home by figures such as Kwame Nkrumah, the founder of pan-Africanism and the first postcolonial prime minister of Ghana, and W. E. B. Du Bois stoked the son's racial consciousness. The world outside of home also schooled Bond about inequality. Life in the North had not entirely shielded him from race prejudice. And in Atlanta, when the young man ventured off the black college campuses where he studied and lived, he experienced the indignities of Jim Crow just like all other blacks, middle class or not. On campus, the intellectually impressive, light-skinned, and strikingly handsome Bond cut a dashing and popular figure. His place in the world of the African-American elite was assured.[27]

Lonnie King's background set him a world apart from Bond. If Bond had escaped some of segregation's sharpest arrows, King had been hit by nearly all of them. Born in Atlanta in 1936, King grew up with the overlapping burdens of race and poverty. His mother was a maid, and his father was a laborer. The King family struggled to pay bills and simply tried to get by week-to-week. Unable even to afford bus fare, the young King walked back and forth to an all-black school. His schoolmates were also low-income blacks, who, like him, read out-of-date books at rickety desks in dank classrooms. Then, at age twelve, King experienced the cruelties of white supremacy in a more overt and violent way. During a walk home from school, King strayed onto the property of a white-owned motor company. First, a dog attacked him. When the overseer of the property came out to investigate, he beat the little boy severely. Frightened for his life, King begged the man not to kill him and was finally able to escape. It would have made no sense for the King family, who were anonymous members of Atlanta's black working class, to call the police and report the assault upon their child. So nothing was done. But the incident was forever etched in King's mind. He never forgot the penalty that Jim Crow could exact for even the slightest racial transgression.[28]

Later, a tour of duty in the navy during the Korean War set King on the path of leadership in the struggle for civil rights. The military, only recently desegregated, altered King's life by opening his eyes to the possibility of life outside Jim Crow. In the navy, King lived and worked in a racially integrated environment. The newfound racial freedom had an enormous and lasting impact on King. His outrage at segregation grew. Steeped in the worldly experiences offered by the navy during his time in Asia, King returned to Atlanta primed to confront Jim Crow. On the Morehouse campus, King, now married and several years older than most other undergraduates, commanded respect. He had an entirely different appeal from Bond. A star player on the Morehouse football team, he was tall and very dark-skinned, an imposing athletic figure. The veteran's standing and self-assurance made a great impression on his classmates, Bond included.[29]

On February 3, 1960, King strolled up to Bond at a campus hangout, the Yates and Milton drugstore. King began a conversation about the Greensboro sit-ins, and then asked Bond if he would help initiate similar protests in Atlanta. Bond eagerly agreed, in part, he recalled, because King was a man that "you just didn't say no to." Moreover, Bond's privileged status, juxtaposed to the humble positions of Rosa Parks and others involved in the Montgomery bus boycott, motivated him to join the movement. "Here I am, a college student," he explained, "in the elite. Here's this…uneducated woman [Parks] and she's making a sacrifice. Why the hell can't I?"[30]

Now a team, the two young men set out to rally a new generation of social activists—a bold, often fearless, collective of dissenters from the racial status quo. King recruited students on one side of the drugstore, and Bond on the other, to meet and discuss the prospect of staging sit-ins in Atlanta. Eventually, the pair enlisted a core group of student leaders, including fellow Morehouse students Benjamin Brown and Morris Dillard, and Spelman College coeds Herschelle Sullivan, Carolyn Long, and Roslyn Pope.[31]

The students then confronted the black power structure: they demanded to move forward with plans to stage a sit-in in Atlanta. The pragmatists again warned the students against precipitous action. Instead, A. T. Walden and other leading black figures, including C. A. Scott, the editor of the *Atlanta Daily World*, L. D. Milton, president of Citizens Trust Bank, Benjamin Mays, president of Morehouse College, James P. Brawley, president of Clark College, and Rufus Clement, president of AU, prevailed on the students to take a lawyerly course of action. Prior to contemplating direct action and certainly before instigating it, the students should write a "bill of particulars" giving the community notice of their concerns. The men promised to help the youth disseminate the statement of grievances to the public once it was drafted. The upstart group of students viewed the statement as yet another "delaying tactic" that "might take the steam out" of the sit-in idea. Lonnie King recalled, "We fully realized that their goal was to stop everything if they could." Yet, the youths could hardly reject the request from the esteemed group of elders. Thus, in February and early March, while black collegians elsewhere took seats at whites-only lunch counters, the Atlanta University Center (AU) students sat preparing a letter to white community leaders. Pope took the lead in drafting, working in collaboration with Bond, Dillard, Sullivan, Long, and King. The students formed COAHR, which included Walden and their other advisers as members.[32]

Notwithstanding the students' resistance to the idea of writing the bill of particulars, they produced an eloquent statement—one that rooted African-American demands for equality in the Constitution and the Declaration of Independence. The COAHR called its bill of particulars "An Appeal for Human Rights." The group published the elegant statement as a full-page advertisement in all of Atlanta's newspapers on March 9, 1960. The *New York Times* published the advertisement a week later. In phrasing and structure, the appeal borrowed from the foundational documents of the American constitutional order to argue its points. The appeal began, "We the students of the six affiliated institutions forming the Atlanta University Center...have joined our hearts, minds, and bodies in the cause of gaining those rights which are inherently ours as members of the human race and as citizens of the United States." Alluding to the ongoing sit-in movement, the AU students pledged "unqualified support" to "those students in this nation who have recently been engaged in the significant movement to secure certain long-awaited rights and privileges." The AU students proclaimed their dissatisfaction with the "snail-like speed" at which racial injustice was being ameliorated. The appeal then enumerated seven areas in which segregation should be "abolish[ed]" or racial disparities eliminated, including education, health care, law enforcement, housing, voting, employment, and public accommodations.[33]

The appeal's eloquence did not belie its stridency in parts. One hard-hitting line read, "We do not intend to wait placidly for those rights which are legally and morally ours to be meted out to us one at a time." The statement continued:

> We want to state clearly and unequivocally that we cannot tolerate, in a nation professing democracy and among people professing Christianity, the discriminatory conditions under which the Negro is living today in Atlanta, Georgia— supposedly one of the most progressive cities in the South.

The students summed up their petition: "We hold that" segregation is "not in keeping with the ideals of Democracy and Christianity," is "robbing not only the segregated but the segregator of his human dignity," and is a gross injustice given black taxation and service in the armed forces. The appeal ended with the students' promise to use "every legal and non-violent means" to "secure full citizenship rights as members of this great Democracy of ours."[34]

The publication of the Appeal for Human Rights precipitated urgent efforts by Atlanta's biracial elite to prevent or limit spontaneous direct action in Atlanta and, at all events, control the students. On the very day that the statement appeared, Mayor Hartsfield held a meeting at Rufus Clement's AU office with Lonnie King and the other student leaders. The mayor offered to facilitate a meeting with the Chamber of Commerce for discussion of the students' concerns about segregation in restaurants and employment discrimination. He urged the students to meet with the city's business leaders before beginning protests. Hartsfield was trying his best to head off the protests with the trusted tool of biracial talks. The students also entertained pleas to postpone the demonstrations from a group of white ministers. The presidents of the black colleges persisted with advice against demonstrations. The editorial page of the *Atlanta Daily World* weighed in against direct action as well. The paper called for continued "communication," a "letter-writing campaign," and "orderly processes of the law" as means of achieving "measured change" in race relations, rather than the "breakdown in law and order" that surely would accompany demonstrations. A chorus of voices importuned the AU students to spurn sit-ins.[35]

## BEGINNINGS OF THE CONTEST BETWEEN DIRECT ACTION AND LITIGATION

In the face of an imposing opposition, the students pushed ahead with plans to dramatize the demands made in the appeal. The dramatic act occurred on March 15, 1960, six days after the appeal had been published and six weeks after the Greensboro sit-ins had begun. At precisely 11:30 A.M. on that cold mid-March day, two hundred African-American students from historically black colleges in Atlanta fanned out across the city. Dividing themselves into small groups, the students, all dressed in their Sunday best under their winter coats, simultaneously targeted facilities that Jim Crow laws forbade them to enter, despite their fancy dress and good manners. The students entered the State Capitol, City Hall, the Fulton County Courthouse, the train stations and bus terminals, and two office buildings patronized by federal employees. The students had targeted facilities that would provide a good footing to lawyers who would mount their legal defenses in criminal court and file legal challenges against segregation in public accommodations. King and Bond had steered clear of facilities unconnected to the government; aware that discrimination by purely private actors did not violate the law, the two men deliberately targeted only facilities that were owned and/or operated by either the state or the municipality and catered to both government workers and the general public.[36]

The city reacted with great dispatch. Citing the state's new antitrespass law, police promptly arrested seventy-seven of the protesters, charging them under state laws banning trespassing and unlawful assembly. Policemen placed the college students—the pride of the black middle-class—in handcuffs, led them to police wagons, and drove them to the city jail. As the patrol cars rolled away, a leader of the student group declared that the collegians were "striving for the freedom that should be ours under the Constitution." The sit-in movement had come to Atlanta.[37]

Hauled to the county jail, the students—including leaders Lonnie King and Julian Bond—posted bonds and were released within three hours of arrest. A. T. Walden and Donald Hollowell represented the students arraigned in *City of Atlanta v. Defendants*. Questioned about the protest, Walden explained that they were designed to test the state's antitrespass law. The Fulton County Criminal Court solicitor responded by saying that he intended to pursue "every angle" in prosecuting the students and their (adult) conspirators. Responding to talk of conspirators, the students explained that they had planned the entire demonstration themselves, without aid from administrators at the AU Center.[38]

After the initial sit-ins, Atlanta's traditional African-American leadership and white racial moderates spoke with one voice in reaction to the students' direct action: enough, they said. Now that the students had gotten the urge to demonstrate out of their systems, they should leave resolution of the problem of discrimination in public accommodations to the lawyers and the legal system. Perhaps the most gracious statement, simultaneously expressing approval and disapproval, came from Borders, the leader of the bus desegregation protest. "I don't think you need to do it again soon, but thank God you did it yesterday!" he declared. Rufus Clement also expressed his "hope that there would be no more demonstrations." The editorial page of the *Atlanta Daily World* disapproved of the students' "attempt at mass, overt protest." The appeal had been sufficient to call attention to racial inequality; the demonstrations went too far. The *World* urged the students to cease demonstrations and instead "follow the due process of law." Attorneys A. T. Walden and Donald Hollowell explained that the students' arrests had, in fact, conferred standing to sue on the issue of segregation in public accommodations. Therefore, the ingredients necessary for filing a lawsuit were in place; further demonstrations were unnecessary. "Inasmuch as they have now joined issues in the law," Hollowell advised the students, they should cease demonstrations, at least until "we get a final judgment." The *Constitution* agreed. Now that a test case for judicial review of the state's segregation laws had been initiated, the students should end "unnecessary and unproductive repetitions." "The processes of law have been started."[39]

The pragmatists' perspective on the law and social change had evolved in a revealing and self-interested way. Threatened with a mass civil disobedience movement by young upstarts, Atlanta's traditional black leaders now championed civil rights litigation as the appropriate mechanism for attacking racial discrimination. Just a few years before, they had viewed litigation as an aggressive form of protest inappropriate in many circumstances; thus, Walden had litigated sparingly. Pragmatic black leaders and white moderates now looked to the "Love, Law, and Liberation Movement" of 1957 as a model for how to defuse the threat posed by the student protests. Borders had responded to the Montgomery bus boycott with a highly choreographed, hours-long "attempt" to desegregate the city buses. Borders's arrest and quick release had been handled by cooperative officers, and a test case was filed soon thereafter. Two years later, the litigation had yielded a court order striking down the segregation ordinances. In Atlanta *Gayle v. Browder* had been implemented without a fuss, not as in Montgomery. The pragmatists now argued that the March 15, 1960, sit-ins could be the predicate for the resolution of the volatile issue of segregation in public accommodations in much the same way that Atlanta had addressed bus segregation. The pragmatists had a sophisticated understanding of law, the courts, and their role in the civil rights struggle. They perceived that litigation's utility turned on the surrounding sociopolitical context and understood that in a dynamic political environment, lawyers could use malleable legal concepts and the courts to shape developments outside the courtroom.[40]

Pushed toward civil rights litigation, the students faced a dilemma. They viewed direct action as a more democratic and effective method of attacking Jim Crow. But they were torn about how much of a break to make with the city's traditional black leaders. Here, at the beginning of the student-led direct action movement, COAHR chose the more cautious course. Just one day after the initial Atlanta sit-ins, Lonnie King acceded to the biracial elites' wishes to call them off. In an obvious response to the biracial power structure's plea to negotiate an end to the current conflict, King said that he "would welcome the opportunity for further discussion" with the city's leadership about the goals set out in the Appeal for Human Rights. Hours after the students announced that they would comply with the pragmatists' wishes to end direct action, the stalwart leaders signaled their approval. At a hastily arranged public meeting, Atlanta NAACP officials and several religious groups "pledged support" for the students' "ideals." Walden and Hollowell praised the students' bravery and called for the community to donate funds to the students' legal defense. At once defensive and self-congratulatory, Walden added, "If it weren't for Negro lawyers we wouldn't be where we are today." Hollowell offered his hope that the 1960 antitrespass law would be "unable to stand" challenge. He and Walden would ensure that it did not, using the orderly processes of law.[41]

Over the next several weeks, however, events pushed the students toward a more confrontational stance toward the pragmatic leadership. A difficult interaction with white members of the biracial elite provided the initial catalyst for the students' change in mood. At the behest of the AU Center presidents and Mayor Hartsfield, Lonnie King and other student leaders attended a meeting with white businessmen about the demands in the Appeal for Human Rights. The session went poorly. The businessmen "listened to the students in silence" and then launched into a litany of criticisms of the students and their statement; the appeal "smacked of Communism," some of the businessmen claimed. Another stated that he was "not even thinking about thinking about doing away with segregation!" The students were "shocked" by the businessmen's attitude; their recalcitrance only proved that direct action was necessary. Then Georgia's political leadership weighed in and buttressed the students' assessment that only extralegal action could topple Jim Crow. In April, Senator Richard Russell took to the floor of the U.S. Senate to argue that the sit-ins were unconstitutional. He proved his point by quoting from judicial opinions, both recent and ancient. The senator drove home the reality that courts were unreliable allies in the struggle for civil rights.[42]

Critical commentary in the national media also had the unintended consequence of encouraging the students' resolve to pursue direct action. Even as some journalists marveled at the courage of sit-in participants, others echoed Senator Russell's contention that direct action violated white businessmen's property rights. *U.S. News and World Report* reported that the sit-ins represented a shift by blacks from "dependence" on courts and characterized direct action as a danger to law and order, and possibly, a "Red menace"—a charge also leveled by former president Truman. *U.S. News* dramatized the few scuffles that had occurred during the sit-ins: "[v]iolence had erupted in city after city" as the sit-downs moved into the Deep South, the magazine insisted. It also reported that the sit-ins had "stirred up" and "agitated" the Ku Klux Klan, whose largest chapter was headquartered in Atlanta. The *New York Times* also questioned whether blacks stood to "gain or lose" from sit-ins when they were "already fighting hard in the courts for school integration and voting rights." The students and their sit-ins were risky alternatives to the NAACP and civil rights litigation, the journalists implied.[43]

This strain of reporting, which depicted direct action as an immense, unpredictable threat to law and order, reached a crescendo in the middle of April 1960, when SNCC sprang into life. An interview with SNCC leader James Lawson, in which he forcefully attacked the NAACP's legal tactics and claimed that the students had "taken the struggle for justice into their own strong hands" provided fodder for those worried about the movement's radical, new direction. Martin Luther King, Jr., added fuel to the fire by calling the student sit-ins a "revolt against those Negroes in the middle class who have indulged themselves in big cars and ranch-style homes rather than in joining a movement for freedom." King also called on student demonstrators to "choose jail over bail." The strategy that King proposed and that SNCC endorsed—choosing jail over bail—suggested that students should only use the legal process to demonstrate the *injustice* of the southern social order. The concept struck many commentators as a sign of the direct action movement's extremism and disdain for law.[44]

Yet, as the students saw it, civil rights litigation, alone—as opposed to equal rights discourse invoked freely outside of court, along with other tactics—had little to offer them. The limited scope of Walden and Hollowell's legal strategy demonstrated the point. The attorneys consistently referred to their effort to bring "test cases," but that term had a different meaning in the context of criminal cases generated under the state antitrespass laws than it did in, say, the school desegregation context. Thurgood Marshall, Walden, Hollowell, and other lawyers for arrested students set the parameters of the test case strategy at a conference held at Howard University School of Law just a few days after the first Atlanta sit-ins. "We're pulling out all of the stops," and "[w]e're really in it," Marshall said of LDF, which was fighting off accusations from student leaders that the organization and the legal tools that it wielded against Jim Crow were inadequate. Marshall promised to defend the students based on states' and localities' use of law enforcement officials to halt peaceful demonstrations; in this sense, the lawyers would test the constitutionality of the antitrespass laws. But at best, the strategy he outlined would generate a ruling that the students had the right to demonstrate—a proposition that the students and many others took for granted. Marshall and the other lawyers also speculated that the arrests could be the basis for a much more profound challenge: the lawyers could frontally attack state enforcement of private actors' racial discrimination. In the same breath, however, Marshall announced that LDF in fact had no plans to challenge the underlying racial discrimination by private property owners.[45]

Marshall's caution was for good reason. As the sit-ins started, most commentators agreed that discrimination by private entities was beyond the reach of the Constitution. Thus, a lawsuit challenging discrimination by private entities that provided services in state- and municipality-owned facilities would be a long shot. To be sure, *Brown*'s mandate had been extended to public transportation provided by private operators; the Warren Court might decide to extend the precedent even further. But few observers thought that it should do so. *Brown* was detested by the white South and even considered legally tenuous by some constitutional scholars who agreed that school desegregation should have been found unconstitutional. As it was, the Court had not been keen to enforce its school desegregation mandate. Under the circumstances, it would be revolutionary—and socially cataclysmic—for the Court to hold that *Brown* upended long-standing precedents distinguishing private action from state action in restaurants, theaters, and the like. Arthur Krock, writing for the *New York Times*, explained the dilemma. "To make this ruling...the Supreme Court would be obliged to hold that implicit in the Fourteenth Amendment's ban against 'state' laws compelling racial segregation are local ordinances protecting its voluntary private exercise." In other words, the Court would have to find a social custom unconstitutional. Krock conceded that sit-in demonstrators who invoked "moral" values rejected such legal reasoning. But, he said, "there are 'moral' values in private rights, too."[46]

Given this legal stumbling block, observers believed that only a federal civil rights law could wipe out Jim Crow from restaurants, theaters, and other "public accommodations." Far from supporting the position of Walden, Hollowell, and others that demonstrations should cease in favor of a legal strategy, the view that the public accommodations issue was not amenable to litigation suggested just the opposite. The walls of segregation in restaurants, theaters, and the many other places that young African Americans wanted to frequent free of the humiliation inherent in segregation could only be attacked through extralegal action. Indicted on April 15, 1960, for "conspir[ing] to take over cafeterias by their numbers and force the managers to serve them" and on charges of trespassing, breaching the peace, and unlawful assembly, the students consented to a legal defense. But they would not give up direct action—the one weapon in their arsenal that might persuade Congress to repudiate the laws and customs that supported discrimination in these social spaces.[47]

## AN ARRAY OF MOVEMENT TACTICS

Indeed, in the coming months, lawyers and political activists—maneuvering in response to one another and jockeying for influence—employed an array of extralegal tactics to advance their preferred pace and objectives in the struggle for civil rights. Direct action, negotiation, media, community education, and the threat of a boycott, together with on-going litigation, all played roles in the summer's lively developments. A contingent of collegians who remained in town over the summer recess precipitated the events. The students rocked Atlanta in June when they attempted a sit-in at restaurants inside Rich's department store, the area's largest locally owned retail establishment. The store's employees refused service and turned out the lights.[48]

The day after the protest, police chief Herbert Jenkins arranged a meeting between the students and the store's owner, Richard Rich, at the police station. The encounter proved a disaster. Rich was Jewish, and he invoked his identity to defend himself and his store from the students' attack. Rich declared that he "understood discrimination" and had sympathy for the students' cause. And he promised that *if* the students ceased their demonstrations, he would desegregate his store's eating facilities *following* the desegregation of the schools. Rich's olive branch was too little too late for the students. The students had found Rich "extremely arrogant" and his declarations of racial liberalism, juxtaposed to his condescending attitude toward them, deeply offensive. When the students rejected his proposal as "a lot of Uncle Tom business" and threatened to boycott his store if he did not agree to immediate desegregation, Rich responded angrily. He upbraided the students for "disrupting commerce in his store," threatened to have them jailed if they returned to his establishment, and in the single greatest insult, exclaimed that he "didn't care if another Negro EVER comes into my store." Rich left the room, promising never to yield to threats and intimidation. The students left just as upset; they were especially incensed by Rich's claim that he could do without black business. "That's something he NEVER should have said," Bond later recalled. The COAHR determined to make Rich eat his words.[49]

Despite the recent establishment of the Student-Adult Liaison Committee (SALC) and talk of an "alliance" between friends and foes of direct action, many established African-American leaders were furious with the students for attacking Rich and his store. Rich did not rank as one of the most powerful members of the business elite, but he was important. Many established, middle-class blacks viewed him as a sympathetic figure and a friend to African Americans—or at least friendlier than others. Many within the African-American community felt "somewhat of a bond" existed between the blacks and the Jews.

Rich was the first owner of a large business in Atlanta to extend credit to African Americans and instructed employees to address black customers as "Mr." and "Mrs."—tremendous departures from local custom. Rich employed large numbers of blacks (although not in managerial positions or jobs where they would have contact with the public). He also supported certain charities that benefited blacks. Moreover, Atlanta's Jews had only recently been under siege themselves. In October 1958, the local temple had been bombed—the "harvest," Ralph McGill wrote at the time, of those white southern politicians, citizens councils, and other extremists who "preached hate" and "defiance of courts." "You do not preach and encourage hatred for the Negro and hope to restrict it to that field," McGill observed. McGill's observation only underscored why the students found Rich's "benign" practice of segregation more—not less—reprehensible than other proprietors' all-out embrace of Jim Crow. He, of all people, had no excuse for appeasing hatred and discrimination. And though Rich touted in-store policies that were less racially restrictive than the norm, the students dismissed these gestures as expedient efforts to gain the business of Atlanta's middle-class blacks, who had considerable purchasing power.[50]

Moreover, there were signs that Rich took his black clientele for granted; they had complained for years about Rich's "substandard" bathrooms and basement-level dining facilities for blacks. And Rich's did not permit African Americans to try on clothes or shoes before purchasing them. Rich's hypocrisy made his store an especially inviting target of protest: he would be made to choose sides in the battle between those who sought equality and those who would deny it. Given Rich's size and its importance in the community, the students figured that if they staged a successful boycott against Rich's, other, smaller merchants would fall, as well. Lonnie King explained, "If we can topple Rich's, all we have to do is just kind of whisper to the others."[51]

Middle-class blacks who supported Rich, together with the white establishment, lobbied mightily for the students to pull back, but at first to no avail. The *World* ran an editorial praising the steps that Atlanta already had taken to remove racial barriers and criticizing "repeat demonstrations" as unwarranted and counterproductive. "The question of eating in certain downtown places is being exaggerated out of proportion to the importance." The paper once again endorsed negotiation and litigation as the preferable tactics for achieving racial advancement. The *Atlanta Journal* seconded the *World*'s opinion, warning that the students had "made their point earlier" and now risked alienating white moderates by belaboring it. The COAHR was unmoved. It responded on June 27 by again attempting a sit-in at Rich's and, on the following day, calling for a boycott of Rich's and other downtown merchants if they did not immediately desegregate. The students rejected Rich's proposal for coupling school desegregation with the desegregation of downtown business. Warren Cochrane, executive secretary of the Butler Street YMCA and secretary of the Negro Voters League, responded with public criticism of the students' methods. He deplored the attack on Rich's, which he called "an institution which has dealt generously with the Negro community." "The race must keep all of the friends it has in the dominant white world and work unceasingly to multiply them." Under intense pressure, the students ultimately acceded to the biracial power structure's demands to delay the boycott.[52]

With the boycott held in abeyance, the pragmatists engaged the problem of segregation in downtown businesses through litigation. On August 3, 1960, A. T. Walden and Donald Hollowell filed three suits in U.S. District Court challenging segregated seating in eating facilities at the State Capitol (*Douglas v. Lee*), the Fulton County Courthouse (*Andrews v. Lindsey*), and Atlanta City Hall (*Gibson v. Hartsfield*). The lawsuits claimed that students were denied service on the basis of race and arrested by state troopers who did not bother to inquire whether plaintiffs would leave upon request. Walden charged that these actions violated plaintiffs' equal protection and due process rights under the Fourteenth Amendment of the U.S. Constitution. In an interview with the press, Walden expressed his hope that lawyers would win a precedent from the court that could be applied all over the South, obviating the need for further demonstrations. Days later, a Southern Regional Council report noted that twenty-nine other southern cities, including Miami, Chapel Hill, Charlotte, Concord, Durham, Greensboro, High Point, Winston-Salem, Knoxville, Chattanooga, Nashville, Austin, Dallas, San Antonio, Alexandria, Arlington, Fairfax, Falls Church, Fredericksburg, Hampton, Norfolk, Portsmouth, Williamsburg, and Richmond, had already desegregated their lunch counters—without lawsuits. But given the objectives of the Atlanta pragmatists, the litigation constituted an immense step forward.[53]

Yet, Walden and Hollowell had avoided targets that were more legally vulnerable than the facilities at the Capitol, the courthouse, and City Hall. The AU students also had demonstrated at the bus and train terminals, but the attorneys had not challenged segregation there, although several precedents had chipped away at Jim Crow inter- and intrastate transportation. The federal court had held segregation on Atlanta's city buses unconstitutional in *Williams v. Public Service Commission*, decided in January 1959; another case, *Coke v. Atlanta*, brought by LDF, had held segregation in a restaurant in Atlanta's airport unconstitutional *Coke* had been decided in January 1960, just three months before the outbreak of the sit-ins. Furthermore, the Supreme Court was set to hear *Boynton v. Virginia* just a few days into the October 1960 term. *Boynton* raised the question of whether a black student's conviction under the

Virginia antitrespass statute for seeking to use an eating facility for whites in an interstate bus terminal could stand under the commerce or equal protection clauses of the U.S. Constitution or under the Interstate Commerce Act. Given the pending case and the favorable bus and airport precedents, it is unclear why the Atlanta attorneys—set on establishing the students' rights to desegregated public accommodations through a lawsuit—would not have challenged segregation in the bus and train terminals as well as in City Hall, the courthouse, and the Capitol.[54]

Whatever the lawyers' logic, the suits they filed would be hard fought. In late August, the defendants in the City Hall, courthouse, and Capitol cases replied; they sought summary judgment in each case. They argued that forced desegregation would violate the constitutional rights of the eateries' owners to conduct their businesses according to their personal preferences. The defendants also claimed that a ruling mandating desegregation would compel the owners to incur financial losses, when, as expected, white customers refused to patronize their establishments. In September, Georgia attorney general Cook offered a defense of a different sort. He asked the federal court to dismiss the cafeteria suit on the ground that the state had closed it (rather than desegregate it) after the sit-in attempt. Hence, plaintiffs' case was moot. The U.S. District Court soon agreed. Judge Boyd Sloan dismissed *Douglas v. Lee* on grounds that "an injunction would serve no useful purpose as there appears to be no likelihood that the condition complained of by the plaintiffs will recur." The thrust and parry between the parties in the remaining two suits, *Andrews v. Lindsey* and *Gibson v. Hartsfield*, continued into the next year.[55]

## THE FALL CAMPAIGN

Just one month after Walden and Hollowell had filed the three public accommodations suits and COAHR's promise to suspend demonstrations in Atlanta, the students reemerged. They again took to the streets, but this time on a massive scale. Beginning on October 19, 1960, COAHR mounted a no-holds-barred direct action campaign against segregated restaurants in downtown Atlanta. The Magnolia Room, the Cockerel Grill, and the Barbecue Grill—all housed in Rich's department store—headed the target list. The students also sat in at lunch counters or picketed several other stores, including the Woolworth's, Kress, Davison-Paxon, Davidson, McCrory, Grant, J. J. Newberry, and H. L. Greene chains. The protesters, approximately seventy-five in all, carried placards reading "Jim Crow Must Go," "The Presence of Segregation is the Absence of Democracy," "Make the World Safe for Democracy and Make Democracy Safe for the World," and "We Prefer Jail to Life in Hell." The demonstrations proceeded peacefully, despite harassment by some white passersby, who shouted racial epithets.[56]

Lonnie King and Dr. Martin Luther King, Jr.—who had reluctantly agreed to join the Atlanta student movement—grabbed national headlines when Rich's management ordered their arrest after they and forty-nine other demonstrators attempted to receive service at Rich's Magnolia Room. The two Kings, and many of the fifty other demonstrators arrested under Georgia's antitrespass law, refused bail. When arraigned by municipal court judge James E. Webb, Dr. King noted that he had spent thousands of dollars at Rich's in the past year, and could no longer countenance its practice of segregation, calling it a "festering sore." "I do not feel we did anything wrong in going to Rich's today and seeking to be served. We went there peacefully, non-violently, and in the spirit of love." King said he would remain in jail for "1, 5, or 10 years," or as long as necessary to affect the "conscience of Atlanta." King and the others pleaded not guilty to the misdemeanor charges and were sent to county jail. The October 19 protest marked the first time Dr. King had chosen jail over bail. King's arrest heightened the stakes of the protests for both the students and observers in the city, the state, and the nation. Lunch counters in 112 other cities and ten other states, including North Carolina, Virginia, West Virginia, Kentucky, Texas, Tennessee, Maryland, Missouri, Florida, and Oklahoma, had already desegregated by mid-October; the protests, with King as a leader, represented a crucial test for the civil rights movement and a showdown that would either reveal Atlanta's New South image as fact or expose it as fiction.[57]

The fall campaign, featuring about three hundred students, continued at a fast pace over the next few days. On October 20, additional waves of students staged sit-ins, expanding the protests to eleven stores and Terminal Station, the city's main train station. White counterdemonstrators lashed out, one spraying an unidentified aerosol mist onto students sitting in at Woolworth's and Newberry's. Police arrested fifty-seven students under the antitrespass law on the second day of protests; they also arrested a white man, charging him with incitement to riot. Judge James Webb again presided over the arraignments, and this time he made clear his displeasure with the protest movement. Webb lectured the students in open court. The judge called the students' actions "unwise and immature" and advised them against following the "wrong leaders." "You were probably out-numbered and if there had been violence directed at you, you might not be alive now," he warned. Over Donald Hollowell's objection that the students had only been engaging in lawful civil disobedience, Judge Webb sentenced twenty-two protesters who had been arrested for seeking service at Terminal Station to ten days in city jail. The judge also announced that future demonstrations "will be dealt with as irresponsible mob action."[58]

The protests continued on October 21, though on a smaller scale. Meanwhile, a group of students and ministers staged a prayer service on a visit to the county jail, where the two Kings and other demonstrators were held. The SNCC and SCLC garnered publicity for the demonstrations by sending telegrams to a host of prominent organizations and individuals. Telegrams went to the 1960 presidential candidates, Senator John F. Kennedy and Vice President Richard M. Nixon, and to Eleanor Roosevelt, Senator Jacob Javits, Governor Ernest Vandiver, Mayor Hartsfield, the U.S. Department of Justice, the NAACP, CORE, and the National Council of Churches, among others. In the telegram, SCLC and SNCC requested help in resolving the stalemate over segregation that divided Atlanta. The telegram to Hartsfield read:

> Urgently request you immediately appoint bi-racial commission reflective of total Atlanta community. Arrests of 50 students and our president (SCLC) provides you with the most creative opportunity in human relations afforded Atlanta in recent years. The moral rights of a customer regardless of racial identity, overshadows in this moment of history any demand of custom or unjust laws. These courageous students and Dr. King have brought segregated lunch counters under scrutiny of Atlanta's conscience. God grant that you, with equal courage, will initiate positive action in this regard for sake of our community.

The cables demonstrated COAHR's intention to push Atlanta's biracial power structure toward corrective action by nationalizing the city's racial dilemma.[59]

Under pressure, the power structure flinched. The *World*'s editorial page, which typically directed its firepower at the students' misguided embrace of radical tactics, now focused on problem solving. The protests demanded immediate action from "leaders of both groups," the paper intoned. The leaders must "move promptly" to maintain "goodwill" and "friendly relations" in Atlanta by resolving the controversy. But Mayor Hartsfield's reaction presented a problem for COAHR. He "sent word" to the students that if they ceased demonstrations, he would personally intervene to resolve the crisis. The mayor had bypassed COAHR, instead consulting with a few handpicked black leaders from the traditional elite. On the afternoon of October 22, Hartsfield called a meeting with SALC. Established as an effort to patch up divisions in Atlanta's black leadership, SALC included pragmatists who disapproved of direct action, as well as students who favored it. But Hartsfield targeted the opponents of protest in his negotiating effort. The *World* anointed William Holmes Borders, who had voiced support for the students of late, as "spokesman" for SALC.[60]

At the meeting, the mayor, who had been "besieged by telegrams from all over the country asking him what he would do about gaining freedom for Dr. King," assumed the role of mediator. He called for a sixty- to ninety-day truce during which the students would "cease further incidents" while Hartsfield reached out to downtown merchants, whom he promised were amenable to the students' demands, including their fair employment complaints. Hartsfield would give the parties a progress report after thirty days. After the meeting, Hartsfield announced that he had reached an "agreement" with a "cross-section" of black leaders, including Rev. Otis Moss Jr., who claimed to stand in for Lonnie King's, to halt the demonstrations. Hartsfield requested that Judge Webb release jailed student demonstrators as a part of the truce agreement, along with Dr. King and the white man held for incitement to riot. In a press conference, Borders called the meeting the "best" he had ever attended at City Hall, and referring to the success of the negotiations and Atlanta's racial equanimity, quipped that the "shortest line to Heaven is from Atlanta, Georgia."[61]

But on the same day, COAHR issued a counterstatement declaring Hartsfield's announcement that a truce had been reached "absolutely inauthentic." "The Mayor has talked to no student leaders. He cannot speak for us," COAHR charged. The *Atlanta Inquirer*, a weekly newspaper managed by leaders of the student movement, had been established in July 1960 as a counterweight to the *Atlanta Daily World*, whose editor opposed direct action. The *Inquirer* promised to cover the movement from a "fair and impartial" perspective and "without fear or favor," and it now countered Hartsfield's "propaganda." The *Inquirer* reported that Dr. King and the rest of the "jail, no bail" group, confined in the Fulton County jail, remained "cheerful" and "confident" about the continued protest. His lie exposed, Hartsfield contacted the students, who met with him at City Hall, along with SALC members.[62]

The students ultimately agreed to the thirty-day truce in exchange for the release of all demonstrators. With this action, the students showed that notwithstanding sometimes heated rhetoric, they were not yet ready to abandon completely the politics of moderation.[63]

With the pressure off, the negotiations stalled. On October 27 COAHR lost its biggest trump card when King left Reidsville State Prison. Though Hartsfield had promised the release of all jailed demonstrators, it turned out that he had no authority over the most prized detainee. Dr. King had been transferred to the maximum security prison in the middle of the night on the orders of a hostile judge. Over the pleas of attorney Donald Hollowell, Judge Oscar Mitchell had sentenced King to four months in prison in connection with a minor traffic infraction: King had been stopped and charged with driving with an out-of-state license while ferrying a white woman—liberal white author Lillian Smith—to the hospital. King's imprisonment became a cause célèbre. Harris Wofford, an advisor to John F. Kennedy's 1960 presidential campaign and later a U.S. senator, explained that the "shocking sentence" "galvanized" the country, especially African Americans. King's release from prison occurred after a phone call from Senator Kennedy to a pregnant Coretta Scott King, and a personal appeal from Robert Kennedy to the presiding judge. After King's release, Daddy King, a long-time Republican, endorsed Kennedy for president. "If I had a suitcase full of votes, I'd hand them over to John Kennedy, hoping he could use them in the upcoming election," King Sr. bellowed from the pulpit of Ebenezer Baptist Church. This series of actions helped Senator Kennedy secure African-American votes, which provided the margin of victory in several states where he defeated Richard Nixon in the 1960 presidential election. But the incident did little to advance COAHR's negotiations with downtown merchants. Dr. King's presence had not been the decisive factor that hopeful students had imagined and the city fathers had feared.[64]

The truce period came and went with Jim Crow intact in downtown Atlanta. Hartsfield's attempts to persuade merchants to settle the dispute on terms amenable to the students went nowhere. Rich refused to negotiate with the mayor, whom he deemed too dependent on the black vote to be an impartial mediator. In an end run around the students, Rich initiated secret settlement talks with several older black leaders whom he counted as opponents of the demonstrations. In the talks, Rich argued that his store should not be a "bell weather [sic] of change." He insisted that school desegregation—set to occur in the fall of 1961—should happen first; then he would desegregate his business and encourage other merchants to do so.

Outraged that blacks holding themselves out as community leaders had met with Rich, Lonnie King issued a broadside in the *Inquirer*. "The era of under-the-counter dealers is over," he cried. "The behind the scenes advocates of 'go slow' and 'not now' must finally realize that their day has ended." He lambasted the moderates' attempts to appease and undermine the students. "During the height of the demonstrations, we heard that this was not the way; that the courts should decide; that businessmen do not yield to pressure...that this is a town of 'good will, peopled with citizens of good intentions.'" The notion that the courts could uproot Jim Crow had proven demonstrably false, he retorted to these statements. He delivered his attack on the courts just a few days after U.S. District Court judge Boyd Sloan issued an opinion declining to dismiss the City Hall cafeteria suit, *Gibson v. Hartsfield*, for lack of evidence that it now operated on a nonsegregated basis. An isolated favorable court ruling could not assuage COAHR's skepticism about a litigation-based approach to ending Jim Crow. Lonnie King concluded his column by giving notice that African Americans would no longer tolerate "a few men, conservative and overprotective of their vested interests, compromising the rights of a people into nothingness." If an agreement was not reached in open negotiations with Hartsfield, Rich and other merchants, he warned, the students would "chart" their "own course."[65]

At the end of the truce period, Hartsfield reported that no progress had been made. The students responded that they would continue their direct action campaign if no settlement had been reached by Thanksgiving. Rich, Dr. Mays, Dr. King, Lonnie King, and other members of SALC met, but to no avail. Rich stood his ground in the face of the students' insistence that the desegregation of schools and private businesses constituted separate issues. In a last-ditch effort to avoid a crisis, Rich and a handpicked group of black leaders scheduled another secret meeting. Lonnie King got wind of the plan and publicly denounced it. The negotiations had reached an impasse—the same one the students had faced several months earlier.[66]

Consequently, the protests began anew. "The merchants have left us no alternative but to renew our efforts," Lonnie King announced, and promised that the students would continue them "as long as it takes." Students attempted sit-ins and picketed with placards reading "Wear Old Clothes With Dignity" and "The Presence of Segregation is the Absence of Democracy." Most merchants responded by closing their eating facilities. But Rich's, continuing to straddle the racial divide, opened its sandwich bars to all comers—so long as they stood. Prominent black moderates continued to oppose the students' tactics, but this time the demonstrations had significant support in the wider African-American community. The jailing of Dr. King had aroused widespread ire among blacks; and the merchants' effort to link the desegregation of schools and businesses struck many as a sign of bad faith and a slap in the face. Some leaders in the older ranks made shows of solidarity by joining the students on picket lines. As many as two thousand attended prayer services and mass meetings held in Atlanta in mid-December in support of the goal of ending segregation at lunch counters and other eateries. Still others expressed support by participating in SNCC's "Christmas Withholding Campaign," a new boycott concept that was unfolded at SNCC's November conference. The organization urged shoppers to avoid segregated merchants with the tag lines "This Christmas Invest in Your Own Dignity" and "This Christmas Give Freedom."[67]

Hostile whites soon pushed back. An organized resistance group, "Georgians Unwilling to Surrender," led by governor-elect Lester Maddox, staged counter-demonstrations at the students' picket line. The Ku Klux Klan, white-robed and white-hooded, also paraded. The Klan marched outside of Rich's "to show support" for the store's segregation policy. The Atlanta police force blanketed the streets to keep the peace. Then on December 12, the sounds of an explosion rang through the air; an African-American elementary school had been bombed. The bomb damaged the school and several homes surrounding it, but no one was hurt. The incident "shocked" city leaders. Mayor Hartsfield blamed the violence on outsiders inflamed by "the silence of most of our substantial civic leaders." "Practically all the rabble-rousing, cross-burning, sheet-flapping, and dynamiting is done by people who do not live inside the [city] limit of Atlanta...the out-house crowd." He implied that the act of violence was a wake-up call for the "substantial citizens" of Atlanta, who, through their silence, were allowing "loud-mouthed racial demagogues" to be mistaken for the "voice of Atlanta." The merchants still did not budge. The Chamber of Commerce and other business concerns rejected the students' pleas for further negotiation, although one hundred other southern communities had desegregated lunch counters by this time. Hence, the demonstrations continued into 1961.[68]

## A SECOND ACT: THE U.S. SUPREME COURT AND SOCIAL PROTEST

The Supreme Court's December 1960 decision, *Boynton v. Virginia*, contributed to an increase in the protests' intensity. *Boynton* reversed a decision by the Virginia Supreme Court upholding the conviction of Bruce Boynton, a black law student who had been arrested under a Virginia antitrespass law for seeking service at a segregated interstate bus terminal. In a seven-to-two opinion written by Justice Hugo Black, the Court held that the conviction, which the Virginia Supreme Court had upheld as "plainly right," violated the student's right under the Interstate Commerce Act, which prohibited discrimination by carriers in interstate transit. The Act's antidiscrimination provision plainly covered restaurants in bus terminals, Justice Black wrote. The *Washington Post* and the *New York Times* hailed *Boynton* as another step by the High Court on the road to rooting out segregation in all areas of public accommodations, which, for Anthony Lewis of the *Times*, included "downtown restaurants." The *Atlanta Constitution* covered *Boynton* in an article headlined "Bus Restaurant Segregation Outlawed by Supreme Court." The article concluded that *Boynton* "will affect bus terminals in large cities throughout the South," including Atlanta. The *Student Voice*, SNCC's newspaper, noted Atlanta police chief Herbert Jenkins's announcement that he would "comply with all decisions of the Supreme Court." Sympathetic onlookers interpreted *Boynton* as a significant victory for Thurgood Marshall, LDF, and the direct action movement: the decision provided legal protection for students arrested while staging sit-ins, at least at interstate bus terminals, and handed civil rights activists a substantive victory in holding segregation in interstate bus terminals unlawful.[69]

But on January 10, 1960, an Atlanta police court judge riled COAHR and SNCC by narrowly construing *Boynton*. Judge Robert Jones remanded to criminal court four students charged under the state antitrespass law for sitting in at Terminal Station. The identity of one of the arrested students, Spelman College student Ruby Doris Smith, a courageous young woman who was well on her way to becoming a legend in the movement for her unflinching bravery in the face of white hostility, caused a stir. Armed with a broad reading of *Boynton*, A. T. Walden argued that the charges should be thrown out. Judge Jones disagreed. "I overrule the motion, Colonel," the judge said, invoking the term of "endearment" that whites used with Walden. "I think that this is a good time to carry the trial up to the Supreme Court," Judge Jones continued. The judge did not explain why he rejected Walden's interpretation of *Boynton*.[70]

However, the Interstate Commerce Act's prohibition against discrimination arguably did not cover the acts of the individuals Walden represented. His clients, all students at AU Center colleges, had sought food at the bus terminal, but were not in transit at the time. They had walked up to the counter from homes in Atlanta, saying "We want steaks," when confronted by police and the restaurant manager. Since the students were not passengers traveling interstate, their actions may not have been covered by *Boynton*; at the very least, it was an open question. By ruling on the statutory, rather than the constitutional, arguments made in *Boynton*, the Supreme Court had avoided the broader rule that Walden's argument suggested—that discrimination by a private actor, when supported or enforced by police officers, became state action.[71]

These legal technicalities mattered little to the demonstrators and their supporters in COAHR and SNCC, however. In court and in comments to the *Inquirer* afterward, Walden had stated that the "law was plain" and "if the judge had followed the law, he would have dismissed the case." Walden's interpretation shaped the students' perception of reality. To the students, Judge Jones's failure to dismiss the charges against Ruby Doris Smith and her comrades illustrated, once again, the unfairness of the courts and the futility of relying on them for social justice.[72]

In the wake of Judge Jones's presumed defiance of *Boynton*, the first anniversary of the student movement in Atlanta, and the merchants' continued refusal to desegregate, COAHR and SNCC implemented the jail-no-bail tactic on a mass scale for the first time in Atlanta. In announcing new protests, set for February 1, 7, and 11, 1961, SNCC promised to "purge the country of the rabies of racism" and, in a slap at legalism, added, "not with the deliberate speed evidenced in school desegregation." Police arrested more than eighty student demonstrators at the February demonstrations, seventy-five of whom refused bail. Seven ministers repeated the protest of the four students whose arrests *Boynton* had not covered, in Judge Jones's estimation. The ministers sought service at the Terminal Station restaurant, police arrested them, and they refused bail, spending the night in jail with students who had previously been arrested. By mid-February, one hundred protesters sat in Atlanta's jails. The "students in jail have said that they can stand it in there as long as other people can stand it [Jim Crow] out there," COAHR leader Herschelle Sullivan announced; COAHR also announced that the boycott would extend through Easter, traditionally an important retail sales period. Around the same time, the group revealed its intention to seek the intervention of President Kennedy and his brother, Attorney General Robert Kennedy, in the Atlanta sit-in movement. The student leaders scheduled a rally in support of the arrested demonstrators at the county jail for February 19, 1961. An air of crisis gripped the city.[73]

## BARGAINING FOR CIVIL RIGHTS

At this juncture, A. T. Walden stepped in. He and Borders asked the students to cancel the rally and instead attend a strategy meeting at the Wheat Street Baptist Church. The students again acceded to these wishes after the pragmatists signed a petition asking the students to do so and pledging adult support "for the duration." At the Wheat Street meeting, Walden asked the students to allow him to act as a "bargaining agent" with white leaders in an effort to resolve the dispute. The students agreed. Walden initiated negotiations, first meeting with Richard Rich's lawyer, Robert Troutman, Sr. Troutman explained that Rich wanted to "get off the hook." Rich had signaled his resignation with a charge to Troutman to "open the goddamned stores and give it to them, if you need to." But Rich stipulated that neither student leaders nor Martin Luther King, Jr., could be involved in the negotiations. Walden and Troutman then initiated talks with Ivan Allen, Jr., the newly appointed head of Atlanta's Chamber of Commerce, which thus far had refused to discuss desegregation. Allen consulted with the chamber's top retailers and returned willing to negotiate a deal based on the view that the "bad publicity" surrounding the ongoing sit-ins threatened to ruin Atlanta.[74]

After reaching the terms of a settlement with the white leaders, Walden went back to the black leaders for their stamp of approval. He invited Lonnie King,

Herschelle Sullivan, and other SALC members, including Martin Luther King, Sr., William Borders, Rufus Clement, Jessie Hill, Jr., Leroy Johnson, and Q. V. Williamson, to meet with Allen and the other white members of the negotiating team. The students upended Walden's plans for a tidy resolution of the problem when they balked at the terms of the agreement. The lunch counters and restaurants of the major retailers, including Rich's, Woolworth's, and Walgreen's, would be desegregated some time *after* the schools were desegregated. In return, the students would halt all sit-ins, pickets, boycotts, or "reprisals" of any sort and return to "complete normalcy as soon as possible." In other words, the terms of the resolution that Walden had reached with the white businesses were precisely the same ones that Richard Rich had proposed—and the students had rejected—as early as June 1960. When Lonnie King protested, Daddy King flew into a rage. "Boy, I'm tired of you! This is the best agreement that we can get out of this," the elder King thundered. Lonnie King chalked Daddy King's "brutal" response up to fear. "[A]n agreement had already been fashioned and had been agreed to by the older Blacks," he said, "they had promised something that they were fearful that they could not deliver." Met with such hostility from their supposed allies, the students acquiesced. Late on March 6, 1961, Ivan Allen, Jr., announced the agreement in an obliquely worded statement:

> We feel that the fine relationship which has existed between the races for a long number of years should be reinstated in Atlanta in every way as soon as is possible. In order to reestablish good relationships, the leading merchants have stated that it is their decision to carry out in lunchroom and other facilities the same patterns as have been recognized and evidenced by...the decision of the Atlanta Board of Education to comply with the orders of the Federal Court—all relating to the public school issues in Atlanta and as are finally decided upon in the public school issues in Atlanta.

Vague on precisely when the stores would desegregate and on details such as whether blacks could now try on clothes and use the same elevators and restrooms as whites, the settlement modeled clarity on one point. The proprietors conditioned their promise to desegregate on the "eliminat[ion] of all boycotts, reprisals, picketing and sit-ins" and the return of "complete normalcy as soon as possible." Even though the merchants had conceded little, COAHR and SNCC had to give up their fight.[75]

The *Atlanta Journal-Constitution* and the *Atlanta Daily World* praised the deal, but a vocal group of African Americans objected to the settlement. As word of the agreement spread through African-American neighborhoods, student activists and their adult supporters were appalled. The merchants had only agreed to desegregate at some uncertain date in the future; in the interim, the status quo would prevail. The settlement's capitulation to gradualism struck many critics like a "cold bucket of water in the face." Writing in the *Inquirer*, Julian Bond quipped, "Waiting for public school desegregation is like waiting for this year to roll around again. The accommodationists…are willing to do just that," but he and others were not. "[T]he time for action is now." Numerous citizens agreed with Bond. Tying the desegregation of downtown businesses to compliance with *Brown* struck many as an escape clause; after seven years, black citizens simply had no confidence that white southerners would ever comply with the Supreme Court's decision. Or, as Carl Holman put it, whites would not stand for "desegregation of any kind at any point short of or beyond Judgment Day." Members of COAHR and SNCC, and many others, denounced Walden, King, and Sullivan as traitors who had "sold out" the civil rights of other African Americans, and for nothing more than a reminder that *Brown* remained a promise unfulfilled.[76]

Though the agreement's time frame constituted its major defect, other problems stood out. The "contract," as Ivan Allen referred to the agreement, did not even specify which facilities it covered. It failed to address the students' demand that the stores increase employment opportunities for African Americans in downtown businesses. This goal was significant to the students, in part because merchants had closed lunch counters during the sit-ins, forcing some five hundred blacks who had worked those counters out of work. The merchants had only agreed "as far as practicable" to "re-employ" employees who had been fired during the picketing. In the minds of many, the agreement signified defeat, not the "major victory" that white-owned Atlanta newspapers had proclaimed. G. Domineck summed up the critics' position in a letter to the *Inquirer*: "It appears that we have been deserted by all our sensible minded leaders, or their sensible minds have deserted them. Do not the students who have withstood violence, humiliation and even jail terms deserve more than this? Do not the boycotters deserve more than the skimpy bone that the Atlanta merchants are tossing us?" The sit-ins, boycotts, and picketing seemed to have been undertaken in vain. Bowing to criticism, Lonnie King and Herschelle Sullivan resigned their positions in COAHR; they soon were reinstated, however. The student leaders were given the benefit of the doubt; opponents of the agreement placed the blame for the debacle squarely on the shoulders of Walden, Daddy King, and other adult leaders, whom they assumed had forced King and Sullivan into acceding to the terms of the agreement.[77]

The controversy grew so heated that SALC called a mass meeting to address the concerns of those who felt betrayed by the settlement. The Warren Memorial Methodist Church hosted the March 10 meeting. Over one thousand people attended. The crowd, described as "openly hostile and disrespectful" even in the *Inquirer*, sat on the edges of crowded pews and jammed the aisles to hear A. T. Walden explain why they should support the agreement. Amid sharp questions, heckles, and hissing, A. T. Walden pleaded with the audience to accept the settlement as a necessary compromise; he cautioned against viewing the resolution as inadequate simply because it did not effect "change overnight." "What difference does a few months make in social progress? We've been fighting for this thing for one hundred years; now we have it within our grasp. Let's have the good sense not to throw it away," Walden pleaded. He clarified crucial elements of the agreement. The downtown stores would be desegregated by October 15, 1961, and the stores would reopen, albeit on a segregated basis until that date, in order to accommodate students' concerns about blacks who had lost their jobs during the sit-ins.[78]

The crowd remained unmoved. Several speakers spoke out against Walden. "No self-respecting Negro can go back downtown under these conditions," one man said, to cheers. Martin Luther King, Sr., a lion in the black community but an unapologetic proponent of the settlement, arose to speak. The crowd booed and shouted him down.[79]

When Martin Luther King, Jr., stepped forward, the crowd finally quieted down. He gave an impassioned address, his best ever, by many reports. "His March on Washington speech was nothing compared to that speech that night," Lonnie King later claimed. In his address, Dr. King strenuously objected to the attack on leaders who supported the agreement, among them his father. As he put it,

> We must move now on the road of calm reasonableness. We must come to a mood of mutual trust and mutual confidence. No greater danger exists for the Negro community than to be afflicted with the cancerous disease of disunity. Disagreements and differences there will be, but unity there must be![80]

After Dr. King's speech, the mood of those assembled at the church changed from defiance to resignation and acceptance. Julian Bond remembered that "all the anger was dissipated and all the harsh feeling had gone away—and the crowd was still." In the days following the mass meeting, leaders sought unity. Criticism of the agreement died down amid calls by religious and civic leaders to end the "irresponsible charges of sell-out and personal abuse" against elders such as A. T. Walden and Daddy King.[81]

But hard feelings remained. Lonnie King complained that the adults had "undercut...the whole thing." He felt he had been "duped" by people whom he "trusted," and that he "had let the students down" and "the Atlanta community down" by "allowing" himself to be "duped by these older men." As for Martin Luther King, Jr., Lonnie King observed, "[H]e ended up trying to run with the foxes and chase with the hounds. He ended up trying to agree with the crowd but at the same time make a defense of his father and all the other older people who basically engineered this thing." In the end, King Jr. saved the day for Walden and the senior members of the black coalition.[82]

Had the students been aware of the extent to which Walden aligned himself, at least privately, with the white power structure, they might not have deferred to King's judgment. In a letter dated March 13, 1961, Walden responded to a local white merchant who had expressed thanks to him for brokering the settlement. He wrote,

> Please convey to the other merchants who were not parties to the agreement arrived at that in all my negotiations, although I had not met any of them in person, I had in mind their concern and interests equally with those of my own group for whom I was specifically authorized to negotiate.[83]

In this letter, which was copied to Chamber of Commerce president (soon to be mayor) Ivan Allen, Jr., Walden seemed to confirm what the students and many of their supporters feared. He had not negotiated an arrangement that put African Americans' interests first. He viewed himself as a nonpartisan in the deal-making, rather than as an advocate for blacks, generally, and the students, particularly.

But Walden may have had an ulterior motive. The consummate politician, Walden may have believed that he gained credibility as a mediator in coming racial struggles if whites viewed him as impartial. He could then spend the political capital that he had earned through his moderate reputation behind closed doors—where he pressed for the rights of African Americans in his genteel manner. Regardless of whether the letter was a true expression of Walden's views or a strategic maneuver, one fact is incontrovertible: the correspondence demonstrates the importance that Walden continued to place on cultivating a genial relationship with white elites.

Details of the plan for implementing the deal also illustrated Walden's continuing concern for allaying the merchants' fears about racially mixed public accommodations. A. T. Walden, Ivan Allen, and others, including Lonnie King and Herschelle Sullivan, formed a "plans and procedures committee" to implement the deal to desegregate. The committee agreed to follow certain principles on the day that the merchants desegregated. The first principle stipulated that "the Negro Participants would help condition the Negro community to insure a peaceful and intelligent desegregation procedure." From this principle followed others, including the merchants' demand that "integration activities" be "limited to off-peak periods."[84]

The merchants and SALC also agreed to limit the number of people permitted to integrate a facility on any given day: there would be a ceiling on the number of African Americans who would be allowed in facilities. For example, in a Rich's dining area with a capacity of 450, no more than eight blacks could desegregate the facility. The committee also agreed to accommodate the store managers' "special request" to "be given an opportunity to meet and know the Negro participants in the controlled desegregation of their stores." In other words, the blacks who desegregated the stores would be handpicked, with Walden designating the participants.[85]

Finally, the parties stipulated that they would enlist the "cooperation of the Atlanta newspapers in an effort to keep the publicity on desegregation to a minimum," on the view that publicity might breed attempts by white resisters at obstruction. The Atlanta Chamber of Commerce would preclear and release any statements regarding the process of desegregation. The plans designated A. T. Walden, Robert Troutman, or Ivan Allen as arbiters of any matters of interpretation of these principles.[86]

Later in the fall, the committee's carefully drawn plans to desegregate Atlanta without further direct action took effect as choreographed. The lunch counters and restaurants of the merchants who were signatories to the settlement and others desegregated on September 28, 1961. In total, seventeen merchants, representing seventy-seven eating establishments, desegregated, restrooms included. At Rich's Magnolia Room—the coveted lunch spot for middle-class whites—four "well-dressed young [black] women in hats, white gloves and high heels" ate at 2 p.m., without incident. No disturbances were reported, though some white patrons left when blacks entered the social spaces that the whites until then had claimed exclusively as their own. The merchants desegregated two weeks before the October 15 deadline that Walden had accepted and about a month after nine African-American students desegregated Atlanta's schools on August 30, 1961.[87]

Atlanta praised itself and was praised by others for its orderly, if deliberate, transition to a desegregated city. But according to the Southern Regional Council, Atlanta was the 104th city to desegregate since February 1, 1960, when the sit-ins began. More tellingly, the vast majority of the city's businesses and government offices remained within Jim Crow's grip.[88]

## HOW DO COURTS CATALYZE CHANGE?

From A. T. Walden's perspective, the desegregation of downtown businesses and the implementation of *Brown*, if on a token basis, had resulted from decades of careful strategizing inside and outside of courtrooms. The settlement agreement constituted a high point of a lifetime of service in the cause of civil rights for Walden, Martin Luther King, Sr., C. A. Scott, Benjamin Mays, William Holmes Borders, and others who had struggled for measures of racial justice in the years since World War II. For these men, those small steps had added up to 1961's giant leap toward equality. The students' concern about the six-month delay in the implementation of the settlement agreement simply demonstrated their immaturity and ingratitude. While the students harped on the six-month delay, Walden and Hollowell had to contend with the threat of prosecution under the state's antibarratry laws for their association with the sit-in movement. Walden found himself in potential legal jeopardy, but thanks to the agreement that he had negotiated, the students arrested and arraigned in *City of Atlanta v. Defendants* would never see prosecution.

Other businessmen and ministers could look back on the initial phase of the student movement and congratulate themselves, as well. Daddy King, whom the students had attacked with the scurrilous label "Uncle Tom," had secured bonds with his personal property to ensure students' release from jail. Walden and his comrades had put their livelihoods, property, and painstakingly cultivated personal relationships with white moderates on the line for the students; this personal sacrifice and racial leadership entitled them, they believed, to make demands upon the students and negotiate settlements that the youth thought less than perfect.[89]

But for COAHR the first phase of the process of uprooting Jim Crow from Atlanta had been bruising. Whereas the pragmatists looked upon Atlanta in September 1961 and saw a city well on its way to revolutionary changes in legal and social norms, the students focused on the fact that the settlement had left Atlanta only partially desegregated and service workers underemployed. The students' complaints about the six-month delay in implementation of the plan bespoke not only a temporal concern but a tactical setback for the direct action movement. The merchants, allowed to set the terms of the settlement, had controlled the movement's agenda. The outcome made the proprietors less likely to accede to students' demands in the future.

Much work remained to be done. For all of Atlanta's self-congratulation, the city remained segregated in most respects. And the students feared that further progress would be delayed by the manner in which the small steps toward desegregation had been achieved.

The settlement left many students embittered and forever frayed their relationship with Atlanta's traditional leadership. After the settlement, Julian Bond explained, the students "no longer trusted" Atlanta's established black leaders "to be our negotiators—we had to do it ourselves."[90]

Despite their disillusionment, the students had taken initial strides toward their conception of freedom—comprehensive desegregation, with attention to the interests of the working class—and had brought the rest of Atlanta along with them. The COAHR had moved the city's traditional black leaders from a vision of equality that accepted racial separation in some areas to one that rejected Jim Crow (at least rhetorically) in every area. Toleration of de jure segregation simply was no longer an acceptable public position, even for the understandable purpose of preserving black capital and institutions. From 1960 onward, Atlanta's leadership joined the chorus of black voices throughout the South that demanded the end of Jim Crow.

The tactical divide remained, though that barrier between the generations also had softened. Many black pragmatists remained opponents of direct action after the students' initial sit-in campaign. But others came to realize the utility of the students' pressure tactics in the struggle against whites' intransigence over ceding basic civil rights for blacks.

Overall, the very character of the civil rights struggle itself had changed under pressure that the students brought to bear. It had become a movement with many dimensions rather than a top-down operation dominated by Walden and a few like-minded people who had come of age at the turn of the twentieth century. The approach was much less paternalistic and much more democratic than it had been under the black pragmatists' control. College students and everyday people could now lay claim, along with civil rights lawyers and Auburn Avenue elites, to shaping the meaning of equality. This transformation in objectives and tactics had occurred in a single year.

But the transformation to a more thoroughly participatory democratic movement was incomplete. The climax of the students' direct action campaign—the imposition of a settlement that many African Americans found unacceptable in terms of both timing and substance—revealed the influence and resilience of the paternalistic brand of racial activism. The pragmatic leadership embraced the student movement, but the relationship between the two remained difficult and sometimes turned volatile. The relationship was fraught with conflict because the black elites kept trying to control the students' tactics, the pace of change, and the movement's priorities. The leaders of important black institutions, including churches, colleges, the local NAACP, and other organizations, sometimes supported the students' initiatives. But they also vied with SNCC and COAHR for strategic dominance over the struggle for racial equality. The pragmatists did not view the needs of the working class as a priority, as the students demanded. Some pragmatists backed desegregation, but balked at pursuing civil disobedience on a mass scale. The pragmatists now embraced litigation, but largely for the purpose of managing the direct action movement. Walden moved toward the court-based legal liberalism of Thurgood Marshall out of expediency.

Under SNCC's leadership, the students maintained direct action as their primary tactic during the next phase of Atlanta's civil rights movement. In addition, they used an array of other tactics—negotiation, media, community education, and boycotts—in their struggle for equality. Moreover, despite their continuing skepticism of the courts, the students found that they could not rid themselves of the influence of civil rights lawyers. In need of resources and legal defense, young activists agreed to modulate their protests in ways consistent with lawyers' tactical objectives. This was not necessarily a negative development.

For this discussion of the sit-in movement's advent in 1960 has shown the many unforeseen ways in which civil rights litigation catalyzed black political activism. With their failure to enforce *Brown*, the justices of the U.S. Supreme Court mobilized and radicalized the students. In their Appeal for Human Rights, these young activists invoked the Constitution and the Declaration of Independence as they called for freedom from discrimination, and then sought redress in the streets from the Court's and society's failure to remedy Jim Crow. The events surrounding *Boynton* tell a different kind of story about the relationship among the Court, society, and the movement than the events surrounding *Brown*. In *Boynton*, the High Court issued a favorable precedent, one that immediately buoyed the student movement. However, the application of that precedent in the lower courts proved an impediment to the activists. A municipal court read the precedent narrowly, and in the process, reignited the students' anger and inspired new demonstrations. Federal district courts' dismissal of public accommodations suits that Walden and Hollowell filed to head off direct action mobilized the students as well. From the streets, the activists called on society to comply with the principle of equal protection articulated in the U.S. Constitution.

Thus, this story teaches, the relationship between the courts, civil rights litigation, and activists was dynamic. Activists exercised considerable agency, notwithstanding the NAACP and pragmatists' attempts to manage the movement. These relationships became even more complex and combustible over time as activists with competing worldviews continued to employ a range of devices against racial discrimination.

CHAPTER 7

# A Volatile Alliance

*The Marriage of Lawyers and Demonstrators, 1961–1964*

If we are expected to pay the bills, we must be in on the planning and launching, otherwise the bills will have to be paid by those who plan and launch. (1961)

Roy Wilkins

Local lawyers have not always acted in the best interests of their clients. We really need about 300 Len Holts. (1962)

Julian Bond

In 1962, Len Holt, a young African-African attorney, wrote to SNCC executive secretary James Forman and proposed a new approach to civil rights lawyering.[1] Holt used military imagery to describe how lawyers could aid the civil rights movement. He imagined roving legal "MASH units" being dispatched to "outpost[s]" where SNCC was engaged in battle.[2] Volunteer "legal corpsmen" would provide "first aid" to SNCC workers just as medical support units aided combat soldiers during the "prosecution of military campaigns." At SNCC's 1962 conference in Atlanta, Holt outlined in great detail the types of assistance that lawyers stood ready to provide. Lawyers would defend civil rights workers after arrest, represent them at trial, and file affirmative constitutional challenges against segregation.[3]

However, the value of Holt's offer of help turned more on the deference he showed to SNCC's methods than the type of legal assistance he offered. Holt considered SNCC the "key catalyst of the integration movement in the South." He believed SNCC's success sprang from two sources: its tactical commitment to direct action and its strategic commitment to a democratic movement, one premised on lay, rather than expert, leadership. Because Holt valued these organizational features of SNCC, he assumed that lawyers would support, rather than attempt to sideline or supplant, SNCC. Legal advocacy would be secondary to, though symbiotic with, SNCC's political activism in the far reaches of the South. Soon, SNCC's leadership wholeheartedly embraced Holt and his style of civil rights lawyering.

Through their association with Len Holt, SNCC and COAHR's conception of civil rights lawyers and the role of legal advocacy in the movement evolved. The students had instigated direct action as an alternative to slow and ineffectual constitutional litigation, and many believed that the continued momentum of the sit-in movement required students' independence from the NAACP and lawyers associated with the NAACP LDF and beholden to its piecemeal, "test case" strategy. Indeed, some critics of the students' tactics counted on civil rights lawyers—and the NAACP—to blunt the impact of the nascent sit-in movement. These naysayers hoped that, in the end, the more moderate legal strategies of civil rights lawyers would prevail over direct action. "There is a conviction among students of race relations that he who controls the legal arm inevitably controls the civil rights movement," noted the *New York Times*.[4]

Neither the students nor their critics had Len Holt in mind when, at the dawn of the sit-in movement, they imagined "the civil rights lawyer" and the threat that he posed to the student wing of the civil rights movement. Holt embodied a kind of civil rights lawyer with whom the nascent student movement could successfully collaborate. Unaffiliated with the NAACP and LDF, Holt worked with more politically militant and less legally orthodox organizations, including the Congress of Racial Equality (CORE) and the National Lawyers Guild (NLG). Holt's style proved synergistic with SNCC and compatible with direct action. His practice proved that lawyers did not necessarily dominate or moderate social movements. It also prefigured the beginning of the student movement's shift from a civil rights agenda to a broader one focused on community mobilization and empowerment, and on economic rights and culture, in addition to civil and political rights. Holt's counsel to social movements in Atlanta and elsewhere constituted a crucial intervention.

Even as SNCC and COAHR students collaborated with Holt and moved toward a broader agenda, the students continued to rely on the NAACP and the lawyers of the NAACP LDF. In a stunning about-face, the student organizations that had lodged searing critiques of these groups in the run-up to the sit-ins spurned neither organization. Out of necessity, SNCC and COAHR tamped down their criticism of these groups. As their direct action campaign evolved, activists found that they could not easily dispense with these organizations.

The law and the courts mattered in multitudinous ways, it turned out, and these organizations had important roles to play in traditional legal venues. Direct activists needed lawyers to defend them after arrest and at trial on trespass charges. The LDF proved a major source of legal representation for SNCC, and the national NAACP was a bountiful source of bail funds. In Atlanta, SNCC and COAHR also relied on NAACP-affiliated lawyers A. T. Walden and Donald Hollowell for legal defense and advice.

But the students continued to bristle under the influence of the two more conventional civil rights organizations. Both the NAACP and LDF objected to the students' new-found ally, Len Holt. The collaboration of SNCC and COAHR with Holt, and later, with the Guild, showcased the persistent tensions in the movement.

Here, the volatile alliance between civil rights lawyers and student demonstrators in the early- and mid-1960s comes into view. Students marched in the streets, but supplemented demonstrations with litigation. The youth groups worked to infuse civil rights lawyering with a democratic, community-centered ethos. In a topical rather than strictly chronological fashion, this chapter discusses the interplay of civil rights litigation and direct action in campaigns to desegregate municipal facilities and health care. In these campaigns SNCC and COAHR collaborated with Len Holt, LDF, and local lawyers. Each campaign demonstrates how a mix of legal, political, social, and economic factors converged, sometimes successfully and sometimes less so, to advance the overarching objective now shared by students, legal liberals, and most pragmatists—ending American apartheid. This chapter shows that all of these actors made strides toward black freedom. But it emphasizes Holt's impact on the Atlanta student movement, and thus the largely forgotten history of progressive lawyers who worked outside of the NAACP and LDF during the height of the postwar civil rights movement. Holt's movement lawyering, like A. T. Walden's pragmatic lawyering, broadens understanding of who civil rights lawyers were and how they related to their clients, to social movements, to adversaries, and to the nation-state.

## THE INDISPENSABILITY OF CIVIL RIGHTS LAWYERS

Civil rights activists reveled in being arrested. The sight of police officers cuffing demonstrators for engaging in peaceful protests against segregation splendidly exposed the evil of Jim Crow. The number of arrests that an activist chalked up became a mark of distinction. Invariably, the most heroic figures in the direct action movement, from Martin Luther King, Jr., to John Lewis, could boast of numerous arrests for their activism. Lewis described his first arrest as "exhilarating." A "large, blue-shirted Nashville police officer" arrested Lewis on charges of disorderly conduct during a February 1960 sit-in in which whites struck out violently against peaceful demonstrators. The arrest and walk to the paddy wagon amid the cheers of a gathering crowd left Lewis feeling "high," "giddy with joy," and "elated." "That paddy wagon—crowded, cramped, dirty, with wire windows and doors—seemed like a chariot" carrying Lewis "across a threshold" to the "purity and certainty of the nonviolent path." In a 1964 interview, James Farmer, national director of CORE, which had been a pioneer in the use of direct action tactics in a campaign to desegregate interstate transportation many years before, explained: "Most people want at some time to have the jail experience—it's become such an important part of the movement." "It's a mystical thing," another CORE official said.[5]

From the inception of the sit-in movement, many of its leaders insisted that demonstrators remain in jail rather than accept bail after arrest. Suffering in jail represented the height of the activists' commitment to Gandhian principles of nonviolent direct action. Rev. James Lawson, one of the most prominent sit-in leaders, had spent three years in India studying Gandhi's teachings. Before and after the Greensboro sit-ins, Lawson held workshops in which he instructed college students in the tenets of nonviolence. The necessity of enduring the ordeal of jail in the cause of civil rights featured prominently in Lawson's lessons. Gandhi had been imprisoned for his beliefs during his struggle against British colonialism, Lawson explained, and the Indian leader had written that a *satyagrahi* who disobeyed an unjust law was compelled to accept "the sanction for its breach," including jail.[6]

Lawson insisted that antisegregation demonstrators follow Gandhi's example. Demonstrators had to pay the price for their principles by enduring confinement. By suffering the consequences of disobeying the laws of segregation, sit-in participants would demonstrate the force of their beliefs to the world. Dr. King preached that the "creative tension" established by the movement through mass arrests and jail-ins would force change. Whites who had ignored or defeated claims for justice made in courts would be driven to respond to the crisis precipitated by the movement in the streets; sympathetic whites would move from being observers to participants. Ultimately, King believed, segregationists would be morally coerced into repudiating Jim Crow.[7]

Even so, no consensus existed within the movement about the use of the jail-no-bail tactic. Activists practiced it infrequently. In Tallahassee, Florida, on March 18, 1960, a group of eight students chose sixty-day jail sentences over bail. At that time, Len Holt, then a CORE field secretary and counselor to the Tallahassee protesters, announced his hope that the group's decision would "set a pattern for other antisegregation demonstrators" to fill the jails. "The impact can only be felt by people suffering unjustifiably, and we are encouraging those who can undergo the hardships to offer themselves as sacrificial lambs," Holt intoned.[8]

Months later, James Lawson chided activists for continuing to accept bail. "We lost the finest hour of this movement when so many hundreds of us left the jails across the South," he said during an October 1960 address in Atlanta. Lawson's advice went unheeded for some time. In fact, Dr. King himself did not always refuse bail. When he and COAHR activists were arrested during the fall campaign in 1960, they at first refused bail, but ended the protest after negotiations with city officials. With charges dropped, the students left jail. Soon thereafter, Dr. King waged a legal and political battle for reprieve from a judge's sentence of four months' hard labor at a Georgia prison in the fall of 1960.[9]

In February 1961 SNCC implemented the jail-no-bail tactic for the first time. Nine students in Rock Hill, South Carolina, received sentences of thirty days' hard labor at the York County Prison Farm after they refused to pay fines upon conviction for trespassing. After the Rock Hill action, SNCC initiated a concerted push to include jail-no-bail as an integral component of all future civil disobedience campaigns. The committee encouraged sit-in participants throughout the South to follow the Rock Hill example by going to jail rather than making bail. After its February 5 meeting, SNCC declared that it "stand[s] behind the belief in 'jail versus bail.'" Edward B. King, secretary of SNCC, even vowed to reject volunteers for the upcoming Freedom Rides who were "unwilling to go to jail and stay there" because, he said, they "damage the morale" of the movement.[10]

Nevertheless, SNCC employed the jail-no-bail tactic sporadically, in Atlanta and many other places. In early 1961 SNCC and COAHR practiced jail-no-bail in Atlanta. But as before, the students disengaged and left jail at the insistence of A. T. Walden. The pattern of protest followed by negotiation and disengagement continued over the course of the students' efforts in Atlanta.[11]

On the national level, the NAACP and LDF strenuously objected to jail-no-bail. It threatened LDF's ability to wage a legal battle against segregation, the groups claimed. In a 1960 address at Fisk University before an audience of four thousand, including sit-in leaders, Thurgood Marshall decried the jail-in tactic in his charming, colloquial manner. "Once you've been arrested, you've made your point. If someone offers to get you out, man, get out!" Marshall also warned the students that their misguided street fight against Jim Crow might "get somebody killed." Students should leave the attack on segregation to lawyers, who could handle the slings and arrows from segregationists. A position paper on jail-no-bail, issued in February of 1961 by Gloster B. Current, the NAACP's director of branches, explained the association's position. Current instructed branch officials that "it is in the best interest of the NAACP" to discourage the practice. He called jail-no-bail "ill-conceived" and "ill-advised." "[I]t is the firm belief of the NAACP," Current wrote, that students should "plead not guilty to the charges and accept bail." Otherwise, they "forfeited their constitutional right[s]" and threw away litigation opportunities. This the organization could not countenance. The carefully planned legal attack on Jim Crow must not be endangered. Hence, all NAACP affiliates should insist that arrested demonstrators "follow the advice of counsel" and accept bail. Only then could they preserve the option of filing test cases about the constitutional issues underlying the sit-ins.[12]

The jail-in tactic also came in for criticism from commentators in the national press. Observers regarded the new tactic as another indication that the civil rights movement had embraced radicalism. Claude Sitton at the *New York Times* noted that the tactic of deliberately going to jail had "aroused criticism in some circles heretofore sympathetic to the Negroes' efforts." Critics thought jail-no-bail was too disruptive of the social order. Burt Schorr of the *Wall Street Journal* wrote that "militant young Negroes" who had "swept into the vanguard of the drive for desegregation" preferred jail-no-bail and other divisive tactics to litigation. Movement leaders who hoped that jail-ins would precipitate a social and political crisis did not shy away from trumpeting this hope to reporters such as Schorr. Slater King, a black real estate magnate who broke ranks with the national NAACP and became a leader of the Albany, Georgia, direct action movement, captured one dimension of the threat posed by the jail-in tactic. Protesters filled the Albany jails in 1962, and King lauded the effect in a 1963 interview. King explained that the tactic's utility began with its unifying impact on disparate elements of the African-American community:

> This jailing was a wonderful thing. Before it happened, I guess we professionals were inclined to go along with the whites. We wanted to keep the masses pacified. We didn't come into contact with day-to-day segregation. The white people we meet are usually interested in selling to us, and we don't use the busing or feel any economic pressure. It was easy to forget the lives most Negroes have to live.

To white and black moderates alike, the specter of mass civil disobedience, arrest, and confinement of such a cross-section of African Americans portended social cataclysm.[13]

External opposition did not alone explain SNCC and COAHR's infrequent jail-ins. Three additional factors militated against the tactic. First, the practice proved difficult to implement for logistical reasons. Jail-ins depended on a steady flow of volunteers. But only a small fraction of the population could be counted on to engage in civil disobedience (much less remain in jail after arrest). The movement would soon collapse if its small corps of volunteers continually refused bail. Second, the cadre of collegians who spearheaded the sit-ins found the prospect of extended time in jail unappealing. The brutal conditions in southern jails quickly became notorious, scaring off all but the sturdiest protesters. While backing the jail-no-bail philosophy, SNCC thus left the decision whether to practice it up to each individual. And third, SNCC's commitment to jail-no-bail wavered in tandem with its outrage over police officers' lawlessness. Abuses ranged from the arrest of protesters on "trumped-up" charges to beatings, gassings, "incommunicado" detention, and the torture of prisoners by officers or surrogates. Such misconduct and brutality bred disrespect for the law and extinguished many activists' commitment to suffering in jail for principle.[14]

The affection of SNCC and COAHR for provocative protests coupled with their inconsistent practice of "jail-no-bail" created a quandary. The students would regularly need legal representation and funds for bail. Volunteers initially looked to SNCC itself for legal aid. But the organization operated on a shoestring budget and sorely lacked the resources to meet the enormous need. Jane Stembridge, a SNCC secretary, responded with the same form answer to the thousands of pleas for counsel and bail funds that streamed into SNCC from students across the South. Unlike the NAACP, SNCC did not collect dues from members; therefore, the organization could not contribute to the legal defense of even the neediest of students. Stembridge's scripted response did not end there. She referred protesters to the NAACP and LDF, which, she said, were "prepared to handle such cases."[15]

In an ironic twist, SNCC, which had begun as a rival of the mainline civil rights organizations, sought assistance from the same organizations. The committee's sworn "enemies" would now help execute its reputedly insurgent strategy. The seeds of the student movement's evolution thus took root.

Invited to play the roles of financier and hired gun, the national NAACP and LDF, at first reluctantly, and then shrewdly, accepted SNCC's invitation. By providing legal defense and supplying bail funds during the early months of the sit-in movement, the stalwart organizations rescued protesters and saved the fledgling student movement from collapse. In August 1960, Thurgood Marshall noted in a letter to Marion Barry, SNCC's chairman at the time, that LDF represented thousands of students arrested for protesting in eight southern states.[16]

A wise calculation motivated the NAACP and LDF's decision to assist the students: their strategic interests demanded a coalition (of sorts) with the youth activists. SNCC posed a mortal threat to the NAACP, Roy Wilkins believed. In 1961, Roy Wilkins called SNCC nothing less than an "effort... to destroy the name and activities" of the NAACP. SNCC had set out to deny the nation's oldest civil rights organization its rightful role as leader of the black struggle for equality by burying it in a "'coordinating' movement." Wilkins cited numerous examples of SNCC's nefarious doings. In Atlanta, he claimed, "NAACP young people have been shut out as an organizational entity." As Wilkins saw it, SNCC hoped to gain dominion and control of the civil rights struggle through three ploys. The group hoped to build itself up by convincing the public that the "NAACP is asleep," by "lur[ing] its young people," and by "soliciting members and money" from it. An NAACP-SNCC alliance could undercut the danger that SNCC posed to the NACCP.[17]

By providing legal representation and financial aid to students who had been deeply critical of their legalism and conservatism, the NAACP and LDF would gain their rival's gratitude and would influence the wayward direct action movement from within. At the same time, the organizations would please donors who clamored, in a torrent of phone calls and telegrams, for the NAACP to help the sit-ins. The public would see that the NAACP remained "on the job" and still out in front, leading black America to the Promised Land. In short, the NAACP and LDF could remain relevant and deflect criticism through a partnership with the students.[18]

But SNCC's dependence on the NAACP and LDF only heightened the divisions between the movement's direct action and legal wings. The reason for the tension was clear. In return for their largesse, the traditional civil rights organizations expected to gain influence, if not outright control, of SNCC's agenda. A 1961 exchange between Roy Wilkins and Edward King illustrated the dynamic. By this time SNCC had launched voting rights campaigns in Georgia and Mississippi. In the process, numerous volunteers had been arrested. When protesters involved in the initiative contacted the NAACP and LDF for assistance, these organizations cried foul. The NAACP "has never agreed to rush in at the call of any organization whose staff or members or cooperators get themselves arrested and jailed carrying out a program devised and launched without consultation with the NAACP," Wilkins protested. The association would only invest in campaigns consistent with the NAACP's own agenda. "If we are expected to pay the bills," Wilkins continued, "we must be in on the planning and launching, otherwise the bills will have to be paid by those who plan and launch." Wilkins accused SNCC of duplicity: the students planned to extract funds from the NAACP and then trap it into supporting any and every item on their agenda. Wilkins expressed his displeasure in no uncertain terms:

> We have received persistent reports...that your Committee has a more or less formal intention of "involving the NAACP whether they like it or not in situations where they cannot escape unless they come along." We don't intend to be

embarrassed . . . and especially in a voter-registration campaign that, so far, seems to have put more workers in jail than it has voters on the books.

Ed King wrote back to Wilkins in apologetic tones. He affirmed SNCC's desire to "work together" and "maintain good relationships" with the NAACP and LDF.[19]

Despite such assurances, conflict endured. Correspondence between the organizations during the heyday of their collaboration documents continuing differences. The students wanted to launch new initiations that required NAACP and LDF support, while the mainstream organizations preferred to limit involvement with SNCC. Jack Greenberg repeated LDF's cautionary refrain in a 1962 letter to SNCC. "I do not think," he wrote, "we can give any specific commitment to represent you and your associates in all cases that may arise in the future. We must retain the flexibility to appraise each case and situation as it arises to determine how it fits in with our program."[20]

The NAACP and LDF refused to fully support the students' agenda, but vetoed SNCC's collaboration with others on numerous occasions. One flashpoint of the continuing strain between SNCC and LDF concerned SNCC's collaboration with the NLG. To many mainstream liberals, the Guild was poison, tainted by association with Communists. The NLG had been "born in revolt." It formed in 1937 to implement the New Deal and oppose the American Bar Association, the all-white, mostly corporate lawyers' group that staunchly opposed much of President Franklin Roosevelt's legislative program. In the preamble to its constitution, the NLG promised "to function as an effective social force in the service of the people to the end that human rights shall be regarded as more sacred than property interests." The group thrived during the 1930s and early 1940s, during its collaboration with New Dealers, legal academics, and civil rights lawyers, including Charles Hamilton Houston and Thurgood Marshall.[21]

But the McCarthy era dawned, and the Guild fell from its lofty perch. Federal Bureau of Investigation director J. Edgar Hoover and the U.S. attorney general targeted it as a "subversive organization." A 1950 report of the House Committee on Un-American Activities called the Guild the "foremost legal bulwark of the Communist Party, its front organizations, and controlled unions." The government's witch hunt succeeded. Fearing for their livelihoods and social standing, thousands of NLG members left the organization. Membership fell from a high of four thousand to a low of five hundred during the mid-1950s.[22]

The Guild "snapped back" to life during the 1960s as a consequence of its partnership with the civil rights movement and with Len Holt. Holt introduced the NLG to the movement. Before joining the staff of the Guild, Holt had been a

CORE field secretary and had collaborated with SNCC; he had counseled students engaged in sit-ins and freedom rides designed to desegregate interstate transportation. Holt brought this wealth of experience to the Guild. At the Guild's 1962 convention, the young attorney made a passionate appeal. He urged Guild members to go to the South and give aid to the civil rights movement; the Guild could be SNCC's legal "MASH unit." Ernest Goodman, former president of the Guild, recalled that Holt provided the "shot in the arm which really changed the whole complexion of the convention and of the Guild itself." Most African-American lawyers, fearful of the taint of black *and* Red, refused to associate with the NLG. Holt bucked the trend and "showed us that we had to play a role," Goodman explained. He convinced the predominantly white, largely Jewish Guild that "This is *our* struggle." "People wanted us, and the South was the place where we could do something useful," Goodman recalled.[23]

The Guild readily accepted the redemptive opportunity that Holt had laid at its feet. The same year, the organization formed the Committee to Assist Southern Lawyers, later the Committee for Legal Assistance to the South (CLAS). Made up of volunteer attorneys and law students, CLAS represented civil rights activists in the trenches of the Deep South. With its service to the movement, the Guild again set itself apart from the ABA. The Guild's assistance to the civil rights movement revitalized the  NLG and shored up SNCC at a time of dire need.[24]

The leadership of SNCC greeted the formation of CLAS with glee. Field secretary Dion Diamond penned a letter to Ernest Goodman soon after CLAS formed that suggested the scope of the legal problem that activists confronted. "With the exception of the metropolises, Negro attorneys do not exist. . . . In the smaller communities, the majority of the attorneys who are at hand refuse to accept cases involving civil rights," Diamond wrote. He concluded, "My thanks to the Guild for establishing this committee. With the addition of it, I am certain that the evils of segregation will be eradicated much faster." Julian Bond wrote to Goodman as well, sounding a similar note. Even in Atlanta, Bond noted, the few attorneys available to represent activists often were "ill prepared." Moreover, Bond wrote, "local lawyers have not always acted in the best interests of their clients." "We really need about 300 Len Holts," Bond lamented, but "lacking this, we greatly appreciate you and your assistance."[25]

The national NAACP and LDF vehemently opposed SNCC's association with the Guild, despite the SNCC's great need and the NAACP's own spotty relationships with SNCC. The NAACP and LDF's institutional history and interests motivated their opposition to the Guild. The NAACP had itself been subjected to Red-baiting. Beginning in the 1930s, segregationists routinely called its campaign against Jim Crow a "Communist plot." The charge no doubt emanated, in part, from highly publicized Communist Party appeals to African Americans. The Party proved attractive to some blacks, and Communists occupied the ranks of a few NAACP chapters. In additional, the NAACP had ties to some popular front organizations, such as the International Labor Defense, with which it competed for representation of the Scottsboro Boys and other black criminal defendants. Moreover, the Guild's membership included prominent LDF lawyers. Given these associations, the NAACP felt vulnerable when the government's hunt for Communists began.[26]

The NAACP responded to the threat by taking an uncompromising stand against the Party, its affiliates, and suspected members, including those within its own ranks. In 1950 the NAACP adopted an anti-Communist resolution to "clean out" the organization; the resolution called for the expulsion of Communists and Party–dominated branches. And LDF refused to represent the Guild when the lawyers faced the attorney general's blacklist. The NAACP's anti-Communist fervor only increased after *Brown*. Segregationists such as Georgia's attorney general, Eugene Cook, embarked on a crusade to destroy the NAACP (and undermine compliance with *Brown)* by alleging that the organization was a Communist front. Cook even claimed that the NAACP's executive secretary, Roy Wilkins, was a Communist. Wilkins and the entire machinery of the NAACP and LDF repudiated the charge. At the NAACP's 1956 convention, Thurgood Marshall made it clear that "there is no place in this organization for communists or those who follow the communist line." Indeed, Marshall went so far as to collaborate with J. Edgar Hoover in his effort to root Communists out of the NAACP. The NAACP and LDF would not risk losing their mainstream liberal constituency's support for their antiracist agenda.[27]

The organizations maintained their institutional hostility to Communists, real or imagined, throughout the 1960s. McCarthyism had receded, but the Cold War lived on. Jack Greenberg, who in 1961 succeeded Thurgood Marshall as LDF's director-counsel, strove mightily to preserve the organization's credibility by distancing it from tainted groups and individuals. The Guild headed the list of suspect organizations. As Greenberg saw it, the Guild existed far outside of the civil rights mainstream. He "worried about giving anyone any slim reason to attribute anything we did to advancing the party line." Greenberg also justified LDF's distance from the Guild in practical terms. The LDF feared that contributions would dry up if it worked with the Guild, given its Red past. Nor did it make sense for LDF to associate professionally with the Guild. The LDF lawyers outdistanced Guild lawyers in expertise and experience in civil rights litigation by a large margin, Greenberg believed. LDF's corps of skilled litigators could learn little from the Guild's band of lawyers, which included upstarts like Len Holt.[28]

Given the presumed risks of associating with the NLG, balanced against the enormous benefits of representation by LDF, Greenberg repeatedly forced client communities to choose between LDF and the Guild. Two examples vividly demonstrate the impact of Greenberg's approach. In 1963, Greenberg issued an ultimatum to African Americans engaged in a tumultuous battle for civil rights in the small mill town of Danville, Virginia. Segregationists had determined to crush the movement through police violence, dragnet arrests, economic reprisals, and "judicial terror." Overwhelmed with the task of seeking the release of hundreds of protesters, Len Holt, the Danville movement's lawyer, sought support from the national NAACP and LDF. It never came. Jack Greenberg and Samuel Tucker, one of LDF's local counsel, promised to help the movement—on one condition. The LDF would underwrite the defense of protesters, but only if they worked with NAACP-approved lawyers. "NAACP money can only go with NAACP lawyers, and Holt is not an NAACP lawyer," Tucker explained. Holt's clients rejected LDF's money, asserting that the Danville movement "was not the property" of LDF. The LDF later helped the residents of Danville, but only after Holt had left the case.[29]

One year later, during Freedom Summer in Mississippi, Greenberg took a similar position. Freedom Summer, SNCC's most ambitious voting rights and community mobilization campaign to date, generated hundreds of arrests in Mississippi and a tremendous need for legal aid in that state. The LDF, in league with Department of Justice officials, unleashed its "sharpest attack" yet on SNCC as a consequence of its decision to work with the Guild during the summer campaign. The LDF and U.S. Department of Justice lawyers "threw a real fit," according to James Forman. Jack Greenberg threatened to "pull out of Mississippi" and never again represent any SNCC activist if the Guild continued to advise and represent SNCC. Answering Greenberg's ultimatum, SNCC's executive committee reaffirmed its commitment to "freedom of association."[30]

Both practical considerations and principle motivated SNCC's audacious response to LDF. The leadership of SNCC could not afford to spurn the Guild's offer of help. The Guild sponsored a broad array of activist lawyers and law students, all willing to provide representation to SNCC. "We were not about to refuse the help of the Lawyers Guild," Forman later explained. "We would take help from anyone, always insisting that no one who gave us help had the right to dictate our policies. There could be no strings attached." Strategic and stylistic differences also influenced SNCC's rebuff of LDF. In SNCC's view, Guild lawyers were "aggressive" litigators with "courage and willingness to openly fight the legal system of the United States." By contrast, SNCC viewed the LDF as tending toward a cautious and "defensive" legal posture. The LDF deployed its resources to steer civil rights lawyers away from direct action and toward a narrow band of legal challenges—school desegregation cases. The vision of black freedom that SNCC held was much broader than that, and the students could not bring themselves to toe LDF's official line. After tallying its misgivings about LDF, SNCC embraced the Guild. The "fights of the thirties and the forties were not really our fight," Forman explained, "although some tried to impose them on us."[31]

Faced with SNCC's defiance, Greenberg relented. For all of the NAACP and LDF's fretting about SNCC's missteps, its headline-grabbing campaigns advanced the interests of the national NAACP and LDF in a crucially important way. SNCC's (and SCLC's) exploits provided excellent fund-raising opportunities. After dramatic confrontations between segregationists and integrationists, the coffers of the national NAACP and LDF filled. Hence, like estranged family members unable to get along but deeply in need of each other, the quarrelsome relationship between and among the NAACP, LDF, and SNCC persisted. The leadership of SNCC continued to accept aid from the national NAACP and LDF.[32]

Yet SNCC also collaborated with Guild lawyers on a wide range of projects. The Guild carried out initiatives designed to secure passage of and implement the 1964 Civil Rights Act and the 1965 Voting Rights Act, protect the rights of black criminal defendants and political dissidents, and assist demonstrators who faced arrest for engaging in direct action and other protest actions. Guild lawyers also filed affirmative litigation, some of it conceived by, and much of it involving, Len Holt. At the same time, Holt's intensifying collaboration with SNCC and COAHR helped to set in motion a new stage in Atlanta's civil rights movement.[33]

## "MOVEMENT LAWYERS" AND OMNIBUS CIVIL RIGHTS LITIGATION

When Len Holt took the podium at SNCC's April 1962 conference, he delivered a hopeful message to the crowd of 250 assembled at the AU Center. In his address, titled "Legal Rights and Responsibilities," Holt outlined a program for a fruitful collaboration between civil rights lawyers and practitioners of civil disobedience. Law and direct action, when practiced in tandem, held radical potential, he said: together, they could transform society. A different type of civil rights lawyer—a "movement lawyer"—could harness the energy of the direct action movement and facilitate the transformation. Driven by the imperatives of grassroots activists, movement lawyers would deploy their professional skills to protect street fighters for racial justice from violence and legal peril. Secondarily, the attorneys would make omnibus legal claims against segregation. The dynamic political environment created by direct action would increase the likelihood that court cases would find success.[34]

In short, Holt advocated a bottom-up approach to lawyering, one in which activists would lead and lawyers would follow. Political activists would define the objectives of civil rights campaigns, and lawyers would solve problems arising out of the strategy as circumstances dictated. Holt encouraged SNCC to form working relationships with any and all attorneys committed to movement lawyering, including the newly formed CLAS of the National Lawyers Guild. In the coming years, Holt reiterated this prescription for sociolegal change at every turn.[35]

Holt's approach to civil rights lawyering emanated from three sources: early adoration of the NAACP and its campaign against segregation, followed by utter disillusionment with the organization; deep connections to clients and community-based organizations across the South; and the repressive sociopolitical context in which he practiced law. A Chicago native, Holt had matriculated at Howard University School of Law in 1952 after an "unpleasant" but "typical experience" with a Las Vegas sheriff's deputy. The officer beat Holt, then a cabdriver, with a club, leaving him to wince in pain from his injuries for more than a week. As a young man on the South Side of Chicago, Holt had often endured the humiliation of "being treated like a black boy by white cops." The Las Vegas brutalization, his harshest encounter yet with police, proved transformative. The officer's savagery politicized Holt. Nothing would ever completely shield black men from racist police officers, but Holt determined to "put [him]self in a position to inconvenience the oppressor." He would fight police harassment with a law license.[36]

Holt attended Howard University's law school during the period 1952 through 1956, a golden age for the institution. At that time, Thurgood Marshall and several other Howard graduates played commanding roles on the national stage as they created the field of civil rights law. Marshall and his staff customarily gathered at Howard to moot arguments prior to each of LDF's appearances in the U.S. Supreme Court. Howard law students who attended these moot arguments could hear the thrust and parry of discussions between LDF staff and the nation's legal luminaries. Second- and third-year students conducted research for LDF lawyers, while first-years found themselves fetching sandwiches and coffee for them. All of the students gained role models, invaluable to African Americans who lived in a segregated society and who hoped to achieve success in a virtually all-white profession. The students could imagine themselves walking in the footsteps of giants. And some did. The successes of Thurgood Marshall, the legendary Howard graduate, attracted Len Holt to the law school. Holt, a "political animal" long before he ever opened a law school casebook, figured that he could go to Howard and learn to "deal with the problems of black people rather than trying to make a million dollars." He was thrilled to be among the students who fetched lunch and researched issues for LDF attorneys, and his admiration for Thurgood Marshall knew no bounds. He conscientiously planned to "join the NAACP team" after he finished law school.[37]

Holt graduated from Howard in 1956 and established a law practice in Norfolk, Virginia. Before long, his hopes to associate with the NAACP were dashed. The world of NAACP lawyers was, he had learned, a "closed society." Much like the initiation process for the black fraternities and sororities, one had to be chosen for membership. Talent and a desire to serve the community were not enough to earn the privilege of collaborating with the lawyers who, by then, had famously won the victory in *Brown v. Board of Education.* A lawyer also had to adhere to the NAACP and LDF's policies and vision of civil rights. This requirement proved difficult for Holt, an independent-minded only child who once had been sent to a school for "incorrigible boys" because of his tendency to speak his mind and act accordingly.[38]

Holt's tensions with LDF had grown out of the school desegregation campaign. The young lawyer disagreed with how the Virginia NAACP and LDF handled aspects of the Prince Edward County, Virginia, litigation and said so. The county responded to a 1959 court order to desegregate its schools with defiance; Prince Edward closed its public schools altogether rather than integrate them. The closure lasted for a remarkable five years. During that time, white students, alone, received publicly supported tuition grants to attend private schools. Holt witnessed the devastating impact of the school closure on local blacks as he crisscrossed the state to represent clients. On drives through Prince Edward County, Holt saw "boys and girls 8 and 9 years old"—the children of black agricultural workers not long removed from sharecropping and slavery—"standing around, doing nothing." Meanwhile, some local NAACP members—people with sufficient financial means—sent their children out of state to receive a proper education. Holt did not blame LDF for the school closure itself, a product of virulent white resistance to the black struggle for freedom. But he concluded that neither the LDF nor the NAACP had taken adequate steps to ensure that all children whom the county denied schooling received compensatory education. The school desegregation litigation imposed extravagant costs on black communities, and NAACP officials had not fulfilled their responsibilities to local blacks to ameliorate those disadvantages. Moreover, Holt questioned whether LDF should focus so narrowly on the school litigation at all given the varied and tremendous material needs of African Americans. When Holt voiced these concerns to Virginia NAACP officials, they were not well received. Holt could collaborate with the NAACP and LDF, he was told, but only on their terms: the organizations demanded full-throttled support of their school desegregation strategy. Holt refused to silence or censor himself. He thus found himself estranged from the NAACP and LDF.[39]

Disillusioned, Holt refocused his energies on building his private practice: he would practice civil rights law in his own way. In his burgeoning practice, Holt represented blacks in Norfolk and other towns in a variety of criminal and civil actions, matters large and small. He soon gained a reputation as a trouble-maker among local whites. Segregationists in cities like Norfolk and in the small Virginia towns where he practiced law reviled him as "that smart nigger bastard who tries to make a fool of white folks." Holt treasured this reputation. He also embraced the nickname that his clients affectionately bestowed upon him—the "Snake Doctor." Both labels captured Holt's role-playing as a rabble-rousing, activist lawyer and champion of racial justice.[40]

The template for Holt's lawyering style and its substance did not derive from his one-time idol, Thurgood Marshall. Holt's mentors included the small band of black lawyers in Danville, Virginia, especially his law partner, E. A. Dawley. Dawley's bravery and passionate commitment to clients in the face of a virulently racist opposition greatly impressed his young colleague. Holt also felt profoundly grateful to Dawley for his unstinting support of a "roving, loud-mouth, theatrical" partner who "would slither into towns wearing patched jeans," "puffing Clint Eastwood–style cigars," and challenge white supremacist norms in unprecedented ways. Later, Holt came to admire William Kunstler and Arthur Kinoy, brash New York lawyers, white and Jewish, who represented civil rights activists during the 1960s, in collaboration with the ACLU and the Guild.[41]

Holt hoped to change the student movement's relationship to civil rights lawyers—developed in interaction with NAACP and LDF lawyers—from one of antagonism to one of cooperation. His vision of a "movement lawyer" sprang from that desire. He lodged a searing critique of the NAACP and LDF. The LDF hewed too closely to a conventional, top-down form of lawyering, and it sought to impose its worldview on everyone else, as Holt's 1963 Danville experience showed. Similarly, the NAACP struck Holt as too "conservative" and "middle-class." The orientation of both organizations contrasted sharply with the more confrontational and antihierarchical student wing of the direct action movement. "[I]f the protest movement was anything," Holt wrote, "it wasn't conservative or middle class."[42]

Holt touted movement lawyering as a "creative" and "dramatic" style of lawyering—one that matched SNCC's political dynamism and philosophy. Holt, who had been present at SNCC's founding, considered the organization's direct action techniques the boldest and most effective means of pursuing racial justice and embraced its commitment to community-driven activism. Consistent with SNCC's philosophy and goals, Holt urged lawyers to play a support role in the movement. Belying the student movement's initial assumptions, Holt saw no contradiction between lawyering and the objectives of the direct action movement. Lawyers were not destined to dominate their clients. Civil rights litigation and political action could be synergistic if lawyers immersed themselves in local communities and learned their strategic objectives. Arthur Kinoy explained the distinction between the conventional civil rights lawyer and the movement lawyer that Holt advocated this way:

> The primary role of people's lawyers in the civil rights movement had shifted from the days before *Brown v. Board of Education*. Lawyers were no longer the central agents fighting to achieve the goals of freedom and equality through their own special arena, the courts of law. Their role now was vastly different. Their primary task was to find ways of helping the Black people themselves resist the efforts of the power structure to derail their own forward movement to enforce the constitutional promises of freedom and equality.[43]

Holt's outlook endeared him to SNCC and local activists. James Forman at SNCC boasted that Holt "offer[ed] more inspiration" to young activists than virtually anyone else. Holt talked to demonstrators about "human and constitutional rights" and endorsed their vision of a youth-led movement. The students "trusted" Holt, a "brilliant" and "aggressive" lawyer, to assist them on their own terms. His approach contrasted with that of the NAACP and even that of the SCLC, both of which tried to steer SNCC in various directions. Forman, arrested with other SNCC protesters during demonstrations in Monroe, North Carolina, in 1961, described a hearing before a "kangaroo court" in which Holt and Kunstler represented him.

> Holt did a magnificent job in court. He took every possible opportunity to make the case political, speaking eloquently about race relations in this country and the need for the type of action in which we were engaged. He gave his summation, a brilliant one, but this was a kangaroo court and his words were like pearls being thrown to swine.[44]

Holt also represented Forman after his arrest in Danville, Virginia, and collaborated with SNCC on numerous other occasions before and after the 1962 conference. Each time, Holt's "knowledge and dedication" to the cause and his respect for SNCC's core beliefs captivated Forman and other SNCC loyalists. Mary King, a SNCC communications office worker, compared Holt to "abolitionists of the underground railroad" when she recalled how the "clever" Holt facilitated her escape from white law enforcement officers in the "war-like" Danville of that time. When vindictive authorities threatened to indict her on unfounded incitement to riot charges under a nineteenth-century statute passed after slave uprisings, Holt sent her across the Dan River to a North Carolina convent run by nuns friendly to the movement.[45]

Future SNCC chairman Stokely Carmichael remembered Holt's defiance of Jim Crow customs in a Mississippi courtroom. The white supremacist judge showed his contempt for the black lawyer by turning his back when Holt spoke. The prosecutor threw documents at his feet rather than hand them over. Holt responded in kind. "Bro Len silently bent down, picked up the papers, calmly made his presentation," and then "deliberately walks across that Mississippi court room, moves around to face the prosecutor, and throws those papers" in his face." Holt refused to play the racist's game. Carmichael and other protesters were euphoric. They found Holt's irreverence in the courtroom, uncommon even in other radical lawyers, inspirational.[46]

Holt's ideas "were far ahead of the conservative legal profession," Forman concluded, and "they earned him the enmity of many lawyers." Holt, said Carmichael, was "certainly one of the great unsung heroes" of the civil rights movement.[47]

Holt endorsed SNCC's philosophy, but he also made a signal professional contribution to the civil rights movement—the "omnibus integration" suit. Holt and Florida attorney Ernest Jackson conceived the omnibus suit strategy. Holt's firm then executed the idea in numerous locales. The omnibus action differed from the traditional civil rights suit in scope. The omnibus suit "infected" the law "with a sense of urgency" by simultaneously attacking every facet of Jim Crow in a local community. "In one complaint, in one suit, it seeks to do the same job of righting wrongs that formerly took a series of suits," Holt explained.

> Instead of just seeking to integrate a library [for example] it attacks racial dis-
> crimination in the cemetery, swimming pool, public hospital, dog pound, parks,
> auditoriums, buses, public housing and you-name-it . . . and it does all this attack-
> ing simultaneously, at one time.[48]

The omnibus suit named as a defendant any public official who managed or otherwise participated in an institution practicing segregation. The litigation might name twenty, fifty, or one hundred public officials as defendants— including local judges who presided over segregated courtrooms. Len Holt filed his first omnibus suit in Danville, Virginia. "The Danville Omnibus Integration Suit asked for the integration of practically everything," Holt recalled: the

Danville Memorial Hospital, the Danville Technical Institute, cemeteries, the City Armory, the nursing home, public housing projects, all public buildings, teacher assignments, all city employment. He and his law partners filed similar suits in other Virginia cities, including Lynchburg and Hopewell, as well as in other southern states.[49]

Omnibus litigation repositioned direct activists as affirmative litigants for racial equality. Typically, activists only appeared in court as defendants after being arrested for protesting Jim Crow. By filing omnibus suits, protesters battled segregation in two different forums, in two different ways. The tactic complemented the spontaneous maneuvers of student demonstrators, while it also undermined the relentless tactical assaults of the racist state. Holt inventoried southern law enforcement and saw a plague of unfair practices: warrantless arrests, denials of jury trials, invalid injunctions, prejudgment of cases, lack of notice, suspension of rules of evidence, segregated seating, and all-white judges, jurors, and police departments. The unfairness that permeated the southern justice system threatened to cripple the protest movement. Hence, Holt championed an unexpected turn: omnibus civil rights litigation, a tactic capable of destabilizing the white power structure and yielding legal victories. Faced with an omnibus desegregation lawsuit, filed against the backdrop of ongoing demonstrations, the white establishment would concede the legal claim in an effort to put an end to disorder in the streets.[50]

Even if omnibus suits failed on the merits, they could achieve an important secondary purpose. The litigation could loosen the mental chains of racism and generate public concern about injustice. In order to trigger this reaction, Holt adopted a confrontational courtroom persona. Rather than ignore the racial repression that characterized southern courtrooms, he called attention to it. Holt's refusal to play along with the social norms of Jim Crow invariably rankled segregationist judges. When these judges took umbrage, which they often expressed in clearly bigoted language, they only illustrated the partiality of the judicial system. A judge's reaction could, in turn, spur communities to action.[51]

Holt's omnibus litigation in Virginia illustrated how the tactic functioned in practice. The full power of the Virginia justice system rained down on Holt after he filed an omnibus suit in Hopewell, Virginia. In 1962, the circuit court of Hopewell found him in contempt of court for accusing a judge of "acting in the capacity of police officer, chief prosecution witness, adverse witness for the defense, grand jury, chief prosecutor and judge." Three years later, the U.S. Supreme Court vindicated Holt. Reversing the contempt finding, the Court held that the Virginia Supreme Court of Appeals had deprived Holt of his Fourteenth Amendment due process rights; the court should not have held an attorney in contempt merely for alleging judicial bias. For Holt, the Supreme

Court's decision did not constitute the most significant victory arising from the case. Holt's greatest achievement lay in having exposed the judge's animosity and bias. The judge's disdain for black rights, encapsulated in the contempt order he issued against the heroic Holt, invigorated the community's direct action drive against Jim Crow. Holt's client community mobilized to fight segregation through participatory democratic action.[52]

Legal action and direct action could work synergistically across the South, Holt believed. Movement lawyering could contribute to the creative tension that Dr. King and SNCC counted on to bring about the demise of Jim Crow. The Snake Doctor brought his provocative style of lawyering to Atlanta in 1961.

## Omnibus Litigation in Atlanta

Len Holt's crusade to marry litigation and direct action tactics had only just begun when he visited SNCC's Atlanta headquarters in early 1961. During an unpublicized meeting with SNCC leaders, among them Julian Bond and James Forman, Holt counseled the group to file omnibus suits. These suits would desegregate all of Atlanta's tax-supported facilities, superseding Walden and Hollowell's piecemeal public accommodations litigation. The time for "one suit at a time" had passed, Holt argued. The one-at-a-time cases undercut the dynamism and core values of the protest movement—especially "Freedom—now!" That demand "of course had stemmed from the slow pace of legalism" in the first place, Holt reminded the Atlanta movement. By resigning itself to piecemeal litigation, the civil rights movement had not "pressed [its] advantages." Omnibus suits, Holt explained, conferred two main advantages over piecemeal litigation: they were more efficient and more "psychologically disturbing to the segregationists." Defenders of Jim Crow had grown accustomed to "ensnaring us with legal delays" and limiting civil rights activists to a defensive posture, Holt said. The scope and procedural boldness of the omnibus suit would bring enormous "pressure to bear" on segregationists.[53]

But the strategy could only be properly implemented by a movement lawyer, Holt warned. If SNCC chose to pursue omnibus litigation, it had to avoid attorneys whose goals differed from its own. Lawyers opposed to the movement's vision might not act in SNCC's "best interests." If an appropriate lawyer could not be found, Holt told the committee to take matters into its own hands: the students should file omnibus suits pro se, that is, without a lawyer's aid. To facilitate pro se practice, Holt offered SNCC a tutorial on civil rights litigation. He explained in detail the form and procedures to be followed in filing a complaint in federal district court. Holt covered everything from the amount of the required filing fee and the form of the case caption to the federal statutes and constitutional provisions providing the cause of action for civil rights suits, and the proper wording of the prayer for relief. He not only tutored SNCC in the basic points of legal practice but also encouraged its leaders to pass along the information to everyday citizens. Holt ended his pitch by recommending that SNCC print information manuals and "do-it-yourself legal kits" outlining federal court practice so that citizens in communities across the South could file omnibus protest suits as well. Forman and Bond responded enthusiastically to the idea of "an offensive legal battle" against segregation.[54]

On May 17, 1961, the seventh anniversary of the Supreme Court's decision in *Brown v. Board of Education*, four Atlanta students, in league with SNCC and Holt, filed an omnibus suit challenging municipal segregation in Atlanta. Lonnie King, Herschelle Sullivan, Benjamin Brown, and Charles Lyles, leaders of COAHR, filed the action, *Brown v. Atlanta*, pro se in federal court. Len Holt had worked closely with the students on drafts of the complaint, but disavowed credit so that Atlanta could become one of the first test sites where community members themselves used the omnibus tactic. The complaint's title, "A Suit to Exhume Much of the Cancerous Racial Segregation That is Festering Within Atlanta," trumpeted its purpose. Sweeping in scope, the suit sought to "abolish racial segregation and racial discrimination in the use and enjoyment of every public facility." The targets ranged from Atlanta's parks, pools, tennis courts, playgrounds, and municipal courts to "everything else the city has anything to do with." The lawsuit described the city's segregation policies as "insulting, degrading, unnecessary, medieval, foolish, septic"— and unconstitutional. Defendants included the City of Atlanta and James Webb, the judge who had passed judgment on numerous COAHR volunteers arrested during the past year's sit-ins.[55]

*Brown v. Atlanta* bespoke the youths' frustration with the strategic calculations of their elders. In the late 1950s, A. T. Walden had declined to push for desegregation of Atlanta's parks, pools, playgrounds, and other recreational facilities, despite the 1955 Supreme Court precedent, *Holmes v. Atlanta*, that invited such a challenge. Black access to the array of recreational facilities open to whites remained a point of contention in 1960, after the sit-ins jolted race relations in Atlanta. In the days before filing the omnibus suit, COAHR lobbied Mayor Hartsfield to desegregate public accommodations. Hartsfield rebuffed the students. He urged them not to "press" for "wholesale desegregation" of park facilities "at this time." By filing the omnibus suit so soon after the unsatisfactory lunch counter settlement of March 1961, the students signaled their intention to strike out on a different path. No longer would they restrict their attack on segregation to the vagaries of biracial negotiation. The omnibus suit

cited *Holmes* to support the contention that the Constitution demanded desegregation of all taxpayer-supported facilities.[56]

With the omnibus suit, COAHR and SNCC had, for the first time, chosen
litigation rather than direct action as a line of attack against segregation. The
editorial page of the *Atlanta Constitution* responded enthusiastically to this
turn of events. "It is good for Atlanta that the Negro students have moved their
activity from the streets to the courts," the lead editorial chirped. Len Holt had
envisioned the omnibus suit as an exceptionally provocative tactic. But Atlanta's establishment greeted the legal case as a welcome departure from radicalism. The students gained goodwill by using the "orderly legal approach." A little
over a year later, they would also gain a resounding legal victory.[57]

On August 27, 1962, U.S. District Court Judge Lewis Morgan delivered the
triumph. Morgan struck down all Atlanta ordinances requiring segregation in
city parks, theaters, arenas, public halls, auditoriums, and other places of public
assembly. The court found these ordinances unconstitutional under the Fourteenth Amendment. The COAHR enthusiastically welcomed the decision.
Plaintiff Ben Brown noted that "it was unfortunate that the federal courts had
to dictate to local authorities the well founded principles upon which our whole
nation was founded," but called the court's ruling a "tremendous accomplishment" for COAHR. Indeed, it was.[58]

A number of recent legal decisions militated in favor of the omnibus suit's
success. A 1961 Supreme Court decision set the stage for Morgan's decision. In
*Burton v. Wilmington Parking Authority*, the Court dealt a blow to segregation by
private businesses that operated in public buildings. The Court found unconstitutional the Jim Crow practices of a restaurant operating in a parking facility
owned by a state agency. *Burton* followed a line of cases, including *Holmes v.
Atlanta*, that applied *Brown*'s antidiscrimination principle to other public places.
*Sanders v. Gray* also indicated that the federal courts would no longer abide
racial discrimination in the public arena. In *Sanders*, decided in April 1962, a
federal district court struck down Georgia's county-unit system—the notorious
apportionment method that ensured rural and white domination of statewide
elections. Soon affirmed by the Supreme Court, *Sanders* paved the way for the
election of African Americans to the state legislature and the U.S. Congress.[59]

The legal victory of COAHR in *Brown v. Atlanta* surpassed A. T. Walden's
litigation record. The students' pro se suit went much further toward desegregating Atlanta than the three state and municipal facilities suits that Walden
and Hollowell had previously filed. Hollowell and Walden had filed suits against
segregation in the state capitol grounds café, in the courthouse cafeteria, and in
the city hall cafeteria in August 1960. The pair had intended to head off demonstrations with the lawsuits.

But they had not won a court-ordered victory in any of the cases. Georgia had closed the Capitol grounds facility rather than desegregate it. As a consequence of the state's maneuver, the federal district court had dismissed the suit. The courthouse cafeteria suit ended with a better result for Hollowell and Walden, but the outcome was still less than a full victory. Fulton County closed the courthouse cafeteria to the general public; at the same time, however, officials opened the facility on a desegregated basis for employees and those with official business in the building. Blacks ate in the cafeteria for the first time on December 1, 1961. Walden and Hollowell had breakfast at the courthouse café before attending the hearing at which Judge Lewis Morgan announced that their case had been mooted by the policy change. Ivan Allen, installed as the city's new mayor in January 1962, personally led a group of black students into the City Hall cafeteria for lunch, desegregating that facility, in May 1963. Allen's action mooted the City Hall cafeteria case that Walden and Hollowell had filed three years earlier. The federal district court had refused to dismiss the suit in October 1960, but apparently had never issued a decree ordering the café desegregated. Allen's action garnered him goodwill, but denied Walden and Hollowell a single victory in their litigation campaign against segregation in state and municipal restaurants. In comparison to Walden and Hollowell's track record, the victory that the students achieved in the omnibus suit looked impressive.[60]

The students victory did not occur by virtue of courtroom action alone, however. The *Atlanta Constitution* had initially welcomed the omnibus suit as an *alternative* to direct action. But the litigation in fact complemented and capped off COAHR's direct action campaign and demonstrated the utility of a many-pronged attack on segregation. The COAHR secured the legal victory within the context of a political mobilization in support of the lawsuit's goals. *Brown v. Atlanta* had been filed and won against the backdrop of protests against segregation in the city's public spaces. The COAHR filed the case soon after the initial phase of Atlanta's sit-in movement. Protests continued in the fall of 1961 and in 1962, when SNCC and COAHR targeted segregation in state and city buildings and facilities. One of the groups' highest profile protests had demonstrators repeatedly challenging Jim Crow in the galleries of the Georgia state legislature beginning in January 1962. One of the largest campaigns featured as many as a hundred AU students; they formed a picket line around the State Capitol and attempted to sit on an interracial basis in the state legislature's galleries. In the months surrounding the August 1962 victory in the omnibus suit, COAHR and SNCC also engaged in protests against privately owned restaurants and hotels. These demonstrations generated dozens of arrests.[61]

The groups also repeatedly attacked segregation in the facilities that were the subject of the omnibus suit. Students tried to use recreational facilities designated for whites only immediately prior to filing the suit and while the case was pending. In fact, two students, Ruby Doris Smith and Frank Holloway, had very publicly been turned away from Piedmont Park's whites-only swimming pool just one week before Judge Morgan sided with COAHR in the omnibus litigation. In short, the omnibus tactic supplemented the street-based political activism of the Atlanta student movement, just as Holt had imagined that it would.[62]

But without more, the court victory did not produce relief. Despite the court order and a subsequent consent decree, the city of Atlanta mostly ignored its duty to desegregate. For the most part, the facilities that the suit targeted remained closed or segregated. It took political and economic pressure, applied by SNCC and COAHR in ongoing protests, to give the court orders teeth. Demonstrations led by SNCC and COAHR in 1962 and 1963, and the negative publicity that they generated, persuaded Mayor Allen to push for implementation of the court order. In Allen's thinking, "Little Rock had virtually died on the vine" because of its defiance of court-ordered school desegregation. Data showed that the protests had already cost his city tourist and convention business. For Allen, the critical question was whether "Atlanta [was] going to be another Little Rock, or was Atlanta going to set the pace for the New South?" The Supreme Court decisions reinforced Allen's thinking. The High Court's cases, beginning with *Brown* and including *Burton*, condemned Jim Crow to death in all public places, the mayor believed. Rather than defy the inevitable and ruin itself economically in the process, the city had to desegregate municipal facilities peacefully.[63]

Progress occurred unevenly, however. Desegregation of the city's pools—an especially alarming proposition for segregationists concerned about the prospect of interracial intimacy—caused an enormous stir. Though Atlanta operated public pools, nothing in Judge Morgan's order required the city to continue to do so. For a time, the possibility of closing the pools was openly considered. Ultimately, Allen found a more prosaic way out. Police patrolled the newly desegregated pools, and the city forbade night swimming to prevent what were termed "disturbances." Other municipal facilities desegregated by early 1964, following the Board of Aldermen's December 1963 repeal of all remaining ordinances mandating segregation in public facilities. The aldermen had waited more than a year to do so after Judge Morgan's order striking down those same ordinances. All told, to obtain and then actually implement the omnibus desegregation decree took more than two years. It would have taken even longer were it not for the widespread mobilization of the black community, the threat of economic ruin, and the prospect of federal civil rights legislation.[64]

Omnibus civil rights litigation had helped to propel Atlanta toward desegregation, as it had Danville, Virginia, Gadsen, Alabama and other cities. Yet the process of racial change remained slow and contested. Unless concerted, extralegal pressure was brought to bear on them, SNCC and COAHR's antagonists conceded little, if anything. The omnibus lawsuit did nothing to change this. This reality, coupled with the fact that there existed no ready legal claim or Supreme Court precedent supporting an omnibus legal attack on discrimination by *private actors*, suggested the limits of the omnibus litigation strategy, if not Holt's vision of movement lawyering in general.[65]

Ultimately, the omnibus integration suit could not meet the great expectations that Holt placed upon it, as he eventually conceded. When it worked, the litigation succeeded in concert with a variety of factors beyond local protest action. Furthermore, like every other form of civil rights litigation, victories in omnibus suits required implementation. And implementation—that is, the actual adoption of new social norms—could never be assumed. Actual desegregation required tedious political work. Moreover, even when the suits forced officials to end segregation, de facto segregation became the problem.

Nevertheless, SNCC and COAHR's use of the omnibus suit and their alliance with the rabble-rousing Len Holt represented an important step in the Atlanta movement's evolution. Student activists—long hostile to civil rights lawyers and litigation—had embraced both. But they had done so on their own terms. *Brown v. Atlanta* constituted an act of defiance against the Atlanta pragmatists on the one hand and the legal liberals of the NAACP and LDF on the other. By filing the pro se omnibus action, the students repudiated A. T. Walden's commitment to biracial negotiation and piecemeal civil rights litigation. But the students' turn to Donald Hollowell, Walden's cocounsel, to negotiate the consent decree in the omnibus case suggested a binding tie between the youth and the black elite. A transitional figure and a bridge-builder, Hollowell would later become the student's trusted ally and a movement lawyer in his own right.

The omnibus litigation also exposed another rift between SNCC and COAHR and the NAACP and LDF. Jack Greenberg dismissed SNCC's relationship with Holt and its use of the omnibus litigation. In the process, Greenberg confirmed the chasm between the NAACP/LDF and the youth wing of the civil rights movement. Greenberg charged that "SNCC went to any lawyer who would help it." He justified LDF's refusal to collaborate with Holt by claiming that "[h]e wasn't a very good lawyer or reliable." Greenberg lambasted Holt's omnibus suit in Danville as "a case so big and complex it could not be litigated" and a "publicity stunt that got nowhere." Greenberg failed to acknowledge the successes that Holt and others achieved using the omnibus tactic. And his assessment of Holt's skills as an advocate differed markedly from those of other lawyers of the era who variously described Holt as "highly competent," "coura-geous," "extraordinary," and "brilliant."[66]

Most significantly, Greenberg's criticism missed, or devalued, the overarch-ing objective of movement lawyering and why it appealed to SNCC and COAHR. Holt's goals differed from those of Greenberg and other conventional civil rights lawyers. Greenberg staked LDF's success on its ability to win cases and to establish formal racial equality under law. For Holt, success did not turn solely on technical maneuvering or prevailing on the legal merits of a case. To be sure, he touted omnibus litigation as a uniquely powerful tactic for securing legal recognition of his clients' rights. However, Holt never considered civil rights litigation a magic bullet. Nor did he consider trained lawyers indispens-able to effective advocacy. Above all else, Holt litigated cases opportunistically, with the goal of empowering local communities to destroy inequality them-selves by tapping their unrealized political potential. The courtroom served as a forum for extending a voice to citizens shut out of formal politics, not neces-sarily as an end in itself. For him, the courtroom could even become a form of political theater.

The difference between the conventional and the movement approaches to lawyering animated the pattern of engagement and conflict between SNCC and COAHR and the national NAACP and LDF throughout the 1960s. That strug-gle, coupled with ongoing tension between the Atlanta student movement and local pragmatists, ensured the city's place as a dynamic laboratory for the evolv-ing strands of civil rights movement.


## CONVENTIONAL LAWYERING AND
## THE STRUGGLE FOR IMPROVED HEALTH CARE

In the battle against segregated health care in Atlanta, LDF's Jack Greenberg took center stage. Greenberg, together with local attorneys A. T. Walden and Donald Hollowell, spearheaded the litigation that challenged Jim Crow at Atlanta's Grady Memorial Hospital. Even though SNCC and COAHR helped lay the groundwork for litigation, the campaign was mainly a lawyer's show.

Initially, the student groups and the local leadership tried to collaborate in the drive to desegregate Grady Hospital. Beginning in November 1961, SNCC and COAHR staged demonstrations against segregation at Grady and against unequal quality of care at the Hughes Spalding Pavilion, an adjoining private black hospital. During the campaign, protesters marched back and forth in front of Grady, carrying placards bearing slogans declaring "Disease and death know no race" and "Grady's policy is backward—speak out for Atlanta's health." The picketers charged that Grady's policies denied African Americans access to an "even share" of medical facilities.[67]

Empirical evidence backed up the claim. In 1962, African Americans constituted 27 percent of Atlanta's population, but only 638 of Atlanta's 4,000 hospital beds were available to them. Grady had no African-American physicians on its staff and refused to grant black doctors working elsewhere practice privileges. African Americans who sought treatment at Grady literally had to leave their black doctors at the door and submit to care by white doctors on staff. Meanwhile, Hughes Spalding suffered from limited funding and a staff inadequate in numbers and training. "'Even a Negro millionaire' could not get proper attention there," where "deplorable conditions" abounded, one commentator asserted. A political cartoon in the *Inquirer* pictured a black patient visiting a "witch doctor" rather than submitting to care at Hughes Spalding.[68]

R. E. Bell, an African-American dentist, invited the students to spearhead protests over health care inequality after his own efforts met a roadblock. Bell was deeply concerned about black physicians' lost work opportunities under segregation. An "outspoken" SCLC officer, he was determined to attack the system at its roots. He filed a complaint with the Fulton-DeKalb Hospital Authority about racial disparities in the public health system. The authority rebuffed him, saying that the U.S. Department of Health, Education, and Welfare (HEW) had jurisdiction over the issues raised. Bell then contacted HEW, only to find that the agency had a "hands-off policy" on hospital segregation; the applicable federal law, the Hill-Burton Act of 1946, did not forbid segregation in federally funded hospitals, the agency noted, placing the matter beyond its reach.

Bell pressed on, with some community backing. The Atlanta NAACP issued a statement condemning Grady's bar against black doctors. With the interests of an influential, if small, segment of Atlanta's black middle class on the line, an interracial group of organizations endorsed the statement as well. Afterward, Bell seized the opportunity to generate more publicity for his agenda; he asked COAHR and SNCC to picket Grady. In the press, Bell claimed that he and the students had been "forced" into using direct action. The *Atlanta Constitution* decried the demonstrations as a breach of Atlanta's customary approach to resolving racial problems. At the time, Atlanta's traditional black leadership said nothing about the protests. For their part, COAHR and SNCC may have thought that the protests—undertaken to protect the interests of an exclusive segment of the black middle class—might earn them admiration and generate support for their broader agenda. After all, the students' protests had reinvigorated a stalled effort to improve black health care that pragmatists originally had pursued more than a decade earlier.[69]

In the late 1940s and early 1950s, Grace Towns Hamilton and A. T. Walden had championed the Hughes Spalding Pavilion as a remedy for unequal access to quality health care. Detractors questioned the construction of the segregated hospital, dedicated in 1952, at a time when Jim Crow's hold on society was loosening. But Hamilton had dreamed of the hospital for years. She began advocating the construction of the pavilion in the years following World War II, when she headed the Atlanta Urban League. The league's 1947 survey titled "Report on the Hospital Care of the Negro Population in Atlanta, Georgia," detailed a public health crisis—for Atlanta's black middle class. Hamilton explained that the pavilion would serve "non-indigent" African Americans and provide employment opportunities for black doctors and nurses. She called the latter objective the hospital's "most important" purpose. The health needs of impoverished blacks could be accommodated at Grady; but the hospital's facilities were inadequate for upper-crust black patrons, who objected to "overcrowded conditions" and "long waiting lists."[70]

Hamilton built support for a black teaching hospital by distributing the league's report to influential whites and blacks. The recipients included Hughes Spalding, Sr., chairman of the Fulton-Dekalb Hospital Authority. Spalding, in turn, wrote letters to 250 of Atlanta's most prominent white citizens, endorsing construction of the hospital as a way of fulfilling their social "responsibility" for "our negro citizens." Over time, Spalding's appeal gained support. The *Atlanta Constitution*, along with other prominent white institutions and individuals, endorsed the Urban League's report and backed the building of the new hospital. Construction began under the supervision of a biracial Advisory Board of Trustees. Upon completion, commentators hailed the pavilion as not only a major advance in health care for blacks but also an example of the benefits of biracial negotiation. Speaking at the hospital's dedication on June 22, 1952, Morehouse president Benjamin Mays lavished praise on the biracial coalition's work. "Distinguished representative citizens sat down together as human beings and planned this project," he noted. "As a result, interracial good will has been generated, interracial respect has increased, confidence has been strengthened, brotherhood has been furthered, and everybody feels better down in his heart."[71]

While Atlanta's African-American leaders crowed about the new middle-class black wing of Grady Hospital, prominent blacks elsewhere saw things differently. Dr. W. Montague Cobb, a professor of anatomy at the Howard University School of Medicine who later founded an organization that advocated hospital desegregation, expressed dismay. As others around the South sought to dismantle Jim Crow, Atlanta's black leadership was celebrating a brand-new segregated hospital facility. Lester Granger, executive secretary of the National Urban League, did not publicly chastise Hamilton in 1952, but he broke with her in the mid-1950s when she rejected the idea of a lawsuit challenging Atlanta's segregated hospital system and condoned residential segregation. Hamilton braved such criticism because she believed that the success of the Talented Tenth, including black doctors, constituted the key to advancement of the race as a whole.[72]

With time, however, Hamilton and other black pragmatists reconsidered their achievement. The pavilion consistently lacked adequate operating funds. The employment opportunities for black doctors and nurses that Hamilton had counted on did not materialize quickly, as the hospital authority delayed instituting a teaching program at Spalding. The pavilion finally became a teaching hospital in 1958, but the instructional program never reached its expected scale. Resistance from white health professionals at Grady, Emory University, and the Fulton-Dekalb Hospital Authority itself stunted the pavilion's growth. Hughes Spalding never lived up to its promise, leaving Dr. Bell and student activists to open a new front in the battle for health care in 1961.[73]

The demonstrations by SNCC and COAHR placed unequal health care on Atlanta's civil rights agenda. But hospital authorities and other white leaders stonewalled in response to black agitation. Hoping to appease those pushing for change, Grady's executives accepted its first African-American intern. This single act of tokenism did not herald a broader policy change, however. In February 1962, the authority voted to make the pavilion a "pay-ward" of Grady Hospital. This administrative change "g[a]ve Grady claim to Negro practitioners and integration." But the racial status quo remained in every aspect of hospital operations; the "combined" facilities continued to operate on a segregated basis. The charade fooled no one. The *Atlanta Inquirer* wrote that "It would take a very good lawyer—or a team of lawyers—to figure out just exactly what the Fulton-Dekalb Hospital Authority is getting at in its announcement concerning the formal adoption of Spalding as a "pay ward of Grady Hospital." The *Atlanta Constitution* conceded that the new system "will mean no more than its administration makes it mean." The SNCC and COAHR called the change a "meaningless" and "meager attempt to pacify the discontented Atlanta community."[74]

The COAHR responded to the hospital's meager efforts with a new round of demonstrations. The group appealed to the community to join it in "showing the Fulton-DeKalb Hospital Authority that we will not settle for anything less than complete integration of the hospital and staff." The pickets returned to Grady on February 6 and 14, 1962. Police arrested thirty-three protesters during the February 14 demonstration. The arrests prompted SNCC and COAHR to send a telegram to President Kennedy with a request that he

introduce legislation to deny federal funds to hospitals that practiced segregation. In a telegram to Mayor Allen, the students decried the Police Department's
mass arrests of peaceful students for daring to challenge Grady's policies; the
arrests violated constitutional guarantees, the students charged. In a letter to
Governor Ernest Vandiver SNCC and COAHR continued their claims on
the Constitution. The letter asked the governor to "declare that segregation in
the State of Georgia is illegal" and "contrary to the spirit of democracy and the
United States Constitution." Vandiver's reply came swiftly. He called the organizations' demand that he outlaw segregation, a "tradition 100 years old," "ridicu-
lous." The campaign had reached a stalemate.[75]

It was this stalemate that soon led SNCC and COAHR to cede the health care
campaign to LDF and Donald Hollowell. Following LDF's lead, the local attorneys turned to litigation to desegregate Grady in mid-1962. The integration of
public health facilities became a prime objective of LDF in early 1962. African-
American physicians, seeking work opportunities and better facilities for patient
treatment, had set their sights on desegregation after *Brown*. In March 1957, 175
black doctors and dentists attended the first Imhotep National Conference on
Hospital Integration, organized by Howard University's Dr. W. Montague Cobb
and sponsored by the NAACP. The conference unanimously passed a resolution
to seek an amendment outlawing discrimination under the Hill-Burton Act.
Such discrimination "now appear[ed] "unconstitutional in light of the recent
Supreme Court decisions," the conference insisted. Subsequently, individual
doctors filed lawsuits challenging hospitals' exclusionary policies.[76]

The year 1962 proved an opportune time for LDF to launch a coordinated
litigation campaign against segregated healthcare. In January of that year,
Republican Senator Jacob K. Javits of New York raised the public profile of the
issue by introducing a bill to amend the Hill-Burton law. The amendment
would outlaw racial discrimination by hospitals receiving federal funds. The
Kennedy administration also voiced support for the concept of nondiscrimination in public health. Javits's bill ultimately died in committee, and the executive branch took no action to prevent discrimination by federally funded
hospitals. Yet, the attention to hospital segregation put the issue in the public
eye. The LDF seized the moment. It struck out against segregation in public
medical facilities in 1962, armed with *Brown* and federal officials' recognition
that hospital desegregation ranked high on the priority list of an important
African-American constituency.[77]

On Lincoln's birthday, February 12, 1962, LDF filed the first ever lawsuit
attacking the constitutionality of the separate-but-equal provisions of the
Hill-Burton Act. The LDF instigated the case, *Simkins v. Cone Memorial Hospital*,
on behalf of doctors and dentists challenging hospital segregation in Greensboro,

North Carolina. The LDF's Jack Greenberg explained *Simkins*'s far-reaching implications: he expected the case to lead to the "integration of health services throughout the South." A few months later, the Kennedy administration took affirmative steps to oppose discriminatory health-care practices. In a coup for LDF, the U.S. Department of Justice intervened in *Simkins* on behalf of its clients on May 8, 1962. The department argued that the Constitution barred the Hill-Burton Act's segregation provision and that Jim Crow hospitals contravened recent Supreme Court precedents outlawing segregation in public facilities.[78]

The LDF's lawsuit redirected the energies of Atlanta activists from protest tactics to court-centered activism. A month after the Justice Department intervened in *Simkins*, Dr. Bell, Dr. Clinton Warner, and others filed a companion suit, *Bell v. Northern District Dental Society*, in Atlanta. Ruby Doris Smith, executive secretary of COAHR, joined the case as a plaintiff. Donald Hollowell, assisted by LDF's Jack Greenberg, filed the action in federal district court in June 1962. The complaint demanded an end to segregation at Grady and the opening of state and local medical and dental societies to African Americans. Like *Simkins*, *Bell* challenged the Hill-Burton Act and also alleged that segregated health care violated the Constitution's Fifth and Fourteenth Amendments. The LDF touted the case as the "broadest legal attack on medical segregation to date." LDF and local lawyers divorced litigation from direct action after filing *Bell*. Thereafter, LDF's professional skills, and the deliberate rhythms of the federal courts' docket, took over. Although their protests against segregation in other areas continued, SNCC and COAHR held no demonstrations in support of *Bell*. Hospital desegregation would be a strictly legal affair.[79]

The lawsuit provided cover for Dr. Bell, who had been subjected to attacks for his noisy brand of activism. A month before Hollowell filed the case, Dr. Bell exposed dissension behind the public scenes of black unity in the fight against Jim Crow at Grady. In a May 19, 1962, *Inquirer* article, headlined "Dr. Bell Blasts Negro Leaders," the dentist revealed that some in Atlanta's black elite opposed and resented his crusade against segregation in public health. He "angrily denounced" the "sniping" against him by "certain Negro leaders" who rejected his militant style and dogged campaign. The Atlanta NAACP had been notably silent after Bell's initial foray into protest; it now turned out that some branch members and leaders, including A. T. Walden, resented Bell's campaign. Critics accused Bell of waging a "lone wolf" battle against the hospital, and decried his direct action tactics. Bell protested that "white benefactors and associates" had been far more supportive of his campaign than blacks, with the exception of the students.[80]

Bell chalked up the black resistance to fear and jealousy. An ally of SCLC, Bell threatened the established method of resolving racial problems in Atlanta.

Dr. Bell hoped to shame critics by speaking publicly about them. "Open season on Roy C. Bell is officially at an end," he said. "And you can tell them that." The lawsuit, backed by Hollowell and joined by several other plaintiffs, ended Bell's run as a "one-man gang" waging battle against Grady. But it did not end some black leaders' pursuit of a negotiated (rather than a litigated or direct-action-induced) end to segregation in public health.[81]

Relief came slowly from the courts. Many months after the filing of *Bell*, LDF prevailed in *Simkins*. On November 1, 1963, the Fourth Circuit struck down as unconstitutional the provision of the Hill-Burton Act that authorized segregation. The federal district court in Atlanta followed suit on January 21, 1964, handing Hollowell and Greenberg a victory. The U.S. Supreme Court weighed in more than a month later. On March 2, 1964, the High Court declined to hear an appeal in *Simkins*. The Court's action had the effect of affirming the Fourth Circuit's *Simkins* opinion. The LDF had achieved success in its legal campaign against Jim Crow hospitals. But as with *Brown* and other landmark cases, LDF's triumphs at the rights-declaration stage constituted only the first battle of a much longer campaign.[82]

Atlanta's traditional leadership took what seemed a curious turn back to negotiation after its victory in *Bell* and the Supreme Court's decision in *Simkins*. At a March 1964 meeting, A. T. Walden—who had not backed Bell's lawsuit or direct action against Grady—lobbied the Fulton County commissioners for an open-door policy at Grady and other county facilities. Many county facilities remained segregated, despite the desegregation of public facilities in the city of Atlanta by this date. Walden arrived at the meeting with a delegation of local leaders. The delegation's lobbying effort constituted an end run around the Fulton County Hospital Authority, which the commissioners appointed. Walden asked the commissioners to establish a special committee to oversee the desegregation of county government. In comments to the press following the summit, Walden took pains to counterpoise the delegation's approach to protest tactics. He noted, "Most of us still feel that this thing [desegregation] can best be accomplished around a conference table like this. We think the atmosphere is getting better to allow the officials to do the things they know to be right. I hope things will move as rapidly as the reality of the situation permits." The commissioners' response to Walden belied his confidence. They committed to nothing. The commissioners counseled the delegation to schedule a meeting with the hospital authority—the very group whose recalcitrance had led Walden to the commissioners in the first place.[83]

Segregation finally fell at Grady as a consequence of the Civil Rights Act of 1964, but whites moved slowly toward desegregation even then. After the Act's passage, Grady desegregated its emergency and nursing school facilities, but continued other discriminatory practices. African-American patients remained in separate waiting and treatment rooms. In February 1965, more than a year after LDF's and Hollowell's victory on the merits, the federal district court finally ordered Grady to end segregation in all of its operations. Still, the hospital stalled. Grady prepared a desegregation plan, yet did little to end discrimination in practice. After the court issued a second order, requiring desegregation by July 1, 1965, Grady announced that all facilities would desegregate by June 1, 1965. Grady did not actually desegregate until June 30, 1965, however, on the eve of the court's ultimatum. Desegregation occurred without public notice, under cover of night.[84]

In the public health context, litigation had fared less well than it did in the municipal facilities context. The lawyers achieved success in *Bell* without coordinating the litigation with direct action leaders or strategies. Yet, the litigation-only approach did not end segregation in federally funded hospitals in the manner that Jack Greenberg had imagined. For all of LDF's faith in legal maneuvers and Greenberg's criticisms of Len Holt, the *Bell* litigation proved less effective in felling Jim Crow at Grady than the omnibus suit and accompanying protests had been in desegregating Atlanta's municipal facilities. The LDF's victory in *Bell* had been achieved in the shadow of congressional debates over, and the impending passage of, the 1964 Civil Rights Act. The legislation, rather than Greenberg's legal strategies, likely served as the most direct cause of Grady's desegregation. By contrast, the legal victory in *Brown v. Atlanta* predated the Civil Rights Act by almost two years.

In both cases, compliance proceeded at a slow pace, but slower still in the public health arena. Mayor Allen initiated the process of municipal desegregation even before issuance of the desegregation order in the omnibus suit so as to avoid economic losses caused in part by SNCC and COAHR's protests. Demonstrators desegregated the public pools, which were some of Jim Crow's most sacred sites, within ten months of winning the omnibus desegregation order. Authorities desegregated Grady at a much more deliberate pace; the process did not even begin until 1965, three years after *Bell* had been filed, notwithstanding two court orders and the new federal civil rights law. White resistance persisted after Grady's formal desegregation. Blacks complained that segregation continued at the hospital "under cover" well after the hospital adopted a nondiscrimination policy.[85]

Moreover, Jim Crow remained intact at Atlanta's other medical facilities, despite *Bell* and the Civil Rights Act. In August 1966, HEW informed eight of the city's hospitals, including Emory University and Hughes Spalding, that they must end segregation or lose federal funds. An HEW investigation had found that in these hospitals there had been "little change in the pattern of assignment of

Negroes to Negro hospitals and whites to white hospitals." In addition, white hospitals seldom granted practice privileges to black physicians. Consequently, African Americans, especially those living in poor neighborhoods, remained underserved. The threat by HEW to cut off federal funds eventually nudged hospitals in Atlanta to desegregate. But access to quality health care remained a problem. White authorities and the white public were acutely vexed by the prospect of blacks mingling with whites in the corridors and wards of hospitals and medical facilities where black doctors as well as white ones practiced medicine.[86]

## WHO ARE THE CIVIL RIGHTS LAWYERS?

The marriage of litigation and direct action strategies produced a vibrant, if fragile, relationship between the civil rights movement, the law, and the civil rights bar during the period 1961–1964. Despite the students' initial misgivings, the law and the courts had provided important sources of energy for SNCC and COAHR's protests. COAHR's filing of *Brown v. Atlanta*, the omnibus municipal desegregation lawsuit, amid continuing protests, synergized civil rights litigation and direct action, just as Len Holt had imagined. The suit actualized movement lawyering, showing that legal and political approaches to pursuing equality were not incompatible. But the omnibus technique and movement lawyering did not, in and of themselves, account for *Brown*'s success. The Supreme Court's piecemeal steps toward dismantling segregation in public facilities, 1961's *Burton v. Wilmington Housing Authority* in particular, facilitated the students' legal victory. The federal court's order striking down segregation in municipal facilities did not, of course, self-implement. Protests made the court victory real. The activists of SNCC and COAHR repeatedly attempted to desegregate the facilities subject to the court order. Desegregation occurred as a consequence of ongoing protests that created political and economic pressure for change.

The students achieved greater success litigating opportunistically than the lawyers' lawyers, A. T. Walden, Donald Hollowell, and Jack Greenberg, achieved litigating conventionally. These attorneys' strategies revolved around the courtroom. Walden, in particular, considered direct action irrelevant or even counterproductive to civil rights litigation. Indeed, Walden, an avowed foe of street protests, initially relied on litigation to deter COAHR from direct action. The suits that Walden and Hollowell filed to challenge segregation in the State Capitol, courthouse, and City Hall eating facilities ended without court-ordered victories for the plaintiffs. *Bell v. Northern Dental*, the hospital desegregation case filed by Hollowell and Greenberg, an opponent of Holt's movement-centered lawyering, had a similarly disappointing trajectory. That litigation, slow to unfold, eventually resulted in a court victory. But it took years to desegregate just one hospital, despite the court order. Outside of the courtroom, LDF and local counsel had brought little political pressure to bear on whites resistant to desegregation. The absence of such pressure from below for desegregation likely mattered most in institutions—like hospitals—where whites found mingling with blacks most distasteful. The pressure for change did not have to take the form of direct action; but the political environment had to become more favorable to racial change to spur desegregation. Congress provided that political lever when it passed the Civil Rights Act; but in a sign of the strength of white resistance to hospital desegregation, Atlanta moved slowly to desegregate even after the Act passed.

The two portraits of civil rights lawyering presented here illuminate the debate over the relationship between civil rights litigation and social change. The LDF's hospital litigation—successful in court but inefficacious until Congress enacted landmark civil rights litigation—substantiates skeptics' claim that civil rights litigation is an unreliable tool of social change.[87]

But my narrative calls into question the idea that court-based social change strategies led civil rights activists astray, whether by diverting intellectual energy, resources, or inspiring a "myth of rights." The history I have told here recovers a form of professional practice that challenges the sharp distinction that those who put forth this argument make between lawyering and politics. Len Holt—a lawyer who openly clashed with the NAACP and LDF and worked in local communities, independently of the civil rights mainstream—is invisible in analyses of law and social change that begin and end with the Supreme Court and national institutions. His work challenges the idea that civil rights litigation undermined political activism. Holt and other movement lawyers had a sophisticated understanding of the utilities and disutilities of law and the courts. Profoundly skeptical of the courts and the judges who presided over them, Holt nevertheless leveraged them to his and his clients' advantage. His court-based strategies were not zero-sum games.[88]

This principle can be generalized. A host of factors determined whether or to what extent law and litigation, whether undertaken by Holt or NAACP-affiliated lawyers, aided or demobilized the struggle for racial justice. These included the style of lawyering that attorneys employed; the degree of unity that existed between lawyers and their client communities; the economic and political incentives for or against desegregation in a given case; and whether the target of protest was a public or a private entity. The changing relationships between lawyers and activists during the historical era explored here show that only a dynamic theory of law and social change can explain whether and on what terms social movements interact fruitfully with lawyers. One verity stands out, however: at best, law, lawyers, and social movements interacted dynamically and with sensitivity to the changing political environment during the civil rights era.

Ultimately, this historical record suggests the advantages and limitations of each of the two approaches to lawyering explored here. Movement lawyering offered a singular benefit: it diversified the tactical arsenal of civil rights advocates. Rather than relying on the courts alone to attain justice, lawyers added the political tool of direct action as a weapon of change.

Beyond that, this approach added another tremendous asset. Movement lawyering held the potential to catalyze social movements. That is, Len Holt's style of lawyering fortified participatory democracy. The bottom-up approach assumed that the attorney should primarily be concerned with politically mobilizing his clients and the citizenry at large. It created opportunities for citizens to express discontent, develop plans to challenge offending authorities, and implement change strategies. Thus, Len Holt exhorted citizens themselves to protest in the streets, and even in the courts, as lay lawyers. He pushed his clients to claim their political voices and confront abusive authorities. His practice rested on the view that the active participation of individual citizens in decision-making, even on a small scale, could reap political dividends; in current parlance, "empowered participation" could yield sociopolitical advantage.[89]

The catalytic potential of movement lawyering did not turn on whether the litigator won or lost his case in court. Indeed, a loss might better facilitate a movement lawyer's goals than a court victory. Moreover, the future dividends from movement lawyering could extend far beyond the original context in which it was deployed. Those who participated in a sit-in linked to a lawsuit might become more highly energized voters, might gravitate toward community organizing or volunteering, or might even run for office long after their initial foray into activism had ended. Leading theorists of law and social change, in their focus on the importance of court victories and implementation to the success of change movements, have missed these important indicators of political empowerment and mobilization.[90]

The characteristics that made bottom-up lawyering an exciting counterpoint to LDF and an attractive tool for facilitating participatory democracy suggest the limitations of the approach. Initiatives such as omnibus litigation and pro se lawyering deemphasized the very technical expertise, based in law and social science, that public interest lawyers had conceived as hugely important tools of advocacy since the Progressive Era innovations of Louis Brandeis. Holt and his cocounsel used the courtroom as political theater as much as forums in which to assert legal claims. This mode of practice, while potentially profitable for political mobilization, posed risks. To the extent that judges perceived omnibus suits or lay lawyering as professionally inadequate, the advocate put his credibility at risk and compromised his clients' interests.[91]

Moreover, bottom-up lawyering was subject to the same criticism that beset all forms of community mobilization activity in the civil rights movement. Holt often styled his approach an alternative to short-term, charisma-driven campaigns such as Dr. King's famous demonstrations in Birmingham in 1963. Yet, the success of Holt's initiatives turned, in part, on Holt's personal magnetism and on his ability to inspire local people. He worked with many different organizations and numerous individuals; he roamed all over the South helping local communities and, consequently, often stayed in one locale on a short-term basis only. Thus, the criticism that Holt and others leveled at King applied more broadly. All activism involving charismatic personas raised a common question: how could social movements involving such imposing personalities, stretched thin as they sought to meet the needs of their constituencies, maintain momentum, grow, and evolve over time?

The advantages of LDF's style of lawyering are evident in comparison to Holt's bottom-up approach. The value of LDF lay in its routinized, meticulous, expertise-driven approach to professional practice, defined by constitutional litigation. None of these traits guaranteed remedial efficacy, as we have seen. Nevertheless, LDF's reputation for professional excellence provided great value to clients. African Americans, long denied access to legal representation and membership in the bar, could look to this small band of attorneys for assistance of a certain type. Communities' ability to rely on these lawyers reinforced democracy, though in a manner different from movement lawyering. Conventional lawyers held forth in court as representatives of the people, making claims on their behalf, in a form and using procedures recognizable to the bench. The reputations of LDF lawyers preceded them, and this reputational good was no small thing for civil rights lawyers. The people themselves could join in as witnesses in the litigators' process, but played no active role commensurate to the one contemplated in bottom-up lawyering. Many black citizens surely found the idea of a representative speaking for them in the corridors of power—a technocrat who could parse legal rules and speak that mysterious legalese—a godsend. Satisfied with such skilled representation, many clients might concern themselves little with the personal agency that movement lawyers so prized.

In the next phase of the battle to desegregate Atlanta, activists who were movers and shakers in the community turned their attention to desegregating private businesses. Whites' sense of entitlement to discriminate in the private context far surpassed their fierce commitment to control the public sector. It would take no less than the Civil Rights Act to dislodge Jim Crow's firm hold on the private sphere.

CHAPTER 8

# Local People as Agents of Constitutional Change

## The Movement against "Private" Discrimination and the Countermobilization

No one leader, no group of leaders, can get your rights. You have to get them for yourselves. (1963)

James Forman

Civil wrongs do not bring civil rights. Civil disobedience does not bring equal protection under the laws. (1964)

Hubert Humphrey

During the summer of 1962, members of the nation's oldest civil rights organization faced the wall of segregation that still stood tall in Atlanta.[1] The national NAACP had chosen Atlanta as the site for its annual convention that year.[2] The association expected the "city too busy to hate" to make its reputation for racial moderation real by greeting NAACP delegates with open arms. In November 1961, eight months before they were scheduled to arrive in Atlanta, national, state, and local NAACP officials staged a press conference in which they called on the city's hoteliers to voluntarily desegregate ahead of the convention.[3]

The vast majority of hotels refused. When the twelve hundred NAACP conventioneers phoned hotels and restaurants seeking reservations, they found that Jim Crow remained rock solid in Atlanta. With a few exceptions, Atlanta's hotels turned away African Americans, including United Nations undersecretary Ralph Bunche. When the NAACP complained, the Atlanta Hotel Association claimed it had no power to intervene. The association did not compel its members to remain segregated, it declared. Each hotel could decide for itself whether to maintain the color line. The law, the hotel owners noted, was on their side. Long-standing constitutional precedent—recently affirmed by the federal courts—deemed discrimination by private businesses perfectly legal.[4]

But the NAACP did not accept the hoteliers' answer. It struck back. Initially, it adopted a resolution urging an end to discrimination by Atlanta's hotels.

Then, some NAACP members took to the streets in protest. As the convention got under way, about one hundred delegates picketed sixteen of Atlanta's segregated hotels and restaurants. A fraction of the total number of delegates in town, the picketers made little impact on local merchants. The reaction of the management of Leb's, a deli that catered to Atlanta's white working class, was typical: the restaurant displayed a sign saying it was "Closed for Alterations."[5]

The stage was set for a showdown. The merchants' hardened response to the NAACP's demand for desegregation generated a new wave of demonstrations by student activists. The students—once again frustrated with what they viewed as the law's complicity in segregation—called for Congress to initiate, at long last, a Second Reconstruction. Together SNCC and COAHR began a campaign against Jim Crow in Atlanta's privately owned restaurants, hotels, and retail merchants. It took off in 1963 and continued for many months. The students' renewed direct action effort was more provocative than any civil rights campaign the city had ever witnessed. The new demonstrations, which coincided with a fresh offensive by Dr. King in Birmingham and other southern cities, ended in victory. Direct action campaigns throughout the South, juxtaposed with the white countermobilization against them, inspired passage of the Civil Rights Act of 1964. The landmark legislation prohibited discrimination by public and private entities alike. The U.S. Supreme Court unanimously rejected a constitutional attack on the Act a few months later, in *Heart of Atlanta Hotel v. United States.*

The story of how events in Birmingham created a more favorable political environment for passage of the Act—with images of young marchers pitted against fire hoses, snarling dogs, and club-wielding police officers—is well known. Dr. King's campaign in Birmingham constitutes the paradigmatic morality tale of the civil rights movement, replete with true heroes and real villains. Birmingham thus became central to the nation's narrative of racial redemption, which culminated with passage of the landmark law and the Supreme Court's decision in *Heart of Atlanta.*[6]

But how did Atlanta, the Southeast's largest city and the home of numerous civil rights organizations and a substantial population of white moderates, figure in the passage of the Civil Rights Act? The account told here features a different portrait—one that contains many more areas of gray than the black-and-white story typically told about Birmingham. In Atlanta, whites played a variety of roles: some fit the image of Bull Connor and official white resistance, while others adopted a more moderate stance (at least rhetorically). Once again, African Americans are central agents of change here, and this story shows that blacks occupied all sides of the battle over desegregation. Some, such as SNCC and COAHR volunteers, aggressively pursued desegregation and sought a federal civil rights bill. Other blacks were ambivalent about a strong federal civil rights bill and about direct action, which had proved so crucial to the civil rights movement's ability to win concessions in the past. Moreover, African Americans realigned their positions as political circumstances changed.

This chapter takes readers inside Atlanta's key communities in the period leading up to passage of the Civil Rights Act. Protests in Atlanta grew increasingly assertive over time. Activists adopted new strategies and tactics in response to the surrounding social, political, and legal environments. The rhetoric and actions of local and national figures, whites and blacks, reactionaries and moderates, politicos and courts, then produced new responses from the activists. In turn, the protesters' actions shaped society. A close examination of civil rights protests during this period reveals just how dynamic, volatile, and violent the situation in Atlanta and the nation had become. Constitutional law framed all of these events. For according to the federal courts, the Constitution did not reach the "private discrimination" at issue in Atlanta and across the nation.

Because some of the most effective architects of white resistance to racial change operated within the law, not outside of it, state and local courts also proved a civil rights battleground. In addition to exploring the agency of demonstrators who attempted to move civil rights forward in the streets, this narrative considers developments in local courts as a window onto the conflict over race, law, and their interplay with gender and counterculture politics. Local actors attempted to sustain racial oppression—even after the U.S. Congress passed the Civil Rights Act and the U.S. Supreme Court affirmed it.[7]

## THE CONSTITUTIONALITY OF PRIVATE DISCRIMINATION

The Atlanta hotels' refusal to loosen Jim Crow's hold generated a controversy within the NAACP over strategy and tactics. The association's executive secretary, Roy Wilkins, represented one end of the spectrum. In the face of the desire of some delegates to expand the protests against the merchants, Wilkins called picketing a distraction. In a press conference, Wilkins damped down expectations of continuing protests and discouraged delegates and media observers alike from elevating the picketing to the "main interest of the convention." But inside the convention halls, speakers hurled recriminations against the city and took a different view of mass action. In his keynote address, Bishop Stephen Gill Spottswood rapped Atlanta for making few racial advances since 1951— the last time the NAACP held its convention in the city. The acid-tongued comedian Dick Gregory, at the convention to receive a citation for his activism, leveled biting criticism at the NAACP itself. "You picked a hell of a place for a convention...the John Birchers don't hold a convention in the Kremlin," he quipped. Gregory encouraged further protests.[8]

Still other speakers focused on the importance of the NAACP's litigation campaign to the achievement of racial progress. Director of branches Gloster B. Current, in a convention report, reminded the audience that the NAACP's "painstaking, well-planned and executed" litigation efforts had jumpstarted the changes that had occurred in race relations to date and remained relevant. But the speech by Robert Carter, the NAACP's general counsel, bucked the message delivered in the other addresses. Carter, whose disputes with the board of the national NAACP and the NAACP LDF soon earned him the moniker "Young Turk," advised conventioneers to broaden their arsenal of weapons. Carter advocated lobbying, picketing, and other forms of mass protest as "adjuncts" to litigation.[9]

The history of an NAACP official's lawsuit against the Jim Crow policies of an Atlanta hotel illustrated why Carter believed that litigation alone would not topple Jim Crow. Dr. Eugene T. Reed, a dentist and the head of the New York state NAACP, sued the Atlanta Cabana Hotel in federal court in July 1962 after the hotel refused to honor his reservation. According to the complaint in *Reed v. Sarno*, Cabana Hotel had refused to honor Reed's reservation because of his race. Reed's attorney, Isabel Gates Walker, argued that the hotel's action violated the Fourteenth Amendment to the U.S. Constitution, the federal Civil Rights Act of 1871, and the Georgia innkeeper statute.[10]

The hotel turned to a cornerstone principle of constitutional law, the state action doctrine, in defense of its actions. The Fourteenth Amendment provided no basis for Dr. Reed's suit because, under settled law, the hotel's owners were not state actors and not acting on behalf of the state. But Walker argued that *Monroe v. Pape*, a 1961 Supreme Court decision, had rejected the notion that a claim under the Civil Rights Act could only be supported by affirmative acts by the state or its officials. State *inaction* also could support a civil rights act claim, Walker argued. Here, the state inaction lay in the refusal of the city of Atlanta and the state of Georgia to enforce the Georgia statute requiring innkeepers to accept all comers. The city and state instead permitted racial separation in public accommodations. This breach violated Dr. Reed's right to nondiscrimination under federal law, Walker explained. The Cabana Hotel's owners disagreed. Walker's conception of "state inaction" constituted an "exercise in semantics" and an "untenable" principle of law, the defendants' attorneys argued.[11]

In the span of a month, the litigants in *Reed* experienced a tangle of emotions as the district court issued opinions in the case. In August, Judge Lewis

Morgan refused to dismiss Dr. Reed's claims. Sufficient factual allegations existed to state a claim for relief, he wrote. Judge Morgan issued this order in *Reed* on the same day that he ruled for the plaintiffs in an omnibus municipal facilities case. The judge's order raised Walker's expectations. She sent off a quick letter to Robert Carter requesting legal and financial support in order to move the case forward. Before Carter could reply, Judge Morgan dashed Walker's hopes.[12]

In September, Judge Morgan granted the defendants' motion to dismiss. Even though state inaction might be a basis for a claim under the Civil Rights Act in certain contexts, the judge concluded, the facts of Reed's suit did not present such a scenario. His argument failed, the court held, because it did not "observe the important distinction between activities that are required by the state and those which are carried out by voluntary choice and without compulsion by the people of the state in accordance with their own desires and social practices." Neither the city of Atlanta nor the state of Georgia mandated segregation in hotels. Proprietors enforced segregation on their own, to satisfy customers' preferences. This fact deprived Dr. Reed of a basis in federal law for his civil rights claim. "The customs of a people of a state do not constitute state action within the prohibition of the Fourteenth Amendment," Judge Morgan concluded. The court cited a long list of cases in support of this conclusion, including the Fourth Circuit's sweeping 1959 decision *Williams v. Howard Johnson's Restaurant*. *Williams* held that neither the U.S. Constitution's commerce clause nor the Thirteenth Amendment, nor the Fourteenth, compelled proprietors to serve African Americans. On appeal, the Fifth Circuit upheld Judge Morgan's decision on Dr. Reed's constitutional claim.[13]

The outcome in *Reed* tells us much about the place of federal constitutional law in the struggle for civil rights. The suit showed that constitutional litigation was unlikely to eradicate Jim Crow from restaurants, hotels, and other private businesses. Judge Morgan's decision repeated the consensus view in the lower federal courts regarding the boundaries of the state action doctrine. The state's acquiescence in discrimination by private businesses did not offend the Constitution, and the private entities could not themselves be considered state actors. The doctrine rested on the Supreme Court's post-Reconstruction precedents, the *Civil Rights Cases* of 1883, in particular. In these cases, the Court struck down the Civil Rights Act of 1875, holding that Congress had no authority under the Fourteenth Amendment to outlaw discrimination by private actors pursuant to custom, as distinguished from discrimination by state actors. The *Civil Rights Cases'* state action analysis failed to persuade many commentators, even at the time. In the cases' solitary dissent, Justice John Marshall Harlan had argued that the state's regulation of railroads, inns, theaters, and the like made them agents of the state—subject to the Fourteenth Amendment's antidiscrimination provisions. In the years preceding the turbulent 1960s, the Court had given some indication, primarily in labor and the restrictive covenant case, that it might reconsider the distinction drawn in the *Civil Rights Cases*. But it had not gone quite so far as to make private businesses vulnerable to suit. Without a major expansion of the state action doctrine by the U.S. Supreme Court, cases like *Reed* could not succeed. Private businesses would desegregate voluntarily, or under the force of a robust new federal antidiscrimination law. In early 1963, neither possibility looked likely to materialize.[14]

## TURNING POINTS IN POLITICS AND LAW

Even as the movement's ability to end private discrimination through court action in Atlanta looked bleak, protests in Birmingham, led by Dr. Martin Luther King and executed by SCLC and Rev. Fred Shuttlesworth's Alabama Christian Movement for Civil Rights riveted the nation. When Eugene "Bull" Connor, the city's brutal police commissioner, used police dogs, fire hoses, and clubs on peaceful demonstrators, including children, and arrested scores of them, including Dr. King, he played into SCLC's hands. Televised images of police abuse, coupled with reports about the bombings of a hotel and a home used by civil rights activists, nationalized the civil rights issue. The events in Birmingham helped to convince whites in the North and West that southern-style segregation demanded a federal solution. President Kennedy captured the Birmingham campaign's significance in late May 1963, when he finally agreed to support a strong civil rights bill. In a meeting with civil rights leaders, Kennedy quipped, "The civil rights movement should thank God for Bull Connor. He's helped it as much as Abraham Lincoln." Within days, the president announced his intention to support passage of a comprehensive civil rights law, one that would ban racial discrimination by nominally private places of public accommodations.[15]

Around the same time, the Supreme Court issued a series of decisions that suggested to some that perhaps it was open to the idea that the Constitution prohibited racial discrimination by private businesses, after all. *Lombard v. Louisiana, Shuttlesworth v. Birmingham, Peterson v. Greenville, Gober v. Birmingham,* and *Avent v. North Carolina,* five decisions announced on May 20, 1963, overturned the criminal trespass convictions of civil rights demonstrators. Four of the cases involved sit-ins at private properties located in states or localities with ordinances or statutes mandating segregation. Such laws "removed" from the "sphere of private choice" the decision to discriminate, wrote Chief Justice Warren in *Peterson*, because the state had implicated itself in private actors' discrimination. "When ... the State's criminal processes are employed in a way which enforces the discrimination mandated by that law," he continued, it constituted a "palpable violation of the Fourteenth Amendment." Consequently, the Court reversed the convictions in *Peterson* and in the other cases involving mandatory segregation, *Gober* and *Shuttlesworth*; it remanded *Avent* for findings consistent with its ruling in *Peterson*.[16]

*Lombard* tantalized observers even more. The Court reversed criminal mischief convictions in *Lombard* that did *not* turn on a segregation ordinance. The reversals instead were predicated on statements by the mayor and the superintendent of police of New Orleans, who had barred challenges to segregation in the city. In effect, the city had a prosegregation policy, even if an uncodified one, the Court held. Under these circumstances, otherwise private discrimination could be subject to constitutional restriction.[17]

News commentary on the five sit-in cases suggested that the Court might, at long last, stretch the state action doctrine to ban instances of merely *state-condoned* segregation. Anthony Lewis at the *New York Times* interpreted the decisions as a boon to the civil rights movement. Had the cases come out the other way, he wrote, the "sit-in movement would have suffered a major blow." Instead, the Court had legitimized the direct action movement. And it had done much more; the Court had advanced the movement's underlying goal of quashing discrimination by private actors by "more and more ... recogniz[ing] that Government and private interests may be entangled." According to Lewis's reading and that of other columnists, the Court stood but one step from reversing the long-accepted rule that private businesses could discriminate at whim. Justice William O. Douglas's concurrence in *Lombard* pointed in precisely this direction. He argued that the Court should outlaw segregation by businesses, such as restaurants, that were subjected to pervasive state regulation. These establishments existed to serve the public, and the Court should demand open access for all members of the public. The Court "should not await legislative action before declaring that state courts [or the police] cannot enforce" discrimination by private businesses. In essence, Justice Douglas wished to extend to the retail business context the rule of *Shelley v. Kramer;* in *Shelley*, the Court found judicial enforcement of racially restrictive covenants in real estate contracts a violation of the Fourteenth Amendment.[18]

But Justice Douglas stood alone in this opinion. The Court had not reached the issue that Justice Douglas wished to address, as the majority opinion pointedly noted. Moreover, Justice John M. Harlan came out strongly against Justice Douglas's conclusion. In a concurring and dissenting opinion, Justice Harlan cautioned the Court against invading the private sphere in the name of equality. "Freedom of the individual to choose his associates or his neighbors...to be irrational, arbitrary, capricious, even unjust in his personal relations are things all entitled to a large measure of protection from governmental interference," he wrote. Harlan continued, "An individual's right to restrict the use of his property...lies beyond the reach of the Fourteenth Amendment."[19]

Thus, even after the sit-in cases, the crucial state action distinction remained in place. The Court had inched toward reevaluating the doctrine, but not as much as hopeful commentary suggested. Suits such as *Reed v. Sarno*, therefore, remained dead ends. Moreover, the sit-in cases indicated that if the Court ever confronted the constitutionality of discrimination by private actors, the case would admit no easy solution. Competing notions of liberty and equality stood in the balance. Meanwhile, Jim Crow remained the norm in private businesses throughout the South.[20]

In the ensuing months, as protests increased in number and intensity, SNCC and COAHR learned that the Supreme Court's sit-in cases had not significantly altered the landscape for civil rights demonstrators. The decisions had a negligible impact on the dynamics of direct action campaigns for two main reasons. First, the Court acted too late to make much of a positive difference in the life of the movement. The convictions that the Court tossed out in the five cases of May 1963 grew out of demonstrations that occurred three years earlier, in 1960—during the initial wave of sit-ins beginning in Greensboro. By this time, the white resistance had developed strategies that restricted the decisions' reach. Many cities, including Atlanta, had repealed segregation ordinances well before the Court found arrests for protesting them unconstitutional. Consequently, the decisions did not threaten the status quo.[21]

Second, Supreme Court decisions could not, in any event, prevent police abuse in the most volatile movement battlegrounds. In theory, segregationists in the Deep South theaters where pivotal skirmishes took place might have pulled back in view of the Court's decisions. In fact, the will to maintain white supremacy vanquished the Supreme Court's rules in many localities. The Court's reversal of convictions, whether based on certain statutory language or failures of due process, left room for future arrests and prosecutions under different circumstances. States or municipalities could modify laws or change police practices in ways that avoided violating demonstrators' rights, as defined by the latest Court rulings. Moreover, officials could, and did, ignore the law altogether. In these places, the decisions were beside the point.

Indeed, after the five decisions, civil rights workers in scores of communities were subject to a degree of harassment that had been in no way diminished by the decisions. Policemen and state troopers used guns, clubs, and handcuffs, and the prosecutors and judges in municipal, state, and federal district courts commanded a panoply of charges—among them trespass, disorderly conduct, breach of peace, and incitement to riot—that they could wield against protesters. Law enforcement and courts continued to be formidable opponents across the South, but especially in Alabama, Mississippi, South Carolina, Arkansas, and Georgia. Rights workers in Birmingham and participants in numerous other high-profile campaigns of the movement—including Danville, Virginia, Cambridge, Maryland, Savannah, Georgia, Selma, Alabama, and Greenwood, Mississippi—faced arrest when registering voters and leading protests to desegregate public facilities or accommodations. In fact, the sit-in decisions may have *encouraged* resistance. In Birmingham, Bull Connor believed so; he predicted that the Supreme Court decisions would only inspire the massive resistance movement. Whatever the truth of Connor's prediction, despite the Court's edicts, the attacks and injustices against demonstrators continued. The potent combination of official and unofficial harassment nearly crippled the movement.[22]

The civil rights movements, in the nation and in Atlanta, reached a turning point amid the explosive forces that converged in mid-1963. The issue of racial equality had pricked the conscience of white citizens as never before. The president had promised to support a potent civil rights bill. The Supreme Court had at once buoyed and disappointed the movement. The sit-in decisions had given direct action the High Court's imprimatur. But the holding of the *Civil Rights Cases* lived on; the Court had refused to address frontally law's sanction for private actors' discrimination. Moreover, the cases provided limited relief from harassment and intimidation. At the same time, segregationists felt besieged, and they were intent on striking out against freedom fighters by using all means at their disposal, violent and nonviolent, official and private. Swept up in these swirling sociopolitical and legal crosscurrents, the youth groups constituting the civil rights movement's leading edge experienced new heights of hope, disappointment, and anger. Change seemed so near, yet so far away.

## THE RADICAL DEMONSTRATION
### PHASE: 1963–1964

Within this context, SNCC and COAHR entered a so-called radical demonstration phase. Unhappy with the pace of change, students turned to aggressive direct action techniques to combat private discrimination. As debates over civil rights legislation raged in the summer of 1963, the organizations intensified their protests. This new round of demonstrations was far more confrontational than ever before. During the early sit-in movement, the overwhelming majority of demonstrations had been peaceful and prayerful; impeccably dressed and well-mannered students had politely requested service in all-white establishments. The protesters often endured incidents of violent white resistance during the early sit-ins. The new tactics contrasted sharply with the old. True, many students remained passive during the sit-ins. But others blocked traffic, obstructed sidewalks and entrances to restaurants, lay prostrate on store floors, and refused to leave establishments when asked or cooperate with arresting officers. Demonstrators targeted the businesses of the most rabid segregationists, seeking out confrontations with Jim Crow's fiercest defenders. Violence became more common, and it was often blamed on protesters.[23]

This shift disrupted the Manichean dynamic that many deemed crucial to the early movement's success. Consequently, SNCC and COAHR's new assertiveness reignited conflicts between the youth groups and Atlanta's pragmatic black leadership. A. T. Walden charged that the students had become *hawks*, leaving him and other stalwarts—*still doves*—to redouble efforts to arbitrate the racial divide. The new demonstrations generated backlash among segregationists and white moderates, as well. The Atlanta chapter of the Georgia Restaurant Association, which represented the main targets of protest, responded to the new campaign with a warning. "Overt demonstrations and pressures" seriously threatened further progress toward desegregation, the association said. Mayor Allen agreed. He personally requested that SNCC and COAHR end the protests. The students ignored the mayor and continued on their uncharted path.[24]

In late May and June, the committees engaged in a series of actions that showed the new face of Atlanta's civil rights movement. One of the highest profile events took place at the Pickrick Restaurant, owned by Lester Maddox, the arch-segregationist whom Ivan Allen had defeated in the 1961 mayoral election. Maddox made his name through racial grandstanding. He ran ads for his restaurant that touted Jim Crow, and he formed Georgians Unwilling to Surrender, a white supremacist group, in response to the sit-in movement. Predictably, Maddox did not take well to black students requesting service in his restaurant and marching outside his store. Maddox grabbed two protesters and pushed them from his restaurant. He then ordered his black employees to finish the job by throwing the other students out. The protesters left the Pickrick rather than continue the confrontation, which had pitted them against poor blacks. In June, SNCC and COAHR staged a cycle of protests at Leb's Restaurant and two restaurant chains, S & W and Krystal. An interracial group of thirty protesters sought service at one establishment after another. Each time managers or police officers turned the group away, citing Georgia's antitrespass law. Each time the students left but returned a short time later, again seeking service and again being turned away. This cycle continued for some time, aggravating and alarming restaurant managers and police officers. But SNCC and COAHR did not pull back. Instead, they upped the ante by making the broad sweep of their demands clear: in two protests, the students demanded more and better jobs and working conditions for black laborers. Then, in early July, 250 SNCC and COAHR volunteers picketed Dobb's House Restaurant in solidarity with three hundred striking workers affiliated with the Hotel and Restaurant Workers Union Local 151.[25]

White counterdemonstrators squared off against SNCC and COAHR in some of the committees' hardest-hitting protests. The biggest confrontation between the opposing camps occurred in late July, when students again targeted Leb's. In their most aggressive actions to date, students blocked traffic at an intersection outside the restaurant. The protest degenerated into violence. Led by the restaurant's owner, Charles Lebedin, white employees physically attacked student activists. The whites beat, kicked, and dragged protesters away. Spectators also grabbed placards bearing antisegregation slogans from the hands of demonstrators, tearing the signs to pieces. When police arrived, officers placed several people, most of them pro–civil rights demonstrators, under arrest. The SNCC and COAHR protesters refused to cooperate after arrest; officers had to pick them up and carry them to the police wagon, where demonstrators swayed back and forth, singing "We Shall Overcome."[26]

The new phase of the protest movement caused a stir. Demonstrations generated hundreds of arrests for trespassing and disorderly conduct, fines, and jail sentences. The behavior of SNCC and COAHR raised the ire of white officialdom and some black moderates. Whites claimed that the students had gone too far. The *Atlanta Constitution* called it a "mistake" for demonstrators to "force arrests" by engaging in "lawbreaking." After all, "This is Atlanta. The police are not out with dogs and hoses eager to make arrests; they want to keep order without arrests." "The people of Atlanta are by and large progressive and fair," the *Constitution* continued, and demonstrators who pushed the envelope beyond the "necessary" were "self-damaging" and "embarrassing people who are actively seeking" solutions to the racial problem. Columnist Eugene Patterson, who had succeeded McGill as the *Constitution's* reputed liberal lion, warned of "riotous anarchy" if demonstrations continued along their present course.[27]

Undoubtedly more distressing to the students was the disapproval of some stalwart blacks, including some bona fide allies. The editorial page of the *Atlanta Inquirer*, usually an ardent supporter of the students, lashed out at COAHR after the Pickrick protest. The *Inquirer* proclaimed itself "shocked and puzzled" by the action: the students had "elected to play right into the hand of" Maddox.

"We think most Negroes would prefer to pass up the right of going to that place, because of the "deep history of insults and race-baiting" the owner has directed, and continues to direct, at Negroes. STUDENTS, WE DON'T GET IT. WE THINK YOU GOOFED. WE SUGGEST THAT YOU REVIEW YOUR STRATEGY," the *Inquirer* screamed. In a July editorial, "A Good Cause May be Sacrificed Upon the Altars of the Wrong Approach," the *Atlanta Daily World* blasted the students for blocking traffic outside Leb's, calling it a "disgraceful scene." The students' actions "tend to intensify hatred, stir up strife and further prolong the chaos in which we have been unfortunately thrust." The *World* urged "restraint" and "reason in attempting to resolve the segregation issue."[28]

In response to the community's censure, Larry Fox, chairman of COAHR, claimed that the "new technique" had been "forced" upon the demonstrators by the "neglect of the city and state." He promised that the "new radical demonstrations will continue." Fox also struck out at "so-called Negro leaders who practice Uncle Tom-ism more than they practice desegregation." And while he protested "negligence and bias in the enforcement of laws," the *Constitution* extolled the civility of Atlanta's police officers. The leadership of SNCC and COAHR would not stray from its new course. The students would continue to court controversy in hopes that the resulting social instability would cause the walls of segregation to buckle.[29]

## RESPONSES TO THE CIVIL RIGHTS BILL

President Kennedy's civil rights bill added to the discord that beset Atlanta during the summer of 1963. Mayor Allen confronted fierce opposition from whites across the political spectrum when he agreed, after entreaties from the president, to endorse the bill in testimony before Congress. Allen relented against his better judgment; testifying would be political suicide, he assumed. The roster of prominent white opponents of the bill featured many erstwhile white moderates and liberals. Ralph McGill, famous as the voice of southern white liberalism, opposed the bill's public accommodations provision on the same grounds as rabid segregationists: it violated whites' property rights. The editorial page of the *Atlanta Constitution* opposed the bill as well, as did columnist Eugene Patterson. Touting Atlanta's "voluntary" progress toward desegregation, the *Constitution* editorialized that "we cannot see the need for the federal law to force actions." The paper called blacks who advocated the bill "intemperate." The board of directors of the Atlanta Chamber of Commerce also opposed the civil rights bill. And Georgia's congressional delegation, led by Senator Russell, and including Senator Talmadge and Representative Charles Weltner of Atlanta, joined the long list of opponents, as did Governor Carl Sanders. Russell called the bill the "most inhuman and sadistic" legislation in U.S. history, an unconstitutional incursion on state and local prerogatives, and a violation of whites' associational and property rights.[30]

The political challenges that Allen encountered did not end with whites, however. Prominent African-American leaders sent mixed signals about Kennedy's civil rights bill. Many objected to Allen's involvement in the debate over the proposed legislation and were ambivalent about the bill itself. Some skeptics in the pragmatist tent opposed a federal, as opposed to a municipal, antidiscrimination law. The Atlanta NAACP called for a municipal antisegregation law in April 1963, just as debates over a strong federal accommodations law heated up. Many black moderates backed the NAACP's proposal. In a letter to the editor published in the *Atlanta Constitution* on June 15, for example, Grace Towns Hamilton explained why she endorsed an antidiscrimination ordinance, as opposed to a federal law. "[T]he prompt passage of a public accommodation ordinance" would be "in the public interest," she wrote. The local ordinance would ward off federal intervention, she noted, approvingly. "Intervention by the federal government becomes a reality only when local government fails to meet its responsibilities." "The strength of the ordinance is not as pertinent as its symbolic value," Hamilton continued.[31]

When Allen informed a group of twenty-four prominent black leaders, including A. T. Walden, Martin Luther King, Sr., William Holmes Borders, Rufus Clement, Benjamin Mays, and Jessie Hill, Jr., of his intention to accept Kennedy's request to testify, ambivalence turned to opposition. "[O]nly four or five out of the twenty-four there" wanted him to testify. The consensus makers in the group claimed that Allen should not "sacrifice" himself for "testimony that wasn't necessarily going to pass the bill." Allen was caught off guard by the skeptical response that his decision elicited among black elites. Even though "[t]he Atlanta newspapers and big television stations weren't for the bill, the political leaders weren't for the bill, the white man on the street wasn't for the bill, and now even the Negro leaders didn't want me to come out for it." Allen eschewed the advice.[32]

On July 26, 1963, Atlanta's mayor strode to the witness table in the Senate Office Building at the U.S. Capitol. In testimony before the Senate Committee on Commerce, Allen broke ranks with every other elected southern official. In his testimony, Allen took a stand for the public accommodations provision of the civil rights bill. He called the legislation a "last resort" to ensure the end of segregation, which he termed "slavery's stepchild." At the same time, Allen requested "reasonable time" for cities and businesses to desegregate before federal intervention. He cited Atlanta's "constructive" and "responsible" black leadership—"realists, not rabble rousers" uninterested in "stir[ring] up demonstrations"—as a factor indicating that his community and others could end segregation with the federal government's help. Under questioning from South Carolina senator Strom Thurmond, who insisted that it would be better to rely on "voluntary action" or a "local ordinance," Allen shot back that localities "had been left up in the air" by Congress and needed "guidance." Congress's failure to take action would by inference be "an endorsement of the right of private businesses to practice racial discrimination."[33]

Allen's testimony met with national acclaim, if not full approval from all quarters. The *New York Times* and other national media hailed Allen's performance. In the wake of such praise for Atlanta's mayor, A. T. Walden went on record praising Allen's "leadership." He called Allen the "voice of the New South." But Walden expressed no direct support for the bill itself. Other prominent black leaders whom the *Atlanta Daily World* routinely quoted on race issues, such as Benjamin Mays and Rufus Clement, made no statement about Allen's testimony or the bill. For its part, the *World*'s editorial page praised Allen's courage in standing up for the "controversial" bill. The *Constitution* also praised Allen, while reiterating disagreement with him on substance. Setting himself apart from many others, Donald Hollowell, by then a frequent defender of SNCC and COAHR demonstrators, made an unambiguous statement in support of the public accommodations bill following Allen's testimony.[34]

Yet, in the coming weeks, some of Hollowell's clients—unabashed supporters of a civil rights law—expressed profound skepticism about the bill. At the August 28 March on Washington, John Lewis, SNCC's newly elected chairman, had to be dissuaded from attacking the bill. The national historical memory of the march has centered on Dr. King's "I Have a Dream" speech. But the address that Lewis proposed to give unmasked the internal battle that raged at this crucial point in the struggle for civil rights. The draft speech articulated a fundamental distinction between SNCC and other civil rights organizations. Rather than a campaign for rights in the courts, the course that the Kennedy administration preferred, SNCC was involved in a "serious revolution" in the streets. The tactical distinction bespoke different philosophies and aims. The courts were an inappropriate forum for mass political activism. "We . . . recognize," Lewis's draft speech declared, "that if any radical, social, political, and economic changes are to take place in our society, the people, the masses must bring them about." Antipoverty activism headed SNCC's list of objectives. Through voter registration and community organizing efforts, SNCC hoped to empower working-class and poor African Americans to become full stakeholders in American society. Because President Kennedy's civil rights bill did not protect the interests of the poor, SNCC could not "in good conscience" support it. Those imprisoned by "political and economic slavery" and inferior educational opportunities would receive no benefit from the bill. It was "too little too late."[35]

Under pressure, Lewis muted his demands. The Kennedy administration and its emissaries persuaded Lewis to temper his rhetoric. In the revised address, Lewis voiced support for the proposed bill. But the toned-down address retained a strident tone and critical punch. Lewis expressed SNCC's concern that the legislation failed to ensure fair employment opportunities and adequate protection for black voters. He charged: "We march today for jobs and freedom, but we have nothing to be proud of. For hundreds and thousands of our brothers are not here." Lewis continued, "They have no money for their transportation, for they are receiving starvation wages...or no wages at all.... While we stand here, there are students in jail on trumped up charges. We come here today with a great sense of misgiving." His address ended with a call to "get in this great social revolution sweeping our nation. Get in and stay in the streets of every city, every village and every hamlet of this nation...until the unfinished revolution of 1776 is complete."[36]

## IMPACT OF THE MARCH ON WASHINGTON

As much as the March on Washington reflected the state of the civil rights movement on the national stage, it also highlighted the state of the movement in Atlanta. During the gathering SNCC had gained prominence. The event solidified SNCC's status as the movement's leading edge. Its commitment to antipoverty activism, as well as civil rights activism, and its resolve to remain the movement's street fighters grew. Increasingly, SNCC undertook projects that tackled intertwined race- and class-based oppression. For example, SNCC and COAHR launched a campaign to improve conditions in South Atlanta. The committees formed a coalition with residents of the impoverished community and an interracial group of adult and youth activists. In early August, the group marched on City Hall and presented a seventeen-page list of grievances to Mayor Allen. The protesters also distributed a leaflet, "South Atlanta: The Forgotten Community," that catalogued the area's many needs, ranging from adequate recreational facilities, parks, libraries, street lights, crosswalks, and traffic signals to proper sewage and garbage disposal, additional transportation facilities, and regular building inspections.[37]

The march had an impact on Atlanta's pragmatic leadership as well. The march's success inspired traditionalists in Atlanta to assume a friendlier stance toward protest actions. Public acclaim for the march propelled the new faith in direct action. The *New York Times* called the march "the greatest assembly for a redress of grievances that this capital has ever seen." President Kennedy hailed the marchers' "quiet dignity" and the "orderly demonstration." The march had clearly advanced the "cause of 20 million Negroes," he added. In the aftermath of such glowing commentary, C. A. Scott's *Atlanta Daily World*, which had opposed demonstrations generally and the march specifically, now praised it. The *World* also unambiguously endorsed the civil rights bill for the first time. A. T. Walden also spoke in a different voice after the march. He had consistently endorsed gradualism in the civil rights struggle. Walden now noted that the Washington demonstration had "put the nation on notice that the Negro and others who love freedom are determined to secure their rights NOW." He stopped short of endorsing the civil rights bill, however. Nor did his approving words about the march imply support for protest action in general. Nevertheless, Walden's change in tone and the *World*'s about-face on the march and the civil rights bill constituted an acknowledgment, albeit implicit, of error.[38]

After the march, SNCC and COAHR, which had demanded freedom now all along, rivaled the pragmatists for leadership of the movement as never before. By the fall of 1963, the student activists had a significant number of allies outside of Atlanta's collegiate community. These allies shared the students' disenchantment with biracial decision-making, their mistrust of courts, and their commitment to integration *now*. But the young leaders' hold on power was constantly questioned and challenged, and their influence fluctuated accordingly. Though SNCC and COAHR made inroads, they could not completely cast aside the pragmatists.

The pragmatists retained considerable power, for two reasons. First, the students' adult allies did not necessarily share their commitment to aggressive forms of direct action. Hollowell refused to give a blanket endorsement to his clients; he expressed personal reservations about blocking automobile and pedestrian traffic, for instance. Second, the white power structure did not consider the students legitimate representatives of the city's black community. When Ivan Allen spoke of Atlanta's "responsible" and "constructive Negro leaders," he had A. T. Walden, Benjamin Mays, and C. A. Scott in mind—not John Lewis, James Forman, and Larry Fox. The use of aggressive civil disobedience tactics by SNCC and COAHR reinforced Allen's perspective. The pragmatists' influence grew in the months ahead whenever student-led demonstrations provoked disorder or violence.

The formation of the Atlanta Summit Leadership Conference (ASLC) on October 19, 1963, signaled this transitional moment in Atlanta's civil rights movement. The conference consisted of a range of local groups, including the

Atlanta NAACP branch, SCLC, SNCC, COAHR, ANVL, and Operation-Bread-basket, a SCLC-backed alliance of employment activists. The ASLC formed to push for "complete integration" in Atlanta. Yet, the umbrella organization consisted of "widely divergent groups" whose agendas conflicted. Opponents of direct action tactics such as ANVL and organizations such as SNCC, committed to direct action above all else, shared ASLC's mantle. Though its formation suggested unity, ASLC masked profound disagreements between disparate elements of the city's black community. These disagreements quickly came to light.[39]

## CONFLICT AMID CONSENSUS

Bowing to pressure from Walden and other opponents of direct action, ASLC first approved negotiation in an effort to end the continuing stalemate over the desegregation of hotels and restaurants. The steering committee of ASLC, cochaired by A. T. Walden and Clarence D. Coleman, set out to pressure officials to implement a plan for "total" desegregation of the city. The committee met with the city's Board of Aldermen and other city and county officials in a bid to secure reform. Defeat came early. The aldermen voted down a resolution, recommended by ASLC and already passed by the Chamber of Commerce, permitting businesses licensed by the city to desegregate. The resolution, enacted against the backdrop of the chamber's continued resistance to a federal public accommodations law, required nothing of proprietors. The aldermen's refusal to cede even this symbolic ground "shocked" the black community, the *Inquirer* reported.[40]

In response to the failed negotiations, direct action proponents within ASLC followed through on a threat to launch new protests, pickets, and boycotts. The most dramatic protest occurred on November 21. Four hundred college and high school students, led by COAHR, SNCC, and SCLC's Ralph D. Abernathy, demonstrated for greater employment opportunities at Rich's department store. The groups framed the protest as a follow-up to the disappointing 1961 settlement agreement and the kickoff of a boycott of Rich's. All signatories to the 1961 agreement now served blacks at their lunch counters, but the establishments still only employed blacks in menial positions. Rich's was a major offender. The downtown store employed just 6 African Americans among its 740 salespersons, even though Richard Rich had promised to hire many more. The SNCC called for a boycott of Rich's to begin during the Christmas shopping season. But A. T. Walden called the Rich's protest a monumental error. He already had initiated negotiations with Rich's over its employment policies. The protests, he feared, would undermine his outreach effort.[41]

Walden's assumption proved wrong. Immediately after the students' call for a boycott, Rich's and fifteen other downtown department stores agreed to hire African Americans in greater numbers and in better-paying positions. Within weeks, the stores had hired 253 black clerks and salespersons. Now COAHR and SNCC had achieved their greatest success yet. The student groups suspended the boycott triumphantly. President Kennedy's assassination on November 22, 1963, also halted talks of further demonstrations for a time, as President Lyndon B. Johnson vowed to push through passage of the civil rights bill.[42]

The Atlanta movement's next action, modeled on the March on Washington, sought to rally the community without antagonizing whites. In Hurt Park on December 16, 1963, ASLC's "Pilgrimage for Democracy" took place. The effort, carefully billed as an interracial "mass assembly" rather than a demonstration, looked to achieve two purposes. The assembly signaled impatience with the pace of desegregation; but it also staved off demonstrations by ASLC affiliates who planned more direct action. Expected to draw ten thousand people, the pilgrimage attracted only forty-five hundred in subfreezing weather. The event's speakers represented a cross-section of philosophies and perspectives within the black freedom movement. Walden, who had reluctantly agreed to support the assembly, boasted of the racial advances that he and other pragmatists had achieved through negotiation with city officials.[43]

But the pilgrimage's main speaker, Dr. Martin Luther King, Jr., offered a different point of view. In pointed remarks, Atlanta's favorite son questioned the city's liberal image and the efficacy of its negotiation tradition. King made a telling comparison of Atlanta—the "city too busy to hate"—with other southern cities. "Something strange and appalling has happened in Atlanta," he thundered. "While boasting of its civic virtue, Atlanta has allowed itself to fall behind almost every major southern city in progress toward desegregation." Charlotte, Chattanooga, Dallas, Houston, Knoxville, Memphis, Nashville, New Orleans, Norfolk, Richmond, and Greensboro all had higher rates of desegregation. Segregation stood as a "glaring reality" in Atlanta. Only one in ten of its restaurants, and just three of Atlanta's 150 hotels and motels, had ended Jim Crow practices. "The cancer of segregation cannot be cured by" the "sedative of tokenism," King charged. The time for resolving the problem through negotiation was "running out" because "the Negro masses may soon lose faith in the negotiations now taking place." Dr. King forcefully endorsed direct action, saying, "If our words fail to move them, then our actions must show them." He closed with a call for unity.[44]

James Forman of SNCC echoed the themes of King's address. Forman stressed the need for citizen-initiated direct action. "No one leader, no group of leaders can get your rights. You have to get them for yourselves," Forman cried. Other speakers agreed that Atlanta had lost its claim as a showcase city for the New South.[45]

On the fringes of the rally, Ku Klux Klansmen stood ominously, as if to underscore the falsity of Atlanta's reputation as a racially progressive city. The pilgrimage reflected the city's racial fault lines and its fractious civil rights movement.[46]

## THE APEX AND NADIR OF THE RADICAL PHASE

The tensions laid bare by the Pilgrimage for Democracy soon became even more profound. In fact, the Atlanta movement nearly collapsed from internal dissension and external attacks when SNCC and COAHR forged ahead with their "drive for an open city." A new stage in the offensive began on December 20, when Oginga Odinga, a Kenyan official and United Nations delegate, visited Atlanta. The students saw the visit as an opportunity to highlight the global reach of the struggle for racial justice. Kenyans had recently liberated themselves from British rule, while segregation still blighted American democracy. In an arranged meeting with the official, SNCC decried the persistence of segregation in America, even as "Third World" citizens overthrew colonial rule. The summit constituted a natural point of departure for renewed protests against segregation in the "First World." After the meeting, student activists requested service at the Toddle House Restaurant, a national chain. When police arrived on the scene and asked the demonstrators to leave, many refused; officers then arrested the students for violating the state's antitrespass law. Many protesters went limp when arrested; police forcibly took them to the police wagon. Two suffered injuries when police officers pulled them feet first from the wagon to the jail. Other protesters claimed that police punched and kicked them during the course of arrest. Inside the jailhouse, many protesters still refused to cooperate. They called themselves "Freedom Now" or "Freeda Now" when booked, declining to give their proper names. Meanwhile, in a telegram to President Johnson, SNCC insisted on passage of a federal public accommodations law to end such embarrassing confrontations.[47]

Around the same time that SNCC and COAHR engaged in this high-profile direct action engagement, ASLC affiliates heatedly debated whether to endorse civil disobedience at all. On January 3, the ASLC steering committee voted to *recommend* mass demonstrations *if* progress did not occur on the desegregation front. The committee's equivocal decision did not signal a new united front on direct action. The recommendation had been voted amid deep divisions. This reality became clear when news spread that ASLC actually had voted to *begin* demonstrations. A. T. Walden called the chatter "erroneous and distorted." Only the committee—not the whole body of affiliates—had voted, he stressed. The committee lacked the power to order demonstrations without the backing of the full body. Walden also made the contingent nature of the committee's recommendation crystal clear; direct action would only be considered if other options failed. A January 7 *Daily World* editorial, following on the heels of Walden's comments, underscored that an influential contingent of the African-American community remained committed to gradualism. The *World* reiterated its long-standing view that "wise political action" held the key to racial progress. Direct action was counterproductive, and unfair in many instances, the daily insisted. Some businessmen refused to desegregate because of "fears" "based on economic losses," rather than "prejudice." Such proprietors should never be subjected to direct action.[48]

But the momentum generated by the new direct action protests was, by now, unmistakable. On January 9, the Council on Human Relations and the Southern Regional Council, long allies in the black struggle for civil rights, announced that they would support mass demonstrations against private discrimination. The groups issued a strongly worded statement that called on other merchants to desegregate. White leaders were on notice: they should move toward desegregation or see demonstrations tear Atlanta apart. On January 11, fourteen leading hotels, including Hilton, Marriott, and Howard Johnson's franchises, announced that they would voluntarily desegregate their facilities. Remarkably, A. T. Walden called the announcement a "major breakthrough" that "justified the wisdom of *our* course of action." Yet, the hotels had taken action in the shadow of SNCC- and COAHR-led protests and on the eve of ASLC's meeting to consider plans, drawn up by SCLC's Wyatt T. Walker, to "totally desegregate" the city through mass demonstrations. The *New York Times*, reporting on developments in Atlanta, underscored cause and effect. The *Times* called the hoteliers' move an "effort to forestall" imminent protests.[49]

Protests continued, nevertheless. Demonstrations begun on the morning of a stormy January 11 meeting—one that resulted in ASLC's split into factions for and against direct action—reached a spectacular climax. Twenty demonstrators staged a protest at the Heart of Atlanta Hotel. The Heart of Atlanta had refused to join the fourteen other hotels that had agreed to desegregate earlier. Police arrested twelve people, including John Lewis, Wyatt T. Walker, other SCLC officials, state NAACP field secretary Leon Cox, three ministers, and a doctor, all of whom had requested service at the hotel. The protest was raucous; one demonstrator sought medical treatment after an employee dragged her over concrete for fifty feet. Other protests—some of which featured standoffs between students and Klansmen—were similarly dynamic. All told, police jailed more than seventy protesters on charges of disorderly conduct and disturbing the peace during demonstrations staged on January 10, 11, 13, 16, 18, and 19.[50]

Atlanta had become a powder keg, or so it seemed. Critics, black and white, were deeply troubled by the development. Disaster loomed, observers charged. The *New York Times* reported that SNCC and COAHR's new drive to desegregate Atlanta threatened a "serious racial crisis" in this "relatively progressive Deep South city." A. T. Walden charged that ASLC's "hawks"—the label now routinely attached to SNCC, COAHR, and the conference's SCLC contingent—threatened to ruin hard-won progress. "We have gotten the best atmosphere that we've ever had in this town for inter-group changes," he said. Just as black Atlanta stood on the brink of victory, the hawks had chosen to change course. "I'm not going to be a party to "Birminghamization" of Atlanta," Walden declared. The *Constitution* weighed in on the controversy as well, aiming its guns squarely at SNCC. On January 21, the paper endorsed a federal public accommodations bill, reversing itself; but the daily took the action in spite of, rather than because of, SNCC's activism, it proclaimed. Its editorial, "For a Public Accommodations Law: Against this SNCC-led Lawlessness," accused SNCC of relying on a "dangerous and utterly cynical" tactic of "deliberate" provocation.[51]

In letters to the editors of the *Constitution* and the *Inquirer* SNCC defended itself. It denied the charge of deliberate provocation and insisted that segregationists and inappropriate police tactics explained the melee. The organization followed up its written defenses of its tactics with a march to City Hall. During the assembly, a SNCC spokesman charged that Atlanta wished to take away a cardinal privilege of American citizenship—the "right to protest peacefully." In this, the city was no different from Birmingham, a fact SNCC's continuing protests would expose. "We demonstrate as a means of communicating our determination that Atlanta will have its reputation a reality, or will admit before the world that it is a carefully constructed fraud."[52]

## CIVIL DISOBEDIENCE ON TRIAL

After even more cataclysmic protests, a full-scale backlash set in. The *Washington Post* defended Atlanta against what it called demonstrators' expectation of "perfection." In Atlanta, police had arrested demonstrators, "but there has been no systematic brutality," no dogs or fire hoses. The constant refrain of white moderates resurfaced. Atlanta was no Birmingham. And the "distinction between Atlanta and Birmingham is a vital one," the editorialist intoned. "It is the distinction between reason and bigotry, between adjustment and conflict." "Hotheads" in the civil rights movement erred in employing militant tactics in a city as racially benevolent as Atlanta, the *Post* argued.[53]

The backlash in the national media reached new heights in the late winter and spring of 1964. A documentary on the Atlanta demonstrations by Walter Cronkite, the trusted newsman, cast Atlanta as illustrative of the problem of destructive and dangerous civil rights protests. The *Wall Street Journal* published an article questioning whether "surprising outbreaks" of racial disturbances in "model" southern cities such as Atlanta threatened passage of a federal civil rights bill. "Some of the more conservative Negroes fret that the timing on the new demonstrations is bad," the *Journal* noted. "They argue that the energy of the civil rights groups would be better devoted to lobbying for the legislation rather than dissipated in the streets of the South." Claude Sitton of the *New York Times* wrote that President Johnson "faces the unpleasant task of wrestling with a reluctant Congress over the civil rights bill in an atmosphere of rising tension." The NAACP, CORE, and the National Urban League joined the chorus of commentators urging orderly demonstrations. Numerous black leaders called for a moratorium on demonstrations while the civil rights bill was pending. Democratic senator Hubert Humphrey and Republican senator Thomas Kuchel, the leading proponents of the civil rights bill, captured the sentiments of the movement's critics. "Civil wrongs do not bring civil rights. Civil disobedience does not bring equal protection under the laws," the lawmakers warned.[54]

### Georgia's "Mr. Civil Rights" and a Cause Célèbre

The unease over civil disobedience came to a head in the courtroom of Atlanta Superior Court judge Durwood Pye. This local judge, unlike many national commentators, was not even a nominal friend of civil rights. Pye personified the face of law that civil rights demonstrators had so often seen in their struggles against Jim Crow—the southern system of injustice: a linchpin of black oppression. Pye boasted a long history of segregationist activism. He had fought to maintain school segregation as secretary of the Georgia Education Commission, formed to circumvent *Brown v. Board of Education* through legal artifice. He also had a hand in Georgia's harassment of the NAACP after *Brown*.[55]

Given his history, it came as no surprise when Pye proved a powerful foe of student protesters. He first manifested his antipathy for demonstrators in an unprecedented way in 1963, during the onset of the "radical demonstration" phase of the Atlanta student movement. On July 15, Pye launched what would become a years-long effort to bring to justice students whom he claimed had "flagrantly" violated the state's antitrespass law. Having decided that he would play the role of both prosecutor and judge, Pye wrote to Atlanta police chief Herbert Jenkins on that date with an unusual request. He asked for the names of "all persons arrested in the City of Atlanta for refusing to leave the premises of another when requested to do so for the last two years." Jenkins responded with a four-page list of names, 302 in all. The list identified protesters arrested between March 1960 and July 1963, complete with dates of arrest, names of arresting officers, and witnesses to events that precipitated the arrests. The roll of protesters in hand, Pye, a sitting superior court judge, set out to ensure that the demonstrators faced vigorous prosecution. First, he ordered the grand jury to investigate all violations of the antitrespassing law—matters of "great seriousness" that had been treated lightly. Then, he commanded the Fulton County solicitor general to seek indictments in the backlog of cases involving student demonstrators who had "flouted, defied, and violated" the law.[56]

In the months after Pye had single-handedly arranged the protesters' indictments, he presided over many of the resulting trials. Pye ruled his courtroom with an iron fist. With his eyes "darting" about and arms flailing, the judge badgered SNCC and COAHR activists with mocking questions, barbs, and taunts from the bench. Judge Pye's courtroom histrionics and displays of contempt for the protesters became notorious among Atlanta activists. His exaggerated mannerisms and intoxication with his judicial power inspired one student to invent a dance mimicking him called the "Pye-Pye Twist." Attorney Donald Hollowell, who frequently defended activists in Pye's court, considered the judge his "archenemy." Before it ended, Pye's vendetta against Hollowell's clients roused elected officials, the U.S. Supreme Court, and the national media.[57]

Hollowell's courtroom skirmishes with Pye earned him the respect of students and set him apart from A. T. Walden, the pragmatic dean of Atlanta's black lawyers. The students mistrusted Walden because of his alliance with powerful whites, his misgivings about direct action, and his "political conservatism." Hollowell, closer to the students in age than Walden, was also ideologically closer to them. A native of Kansas, Hollowell was born in 1917, just as Walden, who was then thirty-two years old, was ending his service in the army. Hollowell was also an army veteran; he had served as an enlisted man in an all-black "Buffalo Soldier" regiment in the late 1930s and in the European theater during World War II, attaining the rank of captain.[58]

Hollowell never aspired to influence or commingle with the white power structure. His physical bearing bespoke self-confidence and pride: he did not fear whites. He was a towering figure at six feet tall, and his skin color was a deep brown. When he spoke, his deep voice filled the room. He carried himself with dignity and brandished his powerful intellect like a sword. He was a commanding presence and an "open" and "encouraging" paternal figure.[59]

By 1961, Hollowell had a growing reputation for making daring inroads against segregation. Hollowell served as Dr. Martin Luther King's personal attorney during his imprisonment at Reidsville State Prison in 1960. And he had filed the suit that overthrew segregation at the UGA. These exploits made Hollowell's star rise among his peers, as well as among students. That year COAHR had also turned to Hollowell to negotiate the omnibus public accommodations consent decree. With his defense of student protesters in Pye's courtroom in 1963 and 1964, Hollowell fully emerged from Walden's shadow.[60]

Hollowell's confrontations with Pye and other judges and police officers soon made him a hero to the students. The lawyer stood with the students at a time when other lawyers quoted exorbitant rates for their services—a practice that "aided the opposition," SNCC claimed. The students returned Hollowell's support with adulation. Benjamin Brown called Hollowell "a model" whom "everyone respected"; "we had all the confidence in the world that he could do anything to protect us." Julian Bond praised Hollowell's "courage" and "brilliant legal mind." Bond continued, "He...out-argued...these famous so-called 'great' constitutional lawyers who had erected this barrier of segregation throughout the South. They had the reputation, but Hollowell had the goods." It is no wonder that Hollowell, feted at numerous community functions, often was introduced as Georgia's "Mr. Civil Rights," an allusion to the title bestowed on Thurgood Marshall. Hollowell returned the students' praise. The lawyer was "greatly impressed" with the students' courage and "superb" organizational skills. His admiration for the students undoubtedly showed as he set about representing them during the heyday of the civil rights movement.[61]

Notably, one of Hollowell's highest profile sit-in cases did not involve the black students who had led Atlanta's direct action movement since its inception in 1960. It involved his representation of a white protester. While Judge Pye showed contempt for African-American demonstrators, he reserved his greatest disdain for white allies such as Mardon Walker.[62]

The daughter of a navy captain stationed at the Pentagon, Walker was an eighteen-year-old Rhode Islander. She was tall, blonde, and bookish-looking. Walker had attended Connecticut College, but in the fall of 1964, she decamped for Atlanta's Spelman College, where she enrolled as an exchange student. Walker had grown up in an overwhelmingly white community. She came South to "see how it feels to be in the minority for once" and to "do something about" inequality. During her time at Spelman, Walker became acquainted with SNCC workers. Soon, Walker herself volunteered to work for SNCC; she participated in demonstrations at three restaurants.[63]

Authorities charged Walker with violating Georgia's antitrespass law during a January 13, 1964 protest at Krystal's Restaurant. She and a group of black friends had sought service and refused to leave the restaurant when asked. Officers also accused the protesters of refusing to cooperate upon arrest. When placed under arrest, they went "limp," like a "sack of flour," refusing to stand or walk on their own; officers were forced to carry each protester to the police wagon.[64]

Walker went on trial in Judge Pye's courtroom. The judge's treatment of Walker illustrated why SNCC and COAHR frequently decried the "jim crow railroaded justice of the Atlanta Courts." During court proceedings, Judge Pye aided the prosecutor at every turn. The problems started during pretrial hearings, when the defense attacked the constitutionality of the antitrespass statute. The statute had been applied in a discriminatory manner, Hollowell and cocounsel Howard Moore argued, delegitimizing the prosecution. The attorneys claimed that the city used the statute to harass civil rights demonstrators: it targeted black protesters and white supporters like Walker for prosecution. In response, the state claimed that discrimination had nothing to do with the prosecution of Walker or any other civil rights demonstrator. In fact, the city's chief prosecutor, William Spence, claimed that the defense's theory made absolutely no sense when applied to Walker because of her race. "How can they complain of the race issue when we are trying a white person," Spence asked during a courtroom exchange with Moore. "I don't know, but they are," Judge Pye offered. Atlanta police chief Herbert Jenkins, a racial moderate by southern standards, supported the prosecutor's (and judge's) claim. He denied that officers targeted civil rights protesters for arrest under the antitrespass law. Yet, when Hollowell pressed the chief to name one white person arrested under the statute who had *not* been engaged in antisegregation protests alongside blacks, Jenkins fell silent.[65]

The city countered by claiming that the overwhelming number of blacks arrested proved not discrimination by the Police Department but blacks' propensity for criminality. The prosecutor called Police Captain R. E. Little of the Atlanta Police Department to the stand to make the point. Little had conceded that 90 percent of those arrested under the antitrespass law were black. Spence asked the captain for an "official percent as to the Negro race with reference to...the crime of rape?" When the officer answered "about 70 percent," Moore sprang to his feet. The attorney objected that the prosecutor's inflammatory question had no place in the trial. But Judge Pye allowed the question. The defense had linked the matters of race and crime, Pye claimed, and Spence's question merely continued the defense's logic. The prosecution could ask the court to "draw an inference" from the rape statistics or any other category of offense. For if the prosecutor could show that blacks "committed" many crimes more frequently than whites, then it would explain why police arrested blacks more frequently than whites for a whole range of offenses, including trespass. In the end, the court heard that Atlanta's finest arrested blacks more often than whites for every possible category of crime—homicide, aggravated assault, larceny. Trespass was no different.[66]

Mardon Walker sometimes responded to the prosecutors' damning questions about her associations with SNCC in ways that did not exactly facilitate her defense. A simple question from her own attorneys illustrated the point. The defense charged discriminatory arrest and prosecution, and Walker's attorneys posed a straightforward question to establish her racial identity. "Miss Walker, are you a member of the white race?" Moore asked. "Well, I would say that I guess, I mean, that is what I have been told," Walker responded—although she had "no conclusive proof" of her race and had no "feelings either way" about it. Walker's answer delighted the prosecution.[67]

From that point on, Spence turned Walker's hesitancy to his advantage. Each and every time a witness stated Walker's race, the prosecutor contested the identification. His purpose was clear. Since the defendant did not concede her race, then officials could not know Walker's race, and the state could not reasonably be said to have targeted Walker for arrest and prosecution for illegitimate, race-based reasons. The state's strategy produced a series of farcical exchanges. When B. F. Marler, one of the arresting officers, declared that the defendant "appears to be a member of the white race," Spence objected. "He can't determine the question," the prosecutor insisted. "I wouldn't swear that I know if you [Marler or anyone else] has one drop of a certain type of blood," Spence continued. Carl Copeland, an assistant prosecutor, seconded his colleague's mystification about race. "You can't tell by looking at a person what race they belong to," Copeland exclaimed. Judge Pye joined the charade. The judge explained that he had represented a gentleman who "came from Barbados to Canada and thence to Georgia." The court had assumed that the man and his family "belonged to the white race." But "[o]ne day they brought other members of the family into the office to meet me, and they were—of the colored race, brothers." The judge's very own experiences, he vowed, showed that there might well "be something to" Spence's point.[68]

Exasperated, Moore asked the court to rely on official police records as proof of Walker's race. Police reports designated Walker a white female, demonstrating, Moore said, that officials perceived her as white—and arrested her because she was a white civil rights demonstrator. Spence objected. The officials had merely relied on Walker's own self-identification, he said. Her statement had been "self-serving," he insisted. Consequently, not even the police records should count as conclusive proof of the defendant's true racial identity. Pye was convinced. He refused to admit the evidence. For purposes of her trial in the Atlanta Superior Court, Walker's membership in the white race had been revoked.[69]

Ironically, in light of the defendant's supposedly indeterminate and irrelevant racial identity, the prosecutor next interrogated Walker about her fraternization with blacks. Spence lobbed questions about her interracial living arrangements. Walker had lived with well-known SNCC activist Ruby Doris Smith and five other people, women and men. "Were they white or were they Negro?" the prosecutor inquired. "Both, and there were even some Japanese people there," Walker said, "they were yellow." Exactly how many white girls lived in the apartment, Spence asked. Just one, Walker responded—her. "And were there Negro men there?" he queried. Yes, Walker retorted. "And they would be mixed up as far as sex is concerned and as far as race is concerned, is that right?" the prosecutor inquired. "Yes," Walker said. "Now, do you know whether any of these people were married to any of those other people who were staying there?" he asked. "I don't know," Walker replied. "We were all together in this one room sleeping sort of shoulder to shoulder," she elaborated. Spence was incredulous. And "there were Negro men there?" he repeated. When Spence persisted with racially and sexually charged questions, Hollowell objected time and again. But the prosecutor had a ready explanation for his inquiries. The questions about sleeping arrangements went "to the credibility of the witness," Spence argued, and to whether Walker had witnessed "illicit or felonious relations." "I think it would be indecent for her to be lying there on the floor with five or six men in one room sleeping," the prosecutor said. Walker, a northern white woman, had defied countless cultural norms, and had maybe even broken a few sexual conduct laws. Judge Pye sided with the prosecution.[70]

## An Audacious Bid to Remove

With no recourse from the prosecutor's bias, Hollowell surprised Judge Pye with a daring legal maneuver. Just as Walker's trial-in-chief was set to commence, Hollowell announced that he had filed a petition to remove Walker's case (and those of several other clients) to federal court. The move enraged Judge Pye. Though a common tactic now, Hollowell's petition constituted a highly controversial, and creative, litigation strategy to employ in a southern courtroom at the time.[71]

A Reconstruction-era statute made Hollowell's action possible. A provision of the Civil Rights Act of 1866 permitted the removal of actions from state to federal court. Actions could be transferred in instances where defendants alleged either that their federal civil rights had been violated or that it would not be possible to enforce their federal civil rights in state court. By 1964, the removal strategy had become a tool that lawyers such as Len Holt, Bill Kunstler, and Arthur Kinoy frequently used to combat segregationists' use of mass arrests, high bail, and criminal prosecutions to stop the direct action movement. When the removal strategy succeeded, it worked brilliantly. The petitions stopped racist state court judges "dead in their tracks." By simply filing legal papers alleging infractions of their clients' constitutional rights, the attorneys secured the release of hundreds of protesters. With state proceedings extinguished, the federal courts, where civil rights litigants typically received a fairer reception, had jurisdiction over the underlying actions.[72]

The removal strategy had its limits, however. The federal district court could remand removed cases to the state courts. This often happened. If a removal petition was thwarted, civil rights lawyers were left to confront the ire of insulted state court judges, who found the procedure a tremendous affront to their authority.[73]

Donald Hollowell saw this firsthand on February 17, 1964. Judge Pye angrily lashed out at the attorney, accusing Hollowell of "playing fast and loose" with his court. The judge claimed that he would comply with a removal order, but expressed antipathy for the concept. Pye called the removal procedure a "striking illustration of the one-sided appeals constantly made to the Fourteenth Amendment of the U.S. Constitution," and a "striking illustration of the aggrandizement of all departments of the federal government which is the real source of all this mischief." He need not have worried about the supposed overreaching federal courts in this instance. Without even scheduling a hearing on the matter, the U.S. District Court denied Hollowell's petition to remove Mardon Walker's case to federal court.[74]

Hollowell faced Judge Pye again. The judge promptly refused to dismiss Mardon Walker's case; he was not persuaded by Hollowell's argument that the city's application of the antitrespass law had been discriminatory. An all-white Fulton County jury would decide Walker's fate after a short trial in which the prosecution established that Walker had refused to leave the restaurant when asked.[75]

The court heard closing statements. Both sides entreated the jury to realize the high stakes riding on the verdict in Mardon Walker's case. Prosecutor William Spence warned, "Every person's property rights depend on the outcome of this case." A not-guilty verdict would threaten the very fabric of the social order,

Spence claimed. His rhetoric reached fever pitch as he cried, "If this jury puts its stamp of approval on violation of this law...property owners can sit by and watch...or get their shotgun[s]." He continued, "Do you want Atlanta to be known as a place all over the United States where civil disorder exists....where mobs take over?" Pointing to Walker, Spence said, "If we don't do something to her, she'll be right back down here leading that pack of wolves into Krystal's."[76]

The "pack of wolves" to which Spence referred, SNCC, emerged front and center in Hollowell's summation as well. The prosecutor had "attempted to try the Student Nonviolent Coordinating Committee," "every demonstration in America," and the "whole civil rights movement" in Mardon Walker's trial, Hollowell complained. He pleaded with the jury to reject that ploy. The jury must not convict Walker for SNCC's alleged sins. The state had "attempted to smear" his young client and in the process had "pervert[ed] the judicial process." Hollowell urged the jury to recognize that the "image of Atlanta is on trial in this case," just as Spence had claimed. But contrary to the prosecutor's suggestion, the watchful eyes of the nation's citizenry demanded that the jury spurn the trumped-up charges against Walker. They must let her go free.[77]

The all-white jury of eleven men and one woman quickly decided which version of events to believe. On February 20, 1964, after less than an hour of deliberations, the jurors found Mardon Walker guilty as charged. Sentencing followed immediately. The Rhode Islander was now at Judge Pye's mercy. Before meting out his punishment, Judge Pye called Walker a "hard-core operator." He relished the opportunity to teach the outsider a lesson. With her father and friends looking on, Pye imposed the maximum penalty. He sentenced Walker to eighteen months on the misdemeanor charge, including twelve months in a public works camp and six months in jail. Pye also fined her $1,000, set her appeal bond at $15,000, and stipulated that only local property could be posted for the bond. Pye had made an example of Mardon Walker—and used "law and order" to demoralize SNCC.[78]

But that was not all Pye had achieved. Walker's sentence generated blistering commentary outside Atlanta. A *Washington Post* editorial, "Jungle Justice," called Pye's sentence "savagery." "The sentence is out of all proportion to the offense of a young girl who protested against something that is morally wrong....The 18 months' imprisonment is a sentence reflecting only the ugly vindictiveness of a segregationist judge." Senator Dodd of Connecticut called the sentence "an outrage." Legislators in Rhode Island passed a resolution expressing dismay at the sentence and called on U.S. attorney general Robert Kennedy to intervene. For her part, Mardon Walker proclaimed that she had no regrets. Her conviction and sentence had only strengthened her commitment to racial equality. "I'd do it again despite having to go to jail for it," she said.[79]

Walker's conviction also stoked the fires of protest in Atlanta's African-American community. At a mass meeting convened at the Friendship Baptist Church on March 6, the ASLC voted to request out-of-state monitors for any trials involving demonstrators charged with violating Georgia's antitrespass laws. "We are concerned about the courts here," the group explained. It also complained to the governor of Georgia and to congressman Charles Weltner. The congressman responded with a statement condemning the demonstrators' conduct, but saying that Judge Pye had denied Walker and others fair trials. Leaders also spoke out against Walker's conviction at a mass rally held on March 8 at Wheat Street Baptist Church. The gathering's featured speaker, veteran labor and civil rights leader A. Phillip Randolph, headed up the list of stalwarts who called Walker's treatment a travesty of justice. The "Constitutional right to petition for redress should be protected" always, Randolph said.[80]

Judge Pye's demonization of Walker and other civil rights activists who appeared in his courtroom mobilized and united Atlanta's often divided black communities, at least temporarily. African Americans remained deeply divided over the wisdom of direct action. But the white resistance to the students pulled ASLC back from the brink of implosion. The most influential moderate leaders decided against publicly abandoning the students as white officialdom attacked. Some in the moderate camp, on record as harboring deep skepticism about SNCC and COAHR's actions, now issued statements in support of them. Martin Luther King, Sr., told a reporter that "all of the organizations are necessary" and that demonstrations were "one of the necessary steps." Yet, King called for a suspension of the present demonstrations. A. T. Walden, who had fought tooth and nail against street protests, called the recent demonstrations "excess[ive] and "disorderly" and argued that such protests "tend to drive people away." But in a great departure, Walden now claimed to support "proper, orderly demonstrations." Around the same time, the ASLC and the Atlanta NAACP called for a boycott during the upcoming Easter season—a "sacrificial Easter"—to pressure more downtown businesses to desegregate.[81]

Within this context, the Board of Aldermen adopted a resolution "urging" all businesses "to give immediate consideration to the removal of racial barriers, rather than wait the forces of legislation." The local community of activists had moved the city toward support for the civil rights bill.[82]

But the backlash to the radical demonstration phase of the Atlanta student movement nevertheless had its intended effect. The leaders of SNCC and COAHR had promised additional protests in Atlanta during the spring and summer of 1964. But the wave of demonstrations that had begun in the city during the summer of 1963 tapered off as activists continued to stand trial in Judge Pye's courtroom and criticism of civil disobedience mounted.

Beginning in June 1964 SNCC turned its attention elsewhere. The Atlanta office continued to coordinate SNCC projects in Georgia and other states, but over the next two years the organization directed much of its energy and resources to the Magnolia State. James Forman, Julian Bond, and John Lewis, some of the most outspoken figures in the Atlanta movement, went to Mississippi during much of this period. Volunteers initially relocated to Mississippi for a summer voter registration and education project—SNCC's most ambitious campaign yet. When SNCC's "Freedom Summer" project in Mississippi, which featured hundreds of white student volunteers, precipitated violent white reprisals, it riveted the nation. The most highly publicized tragedy occurred when SNCC workers Michael Schwerner, Andrew Goodman, and James Chaney went missing in June 1964; their bodies were found two months later near Philadelphia, Mississippi.[83]

## THE CIVIL RIGHTS ACT IN THE HEART OF ATLANTA

The Civil Rights Act became law against the backdrop of resistance to the movement, waged inside and outside of the courts, in cities such as Atlanta as well as in remote areas of the Deep South. Congress passed the Civil Rights Act on July 2, 1964. Over the opposition of the southern Democrats, led by Georgia's Senator Richard B. Russell, the House and the Senate passed the statute by overwhelming margins. The omnibus law forbade discrimination in employment, education, and public accommodations, defined to include municipal facilities, as well as hotels, restaurants, and other businesses.[84]

Atlanta then took center stage in the battle over the constitutionality of the new legislation. Two familiar figures leveled legal attacks against the Civil Rights Act. Moreton Rolleston, Jr., owner of the Heart of Atlanta Hotel, had clashed with demonstrators in 1962, when Atlanta hosted the NAACP's national convention, and on several occasions in 1964 before passage of the Civil Rights Act. This businessman, who was also a lawyer, challenged the constitutionality of the Civil Rights Act exactly two hours and ten minutes after President Johnson signed it into law—lodging the first major test of the new law in *Heart of Atlanta Hotel v. United States.*[85]

If Rolleston presented the legalistic face of segregation, Lester Maddox presented the bombastic and confrontational side of white resistance. Maddox, the perennial foe of SNCC and COAHR, relished his role as the public face of small businessmen's resistance to the Act. If blacks visited the Pickrick, Maddox

promised, "I'll…throw the Negroes out—even if it falls my due to go to jail."
Sure enough, when civil rights testers set upon his restaurant, Maddox refused
to comply with the law. The LDF soon filed suit against him for violating the
Civil Rights Act, and the U.S. Department of Justice intervened in the case,
*Willis v. Pickrick Restaurant*, just as it had in *Heart of Atlanta*, to enforce the
new law.[86]

Rolleston and Maddox's defiance gave rise to a constitutional battle featuring two distinct faces of white supremacy—one sober and legalistic, the other
rabid and violent. The eyes of the nation looked upon the city in mid-July,
wondering how the federal court would respond. In July 1964, a three-judge
panel unanimously sided with the government. Both of Atlanta's standard-
bearers for white resistance had lost. Yet, they battled on. Rolleston appealed,
and Maddox closed his restaurant rather than integrate. (In 1966, Maddox, still
a standard bearer of white resistance, was elected governor of Georgia).[87]

The U.S. Supreme Court heard arguments in *Heart of Atlanta v. United States*
at the very start of its new term. On December 14, 1964, the Court unanimously upheld the public accommodations provisions of the 1964 Civil Rights
Act as a valid exercise of Congress's authority to regulate interstate commerce.
The majority opinion, written by Justice Thomas C. Clark, concluded that "The
power of Congress in this area [interstate commerce] is broad and sweeping.
Where it keeps within its sphere and violates no express constitutional limitation it has been the rule of this Court, going back almost to the founding days
of the Republic, not to interfere." The early commerce clause cases *Gibbons v.
Ogden* and *McCulloch v. Maryland* underpinned the decision. The Court cited
New Deal–era commerce clause cases as well, making clear connections between
the civil rights movement and the constitutional revolution of the 1930s. Segregationists such as Lester Maddox had long castigated civil rights activists and
New Dealers alike as Communists bent on eradicating personal liberty in the
guise of regulation. *Heart of Atlanta* only confirmed their suspicions that the
Far Left had captured Washington.[88]

Yet, the Court's opinion constituted far less of a victory for civil rights than
it might have been, some believed. The Act easily passed muster under the commerce clause, but the Fourteenth Amendment question posed great difficulty
for the Court. The majority opinion avoided discussing the Act's validity under
the amendment, which stipulated that Congress had the power to enact legislation appropriate to enforce the equal protection guarantee. The difficulty lay
in the *Civil Rights Cases* of 1883, in which the Court had invalidated a Reconstruction-era civil rights act that regulated private discrimination. The *Civil
Rights Cases* had "no relevance to the basis of the decision" in *Heart of Atlanta*,
the Court wrote. The Court had missed a tremendous opportunity to overturn

the 1883 *Civil Rights Cases*—long the legal underpinning of Jim Crow in much of American social life—and the constitutional edifice that had propelled civil rights activists into the streets to protest discrimination by private actors in the first place.[89]

Outside the Court, various actors responded as expected to *Heart of Atlanta*. For Moreton Rolleston and other segregationists, the decision said more than enough as it stood. He called December 14 a "sad day for individual freedom." The *Atlanta Constitution* editorialized that the public should accept the Act and the Court's decision. "Further defiance means anarchy and disorder," the *Constitution* counseled. Donald Hollowell, who had a hand in the litigation challenging segregation at the Pickrick, called *Heart of Atlanta* "extremely gratifying." In New York, the NAACP's executive secretary, Roy Wilkins, asserted that the Supreme Court's action "reinforces public confidence in the orderly processes of the law." The decision "should promptly end discrimination in public accommodations," Wilkins predicted. President Johnson, in an allusion to the Act's backing by two presidents, its overwhelming passage by Congress, and the Supreme Court's unanimous decision upholding it, declared that the "nation has spoken with a single voice on the question of equal rights and equal opportunity." He predicted that *Heart of Atlanta* would increase and speed compliance with the Civil Rights Act.[90]

Nearly four years after A. T. Walden's March 1961 agreement to partially desegregate downtown Atlanta, Jim Crow finally fell in Atlanta. Hotels, restaurants, theaters, and other public accommodations desegregated after *Heart of Atlanta*. The heads of the Atlanta motel and restaurant associations urged compliance with the Supreme Court's decision, and most proprietors did comply. Scattered reports of defiant businesses persisted in the months—indeed years—ahead. But with the constitutionality of the act confirmed, African Americans who faced discrimination in public accommodations could now sue in court. The federal government could, and did, sue businesses engaged in patterns and practices in violation of the Act. The battle for an open city had finally ended.[91]

But the fate of Mardon Walker and others like her remained uncertain, even as President Johnson and Roy Wilkins delighted in Atlanta's relatively smooth transition to an open city. This was true even though the U.S. Supreme Court had vindicated her and other young collegians who had done so much to bring about passage of the law on the same day that the Court decided *Heart of Atlanta*. At the same time, it announced its joint decision in *Hamm v. Rock Hill* and *Lupper v. Arkansas*, cases in which demonstrators who had participated in sit-ins appealed their convictions. The demonstrators charged that the businesses targeted in the sit-ins had practiced racial discrimination unlawful under both the new Civil Rights Act and the U.S. Constitution's Fourteenth

Amendment. Consequently, the demonstrators should not have been charged with lawbreaking, and their convictions were void. In a consolidated opinion, a majority of the justices agreed that the Civil Rights Act abated the protesters' criminal trespass convictions. The Court's decision delighted SNCC, COAHR, SCLC, and other practitioners of direct action. *Hamm* promised to cleanse the nation's court dockets of an estimated three thousand pending cases involving civil rights demonstrators. At long last, it seemed, the civil rights movement had beaten southern justice.[92]

Reality defied these expectations, at least for a time. *Hamm* formally vindicated demonstrators, but the Court's opinion did not prevent local judges and prosecutors from evading its rule. Harassment continued and convictions stood because *Hamm* preserved prosecutions for demonstrations not considered "peaceful" or "non-forcible." Moreover, the Civil Rights Act did not cover some venues targeted by protesters, some judges claimed. These caveats jeopardized countless protesters—not only those who had actually engaged in truly disorderly protests but also those merely accused of doing so. Both groups were at the mercy of the same prosecutors and judges who had initiated and presided over sit-in cases before passage of the act—men like Durwood Pye.[93]

In Atlanta, Pye continued his vendetta against Walker well after passage of the Civil Rights Act, despite *Hamm*. In 1965, Donald Hollowell appealed Walker's case to the U.S. Supreme Court. In a per curiam opinion issued in May 1965, the Court granted Hollowell's appeal. The justices reversed a unanimous decision by the Georgia Supreme Court upholding Walker's conviction. The justices cited *Hamm v. Rock Hill* and *Lupper v. Arkansas*, finding that the Civil Rights Act nullified the convictions of peaceful protesters of segregation. Though Justices Black, Harlan, and White—dissenters in *Hamm*—indicated that they would have affirmed the decision of the lower court, commentators welcomed the opinion as a well-deserved victory for Walker. Her treatment in the state courts had given "Georgia justice a black eye," the *Atlanta Constitution* declared in welcoming the conclusion of *State v. Walker*. The *Constitution* deemed the Supreme Court's decision the "final act in Miss Walker's ordeal." In a gesture of gratitude to Donald Hollowell and Howard Moore for bringing the case against his daughter to a successful conclusion, Captain Donald Walker sent the attorneys Air Force wings.[94]

The celebrations proved premature. Mardon Walker soon suffered a stunning reversal of fortune. The Supreme Court's decision had not fully checked Durwood Pye's vendetta against her and other civil rights demonstrators. Judge Pye interpreted the Supreme Court's decision merely as mandating a new trial for Walker, rather than as reversing her conviction. She stood trial again and, once more, was convicted.[95]

It took several more rounds of federal court litigation—including a second removal action and appeal to the U.S. Supreme Court—before Hollowell saw success. The U.S. Court of Appeals for the Fifth Circuit announced its opinion freeing Mardon Walker from the grip of the Georgia courts on September 29, 1969, more than five years after passage of the Civil Rights Act of 1964, and more than five years after her one-time protest in Atlanta. Judge Pye would have no further chance to ensnare Mardon Walker using the courts and the law as his weapons of choice. Finally, she had prevailed.[96]

## HOW DO CITIZENS SHAPE LAW?

SNCC and COAHR's advocacy left a strong imprint on the civil rights movement. The students had catalyzed social, political, and constitutional change. Atlanta's disparate constituencies, the young and the old, pragmatists and liberals, managed to develop a working relationship. The youth organizations pushed the pragmatists toward a commitment to society-wide desegregation and toleration of mass demonstrations. Indeed, significant numbers of African Americans transferred loyalties from the pragmatists and the politics of moderation to the more insurgent brand of politics favored by SNCC, COAHR, and SCLC. The pragmatists' grip on power had been loosened. The youth organizations became the vanguard of a more democratic civil rights movement.

The nation also became more democratic under the pressure that the activists had brought to bear on the political system. The challenge of democracy "cannot be met unless and until all Americans, Negro and white, enjoy the full promise of our democratic heritage—first class citizenship," SNCC stated at its founding. Just four years later, SNCC and its Atlanta affiliate had been an integral part of the maelstrom of black protest and violent white resistance to it that created the political environment favorable to passage of the Civil Rights Act of 1964. Atlanta did not play the direct, causal role in Congress's consideration and passage of the law that Birmingham did.

Yet, developments in the city's protest movement, covered widely by the national press, served as a crucial barometer of race relations in the South. If segregation remained an intractable problem in "the city too busy to hate"—if Atlanta could not solve its race problems—then Congress had to step in. President Kennedy turned to Ivan Allen to break the congressional logjam that impeded enactment of a strong civil rights law precisely because of Atlanta's symbolic importance. Protests led by SNCC and COAHR played a causal role in Allen's embrace of federal intervention. Hence, the Atlanta demonstrations indirectly pushed Congress toward passage of the 1964 Civil Rights Act. Contrary to the claims of the Act's sponsors, civil disobedience *did* help to bring equal protection under the laws.[97]

Whereas SNCC and COAHR's activism laid the groundwork for civil rights legislation on the national level, the effort to desegregate Atlanta itself proved extraordinarily difficult. Sporadic incidents of white violence, perpetrated by Lester Maddox, Charlie Lebedin, and others, including those hidden by white sheets, marred Atlanta's racially moderate reputation. Even so, Atlanta continued to look racially moderate in comparison with cities such as Birmingham, where whites, including government officials, violently repressed civil rights workers as a matter of course. Therein lay the source of the Atlanta movement's difficulty. The city's white political, civic, and business leaders deployed the rhetoric and reality of racial moderation as a device to demobilize and moderate the civil rights movement. Activists were bedeviled by white Atlantans' appeals to social custom, property rights, and an inviolate state action doctrine long embraced by the courts. These factors, coupled with the white power structure's decades-long alliance with black pragmatists, constituted formidable barriers to "freedom—now!" The white business and political establishments made small concessions to SNCC and COAHR, peacefully desegregating certain municipal facilities, restaurants, and schools, on a token basis, in 1961. But segregation endured in the city as a whole. Ultimately, it was the Civil Rights Act that forced the desegregation of public accommodations in Atlanta, just as in Birmingham.

The more aggressive demonstration tactics that SNCC and COAHR employed beginning in the middle of 1963 were a double-edged sword. The tactics created tension, but they also appeared to substantiate opponents' allegations that the movement threatened the social and legal orders. Observers tended to hold civil rights demonstrators responsible for any violence that occurred during the more raucous protests, even when whites committed or instigated the violence. By contrast, little or no actual violence attributable to the protesters occurred during demonstrations staged by SNCC and COAHR in Atlanta from 1960 through early 1963. Then, protesters' claim to equal treatment had been beyond serious reproach. The protests staged during the radical phase nevertheless produced numerous concessions from segregationists. But SNCC and COAHR walked a thin line during the radical phase, veering dangerously close at times to producing chaos rather than creative tension.

The law framed and facilitated the course of the direct action movement in multiple ways—often to the advantage of opponents of change. Segregationists employed the law deftly during both phases of the direct action protests. The antitrespass laws helped to preserve segregation in two ways. First, the Atlanta

Police Department arrested antisegregation demonstrators at the behest of business owners who wished to maintain Jim Crow. Second, the statutes provided a legal bulwark that conferred credibility on the Jim Crow policies of private businesses. A broad cross-section of Americans—including Thurgood Marshall at the dawn of the sit-in movements—believed in the sanctity of property rights, even when owners chose to discriminate. To these observers, a person had a right to prevent another from entering his property uninvited, regardless of the reason. Use of the antitrespass law against civil rights demonstrators looked like a reasonable application of a generally accepted rule. The more boisterous the demonstrators became, the more reasonable the use of the trespass law appeared to observers.

Constitutional law supported private actors' segregation. The line of Supreme Court cases extending from the *Civil Rights Cases* erected a constitutional bar to court-ordered desegregation of public accommodations, or so jurists thought. *Reed v. Sarno*, the NAACP's effort to end segregation in Atlanta's restaurants and hotels, illustrated the constitutional impediment to racial change. In view of the broad legal and social consensus favoring a right of private discrimination, the Civil Rights Act constituted a truly remarkable restructuring of the nation's public and private institutions, its commercial and social spaces. Congress transformed private businesses that had free rein to restrict whom they served into "public accommodations" barred from discriminating on the basis of race, sex, religion, or national origin. The breadth of the Act's definition of public accommodations tore down the time-honored boundary between civil and property rights.

During the racial maelstrom leading up to the Act, when legal precedent disfavored change, the Supreme Court largely remained a bystander. Civil rights activists led, the white resistance responded, Congress followed, and the Court affirmed legislative action in *Heart of Atlanta Hotel*. The Court unanimously upheld the Civil Rights Act under Congress's power to regulate commerce, dodging the constitutional question of whether the *Civil Rights Cases* should be reversed pursuant to Congress's powers to enforce the Fourteenth Amendment.

The justices' caution was not surprising. It had justification on the familiar ground that the Court should avoid reaching broad constitutional issues when not compelled to do so. Even setting aside the prudential concern, the Court's pursuit of the narrower path was predictable, if not inevitable, given its track record in race cases and tendency to follow majority public opinion. The South's massive resistance to the Court's most daring racial decision, *Brown v. Board of Education*, militated in favor of the more conservative course. By averting the Fourteenth Amendment issue in *Heart of Atlanta*, the Court avoided the accusation that it had usurped or invaded powers belonging to the legislature.

Yet, the series of pre-Civil Rights Act sit-in cases, including *Lombard v. Louisiana* and *Peterson v. Greenville*, affirmed the Court's secondary, if important, role in the struggle for civil rights. Narrowly focused edicts primarily about procedure, the sit-in cases conferred legitimacy on demonstrators ex post. But they had little ability to prevent future judicial, police, or private actors' harassment of civil rights activists.

The courts' failure to vigorously protect black civil rights, with the exception of the sit-in cases, exacerbated SNCC's long-standing skepticism about the courts and its growing doubt that the nation would ever live up to its stated commitment to interracial democracy. During the trial of Mardon Walker and others like it SNCC's doubts about the quality of justice available in the nation's courts peaked. Walker's trial showed that determined local judges, prosecutors, and police officers could and did countermobilize against civil rights protesters and flout the federal government.

But Georgia's witch hunt against civil rights demonstrators eventually backfired. Donald Hollowell achieved mythic status for waging battle against Georgia justice in the Walker trial (and many others). In Hollowell, the students found the trusted ally that they never perceived in A. T. Walden. Walden had litigated cautiously. Hollowell litigated with abandon. Faced with Judge Pye's harassment, Hollowell challenged his authority under the federal removal statute  and eventually prevailed. In this, Hollowell followed a path pioneered by movement lawyers who had experienced law enforcement and judicial harassment in communities all across the South. Judge Pye's witch hunt also failed in another important way. His stand against civil rights demonstrators inspired many of Atlanta's black pragmatist leaders to rally in defense of the students and direct action. A. T. Walden expressed qualified support for direct action for the first time.

The unintended beneficial effects of Judge Pye's campaign against civil rights activists illustrate an important theme of this overall discussion. Court action both mobilized and demobilized the civil rights movement. The unexpected outcomes sometimes produced by legal interventions underscored the necessity of tactical flexibility in the movement. This reality made the practices of local counsel, such as Donald Hollowell, and lawyers outside of the civil rights mainstream, such as Len Holt, Bill Kunstler, and Arthur Kinoy, all the more crucial to the movement's success.

In the long term, however, the white backlash weakened the movement in important respects. Judge Pye's use of the courts and the law to undermine the movement, even after passage of the Civil Rights Act, suggested a sobering reality, the truth of which became more apparent over time. Changes in formal law—the end of de jure segregation—would not necessarily end inequality, whether in the judicial system or in society writ large. The movement still had to fight for real change in the lives of African Americans—in housing, schools, health care, the economy, and the political system.

Yet, by the time that Mardon Walker won her battle against Judge Pye, SNCC, the organization that done so much to slay Jim Crow, had just about petered out. After Pye's trials of civil rights demonstrators and charges by other prominent whites that student activists threatened "law and order," SNCC and COAHR's direct action efforts in Atlanta diminished markedly; SNCC never recovered from the damage done to its reputation during the radical demonstration phase. The accusations that prosecutors, judges, journalists, and politicians hurled against the organization during the trials of Mardon Walker and other demonstrators—the narrative of disorder and debauchery that echoed in the courtroom and in the news—discredited SNCC in the minds of influential citizens. In response to what it perceived as unfair criticism, SNCC grew disenchanted with racial liberals, especially whites who criticized students from the safety and comfort of home and office. Its members' alienation and internal dissension, along with its blemished reputation, undermined SNCC as it embarked on its next and perhaps most important and ambitious programmatic phase: its antipoverty and antiwar campaigns.

CHAPTER 9

# "New Politics"

*Law, Organizing, and a "Movement of Movements"*
*in the Southern Ghetto, 1965–1967*

[T]he day-to-day lot of the ghetto Negro has not been improved by the
various judicial and legislative measures of the past decade. (1965)

Bayard Rustin

Imagine 10 SNCC guys in the Georgia House committed to organizing
their districts[,] to using the seats in the House to meet community needs
[as] defined by the community. (1965)

Charles Cobb

"[T]oday, we strike away the last major shackle of the chains of oppression that
had tethered Africans to America," President Johnson proclaimed.[1] He spoke
on August 6, 1965, when Congress overwhelmingly passed the Voting Rights
Act of 1965.[2] John Lewis of SNCC captured the poignant moment in similarly
sweeping terms. He called the voting rights law the "nation's finest hour" and
the "crowning achievement" of the civil rights movement. The law promised to
fulfill the black freedom struggle's central objective: political power and meaningful representation in government.[3]

In Atlanta, passage of the Act also seemed to vindicate A. T. Walden, the
pioneering civil rights lawyer. He died at the age of eighty, just a few weeks
before the momentous day when President Johnson signed the Voting Rights
Act into law. Walden had prioritized voting rights in the pursuit of racial equality, and his vision of black political power now appeared within grasp. The
Voting Rights Act capped off Walden's decades-long effort to place political
power—not desegregation—at the top of Atlanta's civil rights agenda. In the
weeks after the Voting Rights Act passed, African Americans lined up all over
Georgia to register to vote.[4]

The power of the votes that African Americans cast to yield representation
in the legislature owed much to *Baker v. Carr*, the U.S. Supreme Court's

landmark 1962 decision. Justice Brennan's opinion for the Court established that voters could challenge state legislative apportionment decisions in federal court. Following *Carr*, voters successfully challenged Georgia's apportionment system, leading courts to reapportion both houses of the Georgia General Assembly.[5]

Reapportionment permitted African Americans who lived in majority black districts to elect candidates of their choice. Black voters sent Leroy Johnson, a protégé of A. T. Walden, to the Georgia senate. Johnson was the first African American to hold a seat in that august body since Reconstruction. Later, voters elected several blacks to the Georgia house. The new crop of legislators spanned the generations of African-American leadership: the old guard claimed a number of seats, while SNCC veteran Julian Bond represented the new.[6]

More than any other individual, A. T. Walden had brought about the sweeping changes in Georgia politics, capped off by passage of the Act. Because of voter registration campaigns that Walden spearheaded, groups that he had founded and led, federal cases that he instigated, and court orders that he implemented, change had come. African Americans had grown from a mere 4 percent of Atlanta's electorate in 1945, or just three thousand voters, to 34 percent of it in 1965, or about sixty-three thousand voters. The Voting Rights Act, coupled with the principles enunciated in *Baker v. Carr*, would protect and expand the monumental shift in the make-up of the electorate.[7]

The Democratic Party had long shunned African Americans, but party leaders eventually acknowledged Walden's place and importance. Walden represented Georgia Democrats as a delegate to the 1964 national convention in Atlantic City—making the Georgia delegation the only integrated group among Deep South states. President Johnson and Vice President Humphrey joined a remarkable array of state and local leaders who rendered tributes to Walden upon his death. An *Atlanta Constitution* columnist captured the spirit of these remarks. Walden was the "[s]outhern Negro's greatest single soldier manning the gap of history between Booker T. Washington and Martin Luther King." The *Atlanta Inquirer* called Walden a "modern day Moses who led his people to the Promised Land." Born "close enough to slavery to hear the tinkle of chains," Rev. William Holmes Borders said in his eulogy, Walden had "set the world on fire."[8]

Walden's legacy can also be measured by the lights of the generation of political activists who inherited it and then remade it. The older man's distaste for direct action had left him estranged from student leaders, including Julian Bond. Nevertheless, the SNCC veteran's election to the Georgia legislature in 1965 tested Walden's strategy of black empowerment in important ways. Walden had struggled long and hard for black voting rights on the premise that if African Americans could elect the likes of Leroy Johnson and Julian Bond to positions in government, the entire African-American community would prosper.

Walden counted on the political system to be fair, functional, and responsive to African-American interests if blacks became players in the machine as voters and officeholders. He presumed that black and white Democrats would form coalitions in support of a liberal agenda, one that included racial advancement. The power brokers would be middle class, the agenda would be achieved through consensus, and its elements would be moderate. Indeed, Walden's theory of black inclusion in the electoral system rested on the "better class" of blacks—the well-educated, the professionals, the veterans—fitting into the system and playing the game, just like whites, but for the benefit of blacks. The benefits of black representation, Walden believed, would flow to the black working class, whose members naturally would strive to be a part of the better class. The question of whether the poorest blacks would also benefit was not explicitly a part of Walden's equation.

Well before he ever campaigned for the Georgia legislature, Bond already had helped to reshape the racial politics of the South and the nation, and he seemed singularly well equipped to make change again in the arena of electoral politics. Yet, Bond's early experiences illuminated the limitations of black bloc voting and political representation—a concept in which he and Walden believed, despite other ideological differences. The system was not always fair or responsive to black interests, and it was especially unresponsive to the needs of the poor. Once the Civil Rights Act and the Voting Rights Act delivered formal equality under law, the issue of black poverty, always present, came to the forefront. Bond could not ignore the pressing matters at the intersection of race and class, nor did he wish to. To the contrary, he prioritized the concerns of destitute citizens of his district in his 1965 campaign for the Georgia House of Representatives. He promised a "new politics" attentive to the interests of the black poor. However, before Bond could fully turn his attention to problems in his own district, the Cold War intervened.

Geopolitical developments in Africa and Asia—lands far away geographically but close to many African-American hearts and minds—reshaped domestic events and upstaged them. A global tide of pan-Africanism and anticolonialism washed over SNCC, leading the organization to lash out against the Johnson administration's policy in Vietnam. Bond found himself taking a stand against the foreign conflict, waged against impoverished South Asians. Around the same time, a faction within SNCC, led by Stokely Carmichael and William Ware, advocated "black power," a cry for political and economic empowerment, particularly for those trapped in ghettos. The organization's antiwar stance and embrace of black power occurred against the backdrop of urban riots and white demands for law and order. The combination made for a combustible environment. Issues of race and class dominated the national and local agendas, but not as architects of the new politics had planned.

While Bond hoped to use the ballot box to focus on the needs of the black poor, Howard Moore, Jr., SNCC's crusading general counsel, yearned to use the law to create the conditions necessary for achieving "revolutionary" change for poor minority communities. Moore intended to aid SNCC's political agenda through his legal practice. His empathetic lawyering style and commitment to community organizing enhanced the possibility for success. But Moore's plans for the courtroom, like Bond's plans in the electoral arena and SNCC's antipoverty efforts, met unexpected challenges.

It turned out that matters of civil liberties and criminal defense consumed Moore's energies. Harassment by state and local police, courts, and sundry other officials intensified as SNCC became more critical than ever of pillars of government and society. During the same period, SNCC became less cohesive and less disciplined, and consequently an inviting target for law enforcement. Officials tagged real and imagined misdeeds on the organization, on hangers-on, and on hapless bystanders presumed to be lawbreakers. Howard Moore found himself constantly on the defense. Yet, he turned the tables on his opponents and achieved constitutional victories in the federal courts that established the indispensability of civil liberties to civil rights. He secured individual rights for Bond, Carmichael, Ware, and other political dissidents. As important as these civil liberties victories were, they did not directly aid the minority poor in their quest for subsistence—the goal that Moore, like Bond and SNCC, had initially prioritized. Meanwhile, lawsuits that might have succeeded, for example cases that Moore brought to prevent summary evictions of low-income renters, met constitutional roadblocks. Change resulted from the visionary leadership of Bond, Moore, and SNCC's Atlanta Project; but for the black poor, it was not enough. An oppressive system had been destabilized but remained intact.

## BOND'S PROMISE OF A "NEW KIND OF POLITICS"

Julian Bond's election to the Georgia legislature signified a moment of great promise. The potential turned largely on contrasts between the SNCC veteran and A. T. Walden. The twenty-five-year-old Bond campaigned as a Democrat, but he rejected the machine-style, broker politics favored by Walden. For most of his life as a community leader, Walden had asked African Americans to vote as a bloc for the least offensive white Democratic candidate in exchange for a promise that the candidate would protect black interests, as elites defined them. In this decision-making calculus, the problems of the black poor—whether matters of work, housing, politics, or schooling—were never a priority.[9]

Bond rewrote the political playbook in his campaign for state representative. He ran in a district composed of both abjectly poor and middle-class blacks. The easy path to election ran through the middle-class households, where voters already engaged in the political process. Bond chose a different route. In addition to appealing to the customary bloc of voters, he set out to reach the district's destitute citizens. He regarded them as important constituents, although the vast majority had never participated in the political process. Long denied literacy and the right to vote, they knew little about politics. Bond attempted to energize the poor and to create a class of new voters through the simple act of speaking to them. He treated the poor as citizens, and made matters of concern to them central to his campaign. Bond advocated an "alternative politics," a "humanitarian politics, a politics based on principle" and "grounded in the hopes and needs of the very poor."[10]

Bond saw the campaign as a chance to prove that the ordinary citizen had decision-making power, and he formulated his platform after conducting "people's conferences." Bond and his staff walked the streets and canvassed neighborhoods block by block, door to door. He asked the poor citizens of Vine City, a ghetto within the ghetto, to describe their problems and how government could address them. Bond "was *seen* and *known*" on the campaign trail. The candidate's forays into the community represented an entirely new experience for the residents of Vine City. "[L]iterally 100 percent of the people" the campaign canvassed had "*never* had anyone come to their house, sit down and seriously talk to them about their community," noted his campaign manager. Very few people even knew what a state senator was, much less that they were entitled to voice their opinions on public policy issues to their senator.[11]

After canvassing, Bond created a platform tailored to the community's problems. The key planks focused on relieving the neighborhood's economic deprivation. He called for a $2 minimum wage that would cover domestic and restaurant work—jobs that a large number of Vine City residents held—and repeal of right-to-work laws, which banned union membership as a condition of employment. Bond also pledged to support reform of the urban renewal process and abolition of the death penalty, among other initiatives. His campaign slogan: "A vote for Bond is a vote out of bondage." Bond inspired fervent support. He cruised into office, trouncing his primary opponent with 82 percent of the vote and then winning the general election.[12]

Many in SNCC greeted Bond's victory as an indication that SNCC could now transform itself into a political party. Bond's brand of community-centered politics could be replicated across Georgia and throughout the nation. Candidates aligned with the SNCC party would "rally mass support" and gain election to local, state, and federal office. This new breed of elected official would be very different from the typical white liberal Democratic Party official who claimed to support civil rights but in practice sacrificed black interests. The SNCC-backed politicians would raise issues of interest to blacks, especially the poor, that elected officials typically ignored. "Imagine 10 SNCC guys in the Georgia House committed to organizing their districts[,] to using the seats in the House to meet community needs [as] defined by the community," said Bond's campaign manager. Others talked excitedly of replicating Bond's success in other southern cities—Memphis, Nashville, New Orleans, Knoxville, Montgomery, and Birmingham. The dreams of SNCC grew bigger still. The Bond campaign would also provide SNCC with a roadmap for organizing urban centers throughout the North and West. All over the county, "radical candidates" would use elections as "opportunit[ies] for disruption" of politics as usual.[13]

Already, the federal government had engaged the problem of poverty, but on terms that crystallized why adherents to SNCC's brand of insurgent politics should infiltrate government. The centerpiece of President Johnson's "unconditional war on poverty," the Economic Opportunity Act (EOA), became law in August 1964. The EOA established a federal job corps and programs for work training, community action, preschools, community health services, legal aid, and volunteer services. Many proponents considered the EOA, passed just weeks after the enactment of the Civil Rights Act of 1964, the chief vehicle for advancing the aims of the landmark civil rights law. Dr. King called the civil rights and antipoverty legislation "twins," part of a dual approach to combating racial discrimination.[14]

Atlanta—one of the first proving grounds for the War on Poverty—showcased both its potential and its pitfalls. In some cities, the community action programs opened up new avenues for leadership by low-income African Americans. In Atlanta, the poor fared less well. Local officials readily accepted federal antipoverty money, but jealously controlled the decision-making process and the allocation of federal appropriations. Meanwhile, the black middle class wanted its share of government largesse, and fought hard to secure it. Black organizations vigorously lobbied state and local officials for federal antipoverty dollars and for black representation at all levels of antipoverty bureaucracies. Atlanta's Summit Leadership Conference made clear: "[W]e want qualified

Negroes on the professional staffs where plans are developed and decisions made." Similarly, the Atlanta NAACP demanded black employment—patronage, essentially—in "high echelon positions." Ultimately, the lobbying effort paid off: black professionals gained lucrative posts in antipoverty agencies.[15]

By contrast, the black poor, the intended beneficiaries of the antipoverty programs, mostly received intangible rewards: promises of able representation and future benefit. If middle-class blacks gained administrative posts, the Atlanta NAACP president promised, the antipoverty program would be "carried out in good faith" and the "racial problem would be solved." This assumption no doubt proved correct in some instances. But the administration of antipoverty programs by the black middle class on behalf of the poor was not the "maximum feasible participation" of the poor in the War on Poverty that had been envisioned.[16]

The poor seldom participated in decision-making positions, or did so on a significant scale, in Atlanta's antipoverty programs. When employed, lower-income blacks, typically single women, usually worked in the field as "trainees" or "aides," far removed from decision-making. The aides often felt unwelcome and undervalued in EOA program hierarchies. At a charged December 1965 forum, a group of Atlanta aides claimed that EOA administrators discriminated against them in pay and benefits. They also charged that EOA agencies employed professional staff in positions meant for neighborhood people. "The only people who benefit from the program are the highly educated people who already had a high paying job," the *Atlanta Inquirer* concluded. "The poverty program is overlooking the people in poverty." The paper called for an investigation of EOA programs out of concern that it was "unfair" to impoverished people.[17]

When antipoverty programs actually involved poor clients in administration, the experiment proved extraordinarily controversial. An *Atlanta Daily World* headline told the story: "Untrained Poor People Said Hampering Poverty Program." Critics called attempts to include program beneficiaries on oversight committees disastrous. Atlanta's Clarence Coleman, southern director of the National Urban League, offered a telling explanation for the supposed problems. "Membership of these committees often contain 'highly articulate' persons, like top city officials, lawyers and teachers," he said. These elites and the "inexperienced" poor did not mix well. Traditional leaders heaped blame for the difficulties on the poor. Elites often reflexively equated the grassroots' lack of education and expertise with an inability to meaningfully contribute to program design.[18]

Within this context, SNCC seized upon the opportunity to elect Bond and others committed to new politics to state and local government. Like no other, the organization long committed to grassroots leadership could expose the folly of antipoverty programs that marginalized the poor. Bond, blazing the trail for future SNCC candidates, would push for a whole new vision of empowered citizenship for the poor.


## NO SEAT IN THE HOUSE

Before Julian Bond could even begin this ambitious agenda, he experienced a monumental setback. Just after New Year's Day in 1966, Bond and seven other African Americans were set to end white domination of the Georgia house of representatives. Then lightning struck. Bond's would-be colleagues refused to seat him.[19]

A few words, uttered off-the-cuff, precipitated this stupefying turn of events. On January 7, Bond, responding to a reporter's query, expressed support for SNCC's just-issued statement on the Vietnam War. Bond had played no role in drafting the document; nor did he, as communication's director, customarily offer personal views about the organization's policy positions—all the better for the newsman who queried the representative-elect. The statement, issued by SNCC's chairman, John Lewis, characterized the United States' activities in Vietnam as "aggression," and blasted the nation's foreign policy. Two sentences summed up its basic thrust: "We maintain that our country's cry of 'preserve freedom in the world' is a hypocritical mask behind which it squashes liberation movements" that "refuse to be bound by the expediencies of United States cold war policies." It continued, "The United States is no respecter of persons or laws when such persons or laws run counter to its needs or desires." With its statement, SNCC placed itself on the leading edge of the antiwar movement; at the time, the majority of Americans supported the Vietnam War.[20]

The antiwar position that SNCC held sprang from domestic sources—from its experiences in poor communities in the South. The declaration recounted civil rights workers' experiences on the front lines of the battle against Jim Crow and painted a horrid picture of the government's failings. "Our work, particularly in the South, has taught us that the United States government has never guaranteed the freedom of oppressed citizens." Federal officials had stood by while segregationists violently attacked civil rights workers and black locals who only sought to exercise their constitutional rights, the statement said. The terror continued even after passage of the landmark civil rights and voting rights acts. Just days before SNCC had proclaimed its opposition to U.S. foreign policy, yet another staffer had been shot to death in Macon, Georgia; on the day of the murder, a county registrar had brandished a knife at the SNCC worker for attempting to help forty local African Americans register to vote. In SNCC's view, the federal government should have protected these and all other voter registration workers, soldiers on the front lines of the battle to make democracy work. This latest incident and numerous others led to SNCC's claim that the government "is not yet truly determined to end the rule of terror and oppression within its own borders." The statement went on to argue that civil rights workers—domestic freedom fighters—should be exempt from the draft, just the same as Peace Corp volunteers. It did not stop there. It expressed sympathy for those who refused to wage war falsely "in the name of freedom" and avoided the draft.[21]

Bond made his own antiwar, pacifist position crystal clear when the reporter asked for his opinion. Wire reports had claimed that SNCC's John Lewis had urged Americans—in particular, African Americans, disproportionately called to service—to burn their draft cards. Bond insisted that reporters had "distorted" Lewis's statement. The chairman of SNCC had not endorsed any such thing. Georgia's representative-elect then expressed admiration for the "courage" of dissidents who burned draft cards, although he would not, he said, follow suit.[22]

In an "utter surprise" to Bond, his statement set off a storm of criticism. The press agent of SNCC had *himself* become the news. Several white legislators from Georgia's rural hinterlands started a movement to bar Bond from the Georgia house within hours of his controversial utterances. The legislators came together over a dinner of wild hog to discuss ways to "get" Bond; by the end of the meal, their campaign to bar Bond from office was afoot. Bond had committed treason, his opponents claimed, by "giving aid and comfort to the enemy" and advocating the violation of the U.S. Selective Service Act. In view of Bond's endorsement of SNCC's "subversive" statement on Vietnam, there was "no way," one proponent of Bond's ouster proclaimed, that he could "honestly" take his oath of office to uphold the constitutions of the United States and Georgia.[23]

Momentum quickly built against Bond. A long list of white officials, headed by Georgia's governor, echoed the legislators' denunciation of SNCC and criticism of Bond. The representative-elect's "appalling" declarations proved Bond "disloyal" to America and "unqualified" for office. The editor of the *Atlanta Constitution* wrote that Bond had ruined his career as a legislator before it had even begun. The newsman skewered SNCC and the calamitous effect of its rash statement on the civil rights movement. "From now on, when Snick speaks, the Negro suffers." Even Lillian Smith, the white Southern writer, a long-standing foe of segregation and ostracized friend of the civil rights movement, condemned SNCC's stance. Bond's "kind of protest is not my way," she wrote. With so many people against him, the speaker of the Georgia house said, the only chance that Bond had to keep his seat was by "begging and apologizing."[24]

Bond stood pat. "I have done no wrong," he proclaimed in a statement released on the very day the Georgia house convened to decide his fate. "I am right in expressing my views on whatever subject I wish to speak," he said.

> I think it is hypocritical for us to maintain that we are fighting for liberty in other places and we are not guaranteeing liberty to citizens inside the continental United States. I think my responsibility is to oppose things that I think are wrong if they are in Vietnam or New York, or Chicago, or Atlanta, or wherever.[25]

Bond chalked up the attacks on his integrity to his association with SNCC and his fight against segregation, long unpopular in Georgia. In fact, he had fought racism in the Georgia house itself. Four years earlier, Bond and other student activists had sat-in at the segregated galleries of the house chambers. The black students were pushed, shoved, and thrown out. Now, Bond intended to claim his rightful place in the house; he had run for state representative to root out the racial injustice that remained in the state and had legitimately secured election to his seat. "I have promised my constituents that I shall not relinquish the struggle for human dignity," he declared, and "I intend to keep that promise." "I hope," Bond said, "that throughout my life I shall always have the courage to dissent."[26]

Bond's defiance sealed his fate. Rather than mollifying his critics, Bond had hardened his position. On the day of swearing-in, a tall and trim Bond, dressed in a coat, tie, and vest, was the picture of the clean-cut young professional ready to take on the world. But by a lopsided vote of 184 to 12, the Georgia house barred Bond from being sworn into office. Directed to remain seated, he looked on from a distance as other representatives-elect took the oath of office.[27]

Memories from years earlier must have flooded Bond's mind. "Mr. Doorkeeper, get those niggers out of the white section of the gallery," yelled one legislator, when Bond had attempted to desegregate public seating in the legislature. Now, when he had earned the right to integrate not just the gallery but the chamber itself, Bond had been banished from it. The house had made a mockery of democracy and cast a shadow over SNCC's political dreams.[28]

## INTRARACIAL DISSENT ON VIETNAM

Bond's ouster from the legislature quickly became a flashpoint of debate over the Vietnam War. The antiwar stance that SNCC held did not just conflict with the opinion of most Americans. Within the civil rights movement and African-

American communities, opinions diverged widely on whether SNCC's statement and Bond's actions had been wise, just as they differed on the war itself.

The legislature's action smacked of racism and retribution, SNCC and other commentators cried. The overwhelmingly white chamber had denied the constituents of the overwhelming black and largely poor 136th District their representative of choice. In addition to disenfranchising these voters, the move punished SNCC for its past activism, many believed. Dr. Martin Luther King, Jr., agreed. "[W]e have no alternative," he said, "but to interpret this as an attempt to punish a Negro" and an organization that had long protested Georgia's flagrant violations of blacks' rights. Just a few days after Bond's expulsion, King—soon to become an outspoken opponent of the war himself and likewise face criticism for "aiding the enemy"—led a protest march of fifteen hundred in support of the beleaguered legislator.[29]

In standing behind Bond, the SCLC leader bucked majority opinion among African Americans in early 1966. At that time, 85 percent of blacks approved of the administration's policies in Vietnam. Three out of four African Americans supported the draft and believed that the government fairly administered the Selective Service System. Numerous civil rights leaders spoke for these constituents in the wake of the Bond controversy. The NAACP's Roy Wilkins called Bond's expulsion unlawful but made clear that the NAACP did not approve of SNCC's criticism of U.S. foreign policy in Vietnam. Similarly, the head of the National Urban League hailed the valor of black soldiers fighting in Vietnam and cited it as a factor in the steady advance of blacks in American society.[30]

In Atlanta, reported the *Inquirer*, African Americans overwhelmingly opposed SNCC and Bond's antiwar stance. So did the editors of the weekly itself, which Bond had edited for many years. The paper chastised Bond for "permitting reporters to more or less maneuver him into the controversy over Vietnam." He had "acted carelessly" in exercising his freedom of speech, an editorial chided. The *Inquirer* did not endorse the legislature's ouster of Bond, but it did echo the views of Bond's opponents. The organization's antiwar position had potentially given "aid and comfort to the enemy" and had "stabb[ed]" "our soldiers" "in the back." "SNCC may have rendered a serious disservice to our community and to Julian Bond," the *Inquirer* concluded, by inserting itself and the 136th District into the heated debate over American foreign policy.[31]

The *Atlanta Daily World*, which had long been skeptical of SNCC's tactics, criticized the organization and Bond in even more biting terms. The *World* expressed its unequivocal disagreement with SNCC's antiwar stance and Bond's statement. No local leaders—not even fellow representative-elect Grace Towns Hamilton, a family friend of the Bonds—supported the group's "ill-timed" antiwar manifesto, the paper noted. The other blacks set to enter the legislature with Bond had offered only tepid public support. Ultimately, black legislators voted to seat Bond. But they did so reluctantly. Privately, the legislators, and every other prominent black, strongly urged Bond to reconsider his position. Howard Moore, Bond's attorney, recalled:

> The leadership in the African American community was a hundred percent against Julian taking the stand which he took....They had a meeting in Senator Leroy Johnson's house in southwest Atlanta...before the hearing. [T]o a man...they encouraged Julian to recant the statement or certainly apologize for having made the statement.

Many African Americans thought Bond's stance "was dangerous, it was un-American, unpatriotic, probably communist," said Moore. Given the depth of public opinion arrayed against Bond, the *World* predicted, the Bond incident would "hurt the Civil Rights cause" and harm "innocent" blacks.[32]

## Legislative Setback as a Catalyst for Mobilization

The *World*'s forecast may have proved prescient in the long term, but in the short term, SNCC capitalized on the controversy. The development reignited the passions of staff members still upset over what many considered a colossal political defeat in 1964. The Democratic Party's failure to seat the integrated Mississippi Freedom Democratic Party delegation at the 1964 Democratic National Convention had enraged SNCC. Backed by able lawyers, SNCC believed that the seating of the segregated slate of delegates violated the U.S. Constitution's Fourteenth Amendment and the spirit, if not the letter, of the newly enacted Civil Rights Act. After the party's capitulation to Mississippi segregationists, many SNCC workers—who had labored for months to mobilize black voters in the face of abuses of governmental power, bombings, shootings, assaults, and endless threats—lost faith in Democrats and white liberals, generally. A "crisis of confidence" and a "spirit of cynicism and suspicion and mistrust" toward the government "began that week in Atlantic City," SNCC's chairman John Lewis explained.[33]

Now, when the ink on the Voting Rights Act was barely dry, SNCC had witnessed yet another example of blatant white hypocrisy—this one bipartisan. Virtually the entire Georgia legislature, except for a few members, most of whom were black, had turned out Julian Bond. The white power structure's attack on Bond—a black "Prince," as he was called—caused outrage. If

Bond, the dashing scion of such a prestigious family, could be willfully denied his constitutional right to "speak his mind," then no black person could expect the law to protect him. Hence, Bond's ouster held meaning for "Black people all over the South." It indicated the depth of white oppression of blacks in America. The Voting Rights Act and the Civil Rights Act, not to mention numerous federal court precedents mandating equality under law, were no match for the rank discrimination that pervaded society. "Once again," Lewis said, "we were getting screwed," and "the system was making a mockery of justice."[34]

The members of SNCC viewed Bond's expulsion from the legislature as a clarion call to action. As had happened so many times before, when one legal or political avenue closed, the students mobilized and sought other paths through which to pursue their goals. The organization rallied support for Bond, freedom of speech, and world peace. It called on mainstream liberals, academics, and state and federal officials to back Bond's right to take a stand, if not SNCC's antiwar position in full. The "right of every citizen to voice public dissent is a keystone of our democracy," it urged.[35]

In its appeals, SNCC pointedly rejected critics' claims that it had no stake in U.S. foreign policy. "International trade had brought us to America," one activist explained, and SNCC, the premier black freedom organization, had an obligation to speak out on all international affairs, including the war. The strikingly high rate at which blacks, both urban and rural youths, fought and died in Vietnam made the conflict a high-stakes proposition, in SNCC's view. African Americans constituted 9.8 percent of the military forces in Vietnam in 1967, but made up 20 percent of combat units. Blacks constituted 25 percent of all American casualties in late 1965, just before the Bond seating controversy. Black soldiers had achieved a kind of integration, a bloodstained variety, in Vietnam, even as black civilians still fought for freedom in the United States. The linkages between domestic and foreign policy could hardly be missed.[36]

For his part, Bond launched a national media tour in which he defended his right to dissent and his pacifism. On the NBC news program *Meet the Press*, Bond located the origins of his pacifism in his education at a Quaker school in Pennsylvania in 1957. "I don't approve of anyone anywhere under any circumstances engag[ing] in violence," he explained. He spoke before audiences at the United Nations, in numerous American cities, and abroad. The young legislator's plight became an international cause célèbre. The Georgia house had given SNCC, Julian Bond, and the antiwar movement a "shot in the arm."[37]

## COMMUNITY ORGANIZING IN THE
## "SOUTHERN URBAN GHETTO"

The legislature's decision to deny Bond his seat also jumpstarted the Atlanta Project, a new SNCC community organizing venture. This particular project began as a result of Bond's unseating, but SNCC had long turned to organizing, a labor movement tactic, to pursue its joint political and antipoverty goals. Organizing—a "slow and respectful" approach to personal, political, and community empowerment—involved several interlocking steps. Workers listened to everyday people discuss their lives and problems; they educated people about their citizenship rights; and they persuaded them to cast off mental chains imposed by Jim Crow that undermined activism. The most effective organizers possessed emotional and interpersonal intelligence in abundance and embraced a range of roles and personas. They had to be "morale boosters, teachers, welfare agents, transportation coordinators, canvassers, public speakers, negotiators, [and] lawyers."[38]

Through community organizing SNCC sought to plant "seeds of change." As they built relationships with the poor, volunteers nurtured citizens' submerged leadership abilities. Workers in SNCC expected that impoverished and poorly educated blacks, if given encouragement and taught the necessary skills, would move from the margins of society and become energetic stakeholders in the democratic process. The poor would become agenda setters and implement public policy. They would pursue needed economic and social supports and educational opportunities. Local people would turn to electoral politics, cooperatives, and alternative or "parallel" institutions, such as new political parties or "freedom schools," to replace dysfunctional state institutions. Ultimately, organized communities would pursue concrete forms of equality, including a bundle of property and personal entitlements: decent jobs, income supports, housing, and education, as well as political representation and participation. The fierce commitment of SNCC to participatory democracy set it apart from virtually every other contemporary black advocacy group. The NAACP, LDF, and SCLC all "operated on the assumption that leadership came from an educated, professional, or clerical class." By contrast, organizing proceeded from the assumption that ordinary people—the grassroots—should lead their own communities in the struggle against injustice.[39]

During the period 1962 through 1965, SNCC's organizing tactic flowered. SNCC organized in rural areas such as southwestern Georgia and the Mississippi Delta. Now, the Bond controversy had created an opportunity to deploy the tactic in the "southern urban ghetto." The Atlanta Project would serve as a test case for organizing in the cities. Like Bond's new kind of politics, the Atlanta Project, if successful, would be replicated nationwide.[40]

In Atlanta's Vine City neighborhood SNCC established the project's base of operations. The filth, squalor, and misery afflicting Vine City's fifteen hundred destitute residents stood out even among slums. The SNCC workers' organizing effort included Vine City and similar neighborhoods, poor black enclaves with names that often suggested the hardscrabble character of life there: Buttermilk Bottom, Mechanicsville, Cabbage Town. Staffers investigated conditions in these "forgotten" neighborhoods of Atlanta. The areas shared none of the characteristics of the places that glossy Chamber of Commerce pamphlets advertised to northern businesses—skyscrapers, industry, and local proprietors providing the goods and services needed for everyday existence. The people of these neighborhoods inhabited overcrowded wooden shacks with leaky roofs on unpaved streets overrun by vermin living in and feeding on the garbage and trash in the streets. Municipal services were almost unknown. Sewage disposal and trash removal were either nonexistent or inadequate. There were few traffic lights, stop signs, sidewalks, or crosswalks. In short, there was a complete lack of the conveniences of modern living taken for granted in other parts of the city. This was not the image of Atlanta about which apostles of the "New South" boasted.[41]

Hopes for success nevertheless ran high. These neighborhoods seemed promising locales for project staff to "tap and sustain the energies of the people locked up in the city ghettoes." If the black poor could gain a foothold in society through political empowerment anywhere, it would be in Atlanta. Unlike the rural backwaters where SNCC typically worked, the poor neighborhoods of Atlanta existed in tandem with significant black wealth, independent black institutions, and a city government with a liberal mayor primed to address racial inequality. Moreover, the systematic violence and intimidation that had undermined organizing efforts in rural areas did not occur in Atlanta. Here, SNCC staffers believed, while it would not be easy to rally the poor in defense of themselves, the task would be less daunting than it had been elsewhere.[42]

## The Project in Action

The Atlanta Project organized the community to demand "economic justice." Bill Ware, codirector of the project, brought deep commitment to the task. He developed an acute sensitivity to the conditions and worldview of working-class blacks in his youth. Born near Natchez, Mississippi, during the Great Depression, Ware grew up in a rigidly segregated rural area. There, he witnessed the indignities of Jim Crow and "economic slavery" firsthand.[43]

Ware was raised by his paternal grandparents, who worked as sharecroppers. As a young boy, Ware stood watch as his family members worked the fields. The workdays ran extraordinarily long. He saw his grandfather "go out and work very early in the morning, even before sun up." The older man plowed rows of crop with only a mule's aid; a tractor far exceeded his means. Lunch breaks were unheard of; from time to time, Ware's grandmother would bring food to the field, where his grandfather would quickly eat to avoid losing time away from work. Even so, Ware's grandparents fared better than some other black agricultural workers in the area. The young boy was "traumatized" by vagrants roaming the countryside in search of food and shelter.[44]

Though his grandparents could not offer Ware material advantage, they did provide "an umbrella of protection" from virulently racist whites. The couple nurtured his ambition, even as they remained mired in the sharecropping system. In a county without public schools for blacks, they ensured that Ware attained an education in parochial schools. The old man counseled his grandson to pursue a better life, even as he labored. Under the glare of the sun, as he tended the crops, the grandfather pushed the youngster toward a higher calling for himself and his people. "He would be plowing the mules," and he would call out to the other field workers. "'See that little boy there?'" he would say. "'He's going to go off to the North, become a doctor and bring medicine back to the people.'" Ware never became a doctor, but he did "go North." He graduated from St. John's College in Minnesota. Thereafter, he dedicated himself to fighting the desperate poverty and racial oppression that plagued the lives of the black poor, whether in rural Mississippi or urban Georgia.[45]

On a typical day, Ware and the project's small staff, mostly black and working class, canvassed the unpaved streets of Vine City. The staff conducted workshops and public meetings in which they educated people about the utility of picketing, sit-ins, rent strikes, boycotts, and political activism. Volunteers explained their intention to "work for the emergence of a series of political candidates of Julian Bond caliber and integrity" in state and county elections. With such people in office, residents would command attention from decision-makers and make the political process work for them.[46]

Project workers also offered practical solutions to specific problems plaguing poor communities. Medical care, education, employment, welfare, and housing policies topped the agendas. To address these problems, the project turned to untapped resources and unconventional tactics. Workers informed the residents about federal work and educational programs. Citizens in Vine City—a target population for War on Poverty programs—often knew nothing about them. The SNCC workers demystified the governmental process for the poor. Since the search for safe and affordable housing dominated the lives of residents, it also consumed much of the project's energies. Again, staff helped Vine City's poor mainly by giving them access to knowledge about government. They informed residents about city agencies charged with hearing complaints about unsafe and dilapidated housing. In addition, they unlocked the legal process for residents by describing the due process rights owed to them before an eviction could occur.[47]

### Attacking Slum Lords Inside and Outside of Court

Project members practiced lay lawyering on a variety of fronts, but especially in the housing context, where the community's need for services was perhaps most urgent. The housing initiative unfolded in the streets and in the courts. Julian Bond aided and energized the project's efforts, even as he battled his colleagues to claim his seat in the legislature.[48]

The project launched a "war on Atlanta's slums" after a cold snap in late January 1966 exposed deplorable conditions on Markham Street—already well known to city government—to the reproachful eyes of a wider audience. The primitive dwellings there lacked basic features that separated human existence from that of animals. Without electricity, heat, or indoor plumbing, inhabitants were left to freeze in subzero temperatures. Bond demanded attention to the plight of his cold, dirty, and hungry constituents. He wired Mayor Allen with a request that the city fulfill its responsibility to ensure that every citizen in Atlanta had adequate housing. "There is no justification," Bond wrote, "for houses without heat." Shrewdly, Bond also reached out to the American Red Cross. Treating the Markham Street crisis like a natural disaster, Bond requested emergency provisions from the relief agency—blankets, food, and generators. Local and national civil rights and relief agencies chipped in and provided emergency resources, and the immediate crisis subsided. The incident demonstrated the advances that an organized community could make with the aid of a politician committed to the poor.[49]

The arrival of Dr. Martin Luther King, Jr., in Atlanta ensured that attention remained focused on the problem of inadequate housing. King recently had visited Chicago, where he decried the "economic exploitation" and "powerlessness" trapping the black poor in urban ghettos and announced plans for a new campaign there. King now toured the ghettos in his own hometown, in the vicinity of his childhood home. He took a walking tour of Vine City, amid SNCC pickets bearing signs reading "Slum Lords Must Go!" Among the sights he witnessed: a building containing eight families who shared a single bathroom; trash-strewn streets; rows of shoddy houses ready to fall down; and a weeping mother in a dimly lit two-room dwelling heated by a woodstove that she shared with her five children. The woman begged the minister to leave, lest her landlord, who "said for me not to talk to nobody," throw her out. King declared conditions in the neighborhood "appalling." They were, he said, the worst he had ever seen, even more horrendous than the worst slums of Chicago. Remarkably, King exclaimed, "I had no idea people were living in Atlanta, Georgia, in such conditions. This is a shame on the community." As if to underscore the point, a day after King departed, a fifty-year-old black man was found dead in an unheated shack within a block of the area that King had visited. The weekend cold had taken his life.[50]

King's visit signaled the urgency of the slum housing situation, and the Atlanta Project capitalized on the attention the minister had drawn to the issue. The staff announced its intention to obliterate the city's slums. The project made a powerful comparison. "Atlanta landlords have the same relation to their tenants as industrial bosses had to their workers before unions, the Taft Hartley [Act] and child labor laws," SNCC declared. In a press conference staged on the notorious Markham Street, Julian Bond hammered the point home. Markham Street, he said, was "symbolic of many streets in the black ghettos of this Nation" where "greedy landlords" made "huge profit" off of the misery of the poor. "[T]he irony," he wrote, "is that Vine City should exist in the geographical boundaries of the United States, the richest country on the globe." The SNCC staff hoped with their campaign to put an end to the unequal power relations between tenants and landlords.[51]

The staff embraced a range of pressure tactics, including demonstrations and boycotts, in its effort to organize the ghetto against "slum lords." But it most favored the rent strike, an audacious and innovative tactic. In a rent strike, aggrieved tenants withheld rental payments until landlords made needed repairs to address substandard housing conditions. The tactic allowed SNCC to achieve three interlocking goals: it sought to empower the poor to seek concrete changes in their everyday lives, to dramatize the injustices of life in the ghetto, and to pressure both private parties and local government to address the need for safe, affordable housing for low-income citizens.[52]

In February, SNCC led a rent strike against one of the city's most notorious slumlords, Joe Shaffer. The SNCC workers exposed the landlord's sordid practices. He made exorbitant profits by crowding numerous families into his buildings and seldom made repairs to his dilapidated properties. Above that, he ran "a plantation-like" economy on his properties, SNCC charged, simultaneously functioning as "landlord, employer, grocer, creditor, sheriff, judge, and jury over the people who live on his property."[53]

However, the rent strike tactic contained serious flaws even when employed against the worst landlords: the law provided limited relief, and the relief provided could be counterproductive. As a rule, renters did not enjoy a contractual right to demand that a landlord make major repairs. Tenants took the premises of rental properties as they were unless a statute imposed enforceable obligations on landlords to maintain property. In the mid-1960s, few jurisdictions imposed such obligations. Atlanta's building code mostly covered building defects. It *did* set minimum standards for occupancy: a supply of running water, watertight roofs, plumbing, and general "cleanliness." Tenants also enjoyed a legal right to property fit for habitation. But the municipality seldom enforced these code requirements. When it did, a different problem arose: housing code enforcement could leave the poor homeless. Tenants could be compelled to vacate property declared unfit for human habitation—an unsatisfactory "solution" for residents with few resources and housing options. The SNCC staff could only hope for the best: that the strike would embarrass public officials and thereby increase access to existing public housing or stimulate the construction of new private developments that included housing affordable for the poor. Meanwhile, the decision to engage in a rent strike was a risky proposition.[54]

And, in fact, SNCC's rent strike produced mixed results. Joe Shaffer, the slumlord that the project targeted, retaliated. He waged a door-to-door campaign against SNCC, promising eviction to those who spoke to SNCC workers. His threats worked. Many residents refused to participate in the strike or otherwise complain about the terrible conditions in which they lived.[55]

Moreover, SNCC's campaign attracted little support, if any, from other civil rights and civic groups. Many considered rent strikes "radical" and a violation of landlords' property rights. Still, few opposed the initiative outright. In principle, more pragmatic leaders supported the students' goal of relieving the suffering of people living in the city's ghettos. A broad consensus existed that poverty, a plague that disproportionately beset blacks, should be addressed. Nevertheless, when SNCC asked the ASLC to support the strike, ASLC responded with a resolution that affirmed the need for "vigorous enforce[ment]" of existing housing codes, but it stopped short of supporting rent strikes themselves. More predictably, the *Atlanta Daily World* openly criticized the tactic.[56]

Mayor Allen, who two years earlier had testified in favor of the Civil Rights Act and boasted of his understanding of the harms caused by Jim Crow, now showed little leadership. He said SNCC's rent strike was not "the American way." Yet, Allen offered few alternatives to the protest. The mayor did not follow through on his promise to rid Atlanta of slums, a vow he had made in early 1965. No massive assault on dilapidated housing occurred under Allen. And steps that the city did take often proved wrongheaded. The city cracked down on some slum areas by condemning numerous properties. But Atlanta razed slums without ensuring replacement housing; predictably, the city's slum clearance policies resulted in "Negro removal."[57]

Meanwhile, SNCC also lost a legal battle to make the eviction process fairer for indigent citizens. Georgia's eviction statute provided for a speedy, summary eviction proceeding. A tenant could only temporarily halt a proceeding based on alleged nonpayment of rent by posting a bond, payable to the landlord for the sum in dispute at trial. If the tenant could not pay the amount in question, he was summarily evicted. Howard Moore, Jr., SNCC's general counsel, attacked the statute in state court. Moore argued that the statute's bond requirement violated the U.S. Constitution's Fourteenth Amendment. In effect, Georgia's law compelled a poor person to pay for access to the courts: one could only challenge an unlawful eviction if one were wealthy enough to afford to do so—an outlandish proposition for tenants in neighborhoods such as Vine City. The Constitution, Moore argued, plainly barred such outright discrimination against the poor. Moore's argument went nowhere in the Georgia courts. The trial courts rejected Moore's claims. And, in perverse logic, the Georgia Supreme Court affirmed the trial courts' rulings on the ground that Moore's clients had already been evicted—making the issue moot. In other words, his clients were too poor to raise poverty as an issue before the court. Moore filed an appeal to the U.S. Supreme Court. But the Court refused to hear the appeal.[58]

Overall, SNCC's initial campaign against slumlords, whether waged in the streets or in the court, did not materially change conditions on Markham Street. But the benefits of community organizing could not be measured by short-term gains, or the lack of them, alone. The campaign had energized the Atlanta Project and its target community. With additional organizing, the Atlanta Project staff believed, it could mount a citywide tenants' rights movement.[59]

The plan never materialized on such a grand scale, however. External attacks and internal dissension hampered SNCC as never before. Julian Bond's seat in the Georgia legislature remained in legal limbo. Because of its opposition to the Vietnam War SNCC remained subject to political attack. Rather than tamping down the controversy, the organization pursued another. Led by the Atlanta Project, SNCC embraced black power in mid-1966. This turn of events further divided the interracial organization, already less cohesive than it had been in its early days. The law and the organizing movement—as well as the poor themselves—took a back seat amid the ideological conflagration, interpersonal conflict, external scrutiny, and state surveillance and harassment that accompanied SNCC's black power phase.

## STOKELY CARMICHAEL AND BLACK POWER COME TO ATLANTA

Stokely Carmichael, a singular presence, stood at the center of SNCC's internal transformation. Perhaps the most charismatic figure in the movement, Carmichael, SNCC's new chairman as of May 1966, was "brash, beautiful, brilliant," one SNCC worker summed up. His fiery, spellbinding rhetoric showcased his immense intellect. Tall, slender, and physically striking, Carmichael was the "person sculptors would seek as a model for a statue of a Nubian god," said another.[60]

Carmichael's background inspired his strong sense of self and nurtured his passion for racial justice. He was born in Port-of-Spain, Trinidad, a British colony that would remain under England's thumb until 1962. Carmichael's working-class family, descendents of slaves, celebrated its African roots and Caribbean identity. His father championed Trinidad's movement against colonialism. When Carmichael moved to the Bronx, New York as a pre-teen, the traditions, tastes, sounds, and activist politics of the distant Caribbean island of his birth lived on in his new home. Yet, the young boy readily adjusted to his new environment. He took pleasure in the cultural vibrancy of New York City and excelled in overwhelmingly white schools. He won a coveted seat at the prestigious Bronx High School of Science and received a remarkable political education there. He attended meetings of the Youth Communist League—even as McCarthyism raged—studied Marxism, attended peace rallies, and embraced socialism. At the same time, he immersed himself in African-American politics, culture, and intellectual life, centered in Harlem.[61]

These formative experiences followed Carmichael to college, where his political passion, intellect, and charismatic personality blossomed. He chose Howard University, the historically black college in Washington, D.C., over Harvard, where many assumed his prodigious talents would take him. Carmichael's pan-African worldview became more firmly rooted amid interactions with ethnic African and Caribbean immigrant students at Howard during the opening years of the 1960s. Carmichael also gleefully witnessed the dawn of the African liberation movement during college. At the same time, Howard gloried in producing the Talented Tenth, not least among them the lawyers who had won the historic school desegregation decision. Its faculty featured a group of esteemed, politically activist black intellectuals. In this environment, suffused with African and African American pride, Carmichael's awareness of parallels in the African and African American struggles against race-based oppression, and his belief in a race-conscious liberation politics, grew.[62]

As a freshman at Howard, Carmichael joined the Nonviolent Action Group a supporter of the nascent civil rights struggle and SNCC affiliate. He could not long observe the movement from afar. He participated in the Freedom Rides. In this the daring campaign, interracial groups tested compliance with Supreme Court decisions that mandated desegregation of interstate transportation by riding together on buses that traveled from D.C. to New Orleans. Carmichael's activism landed him, at age nineteen, in Mississippi's notorious Parchman prison farm. After college graduation, Carmichael went to work full-time for SNCC.[63]

Carmichael made an indelible mark on the movement through community organizing. In 1965, Carmichael organized an independent political party among destitute and disenfranchised African Americans in Lowndes County, Alabama. Initially called the Lowndes County Freedom Organization (LCFO), the group later became known as the Black Panther Party because of its ballot symbol. The LCFO advocated armed selfdefense against white racial terrorists and, in a state where a plantation economy and mentality persisted, demanded blacks' rightful share of political and economic power.[64]

Carmichael's audacity, his agile intellectualism, and his unabashed race-consciousness contrasted sharply with the ways of John Lewis, whom the twenty-five-year-old organizer succeeded as SNCC's chairman in May 1966. Lewis, a mild-mannered, plain-spoken, religious son of a Tennessee share-cropper, personified the courage, simplicity, and gentle spirit that SNCC found in many black southerners. Lewis had emerged as SNCC's chairman in 1963, after his leadership in the Nashville group of activists who had zealously embraced nonviolence, and gave SNCC its direction during the initial sit-ins. But by the middle of 1966, Lewis looked like a leader of the past rather than of SNCC's future. A vocal contingent of SNCC's staff—headed by the Atlanta Project—now embraced an ideal of black-controlled groups allied in struggle against persistently racist institutions. They called SNCC's initial goal of building an interracial democracy in coalition with enlightened whites impossible, and nonviolent direct action, the strategy pioneered by Lewis, irrelevant. Lewis lost favor as a consequence of this ideological shift. Stokely Carmichael, the LCFO organizer, embodied SNCC's future. Many staffers felt an unrepresentative "mob" deposed Lewis in an unfair election and denounced the changing of the guard as "tragic."[65]

Under Carmichael, SNCC embraced "black power." Carmichael first popularized the slogan during a June 1966 march staged after a racist mob shot James Meredith, who had won acclaim when he desegregated Ole Miss (the University of Mississippi) four years earlier. Before an audience of six hundred, Carmichael expressed his frustration over persistent racism and called for "black power for black people." He galvanized the crowd, which roared its approval, chanting "black power" in response to each call. The voice of black dissent now had a name, but what did it mean? Different observers imputed different meanings to black power, prompting Dr. King to call it an unfortunate choice of words. Carmichael equated black power with cultural pride, political autonomy, and institution building. At the same time, he stressed that the new philosophy took a tone appropriate to the oppression of "young black people in the urban ghetto." The integrationist rhetoric of the old civil rights movement had hidden, or ignored, the suffering in the ghetto and black disgust with white hypocrisy. On other occasions, Carmichael associated black power with an economic critique of the country. He emphasized that the process of black liberation required the country's "economic foundations" to be "shaken." Carmichael also insisted that black power was not antiwhite or revolutionary. Rather, it was a call for blacks to travel down the same path that white ethnic groups had taken to gain a foothold in politics and the economy. Blacks likewise had to "close ranks" before "enter[ing] the open society." An empowered and unified black community could then form political coalitions with whites and negotiate from a position of strength.[66]

Even before Carmichael embraced "black power," the Atlanta Project had written a position paper advocating race-consciousness. In the paper, Ware argued that racial appeals and organizing the ghettos went hand in hand. A year in Africa, a "turning point" in Ware's life, inspired his point of view. In 1962, Ware had joined the Peace Corps. He was posted in Ghana five years after it became the first African nation to gain independence from the British Empire. The "dignity" of the Ghanaian people and their vibrant culture impressed Ware. He witnessed numerous celebrations of kinship, replete with the dancing and festiveness that is a part of the rhythm of African life. When Ware returned to his native Mississippi a year later, his African experience followed and shaped him. His memories of Ghana formed the core of his understanding of African-American freedom. Well before it became fashionable, he wore African garb and valued culture as an arena of struggle against racism. In Atlanta, Ware did not initially organize the group around a cultural agenda, but in 1966, his cultural agenda emerged. His love for African cultures and the idea of African unity translated into a call for race-consciousness in the American movement for racial justice.[67]

With African nations' struggle against colonialism in mind, Ware wrote that the dismal conditions of the ghettoes laid bare the brutality of a white-controlled society. Whites had left blacks to wallow in slums. People consigned to ghettos would only respond to rhetoric that recognized their racial subordination and appreciated their cultural contributions: they would heed the call to unite to gain "black power." Black power would mean black control of all institutions that shaped black life—the police department, the school board, the welfare department, the housing authorities, credit unions, corner groceries. Blacks must move from subservience to dominance in all of these contexts, the position paper argued. Hence, he concluded, the "biggest obstacle" to the pursuit of black liberation was white participation in, and bankrolling of, the civil rights movement. "If we are to proceed toward true liberation, we must cut ourselves off from white people," Ware wrote. No white person could be trusted because all whites in the United States, long a violently white supremacist regime, had been born and bred in racism. Ware advocated expelling whites from SNCC— each and every one of them, no matter how seemingly loyal. Before 1966 closed, he would get his wish.[68]

It came as no surprise that the overwhelming majority of whites greeted the advent of black power with shock and outrage. The rhetoric, all of it—whatever the fine distinctions made by Stokely Carmichael, Bill Ware, or the countless other interpreters of the term—stung and offended. The *Washington Post* called black power an "expression of race hatred," its proponents "black supremacists." Many commentators, who had long warned of the movement's excesses, seemed eager to view black power in the worst possible light. Many black leaders leapt to the defense not of SNCC's black power faction but of whites who viewed black power as a scourge. The NAACP headed the list of SNCC's detractors. Roy Wilkins charged, "No matter how endlessly they try to explain it, the term 'black power' means antiwhite power." Thurgood Marshall, now solicitor general of the United States, echoed Wilkins's sentiments. He called black power "Jim Crow thinking." Dr. King was sympathetic to SNCC's call for black empowerment, but said its terminology seemed to endorse the "evil" of "black supremacy." Bayard Rustin, an architect of the acclaimed 1963 March on Washington, called black power a devastating development that would "ravage" the entire civil rights movement.[69]

In Atlanta, the mainstream leaders with whom SNCC had long been in a fragile alliance spoke out against black power, as well. The ASLC and the NAACP branch categorically condemned violence and lawlessness, and black power's association with them. "The way to protest is set forth in the framework of the Constitution and all should work to see that it is preserved and honored," the groups declared. A long list of community stalwarts, including Senator Leroy Johnson, Walden's protégé, signed the statement. They concluded with a warning to black power advocates: "No man" and "no group" can "go it alone." Both the *Atlanta Daily World* and the *Atlanta Inquirer* published editorials slamming black power as well.[70]

However, the most devastating criticisms of black power came from within SNCC itself. John Lewis, who resigned from SNCC a few months after Carmichael ousted him as chairman, deplored his beloved organization's descent into talk of separatism. Reports surfaced that Julian Bond, absorbed in a legal battle with the Georgia legislature over his endorsement of SNCC's antiwar statement, also was deeply concerned about the organization's direction. In a conversation with Lewis, Bond was more direct: "The crazies are taking over," he quipped, and vowed to soon resign from SNCC. In the months ahead, numerous other volunteers would turn away from the organization.[71]

Whatever the conceptual merits of black power, much of the rhetoric undermined SNCC. Many shapers of public opinion viewed the term as inflammatory and recoiled against it. The backlash impeded the organization's ability to reach its programmatic goals, in particular community organizing in the ghettos of Atlanta and other cities. Donations to SNCC drastically decreased after its turn to black power, leaving the organization barely able to function. Carmichael, the consummate organizer, spent most of his time explicating the new terminology rather than engaging in fieldwork. The question of whether SNCC now condoned violence dominated many of these conversations. Goaded and goading, Carmichael made contradictory statements on the matter. He merely justified self-defense against violent whites, Carmichael claimed. But in the same breath, he lambasted "violent white power" cloaked in the authority of law enforcement. He sometimes used the term "white racist cops," but other times called law enforcement "dirty cracker cops." He also said that he hoped that SNCC's programs would make blacks' "initiation" of violence "unnecessary," leaving open the possibility that violence might be necessary. Ultimately, Carmichael said, SNCC could not control black communities. He laid final responsibility for black-initiated violence on whites.[72]

Within the context of ongoing urban riots, Carmichael's ambiguity struck a nerve. The riots had begun in Harlem in 1964 and spread to dozens of cities, generating millions of dollars in property damages, not to mention injuries and loss of life. Critics feared that Carmichael's rhetoric would spark more unrest. "Pouring gasoline on a blazing fire can lead only to a conflagration," one editorialist warned. Whatever the problems of the urban poor, "[t]hey are not licensed to riot." Indeed, a *Newsweek* poll, commissioned in the wake of persistent rioting and of SNCC's cry for black power, showed that 63 percent of whites now opposed even peaceful civil rights demonstrations. Whites' already thin patience with black demands for redress had become thinner still. As the summer of 1966 turned to autumn, the controversies over black power, urban riots, and the continued legitimacy of blacks' grievances converged and boiled over in Atlanta, with Stokely Carmichael on the scene.[73]

## Riot

The powder keg exploded on September 6, 1966, in the Summerhill neighborhood, a slum area that sat in the shadow of a new $18 million sports stadium. The police shooting of an unarmed black man—Harold Prather, a father of four—triggered the chaos. A consensus soon emerged within the neighborhood that the officer had shot the young man without justification. In the minds of local residents, the situation fit a pattern of police brutality: the shooting was just one of a long list of recent incidents in which trigger-happy cops devalued black lives. The residents determined to stage a protest march against the police and the shooting.[74]

After he learned of the episode, Carmichael visited the area and issued a statement for a radio broadcast decrying the shooting and urging citizen protest. "We are tired of these shootings," he said, and promised to "mount a protest and tear up and turn inside out the city until these incidents have stopped." When asked to clarify his comments, he explained: "Well, I think the black people of this country are afraid to protest, and legitimately so.... [T]hey must be urged... to come out of that fear, to wake up, to tear up that fear." Back at the office, SNCC staff urged the chairman not to return to the scene of the Prather shooting. They were afraid that Carmichael, well known and already a flashpoint for criticism, would become a target for police retribution.[75]

Bill Ware arrived on the scene instead. Ware cruised the neighborhood in a SNCC sound truck. Over the loudspeaker, he invited residents to share their observations about the Prather shooting and police treatment of blacks. A few people took the microphone and denounced police brutality. By some accounts, Ware also expressed support for the protest demonstration already in the works; by other accounts, he actively drummed up support for a protest against police "killing black people." Like everyone else, he assumed that Prather had died from his wounds. Ware continued his pronouncements for only a short time. Before he knew it, police officers had arrested him for operating the truck without the proper permit and placed him in a police wagon.[76]

Later that afternoon, when four hundred angry residents of Summerhill marched in the streets, the city dispatched black officers to the scene to control the crowd. The officers failed in their efforts to disperse the crowd. The police then sent in reinforcements—an all-white contingent of officers and state troopers who wheeled into the neighborhood with lights flashing and brandishing guns. The white officers' arrival unleashed the residents' fury. "Why the guns?" "Why the guns?" crowd members shouted repeatedly. Some again hurled rocks, bricks, sticks, and bottles.[77]

Mayor Allen soon arrived on the scene, but ultimately, force tamed the crowd. Officers in riot gear fired arms into the air, drove their vehicles into the crowd, clubbed bystanders, and teargassed residents. The gas knocked people to the ground and left others gasping for air. Children cried and choked on the gas, along with others uninvolved in the fracas, as the gas wafted into their homes. The police entered the homes of some residents, fired more tear gas guns, and dragged people into police wagons.[78]

At day's end, fifteen people had been injured, several cars had been damaged, and seventy-five people had been arrested. But no one had died, including Prather, who eventually recovered from his wounds. And there had been no looting or shooting. Atlanta's first taste of social disorder during the 1960s had not approached the level of destruction that had gripped Los Angeles and other cities since 1964.[79]

Nevertheless, recriminations were swift, and SNCC bore the brunt of criticism. Mayor Allen led the charges. He accused "outside agitators" in SNCC of deliberately instigating the violence in Summerhill. Allen fingered Carmichael as the source of the problem. The mayor accused SNCC's chairman of "stir[ring] the residents up" with "lies" about the police. He promised to put SNCC "out of business." Police Chief Jenkins also placed blame squarely on SNCC's shoulders. He claimed that the "present" SNCC consisted "mostly of criminals, hoodlums, and outlaws of all types." "It is now the Non-student Violent Committee," he sneered. Governor Sanders called on the courts to punish the "merchants of discord and violence." Eugene Patterson, editor of the *Atlanta Constitution*, wrote: "When Stokely Carmichael's crowd finally got a police shooting to play with, they stirred up" the crowd "as skillfully as white demagogues used to get a night ride going." Hearing these reports, Congressman Wayne Hays, a Democrat from Ohio, called for a federal crackdown on Carmichael and his "anarchist group," which he claimed had also incited riots in Cleveland. Carmichael "belongs behind bars," the Congressman said to applause in the House, and the "quicker we get him there the better off this country is going to be."[80]

The most influential African Americans echoed the reactions of the white establishment. The most direct attack came from a minister, Rev. O. W. Davis, who labeled Carmichael "an albatross around our necks—a parasite on the community." Rev. William Holmes Borders agreed. "One man is giving us hell. We've got to stop him before he stops us." The ASLC voted overwhelmingly to express confidence in Mayor Allen's leadership. The group warned Summerhill residents not to be "use[d]" as "pawns in any evil plot." Heartbroken, Dr. Martin Luther King, Jr., called the riot morally unjustifiable, as well as counterproductive. Yet, he understood riots as the "desperate language of the unheard" and did not assign blame to SNCC for the confrontation.[81]

But residents of Atlanta's ghettos—the very people in whose name SNCC now championed black power—leveled the most poignant rebuke of the organization. Within days of the riot, a group of Summerhill citizens formed a committee to "save" their neighborhood from further violence. In a meeting with city aldermen, the group resolved to keep "outside agitators," thinly veiled code for SNCC, from interfering in neighborhood affairs. Black workers in an antipoverty program near Summerhill formed a "Good Neighborhood" club, pledged to uphold "law and order," and indicated that SNCC was not welcome in the area. By far the most dramatic repudiation of SNCC occurred in Vine City—home of SNCC's Atlanta Project. There, residents staged an "anti–black power rally," signed petitions urging SNCC to decamp from the neighborhood, and burned a table set up to collect bail money for SNCC staff arrested during the Summerhill disturbance.[82]

Another blow came when Julian Bond—a cofounder of SNCC—resigned from the organization. Bond called the Summerhill disturbances "unfortunate," but claimed to have quit SNCC for "personal reasons." Newspapers reported that Bond resigned under "sharp pressure" from constituents and family to dissociate himself from SNCC, which was seen as spiraling out of control.[83]

On the same day that Bond resigned, police officers descended upon SNCC's office in the dark of night. They arrested Carmichael at midnight, confined him to the city jail, and charged him with disorderly conduct and inciting to insurrection and riot. The police also charged other SNCC workers, including Bill Ware, with inciting to riot. Later, the police department announced that it might also charge Carmichael with insurrection itself—a crime punishable by death.[84]

Released from jail pending trial, Carmichael—now famous the world over and constantly in demand—embarked on a nationwide speaking tour. Instead of toning down his rhetoric, he ramped it up. Carmichael castigated "black traitors" and "white racist cops." And he lambasted "courts full of white hate."[85]

## CIVIL RIGHTS AND CIVIL LIBERTIES
## IN THE FEDERAL COURTS

The fates of Stokely Carmichael, William Ware, Julian Bond, and SNCC itself intertwined in the fall of 1966. The officers of SNCC looked at the legal troubles of both Carmichael and Bond and saw a racist plot against SNCC's dissident politics. Executive secretary James Forman claimed that SNCC confronted nothing less than a national conspiracy to undermine it. The organization's civil rights work and its stand against the "sending of black mercenaries to fight an illegal war" in Vietnam had set the power structure against it.[86]

True enough, both Carmichael and Bond had taken stands that riled majority opinion. Each had been mouthpieces of SNCC, as the organization experienced a precipitous decline in favor among opinion makers. State and local authorities tagged both the black pacifism of Bond and the black power of Carmichael as socially deviant, unpatriotic, and illegal. It fell to the federal courts to determine whether the legal norms embodied in the U.S. Constitution's First Amendment and the social norms of the state of Georgia could be reconciled. As the trials of these two symbols of the black counterculture took center stage SNCC's antipoverty agenda and the citizens in Atlanta's ghettos receded into the background.

## "The Tenth Black Lawyer in the State"

Howard Moore, Jr., SNCC's lawyer—a charismatic native son of Atlanta—anchored the legal teams in each case. Until the mid-1960s, Moore had been an important but less well-known figure in the local civil rights bar, as he worked his way from the status of newly admitted attorney to that of Donald Hollowell's protégé. Now, however, he undertook the cases of a lifetime and played a leading role in the black freedom struggle.

Born in 1932, Moore grew up on the city's East Side, in the Fourth Ward, where the famed Auburn Avenue—the heart of the black business district—was located. The homes of black bankers, entrepreneurs, doctors, and civic leaders dotted the ward's neighborhoods. Many working-class and poor families also lived there, in shotgun houses and on unpaved streets. Moore came from one of the ward's working-class families, a supportive and stable one. His father was a tailor and semipro baseball player who was away from home from May through September. Moore's "salt of the earth" mother worked in a steel plant and as a practical nurse. Fannie, Moore's aunt—and the strongest influence on him—was a school principal. "She knew something about everything," according to Moore, "and she'd teach it to me."[87]

His close proximity to the black elite, and Fanny's tutelage, made a strong impression on Moore. He set out to make something of himself. In an effort to prepare for the journey ahead, Moore imitated elite mannerisms and speech patterns. Indeed, at first, the teenager exaggerated genteel mannerisms and "proper" English. On his newspaper route, Moore announced his presence to subscribers with a haughty "It is I, your *Atlanta Journal* paperboy."[88]

Like friends from wealthy neighborhood families, Moore planned to attend college and had his sights set on Morehouse for "as long" as he "could remember." He matriculated in 1950. After flirting with journalism, Moore majored in political science. Thurgood Marshall inspired his interest in law. Moore had encountered the eminent lawyer in Atlanta, in the offices of A. T. Walden, Georgia's own legend. Walden commandeered Moore to fetch lunch for his guest and permitted him to observe interaction between the two men around the office. "Marshall was always telling stories to Walden and others who were gathered in their meetings and discussions, and he'd have a cigarette and cheap beer." Marshall was, Moore remembered, a "fun-loving fellow." Later on, Moore heard the NAACP counsel speak; Marshall wowed the crowd. "I can talk like that," Moore thought. The very next day, he visited the dean's offices at Morehouse for counseling about the steps required to attend law school. After his 1954 graduation from college, Moore was bound for law school; a two-year stint in the army delayed his start.[89]

The young man reached his educational and professional destination, but not without another detour. Moore had to leave his home state, where he had such deep roots and a substantial support network, to pursue his law degree. When Moore submitted his application in 1956, no law school in Georgia would consider him: the institutions, public and private, excluded African-American applicants, without exception. He had "no choice" but to leave. "They didn't want black lawyers in Atlanta," Moore said. Thus, like A. T. Walden decades before him, Moore applied to out-of-state law schools. He settled on a decidedly Yankee institution, the Boston University School of Law.[90]

When Moore returned to Atlanta in 1962 and joined the Georgia bar, his monumental achievement exposed the slow pace of racial change in the professions. Moore was only the tenth black lawyer—not in the city of Atlanta but in the entire state of Georgia. The statistics looked strangely similar to those that Walden had gathered in 1948, when he had founded the Gate City Bar Association to encourage blacks to study law. (The number of black lawyers in Georgia remained small until the 1970s.)[91]

A coveted position awaited Moore upon his arrival in the city. Donald Hollowell, the venerable attorney, offered Moore a job at Hollowell and Ward, the preeminent black law firm in the Southeast. Hollowell had cultivated the young man's interest in law. Moore had met Hollowell by happenstance and had not known who he was. Hollowell had given the college student a ride home from campus one day. During the journey, Moore recalled, Hollowell "said to me that he was a lawyer, and I said to myself, bullshit!" So few blacks practiced law that Hollowell's claim provoked disbelief. "But we talked, and he told me where he was, and to come and see him anytime." Thereafter, Hollowell cultivated Moore's interests, and after law school, his career. Moore, after a clerkship with an esteemed federal judge, would work a docket at the Hollowell firm uncommon for seasoned lawyers. He would litigate cutting-edge constitutional law cases, and in just a few years, he would chalk up numerous appearances—and victories—in the federal courts.[92]

Moore's criminal defense work shaped him as a lawyer, as a citizen, and as a man more profoundly than any of his other endeavors. He handled criminal matters for Hollowell and Ward in which men's lives—black men's lives—hung in the balance. The cases, typically set in rural backwaters, involved common casts of characters: the hapless young black man, often a teenaged agricultural worker; a white employer or other authority figure; a real or alleged theft or assault; a draconian criminal charge, including felony murder punishable by death; an all-white jury, seated despite a large black population; a prosecutor who openly trafficked in racial epithets and stereotypes; and an unsympathetic, and sometimes openly hostile, judge. Prejudice pervaded the criminal "justice" system. "One very seldom meets the truly objective and imaginative mind on the local bench," Moore noted. "I appeared before judges who'd as soon call me 'nigger' as look at me." "One time in court, a prosecutor picked up a chair to hit me. When I called the judge's attention to it," Moore explained, "he damn near put *me* in contempt." Moore's life often was at risk for merely agreeing to defend his clients. He was "run off the road, shot at."[93]

Moore carried with him memories of criminal injustice in rural Georgia as he matured as a lawyer. His representation of poor black men in desperate situations, coupled with his own experiences of discrimination, had a profound impact. They drove him professionally. As Moore crisscrossed the state, visiting his clients, he felt inspired. The young lawyer funneled enormous intellectual, mental, and physical energies into protecting his clients, each and every one of them, men whose lives society devalued, as a matter of course. In the crucible of Georgia's color-conscious courtrooms, Howard Moore, Jr., one of a handful of black lawyers in the state, absorbed the significance of his membership in the bar. With each passing day, Moore grew to embody the archetypal civil rights lawyer: sympathetic, undaunted, and a vital protector of his client's existence by virtue of his presence alone.

As a young associate in Hollowell's firm, Moore also handled his share of cases involving civil rights activists. He transferred the determined spirit he learned in the context of criminal defense to his representation of a different kind of underdog. Like Hollowell, Moore earned enormous respect from student activists. During the early 1960s, he defended SNCC in several trials, squaring off in Atlanta against the notorious racist Judge Durwood Pye in a series of high-profile cases. Moore's docket soon overflowed with SNCC cases, and he became the organization's counsel of record. He worked more closely with SNCC activists than any attorney since Len Holt, who had been so integral to the group's development during the early 1960s. The students liked Moore partly because he, like Holt, was closer in age to them than other authority figures. Moore also shared Holt's fierce commitment to the students' cause. But, in important respects, Moore was no Len Holt. Moore did not swagger into courtrooms, and he waited for confrontations to find him, rather than seeking them out.[94]

Moore—nicknamed "the Lamb"—projected modesty. He exuded warmth. One SNCC volunteer called him a "big lovable teddy bear." But Moore's low-key personality could be disarming. It belied his intensity, daring, and talent. Moore represented a roster of high-profile activists involved in deeply unpopular causes: along with Carmichael and Bond came a coterie of antiwar activists, Black Panthers, pacifists, socialists, and Communists. His cases and clients demanded much of him. He handled both with "superb skill." Indeed, Moore viewed the practice of law as requiring "total commitment"; his work constituted a "crusade" for racial, social, and economic justice.[95]

Many of Moore's clients—steely in public under the pressure of arrest, indictment, and trial—needed tremendous support behind closed doors. Moore provided it, and in no small measure. He brought great empathy to client interactions. And he could lighten even the tensest situations with humor. In short, Moore "held it all together" for activists under pressure. "If Howard Moore hadn't worked with me, tried to help me get myself together, I don't know what I would have done," said one activist, in a typical testimonial. Moore gave his clients the sense that he carried the weight of their cases on his shoulders, and that he would passionately defend them from the excesses of state power. He was beloved.[96]

Moore carefully crafted legal arguments to advance his clients' rights, usually in collaboration with a small network of lawyers involved in defending social activists. In the courtroom, the soft-spoken Moore presented an effective contrast to his clients, who were often confrontational. He frequently impressed observers with his eloquence, and could coddle or confound witnesses and persuade judges and juries alike of the credibility of his arguments. Moore's diligent representation produced a stable of devoted clients and a raft of legal victories for activists in trouble with the government.[97]

The Stokely Carmichael and Julian Bond cases launched the young lawyer onto the national stage. The cases made him a rising star among a new generation of civil rights lawyers—civil libertarians above all else.

## CARMICHAEL V. ALLEN

Moore wasted no time in defending Carmichael against the charges leveled against him after the Summerhill disturbances. Just one day after the Atlanta Police Department hauled Carmichael off to jail, Moore counterattacked. He turned the tables on officialdom. Those who put SNCC on trial would stand trial themselves. Moore filed a lawsuit in federal court that accused Atlanta's mayor, police chief, and chief prosecutor, the presumed guardians of the law, of maliciously using the law against SNCC. Lawyers Bill Kunstler and Dennis Roberts, along with a host of staff lawyers from the National Lawyers Guild, helped in the effort.[98]

*Carmichael v. Allen* would be a case about formalities of constitutional law, but more than that, it would be a political trial. No one disputed the basic facts—disturbances had occurred. But Moore and his cocounsel had filed a case that would make local authorities answer in open court for rushing to judgment and fingering SNCC—as opposed to white police, citizen provocateurs, slumlords, or the city itself—for Summerhill's long-brewing chaos. In Moore's hands, the courtroom became a forum for showing that the white power structure had abused its power and perverted the rule of law.

The past powerfully framed Moore's claims of racial harassment. Stokely Carmichael stood charged with violating provisions of the very same insurrection statute that Georgia had wielded against earlier waves of black freedom fighters. Memories of the state's vendetta against black Communist Party organizer Angelo Herndon had not receded. Herndon had been arrested for insurrection in 1932 after he solicited blacks and whites alike for membership in an integrated Communist Party of Atlanta. The state had labeled Herndon's activities unlawful under the insurrection statute on grounds that Party literature reportedly espoused overthrow of the U.S. government. The prosecution resulted in Herndon's conviction. But a 1937 Supreme Court decision repudiated Georgia: the Court held that the state's insurrection statute violated the First Amendment of the U.S. Constitution. The statute, as construed and applied, amounted to a "dragnet which may enmesh anyone who agitates for a change in government," the Court held. To Moore, Carmichael's arrest under the same law, more than thirty years later, on even flimsier evidence, demonstrated Georgia's cavalier determination to ignore the law whenever racial injustice demanded it.[99]

The First and Fourteenth Amendments to the U.S. Constitution provided the legal architecture for Moore's case. The laws that state and local officials had wielded against Carmichael and his comrades flagrantly violated the U.S.

Constitution, the attorney argued. Broad in sweep and indefinite in their characterizations of prohibited activity, the statutes contravened the First Amendment's prohibition against impermissibly vague statutes. Conduct that could constrict Carmichael's First Amendment rights of free speech, assembly, association, and petition for redress of grievances might fall within the riot and disorderly conduct bans. The charges violated SNCC's Fourteenth Amendment due process rights for the same reason, and because they had been filed in bad faith. The state had engaged in a campaign to intimidate and harass SNCC and, ultimately, to hinder the organization's struggle against inequality. Already, the scheme had seen successful: SNCC had experienced an onslaught of bad publicity and—with $21,000 tied up in bail bonds—a precipitous loss in income as a result of the charges leveled against it.[100]

## The Trial

The initial hearing in *Carmichael v. Allen* took place within weeks of Carmichael's arrest and weeklong stay in the Atlanta city jail. The proceedings began with Moore's impassioned argument that the charges against his client stemmed from a vendetta against SNCC. Ivan Allen had made SNCC a "scapegoat" for long-simmering problems that erupted in Summerhill on September 6, the day of the Prather shooting. The prosecutions amounted to a "scheme to suppress the political views" of Stokely Carmichael and SNCC. The state had set about to punish the group and its leader for exercising their free speech rights. The claim that Carmichael had incited a riot, Moore continued, was specious. Carmichael's presence at Summerhill had been brief, Moore contended, so fleeting that the court could only conclude that the prosecutors had maliciously filed riot charges against SNCC's leader.[101]

Ivan Allen was the star witness in Moore's case against the city. Moore put the mayor on the stand to answer for his role in the anti-SNCC conspiracy. Questioning focused on Allen's statements at the September 7 press conference, during which he had accused SNCC of fomenting the riot. At first, the mayor defended his actions during and after the disturbances. The mayor insisted that the conference had been a "routine" response to a tragedy. His goal was to reassure the public that the city had been cleaned up and put "back in order" after the preceding night's fracas. He had not, Allen claimed, called the conference to persecute SNCC.[102]

But after further questioning, Allen flinched. He admitted that the conference, packed with local and national media, had in reality been a vehicle for pointing the finger of blame at SNCC. There, he had claimed that the "disorders were the results of the deliberate attempt" by SNCC "to create an incident of this very nature." The mayor conceded to Moore that information from "various sources," as well as a feeling in his "heart and mind," had prompted him to blame SNCC for the disorders. Pressed about the identity of his sources, Allen noted that he had not personally seen people whom he believed were SNCC workers in Summerhill that day. He also testified that he "may" have seen Stokely Carmichael in a car leaving the scene. However, the mayor later retracted that statement: in fact, he could not be sure that Carmichael had been in the passing car and "would not testify under oath" that he had actually seen SNCC's chairman. What is more, Allen admitted that he "was not familiar with the membership of SNCC." Thus, he could not definitely link any SNCC worker to the disturbance—never mind the fact that he had done precisely that in his press conference.[103]

Moore called several witnesses to substantiate his charge that Atlanta had manufactured a case against SNCC. A television news cameraman presented eight hundred feet of film of the disturbances. Carmichael appeared in only two frames. Another journalist testified that Carmichael had long been gone from the scene by the late afternoon, when the violence began. An Episcopal priest stated that he had not seen Carmichael in the area; he insisted that the press had manufactured a riot out of a demonstration. The three-judge panel hearing the case watched a thirty-five-minute film of the scene, which featured Carmichael in two brief instances.[104]

Carmichael and Ware took the stand as well. They testified that no one affiliated with SNCC had thrown rocks, bottles, or other objects, assaulted police officers, or obstructed movement. Nor had they urged anyone else to do any of these things or to riot. To the contrary, testified Cleveland Sellers, another SNCC officer, the organization fervently hoped for calm and tried to maintain it in a combustible situation. "If anything happened," SNCC's leadership believed, "we were going to be blamed."[105]

During his testimony, Carmichael insisted that the people of Summerhill—not he—had instigated the protest. He had only endorsed the protest *after* locals had already planned it and after it had begun. Once on the scene, Carmichael said, he had attempted to "simmer down" the crowd. In fact, he had suggested to a black police officer on the scene that if white policemen left, the crowd's anger would subside and "we could begin to try and talk" to them. The officer confirmed Carmichael's account.[106]

Ultimately, a policeman's statement about the day's events undermined the government's credibility. In court, Sergeant Claude Dixon testified that on the day of the riot, he had heard a voice that he believed was Carmichael's utter the phrase "Baby burn" over the SNCC sound truck loudspeaker. The same voice had urged people to remain in the streets during the fracas, the officer said. At the same time,

Dixon conceded that in the "flashing moment" that he had seen Carmichael, SNCC's leader had not thrown rocks or engaged in "anything disorderly." Even with the concession, there was a problem: Dixon's courtroom testimony differed dramatically from the perfunctory statement that he had made earlier in an affidavit supporting Carmichael's arrest. In the affidavit, Dixon stated that he had merely seen Carmichael on the scene, nothing more. On that basis, the judge issued a warrant for Carmichael's arrest on incitement charges, and Dixon executed the warrant.[107]

The implication of Moore's questioning of the officer was clear. Dixon had not actually witnessed Carmichael engaging in misconduct, much less inciting others to behave in a disorderly fashion. But in the context of a lawsuit attacking the charges, the officer had recalled statements that might plausibly support the incitement charge. However, no one else corroborated Dixon's new and improved story about Carmichael. Other officers did testify that they had seen other SNCC workers throw objects at the police. But no evidence showed that the people identified by the police as having done so actually belonged to SNCC. Moore believed that he and his team had been able to show that blacks "were not instigators of violence but rather were the victims of violence and that the violence was instigated and carried out by the police." By the time the trial ended, the charge made by one SNCC supporter that the prosecution had "all the earmarks of a frame-up" seemed more credible than ever.[108]

## Judgment

In the end, Carmichael and Moore defeated the prosecutors. In mid-December, the U.S. District Court enjoined prosecution of most of the counts pending against the SNCC workers. Howard Moore had convinced the Court that the prosecutions chilled freedom of expression.[109]

*Dombrowski v. Pfister*, a one-year-old Supreme Court precedent secured by two of Moore's cocounsels, powered the plaintiffs' victory. The lawsuit had been prompted by the ruthless harassment of civil rights activists by the Louisiana Un-American Activities Committee. On the committee's orders, gun-toting state police officers raided the homes and offices of putatively "un-American" civil rights activists. Officers placed prominent leaders of the Southern Conference Educational Fund under arrest for violating state laws banning subversive and Communist activities. Lawyers Bill Kunstler and Arthur Kinoy sued in federal court to end the state's witch hunt. The attorneys argued that the broadly worded statute discouraged constitutionally protected protest activities. After the U.S. District Court upheld the laws out of deference to the Louisiana state courts, the attorneys turned to the U.S. Supreme Court for relief. The stakes were high for any and all who represented unpopular causes.[110]

In a five-to-two opinion, the Supreme Court struck down the Louisiana law. It violated the activists' rights of due process and free speech. The overly broad statute, the majority held, threatened irreparable harm to those prosecuted, or threatened with prosecution, under the law. It chilled freedom of expression, Justice Brennan wrote, by "frighten[ing] off" potential members of and contributors to the organization and individuals that officials had targeted for harassment. The ill effect remained even if those prosecuted ultimately were not found guilty of the underlying charges. A tremendous innovation in the law, *Dombrowski* made clear the symbiotic relationship between civil liberties and civil rights. After the landmark decision, litigators could turn to the federal courts for immediate relief from an ongoing state court prosecution that interfered with a client's federally protected constitutional rights. Prior to the case, the client had to endure prosecution and appeal after trial.[111]

The district court in *Carmichael v. Allen* looked to *Dombrowski* for guidance. The prosecutions of Stokely Carmichael and others charged along with him could not stand under the precedent, the court held. No meaningful distinction could be made between the issues involved in *Carmichael* and those in *Dombrowski*. In fact, the court found the case for intervention to stop the prosecutions stronger in the Georgia case. The victory hinged, in part, on the Angelo Herndon case. The past was prologue. The U.S. Supreme Court had found one of the laws that Moore had attacked, the state's Reconstruction-era incitement to insurrection statutes, unconstitutional in the 1937 case involving Herndon. But Georgia had left the statute on the books. Now, prosecutors blithely ignored the Supreme Court's ruling and brought incitement to insurrection charges against Carmichael under the same law. The district court declared all provisions of the insurrection statute void. In doing so, it found the city's failure to follow through on its threat to charge SNCC's chairman with insurrection itself irrelevant; the prosecutor had not disavowed any intention to do so in the future. "It is hardly necessary to point out the 'chilling' effect upon the exercise of the freedom of speech," the judges wrote, of a statute "prescribing punishment by electrocution." The court also struck down Atlanta's sweeping disorderly conduct ordinance on the ground that it chilled speech.[112]

In the end, Moore had marshaled evidence of a local vendetta against his client and SNCC, and the federal courts vindicated Carmichael and SNCC. Carmichael's claim that the judiciary's racism rendered the legal process uniformly unfair had been overstated. However, the damage that SNCC's reputation suffered before and during the trial, as a consequence of misjudgments and rhetorical excesses by both opponents and proponents of black power, could not be undone.

## BOND V. FLOYD

Carmichael's blanket condemnation of the courts contrasted with the more tempered rhetoric that SNCC had employed on other occasions. Always impatient with the civil rights lawyers and courts, SNCC had nonetheless used both opportunistically and in tandem with political tactics. The organization invoked concepts embedded in the Declaration of Independence and the U.S. Constitution to persuade courts to affirm the citizenship rights of African Americans, even as it lodged searing critiques of the body politic. Notwithstanding Carmichael's skepticism of the courts, his attorney had followed this pattern in *Carmichael v. Allen*. But Moore had walked a thin line; he had questioned the credibility of Ivan Allen, a man whose reputation for racial liberalism left open the possibility of judicial backlash against SNCC.

In the Julian Bond case, Moore had a more inviting opponent. The legislators who had refused to seat Bond were perfect foils, the stereotypical unenlightened southerners. The attorney repeatedly invoked the rhetorical frames of democracy and equality in his courtroom battle against them and their reactionary actions. A cocounsel's rhetorical question, thundered at a community meeting, signaled the frame: if Bond remained unseated, he asked, "how can we tell the people in Vietnam we are fighting for democracy?" Yet, Moore treated the war itself as incidental to the bedrock principles that framed his case. Moore's choice was prudent: antiwar sentiment was growing, but still thin. The lawyer wisely focused as much on the broader political significance of the Bond controversy as on his client's pacifism.[113]

Moore's strategy to ensure that Julian Bond regained his seat in the Georgia legislature involved two prongs, one for inside the courtroom, one for outside. He filed a legal action in federal court against the Georgia house. Then, he sought to build support for his client's reelection, and thus his legal strategy, in the court of public opinion. His wife, Jane Bond Moore, who was Julian Bond's sister, helped to map out a strategy to secure her brother's reelection; the state of Georgia forced Bond to stand for reelection while he challenged his unseating through the legal process. The Atlanta Project then implemented the political or "street strategy" necessary to demonstrate that Bond's constituents continued to support him. With so many commentators, including blacks, critical of Bond's antiwar stance, electoral defeat might force him out of the legislature—mooting his legal case. With the aid of the project and his spouse, Moore would show that Bond maintained political support as the legal case slowly wound its way through the federal courts.[114]

## Politics

The Atlanta Project staff, along with other SNCC workers, gamely supported Bond's bid for reelection. By aiding Bond, the project could promote itself. Staff members sought to use the Bond incident to encourage a "voice of protest and rebellion" within his district and thereby support the project's community organizing effort. The staff distributed a mountain of letters and leaflets that tied Bond's fate to the residents' plight. Bond had intended to fight for his low-income black constituents in the legislature. The house's vote to turn him out was an attempt to nullify the political power of Vine City residents. It was the most blatant form of disrespect. "Remember how long white was right," one leaflet read. "Change has been happening in the South because people like you have been saying 'no' to what they believe is wrong," it concluded. By rising up in support of Bond, soon to run again in a special election called to fill the seat that he had been denied, the community would further its own interests.[115]

Project members, the "foot soldiers" for Bond's campaign, diligently worked to turn out voters and ensure Bond's reelection, without opposition, to the very seat that his colleagues had denied him. Through their vote, the citizens of the 136th District sent a clear message: Julian Bond was "the people's choice," and his expulsion from the legislature disfranchised the district's sixty-five hundred registered voters. Ultimately, the House "couldn't win" the battle to remove Bond from office" without "nullifying and destroying" the will of the electorate. The people of his district would reelect Bond, time and time again if necessary, until he regained his seat.[116]

Sure enough, Bond prevailed in his reelection bids. His constituents remained in his corner throughout his legal ordeal. The revotes showed that the integrity of the democratic process itself—not merely the fate of one young legislator—hung in the balance.[117]

## Law

The court battle remained, and it promised to be an uphill one. The lawsuit that Moore filed to enjoin the legislature from excluding Bond was far from an open-and-shut case. *Bond v. Floyd* raised novel and thorny constitutional issues.

Moore asked the federal court to void a state legislature's decision regarding a most crucial matter: the qualifications and conduct of one of its own members. Federal courts often regarded such matters as outside their jurisdiction. Race made the political thicket even more treacherous. Nothing guaranteed that the judges—far removed from the world of the 136th District—would see the issues in the case as SNCC, Bond, and his constituents saw them. The state of Georgia, supremely confident that it was within its rights to find Bond unqualified for office, intended to make states' rights and separation of powers—not individual rights or abstract notions of equality and democracy—the dominant narrative frame of the litigation.[118]

Moore, assisted by cocounsel Charles Morgan, Jr., pushed back against the state sovereignty claim with a battery of constitutional arguments. First, they relied on *Baker v. Carr* to persuade the court of its authority to review Bond's challenge to the legislature's decision. *Baker* made clear that federal courts could resolve federal constitutional questions, even in an area that a state traditionally considered its exclusive prerogative.[119]

Next, the lawyers made a contention plain to everyone in SNCC and many outside of it. "Bond was a typical example of Southern justice," Moore argued, and his case was an illustration of selective law enforcement. Bond had been punished for expressing dissent when no white man would have been under similar circumstances. "In almost 100 years, only a Negro who is a pacifist, employed by a militant interracial civil rights organization, was directed to stand aside and humiliated in the presence of family, friends, and constituents," the lawyers argued. The hypocrisy of the situation was apparent. White men who had "railed against the laws and policies of the United States government" from the floor of the General Assembly had expelled Bond from office. Many of the Georgia house members who had voted to unseat Julian Bond for "treasonous" conduct had supported a drive to nullify the Supreme Court's 1954 decision in *Brown v. Board of Education* and to impeach justices who supported the civil rights landmark. The conclusion was "inescapable," Moore argued: the same rationales—racial prejudice and the desire to punish those who subverted the racial order—animated both movements.[120]

The Georgia house had also infringed the rights of Bond's constituents, Moore claimed. The legislature had "taken from the people of the 136th District the ultimate power to determine who shall represent them." The citizens had been without representation in the General Assembly since early 1966, a denial of equal protection and a republican form of government.[121]

Moore coupled his racial critique of the legislature's action with a First Amendment argument. The attorney contended that the oath of office, including the phrases to "support the Constitution" and "conduct myself, as will, in my judgment, be most conducive to the interests and prosperity of this State," should be void for vagueness. Bond had been "ready and willing" to swear the required words, but the Georgia house adjudged his conduct incompatible with the oath. This determination put Bond and all aspiring legislators in an untenable position. In essence, Georgia required "an attitude test" for the office, forbidden by the First Amendment.[122]

The state saw no contradiction between the First Amendment and its treatment of Bond. The Bond case did not involve pure speech, insisted Arthur Bolton, Georgia's attorney general. Moreover, legislators did not enjoy the same right to speak as ordinary citizens. The case concerned a more complex matter—a public official's qualifications for office. Bond's putative support for evasion of military service in Vietnam disqualified him for office, Georgia argued. The First Amendment did not bar the state's determination that Bond's words were "dangerous." "Freedom of speech does not embrace the right to encourage others to violate the law."[123]

Inside the stately halls of the federal district court, Moore's arguments about democracy, equality, and free speech fell flat. Race still shaped Georgia politics, but the court quickly dispensed with the claim that racism had animated Bond's ouster from the legislature. True enough, the Georgia house had barred Bond from office. But January 10, 1966, had been a historic day for the august body, the court recalled. "Seven Negro representatives" had taken the oath of office on that day. Moreover, two black legislators had spoken on Bond's behalf from the floor of the assembly before the vote to unseat him. Hence, the Georgia house had not excluded all blacks from the process. Rather, Bond—one particular Negro, deemed unworthy for office—had been excluded. Without "smoking gun" evidence that those who had spearheaded Bond's ouster did so on account of race, the court would not credit the discrimination argument.[124]

The court's decision also focused on Moore's free speech arguments, but he fared no better there. Georgia had insisted that First Amendment rights must bend to a sovereign state's right to determine legislators' qualifications for office. The judges agreed, and cited a nineteenth-century constitutional treatise for the proposition that "no other body" but the legislature itself could "preserve and perpetuate" its attributes and character. Moore had brought racial developments within America since 1954 to bear on the case, but in the end, age-old traditions determined its outcome. In light of these precepts, the court concluded, the Georgia house had every right to determine that Bond's antiwar statements were "repugnant to his oath of office," the First Amendment notwithstanding. "We are committed in Vietnam," wrote the court, and the "SNCC statement is at war with the national policy of this country." Such rhetoric suggested little space between the majority's subjective beliefs and its constitutional interpretation. Bond had lost in the district court, and his biggest test still lay ahead.[125]

## Bond v. Floyd at the Supreme Court

Moore immediately appealed the district court's decision to the U.S. Supreme Court. The stage was set for a showdown at the Supreme Court over civil liberties during a time of war. The state of Georgia confidently wore its victory in the lower court and expected the High Court to affirm its right to discharge unruly legislators as it saw fit. Bond's lawyers also prepared for a confrontation of the first order. In addition to Howard Moore, Bond's defense team now included Victor Rabinowitz and Leonard Boudin. Partners in a labor law firm, the two attorneys had defended men and women smeared by the House Committee on Un-American Activities during McCarthy-era witch hunts. Rabinowitz and Boudin thus had deep personal and professional experience in high-profile cases involving free speech and civil liberties. Their involvement in Bond's case signaled the importance of the litigation and the Cold War politics that infused it. Bond's critics pointed to his hiring of "two Communist lawyers" as proof of his guilt. Friends, as well as long-standing enemies, questioned Bond's association with Rabinowitz and Boudin. Remarkably, even the ACLU withdrew from Bond's case rather than work with these two lawyers—an act that the pair called "unforgivable." The rift highlighted the litigation's extraordinary stakes.[126]

When the time arrived for argument, the parties' Supreme Court briefs cast the case in stark terms. Which was paramount: freedom of speech or separation of powers? The legal papers refined points made in the district court, often in sharper tones and telling ways. The state once again claimed that the First Amendment did not apply to Bond's speech because he had encouraged draft card burning. Bond's lawyers countered that Bond's "mild observations" quite obviously fell within the zone of constitutionally protected speech. Bond had not incited violent overthrow of the government. He had not even drafted the SNCC statement opposing the war. He had not issued a call to others to support his point of view. Rather, he had merely responded to a press inquiry. Georgia's entire case verged on farce, Moore and Boudin intimated. "A large section of the intellectual community is openly critical of the Administration's conduct of the war," they noted. "Such opposition is not unusual in a democracy." The district court's opinion condoning the state's conduct disregarded Bond's expressive rights. The court's reference to "national policy" in Vietnam and its conclusion that Bond's antiwar utterances had flouted that policy struck the attorneys as "a very strange statement for a court to make."[127]

## Oral Argument

The Court heard arguments in the case on November 10, 1966. Moore and Boudin argued Bond's case. They reprised the arguments made in their briefs: Georgia had engaged in viewpoint discrimination. The speech of pacifists was "no more un-American" than that of segregationists, Moore argued. The legislature had no more right under the First Amendment to expel Bond for his antiwar views than they would have to expel a segregationist for his opposition to the national policy of racial equality, now enshrined in the Civil Rights Act and Voting Rights Act. "Refusal to seat a duly elected official is opposed by our history," Boudin declared at the counsel's podium during his portion of the argument. "[The] people must be represented!"[128]

During his turn at the podium, Arthur Bolton, again representing Georgia, appeared determined to ignore the facts of the case and refashion the law to his liking. Bolton insisted that Bond had counseled lawlessness. Bond expressed "sympathy" for those unwilling to respond to the draft; "horror at the inconsistency of a supposedly free society that drafted Negroes to preserve a democracy that does not exist for them at home"; and "admiration" for the "courage" of those who burned their draft cards. The legislature—the "sole judge of qualifications"—had rightly exercised its authority to prohibit Bond from assuming his seat, Bolton averred: no one who advocated such "lawbreaking" could swear to uphold the Constitution and its laws. The attorney general had assumed that Bond's words—recited in the hallowed chambers of the U.S. Supreme Court—would surely offend the patriots on the bench, making plain the rightness of the state's position.[129]

He miscalculated. "Is that all you rely on?" Justice Brennan—incredulous— asked Bolton. "Is that it?" The attorney general's recitation made it painfully obvious that the case concerned little more than *talk*. Bond had repeatedly denied any intention to advocate lawbreaking, said Chief Justice Warren, and the record indicated no such action. As for Bond's words, they were mild compared to the incendiary language involved in other First Amendment cases that the Court had entertained. The young man had not even mentioned, much less threatened or encouraged, violent overthrow of the U.S. government or other imminent danger to the nation—the kind of language that could be excluded from First Amendment protection. Bolton's recitation of SNCC's antiwar statement had backfired. Justice Abe Fortas made the nature of the state's

constitutional dilemma clear. Georgia's position came "perilously close to suggesting that" a person is "unqualified to sit if he opposed the war in Vietnam."
Georgia had gotten a cold reception from the justices.[130]

## Resolution

The Supreme Court's unanimous December 5 opinion ended the dramatic first
chapter of Julian Bond's political career. The Georgia legislature had violated
the representative-elect's First Amendment rights, the Court decreed, when it
expelled him from its ranks. The discussion at oral argument anticipated the
major points of the Chief Justice's opinion. From the start of the litigation,
Moore had contended that Bond's willingness to swear to uphold the Constitution should extinguish the legislature's inquiry into his fitness for office. The
Court agreed. The legislature had no authority to question the genuineness of
Bond's oath. The justices found no evidence for the state's charge that Bond
had incited lawbreaking. Nor could he have been convicted of treason, as the
Georgia legislature had charged. Without a doubt, the justices concluded, the
First Amendment covered Bond's speech. Its "manifest function" in a "representative government requires that legislators be given the widest latitude to
express their views on issues of policy." The amendment's "central commitment" was to create "uninhibited, robust, and wide-open" debate on public
issues, the Court wrote.[131]

The U.S. Supreme Court had thoroughly vindicated Julian Bond. For the first
time in history, an American court had overruled a state legislature's decision
regarding the qualifications of a member. With the exception of Bond's antagonists in the Georgia house, commentators accepted the Court's decision. The
Justices looked like paragons of reason who, once again, had protected democracy from the parochialism of the South. Atlanta's leading newspapers signaled
that the city, the state, and its people had suffered enough embarrassment. "We
have a government of laws, not of men," said an *Atlanta Journal* editorial in the
wake of the Court's decision. "The law says seat him," and that "is not only the
legal but the smart thing to do." Three times elected to the Georgia house, but
twice denied his seat, Bond could finally join the other members of the chamber.
It was a victory, he said, for the people of his district.[132]

Bond's stature, and that of all of the victors in *Bond v. Floyd*, had increased
tremendously. Thanks to his colleagues, Bond certainly was the most famous
state legislator in the nation and was now celebrated on the antiwar Left. His
ordeal had raised public consciousness about the war's inequities and the
authoritarian mindset of some of its supporters. Howard Moore had won his

first Supreme Court argument, and in the process, had made important new constitutional law. Moore quickly earned a reputation as a "splendid" go-to lawyer for peaceniks and leftist radicals caught in the clutches of the ascendant Right. Leonard Boudin and Victor Rabinowitz had chalked up yet another victory at the Court, adding to their stellar track record as civil liberties lawyers. Each man had elevated his status in his own circle.[133]

## RACE, REPRESENTATION, AND NEW POLITICS AFTER *BOND V. FLOYD*

But what had the community—including Vine City, that ghetto within a ghetto—gained as a result of the legal victory? The benefits were indirect. The courts' treatment of the race issue in *Bond v. Floyd* demonstrated the point. Both courts had entertained Moore's frameworks of democracy and liberty, but the matter of equality had received little attention. The district court had dismissed out of hand the idea that racial animus had played a role in Bond's downfall and in the treatment of his constituents. The only racial issue the district court majority perceived was the race-conscious language with which SNCC described its antiwar sentiment and the government's civil rights record. The unanimous Supreme Court had avoided the questions of race and representation as well. Given its disposition of the First Amendment issue, the Court had written, it "need not decide" the other issues. *Bond v. Floyd* had only a tangential relationship to issues of racial justice, and that oblique link was Julian Bond.[134]

The Atlanta Project had viewed Bond as an instrument for achieving economic justice, but the case and the surrounding dynamics had suggested how difficult it would be to translate political representation into political influence, much less achieve ambitious antipoverty and community-building goals. The Court had functioned ideally; it had forced Bond's opponents to seat him. But in the interim, as the legal process worked and political energies poured into redressing Bond's expulsion from the legislature, some of the momentum surrounding Bond's initial election to the legislature had been lost. The breakthrough year for Bond, SNCC, the Atlanta Project, and Georgia's new black legislators was also a year of setbacks. The political and social space for making change narrowed, amid the antiwar struggle, divisions within SNCC and the community over black power, and the domestic turmoil caused by the Vietnam War.

The Atlanta Project had petered out before Bond even settled into state government. The project staff's relationship with SNCC, long tense, officially ended in early 1967 when the national office fired Atlanta Project staff members for "insubordination." The project would not realize its big dreams of organizing Atlanta's ghettos.[135]

Even Julian Bond, the political star who personified SNCC's dream—in which political radicals won elective office and effected change from the inside out—struggled to gain his footing in the aftermath of his Supreme Court victory. He quietly integrated himself into the Georgia house. The chamber absorbed Bond and carried on, more or less as usual. One legislator, no fan of Bond, captured the early reality with this observation: "I sort of expected him to try to stir things up by introducing Vietnam and civil rights legislation," he said. "But he's off to a good start. He's listening, but isn't saying much." Bond laid low during his first years in office. "I lived through a period of bewilderment, despair and searching," he acknowledged. Even after he was ready to emerge, Bond found himself hamstrung by his antiwar stance. He encountered "enormous resentment" from his colleagues for quite some time, and it impeded his ability to make an impact in the legislature, at least in the short term. Race and inexperience also shaped Bond's experience and efficacy as a legislator. "For a newly elected black official those first few months are lonely and frightening," he explained. "When I was first elected to the Georgia State Legislature, I had high hopes for constructive change but real doubts, too. Would I learn the ropes? Would I be effective? Would I be able to deliver the goods?" The black "prince," like everyone else, was human.[136]

After Bond's court victory SNCC's national office also faced setbacks. The last straw for SNCC in Atlanta came in mid-June 1967. History repeated itself, but with a twist. Stokely Carmichael again was on the scene during a confrontation between residents of the Dixie Hills neighborhood and police over an apparent incident of brutality. The disturbance left a forty-six-year-old black man dead and three other African Americans wounded, including a nine-year-old boy. Approximately five hundred people gathered at the site of the shootings, Carmichael among them, and he and four others were arrested for failing to disperse at officers' command.[137]

Police claimed that Carmichael had attempted to "excite" the crowd and foment ill feelings toward the police. Carmichael retorted that he was in the neighborhood to ensure that people arrested by the police obtained legal representation. "Stokely Starmichael"—as some of his detractors called him—had claimed the center of attention yet again.[138]

The incident culminated in what, for SNCC, was likely the most painful of ways. One thousand residents of Dixie Hills signed a petition asking SNCC and Carmichael to leave their neighborhood. The organization's effort to empower the residents of Dixie Hills had worked. The citizens of the ghetto had risen up as a united voice—only the object of their passion was not the police, the city, land-lords, or discriminatory businesses but SNCC itself. But this was not the SNCC of old. The petition signaled how much SNCC had changed and how much ground SNCC had lost since the early 1960s, when its expression of dissent from the legalism of the NAACP LDF and the mobilizing tactics of SCLC had so energized the civil rights movement. To be sure, SNCC retained some of its old ideals and support in some quarters. But the organization could no longer translate its ideas into effective, mass political action. It had lost much of its leverage and its con-nection to some of the poor black communities it sought to serve.[139]

Senator Leroy Johnson greeted SNCC's departure from Dixie Hills, which he represented, with glee. Leaders in SNCC were "telling the folks what they did not have," he explained, pointing out that the projects were "infested with rats," and had "no athletic facilities, no playgrounds, no anything." What SNCC viewed as organizing and a path to empowerment, Johnson viewed as counter-productive and incendiary. "It's not burn baby burn. It's vote baby vote" that SNCC ought to preach, Johnson urged. Nevertheless, he looked for a way to appease his constituents. He turned to Mayor Allen for help, explaining, "I gotta make some promises out there." Since a young child had been hurt during the Dixie Hills disturbance, Johnson thought that a playground would work as a "tangible commitment" to the community. Allen agreed to bring "earth moving machines" into the neighborhood within a few days so that things would "quiet down." The plan succeeded. "[I]t stopped the folks from just going ape," Johnson remarked.[140]

Meanwhile, others attempted programmatic antipoverty initiatives. Black legislators lobbied for additional federal antipoverty dollars, but with limited success. Some EOA-funded programs provided valuable educational, employ-ment, social, and family services to thousands of poor citizens. Nevertheless, the city of Atlanta and units of local government such as the school system, the housing authority, and the parks and social services departments—all known perpetrators of racial discrimination—continued to discriminate in the fund-ing and operation of the poverty programs.[141]

Moreover, critics continued to charge the EOA's professional staff with draw-ing high salaries from plush offices at the expense of the poor. The dispute spilled into public when pickets charged the Atlanta EOA office and asked God to "have mercy on the poor people of Atlanta" whom the rich "kept on the out-side of the EOA program." Later, four representatives of the poor, all of whom were black, gained seats on the local EOA board of directors. Notably, even after blacks achieved administration positions within EOA, lower-income blacks still complained of underrepresentation, lack of information, discrimination, and inadequate service.[142]

Mayor Allen sought federal dollars to construct additional affordable housing units in the city. And the city improved some services in some poverty-stricken areas under pressure. But these efforts were paltry in comparison to the need and in comparison to the city's investment in infrastructure designed to stimulate economic growth.[143]

The Vietnam War posed the single greatest threat to the success of the poverty programs. As the war dragged on, appropriations dried up. In fiscal year 1967, Congress slashed Atlanta's War on Poverty funding by 40 percent, and the city ended eight antipoverty programs. Dr. King condemned the nation's priorities. "If our country can spend $800 a second, $2 billion a month, $24 billion a year to fight a war in Vietnam," he said, "it can spend billions of dollars to put God's children on their own two feet." Yet, appropriations for the War on Poverty never amounted to more than 1.5 percent of the federal budget. In the end, the "war" on poverty looked like nothing more than a skirmish. The underfunded effort fell far short of the "massive 'crash' attack" on poverty that President Johnson had promised and King imagined.[144]


## CAN THE POOR SHARE IN POWER?


The year 1966 spawned a movement of movements—a maelstrom of dissent within the civil rights movement. Julian Bond's pacifism shook three social movements. It remade the civil rights movement, expanded the antiwar movement, and energized the antipoverty movement. The daring antiwar statement of SNCC, and Bond's reaction to it, encouraged an antiwar culture and global perspective within the civil rights movement. The connections between the war in Vietnam and the war against poverty and racism were made clearer than ever. Victims of the cuts in antipoverty programs and relatives of troops stationed in Southeast Asia could appreciate the link. Increasingly, blacks criticized and resisted the draft precisely because they saw the overlap between domestic and foreign policy. The foray by SNCC into global politics thus helped to reshape conceptions of equality and democracy. Yet, Bond and SNCC's pioneering role in the peace movement have been underappreciated. Many scholars have chosen to emphasize the role of patriotic black soldiers as catalysts of the postwar civil rights movement; this narrative, popularized by mainstream civil rights organizations, has left little room for sustained consideration of black *antiwar* sentiment. In fact, SNCC, and Julian Bond, as its public face, were leading edges of constructive anti-war sentiment within the civil rights movement. That legacy should not be lost.[145]

Nevertheless, Roy Wilkins's warning that the merger of the civil rights and peace movements would be a "serious tactical mistake" for SNCC had an element of truth. The global perspective SNCC held on domestic race relations broke radically with liberal thought. In the postwar era, the NAACP had advanced its civil rights agenda by consciously embracing America and the Cold War. The NAACP warned that America's mistreatment of returning soldiers and southern blacks threatened its claims to leadership of the free world and thus its fight against Soviet domination of Europe, Asia, and Africa. The leadership of SNCC adopted the opposite approach, and its blistering critique of U.S. foreign policy came on the heels of passage of the most far-reaching civil rights laws the country had ever known. Predictably, many Americans, including those generally sympathetic to SNCC, viewed its uncompromising antiwar stance as untimely, unwise, and even unpatriotic. Consequently, SNCC's antiwar position, and Bond's embrace of it, did entail costs as well as benefits for the civil rights movement.

The birth and evolution of the Atlanta Project illustrates how Bond's courageous act of dissent spurred events that both mobilized and demobilized the black freedom movement. Initially, Bond's unseating generated a beneficial backlash among activists, who created political opportunity out of the setback. The Atlanta Project, an outreach effort in Atlanta's ghettos, was born of Bond's dissent.

The project left an important legacy in law and politics. The staff's organizing efforts politically energized a desperately poor community. Howard Moore litigated innovative cases on behalf of renters desperate for a place to live. With Julian Bond's help, the project also raised awareness about substandard housing. Statutory and legal systems weighted in favor of property owners ultimately limited the project's effectiveness in the housing context. Even so, later advocacy groups profited from the project's organizing efforts. The staff's activism made the political environment more favorable to tenant-side housing litigation undertaken by the Georgia Legal Aid Society in the months and years ahead. The project's generative role in the legal arm of the antipoverty and welfare rights movements has been unappreciated.[146]

But the short-lived project—characterized by fits and starts and unfinished agendas—did not reach its loftiest goals. The project failed to organize the ghetto en masse and vest the black poor with political power of a new order of magnitude. It failed, in part, because of the scale of its ambition. No organization since has managed to overcome, on a sustained basis, the multitudinous factors that inhibit electoral participation and political consciousness among the poor.

In addition to being overly ambitious, the project did not achieve all of its high aims because it dissented so much, in so many directions, all at once. At a moment dominated by the alliance between cold warriors and civil rights moderates, the project's simultaneous embrace of black power, antiwar politics, and a new antipoverty agenda doomed it. The public image of SNCC suffered, and it became a less cohesive organization, after it embraced the ideology of black power. Imprecise language and inflammatory sloganeering obscured the project's pointed assessment of society's debt to the black poor. At the same time, project members led antiwar protests outside of military induction centers. These protests energized the peace movement. But project members found themselves jailed and targets of government repression. Howard Moore's docket filled with antiwar protester cases. His battle against the government's attempts to repress the antiwar movement consumed his time. This was an important, even heroic battle, but it was not the affirmative fight *for* economic justice that SNCC had initially desired.

Moore's most significant fight against government repression of antiwar dissidents, *Bond v. Floyd*, shows how Moore, Bond, and the Atlanta Project made change, even as events overtook their aspirations to create space in law and politics for an antipoverty agenda. The project provided political support for Moore's constitutional litigation and aided Bond's campaigns for reelection. Bond won his court case, and his protest remade constitutional law. *Bond v. Floyd* secured public officials' First Amendment rights. In the process, it expanded federal jurisdiction over state politics, already stretched far by *Baker v. Carr*, the case that sent Bond into the Georgia legislature in the first place. The resounding Supreme Court victory lifted the careers of Moore and Bond. But the legal win did not change the everyday lives of the representative-elect's constituents or substantially enhance the antipoverty goals of the Atlanta Project. In fact, by the time the Supreme Court decided the case, Bond had resigned from SNCC, and his strained relationship with the Atlanta Project no longer existed.

Ideology and personality conflicts had caused tension between Bond and the project's staff. The project's strident voice of protest left it open to charges of "reverse racism." Bond also harshly criticized white-controlled institutions. But his presupposition that equality required biracial coalition, integration, and power-sharing remained clear. Bond now operated within the framework of majoritarian politics, and that context demanded a more restrained voice and compromise, especially after he finally took his seat in the Georgia house.

Thus, SNCC's attempt to infiltrate the political system—personified in Julian Bond's entrance into the state legislature—posed a pressing question. Could an organization of outsiders, committed to representing the interests of those on the very bottom of society, exist uncompromised within the system?

Or must it exist on the outside, as an irritant to the body politic, hoping to generate what Dr. King called "creative tension"? Long after Bond's Vietnam protest, SNCC, and its Atlanta Project have faded into the past, the question remains unanswered.

Bond's brand of Democratic Party politics differed in important ways from A. T. Walden's. A vital transformation had occurred. Now, local black communities could elect their own representatives. Howard Moore captured the scale of the change when he measured Bond's feat by noting that twenty years earlier blacks in the South "couldn't even register to vote." "The idea of holding office was a great...fantasy."[147]

But the continuities between the generations of black leadership were striking. The right to be represented in the decision-making process—and the right to participate in decision-making—were distinct concepts. SNCC workers had long recognized that distinction; they had organized communities because of their belief that the black poor could only win the political process if they themselves participated in it as stakeholders. Ironically, the election of same-race politicians obscured that distinction and kept the spokesperson dynamic in black politics, so lamented during the Walden era, in place. The black community's prerogatives now would be defined by a small cadre of black leaders in the Georgia General Assembly. And those black representatives would set agendas without the aid of SNCC—the organization whose insistence on dissident and participatory politics had so energized the civil rights movement. Just as founders like Bond took office, SNCC went into decline—a victim of the maelstrom of dissent that it had unleashed.[148]

The struggle for equality suffered in SNCC's absence. A champion of the "little people," SNCC nevertheless had exercised a measure of influence in the corridors of power. It could make trouble for officials in Washington or Atlanta, or, more likely, influence or provoke Dr. King, Roy Wilkins, Thurgood Marshall, Jack Greenberg, A. T. Walden, and black elites in Atlanta and other cities. After the events of 1966, SNCC no longer held much sway over liberals in government and in the civil rights bar. Once again, just as was the case before blacks gained access to the voting booth, insiders—members of the bar, elected officials, and self-appointed power brokers—would play outsized roles in the struggle for racial justice.

The black struggle continued in Atlanta in the absence of SNCC, but it became more consensus-driven and even less inclined to prioritize the interests of the poor. Organizations for which antipoverty work and community organizing were not priorities set the agendas. Many of these organizations found it difficult to move beyond the "civil rights" paradigm. One such group, the Council on Human Relations, disbanded. The council had achieved its goal of eliminating de jure segregation, and it proclaimed itself incapable of "adapt[ing] to a new purpose—...promot[ing] integration in a legally desegregated society." Of all civil rights organizations, SCLC held out the best hope for a sustained emphasis on poverty; however, the murder of Dr. King in April 1968 greatly diminished the ability of the SCLC to move forward with his goal of waging an all-out campaign against poverty and for full employment.[149]

Thereafter, lawyers allied with social activists in the welfare rights movement and neighborhood groups became the main representatives of the poor in the corridors of power. While the lawyers pursued due process and substantive rights for indigent clients, the activists sought legislation and funding increases to ameliorate poverty. Welfare rights activism overlapped to some extent with SNCC's embryonic antipoverty agenda, as ensuing chapters will illustrate. In important ways, however, no group could replace SNCC, the visionary organization that simultaneously organized the grassroots and influenced elites.

A.T. Walden in the Army, 1915. Photo Courtesy of the Atlanta History Center.

A.T. Walden Portrait, n.d. Photo Courtesy of the Atlanta History Center.

A.T. Walden, attorney, listening as atlanta election official returns his ballot. walden and other negroes attempted to vote and were told their names were not on the registration lists. July, 1944. Photo Courtesy of Corbis.

Voter Registration in Atlanta in May 1946. Photo Courtesy of the Atlanta History Center.

Judge Walden and the Original Gate City Bar Association, 1948. Photo
Courtesy of the Gate City Bar Association. [also cover photo]

A.T. Walden representing unidentified young male during the trial against
racist hate group called the "Columbians." Undated. Photo Courtesy of
Griffith J. Davis and the Atlanta History Center.

Woman throwing wash water into the street from the porch of a substandard house near Capitol Homes Housing Project in downtown Atlanta, Georgia, 1952. Photo courtesy of Bill Wilson and the Atlanta History Center.

First African American Golfers at Atlanta's Formerly All-White Municipal Course, C.T. Bell, Alfred Holmes, and Oliver Holmes, Dec. 28, 1955. Photo Courtesy of Corbis.

Morehouse College President Benjamin Mays in his office in
Atlanta, Georgia, circa 1975. Photo courtesy of Joe McTyre
and the Atlanta History Center.

First Day of Integration in Atlanta Schools, August, 1961.
Photo Courtesy of Getty Images.

Portrait of Constance
Baker Motley, 1963. Photo
Courtesy of the Sophia
Smith Collection, Smith
College Archives.

Lawyer Len Holt On His
Way to Court, Birmingham,
Alabama, 1963. Photo
Courtesy of the *Liberator*
Magazine, L. Pete Beveridge,
Jr., and Len Holt.

KKK Members and Civil Rights Protesters in Atlanta, January, 1964. Photo Courtesy of Corbis.

Donald Hollowell and Howard Moore with Client, a Student Demonstrator, 1964. Photo Courtesy of Corbis.

Julian Bond is Expelled from the Georgia Legislature, 1966. Photo Courtesy of the Julian Bond Collection, University of Virginia Archives.

Georgia Representative Julian Bond Visits the Vine City neighborhood, 1966. Photo Courtesy of Getty Images.

Atlanta Police Officers and an Unidentified Man during a riot in the Summerhill neighborhood of Atlanta, Georgia, 1966. Photo courtesy of the Atlanta History Center.

Lonnie King, President of the Atlanta NAACP and Student Sit-in Leader, circa 1970s. Photo Courtesy of Boyd Lewis and the Atlanta History Center.

Ethel Mae Mathews, the
founder of the Atlanta
Chapter of the National
Welfare Rights Association,
circa 1970. Photo Courtesy
of Boyd Lewis and the
Atlanta History Center.

Ethel Mae Mathews during a welfare rights march in downtown Atlanta, 1976.
Photo Courtesy of Boyd Lewis and the Atlanta History Center.

Father Austin Thomas Ford, the founder of Emmaus House, seated on the steps of the Georgia State Capitol building in downtown Atlanta with an unidentified boy during a demonstration against Governor George Busbee's refusal to increase state welfare assistance levels, circa 1976. Photo Courtesy of Boyd Lewis and the Atlanta History Center.

View of Eva Davis (left), head of the East Lake Meadows Tenants Association, and the Reverend Joseph E. Boone (second from the left), civil rights organizer, at a protest against a police raid in which officers stormed the wrong apartment at Atlanta's East Lake Meadows housing project, March, 1973.

Margie Pitts Hames at the Georgia State Capitol, n.d. Photo
Courtesy of Fulton County, Georgia *Daily Report*.

# PART III

# Questioning *Brown*: Lawyers, Courts, and Communities in Struggle

CHAPTER 10

# A Curious Silence

*Community Activism and the Legal Campaign*
*to Implement* Brown, *1958–1968*

[N]egro students do not desire to change. (1962)

Judge Frank Hooper

Isn't it true that the NAACP is a middle-class organization, unconcerned with the problems of the masses? (1966)

Rev. Joseph E. Boone

At the December 1963 "Pilgrimage for Democracy" in Atlanta—a follow-up to the March on Washington—Dr. Martin Luther King, Jr., chastised his hometown for its delay in desegregating public schools.[1] A little less than ten years ago, he noted, the U.S. Supreme Court's decision in *Brown v. Board of Education* had brought "new rays of hope to millions of disinherited Negroes who had formerly dared only to dream of freedom."[2] Soon, however, "deep rumblings of resistance" had developed in white communities across the South. Initially, Atlanta had followed a more reasonable path. But "something strange and appalling has happened in Atlanta," King argued. A gulf now existed between its profession of racial liberalism and its practice. "Atlanta says her schools are integrated," King intoned, but "[n]ot a single Negro child attends a public elementary school with his white brothers." And Of the more than 14,000 blacks enrolled in high schools, only 153 attended classes with whites.[3]

King warned that blacks in Atlanta and throughout the South had grown weary of such "hard and ugly facts." He reminded the audience of the "urgency of now" and encouraged them to pursue freedom through "creative pressure"— the only method through which blacks had ever made gains in American history. "In the absence of legal, political, economic and moral pressure," the minister insisted, "not even a city as enlightened as Atlanta is likely to grant the Negro his constitutional rights." "Atlanta needs an Amos to cry out, 'let justice roll down like waters and righteousness like a mighty stream.'"[4]

For many years, NAACP LDF lawyer Constance Baker Motley—later the first African-American woman appointed to the federal bench—tried to play the role of "Amos" in the struggle to implement *Brown v. Board of Education* in Atlanta. A critic of A. T. Walden's willingness to compromise with segregationists, Motley took the reins of leadership in the struggle for quality education in 1958. Walden, local black teachers, and other leading members of the black middle class had embraced gradualism as the best course for implementing *Brown*. In 1954, Walden had made headlines in the *New York Times* for advising African Americans to "move slowly" toward an end to school segregation so as not to add to the "emotional instability" of white resisters. By contrast, Motley, like King, fiercely opposed Jim Crow with a sense of urgency and without concern for white prerogatives. She insisted that the constitutional rights of black students could not be made "forever contingent" on white public opinion. She blasted the "white supremacy" that impeded "immediate" desegregation of the city's schools. The Atlanta school case represented one of LDF's highest profile assaults on resistance to *Brown*, and the nation's premier civil rights law firm meant to win the fight.[5]

As much as her views overlapped with King's, Motley's battle plan differed substantially from the one that Dr. King recommended to Atlantans in 1963. The minister prescribed a peaceful "revolt" waged partly in the streets, one in which blacks engaged in direct action and "demanded" freedom. Motley, by contrast, fought segregation in the courtroom, and there, she abjured talk of "demands." An attorney did not make demands to the court; one "prayed for relief" or respectfully "moved" for an order. Motley—a woman who shattered race, gender, and class norms and offended many simply by appearing in the courtroom and claiming to be a lawyer—used less defiant and more technical words to persuade.[6]

No one expected Motley herself to protest in the streets. Others could play that role. A vibrant direct action movement flourished in Atlanta beginning in 1960. The law, the Constitution, and legal precedents—*Brown*, above all else—energized these protests. The Supreme Court's failure to enforce *Brown* inspired disaffected college students to turn away from litigation and to pursue alternative, nonjuridical protest strategies, such as sit-ins. The Atlanta-based SNCC and its local affiliate, COAHR, waged a dynamic battle against segregated public accommodations and for black political power. But these organizations did not wage a similar battle against school segregation during the period that Motley and other LDF lawyers fought in the courtroom against Jim Crow public schools.

In the education context, the twin avenues of civil rights protest—legal and direct action—did not have a catalytic effect on each other. Quite the contrary was true. The spirit of protest seldom touched LDF's school desegregation campaign. This was true despite the national NAACP's awareness that *Brown's* successful implementation would turn on "community action." The law—the courtroom, judges, lawyers, legal precedents, and legal norms—defined, indeed enveloped, the school desegregation campaign. The collaboration between lawyers and activists evident in other areas gave way to a lawyer- and court-driven effort managed at arm's length from the community and local organizations. Neither SNCC nor COAHR devoted significant energy to school desegregation. The most obvious ally in LDF's school desegregation struggle, the Atlanta branch of the NAACP, proved organizationally ineffective and particularly unsuccessful in connecting with the black working class. Neither direct action nor LDF's vision of *Brown* captivated the ASLC.[7]

White resisters to desegregation had a tremendous advantage. Without the aid of politically empowered local organizations, Motley and her colleagues had only law at their disposal in battles over segregation. And the law, it turned out, was not enough to generate the kind of change that LDF sought.


## "A CENTURY OF LITIGATION"


In the first four years after *Brown*, the Atlanta Board of Education did nothing to desegregate its schools. During this four-year span, A. T. Walden did not file a court case to push the board to act, despite his public assurances to the NAACP that Atlanta would lead the school desegregation fight. Walden preferred to "sit down with local officials to map plans" for desegregation in order to "lessen the need for litigation," the *Atlanta Daily World* reported. Walden, it appeared, was content to indulge the board's evasion of *Brown*.[8]

In January 1958, LDF resolved to end the Atlanta Board of Education's years of foot-dragging over *Brown*. For too long, the board had been merely "studying" the problem of how to comply with *Brown*. "Negroes in Atlanta had been waiting for some sign that their rights would be recognized," Marshall declared, but had "received not a scintilla of evidence of any good faith move toward compliance." Nine black students had filed petitions to enter all-white schools in June 1955, but the Atlanta Board of Education had taken no steps to comply with *Brown*. The national NAACP had counseled a prompt and decisive response to such delay. "If no plans are announced or no steps taken toward desegregation" by September 1955, the NAACP directed, "the time for a lawsuit has arrived." Hence, black parents finally turned to the federal courts to decide their grievance. Constance Baker Motley and Thurgood Marshall filed suit to end the city's practice of segregating students by race in the public schools, once and for all.[9]

Given Walden's conciliatory approach to the school board, Motley and her boss would not entrust the task of shepherding the Atlanta school suit through the federal courts to LDF's longtime local counsel. Walden had generally disfavored aggressive civil rights litigation. In fact, one local black leader, in requesting the "strong arm of the National legal staff," complained "that here in Atlanta, throughout the years, we have not been successful in winning a single case in the matter of civil rights." *Calhoun*, which was LDF's "first serious assault on the scaffolding of resistance erected by the hard core of the Southern states," demanded the most tenacious lawyers and the truest believers in the cause of desegregation. A 1955 *Crisis* article directed to branch leaders had underscored the stakes involved in the selection of personnel to lead the fight for equal education: "The kind of person you elect or appoint...to head NAACP delegations to school boards is [of] the utmost importance. The...placement—for any reason—of what sociologists call an 'accommodating' Negro (whom we know, or even suspect as being, an 'Uncle Tom') in such a position of responsibility is virtually inexcusable." It continued, "There can be no compromise, whatsoever, with the principle that segregation and discrimination in public education is subversive, immoral, and illegal." In light of his mixed reputation, Walden did not meet these stringent standards. He was one of the attorneys of record in *Calhoun v. Latimer*, but the case belonged to LDF. Motley directed the litigation, made the appearances in court, argued the motions, and spoke about the matter to the press. E. E. Moore, and later, Donald Hollowell, assisted Motley, as chief local counsel in the case.[10]

Motley—an attractive and elegantly dressed brown-skinned woman who stood nearly six feet tall—made an indelible impression in the southern courtroom. The daughter of a chef for Yale University's "secret" society Skull and Bones, Motley first joined the legal staff of LDF as an intern in 1945, a year before graduating from Columbia Law School. By the time Motley filed the Atlanta school desegregation case, she had already made a singular mark on a profession dominated by men. Motley had been a principal assistant to Thurgood Marshall in *Brown* and lead counsel in numerous teacher salary equalization and higher education desegregation cases. Peers considered her an "excellent" trial lawyer. Perhaps her single most famous legal victory occurred in 1962, when her client, James Meredith, broke Jim Crow's hold on the University of Mississippi. Over the span of her career, she won nine of ten cases she argued before the U.S. Supreme Court.[11]

Motley "knew her stuff" and routinely confounded the expectations of judges and counsel, some of them "perfectly hostile and not particularly well qualified." Often refused the honorific "Mrs.," she grew accustomed to hearing herself called "that Motley woman." She once endured a hearing before a federal judge in Birmingham that began with his observation: "Well, you're a woman." Another judge before whom she appeared routinely closed his eyes rather than view black attorneys; the sight of Motley, black and female, was truly insufferable. Women lawyers rarely appeared in the courtroom, especially in the Deep South. During the 1950s—the height of Motley's career as a civil rights litigator—women constituted merely 3 percent of America's approximately 180,000 lawyers. Black women were a tiny part of this group, less than one-half of 1 percent of the nation's little more than sixty-two hundred female lawyers. These numbers made Motley virtually invisible within the legal profession, but all too conspicuous in the courtroom.[12]

Despite the outrages occasioned by her singularity, Motley had earned her place at counsel's table and she demonstrated great skill in the courtroom. In the process, she exerted an authority unknown to black women over white men. Motley cross-examined state and local officials—who by custom did not deign to acknowledge her, much less speak to her—and forced them to answer questions about their treatment of blacks. She never failed to note disingenuousness, and inevitably made officials "squirm" on the witness stand. "She was a dogged opponent of Southern segregationists who found her tougher than Grant at Vicksburg," colleague Jack Greenberg observed. Others provided similar descriptions. They called her "hard-charging," "unyielding," "indomitable." Black citizens who packed the courtrooms to marvel at the "Negro woman lawyer from New York" as she turned the tables on the white establishment took great pride in the most unusual sight. After Motley's first trial in Jackson, Mississippi, in 1949, local blacks "reenacted scenes from the trial in barbershops and beauty parlors, at parties, in backyards, wherever groups gathered." Motley and other LDF lawyers were extraordinary role models for black southerners.[13]

Yet, Motley fought segregation on her own behalf, as well as for her clients. During her travels across the South to litigate civil rights cases, Motley personally confronted the quotidian injustices that Jim Crow visited upon all blacks. Whites barred her from hotel rooms, restaurants, and restrooms, just as they barred local blacks. Deprived of overnight accommodations in cities where she litigated cases, Motley suffered "hardship" and "sheer physical exhaustion." She drove hundreds of miles to sleep in cities with hotels that rented rooms to blacks, and then drove back to the sites of her trials early the next morning. Sometimes Motley feared for her safety—she lay awake at night, unable to sleep, or slept under guard by men armed with machine guns and rifles—all because of her race, her social activism, and the threat of white lawlessness.[14]

White resistance to her activism was as pronounced in Georgia as in Mississippi or Alabama. Long before she filed *Calhoun*, the state's political leaders had denounced *Brown*. "Come hell or high water, races will not be mixed in Georgia schools," said the governor. Every member of the state's congressional delegation had signed the "Southern Manifesto." This March 1956 document called the Supreme Court's school desegregation decision an "abuse" of judicial power; signatories promised that the South would resist the Court's tyranny through every "lawful means." The state's arch-segregationist attorney general, Eugene Cook, declared that the Supreme Court's "psycho-political" decision "left the door open for a century of litigation" to combat integration. He then launched just such a legal counteroffensive against *Brown*, the NAACP, and its members. Even Atlanta's Mayor Hartsfield, the putative racial moderate, joined the assault against *Brown*.[15]

The school board's response to LDF's complaint made clear its intention to follow this plan of massive resistance by aggressively litigating the case. The lawyers, led by B. D. Murphy and Newell Edenfield, filed a motion to dismiss the complaint that attacked the representativeness of the plaintiff class. Murphy argued that the plaintiffs should be precluded from maintaining a class action because the named parties, ten students, could not show that the approximately forty thousand Negro school children in the City of Atlanta and about twelve hundred Negro teachers had "authorized the complainants to act on their behalf." This calculating argument reflected the school board's awareness that many black Atlantans—especially educators and administrators—were wary of desegregation. In civil rights actions, however, courts permitted cases to proceed without showing that all members of a putative class that had consented to the suit and had precisely the same goals. Nevertheless, the question of whether LDF's clients fully supported its school desegregation campaign was vital and loomed over the proceedings for years. But for now, it had no traction in the district court. In May 1958, U.S. District Court Judge Frank A. Hooper rejected the school board's motion to dismiss the case in its entirety.[16]

If Judge Hooper's decision to deny the board's motion heartened the plaintiffs, so, too, did his preliminary order in the case. The order made clear that the district court would not countenance open political defiance of the Supreme Court. Judge Hooper issued the order against the backdrop of school desegregation battles in Arkansas and Virginia in which federal district courts *had* facilitated outright resistance to *Brown*. Georgia seemed poised to engage in similar resistance. *Calhoun v. Latimer*, the first suit to challenge segregation in Georgia's elementary and secondary schools, had unleashed a political firestorm. Governor Vandiver threatened to close the state's schools rather than "bow to integration." In his order, Judge Hooper acknowledged the passions of the resistance, but insisted that the Supreme Court had tied his hands on the essential question of whether his state could lawfully continue to segregate its schools. "[T]his Court is bound by the decision of the U.S. Supreme Court as announced not only in the *Brown* case, but in many other cases subsequent to the *Brown* case, arising in Little Rock, Arkansas, in Virginia and in other localities," he wrote. "Even the most ardent segregationists in the land, though bitterly opposed to such ruling, now recognize that racially segregated public schools are not permitted by law."[17]

But the Board of Education was undaunted and its legal arguments became increasingly creative. The defendants next argued that *Brown* was immaterial to the suit. The school board's attorney, B. D. Murphy, "categorically denied" that Atlanta had ever erected a system of Jim Crow schools. Children in Atlanta were not "segregated by direction or order of the Board of Education," he explained. Racial "separation"—Murphy's preferred word—had, he explained, originated during Reconstruction. It all began, he declared "about eighteen sixty-five or six when the Freedman's Bureau established public schools here and wouldn't let white children go to them. That's where it started."[18]

Even Judge Hooper—born and bred in rural Georgia, and a man who never "convinced" Motley that he "believed blacks had rights that whites were bound to respect"—responded skeptically to Murphy's claim. At oral argument on the issue, Judge Hooper declared, "It surprises me that the defendants could contend that segregation is not practiced in Atlanta schools." "Do you or do you not concede," he asked Murphy, "that for the last ninety years that the Atlanta Schools have operated by separate schools for white and colored?" "Your Honor," Murphy explained, "I don't have any recollection back as far as ninety years." The judge pressed the school board's attorney. Hooper stressed that he asked not for the attorney's personal remembrances, but for evidence admissible in a court of law about whether "since 1870 there has been any mixing of the races in Atlanta schools." Murphy then conceded that black and white children attended separate schools. But, he insisted, they *voluntarily* attended separate schools: official board action had nothing do with the racial make-up of the city's schools.[19]

The board's defense intended to put Du Bois's separate schools theory to the test. The officials hoped to divide the black community. The board had concluded that "black teachers and administrators wanted segregation to continue so that they could keep their jobs," Motley believed, and "that most black parents were of the same view." Blacks would be willing to keep the separate school system intact because in Atlanta, the school board did not discriminate against Negro students or Negro teachers, as was done in Topeka, Kansas, Clarendon County, South Carolina, and elsewhere—or so it claimed.[20]

Murphy advocated his client's case by advancing a debatable, but ultimately effective, interpretation of both *Brown* and the factual record. Judge Hooper had "misconstrued" *Brown*, the attorney argued. The justices had not mandated school desegregation. Rather, *Brown* "simply held that no child could be denied admission to a school on account of his race or color." Here, Murphy recapitulated the position of Judge John Parker of the district court in the South Carolina case *Briggs v. Elliott*. *Brown* "did not require integration, it merely forbade segregation," Judge Parker held in 1955. School boards throughout the South seized on the holding to claim that they had limited, if any, affirmative obligations to desegregate their school systems; rather, they had only to use race-neutral assignment criteria. Parker's conception of *Brown*'s meaning, recited by Murphy, could be traced back to the Court and the lack of specificity in its original remedial decree and the lack of subsequent decisions robustly implementing the 1954 decree. *Brown I* plainly struck down *all* laws mandating or permitting school segregation, and *Brown II* commanded "nonracial school districts" to be achieved through the revision of attendance areas. But in *Brown II* the justices had, in fact, declined to address when and how school districts had to comply with its edict.[21]

Ominously for the plaintiffs, Judge Hooper warmly received Murphy's legal argument. "If the Defendants would state that they have no intention of denying a colored child admission to a white school on account of his race or color, why I would be inclined to take the case off the calendar and let things proceed on that basis," he stated. Murphy disclaimed authority to make such a statement on the school board's behalf. But he persisted in attempts to show that Atlanta operated a facially nondiscriminatory system. "The *Brown* case decides that it operates to discriminate against the Negro children to deny them admission to schools with white children," Murphy explained, "because it would adversely affect their personalities and put them in a position of inferiority." But, "we expect to prove that ain't so as regards Atlanta." Segregation did not stigmatize Atlanta's blacks.[22]

At first, Murphy's argument proceeded smoothly. Ira Jarrell, the superintendent of schools since 1944, testified that Atlanta had a system of "community schools." The "community," she insisted, "determines the school [assignment], more or less." The Board of Education had not promulgated rules or regulations that compelled students to attend separate schools by race. Edward S. Cook, the longest serving member of the Atlanta Board of Education, buttressed Jarrell's explanation. During the twenty-five years that *he* had been a member of the board, blacks had *never* complained to *him* about their school assignments, Cook testified. They had attended segregated schools by choice, he declared. The 1955 desegregation petitions had been filed only at the bidding of the NAACP.[23]

One of Murphy's own witnesses undermined the board's defense. Initially, Dr. Rufus Clement—the sole black member of the Board of Education and a racial moderate—appeared to be a harmless witness. He disavowed involvement with the NAACP and its push to desegregate Atlanta's schools. He supported other witnesses' claims that the Board of Education did not segregate students by any formal, written rule or regulation. He admitted that he had supported the board's 1955 resolution to take no action in response to the desegregation petitions other than to conduct a "study." But, under cross-examination by Motley, Clement made several damning admissions. In practice, if not by explicit policy, the board *did* assign students to schools by race, he stated: black students could not, for example, attend the schools nearest to them if the board had designated the neighborhood schools for whites. By default, the board assigned such blacks to the nearby "community school" that other blacks attended. Moreover, the board assigned teachers, and even administrative staff, to schools according to race. Most tellingly, Clement testified that since 1954, when he had first joined the board, the city had built separate schools for black and white students. Clement's testimony on crossexamination devastated the board's case. Following it, Motley forced Jarrell to confirm Clement's basic contentions. Between 1944 and 1959, Jarrell conceded, Atlanta had constructed twenty-five new schools to accommodate black population growth; all of the schools had been constructed in black neighborhoods, and only black students had been assigned to the new school buildings.[24]

Murphy had been outmaneuvered. Just two weeks after the initial hearing ended, Judge Hooper rendered the inevitable judgment. The Atlanta Board of Education did assign students to schools by race, Murphy's claims to the contrary notwithstanding. After all, Georgia statutes not only required school segregation, but expressly denied appropriations to integrated schools. The city had in fact segregated its public schools in violation of the law. Hooper enjoined all racially discriminatory practices in admissions. He ordered the Board of Education to formulate a plan that would systematically and effectively desegregate Atlanta's schools by December 1, 1959.[25]

The order precipitated howls of protest from whites, in positions high and low. Governor Vandiver vowed to close the public schools if necessary to avoid desegregation. "No, not one Negro" would attend school with whites, he promised. He emphasized that the Constitution and laws of Georgia gave him no other choice than to end public education in the state. Senators Herman Talmadge and Richard Russell called on the state to hold firm on Jim Crow. Eugene Cook termed the situation "explosive" and called on NAACP lawyers to drop the suit or risk "violent and frustrating results to both races." Other politicians asked white citizens to organize, resist desegregation, and create private, whites-only schools. Primed for resistance, segregationists picketed in the streets, singing "Two, Four, Six, Eight; we don't want to integrate."[26]

In Atlanta however, Mayor Hartsfield had moderated his position. He criticized the decision, but also insisted that the school board would not defy a federal court order. Court-ordered desegregation and de facto segregation could coexist, Hartsfield and other sophisticates implied, even as the Atlanta Board of Education appealed the district court's ruling.[27]

## The Plan of Attrition

Meanwhile, on November 30, 1959, just before the deadline set by the court, the board submitted its desegregation plan. In no hurry to implement *Brown*, the city proposed a twelve-year timetable for assigning students to schools "without regard to race." The board planned to desegregate one grade per year, beginning in September 1960. Twelfth-graders would be eligible for reassignment in the 1960–61 academic year. Those in the eleventh grade could apply for reassignment in 1961–62, and so forth. It would be twelve years—the 1970s—before black first-graders could hope to be assigned to a desegregated school.[28]

Beyond the extended time frame, numerous other barriers awaited students who sought to assert their rights under *Brown*. The board had no intention of reassigning students en masse. A general reassignment plan, the board asserted, would be "disruptive" of "orderly administration" of the school district. If it occurred at all, desegregation would take place through the initiative of individual black pupils, because the plan required black students, if they wished to attend a desegregated school, to apply for transfers to white schools.[29]

But application did not, by any means, guarantee admission. The board claimed "inherent power" to determine whether applicants merited reassignment. The plan subjected transfer applications to a plethora of admissions criteria, and spelled out numerous other factors that the board would use to assess reassignment requests. Some criteria, such as space limitations, teaching capacity, and the availability of transportation, were logistical in nature. However, other criteria permitted the board to thwart desegregation through subjective assessments of questionable legitimacy. The plan permitted the board to consider how a requested transfer would affect white students and the school community itself; how new pupils would affect established or proposed academic programs; the possibility of friction or disorder among pupils or others; the possibility of breaches of the peace, ill will, or economic retaliation within the community; the effect of the admission of a pupil upon the academic progress of other students in a particular school; and the effect of admission upon prevailing academic standards at a particular school.[30]

Still other criteria, described in exquisite detail, made transfer applications contingent upon the board's assessment of black students' academic achievement, morals, and other personal characteristics. Among the topics the plan permitted the board to consider were "academic preparation," "scholastic aptitude," "relative intelligence," "mental energy," "psychological qualifications," and "home environment." The board could assess these variables through interviews of the child, parents, or guardians, and through whatever "tests, examinations, and investigations" it deemed appropriate.[31]

An assortment of procedural hurdles made this already burdensome application process even more arduous. Students could apply for transfers only during a two-week period. A student, parent, or guardian could obtain applications only in person. What is more, they had to obtain applications directly from a school principal or the office of the superintendent of schools. The board accepted only notarized applications. A student had only fifteen days to appeal the board's denial of his transfer request. And, in a move that could only dissuade appeals, the board reserved the right to "investigate" and "examine" pupils who challenged its initial decisions.[32]

Change had come to Atlanta, but not the kind that Motley and LDF sought. Before Judge Hooper had declared the schools unconstitutionally segregated in June 1959, Superintendent Jarrell had boasted that the "community," the populace itself, decided where students attended school. After the federal court ordered desegregation, the board established what amounted to a selective admissions process—akin to college application—for blacks alone. Desegregation was, by design, an onerous and risky undertaking whose burdens fell onto the shoulders of the victims of discrimination.[33]

Motley quickly filed a brief objecting to the board's plan. It was, she charged, completely inadequate. She matched the numbing details of the plan with countless arguments opposing them. Motley protested the "unreasonable and manifestly unnecessary" delays inherent in the complex grade-a-year assignment plan. She objected to the plan's exclusive focus on pupil assignment; *Brown* required desegregation of the entire system, including faculty and staff. Most significantly, she attacked the plan as an ineffective method of dismantling segregation: it placed no obligation whatsoever on the school board to disestablish Jim Crow. The city had ignored the Supreme Court's statement in the Little Rock case, issued in 1958, that authorities must "devote every effort toward *initiating* desegregation and bringing about the *elimination* of racial discrimination in the public school system." Atlanta's approach left the plaintiffs in an untenable position. "[T]he continuance of a completely segregated system will obviously deter individual Negroes from seeking a change in the status quo," she explained. "The bravest citizen would shield his tender young child from such an ordeal." And those intrepid students who did undertake the application process encountered twenty-four unjustifiably complex, vague, or irrelevant criteria— factors employed for the first time in Atlanta public school history.[34]

Judge Hooper found the vast majority of LDF's arguments unpersuasive. He expressed sympathy—not for Motley's clients—but for the Board of Education, tasked with devising a desegregation plan for a large, urban school system. The court rejected Motley's premise that the plan failed in its basic obligation to produce a constitutionally adequate remedy for segregation. Hooper embraced Judge Parker's understanding of *Brown*'s remedial scope. He wrote: "The Plan of the Atlanta School Board...is not invalid merely because it prohibits racial discrimination rather than requiring a mixing of the races." He rejected the plaintiffs' attack on the plan's twelve-year time frame. No legal authority substantiated LDF's claim that the board must proceed more quickly. Finally, the court rejected the plaintiffs' characterization of the reassignment criteria. The psychological, academic, and other assessments did not discriminate per se against applicants. The court did offer, however, to entertain future claims that the board applied the criteria to certain applications in a discriminatory manner. In addition, Judge Hooper agreed that threats, disorder, or retaliation could not impede the desegregation plan, and he extended the timeline for students to appeal rejected transfer applications. Otherwise, the school board won sweeping approval of its desegregation plan. Tellingly, the board withdrew its appeal of Hooper's initial ruling.[35]

What is more, Judge Hooper's order contained language that seemed to encourage open resistance to its terms. The judge made his order "contingent upon the enactment of statutes permitting such plan to be put into operation." He then beseeched lawmakers to confront the conflict between his court order and state law. The judge had commanded Atlanta to desegregate, beginning in September 1960. Yet, Georgia statutes forbade the disbursement of funds to public schools that permitted "the mixing of the races." The state and its school districts faced a crisis because of the Atlanta school desegregation order, and Hooper called on legislators to address this urgent matter before the start of the next academic year. He left it to them how to resolve the federal constitutional matter. "The people of Georgia through their chosen representatives in the Legislature should be allowed to make the important decision as to whether they would prefer the closing of their schools on the one hand, to the gradual desegregation of the schools on the other hand."[36]

Motley was incredulous. The court, she argued, had made the plaintiffs' constitutional rights "forever contingent" upon legislative approval of its order.

Hooper's solicitousness toward the General Assembly defied *Brown II* and *Cooper*, she asserted. Both precedents expressly forbade lower courts from considering public hostility to black students' constitutional rights as a factor in complying with *Brown*. The Supreme Court's October 1958 opinion in *Cooper* commanded the Little Rock School Board to desegregate *despite* opposition to a federal court desegregation order. The Little Rock board had suspended desegregation after the Arkansas General Assembly enacted laws to prevent racially mixed schools and the governor of Arkansas called in the Arkansas National Guard to physically block blacks from entering Central High School. In the face of this defiance, the justices had categorically rejected the board's action and the district court's countenancing of delay. "[T]he Constitutional rights of children not to be discriminated against in school admissions on grounds of race," stated the Court's per curiam opinion, "neither can be nullified openly and directly by state legislators or executive or judicial officials, nor nullified indirectly by them through evasive schemes for segregation." In light of events in Little Rock and the Court's unambiguous response to them, Judge Hooper, Motley insisted, needed to appreciate—and retract—the mixed signals he had sent to the forces of resistance within Georgia.[37]

But Judge Hooper understood perfectly well. In the preliminary order, the court had stressed: "The decision of closing the schools, that is on the people of Georgia. It's not on the court." Judge Hooper intended to permit "different communities" to "speak for themselves as to what they wanted." "This Court will not attempt to say to the people of Georgia or say to the Georgia Legislature or say to any School Board what they should do." Judge Hooper felt compelled to *order* school desegregation, but he did *not* feel obligated to force citizens actually to desegregate. Hooper's actions made a powerful impression on Motley. She "sized him up not as one of the worst federal judges we had to confront (he was always dignified and courteous) but as one who believed that you make promises to black people and do not keep them—a typical segregationist view."[38]

School board lawyer B. D. Murphy had lost the battle, but won the war. Motley, who had relied on the U.S. Supreme Court and its law as weapons of warfare, found herself cornered. The federal district court, a creature of local culture, had subordinated her clients' rights to the will of the majority. The next phase of the litigation—directed by an all-white Georgia General Assembly populated by many who professed hatred of the NAACP, civil rights lawyers, and *Brown*—ensured that LDF and its clients would remain marginalized. On the eve of the upcoming legislative session, Motley could only stand in court and proclaim her "hope" that the "people of Georgia will elect to keep the schools open" and "commence the process of desegregation in peace and harmony." Motley no longer controlled her case. And the named plaintiffs had little, if any, voice. In stark contrast to the collegians who critiqued the inadequacies of litigation, then launched the sit-ins, and eventually boycotted the "racist" Georgia legislature, the student-plaintiffs in *Calhoun* remained out of public view. They awaited further instructions from their lawyers, the courts—and the Georgia legislature.[39]

## STAGECRAFT

The assembly convened less than a week after Judge Hooper made it a partner in carrying out the court's duties. The General Assembly session, called the "most important since Reconstruction," established the Committee on Schools to determine how Georgia would respond to *Brown*. The legislature charged the committee with discerning the public's attitude toward desegregation. Motley protested that blacks did not consider the committee "an acceptable answer" to the school desegregation lawsuit. The committee ignored the criticism. It performed its duties by holding public hearings in the state's ten congressional districts; it promised to report its findings and then make recommendations to the legislature.[40]

The committee's establishment garnered significant coverage in the national broadcast and print media, otherwise obsessed with the spread of the student sit-ins. To distant observers, it looked as if the state's white majority was engaged in public soul-searching about the issue of segregation. Ultimately, however, the hearings were faux populist political theater; highly choreographed events, the sessions revealed little about whites' racial views and permitted little improvisation. Judge Hooper already had set up the framework for discussion. Political leaders would either defy the court and close the schools or comply with the court's order and permit token desegregation.[41]

The hearings did not alter white citizens' stance on segregation; nor did the legislature expect them to serve such a purpose. The committee's chairman, John A. Sibley, a partner at the venerable Atlanta firm King and Spalding, began each proceeding by declaring his confidence that "everyone, black and white, preferred segregation." Speakers then confirmed virtually unanimous resistance to black social equality in rural Georgia and areas around Atlanta. The testimony of Rev. W. F. Abernathy of Cobb County exemplified this view. "God is a segregated God," Abernathy said. "He separated people yonder in days past, and he still wants it to remain that way. I love the colored fellow—I certainly do-but I love him in the place that God gave him."[42]

The one perhaps unexpected development during the hearings troubled the NAACP and LDF. Many blacks refused to endorse school desegregation—even as students protested segregated public accommodations in numerous states and racial equality appeared to be on the rise all around them. To be sure, African Americans appeared before the committee much less often than whites, and rural areas, where white domination was strongest, were the bastions of black ambivalence about *Brown*. Nevertheless, that those blacks who did testify so consistently failed to express support for even token desegregation buttressed whites' claim that the NAACP and LDF did not credibly speak for blacks. Instead of desegregation, the black witnesses preferred equal resources. They expressed pride in separate schools (many recently built by the state in an effort to stave off desegregation) and concern about teacher quality and employment opportunities for black educators after desegregation. Georgia Banks of rural Elbert County, who spoke for her church and PTA, noted, "[w]e have a beautiful school building" and "wonderful buses" and prefer "unmixed" schools. Ann Daniel, a supervisor of the Columbia County Schools, also made the case for separate schools. She explained that black principals, teachers, and presidents of parent-teacher organizations in her county "are very proud of our schools." "Inasmuch as our building, facilities and school programs are equal, relationship between the races is very good," Daniel said, and "we would not like to see the educational progress of our future citizens impeded." She concluded by declaring that she was "strenuously advocating equal but separate schools." Daniel and many others like her articulated Du Bois's argument against LDF's sweeping litigation campaign: separation unaccompanied by discrimination did not harm black students; in fact, it benefited black communities.[43]

Indeed, a significant number of blacks who favored separate schools worked as educators or administrators and conceded their economic interest in preserving this state of affairs. And many had no reservations in saying so. Clinton Tally, a school principal in Calhoun County, noted that blacks in his district received 92 percent of the county's educational budget; this, alone, justified continued segregation. More pointedly, L. H. Hardy, Jr., a principal of the Carnersville Trade School, said he supported the status quo "because I'm a teacher and that's my living." Many other teachers echoed his sentiments. Dr. R. W. Greene of Columbus, Georgia, a minister and president of the Race Relations and Public Relations Council, was by far the most outspoken African-American advocate of separate schools. Greene claimed to speak for black educators reluctant to voice opposition to the NAACP's campaign. He cited job losses among teachers and administrators and recent improvements in segregated schools as rationales for opposition to desegregation. "It is my candid opinion that 95 percent of these teachers would rather maintain the present school pattern, the segregated school, with continued improvements along all lines, on the secondary and college level," Dr. Greene wrote in a pamphlet entitled "Integration Is not Inevitable."[44]

The NAACP pushed back. In a dramatic development, the state NAACP insisted that the commission strike all testimony favoring separate schools by black teachers and principals who resided in Judge Hooper's hometown. Each and every black witness there who supported separation had succumbed to white pressure, the organization insisted. Sibley retorted that the NAACP had unclean hands. *It* had coached black witnesses to testify in favor of desegregation. Chastened, the NAACP dropped its protest. In reality, some black witnesses who testified in favor of separate schools surely had done so under pressure, but many others likely had expressed genuinely favorable feelings toward separate schools, even if the NAACP did not want to hear them. The Sibley committee's hearings provided a window onto a problem that dogged the NAACP and LDF in Atlanta and other cities as the school desegregation campaign unfolded: local people and national leaders did not necessarily agree on what equality required in the educational context.[45]

Nevertheless, as planned, the argument for token desegregation gained momentum when the hearings shifted to Atlanta: advocates for "open schools" dominated the Atlanta hearings. While most of the eighteen hundred Georgians who testified during the Sibley hearings supported Jim Crow schools (1,003 to 575), in Atlanta, 85 of the 114 witnesses favored open schools. Members of Help Our Public Education (HOPE) and the League of Women Voters, along with a few prominent African Americans, including Rev. William Holmes Borders, John Wesley Dobbs, and Donald Hollowell, testified in favor of open schools. The testimony held no surprises. By the time Sibley arrived in the city, Mayor Hartsfield and business leaders had determined to preserve Atlanta's image and marketability. Atlanta could not "afford" to resist. They looked to Little Rock and saw what they did not want their city to become. The standoff between Arkansas's governor and the federal courts had devastated the state's economy. These consequences, decision-makers reasoned, must be avoided in Atlanta. Faced with Hooper's order, Hartsfield and a coalition of business leaders, white moderates, and liberals now framed the state's options as a choice between saving public education and destroying it altogether. School closure would leave all but the wealthiest of Georgia's children without the opportunity to attend school. Consequently, this group favored "open schools" (or in plain language and effect, token desegregation).[46]

In practice, open school advocates knew, only a few African-American students—those who passed the Board of Education's rigorous and subjective evaluation process—would gain admission to a few white schools. This trickle of black students would appease the federal courts and resolve the problems created by *Brown*. Residential segregation would confine the rest to black schools. A. C. Latimer, the president of the Board of Education, expressly supported open schools on this basis. Whites could rest assured that patterns of residential segregation would "deter any mass mixing of the races more than any other single factor," he explained during the hearing. Rev. Borders likewise emphasized that "less than 100 Negro students would be involved in desegregation" and "where they live will determine where they attend school." Neither the *Calhoun* plaintiffs nor their parents spoke at the hearing.[47]

After completing public hearings and considering the options before it, the Sibley committee issued a sharply divided report in April 1960. An eight-person minority of the committee insisted that the state stand pat on segregation, while an eleven-person majority endorsed a local option, or "freedom-of-choice" desegregation plan. The majority lambasted *Brown*, but believed that the state could comply with the law in principle while resisting it in substance. The majority cited Judge Parker's decision in *Briggs v. Elliott* in support of its recommendation. Numerous federal courts, accepting Parker's interpretation of *Brown*, had instituted extraordinarily limited school desegregation plans, the majority report noted. Georgia also could have it both ways. The General Assembly did not adopt the majority's recommendation, however; after all, an eight-person minority on the committee had recommended continued resistance even to token desegregation. In the wake of the two committee reports, the legislature took no steps to repeal the state's laws against school desegregation.[48]

The ball was back in Hooper's court. As a first step, in May 1960, the judge rejected Motley's motion that desegregation commence by the fall. Referencing the split Sibley report, the judge instead gave the General Assembly "one last chance" to amend its laws. Hooper made the Atlanta desegregation plan effective May 1961, a full year later than LDF had requested. The court justified the one-year delay by pointing to a factor that the Supreme Court had expressly banned from consideration in *Cooper v. Aaron*. He cited continued resistance to *Brown* in rural areas of the state, documented during the hearings. In these parts, the court observed, residential patterns did not ensure that desegregation would occur on a token basis. "The danger which Georgia now faces [is that] representatives of the rural communities will not permit the Atlanta Plan to become operative," Judge Hooper declared.[49]

Such delay might have continued to plague *Calhoun* if not for a second suit filed by Motley. The LDF's attack on segregation at UGA tested the federal courts' willingness to confront rather than appease the resistance. The showdown occurred in January 1961, when the U.S. District Court ordered the admission of two African-American students to the flagship campus in Athens.

Whites rioted when the two students, Charlayne Hunter and Hamilton Holmes, arrived on campus. Mobs, including Klansmen, surrounded Hunter's dormitory room, hurled stones, brandished weapons, and committed acts of violence against bystanders. Governor Vandiver vowed to cut off appropriations to the university to prevent desegregation and ordered the university closed. More rioting ensued, amid legal and political maneuvering over the fate of the black students, whom the university suspended on the grounds that their presence on campus endangered the community.[50]

The saga ended after a federal district court declared unconstitutional a Georgia law that would have denied state funds to any integrated school. The court's action provided momentum for white moderates who had grown worried that Georgia would be labeled "another Little Rock" if the crisis at the university continued. The governor caved to pressure from the moderates. In mid-January 1961, after an emotional address by Governor Vandiver, the state legislature abandoned massive resistance to desegregation. Vandiver warned that if the state did not settle the crisis between federal and state law, the confrontation would spread "like a cancerous growth" and stifle the state's economic growth. The Georgia General Assembly then repealed all laws that mandated closure of racially mixed schools—an action that covered public education at all levels.[51]

The resolution of the crisis at UGA paved the way for the token desegregation of Atlanta's public schools in the fall of 1961. The school board, relying on the complex criteria in its pupil placement plan, selected 10 black students—reduced to 9 when one decided to accept early admission to Spelman College instead—from among 129 who applied to serve as desegregation pioneers. On August 30, 1961, the brave students, teenagers aged fifteen to seventeen, broke the racial barrier at four city high schools. The Atlanta Police Department took elaborate security precautions to avoid disorder. Dozens of uniformed officers with K-9 police dogs patrolled the school grounds. In addition, FBI agents kept watch. Law enforcement arrested six people, among them a member of the American Nazi Party. At the appointed hour, the Atlanta Nine quietly entered the school buildings. No violence occurred. Nor did any serious disturbances occur once the students took their places inside; students had been urged to avoid trouble, and meddlesome parents had been barred from campus. The two or three black students in each of the four high schools ate alone during lunch, however, and mostly found an indifferent or "stand-offish" reception in the classrooms and hallways, manned by law enforcement. Some whites were "actively hostile." Teachers and school administrators nevertheless congratulated themselves: the day had been "wonderful," "devoid of tension," "normal," "just perfect."[52]

Journalists from newspapers, magazines, television, and radio observed the scene from large media clearinghouses and hospitality centers set up by the city of Atlanta near the schools. The city staged a show—a sight apart from Little Rock—for the world to see. Mayor Hartsfield, who hosted a press party and took reporters on a tour of the city, did his best to influence media coverage of the big day. He expressed "every confidence that the story" reporters would "flash to the world" would be a "positive, dramatic picture of a great City facing profound change with dignity; a City continuing to be a credit to the Nation; a City too busy to hate." Echoing the mayor's press statements, journalists reported the uneventful matriculation of the Atlanta Nine in tones that painted the city as uniquely progressive. The *New York Times* praised Atlanta as a "new and shining example of what can be accomplished... [b]y people of good will and intelligence." Writers for publications as varied as *Life*, the *Christian Century*, and *Newsweek* also hailed Atlanta as the paradigmatic New South city—one that not only accepted, but embraced, racial equality. President Kennedy followed suit: he opened his daily press conference by "strongly urg[ing] all communities which face this difficult transition [to desegregated schools]...to look closely at what Atlanta has done." Then Kennedy congratulated Governor Vandiver and Mayor Hartsfield on Atlanta's peaceful conversion to a desegregated school system.[53]

Yet, what had actually occurred in Atlanta? By the time the city transitioned to a nominally desegregated school system, numerous other locales had already adopted token desegregation as a method of *resistance* to *Brown*. Despite formal desegregation, the racial integrity of most schools in Atlanta and all schools outside of the city remained unblemished. The school board had assigned the nine blacks who broke the color line to schools that were far apart and scattered the nine amid a sea of white students. On the inaugural day of the desegregation experiment, under the glare of media lights, the model students had boasted of their pride in being racial pioneers. Years later, many of the Atlanta Nine spoke of having to endure taunts, pranks, alienation, loneliness, social exclusion, and the enormous "stress" of having to "prove that all blacks were equal." One of the students, fed up with the scrutiny and unpleasantness, had returned to her old school. The desegregation plan had disillusioned the few blacks involved in it and empowered the school board to delay meaningful.[54]

LDF was undaunted. The period of "massive resistance to integration" had ended, Thurgood Marshall declared in February 1960; it had been replaced by "hard legal maneuvering." Indeed, it had. Judge Hooper crystallized the dilemma that LDF faced during a hearing on Motley's motion to amend the desegregation order. The judge had remarked: "As far as I personally have any part" in *Calhoun*—a bizarre understatement for the presiding judge in the case to make—he intended to ensure a "gradual" rather than a "sudden, explosive" desegregation plan. He would "*never* go along with" Motley "in any rapid integration" plan; instead, the judge would "put as much emphasis on deliberation as speed."[55]

In the years to come, Judge Hooper remained true to his word. Few social or political forces pushed Judge Hooper to rethink his orientation to the case. The LDF—overburdened with casework and untethered to a social movement for desegregation—could not find a way to bring about structural change. Those intransigent to *Brown* controlled state and local government. The majority of whites remained opposed to desegregation, and ambivalence even reigned among blacks, as the Sibley hearings had demonstrated. In this environment, the litigation dragged on, and the court embraced tokenism again and again.


## "EASIER TO GO TO YALE"


Motley fought back against the judge's cramped understanding of the law with carefully crafted arguments. In July 1962, she and local counsel, Donald Hollowell and E. E. Moore, hauled the Board of Education back into court. In a motion for further relief, the lawyers complained that too little had changed in the way the board operated. The lawyers cited overcrowding in black schools, which, they claimed, was caused by segregation. During a hearing on the motion, a witness for the plaintiffs, Mrs. Lottie Harris, testified that she had complained to the board about the overcrowded conditions at her daughter's high school, built for one thousand students but attended by two thousand. Mrs. Harris received no reply and no remedy. In response to Motley's complaint, school board lawyer Edenfield insisted that overcrowding was not a "racial problem." It "applies to all—in many schools." Judge Hooper agreed and denied the plaintiffs' motion.[56]

Motley's criticisms of the plan did not end there. During the hearing on the motion, she had forcefully questioned the city's continued practice of subjecting black transfer applicants to tests and other "merit" criteria. "You have whites applying for transfer every day in the week. And to those whites no test is applied." The school board's practice penalized blacks for seeking transfers, she argued, and violated equal protection.[57]

Judge Hooper perceived the situation differently. Motley had not offered a "scintilla" of evidence of discrimination. The same standard applied to both races. "The plan of transfer has operated in regard to the colored primarily," he explained, merely "because they are the only ones that have asked for a transfer." "It so happens that whites do not wish to transfer." On similar logic, Hooper rejected Motley's request to enjoin the board from considering a transfer applicant's aptitude or achievement. The school board asserted that it no longer required transfer applicants to submit to tests that other students did not have to take. In order to prevail against the board, Motley would have to allege specific instances of discrimination; the court would never entertain blanket claims of discrimination against black transfer applicants.[58]

Motley then took a different tack. She requested an accelerated and more comprehensive desegregation process. Under the current plan, she pointed out, only forty-four of fifty thousand blacks had been placed in formerly all-white schools, an inexcusably low number. The board had not shouldered its burden under *Brown II* of showing that it needed additional time before substantially desegregating the system. Rather than desegregating one grade each year and by so-called freedom-of-choice, the board should redraw attendance lines, desegregate faculty and staff, and take other affirmative steps to disestablish Jim Crow by 1965. Hooper disagreed with Motley's interpretation of the law. The plaintiffs—not the defendants—bore the burden of speeding the desegregation process along. That is, he laid the blame for the numbers she cited at black students' feet. The system had not fully desegregated because only 266 blacks, rather than the full 50,000 black students in the system, had requested transfers. "[N]egro students do not desire to change," he stated. Of the 266 who did seek change, the board had found only 44 qualified to transfer. To Judge Hooper, the numbers that Motley cited proved nothing nefarious. The lawyer retorted: "Negroes cannot be required to apply now for something the Supreme Court says that they are entitled to." Yet, in Hooper's court and in so many others, they certainly could.[59]

Motley and the court had reached an impasse over the obligations of her clients and the school board. The judge held firmly to a conceptual distinction between race-neutral and race-conscious state action. The former remedied the violation found in *Brown*. "What the Court should do," he said, "is to prevent discrimination and not to force mixing." Motley found the pace of the suit deeply frustrating, while the court boasted that the Atlanta school desegregation case had evolved in a "highly satisfactory" manner. Atlanta had nothing to be embarrassed about; she should be proud of her progress. "There has been harmony and there has been cooperation and it's been commended in a great many news articles and other matters throughout the country," Hooper noted, sounding like a city booster. "I have personally felt that that was more important than just a little bit more speed." Consequently, the judge concluded, "I'm willing to let it go as it is." Motley's objections appeared unreasonable to him, and Judge Hooper categorically rejected her motion challenging the desegregation plan in a November 1962 opinion.[60]

Undaunted, Motley turned to the Fifth Circuit Court of Appeals for relief. She found a measure of success in a June 1963 opinion by Judge Griffin Bell, a storied figure in Georgia politics who had helped to initiate the Sibley hearings. In a partial vindication of Motley, Bell found aspects of the school board's admissions policies unlawful. The board discriminated by requiring only black transfer applicants to submit to interviews and to meet or exceed the average achievement test scores of the class into which they sought transfer. These practices the appeals court ordered stopped. But in a blow to LDF, the Fifth Circuit affirmed the bulk of the district court's decision. The appeals court agreed that Atlanta had made sufficient progress toward desegregating the school system. Judge Hooper had correctly determined that no "circuit-wide formula or minimum by which to measure steps forward or backward" existed. Hence, LDF had no basis in law for contending that the process must accelerate. Gradualism prevailed.[61]

As a result, in 1964, ten years after *Brown*, the Atlanta school district looked much the same as it did pre-*Brown*. The school board assigned black children to all-black schools as kindergartners. It funneled those students into all-black schools for the duration of their school careers. Black teachers taught in black schools, black principals led them, and black staff worked in them. Many of the black schools overflowed with students, necessitating double or triple sessions. Meanwhile, many white schools contained vacant classrooms and empty seats. Nevertheless, only blacks in grades nine through twelve could even apply for transfers to white schools under the district's grade-a-year desegregation plan. If a black student took the initiative and applied for a transfer, she might avoid the district's default, race-based assignment policy. However, the odds ran against her. The Board of Education denied the overwhelming majority of transfer requests. Indeed, the board's stringent application process had yielded a saying among African Americans that it was "easier to go to Yale than to transfer from one public school to another in Atlanta." Only 150 of the 56,000 blacks in the district attended school with whites, and those few blacks were dispersed among twelve white schools. These numbers inspired the *Atlanta Inquirer* to call the school board's desegregation plan a "joke."[62]

Motley decided to put Atlanta's desegregation plan to the ultimate test. she appealed the Fifth Circuit's opinion upholding the city's desegregation process to the U.S. Supreme Court. The lawyers asked the Court to declare grade-a-year plans and the token desegregation that they produced unconstitutional. The appeal represented a tremendous test for the city, and the nation as well. Similar plans existed in school districts across the South. Like Atlanta, most districts covered by *Brown* remained segregated in fact, even if not by law. On *Brown*'s tenth anniversary, merely 1.2 percent of blacks in the South attended school with whites. District courts had followed the dictum that *Brown* commanded desegregation, rather than integration. The LDF's appeal in *Calhoun v. Latimer* provided the justices with an opportunity to reevaluate how lower courts had interpreted its landmark precedent.[63]

The entry of the United States into the case made the stakes of the *Calhoun* appeal clear. The Department of Justice filed an amicus brief in support of LDF, calling the issues raised in *Calhoun* a "matter of national concern." The federal government's action enraged Georgia officials, who protested that they had "bent over backwards" to comply with the federal court's desegregation orders. Burke Marshall, the assistant attorney general for civil rights, voiced an altogether different perspective on the city's response to *Brown*. He urged the justices to declare unconstitutional all pupil assignment plans that, like Atlanta's, funneled black and white students into separate schools beginning in first grade. If the justices accepted the arguments of the Department of Justice and LDF, they would fundamentally change the Court's post-*Brown* jurisprudence. A school desegregation process that the High Court had left undefined at its core would now feature a tremendously meaningful judicial presumption: all students should launch their public educational journeys in integrated schools. Atlanta, hailed in 1961 for its peaceful transition from Jim Crow schools and a leader of the "New South," seemed a useful point of departure for the Court to reconsider the contours of its school desegregation jurisprudence.[64]

In sharp exchanges during the April 1964 oral argument at the Supreme Court, the attorneys for each side debated whether *Brown* required affirmative school board action to disestablish racially identifiable schools. A. C. "Pete" Latimer, a former member of the Atlanta Board of Education who now represented it, admitted the obvious: the city had long preferred to proceed slowly on "race mixing." But, he proclaimed, the board had recently taken dramatic steps toward compliance. After the Fifth Circuit upheld the school desegregation plan that Motley so strenuously attacked, the Board of Education had made significant changes. It had eliminated the requirement that transfer applicants submit to a special battery of tests not required of other students. Furthermore, he revealed, henceforth all high school students would be able to register at any school, regardless of race. Latimer sold these disclosures as far-reaching adjustments in district policy. Atlanta always had stood for "compliance, not defiance," the lawyer claimed. "Atlanta points with pride to its accomplishments." Latimer then asked for the Court's patience and trust in the board's good faith efforts to continue the city's "evolutionary" movement toward comprehensive desegregation.[65]

Motley saw a ruse. The policy shifts might appear to be significant. But she found them much less than what was constitutionally required. So-called freedom-of-choice still drove the high school assignment policy. Desegregation would occur only if individual black students were brave enough to attempt to insinuate themselves into white schools, where they were unlikely to be welcomed. Other constraints on students' ability to transfer remained as well. Even if students preferred a desegregated school, the board did not guarantee admission to one. School capacity and proximity to residence still limited high school students' freedom to choose desegregated schools. Furthermore, Atlanta's initial, race-based assignment policy—unchanged by the board—constituted the single biggest impediment to desegregation. At the current rate, first-graders would not even be *eligible* for transfers until 1971, and vestiges of the race-based assignment policy would not end for many years thereafter. Rather than disestablishing segregation, Atlanta instead was preserving it through a "war of attrition" waged by the state against school-aged children "enmeshed in" an "administrative net." "After one hundred years of segregation," Motley argued, the "free transfer program would not suffice." The Court should end Atlanta's scheme of evasion; it should require the Atlanta School District to rezone attendance lines and to mandate transfers to achieve complete desegregation by September 1965. If the board refashioned attendance lines for the system as a whole and desegregated faculty, staff, and other aspects of school life, LDF argued, individual students such as the Atlanta Nine would no longer bear the burden of implementing *Brown*.[66]

When the Justice Department's Burke Marshall rose to the podium, he rebutted Latimer's claim that Atlanta had a progressive school desegregation record. He noted that Washington, Baltimore, St. Louis, and Louisville, as well as paradigms of massive resistance to *Brown* such as New Orleans, Norfolk, and Little Rock, had desegregated at a faster pace than Atlanta. Thus, Marshall explained, while Latimer rightly insisted that the city had not "stood for defiance," Latimer wrongly concluded that it had stood for "compliance." The city had mastered public relations and reconfigured discrimination.[67]

The Supreme Court issued its decision two months later. The justices, believed to have granted review in *Calhoun* to break new ground, did no such thing. Latimer's surprise announcement that the school board had adopted new policies, made after the Court granted certiorari, had its intended effect. An exchange during oral argument, when Chief Justice Warren declared the Court "confused" by the changes in Atlanta's school desegregation plan, foretold LDF's misfortune. Warren had required the attorneys to submit additional legal papers clarifying the facts. Then, in June 1964, rather than announcing a sweeping jurisprudential change, the chief justice read a brief unsigned opinion. The Court recognized the city's "commendable effort to effect desegregation" and returned the case to the district court for further evidentiary hearings, in light of recent school board actions. The justices directed the court below to "test" the Atlanta plan against recent legal precedents; the "context" in which the district court should "interpret and apply" the language of *Brown II* had been "significantly altered." Times had changed, the justices politely admonished the city.[68]

The Court had dashed Motley's hopes and those of civil rights advocates across the country who had observed her appeal. The Atlanta case had not provided a turning point in the school desegregation fight. "Apparently," Motley observed, "the Supreme Court was of the view that as long as Atlanta was moving it could move as slowly as it pleased." The decision "left something to be desired," lamented Hollowell. Georgia officials declared themselves "relieved." "All it adds up to," a deputy school superintendent crowed, "is delay." Desegregation at a snail's pace would continue unless Judge Hooper suddenly changed course.[69]

At the time, however, LDF—commemorating both its twenty-fifth anniversary and the tenth anniversary of *Brown*—determined to frame the outcome in the Atlanta appeal as a victory. *Calhoun*, when coupled with the Court's decision in *Griffin v. Prince Edward County*, Virginia decided in the same term, *did* open a new path to accelerated desegregation, LDF's director-counsel, Jack Greenberg, insisted. Prince Edward County, Virginia had famously closed its schools rather than desegregate; it funneled public funds to whites, who opened private "segregation academies" to avoid desegregation. In *Griffin*, the Court declared such acts unconstitutional; previously, the justices had only made clear that the Court would not tolerate outright defiance of federal court orders to desegregate. The Supreme Court took an important step forward when it ordered the Prince Edward schools reopened. In a key phrase, the majority wrote: "The time for more 'deliberate speed' has run out, and the phrase can no longer justify denying these Prince Edward County children their Constitutional rights." Greenberg and Motley hailed this language; they claimed arguing that the justices had sent a message to school districts throughout the South. Indeed, LDF interpreted the Court's brief directive to Judge Hooper in *Calhoun* as a mandate to apply the principles of *Griffin* in Atlanta, and thereby order "complete and immediate desegregation." Together, Motley claimed, the two cases showed that "grade-a-year plans no longer meet the requirement of 'all deliberate speed.'"[70]

While these characterizations of the precedents represented what LDF had wanted from the Court, the Justices had not gone nearly so far. In *Calhoun*, it had expressly declined to consider whether grade-a-year plans passed muster under *Brown II*. And these plans had not even been a subject of discussion in *Griffin*.

Judge Hooper certainly viewed Motley's reading of the Supreme Court's instructions as fanciful. True to form, after holding the new round of evidentiary hearings directed by the Justices, Hooper refused to modify Atlanta's plan.

The judge reached his decision despite the fact that the board's straightforward promise to the Justices to end race-based high school assignments suddenly sounded more complicated. Now, the board emphasized the limitations on student choice: not only capacity and proximity, but also "justifiable educational reasons," "hardship," "discipline," and "other factors." Moreover, the board still refused to budge on faculty desegregation; and it continued to assign first through seventh grade students to same-race schools. Desegregation may be a "little slow" in Atlanta, Hooper wrote in his order denying relief, but "it has been peaceable." The board's new policies, the ones that had confounded the Supreme Court, would not change that.[71]

## "LET'S DESEGREGATE THE SCHOOLS"

Long before LDF appealed the lower court decisions in *Calhoun* to the U.S. Supreme Court, an outspoken few in Atlanta's civil rights movement—invariably, collegians who favored direct action over litigation—had grown profoundly frustrated with the Board of Education. The board had "done nothing on its own initiative to desegregate the schools," student activist Maurice Pennington wrote in the *Atlanta Inquirer* in early 1963. Like Dr. King, Pennington proposed a solution to the problem: direct action. Black students had protested inequality in other areas, but "too feebly overcrowded schools and the lack of quality educational conditions in the Negro schools." The time had come to protest token integration, just as activists had attacked segregation in parks, on playgrounds, at lunch counters, in restaurants, government buildings, and in the public square. "Let's desegregate the schools," the writer pleaded. "LET US STOP THIS DOUBLE DEALING AND BAD FAITH NOW."[72]

The student's plea did not generate much of a response from the black community, let alone direct action. A year later, an *Inquirer* editorial complained that the "Negro community let off the pressure and permitted lunch counter desegregation alone to be the only critical goal." School desegregation was not a majority priority for ASLC or COAHR. No organized political strategy to secure school desegregation ever materialized. The Board of Education's policies precipitated few public fights on par with those in other areas; on the limited occasions when problems erupted, leaders resolved them through negotiation. The occasional protest did not compare in character to the numerous sit-ins, boycotts, and demonstrations that activists staged against segregation in public accommodations and discrimination in politics. The goal of school desegregation did not generate the requisite level of interest, consensus, and institutional support necessary to inspire significant political mobilization outside the courts. Without these ingredients, no social movement can bloom and evolve.[73]

Community members who *did* value school desegregation mostly left the strategizing to the civil rights bar. The Atlanta NAACP branch president, Samuel Williams, summed up this point of view in 1962, after he attended a federal court hearing with Motley. The lawyer had argued in support of LDF's motion to accelerate desegregation. Williams did not believe that the audience "completely understood the points Mrs. Motley was trying to get across," he commented. "But," Williams insisted, "they'll understand when she hits them over the head with the law in the briefs she is to file."[74]

Williams's analysis might have struck veterans of courtroom combat and direct action campaigns alike as odd. He failed to appreciate that only one person's assessment of Motley and her argument really mattered: Judge Hooper's. The judge did not fail to understand Motley's arguments; he utterly disagreed with them. During pointed exchanges, Judge Hooper had made his disposition toward the case perfectly clear. He complained that Motley had not offered a "scintilla" of evidence to support her claim of systematic school board discrimination against black students. He had ruled against her time and again. This judge was unlikely to be persuaded by Motley's arguments, no matter how impressive. Hence, it would be a huge mistake for Williams and others who hoped for desegregated schools to rely on the bar and the courtroom for victory. Civil rights litigation alone would not bring change.

If Motley hoped to achieve her goal—complete school desegregation by September 1965—she needed leverage. That influence might have come in the form of an unequivocal Supreme Court precedent, preferably one backed up by the powers of Congress and the president, but it had not. Or it might have come in the form of pressure from the black community, engaged in an epic struggle with white resisters over school desegregation. The postwar civil rights movement had waged numerous battles by means of a fractious collaboration between community-based politics and law. Activists created leverage through confrontation; they invited federal intervention through dramatic political confrontations (SCLC) or sustained engagement (SNCC) with the white power structure. Only recently, Samuel Williams had witnessed such conflagrations in Atlanta. Yet, city fathers often boasted that Atlanta had "voluntarily desegregated" prior to passage of the Civil Rights Act of 1964. This claim was fiction, student activists insisted. "Voluntary" desegregation only occurred after restaurants and motels had been "internationally embarrassed," "Negro and white Atlantans withdrew their dollars from downtown stores," and citizens had "worn out their shoes" on picket lines. Comprehensive public accommodations desegregation took place only after Congress passed the Act.[75]

Experience and logic suggested that comprehensive school desegregation would only occur if black communities demanded it, and did so in multiple ways. The national NAACP, the original sponsor of the school desegregation litigation, appreciated the point. It knew it needed community support to implement *Brown*. In the wake of the decision, the organization had called on branches to support LDF's school desegregation campaign through community-based programs "designed to involve the entire membership of the NAACP and influence large circles of citizens beyond our ranks." Curiously, Williams's prescription for educational change ignored the community's vital role; instead, he spoke as if Motley, alone, could bring about change.[76]

## The LDF, the NAACP, and Community Relations

The Atlanta NAACP's actions mirrored Williams's rhetoric. Although the national NAACP and LDF viewed Atlanta branch members as natural allies in the struggle to implement *Brown*, local residents offered little support for the school desegregation campaign. In fact, the Atlanta branch experienced a period of decline just as LDF launched the *Calhoun* litigation. Branch president John H. Calhoun retired under a cloud of controversy in December 1958. His remark, published in local newspapers, that the "atmosphere in Atlanta is not right for integration" had embarrassed the NAACP and sparked rumors that Calhoun had "made some sort of deal with public officials" to undermine the battle for desegregation. However, Calhoun understandably bore scars from attorney general Eugene Cook's effort to harass the NAACP into submission. In 1956, Cook had initiated an investigation of the branch's tax records. Before the saga and the protracted litigation it produced ended, a segregationist judge had held Calhoun in contempt of court and confined him to jail for hours until the branch opened its records for inspection.[77]

Following Calhoun's "retirement," it proved exceedingly difficult to find a new branch leader. Few expressed any interest in the post. In late February 1959, when the local branch finally did hold an election, the new president resigned without explanation the day after his appointment. Within this context, the tensions that had characterized the relationships between the national NAACP, LDF, and the local NAACP during A. T. Walden's branch leadership now fully came to the surface. Given the depth of talent and resources in the Gate City's black community, national and state NAACP officials' expectations ran high. When local residents disappointed, they complained bitterly and loudly. Roy Wilkins, the NAACP's executive secretary, protested that Atlanta, a city where the battle over desegregation had reached a critical stage, urgently needed a branch leader of "stature, independence, and considerable leadership ability." It profoundly disappointed Wilkins that no black Atlantan was willing to "carry on the heavy work of one of our most important branches in the South. Gloster Current, director of NAACP branches, and Wilkins cited a perplexing lack of "enthusiasm," "action," and "results" in Atlanta. He and Wilkins demanded "reform."[78]

Samuel Williams—the same man who later vested so much faith in Motley's ability to implement *Brown* through courtroom tactics—came to the rescue. In December 1959, almost a year after Calhoun's resignation, the branch selected Williams as its president. Williams held the post until 1967, a long tenure that gave him an opportunity to make a strong impact on the organization. When he entered office, Williams promised to correct the branch's course and "overcome" the "internal difficulties which ha[d] afflicted" it. For a variety of reasons, he did not deliver on his promises. Williams devoted only limited time and energy to the branch. In addition to serving as NAACP president, he worked full-time as a professor at Morehouse College, served as the pastor of the Friendship Baptist Church, and was a vice-president of SCLC. He also advised SNCC and AU center activists, groups whose priorities differed from the NAACP's, and cochaired ASLC. These other endeavors took much of Williams's attention, and challenges persisted in the branch. The Atlanta NAACP consistently missed fund-raising and membership goals throughout Williams's tenure.[79]

National and state NAACP officials fumed when Williams could not resurrect the branch. By 1966, problems had worsened to the point that Gloster Current contemplated disbanding the Atlanta branch and reorganizing it, perhaps as multiple branches. The Atlanta branch's membership had declined from 3,547 in 1964 to 1,973 in 1965. According to the national NAACP, a city of Atlanta's size should have yielded between ten thousand and fifteen thousand members. The NAACP's field secretary for Georgia, Amos Holmes, blatant in his assessment, accused Williams and the branch of "inactivity." Ruby Hurley, secretary of the NAACP's Southeast regional office, accused Williams of having "divided loyalties" that undermined the branch's effectiveness. In addition, Hurley decried the influence on the branch of the city's black middle-class "power structure," which she believed "d[id] not *want* a vibrant branch." Williams reacted to criticisms of his stewardship with criticisms of his own, which dovetailed with Hurley's comments about black Atlanta's class structure. The "socioeconomic background" of the membership made true branch leadership impossible, he claimed: black elites, accustomed to exercising outsized influence on political and policy matters, did not wish to cede authority, or to cooperate with him. Tellingly, the national NAACP, which had long endured A. T. Walden's independent streak, agreed with the contention that "old guard" domination constrained his leadership; the national NAACP proposed to assist Williams with the problem.[80]

But change proved elusive. Despite the national office's pledge to help the branch right itself, relations between the branch and the national office remained deeply strained. Current declared that the branch simply was "not progressing" and bemoaned the unreliability of the "upper middle-class and well-off personalities that had traditionally carried the branch." The branch held few meetings, and few attended the meetings that were called. The Atlanta NAACP was "nothing more than a name," Tucker wrote. Rev. Joseph Boone, a minister with deep connections to the grassroots who had secured jobs for the black poor in War on Poverty programs, attempted to revitalize the branch by reaching out to Atlanta's working people. His mission proved difficult due to persistent class tensions. Boone repeatedly confronted the perception that the NAACP was a "middle-class organization, unconcerned with the problems of the masses." By 1967, when Dr. Albert Davis became the new branch president, plans to reorganize the branch had been abandoned. The pattern of under-achievement continued. The branch never became the prominent force in the fight for school desegregation that the national NAACP desired.[81]

Although the national and state NAACP officials directed their ire at the local branch, the Atlanta NAACP's ineffective political leadership, particularly on the school desegregation issue, was not solely a function of local dynamics. In 1958, Thurgood Marshall and Constance Baker Motley had removed A. T. Walden, the most influential skeptic of an aggressive push for school desegregation, from the front lines of the case. Motley now cocounseled with attorneys who shared her commitment to aggressive litigation to implement *Brown*. The shift in control meant that LDF (and the national NAACP) now shared responsibility for generating political support for its strategy. The LDF thus shared the blame for failing to cultivate grassroots support for the school desegregation campaign. Preoccupied with legal strategy and an extensive docket, lawyers from the national office neglected community building. That LDF attorneys overlooked the development of relationships with client communities might seem odd at first. After all, the national NAACP had warned early on that *Brown*'s success would turn on community backing. "[T]he enjoyment of many rights and opportunities of first class citizenship is not dependent on legal action," the association had resolved in 1954, "but rather on the molding of public sentiment and the exertion of public pressure to make democracy work." The NAACP's concerns about the Atlanta branch had stemmed in large part from the national organization's commitment to school desegregation.[82]

The NAACP's concern about community support reflected the values of the NAACP special counsel Charles Hamilton Houston and his protégé, Thurgood Marshall. Both men appreciated the need for civil rights lawyers to cultivate relationships with African Americans on the local level who served as plaintiffs in test cases or otherwise supported the organization's initiatives. In describing the relationship of a civil rights lawyer to his constituency, Houston called the attorney "not only lawyer but evangelist and stump speaker." Marshall, in turn, encouraged LDF staff attorneys to "serve the branches—that is our responsibility." But the staff did not always—or effectively—put these principles into practice.[83]

An important restructuring of the NAACP that took place in 1956 made the task even more difficult. In that year, the NAACP and LDF formally became separate organizations. The split came about because of an Internal Revenue Service investigation into the close working relationship between the tax-exempt LDF and the non-tax-exempt NAACP. The change had profound effects. It reduced communication between LDF lawyers and their constituents in the branches. After the split, Marshall spent less time in the field, in direct contact with the clients he represented. As Motley saw it, the split had a grave impact on organizational efficacy and spirit. The "separation of the two organizations was the most wrenching episode for us in the entire civil rights struggle" because "manpower and resources for implementing Brown became divided." Yet, when Motley took charge of the Atlanta school desegregation case, she did little to rekindle these relationships and stoke the community's fires. Under her watch, LDF did not hold forums, encourage protests, or otherwise invite citizens to participate in *Calhoun* as it unfolded. Rather, as Williams put it, Motley and her cocounsel owned the case and worked to "beat people over the head" with the arguments in their legal briefs. This courtroom-based strategy may have cost LDF potential allies in the struggle to implement *Brown*.[84]

## Community-based Groups and School Desegregation

Even without an invitation from LDF, local community groups might have initiated an extralegal campaign to desegregate the schools. However, the most vibrant organizations, student groups such as SNCC and COAHR, did not take up the challenge. The student groups poured their energies to areas where direct action, rather than law, appeared most appropriate tactically. During the early to mid-1960s, they focused on public accommodations discrimination and voting rights. After the passage of the Civil Rights Act, they continued to pursue black political empowerment and turned to antipoverty initiatives.[85]

The students did take an interest in education, however. They commemorated *Brown* and called for its enforcement on several occasions. Students staged a few isolated protests against overcrowding in black schools. But they did not personally engage the issue on the streets, in community forums, and in planning sessions with the same frequency or intensity that they deployed on other issues. In short, LDF's school desegregation campaign never attracted student activists' *sustained* attention. Of the many reasons for the students' failure to engage the issue of school desegregation, two stand out: LDF's sense that school desegregation was its special preserve, coupled with strategic and ideological ambivalence about school desegregation among student activists.[86]

The ongoing tension within the movement over goals and tactics explained much of the lack of synergy between SNCC and LDF on school desegregation. As I have already explained, Thurgood Marshall and LDF had misgivings about the sit-ins during their initial stages. When it became clear that the students had an important role to play in the effort to end Jim Crow, Marshall and the national NAACP accepted them. But tensions persisted. A flashpoint occurred when SNCC collaborated with Len Holt, the irreverent movement lawyer who criticized LDF for its narrow focus on school desegregation and its top-down relationship to local communities. The students favored "movement lawyers" such as Holt, whose legal strategies were driven by SNCC's own prerogatives and whose penchant for political theater matched their own. Motley did not share Len Holt's views about how lawyers should behave in court or relate to activists. Like her mentor, Thurgood Marshall, and Jack Greenberg, his successor as LDF's director-counsel, Motley, a paragon of lawyerly formality, held a court-centric vision of the civil rights movement. "The achievement in the Court was the main catalyst" for the movement, Motley believed. To be sure, she appreciated the contributions of Dr. King and the student wing of the civil rights movement. But in her view, the U.S. Supreme Court, and civil rights lawyers, through their victory in *Brown*, generated the civil rights movement. The activists had no credibility independent of lawyers. She explained:

> [T]he Black community was stirred to action by...*Brown*, a realization that society was changing in the sense that the Supreme Court appeared to them to be on the side of blacks. And that gave them courage to follow Martin King. Otherwise, he might have been regarded as just a crazy minister.

In Motley's universe, lawyers led activists. Her understanding of the relationship between the civil rights bar and community-based movement for social change did not create a favorable environment for collaboration with SNCC. It crowded students out of the school desegregation campaign and made the implementation of *Brown* exclusively lawyers' work.[87]

Moreover, as the sixties progressed, the likelihood that SNCC would collaborate with LDF to implement *Brown* decreased because some students became skeptical of school desegregation, strategically and ideologically. Mere improvements in black schools of the type proposed by the ASLC would "never eradicate the injustices of Negro education in the city," SNCC activists believed. However, by the mid-1960s, they questioned whether the white power structure and "wealthy Negro politicians" would ever fulfill *Brown*'s promise. The black leaders did not "fully support the demands" of the community. Atlanta would never desegregate without a push from the federal government. Yet a 1966 SNCC special report on southern school desegregation noted that the federal commitment to *Brown* was anemic. The report found several problems with federal policy: the government still permitted freedom-of-choice; it did not demand teacher desegregation; and it did not require immediate desegregation of all grades. "The more we see what happens when 'desegregation' occurs," the report concluded, "the more we don't want [it]."[88]

The strategic frustration of SNCC with the desegregation process fed the flagging ideological commitment to integration among a vocal contingent of the organization—based in Atlanta. This group embraced black power, an ideology deeply in tension with the goals of LDF's campaign to implement *Brown*. In 1966, SNCC's black-power-oriented Atlanta Project began a drive for community "liberation" or "freedom-schools" that emphasized black history and African culture. The short-lived project's concept did not materialize into a working initiative. However, the idea suggested that this faction within SNCC, dominant in Atlanta, did not share LDF's vision of equality in education.[89]

## Moments of Possibility

Despite the absence of direct community engagement with LDF and its litigation campaign, the consortium of civic groups led by ASLC did register complaints about educational inequalities in black schools during the mid-1960s. These episodes revealed community priorities, but ones different from LDF's. These episodes also demonstrated the extent to which black leaders continued to view deliberation and negotiation—not direct action or litigation—as the most attractive modes of dispute resolution.

A series of events in 1965 illustrated these dynamics. That year, the moment seemed ripe for desegregation. For the first time, the federal government had indicated its intention to insist upon compliance with *Brown*. The Civil Rights Act, passed in July 1964, contained provisions that promised to accelerate enforcement of *Brown*. Title IV authorized the U.S. attorney general to initiate school desegregation suits upon a meritorious complaint from a parent or child in a segregated school district. Title VI permitted the federal government to withhold federal funds from any program administered on a discriminatory basis. In the wake of the new law, the U.S. Department of Health, Education, and Welfare promulgated regulations demanding that state and local officials certify an intention to desegregate. Across the South, school officials reacted with urgency to the new law and rules; administrators felt pressure to respond to the threat of federal enforcement action. In Georgia, the Board of Education called meetings to advise local districts that they must pledge to desegregate, or risk loss of the more than $50 million in federal dollars that the state received annually. In late January 1965, the board signed a pledge to desegregate its schools.[90]

But the formal policy changes would be meaningless unless enforced on the ground. Consequently, the national NAACP announced a North-South school drive and encouraged local people to seize the moment. Against the promising backdrop created in Georgia and many other states by the Civil Rights Act and HEW's new regulations, the NAACP advised community leaders to leverage the new law to end school segregation once and for all. When litigation and negotiation failed, the NAACP authorized demonstrations, "study-ins," and school boycotts to insist on "maximum desegregation."[91]

Atlanta's ASLC and All-Citizens' Registration Committee appeared to rise to the challenge. When the Atlanta Board of Education, in concert with City Hall, proposed to close the all-black Charles W. Hill School to build a municipal auditorium—part of an urban renewal plan—these groups objected. The project would have resulted in the transfer of eight hundred black students to portable classrooms, located across town. The elementary students could only have reached the "inferior and substandard" mobile classrooms at the Howard High School Annex after traveling over a hazardous expressway. Jessie Hill, Jr., a black insurance executive and publisher of the *Atlanta Inquirer*, went before the Atlanta Board of Education and read a statement objecting to the plan on behalf of the Hill School PTA. The president of the board, Oby Brewer, did not respond favorably. Brewer accused Hill of "grandstanding." Affronted by the "personal attack" on Hill and the familiar phenomenon of "Negroes getting the short end of the stick," the civic groups announced support for the Hill School PTA. They said, "The children of C. W. Hill are not getting equal treatment under the law." C. T. Vivian, director of SCLC's Atlanta affiliate, threatened a full-scale direct action campaign, including boycotts, demonstrations, and sit-ins, if the board did not reverse its plan. "Demonstrations are not a cheap thing, but a coming fact," Vivian announced. The demonstrations would "indicate our problems to the court" and represent an impressive demand for complete desegregation, notwithstanding the federal district court's heretofore refusal to order it.[92]

Once again, a dynamic moment of possibility had arrived. Riled by the white resistance, activists had decided that court litigation was only one piece of a larger puzzle and that litigation must be supplemented with direct action.

In the end, however, the Hill School controversy generated much less change than it promised. For no consensus had, in fact, formed around the goal of "complete desegregation," or around mass political action to achieve that goal. Even as Vivian pushed for demonstrations, Senator Leroy Johnson, A. T. Walden's protégé, emerged to soften the tenor of the debate. "We have some fine public officials," he said. "I don't see why we can't get together without the Negro always being the loser." Johnson suggested that the parties settle their differences at the negotiating table. The Board of Education then appointed one of its own—Rufus Clement, the black school board member and Walden acolyte—chairman of a committee to address the Hill School problem. The choice of Clement was significant. Only recently, the *Inquirer* had questioned Clement's commitment to school desegregation and whether he adequately represented the interests of "down-trodden black children'" on the school board. In any event, after Clement's appointment, ASLC changed its tune. The organization called the Hill School situation "grave," but argued that the problem should be resolved through negotiation rather than pressure tactics. Vivian receded into the background, no longer a public voice on the matter.[93]

Soon, the school board brokered a behind-the-scenes agreement with Jessie Hill, Jr., and proclaimed the problem resolved. Pursuant to the deal, the board of education continued with its plan to demolish the Hill School. And the city proceeded with its plan to build a new auditorium on the razed land. Hundreds of black students still would be transferred. The board did promise to build a new school for dislocated students. However, the new Hill School would be built in an all-black area of the city; hence, the student body would be all-black. Meanwhile, the board agreed to permit Hill students transferred to the annex to apply for admission to less crowded schools, including those designated for whites only. At the same time, the board announced that any student could now apply for a transfer based on hardship , subject, of course, to space availability. In other words, the Atlanta school board had extended freedom-of-choice to all lower school grades, beginning September 1965. The board had desegregated ahead of a federal court mandate, it boasted. The Hill School controversy had resulted in a huge step forward in the school desegregation controversy, the city claimed.[94]

A closer inspection of the facts told a different, less impressive, and far more familiar story about social change in Atlanta. First and most striking, the linchpin of the bargain had preserved segregation; the new Hill School, sited in a black neighborhood, would be all-black. Second, the school board had merely promised to take steps already mandated or suggested by the federal court. In April 1965, a month after the Hill controversy broke, the district court responded to yet another LDF motion to amend the desegregation plan by expanding the grade-a-year plan to include several lower school grades as of September 1965. Under the amended plan, the burden to desegregate remained with students, and space availability, proximity to a student's residence, and vaguely defined "hardship factors" remained barriers to transfer. All grades would desegregate on a freedom-of-choice basis by the fall of 1968. Thus, the school board was only half right in claiming that it had acted before Judge Hooper required it to extend the grade-a-year plan to the lower grades. The court had already extended the plan, although not to each and every elementary grade. True enough, the board did open the transfer plan to elementary students ahead of the court's September 1968 deadline. But even the *Atlanta Constitution* found that fact unremarkable. The "federal courts had already ordered the speed-up," an editorial noted, and "the grade-a-year plan had run its course anyway and outlived its usefulness." Moreover, Atlanta *followed* most other Georgia school districts, which already had agreed to desegregate by the September 1965 deadline as a result of the looming threat posed by the Civil Rights Act and HEW's desegregation regulations.[95]

Atlanta had not come close to mandating "complete desegregation"—the goal that activists originally had articulated. The Board of Education and federal district court had merely extended desegregation within the freedom-of-choice framework. "Victory" on these terms hardly consoled those who sought meaningful implementation of *Brown*. Thus, it came as no surprise that Constance Baker Motley remained silent in the face of the putative leap forward toward school desegregation in Atlanta. For years, she had condemned "freedom-of-choice" desegregation as patently unconstitutional—a subterfuge designed to give the appearance of compliance with *Brown* without the substance. Jim Crow would only truly be disestablished in the public schools when school boards redrew attendance lines on a nonracial basis and built schools in non–racially identifiable neighborhoods. These things Atlanta did not do. And the black community groups did not follow up on the threat to demand them through demonstrations, sit-ins, and boycotts, backed up by litigation. It was hard to escape the conclusion that leading advocacy groups felt no urgency about pupil desegregation.

Some activists did speak out against the board's claim—supported by ASLC—that the Hill School settlement constituted a leap forward for civil rights. In January 1966, Benny T. Smith, a leader of the Metropolitan Atlanta Civic Council, an upstart group in comparison to ASLC, dismissed the Hill settlement as "sickening." He called for the firing of the superintendent of schools, John Letson, whom Smith held responsible for persistent inequalities in the school system. More tellingly, Smith called on "leading Negroes" such as Jessie Hill, Jr., and Rev. Samuel Williams, along with leading civil rights organizations, including the ASLC and SCLC, to protest segregation in public schools. The Metropolitan Atlanta Civic Council had no patience for the board's professions of good intentions and could not imagine negotiating with its members. These dissident voices demanded—without effect—protest in the streets against the board to desegregate the schools.[96]

Instead, in May 1966, the leading civil rights groups backed a $21 million school bond issue for school construction and renovation vigorously championed by Superintendent Letson. The superintendent talked up the bond at a mass meeting held at a black Baptist church. Approval of the bond measure would resolve the double session problem, he promised. The organizations endorsed Letson's plan. They seemed to prefer school reform to school desegregation. The bond issue did not resolve the inequalities in the school system, however. Numerous battles erupted over site selection, speed of school construction, and other aspects of the board's building plans. One prolonged struggle over a school site pitted middle-class black homeowners against black students set to attend a new school slated for their Vine City neighborhood. As the board, black leaders, and other constituents worked out these problems, black students remained in overwhelmingly one-race schools and double sessions continued. This state of affairs seemed likely to continue.[97]

The volatile political and social context of 1966 framed how leading civil rights organizations set their agendas and whether and how they decided to contest educational inequality. After the wave of riots that had begun in Atlanta in September 1966, "respectable" leaders—those who saw themselves in a class apart from provocateurs such as Stokely Carmichael—feared direct action more than ever. And whatever their position on school desegregation, ASLC, the Atlanta NAACP, and civic groups such as the Community Relations Commission feared racially "hot" summers. The two fears merged: these groups determined to thwart the possibility of disturbances by ruling out street protests, including protests directed at the board. These leaders—the civil rights mainstream—pledged to restore "peace" and "order" and to collaborate rather than confront city officials. In addition, many organizations shifted away from protest to community service models that presumed to correct blacks' personal shortcomings and to ameliorate the worst of their squalid living conditions. They hoped to provide services to black youths in working-class and poor neighborhoods, rather than fight to give these youths access to integrated schools.[98]

## A Turning Point in the Circuit Court

The mainstream civil rights advocates' cautious approach became more apparent after the Fifth Circuit's sweeping December 1966 decision in *United States v. Jefferson County Board of Education*. The decision, penned by the circuit's liberal lion, Judge Minor Wisdom, established a new, uniform standard by which district courts should measure compliance with *Brown*. Henceforth, courts in the circuit should consider school systems' progress toward eliminating segregation and its effects. Districts must convert, Wisdom wrote, from "dual systems" to a "unitary, nonracial system, lock, stock, and barrel." Boards would now labor under an affirmative duty to formulate school plans that *encouraged integrated* schools. The court did not rule freedom-of-choice plans unconstitutional across the board, but it specified a set of criteria for acceptable ones. And it stated: "The only school desegregation plan that meets constitutional standards is one that works." There should be no "white schools or Negro schools—just schools." To facilitate the new standard, the court of appeals placed new limits on school boards. It curtailed boards' discretion over transfer applications. The court commanded school systems to take affirmative steps to desegregate faculties, facilities, and extracurricular activities. And it required schools to submit progress reports detailing compliance with its mandates. "The clock has ticked the last tick for tokenism and delay in the name of 'deliberate speed,'" Wisdom wrote.[99]

*Jefferson*—a landmark decision—presented another opportunity for civil rights lawyers and activists to push for desegregation. In *Jefferson*, Constance Baker Motley had finally gotten the precedent that she had long sought to implement *Brown*. But she observed the victory from a distance and would not lead the charge to implement it in Atlanta. In January 1966, President Johnson announced his nomination of Motley to the federal district court; by the time Judge Wisdom announced his decision, Judge Motley had herself ascended to the federal bench. Howard Moore became LDF's local counsel and lead plaintiff's lawyer in *Calhoun* after Motley's resignation from LDF to accept her new appointment.[100]

Moore put the new precedent to use in the Atlanta school desegregation case. The LDF's new local counsel filed a motion arguing that the city's desegregation plan failed the standards set forth in *Jefferson*. Moore complained that the city's plan lacked provisions for reporting progress in meeting desegregation goals, that it failed to ensure that school construction would facilitate desegregation, and that it did not address faculty and staff desegregation at all. The school board's response indicated the depth of its recalcitrance. Its recordkeeping practices made it impossible to comply with *Jefferson*. The board no longer maintained records designating students' race; therefore, it could not indicate how many black students' requests for transfers it had granted or denied.[101]

Judge Hooper also reacted indifferently to *Jefferson*. Despite the circuit court's decree—meant to remove discretion from district courts, as well as school boards, to impede compliance with *Brown*—the Atlanta school desegregation plan would retain its basic structure. Race-based attendance zones remained. Freedom-of-choice endured. Complaints about overcrowded, under-resourced black schools persisted. For Judge Hooper, the *Jefferson* decision had not changed the legal landscape of desegregation decrees much, if at all.[102]

If LDF's school desegregation campaign ever needed action both inside and outside the courtroom, this moment—the months after *Jefferson*—was the moment. But the well-timed protests never materialized. To be sure, African-American concern about educational inequality persisted. In fact, it had grown among "grassroots elements," reported the *Atlanta Daily World*, who expressed dissatisfaction with ASLC's decision-making. "Certain elements of the Negro community felt left out," one leader explained, "when it comes to ways and means of approaching city officials." Representatives of the grassroots suggested a boycott of downtown stores to register disapproval of school board policy. These elements, led by Rev. J. A. Wilborn, called Letson a "staunch segregationist" and asserted that the black community needed "action" rather than "more talk" to demonstrate its seriousness about discrimination. The boycott idea met with strong opposition.[103]

Instead, following Atlanta's decades-old traditions, Jessie Hill, Jr., and others continued to plead with the Atlanta Board of Education for relief—practical relief. A list of "ten commandments" to the Atlanta Board of Education drafted by a coalition of major black organizations, including ASLC, NAACP, SCLC, and Operation Bread Basket, omitted school desegregation as an objective. The groups demanded that by January 1968, "Thou Shalt Not Have Discrimination in Hiring Chief Administrators and Departmental Heads," "Thou Shalt Not Eliminate Negro Principals;" and "Thou Shalt Not Have Double Sessions." The conference showed no desire to expend the community's limited political capital on an all-out push for pupil desegregation. As the federal appellate courts inched toward compulsory pupil transfers for desegregation, evidenced by *Jefferson* and similar cases, several ministers insisted that black students and parents—not the courts—should decide whether to transfer their children outside neighborhood schools. The *Atlanta Daily World* agreed. Even as LDF slogged it out in court for a massive pupil desegregation plan, Atlanta's civil rights main-stream endorsed freedom-of-choice.[104]

### Educators' Fear of a "One-Way Stream"

If the coalition splintered over direct action and pupil transfers, it coalesced around another goal:  ASLC's member organizations demanded equal employment opportunities for blacks in white schools. Indeed, black concern about the matter of employment for black educators remained atop the educational agenda throughout the 1960s and into the 1970s. Black leaders repeatedly complained about rank discrimination by the Atlanta Board of Education and the Georgia Board of Education. The boards simply did not hire African Americans in administrative, staff, or even clerical positions in white schools. The GTEA led the charge against the boards' "damnable" policies. The GTEA predicted that court-ordered school desegregation would exacerbate systemic employment discrimination, especially in "higher echelon" positions. Just as in the immediate aftermath of *Brown*, the union feared that school boards would fire or demote black teachers and administrators. Desegregation would not occur on equal terms.[105]

The GTEA's executive secretary, Horace Tate, grew so concerned about this issue after passage of the Civil Rights Act that he reached out to President Johnson and the U.S. Department of Justice. He called on the executive branch to ensure that school desegregation did not result in "injustice[s]" such as the "elimination" of black educators' jobs, "tokenism," or a "one-way stream." Allies, including the National Urban League, the NAACP, and the LDF, supported the GTEA's goal. The groups noted that by August 1965, thousands of black teachers across the South had already been pushed out of school districts during the process of pupil desegregation. Perversely, passage of the Civil Rights Act, with its mandate to accelerate desegregation, was resulting in the wholesale removal of blacks from newly "integrated" school systems. Desegregation, these groups charged, provided a guise for discrimination, demotion, and dismissal in a bid to keep black teachers from contact with white students and teachers.[106]

The Atlanta Board of Education's statements about black faculty, and its actions, thus far, had only exacerbated the GTEA's concerns about employment discrimination. During a heated discussion between members of the Board of Education and ASLC in 1963, Superintendent Letson explained that the board had no plans to desegregate faculty. If the board employed identical, "across the board" standards in the hiring of teachers, he explained, black teachers might only constitute 10 percent of teachers in the school system, rather than 50 percent. Letson's claim about qualifications struck a nerve; it refocused attention on the competing interests of black teachers and students. Dr. Tilman Cothran, a professor of sociology at AU, fired back: "If a Negro teacher is not good enough to teach White children, then he's not good enough to teach Negro children." Dr. Rufus Clement, who noted that, as the only black on the board, he was "wearing two hats," also expressed concern about the impact of faculty desegregation on the "quality of education" in public schools. Tate insisted that Letson and other segregationists misrepresented black teachers' qualifications.[107]

In court, the board avoided the matter of faculty desegregation even as LDF attempted to make it a priority. Constance Baker Motley had always insisted that *Brown* required integration of all aspects of school life, and she had repeatedly pressed Hooper to mandate faculty desegregation. He refused. "[W]e intend...to do that last," the judge had insisted in 1962, "after pupils [have] been reassigned." Given how slowly the pupil reassignment process proceeded, Motley did not find Hooper's promise reassuring. When she appealed this issue, the Fifth Circuit upheld the district court's decision to defer the faculty assignment matter. Even after the Fifth Circuit handed down its decision in *Jefferson* in 1966, which demanded faculty desegregation, Judge Hooper was uninterested in the topic and he never made it a priority for the board.[108]

Meanwhile, the GTEA and ASLC continued to voice concerns about the board's employment policies. They carefully monitored personnel changes involving African Americans for signs of unfair demotions. And after Horace Tate won a seat on the Board of Education, he spent considerable energy lobbying for greater black representation in the school system and against persistent teacher salary discrimination. He argued so fervently for black inclusion and equity, some white board members claimed that he had a conflict of interest. Tate did not alone insist on black access to district jobs, however. A September 1966 *Inquirer* investigation revealed that the city lagged behind in faculty desegregation, even in comparison to other Georgia counties. When reporters confronted school superintendent Letson with these statistics, he again insisted that the board assigned teachers and administrators "according to qualifications and without regard to race." Black faculty protested such attacks on their credentials. One black teacher summed up the feelings of her colleagues this way: "What's so all-sacred about white children that they cannot be taught by teachers who are Negros? I am ready now."[109]

By 1967, the GTEA and other advocacy groups increasingly focused on the ceiling that prevented blacks from reaching top administrative posts. In February, after two black men whom ASLC recommended for jobs did not secure the positions, Jessie Hill, Jr., requested an immediate review of the board's hiring practices. "It appears that there is a policy, an understanding or an unwritten agreement to restrict Negroes to traditional jobs with school principalships of all-Negro schools being the basic top job for Negroes." Only five blacks held "token" administrative positions in the school system. Hill specifically deplored the district's unwillingness to promote black men with unimpeachable qualifications: doctorates, long experience, strong references. Whites with less training and experience gained appointment to higher positions. These practices amounted to a board plan to "keep the Negro down." In August, after an annual meeting, GTEA members "were incensed" over reports that all across Georgia, black principals and curriculum directors had been dismissed from their positions "for no other reason than that they are Negro."[110]

In the most raucous response yet, SCLC's Hosea Williams and Rev. Joseph Boone disrupted Board of Education meetings in September and October with loud complaints about employment discrimination, overcrowding, and other matters. Decisions regarding appointment or promotion, Letson declared, "fall...under the jurisdiction of the Board." Vacancies "are widely publicized and have nothing to do with race," he insisted. Subsequently, the board did hire a black administrator. However, the single appointment did not arrest simmering resentment over discriminatory hiring. The tokenism only exacerbated the bitterness. Black leaders monitored the board's transfers and promotions of teachers and administrators more closely than ever.[111]

In April 1968, two years after *Jefferson*, Judge Hooper issued an order that, at first blush, appeared to resolve the contentious matter. The court prohibited the assignment, dismissal, or demotion of faculty and staff on account of race. Upon further inspection, however, the decree only invited further strife. The order avoided concrete requirements. The Board of Education had been left with ample discretion to configure the workplace as it liked. The battles over jobs would continue. In fact, the Atlanta school desegregation case had been transformed into a fight over employment discrimination and socioeconomic class as much as a fight about race and pupil education. The GTEA's unanimous vote, weeks later, to stage a march on the office of the state superintendent of education in protest of "systemic phasing out of black educators in Georgia" showed that a crucial point had been reached. Atlanta's civil rights leaders had tolerated token desegregation, overcrowded schools, broken toilets, inadequate supplies, and double sessions in schools—all without resort to direct action on a sustained basis. But union members had become so distressed over this one issue—the peril that desegregation imposed upon them—that they were willing to take their fight to the streets.[112]

Employment discrimination became a predominant concern even as the Supreme Court issued its most important pupil desegregation decision since

*Brown*. In *Green v. County School Board of New Kent County*, decided in May 1968, the justices commanded school boards to desegregate classrooms not through so-called freedom-of-choice plans but by designing affirmative desegregation plans. The justices, who borrowed heavily from the Fifth Circuit's opinion in *Jefferson*, expressly rejected the New Kent County school board's argument that the Fourteenth Amendment did not command affirmative action. Justice Brennan wrote that school desegregation plans must place the burden of taking affirmative steps toward establishing a unitary system on the school board rather than on black parents. The Court no longer would tolerate a school board's delay in coming forward with a plan "that promises realistically to work now." "The time for mere deliberate speed," the Court declared, "had run out." The Supreme Court had spoken to New Kent County, Virginia, and to recalcitrant school boards and district courts across the South. Freedom-of-choice plans could withstand constitutional scrutiny in an exceedingly narrow category of circumstances: only where they offered "real promise" of establishing a "unitary, nonracial" school system. Boards must adopt the most effective desegregation plan, one that remedied discrimination "root and branch." In Georgia, Governor Lester Maddox responded to the sweeping decision by ordering the American flag lowered to half-mast for mourning.[113]

*Green*, it appeared, would provide LDF with a path to victory in *Calhoun*. Howard Moore cited the Supreme Court's unambiguous new directive, in addition to *Jefferson*, in a motion for further relief, filed in October 1968. Elizabeth Rindskopf, a recent addition to LDF's local legal team, aided the effort to convince Judge Hooper, at long last, that Atlanta no longer could avoid meaningful change. In view of *Green* and *Jefferson*, the lawyers argued, the school board must formulate an entirely new plan for desegregation. Like the school district in *Green*, the Atlanta Board of Education had posted only dismal results in its efforts to desegregate pupils and faculty. Fourteen years after *Brown*, the board still operated fifty-two all-black elementary schools and ten all-black high schools. It maintained sixteen all-white elementary schools and one all-white high school. Only 6 of 120 schools in the entire system had more than two teachers of a race different from the majority of its students. These statistics, the lawyers asserted, made the case for a new and drastically different school board plan to implement *Brown*.[114]

Judge Hooper responded skeptically to LDF's latest effort. He reprimanded the plaintiffs for "constantly filing motions." The judge reminded the attorneys that he had issued an order in the case in April 1968. He would not "reopen" the matter so soon merely because integration had not been achieved "to the extent that petitioners think should have been done." The Supreme Court's "landmark" pronouncement had changed nothing.[115]

Black community groups in Atlanta offered little help to LDF's case. After *Green*, an *Atlanta Daily World* headline blared that the decision constituted a "death blow" to "All Negro Schools." But neither the NAACP branch nor ASLC offered a reaction to such a momentous decision. Then, it appeared that ASLC might leverage the new precedent for change. Two weeks after the Court's action, Rev. Samuel Williams, as cochairman of ASLC, led a group of twenty-five citizens to the office of the Board of Education to complain about over-crowded schools. The group, though small, engaged in the type of protest that ASLC had employed infrequently in the school fight. But Williams did not demand immediate desegregation and an end to freedom of choice. He instead requested additional neighborhood schools.[116]

Another clue that *Green* had not changed ASLC's mindset came in July, when the organization requested an "immediate end to bias" in the city schools during a Board of Education meeting. The majority of ASLC's specific requests concerned the board's employment practices. The group sought a "formula" for assigning school principals to ensure black representation. It sought additional black teachers. It also demanded access for black students to the full comple-ment of extracurricular activities and a curriculum review at an area technical school. These demands—ASLC's "crash program to end racial discrimination in the schools"—were remarkably specific, yet excluded mention of *Green*'s chief subject, pupil integration "that worked." Nor did ASLC weigh in after LDF filed its motion arguing that, in *Green*'s wake, Atlanta must formulate a new, more effective school desegregation plan. Instead, ASLC focused on defeating an annexation effort that would dilute black representation in city government. And GTEA lobbied for a new teacher tenure law. Finally, the Supreme Court had given its imprimatur to all-out pupil desegregation; however, leaders of Atlanta's black establishment had more pressing priorities.[117]

## WHAT IS EDUCATIONAL EQUALITY?

In a 1977 address to the Gate City Bar Association, Constance Baker Motley, then a judge on the U.S. District Court, hailed LDF's commitment to the rule of law. "Not too many years ago," she said, "the law, the courts, and lawyers were viewed as enemies by many blacks." Ultimately, however, black attorneys had spearheaded a racial transformation of society; they had used the law and the courts as weapons of change. "There have been many factors that contrib-uted to the creation of a new social order in Atlanta since 1954," Motley pro-claimed, "but the single most important is law." The judge then saluted Atlanta's preeminent role in the legal struggle for racial equality. "No community in the nation can better illustrate how the law and legal institutions can be used to effect change."[118]

Motley justifiably honored the efforts of black attorneys in the fight against racial oppression. At the same time, however, her comments reflected a particular conception of law and social change, one that is contestable. Motley's remarks revealed a court-centric understanding of how racial change had occurred during the postwar civil rights movement. The LDF's strategy to implement *Brown* in Atlanta had embodied this view. Yet, the story of *Calhoun v. Latimer* and Motley's battle to desegregate Atlanta's schools reveals the limitations of court-centric models of law and social change.

In Atlanta, LDF's best-laid plans fell far short. True, *Calhoun* had ended de jure segregation in the system and desegregated a few schools. But the litigation had not substantially changed the racial make-up of the school system. And it had not begun to dismantle the effects of Jim Crow schools, including real racial disparities in academic preparation and achievement. Several factors, many external to the courts and the law, explained LDF's failure: black ambivalence about mandatory pupil integration, particularly among teachers and administrators; local whites' nonviolent forms of resistance to desegregation; Judge Hooper's minimalist readings of school desegregation precedents; LDF's tenuous connections to its clients; the failure of proponents of school desegregation to politically mobilize, especially through direct action; SNCC's absence from the debate over school integration during the mid-1960s; and the Supreme Court's focus on violent resisters to court orders rather than on districts that more creatively—and effectively—undermined black students' rights. Of all the factors that militated against LDF's school desegregation campaign in Atlanta, the political dynamics proved particularly detrimental. Yet, LDF devoted few of its limited resources and little of its energy to addressing political dynamics that the lawyers may have had some ability to influence.

The Du Bois conundrum—what did equality require, and could it be found in separate schools—remained. The LDF lawyers had answered this question for themselves in 1950 after their victory in *Sweatt v. Painter*—equality demanded desegregation in elementary and secondary education, just as it did in higher education. This truth they asserted to the Supreme Court, culminating in *Brown*. But the lawyers had neither worked through the nuances of this question with local client communities nor secured a remedial decree from the *Brown* Court that ensured swift implementation of their remedial vision. Thurgood Marshall, who pointed to educators' self-interest in the status quo and questioned other critics' commitment to racial justice, felt no obligation to meaningfully engage black skeptics of desegregation. Marshall's position may well have been justified in some instances, but it did not respond to conditions on the ground that had given rise to doubts about LDF's program.

The matter of how different segments of the black community interpreted equality coursed through the Atlanta school desegregation litigation, long after integrationists drove Du Bois out of the NAACP, and well after Motley and Marshall took control of the Atlanta school fight from A. T. Walden, the much-maligned moderate. It lived on among community members.

White authorities capitalized on blacks' struggle to define equality. School board lawyers dared blacks to debate the Du Bois question in the courtroom. They did so in full knowledge that black ambivalence about whether segregation stigmatized blacks worked in the board's favor. From the earliest days of the school desegregation litigation, the city muddied the crucial distinction between whether the school board discriminated against blacks—it most certainly did—and whether blacks could feel stigmatized by separate schools free of discrimination. In the school board attorney's hands, Du Bois's hypothetical, his intellectual puzzle, became one more tool of racial subordination.

The plaintiffs prevailed during the rights declaration phase of *Calhoun*, but the true test of how much ground Motley had won turned on the remedial phase of the litigation. There, LDF experienced repeated setbacks. The problems began in 1959. During the Sibley hearings, staged with the federal district court's ringing endorsement, Atlanta powerfully shaped its image and LDF's remedial options for years to come. The city, already adept at manipulating its racial image, came out as a champion of desegregation among retrogrades, a class apart from Little Rock and rural Georgia. But the reality was more complicated: Atlanta's "open school" advocates supported admission of just a few blacks to white schools and promised that residential segregation, perpetuated by private actors and facially race-neutral transactions, would maintain so-called de facto school segregation. The hearings marginalized LDF, its clients, and black proponents of meaningful desegregation. In short, Atlanta erected an ingenious model of token compliance with the federal district court's order, but effective resistance to *Brown*. All the while, it burnished its image as "a city too busy to hate."

The city's stagecraft bamboozled observers, since opinion makers measured resistance by the standards of Little Rock and Prince Edward County, Virginia. The Supreme Court's disposition of Motley's appeal of Atlanta's grade-a-year plan underscored the point. The justices, impressed by Atlanta's professed commitment to eventual compliance with *Brown*, congratulated the city on its progress and gently encouraged the district court to consider how times had changed since *Brown II*. Meanwhile, the Supreme Court issued a forceful opinion in *Griffin*; the justices required Prince Edward County to reopen and desegregate its schools. Thus, until *Green v. New Kent County*, a logical, if perverse, incentive structure undergirded the Court's school desegregation jurisprudence. The Court reacted most forcefully to protect black students who lived in localities with the most reactionary politicians. Violent and open resistance to *Brown* merited censure and remedy; subtle and politic racists profited from subterfuge. The Court sensibly showered attention on localities where massive resistance to school desegregation was greatest. But it did not necessarily follow that the justices should have abstained from acting in cases arising elsewhere. The LDF could claim particular disappointment with the justices' treatment of its appeal from Atlanta. The city had captured the nation's imagination precisely because of its reputation for racial progress and its apparently smooth transition to formally desegregated schools. When confronted with claims by LDF and the U.S. Department of Justice that the city had not, in fact, lived up to its public image, the justices had a golden opportunity to clarify *Brown*'s remedial scope. They did not accept the challenge.

Legal developments such as these suggested that without extralegal leverage, Motley stood little chance of securing her remedial objective. Despite the national NAACP's acknowledgment that *Brown* could only be implemented with community support, LDF had few deep connections to the black community. It acted independently of local civic organizations. The Atlanta NAACP foundered as LDF's campaign to end segregated education escalated. Motley did not bridge the gap created by the Atlanta NAACP's inertia by cultivating relationships with other groups. She did not collaborate with the social movements that strengthened and catalyzed the national bar's civil rights litigation in other areas. The student activists who had been front and center in the struggle to desegregate public accommodations stood on the sidelines of the fight for school desegregation. Some, under the influence of black power, had ideological qualms about school desegregation. But others were crowded out of the fight to implement *Brown*. In Motley's understanding, civil rights lawyers catalyzed the civil movement, powered it, and formed its core. To be sure, Motley appreciated activists' contributions; however, as a lawyer, she very sensibly viewed the work of lawyers as the critical factor in bringing about legal change. At the height of the school desegregation campaign SNCC, previously the most creative dissenter from LDF's court-based approach to racial struggle, offered little resistance to LDF's vision. Without SNCC and COAHR's political dynamism and participatory tactics, and without significant support from other civic groups, the school desegregation campaign proceeded primarily in the courts.[119]

There, Motley faced a disadvantage. White resistance dominated most political pressure points—the legislatures, the streets, and the courts. The same was
true in other areas, of course; but unlike in other areas, there was little effort by
civil rights activists in Atlanta to undermine white domination in the school
context by applying "creative tension" through the sustained pressure of boycotts, demonstrations, sit-ins, or other public forms of contentious politics.
Even the most talented civil rights lawyer could not prevail under these circumstances, and certainly not in Judge Hooper's courtroom. From the earliest days
of the litigation, Judge Hooper struck Motley as being averse to her claims and
her clients. Her assessment proved accurate; the judge repeatedly ruled against
LDF, issuing the narrowest possible readings of doctrine. Motley's quick assessment of Hooper and his courtroom made LDF's estrangement from the community and its political capital even more remarkable.[120]

Because of citizens' nuanced views about educational equality, LDF's weak
relationship to local communities presented a particularly pressing problem in
Atlanta. Had Motley been in closer contact with local African Americans, she
would have found much common ground. Many citizens shared LDF's outrage
at overcrowded, poorly equipped, and dilapidated black schools. Motley, like
local blacks, believed that black teachers and administrators should have access
to employment in white schools. Yet, the courtroom provided little space for
LDF to drive home how many blacks prized sympathetic and effective teachers
and administrators. Moreover, LDF lacked GTEA's fervent commitment to protecting union members' jobs; the two organizations had distinct, if sometimes
overlapping, priorities. Faculty desegregation constituted a second order priority in LDF's school desegregation litigation. For the GTEA, ASLC, and other
organizations, maintaining opportunities for employment in the single profession that had long formed a core of the black middle class constituted a matter
of the highest priority. Moreover, black leaders sought a voice in decision-making and leverage to shape the Board of Education's choices about how to allocate resources, select sites for school construction, and place personnel. These
matters did not arise in litigation in meaningful ways.

The sharpest difference between Motley and her clients in Atlanta struck at
the heart of LDF's view of *Brown*. Citizens seldom cited pupil desegregation as
a remedial priority of the first order. If local community leaders touted pupil
desegregation—and few did so without qualification, even after passage of the
Civil Rights Act, when it actually appeared within grasp—they did so as a means
to another end. Leaders advocated desegregation as a means of achieving equality, defined in specific ways such as ending overcrowding in a particular school
or neighborhood or gaining employment for black teachers in white schools.
That is, they employed the term strategically, to define and pursue the commu-

nity's daily needs. By contrast, LDF interpreted *Brown* as a case primarily about pupil desegregation in each and every school. This difference in emphasis and priorities between lawyer and client had existed since the earliest days of LDF's campaign against segregated education. But it never received a public airing. After 1950, when LDF decided to attack *Plessy* frontally, Thurgood Marshall discouraged negative client feedback about its pursuit of desegregation.[121]

Instead of communicating with LDF, influential leaders of Atlanta's civil rights struggle dialogued with the defendant in *Calhoun v. Latimer* at critical moments in the battle over school desegregation. Time and again, ASLC pleaded with the Atlanta Board of Education for relief, rather than engaging in more confrontational tactics. The lessons of the intervening years, in which direct action, staged alone or in combination with litigation, had yielded great progress, seemed lost on these activists. That the most influential black leaders had little will to protest educational inequality in the streets and at the bar became increasingly obvious after mid-1964. In the wake of the Civil Rights Act, all three branches of the federal government supported school desegregation to varying degrees. Activists could leverage the Act, HEW regulations, and Judge Wisdom's far-reaching opinion in *Jefferson* to their advantage. But they did not seize upon these opportunities as mandates for change.

And, ironically, just as LDF garnered *Jefferson*, the most favorable precedent yet from the Fifth Circuit, Constance Baker Motley, one of LDF's most talented lawyers, took a seat on the federal bench. To the extent that any hope had ever existed for one outstanding lawyer to single-handedly bend the presiding court and the community to LDF's vision, it was extinguished. Atlanta had lost its "Amos."

These developments revealed a sobering paradox. For years, the federal government had been an unwilling partner in the struggle to implement *Brown*. Now, at the most propitious moment to date, LDF's legal team in Atlanta changed abruptly and pupil desegregation ranked low among the priorities of black power brokers in Atlanta.

The city's black leaders had not been energized by LDF's remedial vision, but they also abstained from educational protest action for an altogether different reason. The disorder that followed black power and the "movement of movements" of 1966 had made social protest less appealing than ever to black leaders intent on membership in the civil rights—and the American—mainstream.

On the few occasions when grassroots activists threatened demonstrations against school board policies, they were outmaneuvered by black establishment leaders. The more moderate views and tactics of higher-status, mainstream blacks prevailed in part because these grassroots leaders—mostly older clergymen—continued to identify with and defer to the black mainstream leaders. All of the older activists were a part of a single social and political network; the network held together under pressure of race-based appeals to group solidarity and in the face of the Board of Education's persistent race-based employment discrimination. The LDF did not intervene in such local, intraracial politics, although it had a heavy stake in them.

All of these dynamics set the stage for an epic showdown. When the U.S. Supreme Court forcefully endorsed LDF's remedial vision in a series of cases that extended the logic of *Green* yet further, LDF finally had to confront a reality that Thurgood Marshall had long resisted: equality held different meanings within the many African-American communities touched by the landmark case of *Brown v. Board of Education*. Furthermore, the few black students who had experienced school desegregation described a bittersweet encounter, at best.

## CHAPTER 11

# End to an "Annual Agony"

*The Black Backlash against* Brown *and Busing, 1969–1974*

If I have to choose between sitting beside whitey and a job that pays money, I want the job. (1973)

Lonnie King

Why should our children be pawned for a few greenbacks? (1973)

Ethel Mae Mathews

In 1970, Lonnie King, former leader of the Atlanta student sit-in movement, and Rev. Andrew Young, former executive director of the SCLC, battled each other to become the Democratic nominee for a seat in the U.S. Congress.[1] School desegregation, a live issue in the federal courts, and "forced busing," a favorite target of the Nixon White House, predictably emerged as topics of debate.[2] The candidates staked out sharply different positions. Young argued that compulsory busing was not necessary to desegregate schools. King castigated him. "If a person agrees that segregation is a destructive institution in terms of human dignity and talents," King railed, then "I do not understand how that person can oppose such a useful instrument for desegregation as busing." King accused Young of providing "ammunition for persons who are still fighting for segregation." "I wonder," King mused, "if he realizes that his attitude toward busing is the same as that of Lester Maddox and other segregationists." King called on voters to sustain efforts "to break down segregation."[3]

King's pitch did not work. Seventy percent of voters in the Fifth District were white. Numerous indicators—including a 60 percent decline in white enrollment in the city's public schools, a corresponding surge in white enrollment in private schools, and school boycotts staged by white teachers and students—demonstrated beyond doubt that a majority of whites disfavored mandatory school desegregation and "forced busing." Moreover, as it turned out, black voters, who made up the remaining 30 percent of the electorate, were not guaranteed to endorse King's position, either. Young beat King in the primary, though he lost in the general election. Two years later, however, Young ran again and made history when he won; he became the first black U.S. representative from Georgia since Reconstruction. Young went to Washington, hailed both for his crossracial appeal and as a voice for blacks in Congress. Yet, he had won his seat in a majority white district partly because he had opposed the conventional black position on *Brown*. And Young won reelection by embracing racially moderate positions that appealed to his white constituents, while reminding his black constituents that "we're only 11 percent."[4]

The King-Young matchup and Young's subsequent election to Congress illuminated the challenges that African American candidates and communities confronted during the 1970s. Black officials served two masters: white and black voters' whose interests could be strikingly different. Since white voters outnumbered black ones, whites' preferences powerfully influenced the positions and actions of even pathbreaking minority candidates. African Americans could only hope to achieve meaningful, as opposed to symbolic, political power in limited circumstances: if blacks and whites formed coalitions and compromised, or if blacks and whites occupied separate political spheres—where blacks could constitute a majority. Otherwise, whites enjoyed an advantage by virtue of numbers alone in an integrated society—not to mention the benefits accrued through social networks, family background, wealth, and racism.[5]

The peculiar position in which African Americans found themselves during this decade—free of Jim Crow but still heavily burdened by systemic disadvantage in the electoral system, the workplace, and the economy—powerfully shaped the era's struggles over school desegregation. Battles for "community control" of schools in Brooklyn and Philadelphia during the late 1960s grew out of the fraught political position that blacks encountered. Typically, scholars have emphasized the racial dimensions of such controversies. They interpret the movement for community control of schools as the natural outgrowth of the black power movement and frustration with white flight from desegregation.[6]

The Atlanta school desegregation litigation also highlights these racial motivations, but it complicates the conventional narrative about community control of schools by analyzing how class dynamics influenced African Americans' educational choices. The Atlanta case powerfully illustrates how the black middle class's aspiration to consolidate not only their political power, but also their economic power, shaped events. It shows a chasm between the aspirations of the black middle and working class—a chasm that courts, civil rights lawyers, and black representatives, elected and self-appointed, addressed inadequately, if at all.

Lonnie King's evolving position on school desegregation sheds light on these dynamic times. By 1973, a scant three years after his failed bid for Congress, King's seemingly unshakable position on desegregation and busing had vanished. As president of the Atlanta branch of the NAACP, King now revolted against LDF and its plan to achieve school desegregation through busing. Together with powerful whites, King negotiated a "compromise" settlement plan that minimized pupil desegregation in exchange for black administrative control of the school system.

The local branch's goal conflicted with long-standing policy of the national NAACP and LDF. Under pressure from the black middle class, leaders of the national organizations at first reconsidered their allegiance to Thurgood Marshall's vision of school integration. Ultimately, however, local counsel Howard Moore and Elizabeth Rindskopf lambasted the Atlanta proposal. Personally, Moore had little faith in school desegregation as a remedy for inequality, but he argued that the compromise foolishly "bargained" for protections already secure under law. King and his allies responded to these critics by shifting the rhetorical terrain away from law. King made claims of authenticity and invoked ideals about community and racial solidarity that the staffs of neither the LDF nor the NAACP could credibly rebut. King, the hero of the sit-in movement, had deep roots in Atlanta and claimed strong support in the black community for the compromise plan. Constitutional law's doctrinal requirements and the legal system's promises of fair play meant little in comparison to that community's present needs.

Yet, as the story that unfolds over the following pages will make abundantly clear, King's claims that he spoke for a "black community" that favored "community" or "local control" were partial truths. Many African Americans, particularly the poor—a new wave of dissenters—challenged King's authority to speak on their behalf. A group of impoverished African Americans, led by Ethel Mae Mathews, a crusading welfare rights activist, challenged the goals espoused by King and his middle-class allies. The group rejected King's conception of racial justice: separate schools governed by black professionals whom these poor activists did not necessarily view as allies. Instead, these parents sought equal education, believed racially mixed schools were a means to that end, and were prepared to bus their children to achieve this goal. Still others entered the debate and staked out different positions in response to King's proposed settlement. Contrary to King's suggestion, no single, monolithic black community existed in Atlanta. The "black community" consisted of multiple communities—often divided by class—with sometimes overlapping and sometimes conflicting values on the question of desegregation.[7]

The federal courts proved no match for such multi-layered problems, which implicated race, class, and divergent views about the responsibilities of minority representatives to their constituencies. The courts were poorly equipped doctrinally, institutionally, and politically to take these complexities into account as the

Atlanta school desegregation case entered its final stages. The battle over *Brown* and busing in Atlanta surely would end with all sides bitterly disappointed with the judicial system, and with each other.

## "INSTANT INTEGRATION" AFTER FIFTEEN YEARS OF DELAY

Two decisions of a newly (and a temporarily) emboldened U.S. Supreme Court galvanized forces in Atlanta and shaped the battle over school desegregation in the early 1970s. First came the justices' October 1969 opinion in *Alexander v. Holmes County Board of Education*. In this decision, issued after Nixon appointee Warren Burger became the new chief justice, the Court held that *Brown II*'s "all deliberate speed" language no longer was a "constitutionally permissible" basis for delay in implementing a desegregation decree. All school districts must end dual systems "at once" and operate unitary systems "now and hereafter."[8]

*Alexander* broke new legal and political ground in the school desegregation fight. The Nixon Department of Justice had petitioned to further delay implementation of the desegregation plans at issue in the cases: "instant integration" in thirty Mississippi districts would only create "administrative confusion." The Court forcefully rejected the government's arguments. Commentators interpreted the decision as a "dramatic slap" at, and a "stunning setback" for, the Nixon administration. The justices had quelled any "false hopes" that the administration had raised in the South by siding with the Mississippi districts. They made clear that the Court no longer would accommodate southern subterfuge on desegregation. The staff of LDF viewed *Alexander* as a crucial victory as well; the lawyers promised to rely on the victory as they sought "immediate integration" in numerous cases.[9]

The full repercussions of *Alexander* soon became clear in Atlanta: above all else, the case inflamed passions over faculty desegregation. Judge Hooper ordered the Atlanta Board of Education to submit new desegregation plans for students as well as faculty. He decreed that student bodies must be "merged" into a unitary school system, but without stipulating specific ratios for pupil desegregation. His mandate with respect to faculty desegregation, by contrast, was specific. Hooper stipulated that the black-to-white faculty ratio in each school must reflect the overall school population (about 57 percent black, 43 percent white), consistent with Fifth Circuit precedent. As a consequence of Hooper's order, the Board of Education announced, it would have to quickly transfer eighteen hundred teachers (nine hundred white, nine hundred black). Most of these teachers would work in schools populated by student bodies "predominantly or entirely of the opposite race."[10]

Reaction was swift. Governor Maddox called the court order a "criminal action by the federal government" against American teachers, children, and parents. White teachers threatened to resign rather than submit to involuntary reassignments. Others organized a group, Teachers of Atlanta, to protect their seniority rights and fight transfers. Students walked out of class. White parents beat a path to the Board of Education; there, they expressed concerns and fears about who would now teach their children. Board members predicted that the decision would backfire; it could only produce white flight and resegregation. An *Atlanta Constitution* reporter summed up the atmosphere in the city: The U.S. Supreme Court's order for immediate school desegregation, "like a spreading fire," had left the public, teachers, and students bewildered and confused.[11]

The fires flamed even more once the Atlanta Board of Education issued its response to Hooper's order to formulate a new pupil desegregation plan. The board—now chaired for the first time by an African American, former Morehouse College president Dr. Benjamin Mays—claimed that *Alexander* should not even apply in Atlanta. The city already had achieved unitary status, the board insisted. Now, housing patterns alone determined where students attended schools. Given the board's stance, it came as no surprise that it proposed a "no-busing" desegregation plan that zoned the city largely along current attendance lines. Still, the plan did end pure freedom-of-choice assignment in Atlanta. It increased black enrollment in predominantly white schools by 8.9 percent, and white enrollment in black schools by 11.9 percent. For the first time, the board proposed to transfer white students to black schools to achieve desegregation. Three thousand students would receive new school assignments. That number represented a small percentage of the city's 110,000 students. Nevertheless, these changes, coupled with the faculty integration order, shocked and dismayed whites accustomed to desegregation in name only. White parents expressed concern over the plan's scale and about children being ordered to attend schools outside their own neighborhoods.[12]

Feeling under siege, whites borrowed tactics of the civil rights movement. They organized against the federal court's order. A group called Hands Across Atlanta delivered a four-inch-thick file of petitions, containing seven thousand names, to the Board of Education. The petitioners urged reversal of court-ordered desegregation. An astounding three thousand students marched in subfreezing January temperatures to protest impending transfers. They paraded in the streets in front of the federal building and the State Capitol. Some waved signs reading "Government is our Servant, Not our Master" and

"Let us Keep Our Teachers." Others staged sit-ins. Several thousand pupils took Governor Maddox's advice to stage a boycott; they stayed away from school. New days brought new protests in which students waved American flags and carried signs saying "We shall overcome!" The speaker of the Georgia General Assembly introduced a bill to outlaw compulsory public school attendance. A social movement against court-ordered desegregation was born, and it posed a serious threat to Judge Hooper's control over *Calhoun v. Cook*, as the case now was known.[13]

As Hooper's orders came down, some community members made efforts to blunt Maddox's continuing showmanship and public concern about the court's edicts. Newspapers ran editorials appealing for calm. A new HOPE formed with sixty members intent on generating support for the court's orders. Now that the federal courts had mandated *faculty* desegregation, the GTEA's Horace Tate issued a statement endorsing complete *student* integration. The *Atlanta Inquirer* reminded white Atlantans that the court order had been imposed after "12 to 15 years of pussyfooting" by the Board of Education. It reminded teachers who complained of being "forced" to transfer that they had been *assigned* to their present workplaces in the first place. Moreover, the paper insisted, "Black students are not the animals they have been pictured to be." Some of those very students—subjects of the school desegregation litigation, but seldom heard from—found a voice in the *Atlanta Inquirer* to simultaneously air their frustrations, seek respect, and allay white fears. Faye Jackson, a fourteen-year-old, did not fear integration, she said; but she demanded that white teachers view her as an equal rather than as an "empty-headed fool." Other students welcomed white teachers to their campuses with promises to treat them with respect. In fact, fifteen-year-old Wendolyn Pyron explained, he likely would "treat a white teacher better" than a black one, "to show them [whites] what they think about the black student is not true."[14]

Nevertheless, emotions remained raw about the "school hassle." A few days after the *Inquirer*'s editorial, 7 percent of Atlanta's teacher corps resigned, all but a few white. Maddox continued to aggravate the controversy. He insisted that white teachers should not have to enter the "foreign" environments of black schools and teach below their "normal level." By contrast, he argued, all black teachers should submit to examinations before being allowed to transfer and teach in white schools; after all, black educators had graduated from "degree mills" and "don't have qualifications" to teach white students. (The examination system that Maddox touted had existed for all Georgia teachers since 1960.)[15]

Many white teachers were petrified on the day that the Board of Education announced reassignment plans. A combination of lottery and seniority determined the "unlucky" few assigned to black schools. Although the transfer process itself went comparatively smoothly, the more pressing problem concerned long-term dynamics. Thousands of white students abandoned the public schools in Georgia after *Alexander* and related court orders. White enrollment declined so dramatically in the Atlanta school district that the system was less racially diverse in the fall of 1970, when the new "immediate desegregation" plan went into effect, than in the prior year. Black high school students outnumbered whites two to one.[16]

The trend would continue, as many whites feared that the worst was yet to come. The specter of a massive, court-ordered school busing plan shadowed the city. No one publicly justified opposition to busing on social grounds; respectable whites did not oppose *Brown* or race-mixing per se. Rather, reasonable citizens opposed "social engineering." The school system "should not be used to develop an artificial society," explained one commentator. Meanwhile, LDF's Howard Moore insisted that Atlanta could achieve "real integration" only if the board used busing as a component of its reassignment plan. Judge Hooper rejected the idea out of hand. The judge would not permit Moore to inject that inflammatory issue into proceedings in his courtroom—not unless and until a higher legal authority commanded it.[17]

## "THE BEGINNING OF THE END OF RESISTANCE"

*Swann v. Charlotte-Mecklenburg Board of Education* came as close as the justices ever would to a full-throttled endorsement of busing as a remedial tool to implement *Brown*. In *Alexander*, the Court had insisted that school boards banish dual school systems. *Swann*, decided in April 1971, considered whether and on what terms school boards could utilize tools such as busing to create unitary systems. In particular, the justices addressed how boards could fulfill their constitutional obligations in large, urban school systems with endemic residential segregation. The school desegregation plan on appeal from the Charlotte school district had been judicially imposed after an earlier one left two-thirds of the district's black students in schools that were 99 percent black. In other words, the old Charlotte plan functioned much the same way as the current Atlanta plan. The Nixon Department of Justice urged the Court to uphold such plans; it should permit local officials to preserve neighborhood schools, even all-black ones, in such instances. Chief Justice Burger's unanimous opinion in *Swann* rejected the administration's argument. The Court emphasized the federal courts' broad equitable powers to create desegregation plans that actually worked. The justices then established constitutional presumptions to guide district courts as they crafted injunctions and reviewed school board plans that were required to cure segregation "root and branch."[18]

The justices authorized broad judicial discretion and robust remedies to redress school board discrimination, but emphasized that it did not mandate "quotas," or demand that school officials remedy discrimination that they did not cause. The Court empowered school boards to prescribe specific ratios of black to white students *in each school* in a district as a "starting point" for dismantling dual systems. It held that officials could gerrymander attendance zones by clustering and pairing noncontiguous areas of a district, even if such practices produced administratively awkward or inconvenient results. The Court upheld race-conscious faculty assignment to achieve a particular degree of desegregation and reaffirmed that nondiscriminatory school systems should not reflect invidious racial differences with respect to faculty, staff, extracurricular activities, facilities, or other aspects of school programming. The justices did not rule one-race or virtually one-race schools uniformly constitutionally impermissible. But the Court held that such schools created a presumption of discrimination; school boards must satisfy presiding courts that such schools were "genuinely nondiscriminatory." The district judge or school authority "should make every effort to achieve the greatest possible degree of actual desegregation and thus necessarily be concerned with the elimination of one-race schools." Finally, the Court endorsed school boards' use of transportation plans if neighborhood school assignment would not dismantle dual systems. "Desegregation plans cannot be limited to the walk-in school," Burger wrote. At the same time, the Court noted that some objections to busing, grounded in concerns for children's health or education, could be legitimate.[19]

*Swann* struck observers as a legal bombshell—the "most historic" school desegregation decision since *Brown*. The justices had "armed federal judges" with a "broad arsenal of weapons" to eliminate the vestiges of Jim Crow, reporters explained. Commentators seized on three aspects of the decision. The Court had sanctioned a measure of deliberate school board "racial balancing." It had approved busing. And in so doing, the justices had unanimously rejected the Nixon administration's criticism of "forced busing" and preference for neighborhood schools, even in places with histories of de jure segregation. With the liberal wing of the Court thinned by departures and ideological shifts among holdovers from the Warren Court, *Swann*'s outcome had been uncertain. But Burger had "refused to take his guidance from the President who made him Chief Justice." The LDF, lawyers for the *Swann* plaintiffs, expressed glee and predicted that the decision had finally set schools across the South on the path toward school integration. Heated criticism of the Justices from opponents of busing—one said the Court should be "abolished" for its "asinine" action, and many white southerners denounced the justices' "discriminatory" treatment of the region—did not dampen advocates' expectation that a "new wave" of desegregation orders would flow from *Swann*. The "Court said this is going to be an integrated country," said LDF's Jack Greenberg. "Most Southern cities will have to increase classroom integration."[20]

In many areas, *Swann* generated the promising results that civil rights lawyers predicted. District courts ordered school systems across the South to use the tools legitimated in the case, specifically, busing and rezoning, to integrate schools. Officials in Charlotte, the birthplace of *Swann* and Atlanta's competitor for capital of the "New South," resigned themselves to busing after the Supreme Court's decree. The decision "marked the beginning of the end of resistance" to school desegregation, as authorities realized that further battles would be futile. Pressure from a few uncompromising African American leaders and a judge who consistently demanded compliance with constitutional requirements pushed white city fathers toward that recognition. Rather than invent ever more clever means of discrimination, Charlotte's Board of Education soon took steps to reduce white flight and comply with the court's order. Within three years, the city had achieved a stable, desegregated school system.[21]

In Atlanta, local elites—a biracial group of decision-makers—gave *Swann* a starkly different reception. *Swann*'s endorsement of busing and rezoning posed a tremendous threat to whites and blacks who had always relied on housing segregation to shield the city from school desegregation. Soon after the Court announced *Brown*, Atlanta school officials described the "location of schools in relation to the Negro population" as a "legal ace" that would preserve separate schools even after the elimination of de jure school segregation. Even as the city debated its response in *Calhoun v. Cook*, school board member and attorney Pete Latimer publicly stated that "geography is probably the one single fact which will prevent any mass mixing of the races." Influential blacks A. T. Walden, Rufus Clement, and Benjamin Mays had made similar statements as the NAACP's campaign against segregation in education made its way through the courts. Atlantans for "open schools" had endorsed token school desegregation during the Sibley hearings while citing their faith that housing patterns would, in reality, moot race mixing in the schools. From the bench, Judge Hooper had repeatedly commented that residential segregation tied the court's hands as it sought to fashion remedies for school segregation. After *Alexander*, the Atlanta Board of Education had even declared itself unitary on the grounds that housing patterns alone determined where students went to school. *Swann* jeopardized the city's long-held plan to preserve school segregation through residential segregation.[22]

It was therefore not surprising that Atlanta's local power structure resisted *Swann*'s mandates. John Letson, superintendent of schools, "reacted angrily" to a statement by an LDF staff lawyer that Atlanta would have to bus students to comply with *Swann*. "There can be no more desegregation in this city than we have already," Letson flatly asserted. A few months after the superintendent's statement, the board revealed the results of a study that it had commissioned. A majority of the city's whites opposed busing. But the same study showed that a majority of blacks *supported* busing. The board's antibusing position nevertheless found plenty of support among influential African Americans, the most important being that of Benjamin Mays, chairman of the Atlanta Board of Education. Even as LDF proclaimed that *Swann* made school desegregation inevitable in Atlanta, members of the Atlanta Board of Education, including its African-American members, voted against designing a new desegregation plan that used busing to achieve greater integration in the school system.[23]

Editors of the *Atlanta Daily World*, the city's leading black daily, came out squarely against busing as well. The paper emphasized that the Burger Court's endorsement of busing had been "permissive" rather than "mandatory." No court should impose busing in Atlanta, the editors concluded. Such "unnecessary pressure or force, even when legal" would be ill considered from an educational standpoint. The Supreme Court's clearest statement to date against freedom-of-choice had hardened black moderates' support for freedom-of-choice. The LDF frontally engaged the dissension among blacks over *Swann*. The organization's lawyers replied that Atlanta's schools remained "separate and unequal." The city's desegregation plan grossly failed *Swann* standards. The law must not yield to expediency. A battle over civil rights that pitted blacks against blacks, and that caused victims to make common cause with their victimizers, had begun.[24]

The crisis only deepened as the federal courts interpreted *Swann*'s meaning in Atlanta. After the decision, the Fifth Circuit vacated Judge Hooper's orders approving Atlanta's no-busing pupil assignment plan. The appeals court remanded the case to the district court with orders to formulate and implement a plan consistent with the new Supreme Court precedent. Hooper did not have the opportunity to respond to the directive, however. A district court panel composed of Judges Sidney O. Smith, Jr., and Albert Henderson replaced Hooper, who had presided in the Atlanta school desegregation case for thirteen years; Hooper's plans for extended foreign travel would have delayed the proceedings for months. When the panel responded to the Fifth Circuit's directive, it parroted the Atlanta Board of Education's recent self-assessment. The judges did not attempt to make *Swann* remedies work in Atlanta. They instead declared *Swann* remedies unworkable in Atlanta. Rather than imposing new forms of redress, the court found the system "unitary." In the estimation of Judges Smith and Henderson, Atlanta no longer operated a dual system. The city had met all its constitutional obligations. The plaintiffs no longer suffered vestiges of discrimination. The case was over.[25]

The court framed its rejection of *Swann* remedies and declaration of unitary status as a pragmatic and sensible resolution to the school desegregation litigation. The "annual agony of Atlanta" should end, the judges explained, for three interrelated reasons: the city's lack of buses, uncontrollable white flight, and black opposition to busing.

The court's discussion of these matters lacked analytical depth. The part of the opinion on busing read peculiarly and disingenuously. Atlanta owned no buses, but, for a long time, it had contracted with local carriers to provide transportation services to students.[26]

The district court's discussion of white flight also missed important facts that should have framed its discussion of *Swann*. The panel relied on white flight from school desegregation to justify its failure to consider *Swann* remedies in Atlanta, rather than as a starting point for a discussion about redress for discrimination. African Americans lived in Atlanta's central city, while white students lived at the city's extreme northern and southern ends, the judges observed. The court traced the racial make-up of the city and its public schools to the *Calhoun litigation itself*. In 1958, when LDF filed the school desegregation litigation, Atlanta's school-aged population had been 70 percent white and 30 percent black. By 1971, the ratios had reversed. In other words, the court causally connected flight and resulting neighborhood patterns to blacks' efforts to obtain desegregated schools. Yet, the panel leaped to the conclusion that "segregated housing, whether impelled by school changes or not" was "the unconquerable foe" of integrated schools. It then leaped again to the insight that any discrimination that now existed in Atlanta was purely "de facto discrimination," and absolved the school board of responsibility for remedying it.[27]

The court's simplistic discussion of white flight occurred in a remarkable historical vacuum. It neglected any consideration of the school board's culpability in segregation and flight. Even had they limited the relevant period to the years 1954–1971, the judges would have drowned in such evidence had they looked for it. The school board's (and state officials') resistance to *Brown*, and later its delaying tactics to avoid *Brown's* implementation, encouraged white resistance to school desegregation and white flight. The Board of Education signaled its resistance to desegregation when it created an elaborate admissions policy, replete with psychological and intelligence tests, to discourage desegregation. It restricted the vast majority of black students to inferior schools. It had taken no systematic steps to cure this discrimination.[28]

At no point did the court seriously discuss how it might comply with *Swann*'s mandate to achieve the "greatest possible degree of actual desegregation" through rezoning and other tools. The court did not attempt to refashion the existing desegregation plan using the whites and blacks remaining in the system. The court did not presume one-race schools discriminatory. Rather, it treated these schools as the result of "resegregation." In fact, the judges intoned that the problem in Atlanta was no longer how to achieve integration but how to prevent resegregation."[29]

The "black community's" perspective on busing, the court said, justified its reading of *Swann*. The court claimed that "a large group of blacks" opposed busing black students from the central city to the white ends of town except on a voluntary basis. The court provided no survey or other data to substantiate its claim about black public opinion. It said nothing of the survey commissioned by the school board, just months earlier, that showed that a majority of blacks supported busing. It did not cite statements of civil rights organizations. Rather, black members of the school board stood in as representatives of the black community. For the court, the two black board members—Dr. Asa Yancey and Dr. John Middleton, and Board of Education chairman Dr. Benjamin Mays, "respected black educator and civil rights leader"—and the "black community" were one and the same. In the court's view, their presence on the board proved that the city had achieved unitary status. "Atlanta now stands on the brink of becoming an all black city," the judges said, and such men, representative of "[i]ntelligent black and white leadership" believed that forced busing would push it over the edge.[30]

Atlanta officials viewed the ruling as a "form of vindication." They declared themselves "relieved" by the judge's order. Benjamin Mays, the board's chairman, welcomed the no-busing decision as "something that all people of good will and who want to see a stabilized school system can live with." The decision, he said, avoided further "community upset." The school district had done all that it could to integrate, Mays insisted. The chairman's views echoed those of members of his board.[31]

But the case was not yet over. The LDF appealed. And, in doing so, it achieved an important victory. In an October 1971 order, the Fifth Circuit vacated the district court's order dismissing *Calhoun*. The appeals court panel, which included Judge Minor Wisdom, author of the 1966 *Jefferson* opinion that had shifted school desegregation jurisprudence in favor of plaintiffs, ordered the district court to allow the civil rights lawyers an opportunity to present an "alternate and superior desegregation plan," consistent with *Swann*.[32]

The appellate court's decision created yet another opportunity for civil rights advance from LDF's perspective, a familiar position for the city and its local leadership. Perhaps, as Jack Greenberg hoped, LDF was on the brink of winning its decades-long effort to integrate Atlanta's schools and to integrate America.

Or the hope might prove hollow. For even as LDF prepared its new plan, the local community lashed out against its actions. Superintendent Letson reacted angrily once more: "People are sick and tired of this issue," he said. The LDF's efforts did not reflect the "wish[es] of a majority of the people of this city, black or white." However, the "black community is afraid to speak out against" busing "for fear of being called Uncle Toms, and the whites are afraid for fear of being called racists." Letson had no such fear. He called court-ordered busing "suicide" and repeated Mays's call for "community stability." Meanwhile, members of the local NAACP branch's executive committee gathered to discuss some board members' discontent over LDF's appeal. And the *Atlanta Daily World* wrote that "local school authorities and local citizens should have the right to decide the busing question in metropolitan areas." Neither the national NAACP nor any other group "has the right to act for the nation's Negroes as a whole, without referring and conferring with the local leaders."[33]

## THE "COMPROMISE"

On December 30, 1971, LDF submitted its desegregation plan to the district court. The plan eliminated all one-race schools in the district using all of the *Swann* techniques, including pairing, clustering, and busing. It proposed to bus students among sixty-four elementary schools and most of the high schools. Overall, however, LDF's proposal was modest in its impact. The LDF had managed to create a plan for a unitary system that would bus fewer than 10 percent of the city's students. The ratios of African-American to white students in many schools necessarily would remain high even under LDF's plan, given the system's demographics. Nevertheless, the lawyers' plan was substantive and more creative than the one that the Board of Education proposed. The LDF had met *Swann*'s mandate. The lawyers' plan would achieve the "greatest possible degree of actual desegregation."[34]

The LDF proposal also addressed faculty and staff assignments. And yet, unlike its recommendations regarding students, this aspect of the plan did not make detailed suggestions. Rather, LDF outlined broad principles regarding the assignment of teachers and administrators. The plan promoted seniority as a governing principle and stipulated that hiring and promotion would be governed by "reasonable, nondiscriminatory and reviewable standards and procedures." Moreover, LDF's proposal required that the ratio of black to white employees in professional positions approximate the ratio of black to white teachers in the school system, as mandated by the Fifth Circuit's two-year-old decision in *Singleton v. Jackson Municipal Separate School District*. Finally, LDF's plan included a provision requiring the district to submit biannual reports detailing district compliance with the plan's goals regarding faculty and staff as well as student desegregation.[35]

As a matter of law, LDF's plan was beyond controversy. Each of its elements had been found constitutional by the Supreme Court and the Fifth Circuit. The lawyers could cite *Swann, Green, Alexander, Singleton, Jefferson*, and even prior orders in *Calhoun* itself to support the proposal. Hence, the Board of Education's response to LDF's new plan did not focus on the letter of the law. Rather, the board attacked the scale of the proposal. In the media and in legal filings, the board charged that LDF sought to impose a "mass busing plan" on Atlanta. And recapitulating a now familiar argument, the board claimed that in Atlanta busing students would be impractical, disruptive, and prohibitively expensive because the city did not own any buses.[36]

At the same time, the board offered an olive branch. In a resolution supported by a biracial advisory committee, the board promised to "increase the number of Blacks in key positions" by "increasing the number of available key positions." It further proclaimed: "In order to perfect a better racial balance in key positions now held mainly by Whites, needed new positions will be created for Blacks immediately, and, further, it will be the policy of this Board to fill the places that become vacant with Blacks until the imbalance in this area is corrected." The same board that rejected racial balance for students embraced it wholeheartedly for administrators. The board's language describing its hiring proposal sounded more resonant of a separate but equal system than of *Brown* and the Civil Rights Act. It stated that "in each functional responsibility there will be both Black and White schools, faculty and services." The board's astounding offer to expend untold funds to expand its administrative force should have been unthinkable for another reason. Just months earlier, it had objected to additional expenditures for busing students to achieve desegregation on grounds that it had no resources to do so. Now, it was apparently flush with enough cash to create a raft of new positions for black professionals.[37]

The board had made a calculated response to LDF's proposal. Black access to faculty and administrative positions had long been a point of tension in the relationship between the Atlanta Board of Education and the GTEA and the ASLC. In the years surrounding Dr. Mays's selection as chairman of the board in 1969, the matter had reached a boiling point. In March 1970, Horace Tate claimed to have documentary evidence that black educators in Georgia had suffered the "brunt" of desegregation; 115 black principals and 800 teachers had been fired or demoted. Tate did not claim that such mass firings or demotions had occurred in Atlanta: he and other black leaders had worked assiduously to ensure that they had not. Most recently, black leaders in Atlanta had focused on employment discrimination in hiring for "upper echelon" positions. The school system could not be considered unitary, Tate argued, until blacks secured "administrative positions" in the "personnel office, the certificates division, the federal projects divisions, assistant superintendents and many others." Over the objections of board members who opposed busing, the Atlanta NAACP ultimately had approved LDF's most recent appeal in *Calhoun* out of concern over a "totally white" administration in a 70 percent black system. The branch had been incensed that Dr. Samuel Nabrit, a nationally known black educator, had been passed over for school superintendent in favor of a white banker. Now, amid the battle over busing, the board capitalized on black middle-class concerns about employment discrimination and professional mobility.[38]

The Board of Education's proposal, designed to appeal to local blacks, struck LDF as nonsensical. It pitted two complementary goals—pupil desegregation and equal employment opportunities for school faculty and administration—against each other. The Supreme Court already had mandated school *and* faculty desegregation. The Civil Rights Act also protected against employment discrimination, if weakly, thus far. In essence, the board offered to honor the rights of only one of two subgroups of the African-American population. Teachers and administrators could win, or students could win, but not both. Alternatively, the proposal rested on the faith that an administrator's race in and of itself added political, economic, and educational value to the black community. Tate exposed both strands of thought when in January, 1970 he conceded: "I think [black] control of the school system is more important than [pupil] integration. Had black people been allowed to control their schools before 1954," he said, the black schools "would have been more productive." "Integration," he went on to explain, "is the best thing that ever happened to the white businessman. He's now getting money that would have [been spent] in the black establishments under segregation." Integration was all about "controlling" and "exploiting" black people. In Tate's view, black school administrators could provide a bulwark against further white domination.[39]

For those who embraced Tate's worldview, the resolution promised something that the Constitution and federal law did not and could not: immediate black administrative power. The board's promise was like money in the bank for those who secured the new posts. For those who prized black administrative influence on ideological grounds, the resolution promised tangible political, economic, and educational benefits as well. They would see more blacks in the district office, and the black community would benefit as soon as the board filled the new positions. The LDF's references to the law on faculty and staff desegregation would pale in comparison to the board's promises of concrete gains.

Indeed, LDF's plan fared poorly. Judges Smith and Henderson had found the views of school board members compelling once before, and they did once again. The board objected that LDF's plan was "unreasonable." The court agreed in an order issued June 8, 1972. "No one wants an all-black school system," the judges concluded, and LDF's busing plan would lead to that result "in a very short time." Moreover, the court reiterated that existing segregation in the Atlanta school system resulted from "de facto forces completely beyond [the board's] control, primarily in terms of housing, population shifts, and the reseg-regation process." Paradoxically, the multitudinous ways in which whites had perpetuated racial discrimination in Atlanta over the years proved advantageous to the perpetrators. The judges had rejected *Swann* remedies and once again declared the Atlanta school system unitary. The Fifth Circuit's command to the district court to seriously consider how *Swann* might work in Atlanta had no discernible impact on the case.[40]

This latest setback did not shake LDF's resolve to obtain a comprehensive desegregation plan in Atlanta. If anything, the organization was emboldened. It responded with a multipronged attack on the school board. It again appealed the district court's unitary status order to the Fifth Circuit Court of Appeals. The LDF also made a motion to amend its complaint in *Calhoun* by adding certain Georgia state actors, including housing authorities, as defendants. Finally, it rebuffed the school board's overture regarding black administrative positions in stark, but legalistic, terms. The lawyers argued:

> Nothing will be rectified by assigning Blacks to new "Black" jobs created espe-cially for them; the proper remedy lies in insuring Black professional person-nel their natural and rightful place in the upper levels of administration in the Atlanta School System. This result will be accomplished, not by broad statements of policy...but by the creation of a procedure by which Blacks may first become aware of administrative staff openings, and then compete for such openings on the basis of their professional qualifications and experience.

The LDF was demanding fair procedures and equal employment opportunity.[41]

The LDF's statement objecting to the school board's offer to increase black administrative positions showed how disconnected it was from the rough-and-tumble reality of black politics in Atlanta. Influential African Americans rema-ined focused, even obsessed, with the reality of employment discrimination in the professional workplace. Horace Tate, a "bulldog" for black teachers' rights and educational equality, a man who had borne witness for years to the Atlanta Board of Education's discrimination, seethed at white supremacy. He demanded proportionate black representation in every school employment category. Lonnie King raged at persistent white domination of the workplace. He found the exclusion of blacks from policy-making positions in the public sector, school systems, and elsewhere especially troubling. "It shocks my sense of justice," King told a reporter. For "no program, however good on paper, is any better than its administrators." Due to its faith that courts, laws, and procedures would ensure equal access to the workplace, LDF's forceful repudiation of the board's proposal was out of step with the priorities of many middle-class blacks in Atlanta. This disconnect between national and local perspectives presaged an even more profound split that was soon to come. For, as it turned out, "new black jobs" could mollify a critical group of LDF's clients.[42]

## Settlement Negotiations Begin

For Atlanta's biracial elites, LDF's aggressive—even dogged—litigation stance proved unsettling. They found LDF's unwillingness to accept the school board's hiring proposal deeply troubling. And they dreaded its plan for busing; mere talk of it had frightened white parents, accelerated the white exodus from the school system, and inspired antibusing protests.[43]

This biracial elite grew even more uneasy when it learned that a second front had opened up in the school desegregation battle. On June 8, 1972, the same day that the district court had declared the Atlanta School District unitary for the second time, largely because the school board bore no responsibility for segregated housing patterns, an ACLU cooperating counsel filed a lawsuit predicated on precisely the opposite argument. The ACLU suit, *Armour v. Nix*, argued that the relationship between school and residential segregation in the Atlanta metropolitan area could be proven. Margie Pitts Hames, the plaintiffs' lawyer in *Armour*, set out to prove that a series of intentional acts—by state and local officials such as school boards on the one hand, and quasi-public and private officials and entities, such as real estate agencies, on the other—had produced Atlanta's pattern of racially identifiable schools and neighborhoods. In light of this conspiracy's scope, the ACLU sought a metropolitan-wide desegregation plan: a "federated" school system encompassing overwhelmingly black Atlanta and the overwhelmingly white suburbs. Soon after the ACLU filed its suit, LDF made a motion in the district court to consolidate *Calhoun v. Cook* with *Armour v. Nix*.[44]

This unsettling combination—LDF's uncompromising stance in *Calhoun* and the ACLU's new effort in *Armour* to create a federated school system—inspired Atlanta's biracial group of decision-makers to take decisive action in July 1972. A small group of Atlanta decision-makers set out to end Atlanta's "annual agony" once and for all. They would settle the school desegregation case out of court and send the interloping LDF lawyers packing. In the process, they would undercut the ACLU's suit as well.[45]

Local leaders launched settlement negotiations to end *Calhoun*, but the settlement process did not proceed in the usual way that litigation is resolved. Negotiation did not take place between lawyers for the Board of Education and lawyers for the plaintiffs acting on the instructions of their respective clients. Rather, a select group of white businessmen and civic leaders met in secret with a select group of black leaders to discuss terms on which to settle *Calhoun*.

These self-selected negotiators shared a critical characteristic: they all opposed the *Swann* remedies that LDF favored. Lonnie King, president of the Atlanta branch of the NAACP, the organizational sponsor of *Calhoun* and representative of the plaintiff class, headlined the black negotiators' group. Dr. Benjamin Mays, chairman of the Board of Education and defendant in *Calhoun*, joined him, along with board member Dr. Asa Yancey. Jessie Hill, Jr., the Atlanta Life Insurance Company executive who cochaired ASLC, and Lyndon Wade, executive director of the Atlanta Urban League and chairman of a "biracial committee" appointed by the district court to advise on the implementation of orders in *Calhoun*, rounded out the group of black negotiators. The white negotiators included school board members and *Calhoun* defendants Frank Smith and William VanLandingham. John Letson, superintendent of the Atlanta Board of Education, architect of the city's strategy of delay in the face of school desegregation orders, and a man who had personally facilitated white flight from Atlanta's public schools also numbered among the white negotiators.[46]

Remarkably, the Honorable Griffin Bell, a sitting judge on the Fifth Circuit Court of Appeals, orchestrated the settlement negotiations. Bell had been intimately involved in Georgia's response to *Calhoun* since 1960. As a former partner at the premier Atlanta law firm King and Spalding, he had helped to engineer Georgia's response to *Brown;* he managed the Sibley Committee hearings and the state's embrace of token desegregation. Subsequently, as a member of the circuit court of appeals, Bell had issued rulings in *Calhoun* itself, presumably as a neutral arbiter of the law. Now, in the settlement negotiations, he took on the partisan role of counsel for the white community at large as it sought to avoid *Swann*'s reach. He took on this role after publicly criticizing the landmark decision. In a July 1972 newspaper interview, Bell stated his preference for a "strict neighborhood school policy" and his disagreement with *Swann*.[47]

Months later, at a meeting of the Atlanta Action Forum, a group of Atlanta's movers and shakers, Bell explained that the legal environment confronting the city had dramatically changed. In the past, the district court had countenanced Atlanta's delay in complying with desegregation orders. Due to recent Supreme Court and Fifth Circuit precedents, the case was on a new legal footing. The judiciary would no longer countenance dilatory tactics. *Swann* remedies and even a metropolitan school desegregation order might be imposed on Atlanta if *Calhoun* remained a live controversy in federal court. Bell thus advised local leaders to remove the case from the judiciary's authority. They should settle the case. And they should begin discussions without the involvement of the attorneys of record. It was imperative to exclude the plaintiffs' lawyers, who were bound to insist on expansive desegregation remedies—precisely what authorities wished to avoid through settlement. Since Bell made his remarks out of public view, no one could question the ethics of a sitting judge playing the role of adviser to a group seeking to subvert the judicial process. Indeed, the public did not know that negotiations were taking place at all—much less the identity of the participants.[48]

Judge Bell provided well-informed advice to the negotiators. For even as they set out to defeat efforts by LDF and ACLU attorneys to win new *Swann* remedies in Atlanta, the Fifth Circuit issued new orders that threatened precisely this judicial intervention. The urgent rulings came in August and October 1972. The Fifth Circuit ordered additional faculty and staff integration. And it again reversed the district court's ruling that the Atlanta school system had achieved unitary status. The appeals court refused to accept Atlanta's claim that it had done all that it could to remedy the wrongs that it had committed against African Americans over the years. The circuit ordered the district court to design a desegregation plan in which "fear of white flight" was not "utilized as a factor" to avoid racial mixing. The circuit court also commanded the district court to pair or group segregated schools in accordance with *Swann* and to provide transportation for students as needed. The panel had run out of patience with the district court. It meant for Atlanta to comply with *Swann*, even as Atlanta opinion-makers greeted the appeals court's order as a "sad" and "painful" decision for the community.[49]

A month after the Fifth Circuit reversed the unitary status finding, Judge Bell, the behind-the-scenes counselor to the settlement negotiators, became publicly involved in *Calhoun*. In his capacity as a member of a three-judge panel presiding over the consolidated metropolitan-wide relief aspects of LDF's suit in *Calhoun* and the ACLU's suit in *Armour*, Bell stayed the proceedings. The rationale for the November 1972 stay order was logical enough: cases involving metropolitan relief were pending in other appellate circuits, in

Detroit, Richmond, and Denver, whose resolution might have an impact on a judge's opinion regarding the advisability of metropolitan relief in Atlanta. Yet, the stay also bought time for those wishing to resolve *Calhoun* in a manner that removed *Swann*-type remedies from consideration. Once the principals settled *Calhoun*, the Atlanta school system—the only one of the six districts involved in *Armour* that included a majority black population—no longer could be a part of the proposed federated school system. As a practical matter, settling *Calhoun* would decrease the likelihood that metropolitan relief would be ordered in the cases that remained.[50]

Around the same time that the stay issued, local newspapers broke news of the behind-the-scenes intrigue afoot regarding the school desegregation cases. An unidentified but "impeccable" source divulged that secret settlement negotiations were under way, reported one daily. The source explained that those involved in the discussions included selected members of the Board of Education—individuals required by Georgia's open meeting (or "sunshine") law to meet in public—who had been threatened with exclusion from further meetings if they divulged information about the talks to anyone outside the circle of self-appointed negotiators. The public was not to know of the discussions. Once they did, some took great offense, though to no avail. Rev. Joseph Boone, one of a small group of black grassroots leaders who had complained about Jessie Hill and ASLC's pattern of negotiating with John Letson, protested. He led a group of fifteen black parents in an attempt to gain entry into a building where a meeting of the negotiators reportedly was being held. Two detectives stationed outside the meeting site turned them away. Negotiations continued "behind a veil of secrecy."[51]

## LDF Is Ousted from Its Own Case and Then Unites with Its Opponents

The negotiations reached a critical new stage when Lonnie King took the remarkable step of firing LDF as counsel in *Calhoun*. The LDF had sealed its fate in November 1972, when New York–based LDF attorney James Nabrit III denounced the ongoing settlement talks. The LDF would never, under any circumstances, broker a deal with the Atlanta Board of Education that failed to maximize pupil desegregation, Nabrit declared. And certainly it would not do so in exchange for job opportunities for administrators. The LDF preferred a plan that bused thirty thousand students. To King, Nabrit's "massive busing plan" threatened progress at an ominous time for the city. White antibusing protesters had begun picketing the headquarters of the Board of Education.

"Hysteria" had set in among white parents fearful of crosstown transfers. Some wrote letters to the court begging it not to order further relief for the plaintiffs. The desperate tones of Mr. and Mrs. James H. Taylor's letter to Judge Smith were typical: "We will go to almost any length to protect and guard our daughter... from attending a heavily integrated (more than 20 percent) school," the couple wrote. Other impassioned white parents had transformed local parent-teacher councils into a full-fledged antibusing movement. These councils argued that busing violated the Civil Rights Act of 1964; and they passed a resolution asking the courts to withdraw their desegregation orders. Several predominantly black parent-teacher organizations also endorsed the same resolution, while other black organizations opposed it. These developments suggested to King that the struggle over school desegregation had to reach a conclusion—and quickly.[52]

King determined that he could only move forward with settlement negotiations by removing Nabrit and LDF from the case. The NAACP president achieved his objective by obtaining powers of attorney—a legal instrument most commonly used by persons at risk of incapacitation to permit another to act on their behalf—from eight of the twenty-seven *Calhoun* plaintiffs. Then, acting as the legal representative of these plaintiffs, King fired Nabrit, Moore, and Rindskopf. He then replaced the LDF lawyers with his own handpicked local counsel, Benjamin Spaulding, a man who was a member of the bar but who had "nothing else to commend him," in Rindskopf's estimation. Spaulding "stepped in" way "over his depth." In the press, King and his supporters claimed that he had fired the LDF attorneys after he had consulted with the plaintiffs and they enthusiastically offered support for LDF's removal. "We don't appreciate a New York yankee coming down here and telling us how to run our school case," one local NAACP official explained. "All the brains in the world aren't concentrated in New York." The LDF had been ousted from its own case—and one of the most important school desegregation cases in the South.[53]

In deposing LDF from *Calhoun*, King was acting as the chief decision-maker and spokesman for the plaintiff class—approximately seventy-five thousand parents of African-American schoolchildren in Atlanta. What gave King this authority? King's stature rested primarily on his post as president of the Atlanta branch of the NAACP. Yet his ascension to the branch presidency had occurred at a time when local membership was declining for lack of interest in NAACP activities, and there had been procedural improprieties surrounding his nomination to the post. Many members of the committee that nominated King and other officers were not members in good standing with the organization. As a result of these irregularities, the branch was required to hold a new nominating session. King, the sole candidate for branch president, was certified the winner of the election in January 1969. Although it is not possible to determine how many people voted King into office, it is clear that those who elected the slate of branch officers in 1969–70 were few in number. At the time, NAACP officials considered the Atlanta branch virtually defunct. Just a few months after King's election, Ruby Hurley threatened to revoke the branch's charter due to a lack of community support, defined by the NAACP's constitution and bylaws as failure to meet the minimum requirement of *fifty* paid memberships. "Are we to assume that the NAACP is dead in your community?" Hurley inquired. Notwithstanding these circumstances, the NAACP's name and cachet suggested to the outside world that King represented a broad and active constituency. For a while, at least, he laid claim to serving as *the* voice of black Atlanta—a voice more credible and more authentically local than LDF, which he repeatedly labeled a group of "outsiders."[54]

King could not have exercised so much influence without the court's consent and, it happened, the aid of LDF. In December 1972, after King's extraordinary request to remove LDF as counsel of record in *Calhoun*, the district court set out to determine which lawyers legitimately represented the plaintiff class. A battalion of lawyers attended the hearing. Howard Moore and Elizabeth Rindskopf represented LDF. Spaulding appeared for King and eight of the *Calhoun* plaintiffs. Margie Pitts Hames attended as counsel for the plaintiffs in *Armour*, the metropolitan suit. Observers of the recent controversy might have expected fireworks. The fissures among the plaintiffs could not have been clearer. Just weeks before the hearing, Howard Moore described blacks who negotiated with the Board of Education "Uncle Toms." He termed the pursuit of administrative jobs in lieu of pupil desegregation a "slave auctioning himself off more or less…literally selling out the rights of children." In response, King had rallied numerous prominent blacks in defense of his proposal. For example, Andrew Young, the newly elected congressman who now was King's ally in opposing busing, had pushed back against Moore and LDF: "If Howard Moore had been around the community for the last year or so, he would understand what Lonnie King and others were trying to do and he would have supported their plan." Relations between the branch and LDF could not have been more tense in the weeks before the hearing.[55]

But no sparks flew. Moore and Spaulding played amicable cocounsel rather than antagonists during the hearing. Both refused to address questions propounded from the bench about the significance of Spaulding's entry into the case as counsel for part, but not all, of the plaintiff class. When Judge Smith implied that Spaulding could not be a legitimate representative of the entire class because it consisted of the approximately fifty thousand African-American children in the school system, rather than only the eight from whom King had obtained powers of attorney, Moore disagreed. He insisted that these facts presented "no controversy about... the make-up of the class, or the relief and scope of the relief which the class seeks." In fact, Moore explained to the court, King no longer wished to substitute counsel; he had withdrawn the motion seeking LDF's ouster and Spaulding's insertion as counsel of record. The LDF had agreed to add Spaulding as counsel in the action. Henceforth, the two would jointly represent the plaintiffs.[56]

The court would not so readily dispense with concerns about the plaintiffs' representation. Judge Henderson suggested that the members of the class should receive notice about these developments in the case. Perhaps, he offered, the plaintiffs should be allowed to "bring their own lawyer[s] in" to ensure that they received "adequate representation." Moore strenuously objected to the suggestion. "[T]here is no dissension" as to "who counsel are in this case representing the class," Moore insisted. He and Spaulding had full authority to speak for all of the plaintiffs in the case; therefore, he claimed, no circumstance had arisen of which the plaintiffs should be made aware. Moore's opposition to notice struck Judges Smith and Henderson as odd. His posture caused the judges to shift the focus of their questions to LDF and its professional ethics in school desegregation cases. Smith offered that "[t]hese school suits... are the only cases really run by the lawyers and not by the class." The judges "had not even seen a member of the class"; "they haven't been in the courtroom, they haven't testified as witnesses or anything." Henderson agreed. The plaintiffs' lawyers, whether Moore or Spaulding, were in the "[m]ost envious position in the world," he said. He continued: "I think we would all have to recognize, to be perfectly honest, that this has always been litigation controlled by the lawyers and not by the class itself." Ultimately, however, the court accepted Moore and Spaulding's argument that no notice was required because the lawyers had worked out the initial problem themselves.[57]

Before now, Moore's decision to join forces with Spaulding has been understood as a simple tactical blunder on LDF's part. The national NAACP and LDF wanted to avoid the embarrassment of a public fight with the Atlanta branch over attorney representation in *Calhoun*, it has been said, and called a truce. During meetings in late November and early December, local LDF counsel Moore, together with New York LDF lawyers Nabrit and Greenberg, had met with influential black leaders in Atlanta who supported Lonnie King. Congressman Young, Benjamin Mays, Jessie Hill, Lyndon Wade, Joseph Lowery, and other black professionals convinced LDF to defer to locals' preferences to settle the case. The two groups had decided to work together on an out-of-court settlement. But LDF planned to demand that any future settlement proposal comply with its key principles. The truce came back to haunt LDF because the organization wrongly assumed that Moore would be able to convince King and local blacks to adopt LDF's point of view on pupil desegregation.[58]

The decision did come back to haunt LDF, but not because Howard Moore had blundered. A sophisticated thinker, Moore had proven himself an excellent lawyer in hundreds of cases by 1972. Far from a careless mistake, Moore's attempt at conciliation with a group opposed to mass busing may well have reflected the fact that—personally—he appreciated King's pursuit of "community control" over schools. Moore's experiences as counsel to political dissidents, including Julian Bond, Stokely Carmichael, and Angela Davis—the black power advocate and Communist professor whom he defended against murder charges at the same time that he litigated the final stages of the Atlanta school desegregation case—proved transformative. During the late 1960s, he embraced black power, which he defined as the ability of blacks the "world over" to "control their resources and to organize themselves in ways that they find appropriate and have the type of government that they feel that's appropriate." Moore called black community control "essential" to empowerment. He respected black autonomy, and he was well aware that "there wasn't a will in the city of Atlanta to desegregate." He thus found himself in a quandary, and he had been troubled by the concept of school desegregation for some time.[59]

A full year before the pivotal truce meeting, Moore published an essay that critiqued *Brown* in terms that resonated with Lonnie King's criticisms of school integration. Moore argued that the landmark decision had merely "modernized white supremacy." The "fault in *Brown*," he wrote, "is the same as that in *Dred Scott* and *Plessy v. Ferguson*. Each of these decisions assumes that whites are racially superior to blacks." *Brown* "accepts without question white domination of the institutional life of the nation." Moore scoffed at the idea that separate schools breed racial inferiority in black children; he called that a "null hypothesis." "The inferiority attributed to Black children attending all-Black schools," he said, "is as much the product of Black children's upbringing in a racist society as it is the product of separate schools." The lawyer conceded that the fight against de jure segregation had been necessary, but in a damning way. Integration was preferable to enforced segregation "to the same extent that prolonged illness is preferred to sudden death," he said. *Brown* had shown the U.S. Supreme Court "irrelevant" to the black liberation struggle. Indeed, he concluded, "[w]hen blacks looked closely at American jurisprudence on questions of race, they find that very little progress, if any, has been made after generations of litigation."[60]

Moore, a seasoned lawyer, certainly could zealously represent his client— LDF, an organization engaged in avowedly political work—without endorsing its views. No rule of lawyer's ethics required him to endorse school desegregation in order to litigate school desegregation cases. Nevertheless, Moore's commentary about *Brown* raised questions about how *zealously* he could pursue a racial balance remedy in a school desegregation case. Years later, the attorney himself conceded that point. "I was not enthusiastic about pursuing wide-scale busing in the city of Atlanta," he recalled, particularly given that "there was no support among the leadership in the city to do that, certainly no support from the local NAACP." He simply "didn't see the value of moving black kids from one place to the other so they could be with the whites." Yet, as LDF's man in Atlanta at the time, Moore was obligated to pursue remedies consistent with LDF's decades-old position that *Brown* required the maximum feasible degree of desegregation, a principle endorsed in *Swann*. Moore had "the highest respect for LDF," he said. The LDF "wanted to finish the job that it had started, [a]nd that [was] understandable." In his view, Moore performed his duties as LDF's local counsel, if with a degree of detachment from the course that he pursued.[61]

But Moore's decision to form a united front with King and Spaulding struck his cocounsel, Elizabeth Rindskopf, as a deliberate and troubling misstep. Rindskopf, the junior attorney on the case, thought that LDF should object to Spaulding's entry into the litigation. The local NAACP's and LDF's positions on school desegregation were too far apart to be reconciled, she believed. Rindskopf thought that Moore was "throw[ing] the case"; he "really wasn't interested" in it. Heated behind-the-scenes conversations informed her perspective. On several occasions, Moore had spoken of his desire to "get rid of" the Atlanta school desegregation case, which he called "nonsense," she said. The litigation not only conflicted with Moore's personal views but also kept him tethered to Atlanta at an inconvenient time. Meanwhile, the Angela Davis case, which garnered international press and promised to dwarf his past work in significance, took place over two thousand miles away, in the San Francisco Bay area. Despite her misgivings, Rindskopf was in no position to question the strategy of Howard Moore—the experienced litigator—not to mention the prerogatives of the local branch of the nation's oldest civil rights organization. Rindskopf—a "white person representing something or someone or some idea" but "certainly not [her]self"—sat at the hearing in silence while Moore formed an alliance with Spaulding.[62]

This hearing proved a decisive moment in the case. After LDF agreed to jointly represent the plaintiffs with the local branch, the momentum had shifted decisively in favor of the Atlanta NAACP and opponents of school desegregation. Lonnie King and Ben Spaulding's credibility, which had been in question, no longer was. If anything, LDF's credibility as representatives of black Atlantans now hung in the balance. The organization's about-face and its opposition to the court's efforts to solicit input from its clients left the impression that

LDF was out of touch with the plaintiffs. The court now had more reason than ever to be skeptical of LDF "outsiders" and their insistence upon imposing "social engineering" on Atlanta.[63]

## A FINAL SETTLEMENT?

Relations between the local NAACP and LDF changed dramatically over the next few months, as settlement negotiations strained the accord between the local and the national organizations to the breaking point. The LDF's Elizabeth Rindskopf participated in many of the negotiation sessions and even drafted parts of the proposal. But she did so, she later said, "under protest" and at the direction of Howard Moore, who was in California. By February 1973, when the local NAACP submitted to the court the "compromise" settlement plan that it had reached with the school board, relations between the local NAACP and LDF had finally ruptured. The compromise, which minimized student integration, could not be reconciled with LDF policy.[64]

The compromise agreement, Dr. Mays explained, would settle the school desegregation case that "had been hanging around the school board's neck like an albatross for fifteen years" by focusing on school administration. It looked much like the hiring proposal that LDF had rejected months earlier. Lonnie King explained how the compromise differed from the typical school desegregation remedies that LDF endorsed:

> I think administrative desegregation to the LDF was secondary. My position was just the opposite. I think I have a responsibility to Atlanta. I'm not a segregationist, but if I have to choose between sitting beside whitey and a job that pays money, I want the job.[65]

The agreement listed thirty-seven administrative positions, twenty-one newly created. It stipulated that blacks would fill the overwhelming majority of these positions—twenty-five of them, including sixteen of the new jobs. Blacks would hold half of the six highest-paying jobs in the school system. For the first time, the superintendent of the school system would be African American. The plan stipulated that this configuration of administrative positions would be maintained for at least three years. The racial set-asides, apparently conceived as a form of affirmative action, were justified "to correct an inequity." The proposal also contained provisions that exempted officials from Fifth Circuit precedent requiring specific ratios of black to white teachers *in each school*;

administrators always had wanted more flexibility over assignments, so that teachers reflected the overall ratio system-wide.[66]

The settlement proposal could not have been more explicit in divvying up administrative positions by race, but the deal-makers eschewed racial ratios for purposes of desegregating pupils. The proposal did not take advantage of any of the *Swann* tools for remedying school segregation. Instead, the proposal seemed designed to minimize rather than maximize interracial contact among students. The agreement left 83 of the city's 153 schools, attended by about fifty-nine thousand students (a majority of the system's pupils), 90 percent or more black. Among the eighty-three schools that would remain segregated, forty-five schools, containing about thirty-three thousand students, would have 100 percent black enrollment. Only about two thousand African-American students and eight hundred white students would be bused under the settlement plan. Those bused would overwhelmingly be the children of working-class and poor black families from places such as northwest Atlanta's Archer School community. Students in middle- and upper-income black neighborhoods would not be bused at all. The settlement did vow that the district would increase support for the voluntary majority-to-minority transfer program already in place; but the Fifth Circuit and U.S. Supreme Court had long found such freedom-of-choice approaches inadequate, alone, to remedy segregation. In essence, the "deal" negotiated and endorsed by Lonnie King and Board of Education member William VanLandingham contained provisions that the Fifth Circuit twice in the previous year had rejected as constitutionally inadequate.[67]

Despite the clear conflict between the local plan and LDF policy, Moore and Rindskopf did not immediately express public opposition to the compromise. Rindskopf did refuse to go to the courthouse to sign the settlement agreement, because, she later explained, it "lack[ed] integrity." But she did so without consulting Moore, the senior counsel who was out of town but still in charge of the case. Rindskopf believed that Moore preferred to settle the case on terms favored by the locals. Media attention on the settlement finally ended Rindskopf's agonizing and pushed the national NAACP, LDF, and thus Moore, to take a stand on the settlement. After the *New York Times* and *Washington Post* noted that the Atlanta compromise represented a major departure from past policy, the national organizations sprang into action. They strongly opposed the settlement and reaffirmed their commitment to maximum pupil integration.[68]

The national NAACP called the compromise "illegal," and LDF termed it "unfair, unreasonable, inequitable and unconstitutional." Moore and Rindskopf, along with the ACLU's Margie Hames, filed objections to the settlement. But the LDF attorneys found themselves in the odd position of repudiating a claim that they had made at the December hearing. Moore had then argued that no dissension existed in the case, that he and Spaulding jointly represented the plaintiffs and agreed on the remedy. Now, just four months later, in a March 1973 filing, he and Rindskopf importuned the court to reject the settlement because their remedial objectives and those of Spaulding and King could not be reconciled. The lawyers argued that King and Spaulding's negotiation of the settlement and request for court approval of the settlement violated the due process clause of the U.S. Constitution. The right of African-American students to attend a desegregated school could not be waived through settlement by the local NAACP, Moore and Rindskopf argued, particularly not when LDF—attorneys of record for the plaintiffs—objected to the waiver.[69]

The lawyers also argued that the pupil assignment scheme endorsed in the settlement violated the U.S. Constitution's equal protection clause. It left the segregated school system substantially intact. Meaningful school desegregation could only be achieved if both African-American and white students, about twenty-three thousand students total, were bused. The burdens of transfers and transportation fell upon poor blacks and, to a lesser extent, low-income white students. The attorneys further objected that the plan to desegregate administrative staff did not comply with Fifth Circuit precedent. The three-year time limit made the proposal's provisions regarding staffing fall far short of meaningful participation for blacks in school administration. Margie Hames endorsed LDF's objections and later would make several more of her own.[70]

The attorneys' about-face dismayed the district court judges. Moore had requested an evidentiary hearing regarding the "adequacy of representation of counsel who negotiated" the settlement a few months after claiming that the question was not an issue in the case. "[I]t is getting extremely frustrating," said Judge Henderson during a hearing on objections to the settlement, "that we seem to get these things resolved and we come back today and nobody is in agreement about anything, not even who represents the plaintiffs in the case." During the same hearing, Hames objected to the plan because it had "been written behind closed doors," a circumstance, she said, that aroused "suspicion" about Spaulding's representation of his clients. Judge Smith reprimanded her for daring to make an issue about Spaulding now, when she had failed to object to his entry into the case in the prior December.[71]

Undaunted, Hames turned the court's focus from her earlier misstep to the traditional requirements in cases involving settlement agreements. She reminded the court that it was customary to give affected parties notice and a hearing prior to approving a settlement of a class action. Judge Smith agreed that the court might need to "poll the class to help us form an opinion about whether it is to the best interest of the class to accept the settlement." But at the same time, he questioned whether the class members in civil rights actions had a "legal right to voice objections." Most of the relevant precedents involved stockholders' derivative suits, cases "about money," the judge noted. Henderson had no response to Hames's argument that the constitutional rights involved in *Calhoun* involved matters "greater than money."[72]

## The Human Face of the Legal Proceedings

Eventually, the court did hear from the plaintiffs. The proceedings first took on this unprecedented character at Hames's insistence. She sought to advance her legal arguments about the unfairness of the settlement by bringing her clients to court and encouraging them to share their views about the proposal. In all of the years that LDF had led the school desegregation effort in Atlanta, it had rarely taken such an approach. Judge Henderson had rightly noted that clients typically had not been a presence in the courtroom. The LDF lawyers had controlled, and been the face of, the litigation. By contrast, Hames attempted to put a human face on the legal proceedings.

Hames's clients—working-class and poor blacks—now captured the court's attention. Ethel Mae Mathews served as the main spokesperson for the *Armour* plaintiffs. The founder and president of the Atlanta chapter of the National Welfare Rights Organization, Mathews was an inspired choice. She had been born in profound poverty in rural Alabama, where she had sharecropped and had received little formal education. Mathews made her way to Atlanta as a young woman, in search of opportunity. A mother of five, she worked as a maid, "scrubbing and mopping," landed in public housing, and subsisted on public assistance in one of Atlanta's poorest neighborhoods.[73]

Yet, she had a strong sense of self and an abundance of practical intelligence, and she was prepared for her role in *Armour*. The experience of moving from a rural to an urban area, and of negotiating the city and an invasive welfare bureaucracy after enduring the injustices of Jim Crow in Alabama, had toughened her. Mathews did not shrink from confronting well-educated authorities. By the time she became involved in the struggle for school desegregation, protest was routine for her. She had grown accustomed to confronting state and local officials and fighting discrimination against poor women. Mathews had engaged in direct action protests, including raucous ones in which she "took over" local welfare offices. She had spent time in jail as a result of her protest activities. She believed poor people had "just as many rights as the rich person." And she "stood up for" her rights. In fact, Mathews had twice run for city council, "to help poor people," and sued the city in federal court for imposing a $500 filing fee on candidates; the practice discriminated against indigent candidates, she successfully argued.[74]

Mathews's experiences as a mother and advocate for poor women also taught her a lesson about race critical in her fight against the *Calhoun* settlement: she did not embrace racial solidarity for its own sake. Welfare mothers faced a profound stigma, and better-off folks routinely made them "feel that [they] were nothing." "Abusive" caseworkers were just as likely to be African American as white, and middle-class blacks were just as condescending as middle-class whites. Hence, Mathews showed no reluctance to point out the transgressions of persons in authority, whatever their race. "We didn't trust nobody. We were just a bunch of welfare mothers, desolated," she said.[75]

Mathews thus strode to the podium in the majestic federal court, undaunted, and offered frank opinions when Judges Smith and Henderson asked whether any onlookers had views about the proposed settlement. She proclaimed the compromise unjust. In Mathews's view, it had resulted from a corrupt process. Mathews explained that "black peoples and poor peoples," as she described herself and fellow *Armour* plaintiffs, had been excluded from the negotiating sessions. Their interests had been ignored by Lonnie King and others who purported to represent Atlanta's black community, despite the fact that the black poor suffered most under the unequal system of education. She exclaimed:

> I am not pleased with the settlement because we black and poor have been sold out for too long, just keep being sold out by our own peoples; so I would like for the Court to [reconsider] and let us poor people be in on the decision as black and poor peoples, because we are the ones can tell, we are the ones that live it, we are the ones that our children go to the ghetto schools....

> I represent poor people.... And I think their children ... need equal education as well as the rich person's children, because when we go to get jobs the first thing we are asked, how far did you go in school, how far did you go in college. So to do the thing right with the poor and the black [give them an] equal chance to express themselves and not just two organizations going to do all the wheeling and dealing, but let all the poor blacks ... do some wheeling and dealing with them.

Mathews expressed support for a remedy that included busing. But she argued that busing should be a "two-way street" so that wealthy white children bore the burdens of leaving neighborhood schools, just the same as poor blacks.[76]

Several other speakers echoed Mathews's call for an expansive remedy. Edward Moody pointed out that he saw "buses running everyday," taking students to and from school; "nobody questions that busing," he noted. Yet, people were up in arms about the possibility that a desegregation plan would mandate a significant amount of busing. He rejected the double standard. Rev. Joseph Boone, the minister who had protested outside of the closed-door settlement negotiations in November 1972, also demanded "reciprocal" busing and voiced support for a metropolitan desegregation remedy. A second minister, Reverend Bernard Lee of the SCLC, saw deliberate malfeasance on the part of those who had negotiated the settlement. The proposal had been "designed to set back" race relations in Atlanta "for the next one hundred years," he said. The attempt to "block school desegregation" in the city was especially pernicious for working-class and poor blacks, whom he believed most needed it.[77]

Two white defendants—members of the Board of Education—broke ranks and lent support to plaintiffs who opposed the settlement. Mrs. Leroy Woodward claimed that the negotiators had played favorites in reaching the agreement. Those who "brought tremendous pressure on the school board" had been exempted from the student transfer and transportation plan, she said. The result had been "discrimination toward certain schools." "I am disturbed and concerned that our schools are being used to satisfy personal and political gains," Woodward added. Howard Klein, a school board member who declared himself concerned about the "blacks and underprivileged," objected to the plan because it was unfair to "poor black" schools. He claimed that many of his African-American constituents had told him of their "upset" over the plan.[78]

This powerful commentary did not go unchallenged. Two plaintiffs supported the settlement. Carolyn Crowder, president-elect of the Fulton High School PTA, deferred to the judgment of black leaders such as Lonnie King. Crowder drew a clear distinction between herself and Mathews. She declared: "I'm not one of these people that feel I have to be included [in the negotiations]." Crowder did not want busing. She wished to see Fulton High improved so that black children would not need to be bused to wealthy white neighborhoods to obtain a quality education. The other unambiguous supporter of the settlement, Edith Hammond, expressed support for it in tones that echoed the rhetoric of many city boosters. The black and white people of Atlanta had a "unique opportunity" to "show the country how we can work together" to achieve a "compromise" that had been negotiated in "good faith," she said. The biracial group of negotiators could not have offered a better justification for themselves. Rev. C. A. Samples, on the other hand, opposed the local NAACP's plan because it would lead to the closure of neighborhood schools. Blacks would "lose identity." The plan would "tear down" "what has been constructed for poor black people."[79]

The court had now entertained plaintiffs' views about the settlement at Margie Hames's behest, but the outpouring of comments had resolved little. Rather, the hearing had exposed long-festering rifts in the black community:

differences over the value of desegregation, the meaning of equality, the salience of class in the black experience, and the priority of working-class interests in the struggle for racial justice.


## Competing Voices

In late March 1973, the district court opened Pandora's box even wider. Judges Smith and Henderson formally convened a hearing for the express purpose of considering class members' views on the proposed settlement. The court alerted members of the plaintiff class (black parents of minors eligible to attend the Atlanta schools) of the opportunity to attend the hearing through newspaper notices. Interested parents could examine copies of the proposal at area schools.[80]

Only thirty-six individuals testified at the hearing on the settlement. Many objected to the settlement. They dismissed the notion advanced by Lonnie King and other settlement proponents that black parents opposed busing. Mamie Dixon asserted that the issue of how far students had to travel to school had been overblown. "We want better education like the whites get." She stated unequivocally that "the Metro suit is the answer" to the problem of black schools' inadequacy. Ethel Mae Mathews, who had spoken so powerfully at the March 8 hearing, again asserted that the settlement would undermine educational opportunity. "[W]hy should our children be pawned for a few greenbacks?" she wondered. Mathews insisted that "our suit is not about busing, but it is about integration for our children to get an equal education." But "if it takes busing for our children to get an equal education, bus, because we have been bused all our lives," Mathews said.[81]

Emma Armour, the named plaintiff in the ACLU suit, *Armour v. Nix*, remarked that her children "don't mind busing" if they could "get the same equal rights as the white children do." Stanley Wise expressed support for a crossdistrict remedy because he viewed it as the only way to ensure that the resources routinely available in the white schools also flowed to blacks. Other settlement objectors believed that the poor gained few, if any, benefits from the settlement. Only the "poor black people" and the "poor white people" would be "moved about and juggled about" under the proposed settlement, explained Walker Moore. Mary Bernice Collins spoke out against the NAACP plan because it would leave black students in educationally inferior schools. "The colored children going to school and come out, can't even write their names."[82]

Others testified in favor of the proposal. Some in this camp, who appeared to have been dispatched by the negotiators to undercut the impact of the settlement's opponents, were not plaintiffs and had no formal connection to the case. Charles Hart, a member of Atlanta's Community Relations Commission, typified these speakers. Hart read a resolution passed by the commission's biracial membership that expressed appreciation to the Atlanta Board of Education, the Atlanta Chapter of the NAACP and the court-appointed Biracial Committee for the agreement in "the court case which has hung over our schools and our city like a threatening cloud for fifteen years." "We are grateful that this settlement has come out of mutual concern to the citizens of Atlanta themselves and has not been imposed by an outside authority or by the Court." The commission's allusion to an "outside authority," a thinly veiled reference to LDF, recapitulated a line that Lonnie King now habitually used to attack the New York–based organization's credibility.[83]

Even as they questioned LDF's authority to represent black interests in court, however, proponents of the settlement manipulated the judicial process to accommodate their own interests. They turned to John H. Calhoun, the former NAACP president and current president of the Atlanta Regional Commission, to testify in favor of the compromise, although he apparently had no children in the school system. Joseph Lowery, SCLC's chairman of the board, also gave extended testimony in favor of the compromise, although he had no standing in the class. Ruby Edwards's support for the settlement rested on her family's employment interests. Two of her daughters taught in the Atlanta schools, she proclaimed, and Edwards was certain that "they are just as competent as white teachers."[84]

Some of the African Americans who spoke in favor of the settlement did have children in the Atlanta public schools, however. Doris Arnold, president of the PTA of L. J. Price High School, revealed her allegiance to her historically black school, as well as her view that anyone who opposed the settlement had fallen under the influence of outsiders. Arnold asked the court to adopt the plan supported by the local NAACP rather than listen to "national organizations" that were "trying to come to our city, trying to disrupt" local decision-makers. Her rhetoric tracked that of the Community Relations Commission's resolution. However, a few settlement supporters offered more organic, unrehearsed views. Gladys Strocier, a mother of nine children and resident of the Perry Homes housing project, supported the settlement because she did not want her children to be bused across town and out of her reach. "I wouldn't feel right," she explained. Strocier wanted "quality education" instead of busing, better teachers, in particular. In fact, she explained, "I think you all should bus some of the teachers away instead of some of our kids."[85]

Many speakers took no position on the settlement and appeared confused about, or dissatisfied with, the available remedial choices. Helen Bell, a former teacher, suggested that the entire school system should be revamped "from head to bottom" so that all students enjoyed equal schools "across the board." But Bell stated that she neither supported nor opposed busing, and neither supported nor opposed the settlement. Likewise, Ruby Clay, another former teacher, stated: "[I] don't think it is important how children...get to school, taxi, bus or car pool. I think it is important that once they get to school their educational needs are being met." The statements of another woman, Mary Lamar, reflected the inaccurate belief that parents would be required to pay out-of-pocket for transportation costs. She objected to any plan that included mandatory busing because she lacked the funds to transport her children to schools across town.[86]

Such misinformed or vague statements highlighted opportunities missed during the March 29 hearing—notwithstanding the presence of three different groups of plaintiffs' lawyers and two presiding judges. The *Calhoun* settlement implicated the rights of thousands of individuals. Yet an abysmal fraction of seventy-five thousand *Calhoun* class members appeared to express an opinion about the compromise. Undoubtedly, many of those whose interests lay in the balance had no experience with the legal process, and thus little inclination or ability to become involved with the proceedings. Indeed, LDF's lawyers had done little to encourage client involvement in the proceedings. The lawyers' sole effort to rally support for its action—a community caucus on the eve of the due process hearing—had been suggested and organized by SCLC, and pitched at black community leaders rather than aimed at class members themselves. The hearing and LDF's actions in the weeks leading up to it once again demonstrated the organization's disengagement from the people whom it represented. Jack Greenberg and his small staff counted "go[ing] around and spend[ing] time talking to people" inefficient. "There was not much contact with the community, and there was not much input." The organization did not believe that politics "made the difference," recalled Jack Greenberg. "Clever litigation" did. To the extent that politics mattered, local communities and local lawyers were responsible for generating political support. In Atlanta, there was a "leadership void" in the community, Rindskopf observed. "Everyone seemed to be "running scared or getting out of it what they could."[87]

Some citizens had shown great interest in the case, however. The preponderance of class members who did participate in the hearing were Margie Hames's clients, members of the *Armour* case. Meanwhile, many of those who testified in favor of the compromise had no formal connection to either case. The parade of nonplaintiffs demonstrated the local NAACP's adept manipulation of the judicial and political processes to achieve its objectives. But the organization had not shown that it genuinely represented black Atlantans or the plaintiff class.

Mary Sanford, a public housing tenant who testified at the March 29 hearing, hinted at the bewildering situation in which everyday people found themselves—at the mercy of power brokers all claiming to stand for them—when she observed: "I keep hearing people talking about the school board, the lawyers and all of this." "But I think we, as parents, can note exactly what we want and how to educate our children" if parents had "some means of letting it [their preferences] be known." Three different organizations had entered the courtroom and claimed to play the role that Sanford so desperately desired: representative of the people and translator of their preferences to those in power. The LDF, attorneys of record for the *Calhoun* plaintiffs for over fifteen years, held itself out as the sole legitimate interpreter of *Brown*'s meaning. But the Atlanta NAACP urged the court to accept it as the people's representatives and approve the compromise that it had negotiated in the people's interest. And the ACLU claimed to offer the best choice of all. Hames represented blacks oppressed by race and poverty—those whose needs had never been priorities for civil rights activists—and held out the promise of a comprehensive remedy for inequality. The competing claims of representational authenticity and legitimacy would have taxed the most patient court.[88]

## Disorder in the Court

Judges Smith and Henderson—who twice had found the Atlanta school system unitary and twice had been reversed by the Fifth Circuit—did not quite fit this description. The numerous organizations and complexities involved in the case left them annoyed. "Everybody else is getting in on the act, so I guess we will hear from Wounded Knee and the Gay Front next," Smith quipped during the March 29 hearing. The judge made the remark when Peg Nugent, president of the Atlanta chapter of the National Organization for Women, asked to offer her perspective on the settlement. Nugent had appeared to criticize the compromise's use of "racial quotas" for the selection of staff, while failing to guarantee equal employment opportunity for women. The judge's dismissiveness of Nugent did not bode well for the settlement's opponents—the plaintiffs who wished to keep *Calhoun* and *Armour* alive in the federal courts. True enough, NOW had no standing in the case. But neither did numerous other individuals, white and black, who had been allowed to speak *in favor* of the settlement. Under the circumstances, Smith's statement spoke volumes. The court's indulgence of the settlement's backers was indicative of its management of the proceedings overall. The stakes of the hearings could not have been higher. But the judges' handling of the hearing often belied the gravity of the situation.[89]

And, in fact, the judges dispensed with all substantive objections to the settle-ment plan on the very same day that they convened the hearings. Attorneys for LDF and several other public interest organizations had filed briefs alleging that the deal brokered by King and Spaulding violated the Constitution. Judges Smith and Henderson rejected all of the arguments. The court rejected Howard Moore's arguments without even granting him the opportunity to argue his points in court. "The facts in this case have been thoroughly tried on numerous occasions and the record thereof is voluminous and complete," the judges said.[90]

The court was equally curt when it refused to permit two other national civil rights organizations to intervene in *Calhoun*. Both the national NAACP and CORE wanted to challenge the lawfulness of the settlement. The national NAACP's motion to intervene argued that neither LDF lawyers nor Ben Spauld-ing, the attorney hired by Lonnie King, adequately represented the interests of the *Calhoun* plaintiffs. Nathaniel Jones, the NAACP's general counsel, argued that the nation's oldest civil rights organization was uniquely equipped to pro-vide leadership in the case. The group had a "special interest" in the matters presented, counsel argued. Judge Smith rejected Jones's motion: "We have more parties and lawyers than we can handle now," he retorted. The judge also rejected the suggestion that more discovery should be conducted in the pro-ceedings. "We have fifteen years of evidence in the case," he said. Smith's remarks skirted Jones's point: the settlement had raised entirely different issues than had ever been presented in the case and thus demanded new evidence.[91]

Judge Smith responded no differently to Charles Conley, CORE's attorney, who objected to the settlement because, he said, of its patent unfairness to the black working class and poor. Conley denounced Lonnie King for "trading off quality education for a few big jobs for a few big Negroes." The client CORE was representing, the Perry Homes Tenant Association, was a group of fourteen thousand poor people in various community organizations who claimed that the NAACP had not consulted them prior to reaching a settlement. Conley argued that poor blacks in Atlanta, particularly the Archer School community, had been targeted for busing, while those in "middle and upper income black communities," who attended prized schools such as Douglass, Harper, and Washington, remained in their neighborhood schools. Parents at Douglass had publicly lobbied for exclusion from the plan, and King had granted the wishes of these middle-class blacks. "It appears quite clearly," argued Conley, "that the plan discriminates in favor of the more well-to-do sections." The black poor also preferred to remain in their neighborhood schools. The district court had no intention of entertaining Conley's complaints. Judge Smith denied CORE's motion to intervene. The "one thing this case doesn't need is a few more law-yers," he informed Conley.[92]

## "Irrelevant" Ethical Conundrums

The objections of ACLU lawyer Margie Hames to the settlement, made on behalf of the *Armour* plaintiffs, added a critical new angle to the case that demanded more attention from the court. Like the other public interest organizations, Hames asked the court to reject the settlement because it prejudiced her clients' ability to obtain metropolitan relief. But she made an additional, explosive allegation. Hames argued that the court must reject the compromise because the process that produced it had been deeply tainted by corruption. Lonnie King, the plan's chief negotiator, had a conflict of interest due to his financial relationship with William VanLandingham, the Board of Education's chief negotiator in the settlement talks. A member of the board of education, VanLandingham also worked as a vice president for public affairs at the Citizens and Southern Bank (C & S Bank).[93]

Hames presented documentary evidence to support her allegation. She submitted a contract showing that King, as general manager and project director of the Onyx Corporation, an educational consulting service, had received $198,857 from VanLandingham's bank. The sum had been paid in connection with a consulting contract that King had been awarded to provide assistance to HEW. During the 1960s King had worked for HEW, where he had helped to design school desegregation plans for several cities. The transaction between King and C & S Bank occurred in August 1972, around the same time that King had begun settlement negotiations with VanLandingham. Benjamin Spaulding, the attorney whom King hired to replace LDF, served as King's counsel during the negotiations with C & S and had been a signatory to the contract. What was more, Spaulding had obtained a personal loan from C & S Bank just as King obtained his loan. Hames argued that the financial dealings between the chief negotiators for the plaintiffs and the defendants raised questions about King and Spaulding's fitness to serve as representatives of the plaintiff class. At the very least, the court should subject King, Spaulding, and VanLandingham to questioning about the transactions. Even if the transactions did not constitute a quid pro quo, the financial relationships between the negotiators—putative adversaries—created a strong impression of impropriety and constituted a conflict of interest.[94]

Hames's ethical objections, however, went beyond these curious financial entanglements. She also questioned the circumstances under which King had gained control of the litigation. Hames brought to the court's attention an allegation, first made in a local newspaper, that King had duped two plaintiffs into granting him the powers of attorney on which he had originally relied in his effort to depose LDF from the case. These two plaintiffs had told a reporter that

King and another local NAACP officer, Jondelle Johnson, had secured powers of attorney by "lying" to them. The pair reportedly said that "the NAACP needed a local attorney" because the LDF attorneys, as outsiders, could no longer handle the case. If the two plaintiffs would simply "sign the papers [granting powers of attorney]," King allegedly said, "this all could be taken care of." The plaintiffs' allegations suggested that King and Johnson had artfully misled them about the status of the case. Contrary to King and Johnson's alleged statements, the Atlanta NAACP's sudden need for new, "local" counsel had nothing to do with any court-imposed limitations presented by LDF's "outsider" status. Howard Moore and Elizabeth Rindskopf already worked in Atlanta as LDF's "local counsel" and had long been admitted to practice in the federal courts. The local branch president's desire for a different lawyer was a product of his own agenda—not the court's insistence.[95]

Hames's extraordinary allegations surely demanded a thorough inquiry by the court. Or so she argued in chambers. During an exchange with Judge Henderson concerning her request that King, Spaulding, VanLandingham, and others submit to questions under oath about their financial dealings, she pointedly framed the stakes for the court. "I represent people who feel like there has been a trade-off of rights of inner-city black children for, whether you call it black jobs or whether you call it the personal gain or benefit of Lonnie King, [or] both." The integrity of the judicial process stood in the balance, Hames insisted. She got nowhere with her arguments. In press interviews, Lonnie King had conceded that he had received a loan from C & S Bank around the time of the settlement, but denied any wrongdoing. In chambers, King remained silent. Spaulding spoke, but he refused to answer Hames's allegations. The court had added him to the case as plaintiffs' counsel months before, he argued, and Hames had no standing to question his representation of his clients. Hames protested that she, as counsel to plaintiffs whose rights were affected by the settlement that he had proposed, had an obligation to raise questions about his professional conduct.[96]

After a lengthy colloquy with Hames, Judge Henderson agreed with Spaulding. The judge remarked that he had grown "weary" of arguments that King and Spaulding did not properly represent the class. The claims were stale; neither Hames nor LDF attorneys had objected to the pair's entry into the case in December 1972—the opportune moment. "I am not going to permit this case to be used as a vehicle for everybody to vent their own personal feelings against everybody in the case, or their suspicions about everything," Judge Henderson concluded. The court did not consider the charges "relevant" to the case. The judges never questioned the negotiators about Hames's allegations of ethical impropriety. In failing to do so, they disregarded precedent that required courts to scrutinize the circumstances surrounding contested settlements and investigate claims of inadequate representation. King, a man who struck LDF's Rindskopf as transparently "on the make" and possibly "on the take," had successfully fended off any inspection of his backroom dealings.[97]

Judges Smith and Henderson finally brought an end to *Calhoun v. Cook*, what they deemed "an ancient class action," on April 4, 1973. The judges called the settlement that King and VanLandingham negotiated "fair, adequate and reasonable." None of the constitutional or ethical objections to the compromise had carried weight with the court. The judges pointedly noted and rejected the claim that Spaulding's late entry into the case invalidated the settlement. They cited LDF's misstep—the failure to challenge Spaulding's entry into the case at the December 1972 hearing—as grounds for rejecting Moore and Rindskopf's "belated attempt" to repudiate the settlement. The LDF's "eleventh hour maneuvering" was "inconsequential and without legal effect," the court determined. The court summarily disposed of the settlement's objectors. The court confined a single reference to these plaintiffs to a footnote, where it characterized the objections as "minimal" considering the size of the class. For the third time in as many years, the U.S. District Court found the Atlanta Public School District unitary.[98]

## A "DANGEROUS" NATIONAL PRECEDENT

The significance of the Atlanta compromise—now approved by federal judges—was not lost on the national press. A small group of negotiators had settled an epic struggle over school desegregation through private channels. The process had marginalized the courts, national civil rights organizations, and all other "outsiders." To some observers, however, the settlement marked a hopeful turning point. To be sure, the local NAACP had broken with past policy, but the change signaled a new freedom. The Atlanta compromise suggested that empowered black communities could now resolve contentious social issues themselves, and in the manner that they wished. The growing number of black elected officials in the city—it would include Maynard Jackson as mayor and half of the city council seats by the fall of 1973—advanced this hopeful narrative about the meaning of the settlement. So did similar racial transitions then taking place in cities such as Gary, Indiana, Cleveland, Ohio and Newark, New Jersey, which also had elected black mayors and other officials. The settlement represented a step on the road toward black autonomy, or so it seemed to many.[99]

But for the national NAACP and LDF, the settlement represented retreat rather than progress. Officials worried that the Atlanta compromise set a "dangerous" national precedent. Roy Wilkins branded the compromise "an unholy mess of hope and fears." He and others feared that it signaled the beginning of the end of the long fight for school desegregation, an attempt "to turn back the clock of history." The backward-looking settlement could only exacerbate the organization's public relations problems. In 1972, 85 percent of white Americans opposed court-ordered busing for school desegregation. Forty-five percent of blacks also opposed busing; black opponents cited school quality as their primary concern and did not believe that busing was the best means of achieving it. White and black opponents of the NAACP's school policies would be emboldened by word that African Americans in the Southeast's largest city had also turned against busing. The NAACP and LDF would be "fighting both races." Moreover, white and black supporters of the organization's school desegregation policies might reconsider their positions as a consequence of Atlanta's deal. The settlement might also undermine the NAACP and LDF in court, as plans like Atlanta's multiplied. By July 1973, the compromise plan already had been cited in several pending school desegregation cases in an attempt to thwart busing remedies. Federal judges might think twice about requiring local school districts to adopt *Swann* principles, officials feared, now that such a prominent group of blacks, Atlanta's respectable middle class, had become opponents of busing and other court-ordered remedies for desegregation.[100]

Incensed national NAACP officials determined to stem the damage from the compromise. To do so, they took decisive action against the local NAACP branch. In March 1973, the national NAACP suspended Lonnie King and other Atlanta branch officials on grounds that the settlement had caused "irreparable harm" to the NAACP. King had claimed broad community support for the compromise, the NAACP's general counsel, Nathaniel Jones, noted. But even if a black majority supported the compromise—and that was by no means clear—it could have no bearing in the school desegregation context. The principle of majority rule did not apply to the enforcement of constitutional rights, Jones argued. "[T]here can be no 'local options' in complying with the Constitution." He continued: "Too vivid in our memories...are the urging of the Barnetts, the Wallaces, the Faubuses to let the race issue in their states be determined by majorities. Constitutional rights are personal, and no person[,] be he Governor, Superintendent of Schools or a Branch President, has any business 'negotiating' away those rights." The tables had turned. During his 1970 race for Congress, Lonnie King, then an impassioned proponent of busing for school desegregation, had accused his opponent, Rev. Andrew Young, an opponent of such policies, of embracing the views of arch-segregationists such as Lester Maddox. Now, King stood accused of the same.[101]

The settlement roiled the national NAACP not only because it violated organizational policy but also because it provided no tangible benefits. In the view of national officials, the plaintiffs gained nothing in the bargain that they had not already won, or could not secure, in court. The "deal" traded away rights protected under the Constitution and Civil Rights Act (pupil desegregation and equal educational opportunity) for other rights protected under the Constitution and Civil Rights Act (faculty desegregation and equal employment opportunity). Indeed, the Fifth Circuit—the very court with appellate jurisdiction over the proceedings in *Calhoun*—had developed some of the most far-reaching precedents yet pertaining to faculty desegregation. Black Atlantans were well positioned to assert their rights in court if violations occurred. The illogic of the deal again raised questions about the integrity of Lonnie King and Benjamin Spaulding. The federal district court that approved the settlement had ignored the claim that greed may have played a role in the settlement negotiations; however, King and Spaulding could not fully escape these sordid charges, and questions about their ethics hovered over their interactions with national officers.[102]

King and Spaulding did not go down without a fight. They protested their suspensions from the organization during an April 1973 hearing before national NAACP officers. The proceedings only reinforced the national NAACP's view that the *Calhoun* compromise had been a product of King and Spaulding's personal prerogatives. Matthew J. Perry, a respected lawyer and chairman of the NAACP Committee on Branches, presided over the hearing. In response to questioning, Spaulding declined to state which local NAACP officers supported the deal that King had negotiated. He declined to indicate which members of the Atlanta NAACP's executive board he represented. The lawyer preferred to stick to generalities. His authority to speak on behalf of the local NAACP had been authorized by a resolution passed by branch members, he said. But the national officers well knew that a resolution passed by an inactive branch could hardly be considered a mandate. Perry pressed Spaulding for the date that the resolution had passed, the number of people who had voted for it, and again, for the names of the Atlanta branch officers whom he claimed to represent at the hearing. Spaulding had no response.[103]

The national officers did manage to elicit information from Spaulding about his and King's justifications for the settlement. The attorney attempted to refute the national NAACP's interpretation of *Brown* and *Swann*, and hence the organization's claim that the local NAACP's settlement agreement had undermined the landmark precedents. Neither Supreme Court case mandated pupil integration; rather, each merely forbade de jure segregation. The theory of educational equality contained in the settlement therefore did not offend the principles of either case, Spaulding argued. The settlement reflected King's conviction that black students could obtain a quality education without white students. In fact, such a view had been endorsed by prominent black educators. Horace Tate, the tenacious leader of the black teachers' union and former member of the Board of Education who retained a high public profile, adamantly opposed busing and strongly supported the compromise. The best plan for integration of Atlanta schools is "no plan at all," Tate had declared.[104]

More important, Spaulding asserted, the compromise reflected King's belief that black administrative control of the school system was more likely than pupil desegregation to yield equality education for two reasons. First, blacks possessed leadership abilities uniquely suited to the school environment, as he had seen as a student at Howard University. Second, King's work at HEW had made it clear that school desegregation plans would be ineffective if white administrators—the same ones who had presided over segregated schools—remained in charge. It was imperative to have nonracist administrators in control of desegregated systems, a qualification that blacks surely met. In sum, Spaulding argued, after fifteen years of "outside influence" on Atlanta's public schools, the national NAACP (and LDF) should permit local citizens, black and white, to resolve racial problems on their own. He echoed King's assertion that LDF's failure to consult its clients may have been "O.K. before," but "there are people who [now] know what they want." The national NAACP should appreciate King as the "man in the middle catching hell from all sides," rather than calling him disloyal to the cause of civil rights for protecting the interests of local people.[105]

Spaulding and King's defense of the compromise featured a mix of rhetoric and themes from all corners of the postwar movement for civil rights. In essence, Spaulding argued—as had proponents of token desegregation during the era of massive resistance—that the Constitution did not command school integration but merely forbade segregation. This may have been a plausible reading of *Brown II*. However, it could not be squared with *Swann*'s mandate to integrate schools to the "greatest possible degree." In fact, it had been *Swann*'s mandate that jumpstarted the secret settlement negotiations. Spaulding and King also asserted a right to local autonomy and invoked a variant on black power ideology to justify the priority that the settlement placed on black school administrators.

King did not recognize or admit, however, the possibility of tension between his passionate concern for, and community members' views about, the value of administrative control. He ignored the refrain of many blacks, summed up by Representative Billy McKinney, a newly elected black member of the Georgia legislature: "It is wrong," he explained, "for the NAACP to continue to negotiate without finding out how black people feel." King—the former student radical who had once damned traditionalists for negotiating with white city fathers without sufficient community support—had spurned litigation and embraced negotiation with white city fathers as a problem-solving strategy, without sufficient community support, many believed.[106]

Moreover, King failed to fully acknowledge how issues of socioeconomic class permeated the terms of the settlement and the social context in which he had negotiated the settlement. Job loss among black teachers and administrators remained a high-priority matter among blacks. The *Atlanta Daily World* religiously covered developments such as the June 1973 release of a National Urban League report indicating that "Southern School Integration Reportedly Cost 31,500 Jobs." Thousands of black faculty and administrators had suffered mightily since the onset of school desegregation, and everybody knew it. King had repeatedly discussed the problem of employment discrimination, in schools and elsewhere, in the months leading up to the deal. But after he negotiated the compromise, he tended to justify it on the basis of its educational value to black students. In one candid moment, he had made a critical concession: that if he, Lonnie King, had to choose between "sitting beside whitey" and a "job that pays," he would take the job. The statement belied the reality that the choice may not have been his to make. And according to the national NAACP and LDF, it represented a false choice; blacks could have and should have both desegregated schools and employment opportunities. Howard Moore—the skeptic of desegregation who nevertheless continued to represent LDF and its commitment to racially balanced schools—found this premise unassailable. The "purpose" of a school desegregation order, he said, "was to create better educational opportunities for our African American students." "If by chance making more administrative positions available to African Americans would do that," he noted, "then I would salute that, but that would not be a . . . quid pro quo that I would take to settle a school desegregation lawsuit."[107]

National officials were unimpressed with the local NAACP's defense. They showed no regard for any of Spaulding's arguments. No one deigned to respond to his claim that *Brown* merely required race-neutral classification. Nor did officials engage his arguments about the utility of black administrators. The NAACP stalwarts considered the goals of pupil, faculty, and administrative desegregation fully compatible. And the organization, biracial from its inception, would never accept the insinuation that only black administrators could properly manage a desegregated school system. The bottom line: King and Spaulding had brokered an unconstitutional settlement. Their defiance of law and organizational policy would not be tolerated. In August 1973, the national officers expelled Lonnie King and all other Atlanta officers from the organization, including prominent figures such as *Atlanta Daily World* editor C. A. Scott, Maynard Jackson, and

Alderman Q. V. Williamson. It then reconstituted the local branch and rebuilt it from the ground up. The national NAACP's action struck a punishing blow against King, the former student movement hero, and signaled to the nation that it remained the leader of the fight for integrated schools.[108]

## QUASHING DISSENT

In reality, however, the federal courts—not the NAACP or LDF—had the final say on the settlement. The Fifth Circuit initially rejected the district court's resolution of the case. An appeals court panel that included Judge Minor Wisdom seemed prepared, once again, to save the day for LDF. In an August 1973 opinion, the Court of Appeals held that Judges Smith and Henderson had given perfunctory consideration to objections to the settlement. The district court had all but ignored the many controversies surrounding King and Spaulding's entries into the case and their handling of the negotiations. "[N]o plan can be approved" where such "widespread and genuine controversy" exists, the court concluded. In addition, the Fifth Circuit noted, it was far from clear that a majority of Atlanta's blacks actually supported the compromise. The district court had not conducted a full evidentiary hearing. Rather, witnesses had appeared and expressed views "in a sort of town meeting." Such musings did not protect class members' due process rights. At the same time, the court noted that the settlement ultimately must meet the test of constitutionality, rather than popularity. Howard Moore had made the point succinctly at the hearing: Even if "everyone in this courtroom agreed to the plan, the court would still have to throw it out because it was unconstitutional."[109]

In light of all of these defects, the panel vacated the district court's decision and ordered the lower court to begin again. The judges must permit all plaintiffs' attorneys (LDF, Spaulding, and ACLU) to present evidence on the merits of the proposed settlement, the Fifth Circuit ruled. In an aside, Judge Wisdom also questioned whether the time had come to settle the question of whether Atlanta should be subject to a metropolitan desegregation order.[110]

But on remand, the district court continued its now familiar pattern. In May 1974, Judges Smith and Henderson found—for the fourth time—that the Atlanta public school system, which now had an 83 percent black majority, had achieved unitary status. And they again approved the settlement. The court specifically found that a black majority—those who occupied administrative and faculty posts—supported the plan. The majority black school leadership could not, by definition, they reasoned, be hostile to minority interests.[111]

In an October 1975 opinion, the Fifth Circuit bowed out of the fight over equal educational opportunity in Atlanta. The court acknowledged that Atlanta had not integrated its schools to the greatest possible extent. Ninety-two of 148 schools remained over 90 percent black. The court also conceded that the Atlanta school system had never fully employed the desegregation tools found lawful in *Swann*. And it agreed with LDF that "substantial precedent" supported its contention that a formerly de jure segregated school system could not be considered unitary if it had never utilized *Swann*-type desegregation techniques. The court nevertheless upheld the district court decision approving the settlement. In essence, the court of appeals exempted Atlanta from *Swann*'s principles because of race—the racial identity of King and others who backed the settlement and now controlled the school system. The court explained:

> [F]or today and in Atlanta, the unique features of this district distinguish [it from] every prior school case pronouncement. The district court found that the black citizens who occupy the majority of the posts on the school board, in two-thirds of the posts in the school administration and staff, and in over 60 percent of the faculty, as well as the numerous non-appealing black plaintiffs who agreed to and support the present plan attest the district's lack of discrimination against black students as well as its freedom from the effects of past race-based practices.... The aim of the Fourteenth Amendment guarantee of equal protection on which this litigation is based is to assure that state supported educational opportunity is afforded without regard to race; it is not to achieve racial integration in public schools. Conditions in most school districts have frequently caused courts to treat these aims as identical. *In Atlanta, where* white students now comprise a small minority and *black citizens can control school policy, administration and staffing, they no longer are.*[112]

In the judgment of the court of appeals, the majority black school administrators and faculty represented the black plaintiffs. Howard Moore's proposition—his restatement of a cardinal principle often articulated by the U.S. Supreme Court—had been rejected. Under the right circumstances, popularity could trump legality. The shared racial identity of the black school power structure and the black plaintiffs triumphed over the letter of the law.

The same court that earlier had remanded the case to the district court out of concern for objectors now dismissed objections to the settlement. The court said nothing about the *Armour* plaintiffs—the working-class and poor African-American families who claimed that they suffered under the compromise while the black middle class gained. These plaintiffs had remained resolutely in opposition to the settlement for three years. They did not merit even a footnote in the Fifth Circuit's opinion.


## DOES DIVERSITY WITHIN GROUPS COUNT?

The Atlanta compromise brought the competing priorities of national and local civil rights leaders—always present but often subsumed amid preoccupation with white racism—into full public light. The clash exposed national organizations' imperious attitude toward local people. Ruby Hurley, the NAACP's southeastern regional director, who testified at Lonnie King's suspension hearing, pointed to these problems and the role that they played in the abrupt conclusion to the Atlanta school desegregation case. For years, Hurley had complained to national officials about the Atlanta branch's inactivity. Now, she redirected her criticism to the national NAACP and LDF. Hurley condemned the national leaders for being detached from the branch, its people, and their problems. She had come to support Atlanta branch officials' intervention in *Calhoun*, she explained, because of her disenchantment with out-of-touch LDF lawyers. Hurley became disillusioned, in particular, with LDF's James Nabrit, the chief New York–based lawyer who worked on *Calhoun* during the early 1970s. She blasted Nabrit's "high-handed" and condescending attitude toward nonlawyers. Nabrit treated lay people like "idiots," Hurley complained. He alienated her and many others with his insistence that LDF alone could make decisions about the school desegregation litigation. Hurley found his approach "very disturbing." She had complained to national NAACP officials about LDF in the fall of 1972, but they had rebuffed her. Hurley, like so many others, felt spurned. Given the national organization's domination and disregard, she could understand why King had repudiated LDF, pushed his way into *Calhoun*, and demanded local control over the case. Officials at the NAACP did not attempt to mollify Hurley. "Whatever the differences" between national and local groups, NAACP general counsel Nathaniel Jones retorted, the local NAACP had flouted the law.[113]

The national NAACP and LDF—the nation's premier civil rights bar—could tolerate no dissent over *Brown*. As they saw it, *Brown* required pupil integration. Indefatigable LDF counsel pursued this goal at every turn. The lawyers, accustomed to litigating in defiance of local norms and customs, had little tolerance for local blacks who "compromised" with segregation because, they asserted, the facts had changed since 1954. For LDF, the matter was simple: the Constitution would not be "put to a plebiscite." Local citizens could not opt out of *Brown* regardless of the circumstances. The LDF's dogma was understandable, but its inflexibility, coupled with its domination of its clients, did not serve it well in Atlanta. Its unyielding policy and arm's-length relationships with clients made implementation of its principle difficult, if not impossible. The lawyers alienated local people who might have supported their unbending position, and inflamed those who opposed it. With most, they failed to cultivate any relationship whatsoever. The LDF's director-counsel Jack Greenberg explained why: "clever litigation"—not politics—made the difference in civil rights litigation. That perspective proved wrong. Significant and lasting sociolegal change requires the political support of clients and community. In the end, local people determine whether constitutional rules are accepted and implemented.[114]

In Atlanta, LDF's political problems began with its own local counsel. Conflict between LDF local counsel Howard Moore and Elizabeth Rindskopf, along with Moore's other professional commitments and deep skepticism of LDF's remedial objectives, further diminished the likelihood that the organization would obtain its goals. Moore's commitment to the black freedom struggle is unimpeachable, but it is hard to escape the conclusion that he held the reins of leadership in the Atlanta school desegregation case long after he could devote full professional, intellectual, or emotional energy to it. Even as he argued against the Atlanta compromise in the federal courts, Moore no longer personally embraced LDF's view that equal education required pupil desegregation, or even believed that the federal courts could bring about change for African Americans. *Calhoun v. Cook* was the last school desegregation case that Howard Moore ever handled precisely because he realized that he no longer had the heart to litigate school desegregation cases. "I just didn't feel that I was into it," he recalled.[115]

Moore's personal views did not disqualify him from representing school desegregation clients, but they may well have made him a less than ideal advocate for those clients who sought desegregation remedies. After all, civil rights lawyers typically litigated school desegregation case out of devotion to the cause. Eventually, Moore's apparent lack of enthusiasm for the cause ruptured his relationship with his cocounsel. Rindskopf concluded that her cocounsel was trying to "throw the case." Moore's decision to represent the plaintiffs jointly with Lonnie King's attorney—a turning point that made the compromise possible—was telling, she believed. In the end, however, Moore *had* objected to the compromise. Personally, he did not believe in school desegregation, but professionally—in representations to the court in March 1973 and thereafter—Moore argued against Lonnie King's settlement proposal.

The compromise quashed pupil integration in the Atlanta schools and conferred financial benefits on blacks who obtained new administrative positions and, perhaps, on King and his attorney. In his writings about *Brown*, Moore had harshly criticized such "tokenism" as "exploitative" and "confusing" to the black community as a whole. In his role as LDF's attorney, he, along with Rind-skopf, also questioned whether the deal conferred benefits on blacks at large. The goal of increasing the number of blacks in administrative and faculty positions was legitimate, they argued, but not mutually exclusive from the goal of pupil desegregation. The law guaranteed both.[116]

These propositions, while true, did not fully capture the stakes at issue in the compromise. The NAACP and LDF viewed the settlement through the narrow prism of the law, the jurisprudence on school desegregation in particular. But the law was abstract and unreliable, while men like King had urgent, tangible goals. By the early 1970s, the school desegregation litigation had morphed into something much larger than a case about students and education: it had evolved into a controversy about political and economic power for the black middle class. Above all else, the determination of a vocal black middle class to secure its fair share of jobs in America's new racial landscape, where whites professed support for racial equality but still dominated the workplace and society at large, had overtaken the school desegregation case. Many members of the black middle class still supported desegregation; but enough powerful blacks opposed the NAACP and LDF— Andrew Young, Benjamin Mays, Horace Tate, Jessie Hill, C. A. Scott, and the city's first black mayor, Maynard Jackson, to name just a few—to ensure that their priorities overwhelmed the case.

*Calhoun* developed into a clash over equal employment opportunity, and raised questions—infrequently posed and still unanswered—about whether and how the black community at large, including the poor, profit from race-conscious hiring policies in the workplace and identity-based political representation. Would the beneficiaries of these policies primarily be black professionals? Would working-class blacks benefit from the political power that resulted from the new black presence on school boards, in town halls, in legislatures? These crucial intraracial questions are seldom discussed because the white majority's concerns about "reverse discrimination" when blacks enter the workplace tend to crowd out all other conversations.[117]

The developments in *Calhoun*, in which the school desegregation case evolved into a public feud rooted in a local black middle-class struggle for political and economic power, had been building for quite some time. The NAACP's school desegregation campaign had never been popular in Atlanta precisely because of the tension between educators' employment interests and the school desegregation campaign. Teachers, a significant part of the black middle class, had long feared that *Brown* would destroy their careers. They "were ambivalent" about LDF's landmark victory, admitted LDF's director-counsel Jack Greenberg. The concern ran deep in Georgia, as elsewhere. A local activist and proponent of school desegregation once quipped to Roy Wilkins:

"Remember when [we] were struggling [for school desegregation] in Georgia? The whites wanted us dead and the black teachers were not far behind." Black leaders, most notably Horace Tate, had worked assiduously to protect educators' interests in the years preceding the settlement. The GTEA painstakingly documented the displacement of black teachers and administrators in the South and throughout Georgia. Lonnie King's own personal experiences and beliefs powerfully reinforced the concerns of the local black middle class about jobs as well. During his time at HEW, King had observed recalcitrant whites undermining the desegregation process in other cities. He readily believed that the fates of black students and black administrators were intertwined. Meanwhile, blacks in Atlanta had begun to attain positions of power in a city and school system that had become majority black. Dr. Benjamin Mays held the chair of the Board of Education, and two other black men had gained seats on it. Blacks won seats on the city council and soon would capture the mayor's office. Andrew Young had become a congressman. All of these circumstances, together with LDF's alienation from the local community and white opposition to meaningful desegregation, created a perfect storm that propelled the settlement negotiations forward.[118]

Ironically, Lonnie King and the local NAACP—who claimed to be more authentic representatives of black Atlanta—negotiated a settlement that many local blacks opposed, some vociferously. As we have seen, King's claims of authenticity were not tethered to any mechanism of accountability. The settlement negotiations had been premised on exclusivity and hierarchy, and kept hidden from the plaintiffs. Dr. Benjamin Mays and the black school board members, elected officials, could more credibly claim to be democratic representatives of black Atlantans, but not necessarily claim to be more accountable or effective ones. As chairman of the Board of Education, Mays served the community as a whole, rather than blacks alone. He had long predicted that local people's preferences would determine whether *Brown* resulted in actual desegregation. In his role as chairman, he helped fulfill this prophecy, even as he professed support for school desegregation in principle. Mays remained conspicuously silent about post-*Swann* survey data showing that a majority of Atlanta's blacks favored busing. Who represented *those* blacks? Neither Mays nor other black members of the board spoke in support of the respondents' perspective, shared by the *Armour* plaintiffs. To the contrary, the settlement removed what Mays called an "albatross" of civil rights litigation and affirmatively undermined black supporters of school desegregation and busing. But it assuaged the long-standing concerns of the GTEA, the ASLC, and Lonnie King himself about employment discrimination. The remedy that they had sought all along for job bias had been achieved: workplace *integration* for black professionals.

Upon close inspection, then, the compromise advanced the priorities and worldviews of the negotiators and the black middle class, but it did not necessarily advance the interests of the large swath of black Atlantans whom the local NAACP leader claimed to represent. The shared attributes of race and place did not ensure that King's views were representative or that community members could hold King accountable. In theory, he was more accountable to local people than LDF, but not always in fact.

After all, King had joined forces with white civic and political elites who had consistently worked to protect the white power structure at the expense of blacks. No single figure better illustrated the manipulative role of white elites in the process than Griffin Bell. Bell, a sitting appellate court judge, pillar of the community, and future attorney general of the United States, proclaimed his disagreement with the U.S. Supreme Court's decision in *Swann*. He endorsed freedom-of-choice. Bell then set in motion the series of events that led to the controversial settlement of *Calhoun*. Rarely have the politics of power been laid so bare.

Yet, history foretold the debacle that emerged over *Brown* in Atlanta during the early 1970s. The Atlanta compromise clashed with the participatory approach to leadership that students had embraced during the direct action phase of the civil rights movement. But it measured up remarkably well with the pragmatic style of leadership favored by A. T. Walden and other black elites in the postwar era. Since the dawn of the modern civil rights era, a small group of Atlanta's black middle class had found politics and negotiation particularly fruitful approaches to solving problems associated with race and racism, and sometimes favored it over civil rights litigation, as they endeavored to cope with racial discrimination. And unlike the national NAACP and LDF, locals in Atlanta had never fully embraced the idea that political equality required interracial social contact. They had jealously guarded black institutions. Walden and his clients had pursued such practical, incremental goals over the objections of others, who preferred the more doctrinaire, integrationist strategy of the national NAACP and LDF. In 1960, Walden met his fiercest critics when students in the Atlanta sit-in movement questioned his moderate instincts, and even his integrity, when he negotiated behind closed doors to end protests against segregation. The students had been particularly upset that Walden had brokered an agreement that did not include their demands that downtown merchants improve conditions for working-class black employees. Remarkably, Lonnie King had participated in these closed-door meetings with Walden, and he and Walden found themselves accused of "selling out" black rights. King's actions in the school desegregation case in 1972 and 1973 were eerily similar to the 1960 episode. Viewed in this historical context, the Atlanta compromise of 1973 seems less exceptional.

The settlement was an outgrowth of familiar patterns of leadership and reca- pitulated old tensions between the priorities of national and local civil rights activists.[119]

The federal courts proved institutionally inadequate for the complex dynam- ics surrounding *Calhoun*. The district court judges made decisions that at once constrained the ability of plaintiffs to object to the settlement and minimized the concerns of the plaintiffs who nevertheless managed to voice objections. The judges dispatched constitutional and ethical objections to the settlement on the basis of a narrow, racial theory of group interest. The most vocal dissent- ers, the *Armour* plaintiff class, asserted a bold claim: that the compromise intentionally disfavored the black poor. Weary of school desegregation, how- ever, the district court judges eagerly approved the settlement. And while the Fifth Circuit had distinguished itself with trailblazing school desegregation precedents in the past, in the end, the appeals court resigned itself to political realities. Indeed, the Fifth Circuit conceded that it could not reconcile *Swann* with those sociopolitical facts that it chose to recognize.

The courts undoubtedly found it simpler to affirm a deal supported by influential blacks (and whites) than to formulate a remedy that addressed the *Armour* plaintiffs' race- and class-based claims of discrimination. In doing so, the lower courts took their cues from the U.S. Supreme Court. The justices had reinforced a simplistic racial calculus in their school desegregation jurispru- dence. Conflict in school desegregation cases, in high-profile places like Little Rock, occurred between the races—the white resistance on the one hand and the African-American victims on the other. At the same time, the Court had rejected poverty lawyers' effort to make wealth a suspect category in equal pro- tection jurisprudence. In sum, class had not been recognized as relevant to adjudicatory and interpretative norms; therefore, it was easy to disregard its relevance to the social realities of litigants, particularly claimants in a race dis- crimination class action. Within this context, the questions about discrimina- tion based on socioeconomic class that the *Armour* plaintiffs raised stood little chance of capturing the judicial imagination. In this way, *Swann*—the case in which the justices finally approved complex remedial solutions to cure the effects of school segregation—failed to take root in Atlanta because simplistic notions about race and group interests prevailed inside the courtroom. Judges wrongly assumed that common racial identity assured racial solidarity, which in turn apparently ensured that all blacks were adequately represented so long as blacks were at the helm of the school system.[120]

Even if the judges could not see it, *Calhoun* revealed enduring divisions among blacks. The case's tortured history—and *Armour*'s as well—demon- strated that the black poor could not count on the black power structure to take notice of, much less press, their interests in corridors of power. Just as officials at the national NAACP and LDF had no answer to locals' criticisms, Lonnie King and the local NAACP had no answer to the *Armour* plaintiffs. The NAACP president remained silent as attorneys for the ACLU claimed that the settlement discriminated against the black poor. Despite making similar claims of class-based discrimination, CORE favored neighborhood schools. Both groups wanted "quality education." Neither cited black administrators as a crucial objective. But after the *Calhoun* compromise, it appeared doubtful that the *Armour* plaintiffs, who continued to press their case for metropolitan relief, could find success on their own terms. Power brokers, now united more than ever across racial lines, had sent every signal that they, and thus the tide of history, had turned against school desegregation.[121]

CHAPTER 12

# "Bus Them to Philadelphia"

*A Feminist Lawyer and Poor Mothers Crusade*
*to Redeem* Brown, *1972–1980*

I feel like [my children] should be able to go to a school of their choice...
a white school. (1976)

> Eva Davis, Plaintiff in Metropolitan School
> Desegregation Case

Are you a married woman? Are you a welfare recipient? Have you ever
been? (1976)

> Robert Feagin, School Board Attorney,
> Questioning Plaintiff Eva Davis

"The...school case will never be over," one Atlantan declared in 1972.[1] This
view summed up the exhaustion and dread with which many in the city greeted
*Armour v. Nix*.[2] *Armour* had been filed in June 1972 by poor black Atlantans
who hoped to supersede the *Calhoun* litigation—then bogged down in its second decade—by claiming larger constitutional violations and seeking bolder
remedies. By order of the Fifth Circuit, the *Armour* case would sit on the trial
court's docket—inactive and pending—until the *Calhoun* settlement was
accepted by the district court. The Fifth Circuit had "pick[ed] up on the mood
of the country" when it affirmed the *Calhoun* compromise and agreed that the
pursuit of pupil integration could be abandoned. The *Armour* plaintiffs, on a
mission to redeem *Brown*, were now ready to march forward. It was clear to
most that they were walking against the wind.[3]

Margie Pitts Hames represented the plaintiffs in *Armour* in cooperation with
the Georgia ACLU. Hames proceeded in the case fearlessly, determined that she
could—and would—win. In the complaint she drafted and filed, she asserted on
behalf of her impoverished clients complex discrimination claims against not
one but ten area school systems and requested that the court order a truly comprehensive remedy, spanning the city of Atlanta *and* its suburbs. Atlanta's history

of "residential apartheid," Hames insisted, coupled with its history of educational discrimination, entitled the *Armour* plaintiffs to a metropolitan-wide desegregation order. The systems would not consolidate but would form a "federation." The federation would collaborate and cooperate to achieve desegregation, but each district would remain separate for all other purposes. Such a geographically comprehensive remedy would defeat white flight, but retain the prized tradition of locally controlled school systems. Students in the city of Atlanta, its poorest areas included, would attend higher quality schools in outlying suburban areas—the places to which whites had flocked. Busing would be equitable. Poor students no longer would bear its brunt; middle-class students, white and black, would be bused, when necessary.

For the ACLU, the relief that Hames requested in *Armour* represented the ideal plan for school integration. Others viewed it far less favorably. The "Metro suit" was a "collage of legalities" that piqued emotions best left dormant, wrote one editorialist. We wonder," nudged the *Atlanta Constitution*, "whether cross-county school transfers represent an idea whose time is no more." An attorney for one of the school boards that Hames sued asked, more pointedly: "How long do we have to pay?" *Armour* invoked a racial past that many whites desperately wished to leave behind.[4]

## A FEMINIST LAWYER

The feared crosscounty school federation would only materialize if Hames prevailed at both the liability and remedial phases of the case, and she believed she could do so despite the highly unfavorable political environment. Hames impressed colleagues as a woman with "bravado," "bold and outspoken," a "bull in the china shop." Just recently, she had surmounted intractable political and legal hurdles in a different area of constitutional law. Hames litigated and won *Doe v. Bolton*, a companion case to *Roe v. Wade*, the landmark case in which the U.S. Supreme Court established that the constitutional right to privacy encompassed a woman's decision whether to terminate her pregnancy. In *Doe*, Hames successfully challenged a Georgia statute that required abortions to be performed in hospitals and only with the advance approval of a hospital committee. The young lawyer called her January 1973 victory in *Doe* a "cornerstone for liberating women." Others called her a "catalyst for women's rights" and a "pioneer" for women's equality as a result of her role in *Doe*. "Fresh from a Supreme Court victory," Hames felt "very able to do about anything," observed Roger Mills, one of her cocounsels in *Armour*.[5]

Hames's story—and how she became a crusading feminist lawyer and civil rights advocate—says much about the sometimes unexpected ways in which people and causes find one another. A southern white woman, Hames grew up on a farm in rural Tennessee in a Christian home with strict, churchgoing parents—not traditionally a breeding ground for liberal causes. Religion alone did not shape Hames's young life, however. Her family was poor, and she lived and worked amid black tenant farmers. "Race really cut across class lines. We had to work together to get the crop in," Hames explained. As a result of her close proximity to blacks, she could see their humanity. Hames acquired an appreciation for black culture during visits to black churches, where she swayed to gospel music.[6]

Indeed, Hames developed the first stirrings of consciousness against both abortion restrictions and racial discrimination in her youth when she heard a schoolteacher say that the only acceptable time for an abortion was "when a black man raped a white woman." This "moral" exception to abortion based on "racial prejudice" "planted the seed of doubt" in Hames's mind about the anti-abortion position. To Hames, it seemed "like an odd exception." She became more skeptical about the ways in which societal norms policed female sexuality when no one would sit next to a pregnant classmate during high school. Hames befriended the girl. The "terrible dehumanization of that young woman" stuck with her. Hames became exasperated with antiabortionists during law school at Vanderbilt University, when her white male classmates recapitulated—albeit in more sophisticated and legalistic terms—her teacher's race-based exception to the antiabortion position. Together, these experiences would help lead her, in 1970, to abortion rights work.[7]

Hames strongly identified with her client, Mary Doe, just as she would identify with her clients in *Armour*, even though by that time she had long since left her humble upbringing behind. A young lawyer, married to a partner in a blue-blood Atlanta law firm, Hames had herself achieved career success. She had practiced labor and employment law for a private firm in Atlanta for several years. She enjoyed the intellectual challenge of the firm. But she was one of only a few women there. The "old boy" network in Atlanta, carefully sustained by exclusive clubs that banned blacks, Jews, and women from membership but catered to the legal establishment, left her with a sense of "professional second-class citizenship and isolation." Nevertheless, Hames broke a barrier: she made partner, a first for a woman at her firm.[8]

Then, Hames encountered sex discrimination in the workplace, and it redirected the course of her professional life. Soon after she made partner at her firm, Hames became pregnant. She intended to continue working full-time after childbirth; however, her colleagues informed her that they intended to reduce her income by 50 percent after she returned to work—regardless of how many hours she worked. Hames would not countenance the "disrespect" and discrimination implied by the decision. She resigned from the partnership and set up her own firm—all before she delivered her first child. This single act of discrimination "cause[d] her to look at the world differently," explained her son. It "awakened something" inside of her. That incident, coupled with her youthful experiences, made Hames into a feminist and civil rights lawyer. She became an advocate for women, blacks, and other outsiders in sex and race discrimination suits and abortion rights litigation.[9]

Hames found a parallel, however imperfect, to her own experience of discrimination in Mary Doe's "poverty and lack of education." Hames made a special effort to treat Doe respectfully and to forcefully assert and protect her client from the negative publicity, hate mail, and threatening telephone calls that the *Doe* litigation provoked. The lawyer sheltered her client, only to arrive at the Supreme Court for oral argument in *Doe* and find herself the object of curiosity and ridicule. "[T]here was much joking among the Court personnel and the press about its being 'Ladies' Day in Court'" because "three of the four attorneys arguing were women, and five of the justices' wives were there.[10]

Gender powerfully shaped *Armour v. Nix* as well. Many of the plaintiffs were women—the poorest of poor black women. Hames's prior work on reproductive and welfare rights cases made women like the *Armour* plaintiffs and their struggles for equality familiar to her. The reproductive and life choices of the *Armour* mothers had been severely constrained, like so many of the clients that Hames had represented in the past. The women lacked resources, education, and more often than not, access to family planning services. They tended to have large families, which exacerbated the women's poverty and social marginalization. Many of the women relied on the state for income support, and Hames had seen the indignities visited upon welfare recipients—black women, in particular—up close. She had litigated welfare cases in which "separate rules existed for black and white women" receiving benefits. The state disincentivized the accumulation of assets and education and undermined relationships and self-sufficiency. Many women on welfare felt a sense of hopelessness.[11]

The plaintiffs in *Armour* were "very motivated" and "very organized" and hoped—through the litigation—to overcome the disadvantages that life had dealt them. They took great pride in their children and struggled to give their offspring a chance at better lives. These women and men "were at the very bottom" of society, but they did not "want their kids to be in the same situation they were in." They sought opportunity for their children, just like middle-class parents, black and white. Hames, a mother of two young children who interrupted her career "when she started having babies," could identify with the impulse. She became the ally of the *Armour* mothers, just as she had been a friend to her pregnant classmate and the champion of Mary Doe.[12]

If Hames felt a close bond with impoverished black female clients, much continued to separate them. Ethel Mae Mathews and her peers embraced Hames's help, but they knew that she "lived way out of town...way out in the rich section" in a "mansion." The lawyer's attire also revealed her wealth. Hames wore a "long fur coat that came down to her shoes." The "baby seal," recalled Marilyn Bright, her paralegal at the time, "would appear every winter." The luxurious fur often elicited comments from onlookers; court personnel were no exception. One unforgettable comment came from the lips of a hostile judge who presided over a police brutality case in which Hames represented the black plaintiffs. The judge eyeballed Hames's coat and lashed out: "That nigger business must pay well, huh?" Hames burst into tears. But she did not stop wearing her prized possession to court, no matter what message it sent to her clients or how distracting it might have been to others. "She loved that coat," Bright noted. Hames's posh wardrobe and manor were just two of many indicators that she did not have "a natural constituency" in the poor, communities of color in which her clients lived. Some thought an African-American lawyer would have been a better advocate for the *Armour* plaintiffs. However, to whatever extent a cultural gulf existed between Hames and her clients, it gave the ACLU lawyer little pause. Hames believed deeply in social justice and the righteousness of her case and her cause. A self-described "strong-willed" woman who enjoyed her "firebrand" reputation, Hames marched forward, unabashed and unafraid.[13]

## IDENTITY POLITICS

Hames and her clients faced off against nineteen lawyers, all white and male, who represented the state of Georgia and the ten Atlanta-area school boards the plaintiffs had named in their complaint. According to Roger Mills, "you had the best school lawyers in the state plus the attorney general's office on the other side" in a case that "was not only a legal case," everyone understood, but also a "political case with enormous implications." The defense attorneys, flush with taxpayers' money, proved tenacious litigators. In their hands, the *Armour* plaintiffs' sex, race, and class became weapons with which to delegitimize the metropolitan desegregation suit.

In pretrial depositions, defense lawyers questioned the women about their marital status, the identities of their children, and the names, whereabouts, and occupations of their children's fathers. In doing so, the school board attorneys sought to underscore how different the plaintiffs were from traditional white middle-class parents of school-age children. When he questioned Mattie Beens, a mother of thirteen children, the school board lawyer asked her to identify each child. "Have you one named Ricky?" "One named Jimmy?" "One named Antonio?" "One named Shirley?" The attorney already knew the names of Beens's children; she had provided the names in writing to him prior to the deposition. But that was the point. The attorney presumably wanted the deposition record to reflect how large her impoverished family was and what unappealing additions her children would make to the suburban schools.[14]

More deliberately obtuse questions followed. The school board attorneys asked for clarification when a woman described her occupation as "housewife." "Where is that? Where do you work?" the disingenuously puzzled attorney wondered. The attorney also asked for clarification when a woman described her occupation as hotel maid. What, precisely, did she do, he wanted to know. In addition, the defense attorneys pointedly asked each plaintiff: "Are you on welfare?" "Have you ever been?" If the plaintiff answered affirmatively, the lawyers inquired how much assistance the plaintiff received per month and for how long they had been receiving benefits. The men also asked if plaintiffs lived in public housing. In sum, virtually all of the state's questions concerned details about the women's personal lives and life choices. For the defense attorneys, *Armour v. Nix* seemed to be as much about family and social arrangements as about the constitutional law of school segregation.[15]

The defendants' effort to explore and expose the personal lives of the plaintiffs contained a certain logic, of course. Hames invariably elicited her clients' desire to attend "white schools" for a "better education." Together, the two lines of inquiry wove a narrative that whites feared: integration would bring the troubles of the black ghetto into the white suburbs. The defense's questions also tapped into the growing backlash against "welfare dependency," a campaign that targeted single black mothers for scorn. Before long, Hames began objecting to the setup. "All this going into people's personal lives" bore no relevance to the underlying issues in the case, she argued. "I don't want any more questions about marriage!" she declared. Her protests were unsuccessful. The personal questions continued.[16]

Intriguingly, however, the defense lawyers abandoned their strategy for three—and only three—of the plaintiffs. One of the male plaintiffs, Edward Moody, resisted the lawyers' efforts to scrutinize his personal life. During his deposition, Moody demanded to know what "bearing" his place of employment and his wife's name had on the case. He refused to answer questions he deemed irrelevant and the attorneys backed off. The defense lawyers did the same when they took the deposition of another male plaintiff, this one of retirement age.

And, most tellingly, they did not badger Ethel Mae Mathews. Certain matters, Mathews insisted during her deposition, were "none of their business." "I don't think you're no better than I am," she announced. Mathews, in an apparent effort to stand up for the female plaintiffs who had come before her, then bitterly criticized the attorneys for questioning these other witnesses about their welfare status. As she continued her tongue-lashing, the school board lawyers interrupted her. They thanked Mathews for her time. She wanted to hold forth, but the defense had heard enough. The lawyers ended Mathews's deposition without propounding further questions.[17]

Ethel Mae Mathews's charisma and experience as a community organizer might have increased *Armour*'s slim chances of success. However, Hames did not seek to mobilize her clients to engage in the kinds of demonstrations and protests that Mathews, Eva Davis, Ed Moody, and other activists among the *Armour v. Nix* plaintiffs customarily led. Hames continued the pattern that LDF's Constance Baker Motley established in the first Atlanta school desegregation case: the clients themselves would play a minimal role in generating community support for the case. Yet, Hames's strategy unfolded in a different social context and with different clients from LDF's. The ACLU lawyer may have identified with the black poor, but the "silent majority" of Americans—"non-demonstrators" and "non-shouters" who had elected Richard Nixon to office after he campaigned to restore "law and order" after ghetto riots, "forced busing," and massive welfare programs—likely would not. The school board lawyers' identity-based questions to Hames's clients appealed to this majority. Civil rights protests were not effective if the target audience did not ultimately find the demonstrators and their cause sympathetic. Perhaps political protest by the black poor during the mid-1970s would have only exacerbated the backlash against them. The *Armour* plaintiffs could best mobilize in coalition with higher-status activists, and that coalition did not materialize.[18]

Hames and the ACLU of Georgia did actively conduct outreach and seek political support from key middle-class players, including women's organizations, nonprofit organizations, and churches. Chronically low on funds, Hames looked to the national and local public interest organizations for resources and political support. Longtime community activist Frances Pauley wrote to Roy Wilkins of the NAACP on Hames's behalf, reminding him that *Armour* represented the last-ditch effort to achieve desegregation in Atlanta. "How can we influence people to give Margie Hames the professional help she needs?" If Wilkins could not influence critical organizations to come to Hames's aid, Pauley wrote, could Wilkins at least persuade them "to be neutral when asked about the case and not stymie financial assistance?" The fund-raising efforts failed to produce needed resources. Racial politics partly explained the lack of success. Many black middle-class groups tagged the ACLU a "white" organization out to "manipulate" the community. Others continued to oppose school desegregation outright. Hames found few institutional backers for *Armour v. Nix* outside of the ACLU.[19]

Some important African Americans did support the plaintiffs, but they did not offset those opposed or indifferent to the suit. Rev. Ralph Abernathy, Rev. Joseph Boone, and others associated with SCLC proved allies. In the wake of Dr. King's assassination in 1968 SCLC had launched an unsuccessful Poor Peoples Campaign and backed striking garbage workers in Atlanta in 1970. Yet, the organization's influence did not compare to that of other stalwart civil rights groups after King's death, and had ebbed by the mid-1970s—at *Armour*'s height.[20]

Julian Bond, a member of the Georgia senate, had always supported school desegregation in principle. But, acutely aware that the transition to desegregated systems had often devastated the ranks of black teachers and administrators, and sometimes harmed black students, he had not been a vocal opponent of the Atlanta compromise. "In the South," Bond once quipped, "the man who'd been principal of Booker T. Washington High School became the assistant-to-the-assistant-to-the-assistant principal at Stonewall Jackson High School." Nevertheless, Bond continued to offer unstinting praise for a robust judicial interpretation of *Brown* during the 1970s, and the *Armour* plaintiffs counted him "very supportive." Bond argued that hysteria over busing, whipped up for "political gain," had obscured the high stakes at issue in the school desegregation debate. "We are talking about equal opportunity in education," he cried. "We are talking about building a democratic society.... We are talking about children and the kind of nation they...will make for future generations."[21]

Notwithstanding Bond's high ideals, many experts viewed interdistrict school desegregation litigation as a risky proposition by the late 1970s, when *Armour* reappeared on the federal court docket after years of delay. The Ford Foundation, a major benefactor of liberal causes, did not fund the litigation. "Integrationists" in the civil rights establishment "felt themselves under attack," explained Robert Sedler, one of Hames's cocounsels. Jack Greenberg, LDF's director-counsel, predicted, as early as 1974, that Hames faced a "permanent setback." He thought metropolitan relief was unlikely given recent court decisions. The single biggest impediment to relief was *Milliken v. Bradley*. In this 1974 decision, the U.S. Supreme Court reversed an interdistrict school desegregation remedy; it held that suburban districts could only be required to remedy segregation in inner-city schools under a limited set of circumstances. Many observers considered *Milliken* the "death knell" of school desegregation. In light of *Milliken*, Greenberg did not think Hames could win her case. He refused to back the "swashbuckling" lawyer's bid for metropolitan relief, despite repeated requests for support.[22]

Greenberg's response provoked a bitter riposte from the director of the Georgia ACLU. The "right opposition is pretty easy to deal with," he said, but "the left opposition" was "much harder" to swallow. *Armour* continued as a "shoestring operation" funded by the ACLU and driven by the energy of Hames and local supporters without the money and clout to defeat the power structure or overcome the hostile political climate.[23]

## TRIALS IN COURT

For all of her daring, Hames litigated *Armour* in a traditional manner. The *Armour* plaintiffs played conventional roles in court. Ethel Mae Mathews, the veteran of raucous direct action campaigns against state and local authorities, provided straightforward testimony during the actual trial in the case. "Black schools are not providing the quality of education that white schools are," Mathews testified. She did not verbally spar with the school board's counsel, as she had when deposed. Eva Davis, whose children had participated in the majority-to-minority program, praised busing as "the greatest thing that has ever happened to my children." Mrs. Armour proclaimed that she would bus her children as far as "Philadelphia, Pennsylvania," if they could find equal opportunity there. Many other plaintiffs spoke of their desires for quality education for their children; they could only find it, they believed, in integrated schools. "In the real world," said Sedler, these "ordinary working-class black people knew that a good education was where the white folks went."[24]

Hames primarily relied on written records—over a thousand documents in all—to make her case. She turned to school board minutes, planning commission reports, maps, and municipal records to support her claims. These documents showed, she claimed, that authorities had periodically disregarded school district boundaries to maintain racial segregation. She proffered evidence that suggested that officials had permitted white students to transfer out of Atlanta schools to suburban schools to escape desegregation. She showed that suburban school officials created attendance zones that had the effect of concentrating the few blacks who lived outside the city limits within a small number of schools. Rather than build new schools or integrate old ones, districts with few or no schools for blacks contracted with schools in other districts to handle the so-called black student overflow. Such practices continued in some suburban systems until the late 1960s, Hames showed.[25]

Evidence about state and local housing policies, however, formed the crux of Hames's case. "Whites live on the north and blacks live on the south (side of

Ponce de Leon Avenue)," Hames explained. "That didn't just happen. It was carefully planned over a number of years by local and state governments." She contended that her evidence demonstrated that school boards, state and local legislative bodies, and planning agencies, such as the Atlanta Housing Authority, the MPC, and the Georgia Real Estate Commission, cooperated in selecting school and housing sites to perpetuate school and residential segregation. Hames turned to history to prove her assertion that these actors had "bottled up" the black poor in the city of Atlanta and reserved the affluent suburbs for whites. Governmental bodies perpetuated Jim Crow through urban renewal and zoning practices, highway and street construction practices, and through boundaries, buffers, and barriers that segregated blacks from whites. Local housing authorities strictly segregated buildings by race and located public housing in racially identifiable neighborhoods. Suburban authorities actively discouraged blacks from moving to outlying areas.[26]

Karl Taeuber, a critical expert witness for the plaintiffs, confirmed the case that her documents made. The sociologist asserted that housing and school segregation in the Atlanta metropolitan area bore a strong correlation. And he claimed that government discrimination had caused both. "A lot of what was done, was done deliberately," he found. Discrimination "severely constrained" housing choices. By 1970, Atlanta was more residentially segregated than it had been in 1940. School segregation logically resulted. Of the twenty-seven new schools built between 1966 and 1972, nine opened with 100 percent black enrollment and sixteen opened with between 92 and 99 percent black enrollment, all because of neighborhood segregation. "There is no way to say there was freedom-of-choice," Taeuber contended, in neighborhoods or schools.[27]

## Two Tales of Biracial Negotiation

In a poignant twist, the ACLU's legal strategy required the court to revisit the decision-making of black business and political leaders in the postwar years as Atlanta confronted its housing shortage. Evidence regarding the role that black leaders had played in shoring up residential segregation provided a compelling subtext when Q. V. Williamson took the stand. Williamson, Atlanta's first black councilman and the realtor who had dominated the black housing market in the city for forty years, testified that blacks had to "get political clearance" before they could "move in and build" on any parcel of land. As president of the Empire Real Estate Board and owner of a realty company, Williamson knew intimately about these practices. For decades, he had acceded to white officials' demands to maintain residential segregation. So had black members of the Westside Mutual

Development Committee and the Atlanta Urban League, Williamson testified, including A. T. Walden, Grace Towns Hamilton, Robert Thompson, and others. They had negotiated with Atlanta mayors William Hartsfield and Ivan Allen to "uph[o]ld the system" that designated land and housing by race. All told, Williamson's testimony made clear, public and quasi-public actors had limited the land and housing available to blacks.[28]

Poor blacks had suffered disproportionately within this rigged system. Hames, however, did not question Williamson about how the system that he described, and in which he played a pivotal role, specifically affected her clients. She would not have wanted to antagonize a witness who provided critical support for her case. It nevertheless was true that Williamson and other black realtors, brokers, salesmen, appraisers, bankers, builders, and developers had profited financially from segregation. They controlled the black housing market. In the process of exercising control, they helped to entrench residential segregation and exacerbated the problems of low-income blacks, in particular, who were afforded the fewest housing options under segregation. Many middle-class blacks could and did live in enclaves apart from poor blacks such as the *Armour* plaintiffs. Williamson acknowledged blacks' "mixed feelings" about working within the system of residential segregation at one point during his testimony. Some blacks believed that leaders should demand "open occupancy," he conceded. But, he went on, pragmatists who preferred to work within the system prevailed. Their decision-making helped to deepen "residential apartheid," and thus, the system of school segregation that Hames now fought in court.[29]

If any one moment embodied the complex array of racial and economic forces at work in Atlanta's housing market, it was the so-called Atlanta wall of 1962. Williamson's testimony about the Atlanta wall riveted the courtroom. During the postwar era, African-American leaders shied away from the courtroom as a forum for addressing the housing crisis. This changed in 1962, when the Empire Real Estate Board turned to litigation to counteract what it considered an outrageous act of white aggression against an African-American surgeon. White residents of the Peyton Forest neighborhood had reacted angrily when a white contractor, in a financial crunch and unable to find a white buyer, sold his home to the black doctor. The angry whites went to the mayor in an attempt to drive the doctor out of the neighborhood. With the approval of Mayor Ivan Allen, Jr., and the backing of the city's Board of Aldermen, the residents literally barricaded the area to physically prevent the surgeon, and any other African Americans who might attempt to invade their neighborhood, from getting in. That is, they erected concrete and steel barricades on Peyton and Harlan Roads to preclude black expansion into their neighborhood and other white areas south of the roadblocks. By comparison, other methods the city had used to cordon blacks off from whites—parks, roads, vacant lots, and cemeteries—seemed subtle.[30]

The "Atlanta wall" of segregation made national headlines and inspired outrage among blacks. African Americans united in opposition to the wall. A coalition of organizations, ranging from the pragmatists of ANVL to the Atlanta NAACP to radical student activists in SNCC, condemned the wall. In this context, the Empire Real Estate Board "organized an all citizens' committee to fight the battle of Peyton Road." At a meeting held at the West Hunter Baptist Church, black leaders, including Q. V. Williamson and Rev. Ralph Abernathy, decried both the practical impact of the wall and its symbolism. It had driven race relations in Atlanta to "an all-time low." Williamson expressed the congregants' views: "These are the darkest days I've seen in Atlanta as far as race relations are concerned. [A]tlanta is the first town in the South to build barricades across public streets" to keep blacks out. "Perhaps we need to send Mayor Allen a copy of the Emancipation Proclamation," another leader cried. After the meeting, the All-Citizens Committee for Better City Planning called for a boycott of white merchants who had supported the roadblocks, hired lawyers, and went into court for an order to "tear down the wall." Ultimately, the Empire Real Estate Board's suit, litigated by Donald Hollowell and Howard Moore, ended the controversy. The city removed the barricades by order of the Fulton County Superior Court. The court found the barrier, which city ordinances had codified, a violation of precedents barring legislation that facially discriminated against residents by race. The Empire Real Estate Board had been moved to activism to protect one of the community's most esteemed members.[31]

But even after the uproar over the Atlanta wall, Williamson and other black leaders continued to take ambiguous positions in response to residential segregation. Their unwillingness to take an emphatic stand against segregated housing was animated, at least in part, by their socioeconomic class. During the summer of 1966, the Lynhurst-Peyton area, the same area in which the wall had been erected just three years earlier, again became a focus of concern. But now middle-class blacks joined with white residents to defeat a rezoning effort that would have brought rental units into the area. At the time, low-income blacks— that is, would-be renters—still faced a shortage of affordable housing units. Q. V. Williamson, the ASLC's Jessie Hill, Jr., and Senator Leroy Johnson headed the list of opponents to rental units in Peyton Forest. The language that the residents used to fend off renters, many of whom the audience presumed would be black, sounded remarkably similar to the rhetoric that whites used when resisting desegregation. At a homeowners' association meeting, Senator Leroy

Johnson urged the assembled crowed to "prevent this invasion" of renters. "You are striving to maintain a community that is worthwhile to live in and you have every right to oppose attempts to destroy it." During the public hearing on rezoning, the question of race surfaced. A white resident denied that additional apartments would accelerate white movement out of the racially transitioning community. Race was not the issue, she insisted, but "maintaining a good community." Q. V. Williamson—who spoke out against the rezoning at the public hearing—was also a member of the committee charged with deciding whether to rezone. The only black member of the committee, Williamson "abandoned his official role for one minute to speak in opposition" to the rezoning, the *Atlanta Daily World* reported. With widespread support from such leading blacks, the biracial coalition opposing rental housing prevailed. There would be no housing for renters in Peyton Forest. In this respect, the black middle-class residents of Peyton Forest were no different from most middle-class homeowners—black and white—in countless subdivisions across the country. One might ask whether the black residents of Peyton Forest, themselves longtime victims of discrimination, should have been more open to those seeking housing opportunities, especially other blacks. But it was not so.[32]

The story presented by Hames in the case—through Williamson and other witnesses—omitted episodes such as the battle over rental housing for blacks in Peyton Forest. It also omitted battles between the national NAACP and the local branch over the desegregation of public housing units, home to many *Armour* plaintiffs, during the late 1960s. In 1967, the national NAACP charged that the U.S. Department of Housing and Urban Development (HUD) had refused to enforce the Civil Rights Act's nondiscrimination provisions in the city's public housing developments. At the same time that it attacked HUD, the national NAACP blasted what it viewed as local black leaders' unwillingness to challenge segregation in public and private housing. The national group even charged that the lone black member of the Atlanta Housing Authority actually supported the agency's segregation policy. According to the national NAACP, prominent members of the local black leadership, including Q. V. Williamson, appeared to support desegregation in theory, but not in fact. These complicating chapters in Atlanta's history were, understandably, not a part of Hames's evidence.[33]

Nevertheless, Williamson's testimony—both the events he recounted and those he left out—suggested the peculiar oppression that the *Armour* plaintiffs faced. They had been subject to race- and class-based disadvantage, sometimes by fellow African Americans, who themselves faced discrimination.

Once Williamson stepped down from the stand, and in the shadow of the *Calhoun* compromise, a looming question seemed to hang over the courtroom:

was the discrimination the *Armour* plaintiffs endured too far-reaching and too complex for a court to remedy? But the parties had only just begun to put on their evidence.

## The Chairman Speaks

If Hames conceived Q. V. Williamson's testimony as a highlight of her case, the *Armour* case reached a low point when Dr. Benjamin Mays took the stand for the defendants. Mays still served as chairman of the Atlanta Board of Education. Few black men in Atlanta could rival Mays's stature. He was the former president of Morehouse College and mentor to Martin Luther King, Jr. He arrived in the courtroom as a "gibraltar of education," a wise community elder who could definitively answer the central question—more political than legal—underlying *Armour v. Nix*: whether school integration, and the metropolitan remedy that it required, was worth the time, resources, and tumult it would cost Atlanta and the surrounding suburbs if ordered by the court.[34]

Mays's mythic status in the community obscured his hopelessly conflicted position in the case. Over twenty-seven years, Mays, the son of South Carolina sharecroppers, had built Morehouse College into one of the nation's preeminent black colleges. He had personally seen success flower in an all-black environment, and he took enormous pride in these accomplishments. "Every time I see an enterprise thriving because of Negro genius, Negro sweat, blood and tears," Mays explained in a 1968 address at historically black Benedict College, "my heart leaps with joy and my soul takes wings." He continued: "I have great pride in Negro banks, Negro insurance companies, Negro churches, the Negro press, Negro colleges, and every worthwhile institution that Negroes run and control." And, Mays said, "I refuse to be swept off my feet by the glamour of a desegregated society." His predispositions were clear. It came as no surprise, then, that, over the years, Mays had made equivocal statements about *Brown*. But the most serious conflict had occurred very recently. Mays, as chairman of the Atlanta Board of Education, had endorsed the compromise settlement of *Calhoun*, a case he considered an "albatross" around the necks of Atlanta's citizenry. Based on that fact alone, Mays seemed unlikely to support Hames's suit.[35]

Rev. Austin Thomas Ford, a white Episcopal priest who actively supported the *Armour* litigation, had other reasons to doubt Mays's support for the plaintiffs. Ford ran a settlement house in Atlanta and had worked for years to help the city's poorest black families gain community services. In 1972, Rev. Ford informed black parents in housing projects of the option to transfer their children to schools outside of the neighborhood; he urged them to take advantage of the court-ordered majority-to-minority program. Ford's efforts attracted more than three hundred prospective transfer students. But, in Ford's telling, the parents encountered stiff resistance from Dr. Mays. The students, many of whom had special educational needs, all wished to gain access to the school district's better schools. Mays and the students' prospective principals "were very upset" about the transfers. Ford personally interceded with Mays. The chairman responded coldly. He was "not interested in the program." When Ford threatened to bring the students and the press to the receiver schools the next day, Mays relented. Ford nevertheless had learned an important lesson. Mays was an "elitist." This encounter and others taught Ford that class differences among blacks "were very intense"; "feelings of real identity" and "fellowship with the poor" were "rare."[36]

Mays almost certainly would have disclaimed class bias, but he nonetheless fervently opposed the claims of the poor black claimants in *Armour v. Nix*. In the press, Mays condemned the suit as a "money-making scheme by lawyers." Notwithstanding the fact that Hames and her colleagues volunteered their services to the penniless plaintiffs and were not guaranteed attorneys' fees, Mays insisted that Hames and her team did not have "the best interest of the child at heart" because "lawyers take cases to make money." Then, in March 1978, Dr. Mays testified for the defendant school boards in *Armour*. He appeared under subpoena as a witness for several of the suburban school districts. The chairman of the Atlanta Board of Education was called as an expert on Atlanta's "ability to provide a quality education without a metropolitan remedy." Mays's testimony began with a disclaimer. "[N]othing I say here," he insisted, "must be interpreted to mean that I believe in a segregated society or segregated education." Mays believed in "quality education," he asserted. But, he claimed, such an education could be found in "segregated" or "integrated" institutions. He clarified: "I think you can have a quality education given equal facilities, equal library, equal buildings, [and] teachers with the same qualifications." Mays appeared to endorse the "separate but equal rule," and Hames condemned his testimony. She objected to his "assault on the holding in *Brown v. Board of Education*." The court overruled her.[37]

The school board lawyers had struck gold. They asked Mays to expound further upon his conclusions. A lawyer again asked Dr. Mays whether it was "necessary for the black children of Atlanta to attend school" with a "substantial portion of white students" in order for them to obtain a quality education. The revered black educator answered unequivocally: "I would have to say I do not believe that [it does] because that repudiates all of my experience as a boy." It defied the experiences of exceptional black men such as Thurgood Marshall and countless other blacks in Atlanta who had attended all-black schools and had "gone on to do well," he explained. They "had self-esteem." Hence, Mays offered, the metropolitan remedy at issue in the case had "nothing to do with quality education." Still, Mays refused to concede Hames's point that he had rejected *Brown*. "The Board of Education is an integrated Board of Education and I don't think you can get that board to argue for segregated education," Mays declared. The logic of the Atlanta compromise had resurfaced, but Mays would not concede its real-life consequences for students. Mays also denied Hames's suggestion on crossexamination that he had once said that the metropolitan remedy would "destroy black political power" in Atlanta. "Politics," Mays testified, had "nothing to do with" his position.[38]

## Finality

Unsurprisingly, the two sides viewed the evidence presented in *Armour v. Nix* differently. The defendant school boards asserted that Hames had presented inadequate evidence of discrimination. Hames believed she had marshaled ample evidence to meet the strict proof standards governing interdistrict school desegregation relief.

The U.S. Supreme Court's decision in the milestone case *Milliken v. Bradley* stood between each litigant and victory. *Milliken*, decided in 1974 by a sharply divided Court, reversed a city-suburban school desegregation remedy in Detroit and outlying areas. The majority held that the plaintiffs had not presented sufficient evidence to prove that the fifty-three suburban districts included in the remedy had affirmatively contributed to the inner-city schools' racial isolation. The plaintiffs had only shown a single suburban district culpable for segregation in the city. Such thin evidence could not support such an expansive remedy, the majority held. Yet, the Court left open the possibility that it would uphold a metropolitan remedy if plaintiffs could prove that acts by suburban school officials or the state had caused or significantly contributed to segregation in the city. Justice Stewart's opinion, in particular, provided a road map for plaintiffs who sought crossdistrict remedial relief. He noted that a metropolitan-wide remedy would be proper were it shown that state officials or political subdivisions of the state had contributed to or fostered school segregation by discriminating in the drawing of school district lines, in zoning, or in housing. Hames thought she had met this evidentiary bar.[39]

The defendants found Hames's claims contemptible. "Madam lawyer's" case was about history—ancient history—the defense attorneys asserted. The attorneys could do little to dispute the historical record, but they asked the court to set it to the side and render it legally meaningless. "We don't want to start with Gone with the Wind and these other historical facts that won't help the Court," said the lawyer for Decatur County. The attorneys found Hames's evidence of recent discrimination weak. The Atlanta Board of Education had been "unitary" for several years. Most of Hames's recent evidence concerned intradistrict rather than interdistrict discrimination. Virtually all of the testimony of her star witness, Q. V. Williamson, fell into this category, the Fulton County attorney argued; therefore, it could not support a metropolitan remedy. Hames had not shown that whites transferred en masse from the Atlanta schools to avoid desegregation; in a free country, white families could move for a variety of reasons. To the extent that Hames did have evidence of white resistance to desegregation, the school board attorneys rejected it in acerbic tones. "The assertion that Georgia has had a history of resistance to education is true," one school district's brief explained, "only to the limited sense that" concepts such as "compulsory racial balance" and "quota[s]" were and still are "contrary to the sociological, philosophical and educational views of most of Georgia's citizens." Another school district's brief invoked a historical analogy to reject Hames's equivalence of "white flight" and discrimination. Parents had only "vot[ed] with their feet" against "extreme racial balance or mixing orders in the public schools," the lawyers wrote, "much as East Germans voted against their intolerable conditions by fleeing to West Berlin before the Berlin Wall was erected."[40]

The federal district court agreed that Hames had not met her burden of proof. In orders issued in March 1978 and September 1979, a three-judge panel granted the defendants' motions to dismiss the case even though the plaintiffs had amassed a staggering amount of evidence. Indeed, the court found strong evidence of state-sponsored housing discrimination. It specifically noted the "agreement between the city and the Empire Real Estate Board, an organization of black real estate brokers and agents, to cooperate" in halting black expansion into white areas. The "race of land" helped determine the "race of schools" within Atlanta and the suburbs. But Hames had made her case against the school boards mostly on the basis of historical wrongs; the court found "this history" a "fascinating topic." However, the panel concluded, evidence concerning events prior to 1960 was not enough to prove liability, particularly since Atlanta had been unitary since 1973, when the compromise took effect. Other defendants were under court-ordered desegregation plans. Government did not cause contemporary residential segregation. In short, the defendants prevailed because the plaintiffs had shown "no significant violations of recent vintage," and certainly none that would "justify the drastic remedy envisioned."[41]

Hames had not expected to win in the district court, however. It had been clear to the plaintiffs' lawyers that the panel of conservative judges were "not sympathetic" to school desegregation. "These three white male southern judges were not about to order the desegregation of the Atlanta schools," said cocounsel Sedler. All along, Hames had pegged her hopes for victory on "get[ting] Stewart's vote." She appealed directly to the Supreme Court. Justice Stewart would see, she believed, the "mountain of evidence" that she had presented in support of a metropolitan remedy. She had some momentum. Many courts had rejected interdistrict remedies after *Milliken*, but a few federal courts had ordered them, including in Wilmington, Delaware and Louisville, Kentucky. Recently, the justices had summarily affirmed the Wilmington remedy.[42]

But it was not to be. In a May 1980 per curiam order, the Supreme Court affirmed the district court's decision *in Armour v. Nix*. It was surely not helpful to the plaintiffs' cause that Justice Thurgood Marshall had recused himself from the case, presumably because of his previous role at the NAACP LDF, in *Calhoun*, specifically. More important, Justice Stewart, the most critical of the eight remaining justices, did not view the case Hames's way. With that, *Armour*— and the legal battle over Atlanta's legacy of Jim Crow schools—was finished, twenty-two years after Thurgood Marshall, Constance Baker Motley, and A. T. Walden had filed the initial case to desegregate the city's schools.[43]

"That was a sad day," Rev. Ford recalled. "I think if Dr. Mays had not been against it, and if Thurgood Marshall had not had to recuse himself," it would have gone the other way. Roger Mills saw the loss in a different light. "We had, staring at us, the *Milliken* case." "Sure the case was wrongly decided," he believed, "but once it's wrongly decided, you have to play by the new rules." After *Milliken*, "it would have taken an awful lot" to win, he admitted. And after the devastating precedent, Mills was "not sure the evidence was there" to prevail. Margie Hames disagreed, and she took the loss "hard." "But she was a strong person," Ford recounted. "She knew it hadn't happened to her, it had happened to the children."[44]

## DOES HISTORY MATTER?

*Armour* brought pragmatic civil rights full circle. For in some ways, the pragmatists' theory of black power in politics, housing, and education had been on trial, along with whites' past discrimination. In the school context, the two fortified each other, as the race of land determined the race of schools: the pragmatists' resignation to residential segregation during the 1940s, 1950s, and 1960s held long-term and, for some, disastrous consequences. On trial during the 1970s, past proponents of the politics of biracial coalition such as Q. V. Williamson all but conceded that the tradition of pragmatic civil rights had not worked out equally well for all members of the black community. By that time, it was too late to repudiate the bargain.

*Armour v. Nix* failed as a matter of law, but the case's full measure cannot be taken in terms of whether the plaintiffs prevailed in court. Grassroots activists had never assumed that courts would do justice in their cases and, consequently had never valued their campaigns in strictly legal terms. Even so, the claims that the *Armour* plaintiffs asserted and the remedies that they demanded are significant. These women upset a growing "conventional wisdom" regarding the perspectives of African-American communities on *Brown*. This truism, advanced in numerous quarters—by adherents to the black power ideology, by former warriors in the fight for integration, and by numerous black spokespersons, elected or self-appointed—held that "the African-American community," especially the working class, no longer agreed with the precepts of *Brown*. Proponents of this "wisdom" characterized the notion that racially separate schools were inherently unequal as sentimental at best and culturally racist at worst. Moreover, they noted, desegregation was impractical to implement. Stokely Carmichael captured part of the sentiment with his quip: "[L]ike communism in Marxist dogma, 'integration' was pure ideal." Law professor Derrick Bell, a former NAACP LDF lawyer who later rejected the NAACP's school desegregation strategy, captured another dimension of the new wisdom. Bell claimed that white liberal idealists had steered LDF away from its true mission; rather than represent poor clients who opposed busing for school desegregation, the lawyers continued to pursue racial balance remedies. Blacks had rejected the NAACP's dogma and now were only concerned about "quality education," matters such as equal resources, good teachers, and control over school governance. He pointed to black Atlantans to support his claim—overlooking the poor blacks, overwhelmingly women, who filed *Armour v. Nix*—and others like them who likely existed in other parts of the country.[45]

The *Armour* litigation exposed a difficult truth, one whose implications advocates on all sides of the school desegregation controversy did not easily accept. During the late 1960s and early 1970s, school desegregation was a deeply contested issue in black communities. It always had been a source of controversy. Class still heavily influenced how individuals and subgroups within black communities weighed the costs and benefits of fighting for integrated education. A 1981 poll revealed the persistent class divide on the issue in Atlanta. Over 64 percent of low-income blacks supported school integration and busing, while 50 percent of middle-income blacks did.[46]

The *Armour* plaintiffs embraced racially integrated schools not because they were romantics or culturally racist. To the contrary, they viewed themselves as the consummate realists. These impoverished women and men thought it was folly to believe that in a racist and classist society, poor black children could obtain quality education outside racially mixed schools. Even if they wanted to, black teachers and administrators would not be able to provide quality education to poor black students in all-black schools. The *Armour* plaintiffs were willing to bear the social costs of access to integrated schools, all because they believed these institutions, on balance, to be higher quality schools. In other words, they sought quality education, and they believed that it was inextricably bound to integration.

With the passage of time, it is clear that both those who sought quality education in same-race institutions and those who sought it in integrated environments made rational choices. Concerns about white intransigence to desegregation and discrimination in desegregated schools, whether it took the form of negative stereotyping of black students or discrimination against qualified black faculty, were legitimate. Yet, substantial social science literature indicates that public schools with high concentrations of low-income minority children—such as those in metropolitan Atlanta and other cities throughout the country—frequently do not produce academically successful students. These schools serve those students with the greatest academic and social needs, and too seldom are able to attract the necessary resources and experienced teachers who are capable of inspiring intellectual growth among at-risk students. In current argot, these schools "leave students behind." High-need schools fail despite black administrative control of school systems and despite black faculties.[47]

One could observe this phenomenon in Atlanta after the *Calhoun* compromise. Time proved that the settlement "was a bad deal," observed Julian Bond. The black superintendent "just really didn't make too much of a difference." The city's schools largely failed. Enrollment declined drastically, test scores plunged, and community support for the schools diminished. Poor students bore the brunt of the system's inadequacies, as even middle-class black students deserted the system. Many black middle-class students moved to the suburbs, where they could attend racially mixed schools, which routinely outperform overwhelmingly black schools. In light of these later developments, the *Armour* plaintiffs' crusade for quality, integrated schools looks entirely reasonable.[48]

The story of *Armour* is also important because it tells us much about the potential agency of marginalized groups in campaigns for change. The *Armour* plaintiffs certainly hoped to prevail on their legal claims and were disappointed when they did not do so. But activists such as Eva Davis and Ethel Mae Mathews achieved a measure of satisfaction simply by identifying how they were wronged and by asserting rights in court. Mathews's verbal jousts with men who first denied her rights and then tried to deny her humanity, she believed, were acts of civic participation rarely seen from the dispossessed. Mathews and her peers were also able to confront power brokers on behalf of those on society's bottom rungs. In so doing, the plaintiffs, many of whom were involved in welfare rights and other forms of political and social activism prior to *Armour*, demonstrated how legal and social movements can fortify one another, regardless of whether plaintiffs achieve victory in court.[49]

In the end, the story of *Armour* is, however, a story of federal court defeat. Because of *Milliken*, Hames's lawsuit stood little chance of success. The case also went up against prevailing political winds. Those opposed to "forced busing" had countermobilized in a wide range of venues. On the streets of numerous American cities, on city councils, and in Congress, opponents of the kinds of remedial devices that Hames sought created a formidable social movement against racial change. Hames's failed crusade to redeem *Brown* revealed how challenging the struggle for social justice had become in an era of federal court resignation to white resistance to school desegregation and divergent black interests over a range of public policy issues. In addition, the campaign brought attention to challenges that the "heroic and clever lawyer" identity—an identity that that successful federal court litigators sometimes may develop—can pose in attorney-client relationships, to say nothing of the challenges that race and class differences can present. Ultimately, however, Hames's "swashbuckling" style exemplified the passion and resolve that lawyers must, at a minimum, summon if they intend—against the odds—to pursue equality through the law.

# Conclusion

The Constitution['s]...language is "we the people"; not we the white people. (1860)

Frederick Douglass

During some of the most contentious hours in American history, statesmen have called the right to dissent fundamental to the political and the constitutional orders.[1] Struggles over slavery, race, and inequality often inspired these expressions of commitment to dissent. President Lincoln, in his first inaugural address, delivered on the eve of Civil War, declared, "This country, with its institutions, belongs to the people who inhabit it." Referencing themes in the Declaration of Independence, Lincoln spoke of the citizens' "revolutionary right" to overthrow the government if it became oppressive or to change it by amending the Constitution. Lincoln affirmed the seceding states' right to rebel and simultaneously endeavored to hold the Union together. Frederick Douglass, the former slave turned abolitionist, also endorsed political dissent, but he sought to assuage no slaveholder. Douglass asserted that the Constitution, as written in Philadelphia, guaranteed blacks the same rights as other men. He proclaimed his ability to "ascertain what the Constitution...is." The document conferred its benefits on "we the people," Douglass noted, "not we the white people," "not we the privileged class, not we the high, not we the low," he said, "but we the people."[2]

This book has told the stories of citizens—descendants of slaves and heirs to Frederick Douglass's tradition of protest—who expressed political dissent by laying claim to the Constitution. These citizens were law shapers, law interpreters, and even law makers. Local people—lesser known lawyers and organizers, litigators and negotiators, elites and grassroots, women and men—in interaction with national institutions and leaders, sought to give meaning to the equal protection clause of the Constitution. These actors contested the constitutional conceptions of equality propounded by powerful judges and celebrated lawyers. A. T. Walden and other leaders within the Atlanta NAACP interpreted the meaning of the Constitution and *Brown v. Board of Education*, often in a manner that fit middle-class prerogatives. When SNCC and members of the Atlanta student movement mobilized a social movement to desegregate public accommodations in defiance of federal courts that provided no remedy for "private" discrimination, they, too, made claims on the Constitution. Prior to launching sit-ins, the students crafted an appeal in which they cited the equal protection clause, as well as the Declaration of Independence, to justify their protests for rights. The students also mobilized against municipal segregation in collaboration with attorney Len Holt, who conceived of the omnibus civil rights lawsuit and taught lay people to file such suits pro se. The students turned to Donald Hollowell and Howard Moore, who crafted novel legal arguments to facilitate the students' political struggle for racial redress. Ethel Mae Mathews, Emma Armour, Eva Davis, and other penniless blacks asserted claims for educational equality with the help of the intrepid Margie Pitts Hames. In all of these instances, local people and unsung members of the civil rights bar actively participated in the making and shaping of constitutional law.

In Atlanta, each wave of civil rights activists insisted on defining equality and the paths toward it in its own way, and each group gave rise to a new wave of activists with different priorities, strategies, and tactics. The gift they pass to the present generation is not a doctrinaire set of goals or methods but the tradition of protest itself, the will to object to injustice, in some way. Julian Bond captured that state of mind and personified that tradition very well in 1966, when the young legislator's antiwar stance imperiled his career. "I hope that throughout my life I shall always have the courage to dissent," a defiant Bond said.[3]

The NAACP and its lawyers shaped the world occupied by other dissenters from the racial status quo. The NAACP's choices, successes, and perceived failures were engines that drove the processes of historical change through which Jim Crow fell. At crucial points, the movement benefited from the conflict that percolated—sometimes intensely—among the NAACP, LDF, and local civil rights groups. Even when conflict did not produce immediate benefits, dissenters pointed out flaws in dominant approaches. They reminded the NAACP and LDF that local activists' objectives extended beyond formal legal equality and its narrow definitions of harm and remedy.

In these ways, the friction between and among lawyers and political activists over ideology and methods often energized the civil rights movement in Atlanta. Friction often had been a factor in black politics, particularly in the era before *Brown*. The African-American community had always defined equality in multiple ways and held diverse views about the best way to pursue it. As it evolved, the civil rights movement enhanced the extent to which the rich diversity of thought within the black community could find greater expression. Consensus—or more accurately, the appearance of consensus—became less plausible as the chains of de jure segregation no longer bound African Americans so tightly together. With Jim Crow's demise, discrimination began to affect different segments of the black community in even more distinct ways. Socioeconomic class—which always had been an important, albeit often submerged, dividing line within the black community—now became more fully visible.[4]

This book's ground-level view of legal history has placed both the civil rights lawyering of the NAACP LDF and the U.S. Supreme Court in proper perspective. As many historians have suggested, the justices played an important role in generating social change in the civil rights movement. But it is also true, as others claim, that the Court did not itself make change. In fact, events in Atlanta show that it was often the justices' inaction and timidity that propelled the direct action wing of the civil rights movement forward. The Court sometimes indirectly gave momentum to the movement by rejecting civil rights claims rather than embracing them, and by disappointing rather than inspiring civil rights activists.[5]

Scholars who emphasize how factors external to the courts drive social change typically also express a cautionary note to public interest lawyers. Such lawyers, it is said, should not put too much faith in the courts as they seek to promote change. Luminaries such as Thurgood Marshall, Constance Baker Motley, Jack Greenberg, and other counsel for LDF had great faith in the courts as they pushed the NAACP's campaign against Jim Crow forward and made the U.S. Constitution's guarantee of equal protection a reality under law. These lawyers embodied the heroic and rightly celebrated federal court litigator—the "clever lawyer," to invoke Greenberg's phrase. But they were not the only civil rights visionaries. Scholars' understanding of how law and social change occurs should be broadened to include a larger cast of lawyers and lay activists.[6]

For the story of the civil rights movement told here shows that not all civil rights leaders of the era focused their energies so exclusively on the Court, and not all shared the same philosophy about equality. Many members of the civil rights bar, and activists who battled segregation in political, social, or cultural arenas, did not fully embrace LDF's approach, or rejected it altogether. Unlike LDF, A. T. Walden and the Atlanta pragmatists believed in the divisibility of political and social rights. Before 1960, they plainly did not overutilize litigation as a tool of social change. Len Holt, the movement lawyer, rejected LDF's primary emphasis on the courtroom, and its focus on school desegregation. So did SNCC. The same was true of Howard Moore, both when he collaborated with SNCC's Atlanta Project, as it organized Atlanta's ghettos, and when he litigated the Atlanta school desegregation case despite deep misgivings about LDF's remedial priorities. A lawyer's fidelity and approach to constitutional litigation existed along a spectrum, and could change over time.

Despite the law's undeniably powerful influence, a diverse array of black Atlantans did not, then, idealize or fixate upon the courts or civil rights lawyers—as much political science and constitutional commentary on the relationship between courts and social change movements would presume. More often than not, they did the opposite. The activists portrayed here were skeptical of the courts and the judges who presided over them. On the ground, political activists—ranging from older Atlanta pragmatists to the youthful idealists of SNCC and COAHR and lawyers such as Len Holt—mobilized outside of the courts in part to avoid the limitations they perceived in civil rights litigation. Law's categories did not define them.[7]

Yet, they did not turn away from the Constitution as a source of inspiration. Even as community activists were skeptical of law and the courts, they sought to leverage the discourse of rights in the pursuit of racial justice. Local activists did not measure racial progress in terms of litigation successes and failures. Under the counsel of lawyer-activists such as Holt, they sought to use the law to their advantage regardless of whether their claims prevailed in court. Activists attached great symbolic significance to the law, and seized political opportunities created by litigation and the language of the law. In their hands, courtroom defeats became pivot points for new strategies and tactics that sometimes yielded advances outside of the courts. Small political victories that were insignificant to lawyers sometimes mattered greatly to community activists. In the end, how the law played out in local context often bore little relationship to how it had played out in court rulings.[8]

Hence, it is scholars, not the historical actors, who fixate upon the Court and certain classes of lawyers as agents of change. The insights that scholars offer about law and social change inevitably grow out of the methodologies and subjects of inquiry we choose. Ultimately, however, to understand law and social change fully, we must closely study how social movements actually evolved over time in real communities. There should be no grand, absolutist theories about courts, lawyers, and social change.

When we remember the past in a way that makes the activism of this wider collection of lawyers and activists visible, it makes a crucial difference in how we view both the past and the world today. It is the difference between seeing and not seeing possibilities, avenues, and tools for change.

While intraracial conflict has been a theme throughout this book, its bottom-up view of Atlanta's civil rights history has revealed a remarkable point of convergence among lawyers and activists for racial change. They seldom gave high priority to the concerns of the black working class. The open clash between middle-class and working-class blacks over school desegregation in Atlanta during the 1970s illustrated a well-rehearsed dynamic in Atlanta, wherein the interests of working-class blacks lost out to other priorities. Whether in the realm of schools, hospitals, public parks, housing, or War on Poverty programs, the interests of middle-class blacks trumped those of working-class blacks.

More than any other groups, SNCC and COAHR engaged the problems of the working class, but their antipoverty work in Atlanta was embryonic and intermittent. The students placed the ills of the working class on the civil rights agenda using rhetoric that indicted the "elitism" of the national NAACP, LDF, and Atlanta pragmatists. Thereafter, they attempted to prioritize the material deprivation of the working class. They demanded fair employment practices at segregated businesses, brought attention to substandard housing conditions, and backed striking laborers. The short-lived Atlanta Project fought slum housing and proposed to do much more in the future.

However, SNCC, whether in Atlanta or elsewhere, did not realize success with respect to its antipoverty initiatives on the scale that it hoped. Without a doubt, white resistance and repression limited what SNCC could achieve for the black working class; so did economic structures beyond its control. But SNCC also fell short of its goals for organizing the working class as a result of factors internal to the organization. It developed projects devoted to a number of issues important to African Americans, such as public accommodations desegregation and voting rights. By contrast, the organization never devoted exclusive and sustained effort to the issues of employment, labor, or welfare rights, despite keen awareness of desperate need in poor black communities. This can be explained partly by SNCC's frayed relations with some of the same poor people whom it had viewed as its primary constituency. Such a rupture occurred in Atlanta's ghettos in 1966, when residents of Dixie Hills asked SNCC's Atlanta Project to leave their neighborhood.[9]

Veteran leaders of SNCC, such as James Forman and Julian Bond, conceded that it fell short of its ambitious goals in the economic sphere. By 1966, Forman observed, "class conflict among blacks had sharpened acutely," even within SNCC. Some college-educated SNCC workers "showed their disdain" toward working-class blacks. In Forman's estimation, the "trend toward middle-class elitism" inhibited SNCC's ability to work closely with the unemployed and with working-class people. To Forman, Bill Ware and other black separatists in SNCC's Atlanta Project personified this destructive turn of events. Julian Bond, who had tense relations with the Atlanta Project, agreed with Forman's analysis. "In spite of our rhetoric," he said, "we never organized people [economically] for the long run and that's a big failure of ours." With SNCC in decline, traditional civil rights organizations—which many in SNCC had accused of being too politically conservative and legalistic—gained greater influence. In the debate over school desegregation in Atlanta during the 1970s, when impoverished blacks complained about the quality of local leadership, SNCC had no presence.[10]

Meanwhile, LDF did champion school desegregation, a position supported by some poor blacks. Yet, these lawyers' support for *Brown* did not translate into close relationships with the LDF's working-class clients, or any class of clients. The lawyers never framed the conflagration over the compromise settlement of the Atlanta school desegregation case in explicitly class-based terms. In fact, LDF proceeded as if the world of constitutional law and the world of local politics existed in separate universes. "The Constitution is not subject to plebiscite," insisted director-counsel Jack Greenberg. Elizabeth Rindskopf, one of LDF's local attorneys, agreed. She responded to the factions that had developed in Atlanta over the compromise with the same formulation: "What the constituency wants…is less important than what the Constitution requires. We don't want to put the Constitution to a plebiscite." Howard Moore, the former attorney for SNCC who had been so solicitous of the autonomy and dignity of student demonstrators during the 1960s, echoed the views of Greenberg and Rindskopf. The presiding judges in *Calhoun v. Cook*—no populists themselves—even chastised Moore for his reluctance to bring his clients into the courtroom. National NAACP counsel Nathaniel Jones had been similarly resistant to client voice. *Brown* was not subject to "local option," he insisted. For these litigators, the messy details of local people's interests and preferences were not things with which courts and lawyers could or should be preoccupied. Yet, those messy details—the complexities of race and class in Atlanta—overwhelmed LDF's case.[11]

The vexing resolution of the Atlanta school desegregation case symbolized all that the legal and direct action strands of the civil rights movement had, and had not, accomplished in America by the 1970s. The dream of black political and economic power, nurtured by A. T. Walden and other black elites, appeared within reach of the black middle class. Atlanta had sent a black man to Congress. Blacks laid claim to several seats in the state legislature, to equal power on the city council, to a majority on the school board, and to the mayoralty. Blacks headed the Board of Education and the superintendent's office. Black teachers held 62 percent of the jobs in the city school system in 1973. Blacks who belonged to the "civil rights network," as congressman Andrew Young called it, had parlayed their connections into positions in government and business. On the strength of black political power and accounts of good race relations, coupled with an economic boom, Atlanta advertised itself as a "mecca" for African Americans. The black-themed popular magazines *Essence* and *Ebony*, printed stories proclaiming that Atlanta provided an ideal environment for black achievement and advancement.[12]

The goal of black access to electoral politics and black representation had indeed been realized, but a pressing question remained: What substantive dividends would this power yield, and for whom? Now, as ever, blacks intent on operating as an effective voting bloc had to define their objectives. How would agendas be set? And what role would whites play in the process? The compromises required in the legislative process would yield winners and losers. How would black majorities determine the losers? Would those with the least status—blacks living in poverty—continue to be neglected when public policy was made? Would black politicians reshape the political process itself to encourage increased voter participation, particularly by blacks? After all, the right to vote was one thing; getting voters to the polls to exercise that right was quite another; and maintaining voters' interest and investment in politics yet another. As the aftermath of the Atlanta school litigation settlement itself confirmed, the black community would not be completely transformed by mere formal political equality, same-race electoral representation, or same-race administrative control of local institutions. The era following passage of the Voting Rights Act signaled the opening of new fronts in the battle over inequality.[13]

The experience of African Americans in Atlanta illustrates the point. Atlanta's new black majority did not prove a "mecca" for all blacks. Like America, generally, the city's political economy functioned best for those who had achieved middle-class status. Or, as Julian Bond once conceded: "[Atlanta] is the best place [for blacks] in the United States if you're middle-class and have a college degree, but if you're poor, it's just like Birmingham, Jackson or any other place." Same-race political leadership did not cure the ills of the city's African-American communities—not their underachieving schools, not their overcrowded and substandard housing, not their inadequate health care, not their rising violent crime rate, or their decaying infrastructure. These conditions persisted despite attempts by some members of the city council, the educational bureaucracy, and the mayor's office to address the problems.[14]

Numerous factors—including deindustrialization, globalization, and other forces far beyond the control of local leaders—accounted for many of the struggles within Atlanta's African-American communities. But whites' ability to exercise considerable power despite the black majority in government was especially critical. Whites had moved out of Atlanta in large numbers, undermining the tax base for schools and services. Even so, white majorities—suburbanites, state and federal legislators, and business owners, domestic and international—retained tremendous power over urban Atlanta. In many instances, these white majorities outside Atlanta's city limits had far more of an impact on urban policy than local black officials. And, just as blacks gained political power in Atlanta, the disadvantage of the working-class and poor became more entrenched. The boundaries of the ghettos, where poor blacks lived physically separated not only from whites of all social classes but also from many middle-class blacks, hardened. Housing shortages increased, and housing discrimination remained common. Residential segregation contributed to black underemployment, as economic expansion tended to occur in faraway suburbs. Rates of joblessness and income inequality among blacks in the metropolitan area increased.[15]

Simultaneously Atlanta's middle-class blacks reaped many of the benefits of the civil rights movement and black power in local government. Black entrepreneurs prospered, due in no small part to their expanded access to contracting opportunities made available during the administration of Mayor Maynard Jackson. Jackson boasted of creating "Maynard's millionaires" during his first years in office—twenty blacks who owed their new-found wealth to his aggressive affirmative action policies. Jackson's policies became a nationwide model (until cities scaled back such programs after adverse Supreme Court decisions). The black middle class also expanded through greater representation in civil service positions during Jackson's administration. Blacks gained high-profile positions as executives at major Atlanta-based companies. Many blacks moved to the suburbs. The black middle class had arrived, but the black poor had—once again—been left behind.[16]

This sobering reality left veteran activist Ethel Mae Mathews, a champion of working-class blacks, weary. In 2000, at the dawn of the twenty-first century, Mathews reflected on her years in the movement and the contemporary situation. She did not like what she saw. She could not count on middle-class blacks who had achieved lofty governmental positions to be caretakers of her interests and of those of her neighbors and friends. "We wasn't just talking about we were sold out by the Board of Education," she said, recalling the settlement of the Atlanta school desegregation case. "We being sold out now. Delete comma!" In Mathews's view, many of those who profess to want change "don't care nothing about poor people." "If they had poor people at heart, they could make it better," she asserted. Five decades after the passage of the Civil Rights and Voting Rights Act, Mathews continued to seek empathy and humane policies from those whom she perceived as callous decision-makers. She criticized powerful people of all colors, but leveled her most searing critique at Atlanta's black leaders. "Our own color exploit us," she said, "that's what makes it so sad and so bad." "They forget about you, they forget about who they are and where they come from, and who helped them get where they is."[17]

For better or worse, Atlanta's story is also a national story. Its racial dynamics looked much like those in many other cities, where even black middle-class leaders who did "care" found their capacity to create change constrained. The stark differences in the experiences of Atlanta's black middle and working class during the 1970s reflected a pattern apparent in urban centers across the country. Blacks celebrated the election of same-race representatives in local and state government, and their perception of government improved. Then, disappointment set in, as blacks learned that black control did not necessarily yield better outcomes for black constituents, the neediest ones in particular. The political ascendancy of African Americans in cities across America, in and of itself, did not seem to undo the material deprivation, social isolation, and discrimination experienced by the black poor. Moreover, the black middle class, and its newfound economic and political power, remained precarious as well. Racial disadvantage persisted for African Americans as a whole. And racial disadvantage overlaid with class disadvantage proved a stubborn reality for a disproportionate number of blacks.[18]

New waves of social change lawyers and social activists who are concerned about persistent racial inequality now face these daunting circumstances. As they confront challenges new and old, they should appreciate that, in the words of pragmatist A. T. Walden, the "struggles of black folk in America are only a counterpart of the fight for disadvantaged people everywhere for…human dignity." Walden—who always chose his words carefully and was never prone to expansive rhetoric—made that observation in 1964. The black struggle for equality is surely still bound up today with the fates of others—the working class, other people of color, religious and sexual minorities, and all people who live on the margins of American society.[19]

At the same time, the struggles over equality, representation, and class, discussed here in the context of the local and national struggles for civil rights, are endemic to all social movements. The women's movement frequently has been highly stratified along lines of class and race. A vocal subgroup of feminists has repeatedly demanded that leaders of the women's movement prioritize matters that affect the lives of working women—issues such the living wage, affordable childcare, adequate healthcare. Equally prevalent in social movements is the question of how lawyers and other experts can best relate to and help communities struggling for social justice. During the 1960s, the women's movement divided when liberal feminists preferred legal strategies, while radicals preferred disruptive tactics. The proper role of lawyers also has been a pressing issue in the gay, lesbian, and transgender rights movement, as it split over whether to pursue a legal right to same-sex marriage. The same has been true within the movement for children with disabilities, as it has struggled to figure out whether inclusion or separation is more consistent with equality education under law.[20]

Perhaps the story of civil rights struggles in Atlanta can provide lessons—or, at the least, cautionary tales—helpful to advocates who are pursuing social justice in contexts well beyond race. One lesson is as inescapable as it may be difficult to implement in practice: Movements should listen to dissenters and should be transformed by thoughtful critiques, particularly those derived from on-the-ground experiences. The leadership should alter organizational structures and strategies to respond to dissenters' concerns, whether about exclusionary processes or substantive goals. Class-based interests and inequities have been a constant source of dissent within movements for social change. It is far from clear, however, that class-based critiques of leadership and priorities have often transformed movements. One could ask, for example, whether leading civil rights organizations have considered matters that disproportionately impact working-class and poor people of color—the isolation of the ghetto, testing and ability grouping policies that lead to dead-end curricula and jobs, chronic unemployment, over-criminalization and "prison overpopulation"— pressing priorities. Meanwhile, it is intriguing to note that class-based critiques span social movements and thus, theoretically at least, present opportunities for coalition-building across barriers of color and gender.[21]

Those keen to make social change can learn to appreciate dissent and, consequently, perhaps learn much from Walden's pragmatic style of lawyering. Walden valued tactical diversity. He believed that the fight for racial justice needed to be waged on many fronts: the ballot box, the courtroom, and the negotiating table. True, he was skeptical of direct action, but his pursuit of racial justice reflected the value he placed on flexibility and strategic choices. Walden's pragmatism grew out of his belief that blacks needed safe social and cultural spaces and that community-based institutions needed a thriving local economy to flourish. The LDF's commitment to integration undermined Walden's pragmatic aspirations for the local community. Walden's own elitism, of course, also marred his conception of community; even as LDF imposed its remedial objectives on Atlanta, Walden and Atlanta's elites imposed their own goals on other members of the local community.

The lawyers of the LDF rightly recognized that self-interested, local leaders could imperil their agenda. Nevertheless, the goal of local autonomy is a worthy aspiration. The question is whether, and under what conditions, public interest lawyers who favor litigation as a tool of advocacy can preserve and enhance community institutions and community independence. National organizations must seek to collaborate with local organizations in ways that both maximize the scale, expertise, and agenda-setting capacities of the national-level organizations, and that promote local knowledge and leadership.

Change agents also can learn much from the concept of movement lawyering. Indeed, the idea may usefully address some of the questions raised above about how national and local organizations can interact most effectively. Communal values and participatory decision-making processes distinguish movement lawyering from other types of advocacy. For the movement lawyer, the connection to community increases the likelihood of accountability. Rather than first identifying a goal and then rallying the community to the cause, the movement lawyer sets an agenda and determines goals only through collaboration with local communities and organizations. In the case of Len Holt, his connection to local people inspired citizens to engage and mobilize around problems. He employed a wide arsenal of weapons as a result of his experiences on the ground: direct action, pickets, and unconventional forms of litigation. Yet, Holt's communal values did not negate his technical lawyering ability. Quite the opposite was true. He litigated a dizzying number of cases, across many subject areas, in numerous venues, and even devised new procedural mechanisms and legal claims as he struggled to address his clients' needs.[22]

The movement lawyering model was not, of course, without its defects. Questions of scale arose. Holt's vision of intensive work in local communities surpassed his manpower. Participatory modes of lawyering predicated on community engagement and organizing, a "slow, respectful" approach to political empowerment, required interpersonal skills that some legal professionals possess or can cultivate, but others do not or cannot. One can also question how far a lawyer could or should go in actualizing a lay community's desires. Nor did movement lawyering remove the problem of hierarchy in social relationships that can beset any problem-solving approach, although it did at least openly engage the matter.[23]

Movement lawyering also does not guarantee particular substantive outcomes. But a major part of movement lawyering's appeal is the process it generates. The legal culture that movement lawyers created was malleable. It was open to goals and approaches developed by local citizens out of the clash of ideas and political dissensus. Indeed, the very point of movement lawyering is to inspire a more vibrant political process through open exchanges about the meaning of equality, rights, legal norms, and the utility of litigation and other forms of social action. This is perhaps the greatest contribution a movement lawyer can make—helping people see themselves as agents of change, and thus helping society avoid the danger of, as Dr. King warned, "an anemic democracy."[24]

# APPENDIX

TABLE 2.1 PERCENTAGE OF AFRICAN-AMERICAN VOTERS, ATLANTA, 1945–1973

| Date | Total number registered | Percentage of electorate |
| --- | --- | --- |
| 1945 | 3,000 | 4.0 |
| 1946 (February) | 6,876 | 8.3 |
| 1946 (June) | 21,244 | 27.2 |
| 1952 | 22,300 | 25.8 |
| 1956 | 23,440 | 27.0 |
| 1958 | 27,432 | 25.3 |
| 1960 | 34,393 | 29.5 |
| 1961 | 41,469 | 28.6 |
| 1962 | 52,000 | 34.0 |
| 1966 | 64,285 | 35.8 |
| 1973 | 101,091 | 49.0 |

*Source*: Compiled from Jack Walker, "Negro Voting in Atlanta: 1953–1961," *Phylon* 24 (1964): 380; Bayor, *Race and the Shaping*, 18.

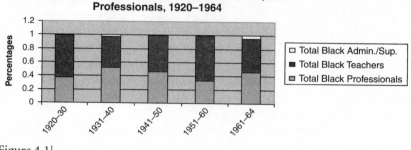

Figure 4.1[1]

[1] Based on data from the U.S. Census Bureau and the Georgia Department of Education; U.S. Bureau of the Census. *Fourteenth Census of the United States Taken in the Year 1920*, vol. 4, *Population 1920, Occupations*. Washington, DC: GPO, 1923; U.S. Bureau of the Census. *Fifteenth Census of the United States: 1930, Population*, vol. 4, *Occupations, By States*. Washington, DC: GPO, 1933); U.S. Bureau of the Census. *Sixteenth Census of the United States: 1940, Population*, vol. 3, *The Labor Force*, part 2, *Alabama-Indiana*. Washington, DC: GPO, 1943; U.S. Bureau of the Census. *Census of Population: 1950*, vol. 2, *Characteristics of the Population*, part 11, *Georgia*. Washington, DC: GPO, 1952; U.S. Bureau of the Census, "Occupation of the Experienced Civilian Labor Force by Color, of the Employed by Race and Class of Worker, And of Persons Not in Labor Force with Work Experience, by Sex, for the State and for Standard Metropolitan Statistical Areas of 250,000 or More: 1960," *Census of Population: 1960*, vol. 1, *Characteristics of the Population*, part 12, *Georgia* (Washington, DC: GPO, 1963), 528–33, table 122; Georgia Department of Education. *Annual Reports of the Department of Education to the General Assembly of the State of Georgia*. Atlanta: 1920–1964. The data for the 1940s excludes three years during World War II, when the Georgia Department of Education did not compile the relevant statistics. The data for the 1960s ends at 1964, when the Georgia Department of Education ceased maintaining relevant statistics disaggregated by race.

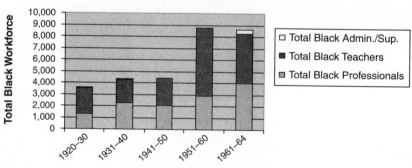

Figure 4.2

TABLE 4.1  AVERAGE PER PUPIL EXPENDITURES BY RACE, ATLANTA,
1943–1947

| School year | Average expenditure per white pupil | Average expenditure per black pupil | White advantage per pupil |
|---|---|---|---|
| 1943–44 | $119.61 | $44.11 | $75.50 |
| 1944–45 | $124.00 | $47.78 | $76.22 |
| 1945–46 | $128.53 | $51.92 | $76.61 |
| 1946–47 | $139.73 | $59.88 | $79.85 |

*Source*: Based on"A Supplemental Report on Public School Facilities for Negroes, Atlanta, Georgia, 1948," Atlanta Urban League Papers, box 23, f. 14.

# Acknowledgments

This project began as a dissertation under the direction of William Chafe at Duke University. Bill introduced me to the study of social movements and to the bottom-up methodological approach to writing history. He then provided a wonderful model of such scholarship in his own landmark community study of civil rights-era Greensboro. I am grateful to him and to Charles Payne, the author of a stunning history of the struggle for civil rights in Mississippi, for teaching me how to be an historian of the movement. Ray Gavins, Steven Lawson, Sydney Nathans, and Nancy Hewitt also were important teachers at Duke.

My education at Yale Law School shaped me as a legal scholar and influenced my thinking about the themes in this work. Reva Siegel, the first brilliant woman legal scholar whom I ever observed, set me on my way. I am a law professor largely because Reva invited me to work as her research assistant, encouraged my intellectual interests, and sponsored my entrée into legal academia. Owen Fiss's passionate teaching about law, equality, and the Warren Court fired a lot of my initial thinking about the relationship between law and social change. Conversations with Paul Gewirtz about constitutional law and with Burke Marshall about the Kennedy administration's response to the movement strengthened my commitment to a bottom-up analysis of the law.

After I graduated from law school, I had the distinct pleasure of clerking for, and learning about lawyers and the civil rights movement from, the Honorable Robert L. Carter. Judge Carter, a lead counsel on *Brown v. Board of Education* and the former general counsel of the NAACP, mentored me. The judge encouraged the critical consciousness about the legal history of the movement that is at the heart of this work. I am indebted to him.

Two fellowships supported the writing of this book. First, as a Charles Hamilton Houston Fellow at Harvard Law School, I met a number of people who provided generous support for the project over time. They include Randall

447

Kennedy, the faculty sponsor of the fellows and a leading scholar of race and the law. I am grateful to Randy for his stewardship during that year. He also offered support thereafter, whether through a helpful note sent to me or a good word passed along to others. I also met Lani Guinier, one of the academy's most creative scholars, during that fellowship year. Happily, Lani took an interest in my work and offered penetrating comments on manuscript drafts. Most important, Lani modeled excellence. When I was the Houston Fellow, Ken Mack, then the Reginald Lewis Fellow, occupied the office across the hallway and provided needed camaraderie. Since that time, Ken has been a thoughtful reader of my work. His terrific scholarship and commentary on this manuscript made it far better.

Second, as a Samuel I. Golieb Fellow in Legal History at New York University School of Law, Bill Nelson welcomed me into the guild of legal historians. I am grateful for Bill's support early in my career. I presented initial chapters of this book at the colloquium and received constructive criticism from Bill, John Phillip Reid, and many others. My participation in the rituals of the Golieb colloquium continued to shape my thinking about this project and my professional identity long after I left the NYU campus.

It is a privilege to work at the University of Virginia, where I enjoy collegial relationships with a supportive and highly engaged faculty. I will always be grateful to my former dean, John Jeffries, who recruited me to UVA, the intellectual home at which my work on this project flourished. I am equally grateful to my current dean, Paul Mahoney, who continued to support my work on civil rights and to recognize my contributions to the law school. I also wish to express gratitude to colleagues Ken Abraham, Lillian Bevier, Vince Blasi, Barry Cushman, Kim Forde-Mazrui, Liz Magill, Julia Mahoney, Charles McCurdy, Dan Ortiz, Mildred Robinson, George Rutherglen, Jim Ryan, Rich Schragger, Paul Stephan, Larry Walker, Ted White, and George Yin. All provided helpful comments on drafts or otherwise offered support for this project. Three colleagues aided me in ways that merit special emphasis. Anne Coughlin gave me the gift of friendship when I most needed it; her visits, with home-baked bread in hand, helped me at a difficult juncture. Risa Goluboff read drafts and provided comments that helped me clarify my conceptual framework. Most important, Risa, an impressive scholar of civil rights and labor, provided intellectual synergy that affirmed my intellectual agenda. Finally, Mike Klarman, my former colleague, offered a tremendous level of support as I worked on this project. Mike read the book from cover to cover and offered countless pages of incisive comments. His invaluable feedback helped me sharpen my analysis of black agency in the civil rights movement. Remarkably, Mike supported this project and offered commentary without imposing his own intellectual agenda, although my work is in conversation with his eminent scholarship.

Julian Bond, the co-founder of the Student Non-Violent Coordinating Committee, former chairman of the NAACP, and professor of history at UVA, graciously provided first-hand knowledge about many subjects discussed in this work. In addition to supplying numerous records, photographs, and other resources, he agreed to an interview, read my work, and connected me to veterans of the civil rights movement. I located Howard Moore, Jr. and Len Holt, two figures who made crucial contributions to my study, through Julian. In addition, Julian invited me to attend SNCC's fiftieth anniversary conference at Shaw University. There, I met numerous veterans of the movement and listened to them, as they shared memories of the movement. For a civil rights historian, this was the opportunity of a lifetime. I am profoundly grateful to Julian for his cooperation with this project—support given without any attempt to exert editorial influence. I am grateful to all whom I interviewed for this project, as well. Special thanks to the Gate City Bar Association.

I began my career in law teaching at Washington University, St. Louis, where two deans, Joel Seligman and Kent Syverud, liberally supported this project. The deans provided a full-time research assistant for an entire year to help me move the project forward. On the faculty, my colleagues Susan Appleton, Chris Bracey, Lee Epstein, Pauline Kim, David Konig , and Ted Ruger provided helpful comments.

I also thank the following scholars at other universities who provided helpful commentary on drafts of this book: Mark Tushnet, whose scholarship laid the foundation for me and all legal historians of the civil rights movement, Regina Austin, Richard Brooks, Susan Carle, Mary Dudziak, Sally Gordon, Winston Grady-Willis, Alton Hornsby, Jr., Darren Hutchinson, David Kairys, Laura Kalman, Kevin Kruse, Matt Lassiter, Peter Lau, Sophia Lee, Serena Mayeri, Gary Orfield, Chris Schmidt, Michael Seidman, and Tom Sugre, as well as anonymous readers for OUP. Special thanks to Claire Priest.

The work of numerous archivists, librarians, and research assistants was crucial throughout this project. Archivists at Emory University, the Atlanta History Center, the Martin Luther King Jr. Center for Non-Violent Social Change, the University of Virginia, the Auburn Avenue Research Library, Georgia State University, Atlanta Public School Archives, Howard University, the Clark-Atlanta University Center, the National Archives and Records Center, Smith College, and the Library of Congress all supported this project. The law librarians at UVA are the best in the business. They already know how much I depend on all of them for my livelihood. I wish to acknowledge, in particular, Kent Olson, Leslie Ashbrook, Jon Ashley, Ben Doherty, Kristin Glover, Xinh Luu, and Amy Wharton for providing especially prodigious assistance. Research assistance from Rebecca Barnes, Tiffany Marshall

Graves, Kelsey Hazzard, Aaron Kleinman, Meghan Largent, Tiffany Nichols, Ben Norris, Rajat Rana, Sonya Reddy, Renada Rutmanis, Andrew Seidman, Joe Tavery, Sarah White, Amy Woolard, Jin Yan, and Herbert Timothy Lovelace also made this work possible. The administrative assistance of Delores Clatterbuck, Karen Spradlin, and Carol Wibbenmeyer was invaluable.

Dave McBride, my editor at Oxford University Press, has been ideal. I could not have asked for greater enthusiasm and care during the publication process. Thanks also to OUP's Alexandra Dauler, Marc Schneider, Alina Smyslova, and numerous others at the press who brought this work together. Thanks to Lynn Lightfoot for her freelance editorial assistance. Bravo to Christy Fletcher for her stewardship of this project.

I am grateful to Sarah Buckalew for the many ways in which she helped my family and me over the past three years. Thanks also to Shirley Heatwole for her support.

Thanks to my friends, Kelli Station Phillips and Kim West-Faulcon, for continued sisterhood over many years. You grounded me as I worked on this project.

My parents, Willie J. and Lillie C. Brown, the first historians of race in my life, provided the seeds of inspiration that eventually flowered into this book. I am eternally grateful to them for their love and for their willingness to share their stories about life under Jim Crow in South Carolina: the dilapidated schools, the tenant farming, the political powerlessness, the "families black and white." These history lessons triggered much of my interest in questions of race, class, and social mobility. My parents' varied experiences of segregated schools and the teachers who taught in them helped me better understand a prominent figure in this book, A. T. Walden, a man whose choices I initially found baffling. In addition to providing these specific forms of help, my parents reared me in a manner that facilitated my present endeavors. They encouraged my love of learning, instilled confidence, demanded discipline, and expected the best from me every single time, all of which enabled me to rise above obstacles and find higher ground in the world. For all of these things and more, I dedicate this book to them.

The affection and support of my siblings, Faith and Marcus, also proved crucial to my ability to write this book. Faith, always fabulous, and now British, encouraged me at just the right moments, and Marcus shared my ambitions. I dedicate chapter 9 to the memory of my brother, a gentle and honorable man, a seeker of opportunity and peace.

I also am grateful to my grandmother, Edna Williams, for her loving care, and to my grandfather, Squire Williams, Jr., a fount of wisdom who passed along knowledge that aided my understanding of America's racial history.

Beyond that, granddad passed along his love of the land and gardening, a pursuit that now sustains my spirit and clears my mind for scholarship.

Most of all, I am grateful to my husband, Danny, who has been my partner and who has taken care of me through all of these years. His love sustained me throughout my work on this project. He skillfully edited countless drafts, often setting aside his own work to read mine. Through the gift of laughter, he bucked me up when my energy flagged. He arranged for our family to take adventures to lovely parts of the world for periods of renewal—respites that I needed to carry on with this work. He also supported my work by preparing our family delicious meals and caring for our sons. In short, my achievement is his, as well. In many ways, Danny models the example set by his late father, Lawrence M. Nagin, a loving supporter of me and all of my endeavors. Larry's guidance, and the support of my mother-in-law, Sherrie, helped me see this project through to the end.

Finally, I am grateful to my sons, Julius and Avishai, whose hugs, smiles, and inquiring minds energized me during the writing process. Julius—seeing me hunched over at my computer with stacks of files and documents at my side—often asked me what the book had to say and why it mattered. Here, at the end of the line, I now see that I might have justified my work by explaining that, ultimately, I wrote this book for him and his brother. I hope that one day Julius and Avishai will read *Courage to Dissent* and find in it inspiration to help repair the world.

# NOTES

## Introduction

1. A. T. Walden, "If I Were Young Today," *Ebony*, June 1963, 74.

2. Ibid.

3. The NAACP formally established its legal arm in 1939, as a successor to its national legal committee. The NAACP and LDF became separate legal entities in 1957. In this text, when referring to the period before 1957, I use the terms "NAACP lawyers" and "LDF" interchangeably and assume a unified agenda except when otherwise noted. The term "NAACP" refers to the national organization, as opposed to the branches. In this text, when I mean to reference the local branch, I refer to the Atlanta branch, the NAACP branch, or the local NAACP. On the history of the NAACP, see Kellogg, *NAACP*, 31–45. On the history of the NAACP legal committee and the NAACP Legal Defense Fund, and their relationships to the NAACP, see Tushnet, *NAACP's Legal Strategy*, 29–32, 55, 100; McNeil, *Groundwork*, 131–36, 140–41, 152, 155, 198–99, 216–18.

4. Professor Mark Tushnet, the distinguished constitutional scholar and historian, characterizes the national NAACP's litigation approach as pragmatic. See Tushnet, *NAACP's Legal Strategy*, 115; see also Tushnet, "Politics of Equality," 884–903. Tushnet's characterization refers to the period prior to 1950, *before* the organization's midyear decision to attack segregation frontally. The lawyers were pragmatic, or experimental, in Tushnet's meaning, because their legal pleadings left open the possibility that equalization, or compliance with *Plessy*, was an acceptable remedy for inequality. I do not challenge Tushnet's characterization of NAACP lawyers. Period. However, in this book I use the term "pragmatic" in a broader sense than Tushnet, and I focus on different actors. My characterization goes beyond the parameters of national legal strategy to include social, political, and cultural ideas that took shape apart from law at the local level. In using the term "pragmatic," I mean efforts to strike a balance between practical concerns and ideals; these ideals did not necessarily include desegregation, but sometimes did. This book shows black leaders in Atlanta embracing such a targeted approach to civil rights that did not revolve around integration *before and after* 1950, well after the national NAACP's strategy became focused on integration in schools and other areas as the path to black freedom. (This book does not mean to engage in a discussion of philosophical or legal pragmatism.)

5. For scholarly accounts that reflect the view that Walden failed to meet the bar of activism set by the national NAACP and LDF, see Tuck, *Beyond Atlanta*, 64–65, 90–92, 98; Ferguson, *Black Politics*, 64, 148; ibid. at 149 (characterizing Walden as "dictatorial"); see also Stone, *Regime Politics*, 53 (noting that Walden and other members of the old guard were considered Uncle Toms who had "done little but feather their own nests").

6. See Bond interview, McGill Papers; Rose and Greenya, *Black Leaders*, 25, 29, 36.

7. See *AC*, 19 Mar. 1960, 1; *AC*, 9 Mar. 1960, 1; Chafe, *Civilities and Civil Rights*, 98–109.

8. See Chafe, *Civilities and Civil Rights*, 98–109.

9. To date, the most detailed discussion of the NAACP's opposition to direct action is Arsenault, *Freedom Riders*.

10. On Marshall's view of King, see Williams, *Thurgood Marshall*, 341.

11. For the King quotes, see King, *Words of Martin Luther King*, 17, 57.

12. On Marshall's reaction to the sit-ins, see Williams, *Thurgood Marshall*, 287, 341. As I explain in chapters 6 and 7, Marshall later modified his public position on the sit-ins.

13. See Lewis, *Walking with the Wind*, 113–14.

14. Mathews interview, 9–12.

15. *ADW*, 12 July 1973, 1; 26 Jan. 1973 1.

16. Mathews and Collins quoted in Transcript of Proceedings, 28, 46–47, Calhoun v. Cook (N.D. Ga., 8 Mar. 1973), NAACP Papers, part V, box 684.

17. See Jacoby, *Someone Else's House*, 383–91.

18. Julian Bond, "Speech Concerning Black Education and the 25th Anniversary of *Brown v. the Board of Education*, Topeka, Kansas," TD, Bond Papers, series I, box 7, f. 11.

19. See Lewis, *Walking with the Wind*, 346–47. On the role of civil rights litigation and interest groups in advancing black equality, see, for example, *NAACP v. Button*, 371 U.S. 415 (1963); Carle, "From *Buchanan* to *Button*"; On voting rights theory and practice, see Guinier, "Triumph of Tokenism," and chapter 9.

20. Quoted in *AC*, 28 Mar. 1973, 11–B.

21. On rivalries among civil rights organizations and debates about equality in the period prior to World War II, see Lewis, *W. E. B. Du Bois*, 2:299–301, 324, 333–35, 339–40, 344–48, 535–40; Harris, "Negro and Economic Radicalism," 130–39; Frazier, *Black Bourgeoisie*; Hare, *Black Anglo-Saxons*; Haines, *Black Radicals*, 18–21; White, *Man Called White*, 42–44, 120–24, 139–43, 166–73, 186–94; Wilkins, *Standing Fast*, 128–36; Kellogg, *NAACP*, 155–275.

22. The pioneering, first-generation scholarship on the NAACP upon which this work builds includes Tushnet, *NAACP's Legal Strategy*; Kluger, *Simple Justice*; Tushnet, *Making Civil Rights Law*; Kellogg, *NAACP*; McNeil, *Groundwork*; Meier and Rudwick, "Attorneys Black and White," 913–46; Meier and Bracey, "NAACP as a Reform Movement," 3–30. See also Kennedy, "Martin Luther King's Constitution" and two important recent accounts of NAACP by Sullivan, *Lift Every Voice*, and Jonas, *Freedom's Sword*. In addition, see recent legal history scholarship on civil rights lawyers in the era before

*Brown*: Goluboff, *Lost Promise*; Mack, "Rethinking Civil Rights Lawyering"; Mack, "Law and Mass Politics," discussed below.

23. I do not mean to suggest that dissensus was or should be viewed as the dominant force in civil rights politics; civil rights organizations shared the common goal of ending racial inequality and often engaged in cooperative endeavors. Nor do I posit that dissensus, when it occurred, always was a productive force in the movement. Rather, I suggest that intraracial conflict, *especially between lawyers and nonlawyers*, was an important phenomenon and central to this particular project's analysis. My perspective has been formed in reaction to scholarship on relationships between "radicals" or "militants" and "conservatives" or "accommodationists" in the civil rights movement, including Haines, *Black Radicals*; Walker, "Functions of Disunity"; Meier and Rudwick, "The Black Revolt of the 1960s," in *From Plantation to Ghetto*, 271–313; Meier, "Negro Protest Movements and Organizations."

Recent works have challenged the perception, popularized by popular media, that black power was a wholly deviant strain in the movement. See Joseph, *Waiting 'til the Midnight Hour*; Joseph, *Black Power Movement*; Countryman, *Up South*. Skeptics of black power within the civil rights movement itself fostered this perception. "It is only with the coming of the term 'black power,'" admonished Dr. King, "that these problems [division] in the civil rights movement came into being." Before black power, the NAACP's Roy Wilkins insisted, African Americans had been united in pursuit of a single goal—integration. Now, rash black youths had killed the dream. See USN&WR, 18 July 1966, 31–34.

24. Pioneering social histories of the civil rights movement include Chafe, *Civilities and Civil Rights*; Norrell, *Reaping the Whirlwind*; Colburn, *Racial Change and Community Crisis*; see also the influential work by sociologist Aldon D. Morris, *Origins of the Civil Rights Movement*. Excellent recent social histories of the movement include Countryman, *Up South*; Self, *American Babylon*; Biondi, *To Stand and Fight*; MacLean, *Freedom Is Not Enough*; Fairclough, *Race and Democracy*; Sugrue, *Sweet Land of Liberty*; Eskew, *But for Birmingham*; Payne, *I've Got the Light*; Arsenault, *Freedom Riders*; Thornton, *Dividing Lines*. For an excellent recent collection of essays that discusses relationships between the national NAACP and local branches, see Verney and Sartain, *Long Is the Way and Hard*; see also Payne, *I've Got the Light*; Eskew, *But for Birmingham*. In addition, see recent urban history studies that focus on grassroots, white counter-movements against the struggle for black advancement in the South and beyond. Lassiter, *Silent Majority*; Kruse, *White Flight*; Sugrue, *Origins of the Urban Crisis*. As noted above, below, and in pertinent substantive chapters, I build on Professor Tushnet's foundational organizational history of the NAACP and biographies of Thurgood Marshall. This work's class analysis builds on the social histories mentioned above as well as works in other disciplines, including Wilson, Declining Significance and The Truly Disadvantaged.

25. See Hall, "Long Civil Rights Movement."

26. Scholars have questioned whether a liberal vision of civil rights ever did, or ever should have, dominated legal practice. See Mack, "Rethinking Civil Rights Lawyering"; Mack, "Law and Mass Politics," 37–62; Goluboff, *Lost Promise*. These legal histories complicate the liberal legal narrative about the NAACP and its legal strategy by arguing that

lawyers used other legal strategies in the era before *Brown*. Mack recovers the history of Marxist, voluntarist, and other strategies outside of the liberal-legal tradition that black lawyers pursued during the 1920s and 1930s. Goluboff focuses on the labor-oriented legal strategy that NAACP lawyers pursued during the 1930s and 1940s, but abandoned, she argues, as a result of *Brown*.

27. See Rosenberg, *Hollow Hope*, 39–40, 74–75, 93, 155–56, 336–43; Klarman, *From Jim Crow*, 363–442, 463–68; Scheingold, *The Politics of Rights*, 5–6; see also Tushnet, *Taking*, 135, 154–76. For alternative views of the Supreme Court's role in race relations, see Kluger, *Simple Justice*, 749–50; Tushnet, "Significance of *Brown*," 174–79, 182–83.

28. My view of the relationship between law and social change resonates with the scholarship of legal mobilization theorists who emphasize that litigation is not a zero-sum game. See McCann, *Rights at Work*, 48; McMahon and Paris, "Politics of Rights Revisited," 63–82; McCann, "Reform Litigation on Trial," 728; McCann and Silverstein, "Rethinking Law's 'Allurements,'" 261–92; Galanter, "Radiating Effects of Courts," 117–42. However, this scholarship claims far more influence and efficacy for lawyers, litigation, and the courts than I do. See Brown-Nagin, "Elites, Social Movements, and the Law," 1488–1501.

29. See Tushnet, *NAACP's Legal Strategy*, 107–11, 113–16, 138–41; Kluger, *Simple Justice*, 3, 7, 12, 70–71, 91–92, 94–95, 116, 170–72, 391–93; see also works that disregard the possibility that blacks were skeptical of the NAACP's goals, with the exception of those who naively embraced Communists or black nationalism. Kellogg, *NAACP*, 183–204, 277–90, 294; White, *Man Called White*, 262–64; see Gilmore, *Defying Dixie*, 7, 9, 19 (criticizing organization as "morally bankrupt" for its failure to pursue anything beyond making "Jim Crow work more smoothly").

30. Some scholars, implicitly or explicitly, reject the negative connotations attached to "accommodationism." See Norrell, *Up from History*; see also Mack, "Rethinking Civil Rights Lawyering," 277–99; Countryman, *Up South*, 7–8, 86–90, 118–19, 198–201; Biondi, *To Stand and Fight*, 4–5, 45–46, 172, 280–81; see generally Pritchett, *Robert Clifton Weaver*, a superb examination of the life of the first black cabinet official. Weaver's work is discussed in relation to the theme of "accommodationism" in chapter 3.

31. The quotes are from Charles Hamilton Houston and Leon A. Ransom, "The George Crawford Case: An Experiment in Social *Statesman* ship," *Nation* 139 (4 July 1934): 19; Carter, "NAACP's Legal Strategy against Segregated Education." Recent works that focus on the NAACP and emphasize its contributions to the movement include Berg, *Ticket to Freedom*; Gilbert, *Freedom's Sword*; Lau, *Democracy Rising*; see, in particular, the discussion of the democratizing impact of the NAACP's litigation in Sullivan, *Lift Every Voice*.

32. This text references numerous books and articles on the history of Atlanta in relevant, substantive chapters. Here, I note particularly important recent scholarship on the city's civil rights history: Grady-Willis, *Challenging*; Hornsby, *Black Power in Dixie*; Kruse, *White Flight*; Lassiter, *Silent Majority*. Excellent works on earlier eras include Ferguson, *Black Politics*; Dorsey, *To Build Our Lives*. These other authors' works, which approach the subject from social, political, and urban history perspectives, provided

invaluable background material and insights for my present analysis of civil rights history from a sociolegal perspective. My own earlier work on Atlanta includes Brown-Nagin, "Class Actions"; Brown-Nagin, "Race as Identity Caricature"; and Brown-Nagin, "An Historical Note on the Stigma Rationale."

33. Statement by Julian Bond, TD, SNCC Papers, 10 Jan. 1966, rl. 53, fr. 531.

## Chapter 1

1. The first two statements in the epigraph by Walden are from A. T. Walden, "If I Were Young Today," *Ebony*, June 1963, 74. The statement in the epigraph by Moore is from Moore interview by author, 4.

2. See "Pay Last Tribute to Georgia's Judge Walden," *Chicago Defender*, 10 July 1965, 3. After Walden retired from active law practice, Atlanta Mayor Ivan Allen appointed Walden an alternate municipal court judge—a bittersweet gesture. Agnew and Haden-Miller, *Atlanta and Its Lawyers*, 58. On the one hand, the appointment did make Walden the first black judge in Georgia, and as such, indicated the esteem in which whites held him. However, Walden's postretirement appointment to the municipal court, a bench that many considered far beneath a man of Walden's stature and achievements, indicated how much race limited his career. Indeed, a black editorial writer complained that had Walden been white, he would have been appointed to the Supreme Court of Georgia or to the Supreme Court of the United States. See *ADW*, 4 July 1965, 4; *AI*, 10 July 1965, 4. Walden and Dr. Miles Amos earned the distinction of being the first blacks to hold public office in Georgia since Reconstruction when they were elected members of the Democratic Executive Committee of the City of Atlanta in 1953. "A Tribute to A. T. Walden," 26 Oct. 1984, 5, Walden Papers, series II, box 2, f. 7.

3. The "gifted" quote is from Pomerantz, *Where Peachtree Meets*, 126.

4. See Article II, Constitution and Bylaws of Gate City Bar Assoc., 1948, Walden Papers, series VI, box 1, f. 7; Richard Atkinson to A. T. Walden, TLS, 3 July 1956, Walden Papers, series VI, box 1, f. 1. On the ABA's discrimination, see Auerbach, *Unequal Justice*, 65–66. On the NBA, see Smith, "Black Bar Association," 654–57; Alexander, "National Bar Association," 1–4; see also Mack, "Law and Mass Politics."

5. See "Tribute," 4–7, Walden Papers, series II, box 2, f. 7; Hine, "Black Lawyers," 38.

6. See A. T. Walden, Commencement Address, Fort Valley State College, 1964, Walden Papers, series II, box 2, f. 8.

7. See Complaint, Thomas v. Louisville & Nashville Railroad Co. (Ful. Cnty. Sup. Ct., 31 Oct. 1955), Walden Papers, series III, box 1, f. 10; A. T. Walden to John Whittaker, 19 Nov. 1958, Walden Papers, series III, box 1, f. 11. The suit was based on precedents secured by Charles Hamilton Houston in 1944, while he was in private practice. At Houston's urging, the U.S. Supreme Court held that unions designated the exclusive bargaining agent for a craft owed a duty of fair representation to all craftsmen; this duty extended to nonunion members, including those excluded on account of race. See McNeil, *Groundwork*, 156–75; Smith and Hogan, "Remembered Hero," 5–13.

8. See Du Bois, "Does the Negro Need Separate Schools?"; Du Bois, "Resigns," *Crisis* 41 (1934): 245. The linkages to Du Bois also are mentioned in chapters on voting and education. Other commentators who supported the black struggle for equality also questioned aspects of LDF's litigation campaign, including its school desegregation litigation. During the period of the Du Bois controversy, see, for example, Bunche, "Critical Analysis," 314–15 (arguing that constitutional rights "more often than not" were "illusory" and that decisions "contrary to the will of the majority cannot be enforced"); W. T. B. Williams, "Court Action."

9. See, for example, Locke, "Dilemma of Segregation" (discussing "basic dilemma" of black leaders who privileged short-term goals, including "self-interested professional ambition," over principle of "progress" inevitable as a result of litigation against racial discrimination in schools and every other public institution). Among legal and social historians, see, for example, the frameworks in the following works, all of which anchor discussions of racial struggle during this period around LDF's litigation campaign and embrace its premises: Tushnet, *NAACP's Legal Strategy*; Kluger, *Simple Justice*; Fairclough, *Race and Democracy*, 46–73; Lau, *Democracy Rising*, 10, 15–33, 187–91, 222–32; Meier and Bracey, "NAACP as a Reform Movement." On Washington's reputation, see Harlan, *Booker T. Washington*, 1:295–304. For recent scholarship challenging the view of Washington, see Norrell, *Up from History*.

10. See Hine, "Black Lawyers," 38; "Tribute," Walden Papers, series II, box 2, f. 7. Jordan's recollections are from Jordan, *Vernon Can Read!*, 33, 48, 55. For Ward's, see Daniels, *Horace T. Ward*, 25–26. On Ward's bid for admission to the university, see ibid., 6–11. For positive accounts of Walden's civil rights activism in the scholarly literature, see Smith, *Emancipation*, 198–99; Pomerantz, *Where Peachtree Meets*, 126–27; Grant, *Way It Was*, 257, 304.

11. See Motley, *Equal Justice*, 81, 136–38; Pratt, *We Shall Not Be Moved*, 6, 11–13, 19, 52–53; Daniels, *Horace T. Ward*, 77–78; Hollowell and Lehfeldt, *Sacred Call*, 112–13; Johnson Interview by author, 1. In 1957, the U.S. District Court dismissed Ward's suit on grounds that he had not exhausted state administrative remedies; the court also ruled that Ward's case against UGA was rendered moot when he enrolled in law school at Northwestern University. Pratt, *We Shall Not Be Moved*, 59–61, 64, 66. Ward went on to become a successful lawyer and federal judge. Walden did file a case against the segregated Georgia State College of Business Administration that in 1959 resulted in a ruling that black applicants could not be denied admission because white alumni had failed to endorse their applications. The case did not, however, result in the admission of the black applicants named in the suit. See Hunt v. Arnold, 172 F. Supp. 847 (N.D. Ga. 1959). A case involving the University of Alabama, which was filed after the UGA case, became the site of the Deep South showdown at a flagship university over segregation. See Lucy v. Adams, 134 F. Supp. 235 (N.D. Ala.), cert. denied, 351 U.S. 931 (1956). The LDF successfully sued for the admission of a black student to the law school at Louisiana State University in 1950. See Wilson v. La. State Univ., 92 F. Supp. 986 (E.D. La. 1950), *aff'd per curiam*, 340 U.S. 909 (1950); see also Sweatt v. Painter, 339 U.S. 629 (1950), in which LDF prevailed in a suit to admit a black student to the University of Texas Law School.

12. The Walden quote is from Statement of A. T. Walden, Co-Chairman, Atlanta Negro Voters' League, 1961, Walden Papers, MSS 614, series VII, box 1, f. 5. For scholarly accounts that reflect the view that Walden failed to meet the bar of activism set by the national NAACP and LDF, see Tuck, *Beyond Atlanta*, 64–65, 90–92, 98; Ferguson, *Black Politics*, 64, 148; ibid. at 149 (characterizing Walden as "dictatorial"); see also Stone, *Regime Politics*, 53 (noting that Walden and other members of the old guard were considered "Uncle Toms" who had "done little but feather their own nests"). Compare Pritchett, *Robert Clifton Weaver*, whose examination documents criticisms that Weaver faced for choosing to pursue racial liberalism within governmental institutions that many blamed for racial inequality, but also attempts to explain Weaver's decisional processes from his own perspective.

13. The focus here on intraracial dynamics contrasts with the classic work on civil rights lawyers, which views them in contest with white lawyers and white communities. See, for example, Meier and Rudwick, "Attorneys Black and White," 913–46; Smith, *Emancipation;* McNeil, *Groundwork.*

14. McNeil, *Groundwork*, 84–85, 134, 137–41, 217–18; Carter, *A Matter of Law*, 24–25, 56. Houston had a sophisticated understanding of politics and law, including a keen appreciation of the degree to which the NAACP's success would turn on public opinion. The nuances of Houston's position have been underappreciated by scholars, as well as by Houston's radical contemporaries, who accused him of encouraging a naïve faith in the courts by the masses. See McNeil, *Groundwork*, 99–103. For a recent article discussing Houston's views and disputing the notion that Houston was naïve about the courts, see Mack, "Rethinking Civil Rights Lawyering" and Mack, "Law and Mass Politics." Accounts of national office lawyering include Carter, *A Matter of Law*, 56–133; Motley, *Equal Justice*, 58–59, 68, 73–76; Ware, *William Hastie*, 152–53; Kluger, *Simple Justice*, 214, 278; Tushnet, *Making Civil Rights Law*, 17–18; Tushnet, *NAACP's Legal Strategy*, 111.

15. Of course, numerous local counsel handled test cases in localities in conjunction with the LDF's core staff, including Oliver Hill and Spottswood Robinson III of Virginia, Louis Redding of Delaware, A. Tureaud, and Loren Miller. All of these lawyers' professional practice lives can serve the same purpose: illuminating how the NAACP's strategy looked on the ground, in local context. For discussions of these lawyers' contributions to the NAACP's campaign, see, for example, Carter, *A Matter of Law*, 56–63, 146; Motley, *Equal Justice*, 62, 66–68, 78–79, 80–82, 119, 142, 153, 197; Ware, *William Hastie*, 32, 45, 52–65, 142–74.

16. See Davis, "Role of Black Colleges," 26; Smith, *Emancipation*, 200–201. The "motto" is from Smith, *Emancipation*, 200. In the early 1970s, African Americans filed a class action suit alleging that the Georgia bar exam was racially discriminatory under the federal constitution, without success. Remarkably, the case, which involved an allegation of intentional discrimination, made no mention of the state's history of purposeful discrimination against prospective black lawyers. See Tyler v. Vickery, 517 F. 2d 1089 (5th Cir. 1975).

17. On discrimination in the bar, see Smith, *Emancipation*, 200–201; see also Hylton, "African-American Lawyer"; Tollett, "Black Lawyers"; Alexander, "National Bar Association," 1–4; Woodson, *Negro Professional*, 221–39; Smith, *Emancipation*, 4–5, 10–15. On Walden's experiences, see "Tribute," Walden Papers, series II, box 2, f. 7; Woodson, *Negro Professional*, 218–19; Smith, "Black Bar Association," 654–60; Smith, *Emancipation*, 200–201; Dittmer, *Black Georgia*, 37; Kuhn, *Living Atlanta*, 314; see also Executive Committee, *History of the Atlanta Bar Association*, 65 (white members only).

18. "Future Cloudy," *Time*, 16 Aug. 1937, 27–28.

19. Minutes, Gate City Bar Association, 25 Jan. 1948, Walden Papers, series VI, box 1, f. 6; Hon. Romae Turner-Power, quoted in in Transcript of "Gate City Bar Association: Upholding a Tradition of Service," DVD recording (1990), 1; Donald Hollowell, quoted in ibid., 2.

20. Article II, Constitution and Bylaws of Gate City Bar Assoc, n.d., Walden Papers, series VI, box 1, f. 7.

21. The lawyers who joined Walden in founding the Gate City Bar Association were Charles Morgan Clayton, Edward D'Antignac, Thomas J. Henry, Rachel Prudence Herndon, Thomas W. Holmes, R. E. Thomas, Jr., Eugene E. Moore, Sylvester S. Robinson, and J. A. Salter. See *ADW*, 26 Nov. 1998, 7; see also *ADW*, 16 May 1954, 7. The quotes are from Hon. Romae Turner-Power, quoted in Transcript of "Gate City Bar Association," 1–2; see also ibid., 3. For a more detailed discussion of the professional world of black lawyers, albeit in a different place and time, see Mack, "Law and Mass Politics."

22. Program, National Bar Association Convention, 16–18 Sept. 1948, Walden Papers, series VI, box 1, f. 3; Minutes, Gate City Bar Association, 10 Mar. 1948, Walden Papers, series VI, box 1, f. 6; Minutes, Gate City Bar Association, 18 May 1948, Walden Papers, series VI, box 1, f. 6; R. E. Thomas to Albert Turner, 13 July 1948, Walden Papers, series VI, box 1, f. 3; see also *ADW*, 26 Nov. 1998, 7; *ADW*, 16 May 1954, 7.

23. For an early account of lawyers' attempts to change society through the courts, see Comment, "Private Attorneys-General," which explores the work of the NAACP, the ACLU, and the National Jewish Congress. The terminology "cause lawyering," used to describe lawyers who worked as partisan for a cause, gained currency well after Walden lived and practiced. However, it is generally apt to his race work and that of other pioneering public interest lawyers. See Sarat and Scheingold, "Cause Lawyering." As the scholarship on cause lawyering explains, a lawyer's representation of a cause in which he has a personal interest can present thorny dilemmas. See, for example, Spillenger, "Elusive Advocate"; Polikoff, "Am I My Client," 443–58; White, "Subordination." This discussion of Walden's activism illustrates the point.

24. On the relationship between the sociological argument against segregation and legal realism, see Tushnet, *NAACP's Legal Strategy*, 117–19; McNeil, *Groundwork*, 47–49, 63–64, 213–14; see also Kluger, *Simple Justice*, 115–16. A number of scholars classify Frankfurter as a legal realist, but others call him an antiformalist, or predecessor of the legal realists. Compare Mack, "Rethinking Civil Rights Lawyering," at 309 and n. 185 with Kalman, *Legal Realism*, 55. Although Houston's reputation as an integrationist is taken for granted, in his private practice he pursued a separate but equal strategy in a school case. See Greenberg, "In Tribute," 265–66.

25. See "Life Begins at 78," *Atlanta Magazine*, Oct. 1963, 43–44.

26. Ibid., 46.

27. Ibid., 43–44; Walden, "If I Were Young Today," 74.

28. See "Questionnaire: If I Were Young Again," Walden Papers, series II, box 2, f. 1; "Life Begins at 78," 43–44.

29. See "Life Begins at 78," 44, 46.

30. See Biographical Sketch, Walden Papers, series II, box 2, f. 1; Commencement Address, Fort Valley State College, 1964, Walden Papers, series II, box 2, f. 8; "Tribute," Walden Papers, series II, box 2, f. 7; see also Smith, *Emancipation*, 198; Bacote, *Atlanta University*, 142.

31. See Biographical Sketch, Walden Papers, series II, box 2, f. 1; "Life Begins at 78," 43–44; Walden, "If I Were Young Today," 74; Agnew and Haden-Miller, *Atlanta and Its Lawyers*, 55; Smith, *Emancipation*, 198. On the University of Michigan, see Elizabeth Gasper Brown, *Legal Education at the Michigan*, 109–13, 202–8, 231–32, 276–79, 477–78, 678; *Law Quadrangle*, 11; "Largest Law Schools."

32. See Biographical Sketch, Walden Papers, series II, box 2, f. 1; "Tribute," Walden Papers, series II, box 2, f. 1; see also Bacote, *Atlanta University*, 422–23.

33. See "Austin Thomas Walden," Hamilton Papers, box 199; A. T. Walden to Directors of Citizens Trust Company, 24 Aug. 1927, Walden Papers, box 22, f. 18; *Pittsburgh Courier*, 14 Jan. 1961, clipping, Hamilton Papers, box 199; "Tribute," Walden Papers, series II, box 2, f. 7. The range of Walden's work on civil matters is demonstrated in the following reported cases: Owens v. Mack, 49 S.E.2d 498 (Ga. 1948); Marshall v. Marshall, 67 S.E.2d 575 (Ga. 1951); Torrence v. American Home Mutual Life Insurance Company, 52 S.E.2d 25 (Ga. 1949); Pilgrim Health and Life Insurance Co. v. Grimmette, 29 S.E.2d 101 (Ga. 1944); Hanley Co. v. Lacy, 26 S.E.2d 136 (Ga. 1943); Bunn v. City of Atlanta, 19 S.E.2d 553 (Ga. 1942).

Although nicknames typically were intended as terms of affection and adoration in the South, and both black and whites referred to Walden as "Captain," "Judge," or "Colonel," these references also permitted local whites to avoid disturbing racial etiquette. They did not have to call Walden, a black man, "Mister." See Bacote, *Atlanta University*, 422–23. Raymond Pace Alexander, an African-American lawyer from Philadelphia and president of the National Bar Association, explained that he "delighted to go South on a case and force white lawyers to call him 'Mister.' 'They'll gladly call you Professor, Colonel, or Doctor, but Mister sticks.'" See "Future Cloudy," *Time*, 16 Aug. 1937, 27–28.

34. Walden quoted in Statement of A. T. Walden, Co-Chairman, Atlanta Negro Voters' League, Walden Papers, MSS 614, series VII, box 1, f. 5; see also Smith, *Emancipation*, 200–201; Dittmer, *Black Georgia*, 37; Grant, *Way It Was*, 257; "Wide Opportunities for Negro Lawyers," *Crisis* 41 (Dec. 1934): 371; Donald Hollowell to Members of the Gate City Bar Association, 22 Mar. 1961, Walden Papers, series VI, box 1, f. 5; U.S. Census Bureau, *Detailed Occupation of Employed Persons by Residence, Race, and Sex: 1970*, tables 171 and 172 (Washington, D.C., 1970).

35. See "Tribute," Walden Papers, series II, box 2, f. 7; see also Annual Report of the Atlanta Chapter of the American Civil Liberties Union, 1948, Walden Papers, series V, box 1, f. 5.

36. A. T. Walden to Members of the Gate City Bar Association, 22 Sept. 1952, Walden Papers, series VI, box 1, f. 5; see also A. T. Walden to Hon. Walter C. Hendricks, 1 Oct. 1952, Walden Papers, series VI, box 1, f. 5.

37. On Walden, see Hollowell interview by Pomerantz; Pomerantz, *Where Peachtree Meets*, 184; Walker, "Sit-Ins in Atlanta," 89. On Houston, see McNeil, *Groundwork*, 3–4, 84–85, 199–200. On King, see Fairclough, *To Redeem*, 5–6, 25–29, 169–70, 232–35. On Marshall, see Tushnet, *Making Civil Rights Law*, 3, 33, 38–41; Tushnet, *Making Constitutional Law*, 4–5, 33, 68, 180–81, 187, 191; Davis and Clark, *Thurgood Marshall*, 3–9, 17, 20, 105, 109, 134–35.

38. Statement of A. T. Walden, Co-Chairman, Atlanta Negro Voters' League, Walden Papers, MSS 614, series VII, box 1, f. 5.

39. See Tushnet, *Making Civil Rights Law*, 11–12; McNeil, *Groundwork*, 88–89, 113–15; Dudziak, *Cold War Civil Rights*. For discussions of other black intellectuals of the era who criticized the NAACP's legal strategy, including for its allegedly inadequate economic agenda, see Sitkoff, *New Deal for Blacks*, 250–53; Harris, "Negro and Economic Radicalism," 130–39; Urquhart, *Ralph Bunche*, 51, 56, 58, 61, 65, 84, 91, 433–36.

40. These statements intend in no way to diminish the virulent white resistance that the national NAACP and LDF encountered. Moreover, I do not mean to suggest that Walden's proximity to resistance and to the local communities that he represented led to particular substantive results. Indeed, a premise of the argument is that Walden's conception of community was more or less limited—to elites, and as we shall see, he was accused of ignoring those with whom he disagreed.

41. On this milieu, see Higginbotham, *Righteous Discontent*, 185–229; Gaines, *Uplifting the Race*, 2–9; Meier and Lewis, "History of the Negro Upper Class," 128–39; Dittmer, *Black Georgia*, 59–61; Ferguson, *Black Politics*, 27–33. For a deft analysis of uplift ideology in late nineteenth-century Atlanta, see Dorsey, *To Build Our Lives*. The first Walden quote is from "Life Begins at 78," 118. The second is from A. T. Walden, Commencement Address, Fort Valley State College, 1964, 9, Walden Papers, series II, box 2, f. 8.

42. See Meier and Lewis, "History of the Negro Upper Class"; Meier, "Negro Class Structure," 262; Bacote, *Atlanta University*, 227, 256–315; Read, *Spelman College*, 55–59, 114–15, 300, 325; Dittmer, *Black Georgia*, 151; Lewis, *W. E. B. Du Bois*, 1:197–98, 211–87, 386–407; Grant, *Way It Was*, 239–41, 243–47. In addition to these five colleges, Atlanta is home to the Interdenominational Theological Center, founded in 1958 as an affiliate of Morehouse College's school of religion. See Mays, *Born to Rebel*, 235–37.

43. On the early uniform emphasis on Greek, Latin, philosophy, and the liberal arts in the strongest historically black colleges and on the values inculcated by the AU system, in particular, see Lewis, *W. E. B. Du Bois*, 1:171–74, 221, 288, 546–49; *W. E. B. Du Bois, Fight for Equality*, 491; Grant, *Way It Was*, 205, 238–53; Jewell, "Black Ivy," 85–108, 111–33; Butler, *Distinctive Black College*, 112; Read, *Spelman College*, 192–93, 198, 210, 255–56, 260; Anderson, *Education of Blacks*, 28–30; Bacote, *Atlanta University*, 15, 25. On respectability, see Higginbotham, "The Politics of Respectability," in *Righteous Discontent*, 185–229; Gaines, *Uplifting the Race*, 2–9.

44. See Martin, *Angelo Herndon*, 98–101; Ferguson, *Black Politics*, 54–70; see generally, Gilmore, *Defying Dixie*, 161–66, 177–78.

45. A. T. Walden, Commencement Address, Fort Valley State College, 1964, series II, box 2, f. 8, Walden Papers; Du Bois, "Talented Tenth," 385–403. Du Bois also was engaged in writing some of the monographs in the AU Studies project during this era. Ibid., 247–52.

46. See Harlan, *Booker T. Washington*, 1:221–27; Harlan, "Secret Life," 110–27; Pete Daniel, "Up from Slavery."

47. See Du Bois, "Counsels of Despair," *Crisis* 41 (June 1934): 182; Du Bois, "Resigns"; Du Bois, "The Anti-segregation Campaign," *Crisis* 41 (1934): 182; Du Bois, "Does the Negro," 417.

48. Harlan, *Booker T. Washington*, 1:205–13; Harlan, *Booker T. Washington*, 2:212–13, 218, 295–304.

49. See Klarman, *From Jim Crow*, 115–16; Carter, *A Matter of Law*, 26.

50. Dittmer, *Black Georgia*, 131; W. Fitzhugh Brundage, *Lynching*, 39–40, 91, 100, 191–94. On Georgia's reputation versus reality, see also Bartley, *Creation of Modern Georgia*, 208–25; Paul M. Gaston, *New South Creed*, 147–50; Tuck, *Beyond Atlanta*, 66–70, 74–80, 101–3.

51. Grant, *Way It Was*, 328, 331; Ferguson, *Black Politics*, 48, 90; Bayor, *Race and the Shaping*, 98; Allen, *Atlanta Rising*, 10; Gilmore, *Defying Dixie*, 106-09. On the NAACP's antilynching campaign, see Kellogg, *NAACP*, 232–45; Zangrando, *NAACP Crusade*, 213–16.

52. On the Klan's revival, see Clement Charlton Moseley, "Political Influence," 235–53. Also see Kuhn, *Living Atlanta*, 313–14, 316; Bayor, *Race and the Shaping*, 177; Allen, *Atlanta Rising*, 10; Ferguson, *Black Politics*, 256; Moseley, "Political Influence," 236; Grant, *Way It Was*, 320–21.

53. Quoted material from "Report on Miscarriages of Justice," 5 Sept. 1940, Barker Papers, box 9, Fulton-Dekalb Committee file; *AC*, 13 July 1940, 18; see also Bayor, *Race and the Shaping*, 173–82; Dittmer, *Black Georgia*, 88–89, 199; Ferguson, *Black Politics*, 24, 29, 143, 149–50, 256.

54. "Report on Miscarriages of Justice," case IV.

55. "Report on Miscarriages of Justice," case II; *AC*, 18 Aug 1940, 7.

56. See Nat G. Long to Friends of the Fulton-Dekalb Committee on Interracial Cooperation, 5 Sept. 1940, Barker Papers, box 9, Fulton-Dekalb Committee file; W. B. Hartsfield to Dr. M. Ashby Jones, 23 May 1940, Barker Papers, box 9, Fulton-Dekalb Committee file; Minutes of the Annual Meeting of the Fulton-Dekalb Committee on Interracial Cooperation, 2 Nov. 1943, Barker Papers, box 9, Fulton-Dekalb Committee file.

57. See "Remember the Klan in the 20s," *Southern Patriot*, July 1946, 2, Barker Papers, box 10, Misc. Printed Matter file; "Danger: Stormtroopers at Work," *Southern Patriot*, July 1946, 3, Barker Papers, box 10, Misc. Printed Matter file; Jim Furniss, "Klan 'Goon Squad' Faces Inquiry of Undercover Men," *Southern Patriot*, 8 June 1946, A1; *AC*, 19 June 1946, A1; "Fighting the Klan on all Fronts," *Southern Patriot*, July 1946, 5, Barker

Papers, box 10, Misc. Printed Matter file; see also Grant, *Way It Was*, 319–20; Ferguson, *Black Politics*, 256–57.

58. "Danger: Stormtroopers at Work," *Southern Patriot*, July 1946, 3, Barker Papers, box 10, Misc. Printed Matter file; see also Ferguson, *Black Politics*, 256; Allen, *Atlanta Rising*, 12–13; Tuck, *Beyond Atlanta*, 18–19, 66–68.

59. See minutes of meeting of the Special Committee on Police Brutality, Atlanta Negro Voters League, 8 May 1962, Walden Papers, series VII, box 1, f. 2; Yarn v. City of Atlanta, 47 S.E.2d 556, 543–46 (Ga. Sup. Ct. 1948).

60. Walden, "If I Were Young Today," 74.

61. King, *Daddy King*, 111.

62. Statement upon Retirement, 20 Sept. 1963, Walden Papers, series II, box 2, f. 20; "Life Begins at 78," 42.

## Chapter 2

1. The statement in the epigraph by Rhodes, president of the National Bar Association from 1933–34, is from Styles, *Negroes and the Law*, xi.

2. The statement in the epigraph by Walden is from Minutes of the All-Citizens Registration Committee and Atlanta Negro Voters League's Leadership Training Clinic, 25 May 1961, 1, Walden Papers, series VII, box 1, f. 5.

3. Leaders of the Democratic Party erected this barrier to black political participation; by excluding blacks from party membership, party leaders excluded them from voting in primary elections. Smith v. Allwright, 321 U.S. 649 (1944); see also Allen, *Atlanta Rising*, 10; Walton, *Blacks and Political Machines*, 67.

4. E. M. Martin, "A Southerner Speaks," *Southern Frontier*, Oct. 1944, 3, Barker Papers, box 10, Misc. Printed Matter file. Martin was the brother-in-law of the NAACP's executive secretary, Walter White.

5. The scope of community need, including the problem of police brutality, is described in chapter 1. The Walden quote is from "Life Begins at 78," 118.

6. On northern blacks' electoral clout after the migrations, see Sitkoff, *New Deal for Blacks*, 84–101; Van Deusen, "Negro in Politics." For accounts of black migrants' encounters with Northern political machines, including efforts to seek civil service positions, police and fire protection, city services, and antidiscrimination legislation, see Du Bois, *Philadelphia Negro*, 373–75, 382, 382–83; Countryman, *Up South*, 13–16, 19–21; Biondi, *To Stand and Fight*, 38–59, 98–111; Drake and Cayton, *Black Metropolis*, 342–77; Higginbotham, "In Politics to Stay," 199–220. Notably, black migrants' votes yielded racial progress, but not enough; leaders turned to lawsuits and protest tactics when local and state politicians did not fully respond to their needs. See, for example, Biondi, *To Stand and Fight*, 79–97; 112–36.

7. On the broad sweep of the NAACP's agenda, including its litigation campaign, see Kellogg, *NAACP*, 183–210; Jonas, *Freedom's Sword*, 11–12, 31–66. On the "indivisibility of rights," see Tushnet, "Political Aspects." For Reconstruction-era views on the concept, see ibid. at 886–89; on views within the NAACP, see ibid. at 891–96. In the

education context, LDF officially ceased representation of those who preferred equalization over desegregation suits in 1950. See Tushnet, *NAACP's Legal Strategy*, 136–37.

8. A. T. Walden, "Address to Fort Valley State College Graduation," 1964, Walden Papers, series II, box 2, f. 8.

9. See Acts of Gen. Ass. of Georgia 446 (1908) (forbidding registration without payment of poll tax and providing that voters' qualification can be challenged for "legal cause"); see also Code of City of Atlanta 2130–33, 2136, 2138 (1910).

10. See Bacote, "Negro in Atlanta Politics," 333–50; Grant, *Way It Was*, 335. For a general discussion of Georgia's legal strategies for disenfranchising African-Americans, see Grantham, "Georgia Politics."

11. Kellogg, *NAACP*, 250–55. On the black experience during World War I, see Meier and Rudwick, *From Plantation to Ghetto*, 238–41; Emmett Scott, *Scott's Official History*, 59–64, 72–81, 97–98, 102–3, 428–30; Franklin and Moss, *From Slavery to Freedom*, 339.

12. Bayor, *Race and the Shaping*, 16–20, 202–4.

13. Ferguson, *Black Politics*, 83–116.

14. See *Spritzer and Bergmark, Grace Towns Hamilton*, 79; Ferguson, *Black Politics*, 95–96, 138–43, 153–55.

15. Ferguson, *Black Politics*, 138–40.

16. Calhoun interview, 6–8, McGill Papers, box 109, f. 8; Ferguson, *Black Politics*, 141, 153–59; Pomerantz, *Where Peachtree Meets*, 125–27, 147–48.

17. See, for example, Strong, "Future of the Negro Voter," 400–407.

18. Of the barriers to black voting, the qualification tests were more effective than the poll tax, judging from some reports, which do not make specific claims about Georgia. See Klarman, *From Jim Crow*, 158–59. On the relationship between the dearth of sympathetic candidates and black voting patterns in the South, see *Matthews and Prothro, Negroes and the New Southern Politics*, 158–59, 161–62.

19. See "Danger: Stormtroopers at Work," *Southern Patriot*, July 1946, 3, Barker Papers, box 10, Misc. Printed Matter file; see "Fighting the Klan on all Fronts," *Southern Patriot*, July 1946, 5, Barker Papers, box 10, Misc. Printed Matter file; Ferguson, *Black Politics*, 256; Tuck, *Beyond Atlanta*, 27–28. On the Monroe lynchings, see *ADW*, 27 July 1946, 1; 27 July 1946, 1; 30 July 1946, 1; 3 Aug. 1946, 1; 31 July 1946, 1; Ira De A. Reid, "Persons and Places," *Phylon* 7 (third quarter 1946): 290.

20. "A Statement by Southern Negroes on a Basis for Interracial Cooperation and Development in the South," TD, 20 Oct. 1942, Barker Papers, box 10, Race Misc., 1940–1956 file, 1–10; see also Rufus E. Clement, "Black G.I. Joe Comes Home," *Southern Frontier*, Oct. 1945, 3, Barker Papers, box 10, Misc. Printed Matter file; Stetson Kennedy, "Is the South's 20% Democracy Enough," *Southern Frontier*, Oct. 1945, 1, 3, Barker Papers, box 10, Misc. Printed Matter file; Brooks, "Winning the Peace."

21. Smith v. Allwright, 321 U.S. 649 (1944); Nixon v. Herndon, 273 U.S. 538 (1927); see also Hine, *Black Victory*, 51, 69, 113–19.

22. Hine, *Black Victory*, 196–98 (discussing Grovey v. Townsend, 295 U.S. 45 (1935)). The *Grovey* case was not litigated by the NAACP, but undertaken by local blacks disenchanted with the strategy of national NAACP lawyers.

23. Nixon v. Condon, 286 U.S. 73 (1932); Hine, *Black Victory*, 142–45, 157–60, 225–28, 232–33; see also Lawson, *Black Ballots*, 42–44.

24. Hine, *Black Victory*, 238–39, 241–42; see also Klarman, *From Jim Crow*, 201–2.

25. See *ADW*, 5 Apr. 1944, 1; 5 Apr. 1944, 6; Hine, *Black Victory*, 238–39, 241–42; see also Klarman, *From Jim Crow*, 201–2.

26. *ADW*, 12 Apr. 1944, 1.

27. Harmon, *Beneath the Image*, 18.

28. *ADW*, 4 July 1944, 1; Pomerantz, *Where Peachtree Meets*, 149.

29. See *ADW*, 5 July 1944, 1; Kuhn, Joye, and West, *Living Atlanta*, 332; Harmon, *Beneath the Image*, 3. On the poll tax, see Harper v. Virginia Board of Elections, 383 U.S. 663 (1966).

30. See *ADW*, 13 Oct. 1945, 1.

31. See *Chapman v. King*, 62 F. Supp. 639, 640, 650 (D. Ga. 1945); see also *ADW*, 13 Oct. 1945, 1.

32. See Harmon, *Beneath the Image*, 20–21.

33. See *ADW*, 13 Feb. 1946, 1; see also Ferguson, *Black Politics*, 95–96, 253; Harmon, *Beneath the Image*, 150.

34. Allen, *Atlanta Rising*, 2–3.

35. *Chapman v. King*, 62 F. Supp. 639 (N.D. Ga. 1945), aff'd 154 F.2d 460, 464 (5th Cir. 1946), cert. denied, 66 S.Ct. 905; see also *ADW*, 7 Mar. 1946, 1; 2 Apr. 1946, 1.

36. See *ADW*, 2 Apr. 1946, 1.

37. See *Hamilton interview*, 6; Jack Walker, "Negro Voting in Atlanta: 1953–1961," *Phylon* 24 (1964): 380; see also *Spritzer and Bergmark, Grace Towns Hamilton*, 112–13; Ferguson, *Black Politics*, 253–54; Bayor, *Race and the Shaping*, 23; Pomerantz, *Where Peachtree Meets*, 151–52.

38. Klarman, *From Jim Crow*, 236. About 250,000 southern blacks were registered to vote prior to Smith v. Allwright. *Matthews and Prothro, Negroes and the New Southern Politics*, 148.

39. But intimidation and fear of economic reprisals continued to be problems, especially outside of Atlanta following *Brown*, when white intransigence to civil rights hardened. See Tuck, *Beyond Atlanta*, 98–101, 106.

40. See Bacote, "Negro Voter," 315–16; *ADW*, 15 Mar. 1952, 1; Roy Wilkins, *Journal of Negro Education* 26 (summer 1957): 424–31. Georgia's rate of black voter registration lagged behind several other states in 1958, including Arkansas, Florida, Texas, and North Carolina. *Matthews and Prothro, Negroes and the New Southern Politics*, 148.

41. On voter apathy in general, see Rosenberg, "Meaning of Politics," 5–15.

42. On the lack of a strong correlation between urbanization and industrialization and black voting in Georgia and other southern states during the late 1950s, see Earl Black and Merle Black, *Politics and Society*, 114–16.

43. See *Matthews and Prothro, Negroes and the New Southern Politics*, 148.

44. See *ADW*, 19 July 1946, 1; 3 Aug. 1946, 1; Tuck, *Beyond Atlanta*, 7, 17, 66, 69, 75–76; *Key, Southern Politics*, 119 and n. 14.

45. See *ADW*, 19 July 1946, 1; Bernd, "White Supremacy"; Tuck, *Beyond Atlanta*, 66–68; Grant, *Way It Was*, 366.

46. See *AJ*, 19 Aug. 1948, 20; 17 Aug. 1948, 6; Jim Furniss, "Talmadge, in North Georgia, Blasts Jekyll," clipping, n.d., Walden Papers, MSS 614, box 4, f. 7.

47. See Furniss, "Talmadge, in North Georgia, Blasts Jekyll"; *Statesman* (Hapeville, Ga.),17 June 1948, 4; *ADW*, 5 Sept. 1948, 1, 4; 7 Sept. 1948, 1; 4 Sept. 1948, 1; 8 Sept. 1948, 1; M. L. St. John, "No Mingling of Races—Thompson," clipping, n.d., Walden Papers, MSS 614, box 4, f. 7; *ADW*, 10 Sept. 1948, 1; see also Tuck, *Beyond Atlanta*, 70; *Spritzer and Bergmark, Grace Towns Hamilton*, 113.

48. See *Walton, Black Politics*, 67; Bacote, "Negro Voter," 311; Bayor, *Race and the Shaping*, 23–24; Allen, *Atlanta Rising*, 35; Harmon, *Beneath the Image*, 36.

49. A. T. Walden and John Wesley Dobbs, Atlanta, Ga., Joint Chairman, Atlanta Negro Voters League, to Voters of Atlanta, TLS, 2 Sept. 1949, Atlanta Urban League Papers, box 23, f. 10; see also Harmon, *Beneath the Image*, 9, 25–31; Pomerantz, *Where Peachtree Meets*, 188; Bayor, *Race and the Shaping*, 25–26; Walker, "Negro Voting in Atlanta," 380.

50. See *ADW*, 9 Sept. 1949, 1; Bacote, "Negro Voter," 311; see also Bayor, *Race and the Shaping*, 26.

51. See *ADW*, 8 Sept. 1949, 1; Bayor, *Race and the Shaping*, 26.

52. See Bacote, "Negro Voter," 311; see also Atlanta Urban League Occasional Papers, no. VII, May 1953, Barker Papers, box 8, Urban League file, 2–3; *AJ*, 9 May 1957, 15; Bacote, "Negro Voter," 311, 313–14. Whites who voted for Clement may not have known exactly whom they were electing: his photo was not printed on his campaign materials.

53. See "An Open Letter to the Negro Voters of Georgia," TD, 4 Sept. 1954, Davis Papers, box 148, Segregation News-Clippings file; Grant, *Way It Was*, 370, 378–79.

54. See Myrdal, *American Dilemma*, 497. Chapter 9 and the conclusion develop the theme that blacks did not benefit in the manner anticipated from the vote following passage of the Voting Rights Act of 1965. For related legal scholarship, see, for example, Guinier, "Triumph of Tokenism," which discusses the difficulties that African Americans encountered in achieving responsive government after the passage of the Voting Rights Act. For an exploration of similar themes in the political science literature, see, for example, Lublin, *Paradox of Representation*, which discusses ways in which post–Voting Rights Act racial redistricting strategies have increased black representation in Congress but minimized minority influence in the legislative process. See also Swain, *Black Faces, Black Interests*, which argues that whites can effectively represent black interests.

## Chapter 3

1. The statement from Stuart in the epigraph is from Testimony of Robert C. Stuart, Director, Metropolitan Planning Commission, in U.S. Commission on Civil Rights, Housing Hearings, 10 Apr. 1959, 480.

2. The statement from Hartsfield in the epigraph is from Testimony of William Hartsfield, U.S. Commission on Civil Rights, Housing Hearings, 10 Apr. 1959, 444.

3. See Testimony of William Hartsfield, U.S. Commission on Civil Rights, Housing Hearings, 10 Apr. 1959, 447–48; Testimony of Arthur Burdett, Jr., President, Atlanta Real Estate Board, 535–36.

4. See Testimony of William Hartsfield, U.S. Commission on Civil Rights, Housing Hearings, 10 Apr. 1959, 447–48; Testimony of Robert C. Stuart, Director, Metropolitan Planning Commission, U.S. Commission on Civil Rights, Housing Hearings, 10 Apr. 1959, 481.

5. See Testimony of Arthur Burdett, Jr., President, Atlanta Real Estate Board, U.S. Commission on Civil Rights, Housing Hearings, 10 Apr. 1959, 535–36.

6. See Testimony of Robert Thompson, Housing Director, Atlanta Urban League, U.S. Commission on Civil Rights, 10 Apr. 1959, 523; Testimony of Q. V. Williamson, President, Empire Real Estate Board, U.S. Commission on Civil Rights, Housing Hearings, 10 Apr. 1959, 540–43; see also "Resolutions Adopted by the Forty-Fourth Annual Convention of the NAACP at St. Louis, Missouri, June 27 1953," *Crisis* 60 (Aug.–Sept. 1953): 438.

7. 245 U.S. 60 (1917).

8. On the laws, see Dittmer, *Black Georgia*, 13; Bayor, *Race and the Shaping*, 54. The cases include Glover v. Atlanta, 96 S.E. 562 (Ga. Sup. Ct. 1918); Harden v. Atlanta, 93 S.E. 401 (Ga. Sup. Ct. 1917); Carey v. Atlanta (1915), 84 S.E. 456 (Ga. Sup. Ct. 1915).

9. See *Atlanta, Georgia Code* 3358–59 (1924); see also Kuhn, *Living Atlanta*, 37; Bayor, *Race and the Shaping*, 54.

10. See Ambrose, "Redrawing the Color Line," 67, 88; Bayor, *Race and the Shaping*, 7.

11. See Ambrose, "Redrawing the Color Line," 37–40; Dittmer, *Black Georgia*, 14; Bayor, *Race and the Shaping*, 6–7; see also Thompson, "Black-white Residential Segregation," 88–90; Thompson, Lewis, and McEntire, "Atlanta and Birmingham," 17–20. Du Bois is quoted in Dittmer, *Black Georgia*, 12.

12. See "Negotiated Expansion and 'Urban Renewal,'" in Ambrose, "Redrawing the Color Line," 88–150; "Report of the Housing Coordinator," TD, 26 Aug. 1960, Atlanta Bureau of Planning Papers, box 1, f. 1; Metropolitan Housing Commission, "Report of the Housing Coordinator," TD, 26 Aug. 1960, Atlanta Bureau of Planning Papers, box 1, f. 1.

13. "The Community Housing Corporation," TD, n.d., Walden Papers, box 43, f. 16; Ambrose, "Redrawing the Color Line," 88–93; Harmon, *Beneath the Image*, 62–63; Bayor, *Race and the Shaping*, 54–55. The 10 percent figure is from 1946; over the period of the fifties, the percentage of land allotted blacks increased as a result of the efforts discussed here.

14. "The Story of Negro Housing in Atlanta," TD, n.d., Atlanta Bureau of Planning Papers, box 1, f. 1; see also Ambrose, "Redrawing the Color Line," 88–150; Bayor, *Race and the Shaping*, 53–92.

15. Deposition of Robert Thompson, Armour v. Nix, no. 16708, 15 Apr. 1975, 6–8, 9–13; Ambrose, "Redrawing the Color Line," 94–98. Atlanta had been the site of the country's first public housing project, and it had been constructed during the New Deal with the support of a biracial coalition. The projects were segregated. See Pritchett, *Robert Clifton Weaver*, 57–61.

16. 334 U.S. 1 (1948).

17. "The Community Housing Corporation," TD, n.d., Walden Papers, box 43, f. 16; see also Thompson, Lewis, and McEntire, "Atlanta and Birmingham," 23; *ADW*, 15 Nov. 1947, 1; *Spritzer and Bergmark, Grace Towns Hamilton*, 93–96; Ambrose, "Redrawing the Color Line," 98–99.

18. Petition from Urban Villa, Inc. to Fulton County Commissioners of Roads and Revenues, Apr. 6, 1949, 2, Walden Papers, series II, box 1, f. 1; Ambrose, "Redrawing the Color Line," 98–100; *ADW*, 30 Jan. 1947, 6.

19. Petition from Urban Villa, Inc. to Fulton County Commissioners of Roads and Revenues, 6 Apr. 1949, 2–3, Walden Papers, series II, box 1, f. 1; see also S. S. Robinson to A. E. Fuller, TL, Apr. 19, 1949, 1–2, Walden Papers, series II, box 1, f. 1.

20. A. E. Fuller to S. S. Robinson, TL, 15 Apr. 1949, 1–2, Walden Papers, series II, box 1, f. 1.

21. Ibid.

22. William Hartsfield to A. T. Walden, E. A. Sewell, Philip Hammer, Richard Florrid, S. B. Avery, T. M. Alexander, and W. H. Aiken, TLS, 8 Dec. 1952, Walden Papers, box 43, f. 17; Deposition of Robert Thompson, Armour v. Nix, no. 16708, 15 Apr. 1975, 46–50.

23. William Hartsfield to A. T. Walden, E. A. Sewell, Philip Hammer, Richard Florrid, S. B. Avery, T. M. Alexander, and W. H. Aiken, TLS, 8 Dec. 1952, Walden Papers, box 43, f. 17; Deposition of Robert Thompson, Armour v. Nix, no. 16708, 15 Apr. 1975, 46–50; *ADW*, 18 Feb. 1949, 1; Ambrose, "Redrawing the Color Line," 99–100, 104–5, 107; Bayor, *Race and the Shaping*, 60, 62–65, 68, 151; Harmon, *Beneath the Image*, 65–66, 91.

24. See "Report of Housing Coordinator," TD, 26 Aug. 1960, Atlanta Bureau of Planning Papers, box 1, f. 1; "The Story of Negro Housing in Atlanta," n.d., Atlanta Bureau of Planning Papers, box 1, f. 1.

25. See *AC*, 27 Feb. 1956, clipping, Davis Papers, box 148, Segregation News Clippings folder; *AJ*, 26 Mar. 1956, clipping, James Davis Papers, box 148, Segregation News Clippings folder; *ADW*, 25 Oct. 1947, 1; 28 Oct. 1947, 1; 30 Oct. 1947, 1; 31 Oct. 1947, 1; 1 Nov. 1947, 1; 23 Feb. 1949, 2.

26. See "Report of Housing Coordinator," TD, 26 Aug. 1960, Atlanta Bureau of Planning Papers, box 1, f. 1; "The Story of Negro Housing in Atlanta," TD, n.d., Atlanta Bureau of Planning Papers, box 1, f. 1; "Report on Grove Park Transition Area," TD, 26 Aug. 1960, 1–2, Atlanta Bureau of Planning Papers, box 1, f. 1; Ambrose, "Redrawing the Color Line," 106.

27. See "The Story of Negro Housing in Atlanta," TD, n.d., Atlanta Bureau of Planning Papers, box 1, f. 1; "Report on Grove Park Transition Area," TD, 26 Aug. 1960, Atlanta Bureau of Planning Papers, box 1, f. 1, 1–2; *ADW*, 23 Feb. 1949, 2; Ambrose, "Redrawing the Color Line," 106.

28. Memorandum from Robert C. Stuart, Director of the Metropolitan Planning Commission, to Robert Allen, Principal Planner, TD, 23 July 1957, Atlanta Bureau of Planning Papers, box 1, f. 1; Metropolitan Planning Commission, "Now—For Tomorrow," TD, Sept. 1954, cited in Memo from Stuart to Allen, Atlanta Bureau of Planning

Papers, box 1, f. 1; Metropolitan Planning Commission, "Neighborhood Improvement List," TD, 13 Nov. 1956, Atlanta Bureau of Planning Papers, box 1, f. 1.

29. Memo from Stuart to Allen, Atlanta Bureau of Planning Papers, box 1, f. 1; Metropolitan Planning Commission, "Now—For Tomorrow," TD, Sept. 1954, cited in Memo from Stuart to Allen, Atlanta Bureau of Planning Papers, box 1, f. 1. See also Ambrose, "Redrawing the Color Line," 88–94, 99; Bayor, *Race and the Shaping*, 60, 62–65, 68, 151.

30. Memorandum from Grace Hamilton to A. T. Walden, 15 Apr. 1955, Atlanta Urban League Papers, box 18, f. 51; William Hartsfield to A. T. Walden, E. A. Sewell, Philip Hammer, Richard Florrid, S. B. Avery, T. M. Alexander, and W. H. Aiken, TLS, 8 Dec. 1952, Walden Papers, box 43, f. 17; "Proposal for Neighborhood Improvement Program," TD, 23 July 1957, Atlanta Bureau of Planning Papers, box 1, f. 1.

31. Memorandum from Grace Hamilton to A. T. Walden, 15 Apr. 1955, Atlanta Urban League Papers, box 18, f. 51; "Wisteria Lane" Advertisement, *ADW*, 18 June 1961, Atlanta Bureau of Planning Papers, box 1, f. 1; William Hartsfield to A. T. Walden, E. A. Sewell, Philip Hammer, Richard Florrid, S. B. Avery, T. M. Alexander, and W. H. Aiken, TLS, 8 Dec. 1952, Walden Papers, box 43, f. 17; see also Ambrose, "Redrawing the Color Line," 96–132; Bayor, *Race and the Shaping*, 58, 64–68, 70–71; Harmon, *Beneath the Image*, 66; *AC*, 30 Apr. 1950, 11-B; Robert C. Weaver, "Recent Developments in Urban Housing and Their Implications for Minorities," *Phylon* 16 (third quarter 1955): 277.

32. See Memorandum from Grace Hamilton to A. T. Walden, 15 Apr. 1955, Atlanta Urban League Papers, box 18, f. 51; Deposition of Robert Thompson, Armour v. Nix, no. 16708, 15 Apr. 1975, 17–18; *Spritzer and Bergmark, Grace Towns Hamilton*, 82–83, 88, 92–100.

33. See Ambrose, "Redrawing the Color Line," 107–9; Testimony of Dr. Taeuber, Armour v. Nix, no. 16708, 16 Nov. 1977, 118–19.

34. See Testimony of Dr. Taeuber, 118–19. For the Thompson quote, see Deposition of Robert Thompson, Armour v. Nix, no. 16708, 15 Apr. 1975, 19.

35. Shelley v. Kraemer, 334 U.S. 1 (1948), was filed by George Vaughn, a St. Louis lawyer acting independently of the NAACP, much to the chagrin of Charles Houston and Thurgood Marshall. The NAACP filed a separate restrictive covenants case, Hurd v. Hodge, 334 U.S. 24 (1948), which ultimately was heard by the Court at the same time as *Shelley*. See Greenberg, *Crusaders in the Courts*, 111–12, 276; Kluger, *Simple Justice*, 247–55. On Corrigan, see 271 U.S. 323 (1926).

36. For Marshall's statements, see *ADW*, 4 May 1948, 1; 4 May 1948, 2. For Walden's statement, see *ADW*, 5 May 1948, 6. *ADW*'s editorial on *Shelley* is "Restrictive Covenants," 5 May 1948, 6.

37. On the Truman administration's support for ending restrictive covenants and promulgation of new regulations banning racial discrimination by federal housing authorities, see Tushnet, *Making Constitutional Law*, 90–98, which notes that the NAACP was not satisfied with the Truman Administration's enforcement policies, even with the post-*Shelley* changes. On discrimination by local housing authorities, see Ambrose, "Redrawing," 104–5, 121–23; Peter Kivisto, "Historical Review," 4–5.

38. See 42 U.S.C. 1982 et seq.; Shelley v. Kraemer, 334 U.S. 1 (1948); Hurd v. Hodge, 334 U.S. 24 (1948); Buchanan v. Warley, 245 U.S. 60 (1927); Birmingham v. Monk, 185 F.2d 859 (5th Cir. 1950), cert. denied, 341 U.S. 940 (1951) (striking down zoning ordinance that had segregative effect); Detroit Housing Commission v. Lewis, 226 F.2d 180 (6th Cir. 1955) (finding that public housing commission's policy of segregating residents and limiting certain projects to whites only was unlawful racial discrimination); Jones v. City of Hamtramck, 121 F. Supp. 123 (E.D. Mich. 1954) (finding municipal housing commission's practice of excluding blacks from low cost housing project on basis of race unconstitutional); Banks v. Housing Authority, 260 P.2d 668 (Cal. D.Ct. App.1953), cert. denied, 347 U.S. 974 (1954) (finding public housing authority's policy of selecting tenants for public housing by race unconstitutional); Seawell v. McWhitney, 63 Atl. 2d 542 (Sup.Ct. N.J.), rev. on other grounds, 67 Atl. 2d 309 (N.J. 1949) (finding practice by municipality and its agents of segregating public housing complexes unconstitutional); see also Glover v. Atlanta, 148 Ga. 285 (Ga. 1918); Carey v. Atlanta, 143 Ga. 192 (Ga. 1915).

39. See *ADW*, 16 Feb. 1949, 1; "Fifth Annual Conference, NAACP, Southeastern Region, Atlanta, Georgia, Feb. 28, March 1–3, 1957," 1–2, TD, Walden Papers, series IV, box 3, f. 10; NAACP Annual Report 1954, TD, Davis Papers, box 151, NAACP file, 34–36. On Walden's defense work against restrictive covenants, see *ADW*, 5 May 1948, 6.

40. See NAACP Annual Report 1954, 34–36; "Resolutions Adopted by the Forty-Fourth Annual Convention of the NAACP at St. Louis, Missouri, June 27 1953," *Crisis* 60 (Aug.–Sept. 1953): 438; "Fifth Annual Conference, NAACP, Southeastern Region, Atlanta, Georgia, Feb. 28, March 1–3, 1957," 1–2, TD, Walden Papers, series IV, box 3, f. 10.

41. See *ADW*, 17 June 1954, 1, 6.

42. The federal housing act is codified at 42 U.S.C. 1401, et seq. See Appellants' Brief at 1–4, 15–18, Heyward v. Public Housing Adm., no. 16040 (5th Cir. n.d.), Walden Papers, series IV, box 2, f. 11. On legislation and the federal public housing authority, see Kivisto, "Historical Review," 1–18; Hubert M. Jackson, "Public Housing and Minority Groups," *Phylon* 19 (1st Qtr. 1958), 21–30.

43. See Heyward v. Public Housing Administration, 154 F. Supp. 589 (D. Ga. 1957) (rejecting plaintiffs' claims), *aff'd* sub. nom. Cohen v. Public Housing Administration, 257 F.2d 73, 78 (5th Cir. 1958), cert. denied, 358 U.S. 928 (1959); see also Heyward v. Public Housing Administration, 135 F. Supp. 217 (S.D. Ga. 1955) (dismissing plaintiffs' claims), *aff'd* in part, rev'd in part, 238 F.2d 689 (1956), on remand to 154 F. Supp. 589 (S.D. Ga. 1957) (dismissing plaintiff's claim). On the threats, see *AJ*, 21 May 1957, clipping, James Davis Papers, box 151, Negro Housing folder. On the trial court's reliance on the separate but equal doctrine, see Heyward, 135 F. Supp. at 220.

44. When the Savannah suit was filed, the *Atlanta Daily World* reported that it might have an impact on Atlanta. See *ADW*, 14 Sept. 1952, 1. But, of course, the suit was not successful, and it did not resolve the problem of racial discrimination by the Atlanta Housing Authority. On continuing discrimination in public housing see, for example, *AI*, 6 Nov. 1965, 1; 29 May 1965; see also Grant, *Way It Was*, 497. The earliest challenges

to housing discrimination include United States v. West Peachtree Tenth Corp., 437 F.2d 221 (5th Cir. 1971); McNeil v. P-N & S Inc., 372 F. Supp. 658 (N.D. Ga. 1973) (Dekalb County).

45. See "The Community Housing Corporation," TD, n.d., Walden Papers, box 43, f. 16; "Report of Housing Coordinator", TD, 26 Aug. 1960, Atlanta Bureau of Planning Papers, box 1, f. 1; *ADW*, 26 Aug. 1947, 1, 3. The statistics on bombings are found in Meyer, *As Long As*, 104.

46. See "Report on Adair Park Transition Area," TD, 26 Aug. 1960, Atlanta Bureau of Planning Papers, box 1, f. 1; "The Community Housing Corporation," TD, n.d., Walden Papers, box 43, f. 16; "Report of Housing Coordinator", TD, 26 Aug. 1960, Atlanta Bureau of Planning Papers, box 1, f. 1; see also *ADW*, 26 Aug. 1947, 1, 3.

47. "Supplementary Report of Coordinator—Housing Relocation," TD, 19 June 1961, Atlanta Bureau of Planning Papers, box 1, f. 1; "Report on Adamsville Transition Area," TD, Aug. 26, 1960, Atlanta Bureau of Planning Papers, box 1, f. 1; Thompson, Lewis, and McEntire, "Atlanta and Birmingham," 30.

48. See Atlanta Urban League, Occasional Papers no. 1, TD, n.d., Barker Papers, box 8, Urban League folder, 1–3; Atlanta Urban League, Occasional Papers no. 3, TD, n.d., Barker Papers, box 8, Urban League folder, 2–3; Deposition of Q. V. Williamson, Armour v. Nix, no. 16708, 24 June 1975, 45–51, 61; Deposition of Robert Thompson, Armour v. Nix, no. 16708, 15 Apr. 1975, 58; Testimony of Robert Thompson, Housing Director, Atlanta Urban League, U.S. Commission on Civil Rights, Housing Hearings, Atlanta, Ga., 10 Apr. 1959: 525–26.

49. Testimony of Robert Thompson, Housing Director, Atlanta Urban League, U.S. Commission on Civil Rights, Housing Hearings, 10 Apr. 1959, 527.

50. See *AJC*, 30 July 1950, clipping, Barker Papers, box 8, Urban League folder; Atlanta Urban League, Occasional Papers no. 1, TD, n.d., Barker Papers, box 8, Urban League folder, 1–3; Atlanta Urban League, Occasional Papers no. 3, TD, n.d., Barker Papers, box 8, Urban League folder, 2–3.

51. *AJC*, 30 July 1950, clipping, Barker Papers, box 8, Urban League folder; *AJC*, 13 Dec. 1959, clipping, Davis Papers, box 155, Atlanta Schools folder; see also see also Parris and Brooks, *National Urban League*, 322.

52. Deposition of Robert Thompson, Armour v. Nix, no. 16708, 15 Apr. 1975, 19.

53. On the Urban League's philosophy, see Moore, *Search for Equality*, 86, 202–3; see also Parris and Brooks, *National Urban League*, 318–21, 322, 339–44.

54. See Drake and Cayton, *Black Metropolis*, 113–14, 201; Rabinowitz, *Race Relations*, 98–100, 102–4; Meyer, *As Long As*, 31, 33, 79. On the class element of housing desegregation litigation, see Pritchett, "Where Shall We Live?"

55. See Pritchett, *Robert Clifton Weaver*, 57–65, 81–84, 121–29, 141–43. Pritchett argues that although Weaver did not object directly to racially segregated projects during his time in the Roosevelt administration, he did fight against efforts to "entrench" segregation. Ibid. at 83. Notably, Weaver favored alternatives to racially restrictive covenants, called "occupancy agreements," in which homeowners' associations could make agreements to limit developments to single-family residences. Critics in the civil rights

community vehemently objected to the proposal. Ibid. at 129. During the 1960s, when Weaver reentered the federal housing bureaucracy, including as secretary of housing and urban development, he administered urban renewal and slum clearance programs that disproportionately displaced, segregated, or otherwise discriminated against blacks. Ibid. at 201–2, 233–324.

56. See Drake and Cayton, *Black Metropolis*, 113–14, 201; Rabinowitz, *Race Relations*, 98–100, 102–4; Meyer, *As Long As*, 31, 33, 79; Pritchett, "Where Shall We Live?" 424–25.

57. See Capeci, "Fiorello H. La Guardia"; Biondi, *To Stand and Fight*, 121–36. As a result of the Stuyvesant Town controversy, activists pressed for and eventually won the nation's first fair housing law, barring discrimination in publicly assisted private housing. However, open housing advocates definitely lost the court battle over the Stuyvesant Town development itself, as explained below, and officials seldom enforced the new antidiscrimination law.

58. See Capeci, "Fiorello H. La Guardia"; Biondi, *To Stand and Fight*, 121–36.

59. On Levittown, see Bressler, "Myers' Case"; Ruff, "For Sale" (discussing first Levittown development in New York); Pritchett, *Robert Clifton Weaver*, 165. Levitt also built housing that excluded Jews. *NYT*, 28 Dec. 1997, 24. Blacks' exclusion from new postwar suburban developments such as Levittown held profound costs: the denial of employment and educational opportunities of which whites could take advantage during the late 1940s and 1950s, a time of tremendous economic growth. On the phenomenon of expanding opportunities for whites beyond central cities and contracting opportunities for blacks within central cities during the postwar era, see Sugrue, *Origins of the Urban Crisis*; Self, *American Babylon*; see also Lassiter, *Silent Majority*. On whites' tactics of discrimination, see, for example, Meyer, *As Long As*, 8, 13–28, 30–47, 64–78, 98–102, 106–14, 116–33.

60. See Dorsey v. Stuyvesant Town Corp., 299 N.Y. 512 (Ct. App. 1949). Marshall also challenged the discrimination at Stuyvesant Town under the Equal Protection Clause of the New York constitution, which was coextensive with the U.S. Constitution's equal protection clause. See Dorsey, 299 N.Y. at 530–31. For discussions of the litigation, see Abrams, *Forbidden Neighbors*, 252–53; McGraw and Nesbitt, "Aftermath of Shelley versus Kraemer"; "Exclusion of Negroes."

61. See Johnson v. Levitt and Sons, Inc., 131 F. Supp. 114 (E.D. Pa. 1955); McGraw and Nesbitt, "Aftermath of Shelley versus Kraemer."

62. The Stuyvesant Town litigation, which Marshall joined on appeal, is Dorsey v. Stuyvesant Town Corp., 299 N.Y. 512, 522–36 (N.Y. 1949), aff'g 74 N.Y.S.2d 220 (N.Y. Spec. Term 1947), cert. denied, 339 U.S. 981 (1950). In the New York Court of Appeals, the Dorsey Court closely divided. The minority would have held that Metropolitan Life had been transformed into a state actor through its cooperative endeavors with the city. In fact, the minority concluded that the city had sanctioned the company's discriminatory policy; 299 N.Y. at 536–45. The U.S. Supreme Court declined to hear an appeal in this case.

63. The Levittown litigation is Johnson v. Levitt and Sons, Inc., 131 F. Supp. 114, 115–17 (E.D. Pa. 1955). For a discussion of cases decided during the same period as

*Dorsey* and *Johnson* that also tested that boundaries of the state action doctrine, see McGhee and Ginger, "House I Live In."

64. On the limitations of *Shelley*, see, for example, Pritchett, "Where Shall We Live?"; "Impact of Shelley v. Kraemer." The Civil Rights Act of 1968 banned discrimination on the basis of race, religion, or national origin in the sale or rental of housing. The law covered public and private dwellings, with some exemptions. One month after Congress passed the fair housing law, the U.S. Supreme Court decided Jones v. Mayer, 392 U.S. 409 (1968). The majority held that the Civil Rights Act of 1866 forbade racial discrimination in the sale or rental of housing by private individuals receiving no public funds. The landmark was based on a remarkably broad reading of the statute. Both government and individuals could seek relief from discrimination. See Meyer, *As Long As*, 203–9, 214–15.

65. See Banks v. Housing Authority, 260 P.2d 668 (Cal. D.Ct.App. 1953), cert. denied, 347 U.S. 974 (1954) (finding public housing authority's policy of selecting tenants for public housing by race unconstitutional); Detroit Housing Commission v. Lewis, 226 F.2d 180 (6th Cir. 1955) (finding that public housing commission's policy of segregating residents and limiting certain projects to whites only was unlawful racial discrimination); see also Seawell v. McWhitney, 63 Atl. 2d 542 (Sup. Ct. N.J.), rev. on other grounds, 67 Atl. 2d 309 (N.J. 1949) (finding practice by municipality and its agents of segregating public housing complexes unconstitutional). The favorable judicial rulings in these cases did not begin to remedy the segregation problem in public housing. See, for example, McGhee and Ginger, "House I Live In," 200–202.

66. Deposition of Q. V. Williamson, Armour v. Nix, no. 16708, 24 June 1975, 8–10; *ADW*, 10 Oct. 1948, 4; Thompson, Lewis, and McEntire, "Atlanta and Birmingham," 28; Ambrose, "Redrawing the Color Line," 117–18. On discrimination against black realtors, see William Brown, "Access to Housing," 66–78.

67. See Deposition of Q. V. Williamson, Armour v. Nix, no. 16708, 24 June 1975, 8–10; *ADW*, 27 May 1949, 4; see also Thompson, Lewis, and McEntire, "Atlanta and Birmingham," 28; Ambrose, "Redrawing the Color Line," 117–18.

68. On the New York fair housing laws, see Biondi, *To Stand and Fight*, 122, 132, 134–35; Capeci, "Fiorello H. La Guardia," 307–10. On the limited impact of the New York laws, see Pritchett, "Where Shall We Live?" 432–41; see also Biondi, *To Stand and Fight*, 135, for the racial breakdown of Stuyvesant Town's population in 1960. On open occupancy laws elsewhere, see Saks and Rabkin, "Racial and Religious Discrimination," 513–16, 522–23.

69. See *Pittsburgh Courier*, 8 May 1948, 1.

70. Discrimination continues to plague African Americans in the housing context. For a discussion of the continuing problem of residential segregation and limitation of court and legislative remedies, see, for example, Meyer, *As Long As*, 212–22.

71. See Thompson, Lewis, and McEntire, "Atlanta and Birmingham," 40–44; Emmett John Hughes, "The Negro's New Economic Life," *Fortune*, Sept. 1956, 251. On the pivotal role of an early pioneer, Heman E. Perry, who purchased land on Atlanta's West Side later used for black expansion, see Henderson, "Heman E. Perry," 228.

72. See Report of Program—Atlanta Urban League, 1957–58, 1, McGill Papers, box 48, f. 1; *AJC*, 13 Dec. 1959, clipping, Davis Papers, box 155, Atlanta Schools folder.

73. See *AI*, 5 June 1965, 1.

74. As chapter 12 discusses, Atlanta was more residentially segregated by 1970 than it had been in 1940; on a scale of 0 to 100, Atlanta's segregation index stood at 87 in 1940, and at 92 in 1970. See Taeuber, "Residential Segregation," 155–57. Hypersegregation in the city undermined the LDF's efforts to eliminate majority minority schools in Atlanta, consistent with its interpretation of *Brown* and subsequent school desegregation precedent.

*Chapter 4*

1. The statement from Marshall in the epigraph is from *ADW*, 25 May 1954, 1. The statement from Greenberg in the epigraph is from Greenberg, *Crusaders in the Courts*, 85.

2. See Brown v. Board of Educ., 347 U.S. 483, 489–93 and n. 11 (1954).

3. For seminal early criticisms and defenses of *Brown*, see Wechsler, "Toward Neutral Principles"; Pollak, "Racial Discrimination and Judicial Integrity," 31–32; Black, "Lawfulness of Segregation Decisions," 421–27.

4. On the chief justice's insistence upon a unanimous decision, see Klarman, *From Jim Crow*, 293–302. On postwar geopolitics and its impact on *Brown*, see Dudziak, *Cold War Civil Rights*, 79–117.

5. The unanimous opinion belied considerable uncertainty among some Justices about the proper outcome in *Brown*; Warren ultimately demanded unanimity to prevent white resistors from seizing upon a split decision in an effort to gain political advantage. See Klarman, *From Jim Crow*, 299–302.

6. The sociological evidence and logic of LDF's school desegregation campaign was subjected to wholesale criticism contemporarily and ever since, within and outside of black communities. On such criticisms, see Baldwin, "Black Self-hatred Paradigm"; Whitman, "Doll Man and His Critics," 48–57; Daryl Michael Scott, *Contempt and Pity*. For discussions of the benefits of separate schools, see, for example, Fairclough, *Class of Their Own*, 59–131. Prior scholarly treatments of particular communities' skepticism of school desegregation include Walker, *Their Highest Potential*; Cecelski, *Along Freedom Road*; Dougherty, *More Than One Struggle*; see also Patterson, *Brown v. Board*, xxiv-xxvii, 7–8. In the legal scholarship, see Bell, "Serving Two Masters." In the political science, see Michael Dawson, *Black Visions*. For a summary of scholarship that challenges the claim that blacks embraced desegregation, see Morris, "Research, Ideology, and the *Brown* Decision."

7. For excellent theoretical perspectives on *Brown*'s limitations as a remedy for racial inequality, see Guinier, "From Racial Liberalism to Racial Literacy"; Bell, "Brown v. Board of Education and the Interest-convergence Dilemma."

8. See Bacote, *Atlanta University* 227, 256–315; Read, *Spelman College*, 55–59, 114–15, 300, 325; Dittmer, *Black Georgia*, 151; Lewis, *W. E. B. Du Bois*, 1:197–98,

211–87, 386–407; Grant, *Way It Was*, 239–41, 243–47. In addition to these five colleges, Atlanta is home to the historically black Interdenominational Theological Seminary, founded in 1959, as an affiliate of Morehouse College. See Mays, *Born to Rebel*, 235–37.

9. On teaching careers at the black colleges, see Dittmer, *Black Georgia*, 144 and n. 13; Bacote, *Atlanta University*, 34, 158; Read, *Spelman College*, 363; Mays, *Born to Rebel*, 185; W. E. B. Du Bois, *Education of Black People*. On the import of teaching as careers for blacks, see Foster, *Black Teachers on Teaching*, xvii (citing U.S. Bureau of the Census, *Negro Population in the United States, 1790–1915* (New York: Arno Press, 1968); Fairclough, *Teaching Inequality*, 5; Anderson, *Education of Blacks*, 110–11.

10. See Act XXXIX, *Earliest Printed Laws*, 46; see also Anderson, *Education of Blacks*, 28, 30–31, 110–11, 239–43; Harlan, *Separate and Unequal*, 5, 210–12; Bacote, *Atlanta University*, 16–17, 25–39, 169–70; Read, *Spelman College*, 210; Fairclough, *Teaching Equality*, 2–8; Jones, *Soldiers of Light and Love*, 61–64, 68.

11. See Irvine, *In Search of Wholeness*; Brown-Nagin, "Transformation"; Fairclough, *Teaching Equality*, 5–8; see also W. E. B. Du Bois, "Does the Negro," 409.

12. See Margo, *Race and Schooling*, 8–9, 84; Anderson, *Education of Blacks*, 113–15; Dittmer, *Black Georgia*, 144; Mays, *Born to Rebel*, 190–91; see also ibid. at 188–89; Bacote, *Atlanta University*, 70–81, 107–21; Read, *Spelman College*, 125, 128, 151, 200, 212–14; Atlanta University, "Negro Common School," 5–8; J. C. Dixon, "Negro Education in Georgia," *Crisis* 40 (1933): 179–80.

13. See Tushnet, *Making Civil Rights Law*, 20–21.

14. See ibid. 20–26, 117–20; Kluger, *Simple Justice*, 214–15, 379.

15. C. L. Harper to Ira Jarrell, TLS, 9 Jan. 1942, Atlanta Education Association Papers, box 2010, Ira Jarrell, 1941–43 folder.

16. Minutes, Executive Board Meeting, Atlanta Education Association Papers, box 2030, folder 5; George E. Manners to Ira Jarrell, 9 Dec. 1941, Atlanta Education Association Papers, box 2010, Ira Jarrell, 1941–43 folder.

17. *ADW*, 8 Nov. 1947, 6.

18. *ADW*, 6 Nov. 1947, 1, 4; 6 Nov. 1947, 4; 12 Nov. 1947, 6; 19 Nov. 1947, 1; see also Fairclough, *Teaching Equality*, 59.

19. See Davis v. Cook, 80 F. Supp. 443, 445–51 (N.D. Ga. 1948); Teachers Equal Pay Suit Bulletin, no. 3, 17 Nov. 1947, TD, Barker Papers, box 8, Atlanta Teachers Union folder.

20. See Davis v. Cook, 80 F. Supp. 443, 445–51 (N.D. Ga. 1948); Teachers Equal Pay Suit Bulletin, no. 3, 17 Nov. 1947, TD, Barker Papers, box 8, Atlanta Teachers Union folder; see also Grant, *Way It Was*, 374; Mays, *Born to Rebel*, 205.

21. See Teachers Equal Pay Suit Bulletin, no. 3, 13 Nov. 1947, TD, Barker Papers, box 8, Atlanta Teachers Union folder; Teachers Equal Pay Suit Bulletin, 17 Nov. 1947.

22. See Teachers Equal Pay Suit Bulletin, no. 3, 13 Nov. 1947, TD, Barker Papers, box 8, Atlanta Teachers Union folder; Teachers Equal Pay Suit Bulletin, 17 Nov. 1947.

23. See Teachers Equal Pay Suit Bulletin, no. 3, 13 Nov. 1947, TD, Barker Papers, box 8, Atlanta Teachers Union folder; Teachers Equal Pay Suit Bulletin, 17 Nov. 1947; *ADW*,

11 Nov. 1947, 1; 12 Nov. 1947, 1, 6; 13 Nov. 1947, 1, 4; 20 Nov. 1947, 1; TD all in Barker Papers, box 8, Atlanta Teachers Union folder.

24. See Teachers Equal Pay Suit Bulletin, 13 Nov. 1947; 17 Nov. 1947; *ADW*, 11 Nov. 1947, 1; 12 Nov. 1947, 1, 6; 13 Nov. 1947, 1, 4; 20 Nov. 1947, 1; TDall in Barker Papers, box 8, Atlanta Teachers Union folder.

25. See Teachers Equal Pay Suit Bulletin, 13 Nov. 1947; Teachers Equal Pay Suit Bulletin, no. 4, 14 Nov. 1947, TD, Barker Papers, box 8, Atlanta Teachers Union folder; Teachers Equal Pay Suit Bulletin, 17 Nov. 1947; Teachers Equal Pay Suit Bulletin, no. 3, 18 Nov. 1947, TD, Barker Papers, box 8, Atlanta Teachers Union folder; *ADW*, 6 Nov. 1947, 1, 4; 6 Nov. 1947, 4; 11 Nov. 1947, 1; 15 Nov. 1947, 1, 6; 16 Nov. 1947, 1; 18 Nov. 1947, 1; TD all in Barker Papers, box 8, Atlanta Teachers Union folder.

26. See Teachers Equal Pay Suit Bulletin, 13 Nov. 1947; 14 Nov. 1947; 17 Nov. 1947; 18 Nov. 1947; *ADW*, 6 Nov. 1947, 1, 4; 6 Nov. 1947, 4; 11 Nov. 1947, 1; 15 Nov. 1947, 1, 6; 16 Nov. 1947, 1; 18 Nov. 1947, 1; TD all in Barker Papers, box 8, Atlanta Teachers Union folder.

27. See Teachers Equal Pay Suit Bulletin, 18 Nov. 1947; *ADW*, 18 Nov. 1947, 1; TD all in Barker Papers, box 8, Atlanta Teachers Union folder.

28. See Teachers Equal Pay Suit Bulletin, 13 Nov. 1947; 14 Nov. 1947; 17 Nov. 1947; 18 Nov. 1947; *ADW*, 6 Nov. 1947, 1, 4; 6 Nov. 1947, 4; 11 Nov. 1947, 1; 15 Nov. 1947, 1, 6; 16 Nov. 1947, 1; 18 Nov. 1947, 1; TD all in Barker Papers, box 8, Atlanta Teachers Union folder.

29. The early cases were Mills v. Board of Education of Anne Arundel County, 30 F. Supp. 245 (D. Md. 1939); Alston v. School Board of Norfolk, 112 F.2d 992 (4th Cir.), cert. denied, 311 U.S. 693 (1940). On these cases, see Tushnet, *NAACP's Legal Strategy*, 61–69, 78–81; Kluger, *Simple Justice*, 215–16, 297, 303, 472, 475.

30. Davis v. Cook, 55 F. Supp. 1004 (N.D. Ga. 1944) (denying defendants' motion to dismiss); Davis v. Cook, 80 F. Supp. 443 (N.D. Ga. 1948), rev'd Cook v. Davis, 178 F.2d 595, 600–601 (5th Cir. 1949) (reversing for failure to exhaust administrative remedies), cert. denied 71 S. Ct. 38 (1950). See also *NYT*, 29 Sept. 1948, 34; Motley, *Equal Justice*, 78; *ADW*, 6 Nov. 1947, 1, 4.

31. *ADW*, 30 Dec. 1949, 4; 20 Sept. 1950, 3.

32. *ADW*, 30 Dec. 1949, 4; 20 Sept. 1950, 3; *AC*, 21 Sept. 1950, A1; 21 Sept. 1950, A8. For a discussion of ways in which school districts perpetuated racial discrimination after forced by salary equalization suits to end facially discriminatory practices, see Tushnet, *NAACP's Legal Strategy*, 90–93, 96–97; Brown-Nagin, "Transformation."

33. See Teachers Equal Pay Suit Bulletin, 18 Nov. 1947, TD, Barker Papers, box 8, Atlanta Teachers Union folder.

34. See Dittmer, *Black Georgia*; Bayor, *Race and the Shaping*, 210–18; Rouse, *Lugenia Burns Hope*, 74–79; see also *ADW*, 14 Sept. 1948, 1; 16 June 1947, 1; 30 May 1948, 1; 11 June 1948, 1.

35. "A Summary of the Work of the Citizens Committee on Public Education Organized by the Atlanta Urban League, 1944 to 1946," TD, Atlanta Urban League Papers, box 23, f. 14; *Spritzer and Bergmark, Grace Towns Hamilton*, 102–8; Dittmer, *Black Georgia*, 148; Bayor, *Race and the Shaping*, 210–18.

36. "A Supplemental Report on Public School Facilities for Negroes, Atlanta, Georgia, 1948," Atlanta Urban League Papers, box 23, f. 14; *Spritzer and Bergmark, Grace Towns Hamilton*, 107–8.

37. See *ADW*, 21 Sept. 1947, 1; 26 Sept. 1947, 1.

38. See *ADW*, 21 Sept. 1947, 1; 26 Sept. 1947, 4; 13 Nov. 1947, 4.

39. See *ADW*, 21 Sept. 1947, 1; 27 Apr. 1946, 1; 9 Sept. 1948, 1; 26 Sept. 1947, 4; 1 May 1946, 6; 13 Nov. 1947, 4; 14 Jan. 1948, 4; 9 Sept. 1950, 4; 5 Aug. 1948, 2; 19 Sept. 1947, 1; 12 Jan. 1949, 4; 11 Jan. 1949, 1; Tushnet, *Making Civil Rights Law*, 121–23, 129–30, 133–34.

40. See *ADW*, 20 Sept. 1950, 1; 30 Apr. 1946, 1; *AC*, 20 Sept. 1950, A1, 4. None of the seminal studies of the NAACP's campaign to end school segregation mention *Aaron v. Cook*.

41. See "The Virginia School Fight—a Clarification," *Crisis* 58 (Apr. 1951): 228–30; Walter White, "Report on Civil Rights in 1951," *Crisis* 59 (Feb. 1952): 98; see also Tushnet, *NAACP's Legal Strategy*, 130–36.

42. See *NYT*, 26 Sept. 1950, 22; *AC*, 20 Sept. 1950, A1, 4; 21 Sept. 1950, A1; 21 Sept. 1950, A1; 21 Sept. 1950, A8.

43. See *NYT*, 26 Sept. 1950, 22; *AC*, 20 Sept. 1950, A1, 4; 21 Sept. 1950, A1; 21 Sept. 1950, A8.

44. *ADW*, 21 Sept. 1950, 4; 28 Sept. 1950, 1; 20 Sept. 1950, 1, 5. On Ward's application to Georgia, which some blacks opposed, see Mays, *Born to Rebel*, 205–8; *ADW*, 11 Nov. 1951, 1; 14 June 1951, 1.

45. See, for example, "An Analysis of Per-Pupil School Expenditures By Race, 1948–1949, 1949–1950," 15 Aug. 1950, TD, Barker Papers, box 8, Urban League folder; Report of Executive Secretary, ANVL, TD, 23 Sept. 1949, Walden Papers, series VII, box 1, f. 4. On the meeting about the school suit and Hamilton's role in it, see *ADW*, 11 Jan. 1949, 1; 24 Sept. 1950, 1; see also *Spritzer and Bergmark, Grace Towns Hamilton*, 108.

46. See *ADW*, 24 Sept. 1950, 1; see also *Spritzer and Bergmark, Grace Towns Hamilton*, 108.

47. See *ADW*, 14 Apr. 1950, 1; 14 Apr. 1950, 3; 10 Feb. 1949, 2; 26 Aug. 1947, 1; 27 Aug. 1947, 1; 31 Aug. 1947, 1. On the organizational history of the GTEA, see Georgia Teachers, *Rising in the Sun*, 27–28, 49, 86–101.

48. See *ADW*, 14 Apr. 1950, 1; 10 Feb. 1949, 2; 26 Aug. 1947, 1; 27 Aug. 1947, 1; 31 Aug. 1947, 1.

49. "October 4, 1950 Hungry Club Broadcast Over Station WERD By Dr. Benjamin E. Mays," TD, Walden Papers, box 43, f. 2; C. L. Harper to "Our Teachers," TLS, 6 Oct. 1950, Walden Papers, box 43, f. 2; Benjamin E. Mays, "Why an Atlanta School Suit," *New South*, Sept.–Oct. 1950, McGill Papers, box 58, f. 4.

50. "October 4, 1950 Hungry Club Broadcast Over Station WERD By Dr. Benjamin E. Mays," TD, Walden Papers, box 43, f. 2; Harper to "Our Teachers"; Benjamin E. Mays, "Why an Atlanta School Suit."

51. See *ADW*, 30 Apr. 1946, 1; 9 Sept. 1948, 1; 21 Jan. 1948, 1; 13 June 1950, 1; 11 June 1950, 1.

52. See *ADW*, 28 June 1951, 1; Greenberg, "Racial Integration," 584–87.

53. See Lester B. Granger, "Does the Negro Want Integration?" *Crisis* 58 (Feb. 1951): 73–79; Guy B. Johnson, "Segregation vs. Integration," *Crisis* 60 (Dec. 1953): 591–66.

54. See *ADW*, 7 June 1950, 4; 6 June 1950, 1; 11 June 1950, 1; "October 4, 1950 Hungry Club Broadcast Over Station WERD By Dr. Benjamin E. Mays," TD, Walden Papers, box 43, f. 2; Harper to "Our Teachers"; see also Allen, *Atlanta Rising*, 46.

55. See Benjamin E. Mays, "We Are Unnecessarily Excited," TD, n.d., McGill Papers, box 58, f. 5; Peeks, *ADW*, 28 Jan. 1954, 1; 27 Apr. 1954, 1.

56. See *ADW*, 7 June 1950, 4; 6 June 1950, 1; 11 June 1950, 1; Allen, *Atlanta Rising*, 46.

57. See Johnson, "Desegregation of Public Education"; *ADW*, 27 Sept. 1951, 1; 17 May 1951, 1; see also *ADW*, 23 Dec. 1951, 1; Greenberg, "Racial Integration," 585.

58. See *SSN*, 3 Sept. 1954; *ADW*, 30 Mar. 1952, 1; 31 Mar. 1952, 1; 28 Feb. 1952, 1; 12 Feb. 1952, 1; 6 Feb. 1952, 5; 19 Jan. 1952, 5.

59. See, for example, *ADW*, 31 Jan. 1952, 1.

60. See *ADW*, 4 June 1955, 1; 5 June 1955, 1; see also Harmon, *Beneath the Image*, 98. On the litigation in the other states and the district, see *NYT*, 10 Dec. 1952, 1; *ADW*, 31 May 1951, 2; 12 July 1951, 1; 12 Aug. 1951, 1; see also Tushnet, *NAACP's Legal Strategy*, 138–41.

61. See Brown v. Board of Education, 347 U.S. 483, 495 (1954) and n. 11.

62. See *AC*, 18 May 1954, A1; 18 May 1954, A4; 18 May 1954, A10; 19 May 1954, A1; 19 May 1954, A1, 6; 9 Jan. 1957, A1; 14 Nov. 1958, A13; see also Lankevich, *Atlanta*, 63; O'Brien, "Georgia's Response," 99, 110–38, 143–50, 160–67, 175; McMillen, *Citizens' Council*, 81–85, 89–90; Grant, *Way It Was*, 378.

63. See *AC*, 18 May 1954, A1; *ADW*, 24 June 1954, 1; 25 June 1954, 1; 26 June 1954, 1; 30 Sept. 1954, 1; see also O'Brien, "Georgia's Response," 99, 110–38, 143–50, 160–67, 175; McMillen, *Citizens' Council*, 81–85, 89–90; Grant, *Way It Was*, 378.

64. *ADW*, 18 May 1954, 1, 5; 18 May 1954, 2; 18 May 1954, 6; 25 May 1954, 6; 26 May 1954, 1; 23 May 1954, 1.

65. *ADW*, 25 May 1954 1; 10 June 1954, 1.

66. See *ADW*, 14 July 1954, 1; 23 May 1954, 1; 27 Apr. 1954, 1; 18 May 1954, 1, 5.

67. See *SSN*, June 1956; *ADW*, 14 July 1954, 1; 23 May 1954, 1; 27 Apr. 1954, 1; 8 Aug. 1954, 4; Nasstrom, "Women, Civil Rights Movement," 131–37; *ADW*, 19 May 1954, 2; Kluger, *Simple Justice*, 391–92.

68. See *SSN*, June 1956; *ADW*, 27 Apr. 1954, 1; 19 May 1954, 2.

69. See *SSN*, 3 Sept. 1954; 1 Oct. 1954; 3 Feb. 1956; May 1956; 1 Oct. 1954; 4 Nov. 1954; Oct. 1955; Jan. 1956; Haney, "Effects of the *Brown* Decision"; Rosenthal, "Negro Teachers' Attitudes"; Kluger, *Simple Justice*, 391–92; Fairclough, *Teaching Equality*, 45, 58, 64.

70. On southern states' efforts to drive the NAACP out, see Tushnet, *Making Civil Rights Law*, 283–300; Carter, *A Matter of Law*, 147–59, 162–63; Greenberg, *Crusaders in the Court*, 217–22; *ADW*, 7 Aug. 1955, 1; 13 July 1955, 1; 16 Aug. 1955, 1; 27 Feb. 1954, 4. Cook's investigation of the local branch resulted in prolonged litigation and

an uncollected fine against the branch. See *ADW*, 31 Mar. 1959, 1; Petition for a Writ of Certiorari to the Supreme Court, 28–30, Williams v. NAACP, General Case Material, 1959–1960, in *NAACP Papers*, pt. 23A, rl. 16, frs. 608–9. The matter is discussed in greater detail in chapter 10.

71. See Fairclough, *Class of Their Own*, 367.

72. *ADW*, 25 May 1954, 1.

73. *AC*, 18 May 1954, A1. *Aaron v. Cook* had been dismissed for lack of prosecution in 1956. *ADW*, 1 June 1955, 1; 1 June 1955, 1; 2 June 1955, 1; O'Brien, "Georgia's Response," 99, 139.

74. See *ADW*, 1 June 1955, 4; 3 June 1955, 1; see also *ADW*, 27 Mar. 1954, 1.

75. Minutes of the Board of Education of the City of Atlanta, 13 June 1955, Atlanta Board of Education Papers, Desegregation File; Minutes of the Board of Education of the City of Atlanta, TD, 11 July 1955, Atlanta Board of Education Papers, Desegregation File; Complaint at 5, Calhoun v. Latimer, no. 71-2622 (N.D. Ga., 11 Jan. 1958), Case File, NARA, box 53, f. 1; *ADW*, 3 June 1955, 1.

76. Minutes of the Board of Education of the City of Atlanta, June 13, 1955, Atlanta Board of Education Papers, Desegregation File; Minutes of the Board of Education of the City of Atlanta, TD, 11 July 1955, Atlanta Board of Education Papers, Desegregation File; Complaint at 5, Calhoun v. Latimer, no. 71-2622 (N.D. Ga., 11 Jan. 1958), Case File, NARA, box 53, f. 1.

77. *ADW*, 16 Nov. 1954, 1; *ADW*, 3 June 1955, 1.

78. See Minutes of the Board of Education of the City of Atlanta, 12 Sept. 1955, Atlanta Board of Education Papers, Desegregation file; 13 Feb. 1956; 11 June 1956; *ADW*, 16 Nov. 1954, 1; *ADW*, 3 June 1955, 1.

79. Minutes of the Board of Education of the City of Atlanta, 8 Aug. 1955, Atlanta Board of Education Papers, Desegregation file; Statement of the Education Committee of the Atlanta NAACP Branch, 11 Sept. 1955, NAACP Papers, part V, box 2562, branch files; *ADW*, 9 Aug. 1955, 1.

80. See Statement of the Education Committee of the Atlanta NAACP Branch, 11 Sept. 1955 NAACP Papers, part V, box 2562, branch files; see also *ADW*, 13 Sept. 1955, 1.

81. See NAACP Annual Report 1954, TD, Davis Papers, box 151, NAACP file, 6–9, 24; *SSN* 1 (1 Oct. 1954); see also Tushnet, *Making Civil Rights Law*, 218–19.

82. *ADW*, 25 June 1954, 1.

83. See *SSN*, 1 Oct. 1954; 4 Nov. 1954; 1 Dec. 1954; 6 Jan. 1955; Jan. 1956; Apr. 1956; Aug. 1956.

84. Du Bois, "Postscript: Anti-segregation Campaign," *Crisis* 41 (Jan. 1934): 182; Du Bois, "Does the Negro."

## Chapter 5

1. The statement from Holmes in the epigraph is quoted in *ADW*, 8 Nov. 1955, 1.

2. The statement from Borders in the epigraph is from *AC*, 10 Jan. 1959, A1.

3. See NAACP Annual Report 1954, TD, Davis Papers, box 151, NAACP file.

4. See *ADW*, 22 July 1951, 4; 22 Jan. 1952, 5; 30 July 1951, 1.

5. See Holmes v. City of Atlanta, 350 U.S. 879 (1955).

6. *AC*, 24 Dec. 1955, A1, 2.

7. See Thomas interview, 4; see also *AC*, 24 Dec. 1955, A1, 2; *ADW*, 8 Nov. 1955, 1.

8. *AC*, 24 Dec. 1955, A1, 2; 8 Nov. 1955, A1; *ADW*, 8 Nov. 1955, 1; 27 Dec. 1955, 1; 25 Dec. 1955, A1, 9. See also Holmes v. Atlanta, 124 F. Supp. 290 (N.D. Ga. 1954).

9. Thomas interview, 5; Moore interview, 2; *AC*, 9 July 1955, A1.

10. *AC*, 8 Nov. 1955, A1; 9 July 1955, A1; see also Holmes v. City of Atlanta, 350 U.S. 879 (1955).

11. *AC*, 8 Nov. 1955, A1; *ADW*, 10 Nov. 1955, 1; see also *ADW*, 11 Nov. 1955, 1.

12. *AC*, 9 Nov. 1955, A1, 13; *ADW*, 11 Nov. 1955, 4.

13. *ADW*, 23 Dec. 1955, 1; *AC*, 8 Nov. 1955, A1.

14. Bayor, *Race and the Shaping*, 151–52.

15. See Report on Parks and Recreational Facilities for the Negro Population of Atlanta, Georgia, Jan. 1954, Barker Papers, box 8, Urban League file; see also Bayor, *Race and the Shaping*, 20, 25–26, 28, 36, 132, 134, 147–52.

16. See Annual Meeting, Fulton-Dekalb Interracial Committee, 5 Dec. 1939, Barker Papers, box 9, Fulton-Dekalb Interracial Committee File.

17. See Report on Parks and Recreational Facilities for the Negro Population of Atlanta, Georgia, Jan. 1954, Barker Papers, box 8, Urban League file; see also Bayor, *Race and the Shaping*, 36.

18. See Report on Parks and Recreational Facilities for the Negro Population of Atlanta, Georgia, Jan. 1954, Barker Papers, box 8, Urban League file; *ADW*, 5 June 1954, 1; see also Bayor, *Race and the Shaping*, 151.

19. See Report on Parks and Recreational Facilities for the Negro Population of Atlanta, Georgia, Jan. 1954, Barker Papers, box 8, Urban League file; *ADW*, 5 June 1954, 1; see also Bayor, *Race and the Shaping*, 151.

20. See Dawson v. Baltimore, 220 F.2d 386, 386–88 (4th Cir.), *aff'd* 350 U.S. 877 (1955); see also Palmer v. Thompson, 403 U.S. 217, 244 (1971) (noting that the Court "resolved any possible ambiguity" about *Brown*'s reach in this area by "ma[king] it clear that state-sanctioned segregation in the operation of public recreational facilities was prohibited in Mayor & City Council of Baltimore v. Dawson, 350 U.S. 877 (1955) and Dawson v. Baltimore, 220 F.2d 386, 386–88 (4th Cir. 1955)).

21. See chapters 7 and 8.

22. See Fairclough, *To Redeem*, 15–18; Garrow, *Bearing the Cross*, 11–82. The legal case is Browder v. Gayle, 142 F. Supp. 707 (M.D. Ala.), *aff'd* 352 U.S. 903 (1956). For an excellent discussion of the case and its social context, see Kennedy, "Martin Luther King's Constitution."

23. Fairclough, *To Redeem*, 18–20, 43; Garrow, *Bearing the Cross*, 66–79, 173–230; Branch, *Parting the Waters*, 145.

24. Klarman, *From Jim Crow*, 369–71.

25. See "Two Southern Cases," *Crisis* 37 (1930): 16–17.

26. See ibid.

27. See "Conference with Georgia Power Officials," TD, 12 Nov. 1942, Barker Papers, box 82, Committee on Interracial Cooperation file.

28. Petition to Georgia Public Service Commission, 6 Oct. 1953, Walden Papers, MSS 614, series III, box 1, f. 8.

29. A. T. Walden to Mayor and City Council, TL, 31 Oct. 1953, Walden Papers, MSS 614, series III, box 1, f. 8. On Blackburn's activism, see Nasstrom, "Down to Now."

30. A. T. Walden to Mayor and City Council, TL, 31 Oct. 1953, Walden Papers, MSS 614, series III, box 1, f. 8.

31. See J. C. Steinmetz to Ruby Blackburn, 14 Oct. 1953, Walden Papers, series III, box 1, f. 9; J. C. Steinmetz to Georgia Public Service Commission, TLS, 20 Oct. 1953, Walden Papers, series III, box 1, f. 9; ADW, 9 Oct. 1953, 1; Robert Sommerville to A. T. Walden, TLS, 1 Nov. 1955, Walden Papers, series III, box 1, f. 9; Robert Sommerville to A. T. Walden, TLS, 17 Jan. 1956, Walden Papers, series III, box 1, f. 9; A. T. Walden to Robert Sommerville, TL, 20 Jan. 1956, Walden Papers, series III, box 1, f. 9.

32. King, Daddy King, 154, 155–56.

33. AC, 11 Jan. 1957, A1, 11; ADW, 9 Jan. 1957, 1, 5.

34. Branch, Parting the Waters, 198–99; AC, 8 Jan. 1957, A1; ADW, 11 Jan. 1957, 1.

35. ADW, 10 Jan. 1957, 1; 11 Jan. 1957, 1.

36. ADW, 9 Jan. 1957, 6; AC, 21 Jan. 1959, A1; ADW, 10 Jan. 1957, 1; 11 Jan. 1957, 1; 10 Jan. 1959, 1; AC, 10 Jan. 1957, 1, 10; see also Harmon, Beneath the Image, 70–71; Robinson, Montgomery Bus Boycott, 53–55; Branch, Parting the Waters, 134–35.

37. Williams v. Georgia Public Service Commission is an unreported case; the decision was read from bench by the presiding judge. ADW, 10 Jan. 1959, 1.

38. See ADW, 13 Jan. 1959; 10 Jan. 1959, 1; AC, 10 Jan. 1959, A1; AC, 10 Jan. 1959, A1.

39. AC, 21 Jan. 1959, A1; see also AC, 10 Jan. 1959, A1; ADW, 13 Jan. 1959; 10 Jan. 1959, 1; 10 Jan. 1959, 6.

40. King, Daddy King, 154, 155–56; Harmon, Beneath the Image, 70–71; AC, 11 Jan. 1957, A1, 11; Pomerantz, Where Peachtree Meets, 217.


Chapter 6

1. The statement from Walden in the epigraph is from ADW, 18 Mar. 1960, 1.

2. The statement from Holt in the epigraph is from Holt, Act of Conscience, 67.

3. See Chafe, Civilities and Civil Rights, 75–79, 82–86, 100–109; Halberstam, Children, 26, 69, 76.

4. See Rosenberg, Hollow Hope, 7, 70, 107, 145; Klarman, From Jim Crow, 377, 466–68.

5. See Brown v. Board of Education, 347 U.S. 483 (1954); Brown v. Board of Education, 349 U.S. 329 (1955); Cooper v. Aaron, 358 U.S. 1 (1958).

6. See Shuttlesworth v. Birmingham Board of Education, 162 F. Supp. 372, 379–84 (N.D. Ala.), aff'd 358 U.S. 101 (1958); SSN, Sept. 1957, 5–7; May 1958, 9; June 1958, 8–9; Dec. 1958, 3–4; see also Manis, Fire You Can't Put Out, xx, 146–54; Klarman, From Jim Crow, 312–20, 329–33; NYT, 30 Dec. 1958, 34.

7. See Martin Luther King, Jr., "The Social Organization of Nonviolence," in *Essential Writings*, p. 31; "Love, Law, and Civil Disobedience," in *Essential Writings*, p. 44.

8. See "October 1960 Conference Editorial," TD, SNCC Papers, box 25, Miscellaneous Statements 1960 Folder; USN&WR, 14 Mar. 1960, 41; "We're So Very Happy," *New Republic*, 25 Apr. 1960, 13; Lewis interview, 2; Bond interview by Fort; Bond interview, McGill Papers, 1; *AI*, 31 Oct. 1960, 2; Halberstam, *Children*, 26, 69, 76; Lewis, *Walking with the Wind*, 45.

9. On relationship between student protests and students' views of inadequacy of law, see Thurgood Marshall, "The Cry for Freedom," *Crisis* 67 (May 1960): 287–90; Roy Wilkins to Presidents of NAACP Branches, TM, 2 Feb. 1961, NAACP Papers, Group III, series A, Sit-ins file, rl. 22, fr. 00001; *NYT*, 15 Feb. 1960, 1; 21 Feb. 1960, E3; 17 Apr. 1960, 32; 6 Mar. 1960, E3; "While Congress Debates," *New Republic*, 28 Mar. 1960, 4; Bond interview by Fort; Bond interview, McGill Papers, 1; Holt, *Act of Conscience*, 67; *AC*, 23 Feb. 1960, 7; Lewis, *Walking with the Wind*, 107–8.

10. See Marshall, "Cry for Freedom"; Roy Wilkins to Presidents of NAACP Branches, TM, 2 Feb. 1961, NAACP Papers, Group III, series A, Sit-ins file, rl. 22, fr. 00001; Roy Wilkins to Kivie Kaplan, TL, 24 Apr. 1961, NAACP Papers, Group III, series A, Sit-ins file, rl. 22, fr. 00001.

11. See Marshall, "Cry for Freedom"; Wilkins to Presidents of NAACP Branches, TM, 2 Feb. 1961, NAACP Papers, Group III, series A, Sit-ins file, rl. 22, fr. 00001; Roy Wilkins to Kivie Kaplan, TL, 24 Apr. 1961, NAACP Papers, Group III, series A, Sit-ins file, rl. 22, fr. 00001; Wilkins, *Standing Fast*, 269–70; see also Williams, *Thurgood Marshall*, 251–52, 286–90, 341; see also Holt, *Act of Conscience*, 67.

12. See Wright, "Doughnuts and Democracy," *Crisis* 60 (May 1960): 277–86; *AC*, 23 Feb. 1960, 7. On SNCC's media and communications strategy, see Murphee, *Selling of Civil Rights*, 2–6, 13–15, 20–23, 28–30, 34–35, 38, 40.

13. See Chafe, *Civilities and Civil Rights*, 100–109; see also Hampton and Fayer, *Voices of Freedom*, 55–57.

14. See Chafe, *Civilities and Civil Rights*, 98–141.

15. Statement by John Lewis, TD, Feb. 1965, SNCC Papers, box 3, f. 2. On SNCC, see Carson, *In Struggle*, 19–25; Ransby, *Ella Baker*, 239–64.

16. See Chafe, *Civilities and Civil Rights*, 99; *NYT*, 15 Feb. 1960, 1; 21 Feb. 1960, E3; Meier, "Negro Protest Movements and Organizations," 437–50.

17. See "Requiem for Jim Crow," *Nation*, 12 Mar. 1960, 218; *NYT*, 15 Feb. 1960, 1.

18. See *Beyond Atlanta*, 74–109, 111; Sokol, *There Goes My Everything*, 47, 83–84; Kruse, *White Flight*, 131–34, 180–83, 219–20; Lassiter, *Silent Majority*, 26–30, 77; Fite, *Richard B. Russell, Jr.*, 331–48.

19. See *SSN*, Mar. 1960, 1. One important recent study of Atlanta places the city in the vanguard of the sit-in movement. See Grady-Willis, *Challenging*, xx, 6. However, many histories note, as I have here, that the Atlanta sit-ins began well after those in other cities. See Bayor, *Race and the Shaping*, 32–34; Tuck, *Beyond Atlanta*, 110–13; Walker, "Functions of Disunity," 342-61; Walker, "Protest and Negotiation."

20. See Bond interview, McGill Papers, 4; Walker, "Sit-Ins in Atlanta," 64–65, 85; Fort, "Atlanta Sit-in Movement," 129–37; *NYT*, 20 Mar. 1960, E8.

21. See *WP*, 29 Feb. 1960, at A1; *AC*, 24 Feb. 1960, 7; 23 Feb. 1960, 7; Bond interview, McGill Papers, 4; Walker, "Protest and Negotiation," 101; Walker, "Sit-Ins in Atlanta," 64–65, 85; Fort, "Atlanta Sit-in Movement," 129–37; King, *Daddy King*, 153–58; Garrow, *Bearing the Cross*, 128–30.

22. See Walker, "Protest and Negotiation," 101; Walker, "Sit-Ins in Atlanta," 64–65, 85; Fort, "Atlanta Sit-in Movement," 129–37; King, *Daddy King*, 153–58; Garrow, *Bearing the Cross*, 128–30.

23. See *SSN*, Mar. 1960, 1; *AC*, 11 Feb. 1960, 10; 19 Feb. 1960, 1;; *Chicago Tribune*, 19 Apr. 1960, 8.

24. *SSN*, Feb. 1960, 1; *AC*, 27 Feb. 1960, 1, 8.

25. *SSN*, Feb. 1960, 1; *AC*, 27 Feb. 1960, 1, 8; *WP*, 29 Feb. 1960, A1; Roche, *Restructured Resistance*, 47–68; Bartley, *Creation of Modern Georgia*, 214–16.

26. See Walker, "Sit-Ins in Atlanta," 63–65; Branch, *Parting the Waters*, 30; Mays, *Born to Rebel*, xxiv–xxv, 90–91.

27. Bond interview, McGill Papers,1; see also Anderson, *Education of Blacks*, 23, 176–77; Rose and Greenya, *Black Leaders*, 25, 29, 36; Urban, *Black Scholar: Horace Mann Bond*, 74–167.

28. Bond interview by Fort; Bond interview, McGill Papers, 1; Rose and Greenya, *Black Leaders*, 25, 29, 36; see also *WP*, 23 Jan. 1966, E3; Branch, *Parting the Waters*, 874; Pomerantz, *Where Peachtree Meets*, 255; Anderson, *Education of Blacks*, 23, 176–77; Halberstam, *Children*, 217, 571, 647, 649; see also Bond, *Education of the Negro*; Fort, "Atlanta Sit-in Movement," 133; Henderson, *Atlanta Life Insurance Company*, 121, 123–26; Bacote, *Atlanta University*, 205–20, 236–42, 276–84, 320; Jewell, "Black Ivy," 67–72, 85–108, 109–33.

29. See King Interview, McGill Papers, box 110, f. 4.

30. See Brown interview; Lonnie King interview by Fort; King interview, McGill Papers, 4, 7; Pomerantz, *Where Peachtree Meets*, 252; Allen, *Atlanta Rising*, 90–91; Mays, *Born to Rebel*, 287; Fort, "Atlanta Sit-in Movement," 131–32.

31. Bond interview by Fort; Bond interview, McGill Papers, 1; Rose and Greenya, *Black Leaders*, 25, 29, 36; Branch, *Parting the Waters*, 874; Pomerantz, *Where Peachtree Meets*, 255; Anderson, *Education of Blacks*, 23, 176–77; Halberstam, *Children*, 217, 571, 647, 649; see also Bond, *Education of the Negro*; Fort, "Atlanta Sit-in Movement," 133; Henderson, *Atlanta Life Insurance Company*, 121, 123–26; Bacote, *Atlanta University*, 205–20, 236–42, 276–84, 320; Jewell, "Black Ivy," 67–72, 85–108, 109–33.

32. King's military training inclined toward a "bureaucratic administrative structure" that replicated the hierarchy of the armed services. This background may have contributed to a controversy that developed surrounding King's leadership of the Atlanta movement in early 1960. Some students claimed that King did not have a "constituency"; yet, he "ignored" that question and continued to recruit students for the movement. He had wanted to hold a sit-in the city on February 12 (Lincoln's birthday) but could not find enough interested students to make an impressive showing; only twenty agreed to participate. Eventually, King and Bond rallied more students to the cause. Fort, "Atlanta Sit-in Movement," 131–32.

33. Fort, "Atlanta Sit-in Movement," 131–32; King interview, McGill Papers, at 10; Fort, "Atlanta Sit-in Movement," 158; Harmon, *Beneath the Image*, 128–29.

34. See *AC*, 9 Mar. 1960, 13; Fort, "Atlanta Sit-in Movement," 125–25, 133; Walker, "Sit-Ins in Atlanta," 65; Fort, "Atlanta Sit-in Movement," 183, 187; Brown interview.

35. See "An Appeal for Human Rights," *AC*, 9 Mar. 1960, 13.

36. See *ADW*, 10 Mar. 1960, 1; *AC*, 9 Mar. 1960, 1; *ADW*, 11 Mar. 1960, 4; Paschall, *It Must Have Rained*, 14–15, 20; Mays, *Born to Rebel*, 290; Walker, "Sit-Ins in Atlanta," 67.

37. See *AC*, 19 Mar. 1960, 1; *ADW*, 16 Mar. 1960, 1; *NYT*, 16 Mar. 1960, 27; *AC*, 16 Mar. 1960, 12; Walker, "Sit-Ins in Atlanta," 67; Walker, "Protest and Negotiation," 102; Fort, "Atlanta Sit-in Movement," 132–34; Brown interview; King interview; Fort, "Atlanta Sit-in Movement," 124, 153; Bond interview, McGill Papers, 4.

38. See *AC*, 19 Mar. 1960, 1.

39. See *AC*, 16 Mar. 1960, 5; 16 Mar. 1960, 12; 19 Mar. 1960, 1; *ADW*, 16 Mar. 1960, 1; *NYT*, 16 Mar. 1960, 27; Walker, "Sit-Ins in Atlanta," 67; Allen, *Atlanta Rising*, 90–91; Walker, "Protest and Negotiation," 102; Harmon, *Beneath the Image*, 132; Mays, *Born to Rebel*, 290; Fort, "Atlanta Sit-in Movement," 124, 132–34, 153; Brown interview; Lonnie King interview by Fort; Bond interview, McGill Papers, 4.

40. *AC*, 16 Mar. 1960, 4; *ADW*, 16 Mar. 1960, 4; 17 Mar. 1960, 1; 18 Mar. 1960, 1; *AC*, 30 Mar. 1960, 7; Walker, "Sit-Ins in Atlanta," 68–69.

41. Benjamin E. Mays to Roy Wilkins, TL, 19 Mar. 1960, Benjamin Mays Papers, Moorland-Spingarn Research Center, Howard University, Installment 2, box 36, Correspondence folder; *NYT*, 20 Mar. 1960, E8; Fort, "Atlanta Sit-in Movement," 158; see also Barnes, *Journey from Jim Crow*, 132–56.

42. *ADW*, 18 Mar. 1960, 1; Walker, "Sit-Ins in Atlanta," 69.

43. See *NYT*, 3 Apr. 1960, E7; 10 Apr. 1960, E6; *WP*, 26 Apr. 1960, A24; *AC*, 31 Mar. 1960, 9; Walker, "Sit-Ins in Atlanta," 69–70; Harmon, *Beneath the Image*, 132; Mays, *Born to Rebel*, 291.

44. See *USN&WR*, 7 Mar. 1960, 44; 14 Mar. 1960, 41; 18 Apr. 1960, 52; *AC*, 19 Apr. 1960, 1; *NYT*, 10 Apr. 1960, E6.

45. See *USN&WR*, 28 Mar. 1960, 4; 18 Apr. 1960, 52; *NYT*, 17 Apr. 1960, 32; 10 Apr. 1960, E6; *ADW*, 17 Apr. 1960, 1.

46. See Thurgood Marshall, "The Cry for Freedom," *Crisis* 67 (May 1960): 289; Hollowell interview by Fort; *ADW*, 20 Mar. 1960, 1; *NYT*, 3 Apr. 1960, E7; 10 Apr. 1960, E6; *WP*, 26 Apr. 1960, A24.

47. See Marshall, "Cry for Freedom," 289; *NYT*, 22 Mar. 1960, 36; *AC*, 16 Apr. 1960, 1; *ADW*, 17 Apr. 1960, 1; 20 Mar. 1960, 1. Important recent scholarship emphasizes that many observers did not know where the Court ultimately would draw the state action line. Schmidt, *Sit-ins and the State Action Doctrine*.

48. See Hollowell interview by Fort; Marshall, "Cry for Freedom"; *ADW*, 20 Mar. 1960, 1; 18 Mar. 1960, 1; *NYT*, 3 Apr. 1960, E7; 10 Apr. 1960, E6; 20 Mar. 1960, E8; *WP*, 26 Apr. 1960, A24; *NYT*, 22 Mar. 1960, 36; *AC*, 16 Apr. 1960, 1; *ADW*, 17 Apr. 1960, 1; 6 May 1960, 1.

49. Walker, "Sit-Ins in Atlanta," 75; Fort, "Atlanta Sit-in Movement," 135, 141.

50. Eliza Paschall to Richard Rich, TLS, 21 Dec. 1960, Paschall Papers, box 37, folder 12b; Bond interview, *Unbroken Circle*; King interview, *Unbroken Circle*; Harmon, *Beneath the Image*, 136; Walker, "Sit-Ins in Atlanta," 75; Fort, "Atlanta Sit-in Movement," 135, 141.

51. See Maxine T. Webb to Richard H. Rich, TLS, 24 Mar. 1958, Rich Papers, box 37, folder 1; Richard H. Rich to Maxine T. Webb, 27 Mar. 1958, Rich Papers, box 37, f. 1; Dolores Robinson to Richard H. Rich, TLS, 11 Apr. 1958, Rich Papers, box 37, f. 1; Richard H. Rich to Dolores M. Robinson, TLS, 16 Apr. 1958, Rich Papers, box 37, f. 1; Jewel Simon to Richard H. Rich, TLS, 14 Apr. 1958, Rich Papers, box 37, f. 1; Richard L. Rich to Dolores M. Robinson, TLS, 19 June 1958, Rich Papers, box 37, f. 1; Eliza Paschall to Richard Rich, TLS, 21 Dec. 1960, Paschall Papers, box 37, f. 12b; Jordan interview, 4; *AC*, 13 Oct. 1958, 1; *AC*, 13 Oct. 1958, 1; Walker, "Sit-Ins in Atlanta," 76–77; Fort, "Atlanta Sit-in Movement," 135, 141.

52. See Maxine T. Webb to Richard H. Rich, TLS, 24 Mar. 1958, Rich Papers, box 37, f. 1; Richard H. Rich to Maxine T. Webb, 27 Mar. 1958, Rich Papers, box 37, f. 1; Dolores Robinson to Richard H. Rich, TLS, 11 Apr. 1958, Rich Papers, box 37, f. 1; Richard H. Rich to Dolores M. Robinson, TLS, 16 Apr. 1958, Rich Papers, box 37, f. 1; Jewel Simon to Richard H. Rich, TLS, 14 Apr. 1958, Rich Papers, box 37, f. 1; Richard L. Rich to Dolores M. Robinson, TLS, 19 June 1958, Rich Papers, box 37, f. 1; Eliza Paschall to Richard Rich, TLS, 21 Dec. 1960, Paschall Papers, box 37, f. 12b; Jordan interview, 4; *AC*, 13 Oct. 1958, 1; *AC*, 13 Oct. 1958, 1; Walker, "Sit-Ins in Atlanta," 76–77; Fort, "Atlanta Sit-in Movement," 135, 141.

53. Richard H. Rich to Lonnie C. King, Jr., TLS, 10 Aug. 1960, Rich Papers, box 37, f. 1; *ADW*, 26 June 1960, 4; Walker, "Sit-Ins in Atlanta," 76–77; Fort, "Atlanta Sit-in Movement," 135, 141.

54. See *ADW*, 4 Aug. 1960, 1; 7 Aug. 1960, 1; *NYT*, 4 Aug. 1960, 25.

55. See Boynton v. Virginia, 364 U.S. 454 (1960); Coke v. City of Atlanta, 184 F. Supp. 579 (N.D. Ga. 1960); Hollowell and Lehfeldt, *Sacred Call*, 117–18; *NYT*, 13 Oct. 1960, 58; 6 Dec. 1960, 1.

56. See *ADW*, 24 Aug. 1960, 1; 15 Sept. 1960, 1; 12 Oct. 1960, 1.

57. *NYT*, 20 Oct. 1960, 39; *Chicago Daily Tribune*, 20 Oct. 1960, B18; *AI*, 24 Oct. 1960, 1; *ADW*, 20 Oct. 1960, 1; 18 Oct 1960, 1; *AC*, 18 Oct. 1960, 13.

58. *NYT*, 20 Oct. 1960, 39; *Chicago Daily Tribune*, 20 Oct. 1960, B18; *AI*, 24 Oct. 1960, 1; *ADW*, 20 Oct. 1960, 1; 18 Oct 1960, 1; *AC*, 18 Oct. 1960, 13; 20 Oct. 1960, 1; Hollowell and Lehfeldt, *Sacred Call*, 132; Walker, "Functions of Disunity," 345; Fort, "Atlanta Sit-in Movement," 136.

59. *ADW*, 21 Oct. 1960, 1; *AC*, 22 Oct. 1960, 1.

60. Lonnie King et al. to William B. Hartsfield, TLS, 1 Nov. 1960, Paschall Papers, box 37, f. 12b; William B. Hartsfield to Rev. Otis Moss, Jr., 2 Nov. 1960, Paschall Papers, box 37, f. 12b; *ADW*, 21 Oct. 1960, 1; *AC*, 22 Oct. 1960, 1; Walker, "Sit-Ins in Atlanta," 77–79; Mays, *Born to Rebel*, 289.

61. See Lonnie King interview by Fort; Bond interview, McGill Papers, 6; Hollowell interview by Fort.

62. Lonnie King et al. to William B. Hartsfield, TLS, 1 Nov. 1960, Paschall Papers, box 37, f. 12b; William B. Hartsfield to Rev. Otis Moss, Jr., 2 Nov. 1960, Paschall Papers, box 37, f. 12b; *ADW*, 22 Oct. 1960, 1; 23 Oct. 1960, 1; *AI*, 24 Oct. 1960, 1; 25 Oct. 1960, 1; *NYT*, 23 Oct. 1960, 77; Walker, "Sit-Ins in Atlanta," 78.

63. See *AI*, 31 July 1960, 1; Bond interview, McGill Papers, 5; *AI*, 24 Oct. 1960, 1.

64. Lonnie King et al. to William B. Hartsfield, TLS, 1 Nov. 1960, Paschall Papers, box 37, f. 12b; William B. Hartsfield to Rev. Otis Moss, Jr., 2 Nov. 1960, Paschall Papers, box 37, f. 12b; *ADW*, 21 Oct. 1960, 1; 21 Oct. 1960, 4; 22 Oct. 1960, 1; 23 Oct. 1960, 1; *AI*, 24 Oct. 1960, 1; 25 Oct. 1960, 1; *NYT*, 23 Oct. 1960, 77; Walker, "Sit-Ins in Atlanta," 78.

65. See King, *Daddy King*, 176; Hollowell and Lehfeldt, *Sacred Call*, 132–34; *AW*, 27 Oct. 1960, 1; Hampton and Fayer, *Voices of Freedom*, 68, 71.

66. See *AI*, 31 Oct. 1960, 2; *AJ*, 30 Nov. 1960, 6; *AW*, 29 Oct. 1960, 1; *Student Voice*, Nov. 1960, 6–7; Harmon, *Beneath the Image*, 139–41; Walker, "Sit-Ins in Atlanta," 78–81, 85.

67. See *AI*, 31 Oct. 1960, 2; *Student Voice*, Nov. 1960, 6–7; Harmon, *Beneath the Image*, 139–41; Walker, "Sit-Ins in Atlanta," 78–81, 85.

68. *AI*, 28 Nov. 1960, 1; *ADW*, 26 Nov. 1960, 1; "Christmas Withholding Campaign," Nov. 1960, TD, SNCC Papers, box 7; *Student Voice*, Dec. 1960, 1; "Adults Backing Boycott," *AI*, 5 Dec. 1960; *NYT*, 26 Nov. 1960, 10; *WP*, 27 Nov. 1960, A16; *Chicago Daily Tribune*, 12 Dec. 1960, 5; Harmon, *Beneath the Image*, 141–43.

69. *Student Voice*, Nov. 1960, 4; *ADW*, 27 Nov. 1960, 1; *NYT*, 27 Nov. 1960, 1; *AC*, 13 Dec. 1960, 1; *ADW*, 16 Dec. 1960, 1; *AI*, 17 Dec. 1960, 1; Walker, "Sit-Ins in Atlanta," 82–83; Harmon, *Beneath the Image*, 141–43. SNCC began publishing its newspaper in June, 1960. Carson, *In Struggle*, 25.

70. Boynton v. Virginia, 364 U.S. 454, 463–64 (1960); *Student Voice*, Jan. 1961, 1; *NYT*, 6 Dec. 1960, 1; *NYT*, 11 Dec. 1960, E6; *WP*, 6 Dec. 1960, A1; *AC*, 6 Dec. 1960, 1. On Robinson's life and legacy, see Fleming, *Soon We Will Not Cry*.

71. *AI*, 21 Jan. 1961, 1; *Student Voice*, Jan. 1961, 1; *AC*, 13 Dec. 1960, 1.

72. For commentary on *Boynton* consistent with the interpretation offered here, see Pollak, "Supreme Court and the States," 39–41; Dixon, "Civil Rights," 216–19.

73. *AI*, 21 Jan. 1961, 1; *Student Voice*, Jan. 1961, 1. The outraged reaction to Judge Jones's interpretation of *Boynton* overshadowed a legal victory for Atlanta's civil rights proponents that occurred around the same time; Don Hollowell's suit to desegregate the UGA saw success on January 6, 1961. See Pratt, *We Shall Not Be Moved*, 76–92.

74. *AI*, 18 Feb. 1961, 2; 9 Dec. 1960, 2; *Student Voice*, Feb. 1961, 1; *NYT*, 29 Jan. 1961, 64; 9 Feb. 1961, 21; 10 Feb. 1961, 31; 12 Feb. 1961, 77; *WP*, 11 Feb. 1960, A4; *AI*, 18 Feb. 1961, 1; Walker, "Sit-Ins in Atlanta," 85–89; Fort, "Atlanta Sit-in Movement," 140; Harmon, *Beneath the Image*, 143–44; News Release, 18 Feb. 1961, Walden Papers, box 43, f. 30. The news release is erroneously dated 1960.

75. *AI*, 25 Feb. 1961, 1; Allen, *Mayor*, 38–39; Pomerantz, *Where Peachtree Meets*, 265–68.

76. Press Release, 7 Mar. 1961, TD, Walden Papers, box 43, f. 30; King interview, McGill Papers, 10, 14–15; Garrow, *Bearing the Cross*, 151; Allen, *Mayor*, 38–39; Walker,

"Sit-Ins in Atlanta," 85–89; Fort, "Atlanta Sit-in Movement," 140; Allen, *Atlanta Rising*, 101; Pomerantz, *Where Peachtree Meets*, 265–68; Harmon, *Beneath the Image*, 143–44.

77. *AI*, 13 Mar. 1961, 1; 13 Mar. 1961, 2; Press Release, 7 Mar. 1961, TD, Walden Papers, box 43, f. 30; Plans and Procedures Committee: Resume of Agreements, 7 Mar. 1961, TD, Walden Papers, box 43, f. 30; Walker, "Sit-Ins in Atlanta," 87–88; Pomerantz, *Where Peachtree Meets*, 264; Harmon, *Beneath the Image*, 144–45.

78. *AI*, 13 Mar. 1961, 1; *AI*, 13 Mar. 1961, 2; 13 Mar. 1961, 2; Press Release, 7 Mar. 1961, TD, Walden Papers, box 43, f. 30; Plans and Procedures Committee: Resume of Agreements, 7 Mar. 1961, TD, Walden Papers, box 43, f. 30; Walker, "Sit-Ins in Atlanta," 87–88; Pomerantz, *Where Peachtree Meets*, 264; Harmon, *Beneath the Image*, 144–45.

79. Statement of A. T. Walden, Co-Chairman, Atlanta Negro Voters League, 8 Sept. 1961, Walden Papers, series VII, box 1, f. 5; Bond interview, McGill Papers, 7; *AI*, 13 Mar. 1961, 1; 18 Mar. 1961, 1; *NYT*, 12 Mar. 1960, 40; Walker, "Sit-Ins in Atlanta," 89–90.

80. King interview, McGill Papers, 14–16; Walker, "Functions of Disunity," 346.

81. King interview, McGill Papers, 14–16; *AI*, 18 Mar. 1961, 1.

82. Statement of A. T. Walden, Co-Chairman, Atlanta Negro Voters League, 8 Sept. 1961, Walden Papers, series VII, box 1, f. 5; Bond interview, McGill Papers, 7; *AI*, 13 Mar. 1961, 1; 18 Mar. 1961, 1; *NYT*, 11 Mar. 1961, 21; 12 Mar. 1960, 40; King interview, McGill Papers, 14–16; Walker, "Sit-Ins in Atlanta," 89–90.

83. A.T. Walden to Harold Yudelson, TL, 13 Mar. 1961, Walden Papers, box 43, f. 30.

84. A. T. Walden to Harold Yudelson, TL, 13 Mar. 1961, Walden Papers, box 43, f. 30; King interview, McGill Papers, 14–16.

85. Minutes, Plan and Procedure Committee Meeting, 18 Mar. 1961, TD, Walden Papers, box 43, f. 31.

86. Ibid.

87. Ibid.

88. *NYT*, 29 Sept. 1961, 1; *AC*, 29 Sept. 1961, 1; *ADW*, 29 Sept. 1961, 1; Harmon, *Beneath the Image*, 144.

89. See *AC*, 29 Sept. 1961, 1.

90. Bond interview, McGill Papers, 7; Fort, "Atlanta Sit-in Movement," 143.

### Chapter 7

1. The statement from Wilkins in the epigraph is from Roy Wilkins to Edward King (exec sec.), TLS, 1 Sept. 1961, SNCC Papers, NAACP Correspondence, 1959–1972, rl. 43, fr. 107. The statement from Bond in the epigraph is from Julian Bond to Ernest Goodman, TL, 4 May 1962, SNCC Papers, rl. 8, fr. 267.

2. Len Holt to Jim Forman, TM, "Legal Corpsmen for Concentration Areas," n.d. 1962, SNCC Papers, box 14, Len Holt folder.

3. Len Holt to Victor Rabinowitz, TLS, 26 Mar. 1962, SNCC Papers, rl. 6, fr. 178.

NOTES TO PAGES 176–183

4. See *NYT*, 24 Apr. 1960, E4; 15 Feb. 1960, 1; 22 Mar. 1960, 36; Meier, "Negro Protest Movements and Organizations," 441–43. For a discussion of precedents suggesting that racial discrimination by private actors was constitutional, barring state action, see, for example, Carl, "Reflections on the 'sit-Ins'"; Henkin, "Shelley v. Kramer"; Van Alstyne and Karst, "State Action"; see also Wechsler, "Toward Neutral Principles."

5. See Lewis, *Walking with the Wind*, 107–8; Martin Mayer, "CORE: The Shock Troops of the Negro Revolt," *Saturday Evening Post*, 21 Nov. 1964, 79.

6. See "Theory and Practice of Civil Disobedience" at 16–17, TD, SNCC Papers, box 25, April 1962 Conference folder; *NYT*, 12 Feb. 1961, 77; Halberstam, *Children*, 11–13, 48–50, 56, 59–64, 77–81, 101; Carson, *In Struggle*, 22–24; see Gandhi, *Non-violent Resistance*, 60.

7. See King, "Letter from Birmingham City Jail," in *Essential Writings*, 291, 294; King, "Suffering and Faith," in *Essential Writings*, 41; see also *NYT*, 17 Apr. 1960, 32; Hodding Carter, "The Young Negro Is a New Negro," *New York Times Magazine*, 1 May 1960, 11.

8. See *NYT*, 19 Mar. 1960, 8; 12 Feb. 1961, 77.

9. See *Student Voice*, Apr. and May 1961, 2; *NYT*, 19 Mar. 1960, 8; 12 Feb. 1961, 77. Also see the discussion of the Atlanta sit-in movement in chapter 6.

10. See *Student Voice*, Apr. and May 1961, 2; *NYT*, 7 Feb. 1961, 36; 1 June 1961, 25; 12 Feb. 1961, 77.

11. See *Student Voice*, Apr. and May 1961, 2; *NYT*, 20 Oct. 1960, 39; Zinn, *SNCC*, 21, 38. Also see the discussion of the Atlanta sit-in movement in chapter 3.

12. NAACP Position on Jail, No Bail, Memorandum from Gloster B. Current to Roy Wilkins et al., 9 Feb. 1961, TD, NAACP Papers, Group III, series A, Adm. Files, NAACP Instructions for Sit-ins, 1960–1961, rl. 22, fr. 00061; Jane Stembridge to J. M. Lawson, TL, 9 Sept. 1960, SNCC Papers, box 25, Oct. 1960 Correspondence; Lewis, *Walking with the Wind*, 113.

13. See *WSJ*, 23 Jan. 1962, 1; *NYT*, 12 Feb. 1961, 77.

14. See *ADW*, 17 June 1962, 6; *Student Voice*, Dec. 1962, 2; Apr. 1963, 1; Aug. 1963, 1; Aug. 1963, 2; Oct. 1963, 2; Jan. 1964, 1.

15. Jane Stembridge to Rev. Thomas Wright, TL, 13 July 1960, SNCC Papers, NAACP Correspondence, 10 Mar. 1959–5 May 1964, rl. 43, fr. 107.

16. Thurgood Marshall to Marion S. Barry, Jr., TLS, 4 Aug. 1960, SNCC Papers, NAACP Correspondence, 10 Mar. 1959–5 May 1964, rl. 43, fr. 107.

17. Roy Wilkins to Kivie Kaplan, TL, 24 Apr. 1961, SNCC Papers, Group III, series A, Sit-Ins, rl. 22, fr. 00001; Roy Wilkins to Hon. Theodore Spalding, TL, 28 Mar. 1961, SNCC Papers, Group III, series A, Sit-ins, rl. 22, fr. 00001.

18. Roy Wilkins to Kivie Kaplan, TL, 24 Apr. 1961, SNCC Papers, Group III, series A, Sit-Ins, rl. 22, fr. 00001; Roy Wilkins to Hon. Theodore Spalding, TL, 28 Mar. 1961, SNCC Papers, Group III, series A, Sit-ins, rl. 22, fr. 00001.

19. Roy Wilkins to Edward King, TLS, 1 Sept. 1961, SNCC Papers, NAACP Correspondence, rl. 43, fr. 107; Edward B. King, Jr., to Roy Wilkins, TL, 5 Sept. 1961, SNCC Papers, NAACP Correspondence, rl. 43, fr. 107.

20. Jack Greenberg to James Forman, TLS, 5 Apr. 1963, SNCC Papers, box 17, NAACP Correspondence; Jack Greenberg to James Forman, TLS, 21 May 1962, SNCC Papers, box 17, NAACP Correspondence; Jack Greenberg to James Forman, TLS, 18 Dec. 1962, SNCC Papers, box 17, NAACP Correspondence; Charles Cobb to Jack Greenberg, TL, 10 Sept. 1963, SNCC Papers, box 17, NAACP Correspondence.

21. See Auerbach, *Unequal Justice*, 158, 198–204; Bailey, "Progressive Lawyers," ii–x, 103–35; Rabinowitz and Ledwith, *History*, 7–10, 17–33; Ginger and Tobin, *National Lawyers' Guild*, 7–13, 30–38, 115–21, 136–37, 158–59; Brown, "'subversive' Southerners," 1–12, 33–36.

22. See Bailey, "Progressive Lawyers," 103–35; Ginger and Tobin, *National Lawyers' Guild*, 115–21, 136–37, 158–59; Auerbach, *Unequal Justice*, 158, 198–204; Brown, "'subversive' Southerners," 33–36.

23. See Ernest Goodman and George Crocket, Jr., to SNCC, TLS, 27 Apr. 1962, SNCC Papers, rl. 8, fr. 267; *National Lawyers Guild Newsletter*, Jan. 1965, 2; Holt, *Act of Conscience*, 18–19, Holt, *Summer*, 55–75, 268–80, 289–91; William Goodman, "National Lawyers Guild," 79; Ernest Goodman, "NLG," 1–5; Rabinowitz and Ledwith, *National Lawyers' Guild*, 33–44.

24. See Ernest Goodman and George Crocket, Jr., to SNCC, TLS, 27 Apr. 1962, SNCC Papers, rl. 8, frame 267; *National Lawyers Guild Newsletter*, no. 7 (Jan. 1965), 2; Holt, *Act of Conscience*, 18–19, Holt, *Summer*, 55–75, 268–80, 289–91; William Goodman, "National Lawyers Guild as An All-White Organization," 30 *Guild Practice* 74 (1972–1973), at 79; Rabinowitz and Ledwith, *History*, 33–44.

25. See Dennis Roberts to Ernest Goodman, TLS, 10 Mar. 1964, SNCC Papers, rl. 43, fr. 129; Dion T. Diamond to Ernest Goodman, 3 May 1962, TL, SNCC Papers, rl. 8, fr. 267; Julian Bond to Ernest Goodman, TL, 4 May 1962, SNCC Papers, rl. 8, fr. 267; Ernest Goodman and George Crocket, Jr., to SNCC; *National Lawyers Guild Newsletter*, Jan. 1965, 2; Holt, *Act of Conscience*, 18–19; Holt, *Summer*, 55–75, 268–80, 289–91; Goodman, "National Lawyers Guild," 79; Goodman, "NLG," 1–5; Rabinowitz and Ledwith, *National Lawyers' Guild*, 33–44.

26. See Biondi, *To Stand and Fight*, 77, 165–75; Mack, "Law and Mass Politics"; see also Wilkins, *Standing Fast*, 157–61, 189–90; White, *Man Called White*, 68, 128–33, 314–16.

27. See Tushnet, *Making Civil Rights Law*, 44–46; Lewis, *W. E. B. Du Bois*, 2:255–65; Biondi, *To Stand and Fight*, 77, 165–75; Woods, *Black Struggle, Red Scare*, 20–23, 58–65, 150–55; Dudziak, *Cold War Civil Rights*, 28–29, 111–12; Williams, *Thurgood Marshall*, 253–59, 282–83; see also Wilkins, *Standing Fast*, 157–61, 189–90; White, *Man Called White*, 68, 128–33, 314–16. Marshall also insisted that the NAACP turn over the names of rank-and-file members to the state of Alabama when it sought to bar the organization from the state in the wake of *Brown*. Robert Carter, Marshall's former chief lieutenant and general counsel at the NAACP, undermined the effort to turn over the NAACP's membership lists to Alabama. Carter argued that doing so would be unconstitutional. His view prevailed in a landmark Supreme Court decision, *NAACP v. Alabama*, 377 U.S. 288, 310 (1964). See also Williams, *Thurgood Marshall*, 258–59.

28. Greenberg, *Crusaders in the Courts*, 349–51; Forman, *Making*, 350.

29. See Greenberg, *Crusaders in the Courts*, 349–53; Woods, *Black Struggle, Red Scare*, 170, 205–6; Holt, *Act of Conscience*, 4, 17–49, 66–70, 196–207, 220–26; Holt, *Summer*, 11; Kinoy, *Rights on Trial*, 187–89; Ely, "Negro Demonstrations," 927, 932–50, 960.

30. See Carson, *In Struggle*, 107; Greenberg, *Crusaders in the Courts*, 349–53; Forman, *Making*, 380–83.

31. See Carson, *In Struggle*, 107–8, 136–37, 182–83; Woods, *Black Struggle, Red Scare*, 206–7, 215–16; Forman, *Making*, 380–83.

32. See Jonas, *Freedom's Sword*, 105–7; Williams, *Thurgood Marshall*, 288; Forman, *Making*, 383.

33. See Memorandum from Ernest Goodman to National Lawyers Guild Exec. Board, 22 Apr. 1965, SNCC Papers, rl. 43, fr. 129; National Lawyers Guild, "Know Your Rights," 1963, SNCC Papers, rl. 43, fr. 88; National Lawyers Guild, "Arrest and Detention—Remember You Have Rights: A Manual for Laymen," SNCC Papers, rl. 8, fr. 267; James Forman to Dean Robb, TL, 2 May 1962, SNCC Papers, rl. 8, fr. 267; Julian Bond to George W. Crockett, Jr., and Ernest Goodman, TL, 26 Dec. 1962, SNCC Papers, box 17, National Lawyers Guild folder; Irving Rosenfeld to George W. Crockett, Jr., and Ernest Goodman, TLS, 7 Jan. 1963, SNCC Papers, rl. 8, fr. 267; Ernest Goodman and George Crockett, Jr., to SNCC, TLS, 27 Apr. 1962, SNCC Papers, box 17, National Lawyers Guild folder; *Guild Lawyer*, Mar.–Apr. 1963; George Crockett, Jr., to James Forman, TLS, 29 Apr. 1965, SNCC Papers, box 17, National Lawyers Guild folder; Holt, *Act of Conscience*, 275–80; see also Hilbank, "Profession," 60–83.

34. Len Holt to Jim Forman, TM, "Legal Corpsmen for Concentration Areas," n.d. 1962, SNCC Papers, box 14, Len Holt folder.

35. See *Student Voice*, June 1962, 3; "SNCC Conference, April 27–19, 1962," TD, SNCC Papers, box 25, April 1962 Conference folder.

36. Holt telephone interview, 1–5; Holt email interview, 12 and 25 Aug. 2009.

37. Holt telephone interview, 4–6; Holt email interview, 12 and 25 Aug. 2009. On NAACP counsels' tradition of rehearsing Supreme Court arguments at Howard, see McNeil, *Groundwork*, 149–50, 182.

38. Holt telephone interview, 2.

39. Ibid., 6–7; see also Kluger, *Simple Justice*, 449–79.

40. See Holt, *Act of Conscience*, 9, 18–19, Holt, *Summer*, 55–75, 268–80, 289–91.

41. See Holt email interview, 17 Aug. 2009; Holt, *Act of Conscience*, 9, 18–19; Holt, *Summer*, 55–75, 268–80, 289–91; Rabinowitz and Ledwith, *History*, 7–10, 17–33; Ginger and Tobin, *National Lawyers' Guild*, 7–13, 30–38, 115–16; Langum, *William M. Kunstler*, 64–67.

42. See Holt, *Act of Conscience*, 9, 18–19, Holt, *Summer*, 55–75, 268–80, 289–91; Rabinowitz and Ledwith, *History*, 7–10, 17–33; Ginger and Tobin, *National Lawyers' Guild*, 7–13, 30–38, 115–16; Langum, *William M. Kunstler*, 64–67.

43. See Holt telephone interview, 13 Aug. 2009, 11; Len Holt to Victor Rabinowitz, TLS, 26 Mar. 1962, SNCC Papers, rl. 6, fr. 178; "October 1960 Conference Editorial," TD, SNCC Papers, box 25, Miscellaneous Statements folder; Holt, *Act of Conscience*, 17–49;

Kinoy, *Rights on Trial*, 192–93; Ginger and Tobin, *National Lawyers' Guild*, 204; see also Hilbank, "Profession," 60–83. The movement lawyer concept bears a kinship to the community-connected approach to legal representation employed by the International Labor Defense, the Communist Party organization, during the early twentieth century. See Goodman, *Stories of Scottsboro*, 7–8, 29, 37–38, 67–68, 82–84.

44. James Forman to Araya Lenske, TL, 2 May 1962, SNCC Papers, box 17, National Lawyers Guild folder; Forman, *Making*, 156, 209, 330.

45. Forman, *Making*, 380; King, *Freedom Song*, 84, 114–15, 117–18.

46. Carmichael, *Ready for Revolution*, 142.

47. Forman, *Making*, 380; Carmichael, *Ready for Revolution*, 142.

48. See "SNCC Atlanta Conference, Apr. 27–29, 1962," TD, SNCC Papers, box 25, April 1962 Conference folder; "Danville Sued on Race Issue," *WP*, 22 Aug. 1962, B7.

49. See Holt v. Commonwealth of Virginia, 136 S.E.2d 809, 809–16 (1964), rev'd 381 U.S. 131, 135–38 (1965); 209 F. Supp. 106 (1962); Wood v. Vaughn, 209 F. Supp. 106 (W.D. Va. 1962); see also Goodman, "Suing the State," 1277–78; *WP*, 22 Aug. 1962, B7.

50. See Len Holt to Victor Rabinowitz, TLS, 26 Mar. 1962, SNCC Papers, rl. 6, fr. 178; Len Holt to Araya Lenske, TLS, SNCC Papers, rl. 6, fr. 178; "SNCC Atlanta Conference, Apr. 27–29, 1962," TD, SNCC Papers, box 25, April 1962 Conference folder; Holt, *Act of Conscience*, 17–49; Ginger and Tobin, *National Lawyers' Guild*, 204.

51. See Holt email interview.

52. See Len Holt to Victor Rabinowitz, TLS, 26 Mar. 1962, SNCC Papers, rl. 6, fr. 178; Holt, *Act of Conscience*, 62, 72–77; Holt v. Commonwealth of Virginia, 136 S.E.2d 809, 809–16 (1964), rev'd 381 U.S. 131, 135–38 (1965); 209 F. Supp. 106 (1962); Wood v. Vaughn, 209 F. Supp. 106 (W.D. Va. 1962).

53. "Memorandum from Atlanta Office to Staff and Friends of SNCC," 25 Jan. 1962, 1–2, SNCC Papers, box 14, Len Holt folder; Len W. Holt to Araya Lenske, TLS, 5 Feb. 1962, SNCC Papers, rl. 6, fr. 178; Julian Bond to Len Holt, TL, 26 Mar. 1962, SNCC Papers, rl. 6, fr. 178; Memorandum from Julian Bond to James Forman, 2 Apr. 1962, SNCC Papers, rl. 6, fr. 178; *Student Voice*, Apr. and May 1961, 1.

54. "Memorandum from Atlanta Office to Staff and Friends of SNCC," 25 Jan. 1962, 1–2, SNCC Papers, box 14, Len Holt folder; Len W. Holt to Araya Lenske, TLS, 5 Feb. 1962, SNCC Papers, rl. 6, fr. 178; Julian Bond to Len Holt, TL, 26 Mar. 1962, SNCC Papers, rl. 6, fr. 178; Memorandum from Julian Bond to James Forman, 2 Apr. 1962; SNCC Papers, rl. 6, fr. 178; Len Holt to Victor Rabinowitz, TLS, 26 Mar. 1962, SNCC Papers, rl. 6, fr. 178; Julian Bond to Ernest Goodman, TL, 4 May 1962, SNCC Papers, rl. 8, fr. 267; Ernest Goodman and George Crockett, Jr., to SNCC, 27 Apr. 1962, SNCC Papers, rl. 8, fr. 267; "SNCC Atlanta Conference, Apr. 27–29, 1962," TD, SNCC Papers, box 25, April 1962 Conference folder; *Student Voice*, Apr. and May 1961, 1; June 1962, 3.

55. Brown v. City of Atlanta at 1–5 (N.D. Ga. May 16, 1961), SNCC Papers, rl. 7, fr. 204; Holt telephone interview, 14; *Student Voice*, Apr. and May 1961, 1; *ADW*, 18 May 1961, 1; *AI*, 20 May 1961, 1; *AC*, 18 May 1961, 1.

56. Brown v. City of Atlanta at 1–5 (N.D. Ga. May 16, 1961), SNCC Papers, rl. 7, fr. 204; *Student Voice*, Apr. and May 1961, 1; *AI*, 13 May 1961, 1; *ADW*, 18 May 1961, 1; *AI*, 20 May 1961, 1; 26 Aug. 1961, 1; 3 June 1963, 1; *AC*, 18 May 1961, 1.

57. *AC*, 18 May 1961, 1.

58. Judge Morgan, however, denied injunctive relief "in the light of progress made in the desegregation of municipal facilities." *AC*, 18 May 1961, 1; *ADW*, 28 Aug. 1962, 1; *AI*, 1 Sept. 1962, 1.

59. See Burton v. Wilmington Housing Authority, 365 U.S. 715 (1961); Gray v. Sanders, 372 U.S. 368 (1963), *aff'g* 203 F. Supp. 158 (N.D. Ga. 1962).

60. *ADW*, 12 Oct. 1960, 1; 5 Dec. 1961, 1; *WP*, 3 Dec. 1961, A6; *AC*, 1 Dec. 1961, 10; 2 Dec. 1961, 1; *AW*, 29 Oct. 1960, 1; Ivan Allen, *Mayor*, 21–22, 52–53.

61. See, for example, "Segregation Abolished in Galleries of Georgia Senate and House," SNCC Press Release, 11 Jan. 1962, SNCC Papers, rl. 19, fr. 105; SNCC Press Release, 1 Feb. 1962, SNCC Papers, rl. 19, fr. 105; SNCC Press Release, 7 Feb. 1962, SNCC Papers, rl. 19, fr. 105; "Negroes Urged to Go Slow," *AC*, 1; *AI*, 13 May 1961, 1; 26 Aug. 1961, 1.

62. *AI*, 25 Aug. 1962, 1. After marriage, Ruby Doris Smith later took the surname "Robinson." See Fleming, *Soon We Will Not Cry*, 103.

63. *AI*, 3 June 1963, 1; Allen, *Mayor*, 21–22, 52–53; Bayor, *Race and the Shaping*, 151; Harmon, *Beneath the Image*, 148–15.

64. "An Ordinance Repealing Ordinances Requiring the Separation of Persons Because of Race, Color or Creed," 18 Dec. 1963, Exh. 19, The State of Georgia v. Mardon Walker, no. 85028 (Sup. Ct. Fulton Cnty 6 Feb. 1964), Moore Papers; *AC*, 28 Aug. 1963; 13 June 1963, 1; 18 May 1963, 5; 30 May 1963, 1; *AI*, 3 June 1963, 1; Allen, *Mayor*, 21–22, 52–53; Bayor, *Race and the Shaping*, 151; Harmon, *Beneath the Image*, 148–15.

65. African Americans in other localities experienced both the promise and the limits of omnibus litigation as well. It worked well in Danville, Virginia, and Gadsen, Alabama, for example, but did not work in Albany, Georgia, as Holt readily admitted. See Wood v. Vaughan, 209 F. Supp. 106, 107–16 (1962); Coleman v. Aycock, 304 F. Supp. 132, 134–47 (1969); Shuttlesworth v. Gaylord, 202 F. Supp. 59 (1961); Holt, *Act of Conscience*, 196–97, 226; see also Sitton, "New Racial Techniques," *NYT*, 12 Mar. 1963, 6; 5 July 1963, at 33; 20 Feb. 1963, at 4; 23 Apr. 1964, 32; *WP*, 16 Sept. 1962, B5; *NYT*, 20 Feb. 1963, 4.

66. See Greenberg, *Crusaders*, 351–53; Tigar, "Lawyers and Social Justice"; Kinoy, *Rights on Trial*, 193–95; Langum, *William M. Kunstler*, 61, 67; Kunstler, *My Life*, 107; Zinn, *SNCC*, i.

67. See *AI*, 18 Nov. 1961, 1; *AC*, 11 Nov. 1961, 1.

68. See "Fact Sheet on Hospitals," 15 Mar. 1962, SNCC Papers, rl. 6, fr. 179; *AC*, 14 Nov. 1961, 4; 12 Dec. 1961, 25; 30 Dec. 1961, 1; Smith, *Health Care Divided*, 46–47.

69. *AI*, 18 Nov. 1961, 1; *AC*, 11 Nov. 1961, 1; 12 Dec. 1961, 25; 30 Dec. 1961, 1.

70. *Spritzer and Bergmark, Grace Towns Hamilton*, 115–16; Harmon, *Beneath the Image*, 81; Bayor, *Race and the Shaping*, 163.

71. Hughes Spalding, Sr. to B. Aurthur Howell, TLS, 30 Jan. 1948, Hamilton Papers, box 177, f. 2; *AC*, 22 June 1952, A1; Harmon, *Beneath the Image*, 67–68, 73; Bayor, *Race and the Shaping*, 163–68, 172–73; Kuhn, Joye, and West, *Living Atlanta*, 246; Mays, *Born to Rebel*, 228; Spritzer and Bergmark, *Grace Towns Hamilton*, 115–31.

72. "History of the IMHOTEP National Conference on Hospital Integration," *Journal of National Medical Association*, Jan. 1962, 116–18, SNCC Papers, rl. 6, fr. 179; "Nurses to Take Drastic Action," *AI*, 2 Dec. 1961, 1; *Spritzer and Bergmark, Grace Towns Hamilton*, 115–31; Bayor, *Race and the Shaping*, 163–65; Harmon, *Beneath the Image*, 58, 61, 67–68.

73. *AI*, 6 Jan. 1962, 2; *Spritzer and Bergmark, Grace Towns Hamilton*, 115–31; Bayor, *Race and the Shaping*, 163–65; Harmon, *Beneath the Image*, 58, 61, 67–68.

74. See *AI*, 10 Feb. 1962, 1; 10 Feb. 1962, 2; *AC*, 3 Feb. 1962, 4.

75. See SNCC Press Release, 14 Feb. 1962, SNCC Papers, rl. 19, fr. 105; SNCC Press Release, 16 Feb. 1962, SNCC Papers, rl. 19, fr. 105; *AI*, 10 Feb. 1992, 1; 17 Feb. 1962, 1; *NYT*, 14 Feb. 1962, 38; *AC*, 7 Feb. 1962, 9.

76. See "History of the IMHOTEP National Conference on Hospital Integration," 116–17; SNCC Press Release, 19 June 1962, SNCC Papers, rl. 19, fr. 105. Imhotep, the architect of the first Egyptian pyramid, also is often recognized as the world's first doctor and the "Father of Medicine" (along with Hippocrates). See Grimal, *History of Ancient Egypt*, 65–66, 107.

77. See Smith, *Healthcare Divided*, 54–63.

78. See Simkins v. Cone Memorial Hospital, 323 F.2d 959, 969 (4th Cir. 1963); *Charlotte Times*, 13 Feb. 1962, clipping, SNCC Papers, rl. 6, fr. 179.

79. See Bell v. Northern District Dental Society (N.D. Ga. 1962, Civ. Action no. 7966); SNCC Press Release, 19 June 1962, SNCC Papers, rl. 19, fr. 105; *NYT*, 20 June 1962, 16; *AI*, 23 June 1962, 1; *ADW*, 20 June 1962, 1; Hollowell and Lehfeldt, *Sacred Call*, 188–89.

80. *AI*, 19 May 1962, 1; 23 June 1962, 1.

81. *AI*, 19 May 1962, 1; 23 June 1962, 1.

82. See Simkins v. Cone Memorial Hospital, 323 F.2d 959, 969 (4th Cir. 1963), cert. denied 376 U.S. 936 (1964); Bell v. Georgia Dental Ass'n, 231 F. Supp. 299, 300–302 (D.C. Ga. 1964); see also *AC*, 11 Feb. 1964, 6; Smith, *Health Care Divided*, 114 and n. 35.

83. See *ADW*, 19 Mar. 1964, 1; Hollowell and Lehfeldt, *Sacred Call*, 188–89; Harmon, *Beneath the Image*, 149–50.

84. See Quadagno, "Promoting Civil Rights"; Smith, *Health Care Divided*, 114–15; Harmon, *Beneath the Image*, 149–50; *AI*, 19 June 1965, 1.

85. See *AI*, 19 June 1965, 1.

86. See *NYT*, 17 June 1966, 33; 7 Jul 1966, 25; 13 Aug. 1966, 8; Smith, *Health Care Divided*, 115–16.

87. See Rosenberg, *Hollow Hope*, 39–40, 74–75, 93, 155–56, 336–43; Scheingold, *Politics of Rights*, 5; see also Klarman, *From Jim Crow*, 94–96, 101–3, 182–84, 192–95, 236–89, 324–26, 314–15, 356–57, 411–13, 463–68; Tushnet, *Taking*, 135, 154–76.

88. McCann, *Rights at Work*.

89. See e.g. Fung, *Empowered Participation*.

90. Compare my conclusions to Rosenberg, *Hollow Hope*, for example, and other works cited in note 87; see Doug McAdam's work on the activist life paths of those involved in 1960s social movements, *Freedom Summer*.

91. See Urofsky, *Louis Brandeis*; Strum, *Louis Brandeis*.

*Chapter 8*

1. The statement from Forman in the epigraph is from *Student Voice*, 16 Dec. 1963, 1.

2. The statement from Humphrey in the epigraph is quoted in *WSJ*, 5 Feb. 1964, 1.

3. See *ADW*, 17 Dec. 1963, 1; *AI*, 18 Nov. 1961, 1; *NYT*, 16 Dec. 1963, 17; Grady-Willis, *Challenging*, 43..

4. *NYT*, 5 July 1962, 14; 2 July 1962, 23; Gloster B. Current, "The 53rd—A Hardworking Convention," *Crisis* 69 (Aug.–Sept. 1962): 377–92.

5. *WP*, 4 July 1962, A7; *NYT*, 5 July 1962, 14; 2 July 1962, 23; Current, "53rd"; see also Kruse, *White Flight*, 207–9.

6. See Klarman, *From Jim Crow*, 433–37, 38–44; Garrow, *Bearing the Cross*, 231–86.

7. See Lassiter, *Silent Majority*; Kruse, *White Flight*; Self, *American Babylon*; Sugrue, *Origins of the Urban Crisis*; Thornton, *Dividing Lines*.

8. *AI*, 18 Nov. 1961, 1; *WP*, 3 July 1962, A4; 4 July 1962, A7; *NYT*, 5 July 1962, 14; 2 July 1962, 23; Current, "53rd"; see also Kruse, *White Flight*, 207–9.

9. *NYT*, 5 July 1962, 14; *WP*, 5 July 1962, A1; Current, "53rd"; Kruse, *White Flight*, 207–9.

10. Originally Reed's attorney sued in tort but recast the suit as a civil rights action after consulting with Carter. See Complaint, Reed v. Sarno, Civil Action no. 7982 (N.D. Ga. 1962), NAACP Papers, rl. 15, fr. 685; Amendment to Complaint, 1–2, Reed v. Sarno, NAACP Papers, rl. 15, fr. 685; Isabel Gates Webster to Robert L. Carter, TLS, 17 July and 27 Aug. 1962, NAACP Papers, rl. 15, fr. 685.

11. Memorandum of Defendants in Support of Motion to Dismiss Amended Complaint, 1–3, Reed v. Sarno, NAACP Papers, rl. 15, fr. 685; Memorandum of Plaintiff in Support of Denial of Motion to Dismiss and Strike, 1–3, Reed v. Sarno, NAACP Papers, rl. 15, fr. 685; Supplemental Memorandum of Defendants in Support of Motion to Dismiss Amended Complaint and in the Alternative to Strike, 1–2, Reed v. Sarno, NAACP Papers, rl. 15, fr. 685.

12. Order, 1–2, Reed v. Sarno, Aug. 27, 1962, NAACP Papers, rl. 15, fr. 685; Isabel Gates Webster to Robert L. Carter, 31 Aug. 1962, TLS, Reed v. Sarno, NAACP Papers, rl. 15, fr. 685.

13. Order, 1–4, Reed v. Sarno, Sept. 24, 1962, NAACP Papers, rl. 15, fr. 685; Williams v. Howard Johnson's Rest., 268 F.2d 845, 845–48 (4th Cir. 1959).

14. For a contemporary assessment of the legality of discrimination in public accommodations, see, e.g., Cobb, "Reflections on the Sit-Ins." Labor cases, restrictive covenant, and voting rights cases from the 1930s and 1940s suggest that the Court may have been poised to reconsider the public/private distinction. See Goluboff, *Lost Promise*, 200–201, 229; Schmidt, "Sit-ins and the State Action Doctrine."

15. Fairclough, *To Redeem*, 111–39; Garrow, *Bearing the Cross*, 220–30; Klarman, *From Jim Crow*, 433–37.

16. See Shuttlesworth v. Birmingham, 373 U.S. 262 (1963); Peterson v. Greenville, 373 U.S. 244 (1963); Lombard v. Louisiana, 373 U.S. 244 (1963); Gober v. Birmingham,

373 U.S. 374 (1963); Avent v. North Carolina, 373 U.S. 375 (1963). In a sixth case, Wright v. Georgia, 373 U.S. 284 (1963), decided on the same date, the Court reversed breach of peace convictions for blacks who had played basketball in a whites-only city park in Savannah, Georgia, on narrower grounds; in that case, the students had insufficient notice that their activities would violate the statute, the Court held.

17. Lombard, 373 U.S. 244 (1963).

18. See NYT, 22 May 1963, 26; WP, 22 May 1963, A4; 21 May 1963, A1; see also Lombard, 373 U.S. at 281–82 (Douglas, J., concurring).

19. See Peterson, 373 U.S. at 248 (Harlan, J., concurring and dissenting).

20. See Peterson v. Greenville, 373 U.S. at 244 (1963); Lombard v. Louisiana, 373 U.S. 267 (1963).

21. AC, 21 May 1963, 1; 21 May 1963, 4; WSJ, 23 May 1963, 1; WP, 23 May 1963, C18.

22. SNCC Third Annual Spring Conference, Apr. 12–14, 1963, TD, SNCC Papers, rl. 19, fr. 105; Student Voice, Aug. 1963, 1; Aug. 1963, 2; Aug. 1963, 3; Aug. 1963, 4; Oct. 1963, 2; WSJ, 23 May 1963, 1.

23. See, for example, AC, 8 June 1963, 10; 15 June 1963, 3; see also Grady-Willis, Challenging, 40–41.

24. AC, 11 May 1963, 5; 18 May 1963, 5.

25. AC, 14 May 1963, 8; 8 June 1963, 10; 15 June 1963, 3; 17 June 1963, 7; 18 June 1963, 11; 19 June 1963, 9; 28 June 1963, 13; 3 July 1963, 5; 27 July 1963, 3; AI, 10 Aug. 1963, 2; Grady-Willis, Challenging, 40–41.

26. AC, 8 June 1963, 10; 18 June 1963, 11; 27 July 1963, 3; 28 June 1963, 25; AI, 3 Aug. 1963, 1.

27. AC, 15 June 1963, 4; 19 June 1963, 4; 30 July 1963, 3.

28. AI, 18 May 1963, 2; ADW, 28 July 1963, 4; 4 Aug. 1963, 4.

29. "Mixed Group Gets 34 Days after Down Town Sit Down," SNCC Press Release, 29 July 1963, SNCC Papers, rl. 19, fr. 105; "17 Face Trespass Charges Could Get 18 Months," SNCC Press Release, 20 Aug. 1963, rl. 19, fr. 105; AC, 27 July 1963, 3.

30. See Allen, Mayor, 101–16; AC, 27 June 1963, 4; 6 June 1963, 4; 20 June 1963, 1; Eugene Patterson, "Law Is Not Needed," AC, 21 June 1963; AC, 25 June 1963, 1; AC, 18 July 1963, 1; AC, 21 June 1963, 1; AC, 5 July 1963, 1.

31. Grace Hamilton to the Editor, AC, TL, 8 June 1963, Walden Papers, series VII, box 1, f. 12; AC, 15 June 1963, 4.

32. Allen, Mayor, 110; Mays, Born to Rebel, 278.

33. ADW, 27 July 1963, 1; NYT, 27 July 1963, 1; AC, 27 July 1963, 4. Months later, after the Allen controversy died down and Walden retired, he endorsed the public accommodations bill. See "Life Begins at 78," Atlanta Magazine, Oct. 1963, 43.

34. ADW, 28 July 1963, 1; 28 July 1963, 4; 6 Aug. 1963, 1; 27 July 1963, 4.

35. Address of John Lewis, Mar. 28, 1963, Washington, D.C., TD, SNCC Papers, box 49.

36. Student Voice, Oct. 1963, 1, 3–4; see also Robert D. Loevy, To End All Segregation, 31–32.

37. "17 Face Trespass Charges Could Get 18 Months," SNCC Press Release, 20 Aug. 1963, SNCC Papers, rl. 19, fr. 105; *ADW*, 28 Aug. 1963, 1; *AI*, 10 Aug. 1963, 1; *ADW*, 6 Aug. 1963, 1.

38. *Student Voice*, 18 Nov. 1963, 4; *ADW*, 30 Aug. 1963, 1; *NYT*, 29 Aug. 1963, 1.

39. *Student Voice*, 18 Nov. 1963, 4; *AI*, 26 Oct. 1963, 1; Debbie Amis, "Atlanta," TD, n.d., SNCC Papers, box 95; Statement by SNCC Executive Secretary James Forman, TD, Dec. 24,1963, SNCC Papers, box 49; *ADW*, 6 Aug. 1963, 1; see also Harmon, *Beneath the Image*, 154–55; Paschall, *It Must Have Rained*, 90, 93–95, 97–100, 102.

40. *Student Voice*, 9 Dec. 1963, 3; *AI*, 16 Nov. 1963, 1; see also Harmon, *Beneath the Image*, 158–59; Kruse, *White Flight*, 214; Grady-Willis, *Challenging*, 42–43.

41. *AI*, 22 Nov. 1963, 1; *Student Voice*, 21 Nov. 1963, 1–2; see also Harmon, *Beneath the Image*, 158–59; Kruse, *White Flight*, 214; Grady-Willis, *Challenging*, 42–43.

42. *Student Voice*, 9 Dec. 1963, 3; *NYT*, 3 Dec. 1963, 1.

43. See *Student Voice*, 16 Dec. 1963, 1; *ADW*, 17 Dec. 1963, 1.

44. See *Student Voice*, 16 Dec. 1963, 1; *ADW*, 17 Dec. 1963, 1; *NYT*, 16 Dec. 1963, 17; Bayor, *Race and the Shaping*, 300 n. 26; Grady-Willis, *Challenging*, 43.

45. See *Student Voice*, 16 Dec. 1963, 1; *ADW*, 17 Dec. 1963, 1.

46. See *Student Voice*, 16 Dec. 1963, 1; *ADW*, 17 Dec. 1963, 1; *NYT*, 16 Dec. 1963, 17.

47. *Student Voice*, 23 Dec. 1963, 1–2; Statement by SNCC Executive Secretary James Forman, TD, 24 Dec. 1963, SNCC Papers, box 49; "What Happened in Atlanta," TD, n.d., Paschall Papers, box 5, f. 11; see also Bayor, *Race and the Shaping*, 115; Paschall, *It Must Have Rained*, 62–63, 72–76.

48. *ADW*, 7 Jan. 1964, 4; *NYT*, 8 Jan. 1964, 28.

49. *ADW*, 11 Jan. 1964, 1; 17 Jan. 1964, 1; 12 Jan. 1964, 1; *NYT*, 12 Jan. 1964, 1.

50. *ADW*, 12 Jan. 1964, 1; "Atlanta 'Open City' Drive Continues," TD, 16 Jan. 1964, SNCC Papers, box 95; *Student Voice*, 14 Jan. 1964, 1, 3; *ADW*, 12 Jan. 1964, 1; 12 Jan. 1964, 2; 19 Jan. 1964, 1; *NYT*, 12 Jan. 1964, 1; 19 Jan. 1964, 1; 20 Jan. 1964, 15; see also Grady-Willis, *Challenging*, 47.

51. *AC*, 21 Jan. 1964, 4.

52. *ADW*, 14 Jan. 1964, 1; 21 Jan. 1964, 4; 22 Jan. 1964, 1; *AI*, 23 Jan. 1964, 1; 25 Jan. 1964, 1; *ADW*, 29 Jan. 1964, 1.

53. *ADW*, 30 Jan. 1964, 1; *NYT*, 29 Jan. 1964, 18; 30 Jan. 1964, 15; 31 Jan. 1964, 12; 2 Feb. 1964, 64; *WP*, 3 Feb. 1964, A14.

54. *NYT*, 2 Feb. 1964, 64; 3 Feb. 1964, 18; *WSJ*, 5 Feb. 1964, 1; *NYT*, 9 Feb. 1964, E3; USN&WR, 10 Feb. 1964, 78; *ADW*, 15 Feb. 1964, 1. See "The Nation," *Time*, 24 Apr. 1964, 17; USN&WR, 27 Apr. 1964, 10; "Negro Riots Will Go on, Unless…" *New Republic*, 5 Sept. 1964, 22; "The Nation," *Time*, 24 Apr. 1964, 17.

55. On Pye's segregationist activism, see *NYT*, 9 Dec. 1954, 38; 7 Dec. 1956, 23; *WP*, 15 Dec. 1956, A5.

56. Herbert Jenkins to Hon. Durwood Pye, TLS, 17 July 1963, Moore Papers, box 14, State of Georgia v. Mardon Walker file; "Mixed Group Gets 34 Days After Down Town Sit Down," SNCC Press Release, 29 July 1963, SNCC Papers, rl. 19, fr. 105; "17

Face Trespass Charges Could Get 18 Months," SNCC Press Release, 20 Aug. 1963, rl. 19, fr. 105; *AC*, 20 July 1963, 3; *ADW*, 28 July 1963, 1; 2 Aug. 1963, 1; 1 Aug. 1963, 1.

57. Hollowell and Lehfeldt, *Sacred Call*, 2, 27, 128–38, 139–52.

58. Hollowell interview by author, 2–4; Hollowell and Lehfeldt, *Sacred Call*, 27–37.

59. Bond interview by author, 10; Hunter-Gault interview, 4–5; quote is from Moore interview by author, 5.

60. Hollowell interview by Fort; Hollowell and Lehfeldt, *Sacred Call*, 3–21, 27–28, 36–37, 49–53, 68–69, 80.

61. Lonnie King interview by Fort; Brown interview, 76; Bond interview by Fort; Hollowell interview by Fort; Marion S. Barry, Jr., and Jane Stembridge to J. W. Hatchett, TL, 12 July 1960, SNCC Papers, rl. 43, fr. 107; *ADW*, 3 Feb. 1966, 1; 17 July 1968, 1; Hollowell and Lehfeldt, *Sacred Call*, 128–38, 139–52.

62. Hollowell and Lehfeldt, *Sacred Call*, 189–93.

63. See *AC*, 14 Jan. 1964, 9; *ADW*, 29 Jan. 1964, 1; Hollowell and Lehfeldt, *Sacred Call*, 138.

64. See Transcript of Trial Proceedings in Fulton County Sup.Ct., 338–40, 349–51, 365, 368, 6 Feb. 1964, Moore Papers, State v. Walker, box 14, Transcript file; Transcript of Trial Proceedings in Fulton County Sup.Ct., 3–4, 17 Feb. 1964, Moore Papers, State v. Walker, box 14, Transcript file; see also *AC*, 14 Jan. 1964, 9; *ADW*, 29 Jan. 1964, 1; *AC*, 21 Jan. 1964, 4; 30 Jan. 1964, 4; *AI*, 8 Feb. 1964, 1; Hollowell and Lehfeldt, *Sacred Call*, 138.

65. Transcript, 14–18, 22–29, 30–38, 6 Feb. 1964, Moore Papers, State v. Walker, box 14; *ADW*, 8 Feb. 1964, 1; 11 Feb. 1964, 1; *AC*, 11 Feb. 1964, 3.

66. Transcript, 210–16, 6 Feb. 1964, Moore Papers, State v. Walker, box 14.

67. Ibid., 345–46.

68. Ibid., 4–9.

69. Ibid., 4–9.

70. Ibid., 350–52, 356–58, 360–63, 366, 374–77, 389, 392–93; *AC*, 13 Feb. 1964, 9. On Smith's exploits, see Grady-Willis, *Challenging*, 16, 35, 39.

71. See Motion to Remand to Fulton County Sup.Ct., Georgia v. Walker, 24 Aug. 1966, 235–37, Moore Papers, box 14, Briefs folder; *ADW*, 18 Feb. 1964, 1.

72. On the removal strategy, see National Lawyers Guild, *Civil Rights*, sections 2–46, 3–60; Amsterdam, "Criminal Prosecutions," 810–30, 842–82; "Removal"; Holt, *Act of Conscience*, 11; Kinoy, *Rights on Trial*, 191–92.

73. The Civil Rights Act of 1964 conferred a right of appeal when removal petitions were remanded. See 28 U.S.C. section 1447(d).

74. See *AC*, 18 Feb. 1964, 11.

75. Transcript, 1–22, 19–29, 17 Feb. 1964, Moore Papers, State v. Walker, box 14; *ADW*, 19 Feb. 1964, 1; *ADW*, 20 Feb. 1964, 1; *AC*, 11 Feb. 1964, 3; *ADW*, 18 Feb. 1964, 1.

76. *ADW*, 1 Feb. 1964, 1.

77. Ibid.

78. "White Girl Gets 18 Months, $1,000 Fine in Sit-In Case," 20 Feb. 1964, SNCC Press Release, rl. 19, fr. 105; *ADW*, 21 Feb. 1964, 1.

79. *WP*, 24 Feb. 1964, A14; *AC*, 24 Feb. 1964, 13; *WP*, 1 Mar. 1964, E3; *ADW*, 6 Mar. 1964, 1.

80. *ADW*, 8 Mar. 1964, 1; 10 Mar. 1964, 1; 21 Mar. 1964, 1. On the Prathia Hall controversy, see *ADW*, 24 Mar. 1964, 1; 25 Mar. 1964, 1; 26 Mar. 1964, 1; 8 May 1964, 1.

81. *AI*, 8 Feb. 1964, 1; *ADW*, 15 Feb. 1964, 1.

82. *NYT*, 16 Feb. 1964, 68.

83. "SNCC Communications Manual," Summer 1964, SNCC Papers, box 35, Miscellaneous folder; "SNCC Shifts National Headquarters," Press Release, 12 June 1964, SNCC Papers, rl. 19, fr. 105; Statement of SNCC Chairman John Lewis, 12 June 1964, SNCC Papers, rl. 19, fr. 105.

84. See Charles Whalen and Barbara Whalen, *Longest Debate*, xviii–xix, 11, 14–16, 25–26, 80–82, 94–95; Loevy, *To End All Segregation*, 123, 153–66, 202–10, 295–304; Chafe, *Unfinished Journey*, 211–17, 228–35; Fairclough, *To Redeem*, 132–34; Franklin and Moss, *From Slavery to Freedom*, 500–508.

85. Heart of Atlanta Motel, Inc. v. United States, 231 F. Supp. 393, 394 (N.D. Ga. 1964); "SNCC Finds Violence Meets Rights Law Testers," Press Release, 9 July 1964, SNCC Papers, rl. 19, fr. 105; *NYT*, 4 July 1964, 1; *NYT*, 2 July 1964, 1; 7 July 1964, 1; 11 July 1964, 23; Cortner, *Civil Rights*, 29–30, 34–36. On uneven local compliance with the Civil Rights Act, see Paschall, *It Must Have Rained*, 104, 113–14, 138–41, 145–54, 168–69; "Scripto's Half Million Dollar Contracts under Investigation, SNCC Told," 9 Jan. 1965, SNCC Papers, box 49.

86. Willis v. Pickrick Restaurant, 231 F. Supp. 396, 398 (N.D. Ga. 1964); *NYT*, 4 July 1964, 1; *WP*, 18 July 1964, A1; *NYT*, 29 Sept. 1964, 26; 2 July 1964, 1; *Chicago Tribune*, 14 July 1964, 3; Cortner, *Civil Rights*, 37–39. In April 1965, an all-white jury acquitted Maddox on criminal charges of brandishing the gun at the divinity students.

87. See Willis, 231 F. Supp. at 398–404; Heart of Atlanta, 231 F. Supp. at 395–96; Mintz, *WP*, 18 July 1964, A1; *Chicago Tribune*, 23 July 1964, 1; *NYT*, 27 Aug. 1964, 24; 12 Aug. 1964, 1; Cortner, *Civil Rights*, 56–62.

88. Heart of Atlanta, 379 U.S. at 254–58; ibid. at 270–77 (Black, J., concurring); *NYT*, 15 Dec. 1964, 1; Cortner, *Civil Rights*, 171–81. In addition to *Heart of Atlanta*, the Court heard arguments in *Katzenbach v. McClung*, in which a three-judge panel in Birmingham had found the Act inapplicable to a barbecue restaurant. The Court upheld the Act in *McClung* as well. See Katzenbach v. McClung, 379 U.S. 294 (1964).

89. Heart of Atlanta, 379 U.S. at 250; ibid. at 279–83, 286 (Douglas, J., concurring); ibid. at 291–93 (Goldberg, J., concurring).

90. See *NYT*, 15 Dec. 1964, 1; *WP*, 15 Dec. 1964, A8; Cortner, *Civil Rights*, 181–82, 188–92.

91. On the aftermath of passage of the Act and uneven local compliance with the law, see Kruse, *White Flight*, 229–33; Paschall, *It Must Have Rained*, 104, 113–14, 138–41, 145–54, 168–69; "Scripto's Half Million Dollar Contracts Under Investigation, SNCC Told," 9 Jan. 1965, SNCC Papers, box 49.

92. Hamm v. Rock Hill, 379 U.S. 306, 306–8 (1964). On the number of cases affected by the abatement decisions, see Transcript of Hearing, 2–4, Hamm v. Rock Hill, no. 2

(U.S. Sup. Ct. Oct. 12, 1964); Petition for Rehearing, 4, Lupper v. Arkansas, no. 5 (U.S. Sup. Ct. Jan. 5, 1965).

93. For cases that demonstrate the room that *Hamm* and *Lupper* left for prosecutions to continue, see Clemons v. Birmingham, 171 So.2d 456, 460 (Ala. 1965); Johnson v. State, 173 So. 2d 817, 823–24 (Ala. Ct. App.1965); see also Adderly v. Florida, 385 U.S. 39, 43–44 (1966); Greenwood v. Peacock, 384 U.S. 808 (1966).

94. Hollowell and Moore first appealed to the Georgia courts. In a November 5, 1964, opinion, the Georgia Supreme Court categorically rejected the claim that Mardon Walker had been wrongly convicted. Georgia's antitrespass statute had no infirmities under either the state or federal equal protection or due process clauses, and the law had not been discriminatorily applied to Walker, the court held. Bill of Exceptions, 1–2 (Ga. Sup.Ct. July 8, 1964), Walker v. State, Moore Papers, box 14; *Student Voice*, 3 Mar. 1964, 1; "Judge Refuses to Grant Coed New Trial," 9 July 1964, SNCC Press Release, rl. 19, fr. 105; *ADW*, 11 Mar. 1964, 1; 14 Mar. 1964, 1. Walker v. Georgia, 381 U.S. 355 (1965); *AC*, 25 May 1965, 1; 25 May 1965, 4; *WP*, 25 May 1965, A5; Hollowell and Lehfeldt, *Sacred Call*, 190.

95. Walker v. State, 417 F.2d 1, 3–4 (5th Cir. 1969); Transcript of Hearing, 6–13, 28 Sept. 1967, Walker v. State (U.S. District Court), Moore Papers, box 12.

96. Walker v. State, 417 F.2d at 4–5.

97. "October, 1960 Conference Editorial," TD, SNCC Papers, box 25, Miscellaneous Statements 1960 folder.

*Chapter 9*

1. The statement from Rustin in the epigraph is from Rustin, "Black Power," 35.

2. The statement from Cobb in the epigraph is from Cobb, "Atlanta," 118.

3. See Kotz, *Judgment Days*, 335–37; Lewis, *Walking with the Wind*, 346–47.

4. See *AI*, 8 Aug. 1970, 1.

5. See Baker v. Carr, 369 U.S. 186, 199–201, 206, 207–9, 235–37 (1962); see also *NYT*, 27 Mar. 1962, 1; 1 Apr. 1963, 46.

6. See Johnson interview, 3–7; *AI*, 10 Nov. 1962, 1; see also McDonald, *Voting Rights Odyssey*, 80–90.

7. See chapter 2.

8. See *AI*, 10 July 1965, 1; 10 July 1965, 4; *AC*, 8 July 1965, 29; Eugene Patterson, "A. T. Walden: A Great Southerner," *AC*, 5 July 1965; *ADW*, 21 Aug. 1964, 2.

9. See *NYT*, 23 May 1965, 80.

10. See Bond, "SNCC: What We Did," *Monthly Review*, Oct. 2000, 24; Cobb, "Atlanta," 116–18; "The Atlanta Project," TD, 10 Jan. 1966, SNCC Papers, box 95.

11. See *Student Voice*, 5 Mar. 1965, 1; July 1965, 1; "The Atlanta Project," TD, 10 Jan. 1966, SNCC Papers, box 95; Cobb, "Atlanta," 116–18.

12. See *Student Voice*, 30 Apr. 1965, 2; *WP*, 5 May 1965, A6; Cobb, "Atlanta," 116–18.

13. See "Friends of SNCC Newsletter #3," 3 Dec. 1965, SNCC Papers, rl. 56, fr. 156; Bond, "SNCC," 24; Forman, *Making*, 443; see also Rustin, "Black Power," 25–31. Some

in SNCC were skeptical of Bond's candidacy, however. For them, grassroots leadership required representation of the poor by the poor and independent politics. The decision by Bond, an archetypal member of the black upper class, to run for a seat in the Georgia legislature as a Democrat, was deeply problematic. Critics accused Bond and his supporters of "selling out" to the "establishment" in a futile attempt to "play the political game." See *Student Voice*, 28 Apr. 1964, 2; 23 Sept. 1964, 1; 20 Dec. 1965, 1; 20 Dec. 1965, 2; Bond, "SNCC," 20–24.

14. See *WP*, 21 Aug. 1964, A1; Clark, *Victory Deferred*, 23–26, 28–31; Kotz, *Judgment Days*, 93–94, 96–97, 181–85, 244; Jackson, *From Civil Rights*, 123–28, 193–98, 203–8.

15. See Clark, *War on Poverty*, 35–36. On CAPS and new leadership, see Piven and Cloward, *Poor People's Movements*, 270–71; Naples, *Grassroots Warriors*, 1–3, 39–61. On local decision-making process, see *AC*, 20 Aug. 1964, 1; Ivan Allen, *Mayor*, 91, 130, 152, 177, 240. On black lobbying, see Economic Opportunity Atlanta Inc. Charter of Incorporation, 17 June 1965, TD, Paschall Papers, box 16, f. 15; *ADW*, 6 Apr. 1965, 1; 4 Dec. 1964, 1; 29 Nov. 1964, 1; 6 Dec. 1964, 4; 4 Apr. 1965, 1.

16. See Economic Opportunity Atlanta Inc. Charter of Incorporation, 17 June 1965, TD, Paschall Papers, box 16, f. 15; *ADW*, 4 Dec. 1964, 1; 6 Apr. 1965, 1; 9 Apr. 1965, 1; 6 July 1965, 1.

17. See *AI*, 11 Dec. 1965, 1; 25 Dec. 1965, 1; *ADW*, 4 Aug. 1965, 1; see also Paschall, *It Must Have Rained*, 128–29; Clark, *Victory Deferred*, 87.

18. See *ADW*, 4 Aug. 1965, 1; 6 Apr. 1965, 1; 23 May 1965, 1; *AC*, 24 May 1965, 8; see also Harmon, *Beneath the Image*, 190–93.

19. "Ga. Legislature Refuses to Seat Freedom Worker," n.d., Bond Papers, series 3, box 56, f. 8; *ADW*, 9 Jan. 1966, 1.

20. "Statement by the Student Nonviolent Coordinating Committee on the War in Vietnam," 6 Jan. 1966, SNCC Papers, rl. 37, fr. 522; Lewis, *Walking with the Wind*, 360; Kotz, *Judgment Days*, 372.

21. See Simmons interview, 6; "Statement by the Student Nonviolent Coordinating Committee on the War in Vietnam," 6 Jan. 1966, SNCC Papers, rl. 37, fr. 522; "SNCC and Vietnam," Feb. 1966, TD, SNCC Papers, rl. 56, fr. 156; SNCC Anti-War Statement, Bond Papers, series 3, box 56, f. 12.

22. *NYT*, 8 Jan. 1966, 3; *ADW*, 7 Jan. 1966, 1.

23. Bond interview by author, 6; *NYT*, 11 Jan. 1966, 1; 8 Jan. 1966, 3; *ADW*, 11 Jan. 1966, 1.

24. See Eugene Patterson, "SNCC Reaches End of the Line," *AC*, 8 Jan. 1966; Lillian Smith, "Old Dream, New Killers," *AC*, 15 Jan. 1966; *AC*, 11 Jan. 1966, 1; *NYT*, 8 Jan. 1966, 3; Lewis, *Walking with the Wind*, 361.

25. Defendants' Trial Brief, 4, Bond v. Floyd, Moore Papers, box 5, Bond v. Floyd file.

26. "Statement by Julian Bond," TD, 10 Jan. 1966, SNCC Papers, rl. 53, fr. 531.

27. See *AC*, 11 Jan. 1966, 1; *ADW*, 11 Jan. 1966, 1.

28. "Statement by Julian Bond," TD, 10 Jan. 1966, Moore Papers, box 7, Bond v. Floyd, News Article file; *NYT*, 18 June 1965, 15.

29. See "Julian Bond Prevented from Taking Oath by Georgia House," TD, 8 Jan. 1966, SNCC Papers, rl. 37, fr. 528; ADW, 12 Jan. 1966, 1; 15 Jan. 1966, 1; WP, 14 Jan. 1966, 2; see also Jackson, From Civil Rights, 308–25.

30. See Lunch and Sperlinch, "American Public Opinion," 22–23; Gartner and Segura, "Race, Casualties," 120; Westheider, Fighting on Two Fronts, 8, 19; see also Roy Wilkins, "SNCC Does Not Speak for the Whole Movement," Los Angeles Times, 13 Jan. 1966, clipping, Bond Papers, series 3, box 59, f. 2.

31. AI, 15 Jan. 1966, 1; 15 Jan. 1966, 4; NYT, 11 Jan. 1966, 1; see also Lewis, Walking with the Wind, 359–61.

32. ADW, 15 Jan. 1966, 4; 12 Jan. 1966, 4; Moore interview at 11, 12.

33. Lewis, Walking with the Wind, 282; see also Lee, For Freedom's Sake, 18–19, 87–88, 95, 99, 100; Hogan, Many Minds, One Heart, 193–96.

34. "The Atlanta Project," TD, n.d., SNCC Papers, rl. 37, fr. 45–602–11; "The Julian Bond Campaign," n.d., SNCC Papers, rl. 37, fr. 45–603; Lewis, Walking with the Wind, 361. "Black Prince" is from Nwangaza interview, 13.

35. See "Petition to Governor Carl E. Sanders," n.d., SNCC Papers, rl. 53, fr. 570; Telegrams in Support of Julian Bond, SNCC Papers, rl. 37, fr. 530; "Emergency Bulletin," 8 Jan. 1966, TD, SNCC Papers, rl. 37, fr. 527.

36. See Williams interview, 12, 20; Tillinghast interview, 5; "Statement by the Student Nonviolent Coordinating Committee on the War in Vietnam," 6 Jan. 1966, SNCC Papers, rl. 37, fr. 522; see also Nalty and MacGregor, Blacks in the Military, 344–48; Baskir and Strauss, Chance and Circumstance, 6–10, 14–61; Murray, "Blacks and the Draft," 57–76; Westheider, Fighting on Two Fronts, 12–13.

37. See Bond interview, Meet the Press, 2; NYT, 22 Jan. 1966, 12; "Petition to Governor Carl E. Sanders," n.d., SNCC Papers, rl. 53, fr. 570.

38. See Payne, I've Got the Light, 236–64; Ransby, Ella Baker, 279–81; 299–322.

39. See Payne, I've Got the Light, 236–64; Ransby, Ella Baker, 279–81; Carson, In Struggle, 62–64.

40. See Carson, In Struggle, 74–82, 99–129; Payne, I've Got the Light, 236–64; Ransby, Ella Baker, 281–91, 301–29. The most comprehensive study of the Atlanta Project to date is Grady-Willis, Challenging. This study focuses on the project's black power politics, as well as its community organizing and antiwar activism. Grady-Willis's excellent work complements this text's focus on the legal dimensions of the project workers' community organizing work and their relationship to Bond, Carmichael, and larger political dynamics within SNCC and in Atlanta.

41. "The Atlanta Project," TD, 10 Jan. 1966, SNCC Papers, rl. 37, fr. 45–602; "Purpose of the Atlanta Project," TD, n.d., SNCC Papers, box 95; "Buttermilk Bottom," TD, 1964, SNCC Papers, box 49; AI, 27 Feb. 1965, 1; 13 Mar. 1965, 1; 28 Aug. 1965, 1; 4 Sept. 1965, 1; 6 Nov. 1965, 1.

42. "The Atlanta Project," TD, 10 Jan. 1966, SNCC Papers, rl. 37, fr. 45–602; see also Carson, In Struggle, 166; Dittmer, Local People, 170–93.

43. Ware interview, 11 Jan. 2008, 1–2, 4.

44. Ibid.

45. Ware interview, 3, 4–5, 7–9, 11–12.

46. See Ware interview, 18 Jan. 2008, 21; Nwangaza interview, 1–5; Simmons interview, 2–5; Williams interview, 3–7, 12, 14–16; see also "The Purpose of the Atlanta Project," TD, 10 Jan. 1966, SNCC Papers, rl. 37, fr. 45–625; "Prospectus for an Atlanta Project," TD, n.d., SNCC Papers, rl. 37, fr. 45–622; Carson, *In Struggle*, 192–96. Project staff included Dwight Williams, Michael Simmons, Margaret Mills (a.k.a. Efia Nwagaza), Heligard Berland, Donald Stone, Frank Holloway, Robert Moore, and Gwen Robinson, codirector of the project. SNCC's work built on work of "civic leagues" and other local organizations designed to aid poor Atlanta neighborhoods. See Harmon, *Beneath the Image*, 180–81, 193–96, 215–16; Bayor, *Race and the Shaping*, 136–38, 144–46; Paschall, *It Must Have Rained*, 113–16, 126–40, 145–54, 157–59.

47. "The Atlanta Project," TD, 10 Jan. 1966, SNCC Papers, box 95; Debbie Amis, "Atlanta," TD, n.d., SNCC Papers, box 95; "Prospectus for An Atlanta Project," TD, n.d., SNCC Papers, box 95; "Tenant's Right to Trial," 9 Feb. 1966, SNCC Papers, box 49; Carson, *In Struggle*, 192–96.

48. For the classic text on the concept of lay lawyering, or informal peer-to-peer problem-solving, see López, *Rebellious Lawyering*, 38–44.

49. See "The Nitty-Gritty: The Reasons Why," TD, n.d., SNCC Papers, box 95; Atlanta Civic Council to Ivan Allen, TL, 19 Aug. 1963, SNCC Papers, rl. 37, fr. 435; "South Atlanta Project: Critical Analysis," TD, 15 Aug. 1963, SNCC Papers, rl. 37, fr. 638; Amis interview.

50. See *AC*, 1 Feb. 1966, 1; 2 Feb. 1966; *AI*, 5 Feb. 1966, 1; see also Jackson, *From Civil Rights*, 280–81. Many commentators expressed surprise at King's claim that he was unaware of conditions in Vine City. See *AI*, 5 Feb. 1966, 12.

51. See *Nitty Gritty*, 23 Feb. 1966, 1, Paschall Papers, box 25, 1963–64 folder; "Purpose of the Atlanta Project," TD, n.d., SNCC Papers, rl. 37, fr. 620; *AI*, 5 Feb. 1966, 1.

52. See *Nitty Gritty*, 23 Feb. 1966, 3, Paschall Papers, box 25, 1963–64 folder; "The Atlanta Project," TD, 22 Jan. 1966, SNCC Papers, box 95. Both CORE and SNCC pioneered rent strikes in Cleveland and New York City in 1963. See *WSJ*, 30 Dec. 1963, 1. In Atlanta, community civic groups had threatened rent strikes months prior to SNCC's efforts. See *AI*, 2 Oct. 1965, 1.

53. *ADW*, 2 Feb. 1966; *Nitty Gritty*, 23 Feb. 1966, 3, Paschall Papers, box 25, 1963–64 folder.

54. See City of Atlanta Building Code, Apartment House Law, sections 266, 270–71, 273–301, 304–7, 310, 313–17, 318–19 (1923). Poverty lawyers used the rent strike in several cities during the 1960s with ambiguous results. See Lawson, *Tenant Movement*, 3, 5, 181–97; Johnson, "Collective Tenant Action"; Fossum, "Rent Withholding."

55. "The Atlanta Project," TD, 10 Jan. 1966, SNCC Papers, box 95; Paschall, *It Must Have Rained*, 164–65; *Nitty Gritty*, 23 Feb. 1966, 3, Paschall Papers, box 25, 1963–64 folder.

56. See *ADW*, 20 Aug. 1967, 1; "SNCC Urges Summit to Support Rent Strikes," *Nitty Gritty*, 1, 4, Paschall Papers, box 25, 1963–64 folder. The cry of disapproval of rent strikes became a roar as the sixties rolled on and the tactic increasingly became a tool of the

burgeoning welfare rights movement. See Kornbluh, *Battle for Welfare Rights*; Martha Davis, *Brutal Need*, 40–55; Piven and Cloward, *Poor People's Movements*, 264–66, 269, 288–307.

57. See *AI*, 28 Aug. 1965, 3; *AC*, 2 Feb. 1966, 1; *ADW*, 5 Feb. 1966, 1; 15 Feb. 1966, 1; Ivan Allen, *Mayor*, 91, 151–52, 241.

58. See Williams v. Shaffer, 149 S.E.2d 668, (Ga. Sup. Ct. 1966); see also Williams v. Shaffer, 385 U.S. 1037, 1039 (1967).

59. "Poor People's Housing Proposal Program," TD, 1966, SNCC Papers, box 95; Grady-Willis, *Challenging*, 79–113.

60. The "brash" quote is from Tillinghast interview, 5–6. The "Nubian god" description is from Holt, *Summer*, 44.

61. See Carmichael, *Ready for Revolution*, 178–215.

62. Ibid. 110–35. Howard was not entirely a positive experience for Carmichael, who chafed under the influence of "Afro-Saxons" on a mission to assimilate blacks and appease whites, including the segregationists who controlled the university's purse strings, and materialistic, apolitical students. See ibid., 116–20, 125–27, 133–34.

63. Ibid. 178–215.

64. See Carmichael, *Ready for Revolution*, 178–215, 241–43, 248–49, 277–322, 460–69, 474–83, 659–72; Carson, *In Struggle*, 162–66.

65. See Carson, *In Struggle*, 191–211; Carmichael, *Ready for Revolution*, 478–83; Sellers, *River of No Return*, 139–40, 146–48, 151–54, 158–59; Lewis, *Walking with the Wind*, 349–50, 352–53, 364–69.

66. On the context for black power, see Carson, *In Struggle*, 158–62, 207–11. The quotations are from Carmichael, "What We Want," *New York Review of Books*, 22 Sept. 1966; Carmichael and Hamilton, *Black Power*, 34–41, 44–48, 58, 60, 80–81, 88; *NYT*, 21 June 1966, 30; "SNCC 1966: Comments by Stokely Carmichael, Chairman," n.d., Bond Papers, series 3, box 56, f. 12.

67. Ware interview, 11 Jan. 2008, 12–14, 17–25; see also "From Peace Corps to Mississippi Jail," *Liberator*, Mar. 1964.

68. Bill Ware, untitled,TD, SNCC Papers, box 7; *NYT*, 5 Aug. 1966, 10. Carmichael and others decried the attribution of Ware's position paper, entitled "Student Nonviolent Coordinating Committee Position Paper: The Basis for Black Power," to the organization; they viewed it as too strident and a distortion or misinterpretation of black power. See Carmichael, *Ready for Revolution*, 567–71. In December 1966, a contingent in SNCC led by the Atlanta faction purported to "expel" whites from SNCC by vote, over the objection of Carmichael, who favored alliances with progressive whites. Only nineteen people voted to expel whites; eighteen voted against and twenty-four abstained—hardly a ringing endorsement of "expulsion." Before long, the few whites who remained in SNCC resigned. See Carson, *In Struggle*, 205–06, 217–18, 240–42; Carmichael, *Ready for Revolution*, 570–71.

69. See *WP*, 29 May 1966, E6; *WSJ*, 24 June 1966, 8; *NYT*, 7 July 1966, 1; 17 Aug. 1966, 13; *WP*, 27 July 1966, 1; Bayard Rustin, "'Black Power' and Coalition Politics," *Commentary* 42 (Sept. 1966): 35; see also Joseph, *Waiting 'Til the Midnight Hour*, 149–52.

70. See *ADW*, 6 Aug. 1966, 1; *AI*, 13 Aug. 1966, 4: 7 July 1966, 4.

71. See *AI*, 21 May 1966, 1; Lewis, *Walking with the Wind*, 368, 372–73.

72. See *NYT*, 23 Aug. 1966, A12; Carmichael, *Ready for Revolution*, 540–41; Carmichael, "What We Want," 22 Sept. 1966.

73. See *Chicago Tribune*, 30 July 1966, A10; *NYT*, 16 Aug. 1966, 24; 23 Aug. 1966, A12.

74. See *ADW*, 7 Sept. 1966, 1; Paschall, *It Must Have Rained*, 155–56; Ruby Doris Smith, "Description of 'Riot' in Atlanta, Georgia on Sept. 6, 1966," TD, SNCC Papers, box 95; untitled, TD, Sept. 1966, SNCC Papers, box 95; Grady-Willis, *Challenging*, 117–20.

75. See Transcript of Hearing, Sept. 29–30, 1 Oct. 1966, 467–68, Carmichael v. Allen, Moore Papers, box 1; Carmichael v. Allen, 267 F. Supp. 985, 988 (N.D. Ga. 1967).

76. See Carmichael v. Allen, 267 F. Supp. 985, 988–89 (N.D. Ga. 1967); Sellers, *River of No Return*, 175–76; Smith, "Description of 'Riot' in Atlanta, Georgia on Sept. 6, 1966," TD, SNCC Papers, box 95; Later, the police charged Ware with inciting to riot.

77. See *ADW*, 7 Sept. 1966, 1; *AC*, 7 Sept. 1966, 1; Smith, "Description of 'Riot' in Atlanta, Georgia on Sept. 6, 1966."

78. See *ADW*, 7 Sept. 1966, 1; Ivan Allen, *Mayor*, 181–91.

79. See *ADW*, 8 Sept. 1966, 1.

80. For the Allen quotes, see Allen, *Mayor*, 183; *ADW*, 14 Sept. 1966, 1; *NYT*, 8 Sept. 1966, 1. For the Patterson quotes, see *AC*, 7 Sept. 1966, 4; 8 Sept. 1966, 4. The Hays quote is from *WP*, 9 Sept. 1966, A4.

81. See *ADW*, 8 Sept. 1966, 1; *AC*, 15 Sept. 1966, 3.

82. See *ADW*, 8 Sept. 1966, 1; 9 Sept. 1966, 1; 10 Sept. 1966, 1.

83. See *ADW*, 9 Sept. 1966, 1; Julian Bond to Stokely Carmichael, 6 Sept. 1966, Bond Papers, series 3, box 56, f. 12.

84. See Transcript of Hearing, 29–30 Sept., 1 Oct. 1966, 476–78, Carmichael v. Allen, Moore Papers, box 1; *NYT*, 9 Sept. 1966, 1; *ADW*, 9 Sept. 1966, 1; *AC*, 8 Sept. 1966, 1.

85. See *NYT*, 19 Sept. 1966, 51; 30 Oct. 1966, 62.

86. See *ADW*, 10 Sept. 1966, 1; *WP*, 10 Sept. 1966, A1.

87. Moore interview by author, 1–2; see also Moore, "Tenth Black Lawyer," 210–11.

88. Moore, "Tenth Black Lawyer," 210–11.

89. Ibid., 211–12; see also Moore interview by author, 6; Howard Moore, "Black Barrister," 154.

90. Moore, "Tenth Black Lawyer," 212.

91. See ibid. 212–13. Moore's recollection may or may not be off by a few. The 1960 U.S. Census lists 12 Georgia "non-whites" as lawyers or judges. U.S. Bureau of the Census, "Occupation of the Experienced Civilian Labor Force by Color, of the Employed by Race and Class of Worker, And of Persons Not in Labor Force with Work Experience, by Sex, for the State and for Standard Metropolitan Statistical Areas of 250,000 or More: 1960," *Census of Population: 1960*, vol. 1, *Characteristics of the Population*, part 12, *Georgia* (Washington, DC: GPO, 1963), 528-33, table 122, http://www2.census.gov/prod2/decennial/documents/37721815v1p12ch7.pdf. That term is not, of course, coextensive

with "black lawyers." In any event, the difference between the number that Moore quoted and the figure provided by the census is insignificant. The UGA's refusal—still—to admit African-American law students contributed to the dearth of black lawyers. As a result of a lawsuit that Moore worked on, the University of Georgia School of Law admitted its first black student in 1963. See Daniels, *Horace T. Ward*, 152, 219.

92. See Moore interview by author, 5; Hollowell and Lehfeldt, *Sacred Call*, 128–80; see also Daniels, *Horace T. Ward*, 165.

93. See Moore, "Tenth Black Lawyer," 214; Moore, "Black Barrister," 157.

94. See Moore, "Tenth Black Lawyer," 214; see also Carmichael, *Ready for Revolution*, 555.

95. Parker interview by author, 10; Bond interview by author, 7; Nwangaza interview by author, 8; see also Davis, *Autobiography*, 289; Moore, "Black Barrister," 155, 159.

96. Nwangaza interview, 8; Parker interview, 10; Davis, *Autobiography*, 289, 307–8, 315–16; Carmichael, *Ready for Revolution*, 515. The testimonial is from Sellers, *River of No Return*, 245.

97. Nwangaza interview, 8; Bond interview, 7; Kunstler, *My Life*, 181; Sellers, *River of No Return*, 226, 241, 252, 260.

98. See *NYT*, 19 Sept. 1966, 51; Moore interview, 9–10.

99. See Herndon v. Lowry, 301 U.S. 242, 242–64 (1937). For a discussion of the circumstances surrounding the Herndon case, see also Martin, *Angelo Herndon Case*, 5–8.

100. Moore made facial and as applied challenges to the statues. See Complaint, 3–7, Carmichael v. Allen (N.D. Ga. 1964), Moore Papers, box 2, Briefs folder; Transcript of Hearing, 29–30 Sept., 1 Oct. 1966, 487–88, Carmichael v. Allen, Moore Papers, box 1. The riot statute read, "Any two or more persons who shall do an unlawful act of violence or any other act in a violent or tumultuous manner, shall be guilty of a riot and punished as for a misdemeanor." The unlawful assembly statute read, "It shall be unlawful for any person to act in a violent, turbulent, quarrelsome, boisterous, indecent or disorderly manner, or to use profane, vulgar or obscene language, or to do anything tending to disturb the good order, morals, peace or dignity of the city." Ibid., Ex. A. Moore made facial and as applied challenges to the statues.

101. See Transcript of Hearing, Sept. 29–30, 1 Oct. 1966, 11–13, Carmichael v. Allen, Moore Papers, box 1; *ADW*, 30 Sept. 1966, 1.

102. Transcript of Hearing, 29–30 Sept., 1 Oct. 1966, 246–47, 250, Carmichael v. Allen, Moore Papers, box 1; *ADW*, 1 Oct. 1966, 1.

103. Transcript of Hearing, 29–30 Sept., 1 Oct. 1966, 241–44, Carmichael v. Allen, Moore Papers, box 1; *ADW*, 1 Oct. 1966, 1; *ADW*, 2 Oct. 1966, 1.

104. See Transcript of Hearing, 29–30 Sept., 1 Oct. 1966, 238, Carmichael v. Allen, Moore Papers, box 1; *ADW*, 30 Sept. 1966, 1; *NYT*, 30 Sept. 1966, 25.

105. See Transcript of Hearing, 29–30 Sept., 1 Oct. 1966, 257, 265, 272–73, 196, 201–9, Carmichael v. Allen, Moore Papers, box 1; *NYT*, 30 Sept. 1966, 25.

106. See Transcript of Hearing, 29–30 Sept., 1 Oct. 1966, 469–70, 474, Carmichael v. Allen, Moore Papers, box 1.

107. See Transcript of Hearing, 29–30 Sept., 1 Oct. 1966, 335, 339, Carmichael v. Allen, Moore Papers, box 1; Brief for Plaintiffs, 17 and n. 10, Carmichael v. Allen, Moore Papers, box 2, Briefs file; *AC*, 1 Oct. 1966, 1.

108. See Transcript of Hearing, 29–30 Sept., 1 Oct. 1966, 325, 327–28, 330–32, 335, 339–40, 475, Carmichael v. Allen, Moore Papers, box 1; Brief for Plaintiffs, 17 and n. 10, Carmichael v. Allen, Moore Papers, box 2, Briefs file; Carmichael v. Allen, 267 F. Supp. 985, 992 (U.S. D.C. 1967); Robert B. Curtis to Stokeley Carmichael, 13 Sept. 1966, TLS, Moore Papers, Carmichael v. Allen file, box 4, Letters and Receipts folder; Moore interview, 10.

109. Carmichael v. Allen, 267 F. Supp. 985, 993–96 (N.D. Ga. 1967); Brief in Support of Motion for Preliminary Injunction, 1–7, Carmichael v. Allen (N.D. Ga. 1964), Moore Papers, box 2, Briefs folder.

110. Dombrowski v. Pfister, 227 F. Supp. 556, 564–67 (E.D. La. 1964); see also Adams, *James A. Dombrowski*, 273–75.

111. Dombrowski v. Pfister, 380 U.S. 479, 486–97 (1965); Adams, *James A. Dombrowski*, 275–79; see also Fiss, "Dombrowski."

112. Carmichael, 267 F. Supp., 993–99; *ADW*, 15 Dec. 1966, 1; *NYT*, 14 Dec. 1966, 37. Moore's success in the District Court did not extend to the state riot charges because the riot statute pertained to conduct alone, rather than to words. The First Amendment's protection of expression had no force in the context of an alleged riot, the Court held. Carmichael was not prosecuted on this charge, however. Moore interview, 10.

113. See Transcript of Committee Proceedings, Contest to the Seating of Rep.-Elect Julian Bond, Atlanta, Georgia, 23 May 1966, 23, Moore Papers, box 5, Bond v. Floyd file; Plaintiff's Trial Brief, 1, 15, Bond v. Floyd, no. 9895 (N.D. Ga., 27 Jan. 1966), Moore Papers, box 5, Bond v. Floyd file; Williams interview, 16; see also *ADW*, 13 Jan. 1966, 1.

114. Moore interview, 11; Parker interview, 26-27.

115. Bond interview by author, 5; Simmons interview, 18 Jan. 2008, 2; Ware interview, 18 Jan. 2008, 19–20; "Support Julian Bond," TD, n.d., SNCC Papers, rl. 53, fr. 573; "Meet Julian Bond," TD, n.d., SNCC Papers, rl. 53, fr. 554; "Julian Bond Prevented From Taking Oath by Georgia House," TD, 8 Jan. 1966, SNCC Papers, rl. 37, fr. 527; "Emergency Bulletin," 8 Jan. 1966, TD, SNCC Papers, rl. 37, fr. 527; "Purpose of the Atlanta Project," TD, 22 Jan. 1966, SNCC Papers, rl. 37, fr. 622.

116. See Transcript of Committee Proceedings, Contest to the Seating of Rep.-Elect Julian Bond, Atlanta, Georgia, 23 May 1966, 23, Moore Papers, box 5, Bond v. Floyd file; Plaintiff's Trial Brief, 1, 15, Bond v. Floyd, no. 9895 (N.D. Ga., 27 Jan. 1966), Moore Papers, box 5, Bond v. Floyd file; Williams interview, 16; *ADW*, 13 Jan. 1966, 1.

117. See Statement by Julian Bond on the Decision of the Federal Court on His Seating in the Georgia Legislature, TD, Feb. 1966, Moore Papers, box 7, Bond v. Floyd, News Articles File; *ADW*, 11 Feb. 1966, 1; *ADW*, 22 Feb. 1966, 1. Bond had to stand for reelection again in the regular election in the fall. First, he defeated a primary opponent, though in a close election. In November, he overwhelmingly won reelection against his Republican adversary. See *NYT*, 16 Sept. 1966, 22; 10 Nov. 1966, 30; *AC*, 24 Feb. 1966, 1; 5 Mar. 1966, 9.

118. See Plaintiff's Trial Brief, 11, 19, 20, Bond v. Floyd (N.D. Ga., 27 Jan. 1966), Moore Papers, box 5, Bond v. Floyd file; Defendants' Brief, 6–19, Bond v. Floyd (N.D. Ga., Feb. 1966), Moore Papers, box 5, Bond v. Floyd file.

119. See Plaintiff's Trial Brief, 11, 13–15, Bond v. Floyd, Moore Papers, box 5, Bond v. Floyd file; Baker v. Carr, 369 U.S. 186, 217–26 (1962).

120. See Plaintiff's Trial Brief, 1, 11, 13–15, 52–54, Bond v. Floyd, Moore Papers, box 5, Bond v. Floyd file; Plaintiff's Supplemental Trial Brief, 17, 32, Bond v. Floyd, Moore Papers, box 5, Bond v. Floyd file; see also *ADW*, 13 Jan. 1966, 1.

121. See Plaintiff's Trial Brief, 47–51, Bond v. Floyd, Moore Papers, box 5, Bond v. Floyd file.

122. See Plaintiff's Trial Brief, 11–51, Bond v. Floyd, Moore Papers, box 5, Bond v. Floyd file.

123. See Plaintiff's Trial Brief, 22–42, Bond v. Floyd, Moore Papers, box 5, Bond v. Floyd file; Defendants' Trial Brief, 7–16, 17, Bond v. Floyd, Moore Papers, box 5, Bond v. Floyd file; *ADW*, 13 Jan. 1966, 1.

124. See Bond v. Floyd, 251 F. Supp. 333, 339 (N.D. Ga., 10 Feb. 1966); *NYT*, 29 Jan. 1966, 9.

125. *Bond v. Floyd*, 251 F. Supp. at 340–45 (quoting Joseph Story, 2 *Commentaries on the Constitution of the United States* (1833)); see also *WP*, 29 Jan. 1966, A2. One judge, Elbert Tuttle, who already had earned a reputation as an unstinting enforcer of civil rights in the reapportionment and voting rights that created seats in state government for African-American officials—including the plaintiff, Julian Bond—dissented from the majority opinion. Bond v. Floyd, 251 F. Supp. at 345, 357 (Tuttle, J., dissenting). The seminal cases that Tuttle ruled in included Sanders v. Gray, 203 F. Supp. 158 (N.D. Ga. 1962), modified, 372 U.S. 368 (1963); Westberry v. Vandiver, 206 F. Supp. 276 (N.D. Ga. 1962), *rev'd sub nom*, Westberry v. Sanders, 376 U.S. 1 (1964); Toombs v. Fortson, 205 F. Supp. 248 (N.D. Ga. 1962), *aff'd per curiam*, 384 U.S. 210 (1966). For Tuttle's account of his role in these cases, see Tuttle, "Equality and the Vote."

126. Rabinowitz was, in fact, a member of the Communist Party from 1942 through the early 1960s, he wrote in his memoir; it is unclear, however, whether he publicly advertised this fact at the time. See Victor Rabinowitz, *Unrepentant Leftist*, 73–90. On the ACLU controversy, see Victor Rabinowitz to Melvin Wulf and Charles Morgan, Jr., TLS, 1 Mar. 1966, Bond Papers, box 92, f. 3; *AC*, 1 Mar. 1966, 10; *NYT*, 21 Feb. 1966, 44; *ADW*, 26 Feb. 1966, 1. The ACLU later filed an amicus curiae brief in support of Bond when his case was heard by the U.S. Supreme Court. See Brief of the American Civil Liberties Union as Amicus Curiae, Bond v. Floyd, no. 87, U.S. Supreme Court (Oct. 1966).

127. See Brief for Appellants, Bond v. Floyd (24 Sept. 1966), 27–37; Brief for Appellees, Bond v. Floyd (21 Oct. 1966), 26–44.

128. "Arguments Before the Court: Exclusion of Legislator," *U.S. Law Week*, 15 Nov. 1966.

129. Ibid.

130. See *NYT*, 11 Nov. 1966, 27; *AI*, 19 Nov. 1966, 1; *WP*, 11 Nov. 1966, A4.

131.  Bond v. Floyd, 385 U.S. 116, 132–37 (1966). The second quoted material is from New York Times v. Sullivan, 376 U.S. 254, 270 (1964).

132.  *AJ,* 5 Dec. 1966, 1; *AC,* 6 Dec. 1966, 20; 6 Dec. 1966, 1; 6 Dec. 1966, 4; *ADW,* 10 Jan. 1967, 1.

133.  See *NYT,* 6 Dec. 1966, 1; *ADW,* 6 Dec. 1966, 1; 10 Jan. 1967, 1. Howard Moore represented thousands arrested during peace movement activities or intent on avoiding military service on grounds of hardship or conscientious objector status. Remarkably, Moore's work for the antiwar movement extended to the U.S. Army itself. He filed an unprecedented First Amendment suit on behalf of soldiers who opposed the Vietnam War. Moore argued that the soldiers enjoyed the same freedoms of speech and protest as civilians. The U.S. Army described the case as "without parallel in American military history." See *NYT,* 2 Apr. 1969, 1; 14 Apr. 1968, 10. More famously, Moore represented black activists in trials where racial bias in the criminal justice system featured prominently, including UCLA philosophy instructor and avowed Communist Angela Davis, who was acquitted of murder and related charges. See *NYT,* 6 Jan. 1971, 17.

134.  Bond v. Floyd, 385 U.S. at 137.

135.  The immediate cause of the firing was project members' failure to return an SNCC car, which national officers subsequently reported missing to the Atlanta police department. See Sellers, *River of No Return,* 185–86; Carson, *In Struggle,* 241–42. However, conflict also existed over the black power ideology; and deep personal animosity existed between Carmichael and Bill Ware. Ware interview, 36–45; Simmons interview, 4–7.

136.  See *NYT,* 3 Feb. 1967, 16; Bond interview by author, 9; *San Fran. Chron.,* 12 Feb. 1967, clipping, Bond Papers, series 2, box 12, f. 6. The "bewilderment" quote is from Draft SEDFRE fundraising letter, n.d., 109, Bond Papers, series 3, box 52, f. 10. The questions are from "Fundraising letter from Julian Bond to SEDFRE friends," n.d., 118, Bond Papers, series 3, box 52, f. 11.

137.  Grady-Willis, *Challenging,* 117–33.

138.  Sellers, *River of No Return,* 184.

139.  Paschall, *It Must Have Rained,* 171–74; Harmon, *Beneath the Image,* 212.

140.  Johnson interview, 27.

141.  See Economic Opportunity Atlanta Inc. 2 year Progress Report, Jan. 1967, TD, Paschall Papers, box 16, f. 18; *ADW,* 3 Apr. 1966, 3; 3 Aug. 1966, 1; 2 July 1966, 1; 11 Sept. 1965, 1; 1 July 1966, 1; 2 June 1966, 1; *AC,* 21 Aug. 1967, 1; Clark, *Victory Deferred,* 47, 53–59, 87–89; Harmon, *Beneath the Image,* 191–92.

142.  See Economic Opportunity Atlanta Inc. 2 year Progress Report, Jan. 1967, TD, Paschall Papers, box 16, f. 18; *ADW,* 15 Feb. 1966; 1 Apr. 1966, 1; 5 Apr. 1966, 1; 9 Apr. 1966, 3; see also Bayor, *Race and the Shaping,* 119. Poor blacks also gained seats on local advisory boards to the EEO program. See *Nitty Gritty,* 23 Feb. 1966, 2, Paschall Papers, box 25, 1963–64 folder.

143.  Economic Opportunity Atlanta Inc. 2 year Progress Report, Jan. 1967, TD, Paschall Papers, box 16, f. 18; Bayor, *Race and the Shaping,* 119.

144. See *AI*, 3 Dec. 1966, 1; 31 Dec. 1966, 1; *AJ*, 4 Dec. 1966, 22; *ADW*, 12 Aug. 1965, 1; Levine, *Poor Ye Need*, 32–39; Clark, *Victory Deferred*, 25–30, 87–89.

145. The "movement of movements" phrase is from Hall, "Long Civil Rights Movement," 1239, 1254–61. For works that focus on black WWII veterans as catalysts in the civil rights movement, see Klarman, From Jim Crow, 444; Dudziak, Cold War Civil Rights, 12, 82–89.

146. See Shepard, *Rationing Justice*, 37–67, an important chronicle of the Legal Services Program in the Southeast that focuses on the challenges that attorneys face as a result of decision-making in Washington. The book does not discuss the Atlanta Project's groundwork around slum housing issues.

147. Moore, "Tenth Black Lawyer," 210–11.

148. See also Payne, *I've Got the Light*, 374.

149. Paschall, *It Must Have Rained*, 175; Bayor, *Race and the Shaping*, 142–46; Fairclough, *To Redeem*, 357–69, 383–97.

## Chapter 10

1. The statement from Hooper in the epigraph is from Transcript of Hearing, Calhoun v. Latimer, 31 July 1962, 128, Walden Papers, series IV, box 1, f. 2.

2. The statement from Joseph E. Boone in the epigraph is from Boone, Atlanta Branch NAACP Fall Renewal Campaign Progress Report, TD, 11 Nov. 1966, NAACP Papers, box C6, 1966–69 file.

3. See Dr. Martin Luther King, Jr., Pilgrimage for Democracy Address, 15 Dec. 1963, Atlanta, Ga., 1–3, Paschall Papers, box 24, SCLC folder.

4. Ibid., 4–5.

5. Transcript of Hearing, Calhoun v. Latimer, 14 Dec. 1959, 104, Walden Papers, series IV, box 1, f. 4; *NYT*, 22 May 1954, 15; *ADW*, 10 Apr. 1964, 1; see also *NYT*, 29 Sept. 2005, B10.

6. See Dr. Martin Luther King, Jr., Pilgrimage for Democracy Address, 15 Dec. 1963, Atlanta, Ga., 5, Paschall Papers, box C6, 1966–69 file. Motley corrected a reporter who had insisted that she made a "demand" in court. She said, "What do you mean 'I demanded the court'? You don't demand, you pray for relief or move for some action." *NYT*, 29 Sept. 2005, B10.

7. On ASLC's activities, see chapters 5, 6, and 7.

8. See *ADW*, 14 June 1955, 1; see also chapter 4.

9. See Complaint, 6, Calhoun v. Latimer, no. 71-2622 (N.D. Ga., 11 Jan. 1958), Case File, NARA, box 53, f. 1; *ADW*, 14 June 1955, 1; 26 Jan. 1958, 1. For the national NAACP's directives, see Thurgood Marshall and Roy Wilkins, "Interpretation of Supreme Court Decision and the NAACP Program," *Crisis* 62 (June–July 1955): 329; "Directives to Branches Adopted by Emergency Southwide NAACP Conference, Atlanta, Georgia, June 4, 1955," *Crisis* 62 (June–July 1955): 339.

10. See Atlanta NAACP to Atlanta Board of Education, Memorandum, 11 Sept. 1955, TD, box 2562, NAACP Papers; E. E. Martin to J. H. Calhoun, 12 Sept. 1957, TL, NAACP Papers, box 2562; *NYT*, 19 Jan. 1958, E9; Wagner D. Jackson, "Working with School Boards

to Implement Desegregation," *Crisis* 62 (Jan. 1955): 5, 7. The local NAACP branch disclaimed involvement in the school desegregation suit. See *ADW*, 31 Dec. 1957, 1.

11. See Motley interview, 253–54, 270–73, 292, 314–22, 687–90; Biographical Sketch, 1–2, Motley Papers, box 1, f. 2; see also Motley, *Equal Justice*, 59, 183; Hill, *Big Bang*, 273; Carter, *A Matter of Law*, 77–78, 99. The tenth Supreme Court argument did not result in a decision. Motley recalled that she was one of ten blacks at Columbia Law School during her time there, and one of four black women. These were unusually strong wartime numbers for blacks and women. See Motley, "Reflections," n. 1; Goebel, *History*, 506 n. 57.

12. See Motley interview, 253, 255, 270–75, 431–32, 471. Judge Motley did not often identify those who insulted her. However, she did note that a federal judge named in Birmingham named "Armstrong" had noted her sex before she argued a motion. Motley also noted that "Judge Duvane" in Florida made untoward remarks when she argued a Florida higher education desegregation case. The figures on women lawyers are from Epstein, *Women in Law*, 4. The figures on black women lawyers are from Smith, *Rebels in Law*, 285–88. By comparison, in 2000, black women still comprised a fraction of attorneys, 1.8 percent; women overall constituted 28.6 percent of U.S. lawyers. See American Bar Association, Commission on Racial Diversity in the Profession, Statistics about Minorities in the Profession, at www.abanet.org/minorities/links/2000census.html.

13. See Motley interview, 253, 255, 270–75, 431–32, 471; see also Motley, *Equal Justice*, 59, 183; Remarks by Mayor Robert Wagner in Honor of Constance Baker Motley, 4–5, Motley Papers, box 1, f. 2. Commentary by contemporaries include Hill, *Big Bang*, 273; Greenberg, *Crusaders in the Courts*, 33–34, 39; Carter, *A Matter of Law*, 76; see also Pratt, *We Shall Not Be Moved*, 128–29; Strebeigh, *Equal*, 175–76.

14. See Motley interview, 271–74, 292–95; see also Greenberg, *Crusaders*, 34; Williams, *Thurgood Marshall*, 248–49; Jordan, *Vernon Can Read!* 140.

15. On Georgia politicians' and Walden's responses to *Brown*, see chapter 4; see also *SSN*, May 1964, 7-B; *AC*, 18 May 1954, 1; 2 June 1955, 1. On the manifesto, see Klarman, *From Jim Crow*, 320.

16. Answer, 1–2, Calhoun v. Latimer (N.D. Ga., 10 Mar. 1958), Case File, NARA, box 53, f. 1; Brief of Defendants in Support of Their Motion to Dismiss, 5–6, Calhoun v. Latimer (N.D. Ga., 10 Mar. 1958), Case File, NARA, box 53, f. 1. On liberal certification rules in civil rights class actions, see also 3b James Wm. Moore et al., *Moore's Federal Practice*, ¶ 23.02 (2d ed. 1996); Johnson v. Bd. of Trustees of Univ. of Ky., 83 F.Supp. 707, 709–10 (Ky. 1949).

17. Order, 8, Calhoun v. Latimer (N.D. Ga., 10 Mar. 1958), Case File, NARA, box 53, f. 1. For Vandiver's statement, see *SSN*, Sept. 1958, 12. On federal district courts and resistance to *Brown*, see Aaron v. Cooper, 163 F.Supp. 13 (E.D. Ark. 1958); Allen v. County School Bd. of Prince Edward County, Va., 164 F.Supp. 786 (Va. 1958), rev'd 266 F.2d 507, cert. denied 361 U.S. 830.

18. Transcript of Hearing, Calhoun v. Latimer, 5 June 1959, 33–34, Walden Papers, series IV, box 1, f. 5.

19. Transcript of Hearing, Calhoun v. Latimer, 5 June 1959, 33–34, Walden Papers, series IV, box 1, f. 5; see also *ADW*, 6 June 1959, 1; Motley, *Equal Justice*, 197.

20. Motley, *Equal Justice*, 142; Transcript of Hearing, Calhoun v. Latimer, 5 June 1959, 36–37.

21. Transcript of Hearing, Calhoun v. Latimer, 5 June 1959, 34–37. The South Carolina case is Briggs v. Elliott, 132 F. Supp. 776, 777 (E.D.S.C. 1955).

22. Transcript of Hearing, Calhoun v. Latimer, 5 June 1959, 35–36; see also *ADW*, 14 Mar. 1958, 1.

23. Transcript of Hearing, Calhoun v. Latimer, 5 June 1959, 81, 119–24.

24. Ibid., 43–50, 116–18; see also Testimony of Louise Simpson, Secretary of the Atlanta Board of Education, ibid., 54–57; Testimony of Jarvis Barnes, Assistant Supt. Adm. Services, Atlanta Board of Education, ibid., 73–80; Testimony of Ira Jarrell, Superintendent of Schools, ibid., 101–4, 115, 121–22.

25. See *SSN*, July 1959; Order, 4, Calhoun v. Latimer (N.D. Ga., 9 July 1959), Case File, NARA, box 53, f. 1.

26. See *SSN*, July 1959; Sept. 1959; Oct. 1959; May 1964, 7-B; Henderson, *Ernest Vandiver*, 82.

27. See *SSN*, July 1959; May, 1964, 7-B.

28. School Desegregation Plan, 5,Calhoun v. Latimer (N.D. Ga., 30 Nov. 1959), Case File, NARA, box 53, f. 1; Minutes of the Board of Education of the City of Atlanta, 30 Nov. 1959, Desegregation File, Atlanta Board of Education Papers.

29. School Desegregation Plan, 1–3, Calhoun v. Latimer (N.D. Ga., 30 Nov. 1959), Case File, NARA, box 53, f. 1.

30. Ibid.

31. School Desegregation Plan, 2–5, Calhoun v. Latimer (N.D. Ga., 30 Nov. 1959), Case File, NARA, box 53, f. 1; see also Hornsby, "Black Public Education," 29.

32. Resolution, TD, 30 Nov. 1959, 4–5, Calhoun Case File, NARA, box 53, f. 1.

33. Southern white families steeped in the norms of Jim Crow could hardly be expected to request transfers to black schools, and they did not. On the NAACP's attempt to mobilize individuals to apply despite obstacles created by the school board, see Nasstrom, "Women, Civil Rights Movement," 198–99.

34. Plaintiffs' Objections to Defendants' Desegregation Plan, 1–2, Calhoun v. Latimer (N.D. Ga., 30 Dec. 1959), Case File, NARA, box 53, f. 1; Plaintiffs' Brief in Support of Objections to Defendants' Desegregation Plan, 1–5, 6–7, 10–14, Calhoun v. Latimer (N.D. Ga., 30 Dec. 1959), Case File, NARA, box 53, f. 1; Transcript of Hearing, Calhoun v. Latimer, 14 Dec. 1959, 75–87, 91–92, Walden Papers, series IV, box 1, f. 4; *ADW*, 2 Dec. 1959, 1; see also Cooper v. Aaron, 358 U.S. 1, 7 (1958).

35. Order of Court on Motion by Defendants to Approve Plan, 5, 6–9, Calhoun v. Latimer (N.D. Ga., 30 Dec. 1959), Case File, NARA, box 53, f. 2; see also *SSN*, Feb. 1960.

36. Motion for Further Relief, 3–6, Calhoun v. Latimer (N.D. Ga., 26 Feb. 1960), Case File, NARA, box 53, f. 2; Order of Court, 2–4, Calhoun v. Latimer (N.D. Ga., 9 Mar. 1960), Case File, NARA, box 53, f. 2; *ADW*, 10 July 1959, 1.

37. See Transcript of Hearing, Calhoun v. Latimer, 14 Dec. 1959, 103–5, Walden Papers, series IV, box 1, f. 4; see also *Brown II*, 349 U.S. 294, 300 (1955); Cooper v. Aaron,

359 U.S. 1, 17 (1958). On the Little Rock saga, see Jacoway, *Turn Away Thy Son*, 13; Freyer, *Little Rock on Trial*.

38. See Transcript of Hearing, Calhoun v. Latimer, 14 Dec. 1959, 105–6, Walden Papers, series IV, box 1, f. 4; *SSN*, Jan. 1960; see also Motley, *Equal Justice*, 197; Motley interview, 277, 497.

39. See Transcript of Hearing, Calhoun v. Latimer, 14 Dec. 1959, 110, Walden Papers, series IV, box 1, f. 4.

40. See *AC*, 17 June 1959, A1; *SSN*, Mar. 1960.

41. Roche, *Restructured Resistance*, 39, 67–68; Harmon, *Beneath the Image*, 97.

42. Roche, *Restructured Resistance*, 97–144.

43. See Statements of Georgia S. Banks, Ann Daniel, Leonard N. Rogers, W. H. Ingram, L. M. Stinson, W. E. Mason, Harry King, and Duncan Bell, TD, 7 Mar. 1960, Washington, Georgia, Sibley Papers, box 145, Witness Testimony folder.

44. See Statements of L. H. Hardy, Jr., and C. L. Tally, TD, 7 Mar. 1960, Washington, Georgia, Sibley Papers, box 145, Witness Testimony folder; Dr. R. W. Greene, "Integration Is Not Inevitable," TD, Jan. 1960, Sibley Papers, box 144, Race folder.

45. Roche, *Restructured Resistance*, 105–6, 139–41.

46. On the political calculations involved in the "open schools" movement, see *ADW*, 7 June 1959, 1; 18 June 1959, 1; see also Roche, *Restructured Resistance*, 90–94, 158–59. For testimony, see Statement of John Wesley Dobbs, TD, 24 Mar. 1960, Atlanta, Georgia, Sibley Papers, box 145, Witness Testimony folder; Statements of Donald Hollowell and William Holmes Borders, TD, 24 Mar. 1960, Atlanta, Ga., Sibley Papers, box 146, Witness Testimony folder; *SSN*, Apr. 1960; see also Roche, *Restructured Resistance*, 58–64, 145, 149, 172–74; 146–48, 150; Nasstrom, "Women, Civil Rights Movement," 138–46, 157–64. The 1,800 witnesses represented 115,000 persons. Of the eighteen hundred, sixteen hundred were white. For statistics, see Majority Report, General Assembly Committee on Schools, TD, 28 Apr. 1960, Sibley Papers, box 145, Report folder.

47. Statement of William Holmes Borders, TD, 24 Mar. 1960; *SSN*, Apr. 1960.

48. Majority Report, General Assembly Committee on Schools; see also Minority Report, General Assembly Committee on Schools, TD, 28 Apr. 1960, Sibley Papers, box 145, Report folder; *SSN*, May 1960.

49. See Order of Court, 1–2, Calhoun v. Latimer (N.D. Ga., 9 May 1960), Case File, NARA, box 53, f. 7; Opinion on Plaintiffs' Motion For Further Relief, 2–5, Calhoun v. Latimer (N.D. Ga., 8 Sept. 1960), Case File, NARA, box 53, f. 7; *SSN*, June 1960.

50. See Motley, *Equal Justice*, 81, 137–38, 145–46; Daniels, *Horace T. Ward*, 150–51; see also Hornsby, "Black Public Education," 23–24.

51. See Daniels, *Horace T. Ward*, 156–57; Hornsby, "Black Public Education," 23–24.

52. See *ADW*, 31 Aug. 1961, 1; *SSN*, Sept. 1961; Ball Interview by author, 2; Welch Interview by author, 2. Damarius Allen, one of the ten selected for the desegregation experiment, decided just two days before the opening of school to attend college instead. See *AJC*, 30 Aug. 1991, 3. The nine students who desegregated the Atlanta public schools were Lawrence Jefferson, Mary James McMullen, Madelyn Nix, Thomas Welch, Willie Jean Black, Donita Gaines, Rosalyn Walton, Martha Ann Holmes, and Arthur Simmons, Jr. See *ADW*, 31 Aug. 1961, 1.

53. See "The 'Deep South'—Land with a Future: Atlanta," USN&WR, 6 Nov. 1961, 68; George McMillan, "Atlanta's Peaceful Blow for Justice: With the Police on an Integration Job," *Life*, 16 Sept. 1961, 35–36; "Glad to See You," *Newsweek*, 11 Sept. 1961, 93; Kyle Haselden, "Too Busy to Hate," *Christian Century*, 27 Mar. 1963, 392; Fuller, "Atlanta Is Different," 15–16, reprint from *New Republic*, 1960, Paschall Papers, box 23, f. 6; see *ADW*, 31 Aug. 1961, 1.

54. See *ADW*, 5 Aug. 1959, 1; *AC*, 30 Aug. 1991, G3; *SSN*, Sept. 1961; Ball Interview by author, 2.

55. See Transcript of Hearing, Calhoun v. Latimer, 14 Dec. 1959, 107–8, 213–15, Walden Papers, series IV, box 1, f. 4; *SSN*, Feb. 1960.

56. See Transcript of Hearing, Calhoun v. Latimer, 31 July 1962, 213–16, Walden Papers, series IV, box 1, f. 2; *ADW*, 1 May 1962, 1.

57. See Transcript of Hearing, Calhoun v. Latimer, 31 July 1962, 228, Walden Papers, series IV, box 1, f. 2; *ADW*, 1 May 1962, 1.

58. See Transcript of Hearing, Calhoun v. Latimer, 31 July 1962, Walden Papers series IV, box 1; f.2; 229–32; see also *ADW*, 1 Aug. 1962, 1.

59. See Transcript of Hearing, Calhoun v. Latimer, 31 July 1962, 128, 241, 244–45, Walden Papers, series IV, box 1, f. 2; *ADW*, 31 July 1962, 1; *ADW*, 1 Aug. 1962, 1.

60. See Transcript of Hearing, Calhoun v. Latimer, 31 July 1962, 241, 244–45, 287–88, Walden Papers, series IV, box 1, f. 2; see also 217 F. Supp. 614, 615–16 (N.D. Ga. 1962).

61. See Calhoun v. Latimer, 321 F.2d 302, 304–5, 307–11 (5th Cir. 1963).

62. *AI*, 4 Apr. 1964, 4; see also *AI*, 13 Apr. 1964, 1; *AC*, 9 July 1963, 1; *SSN*, June 1961, 8.

63. See *SSN*, Apr. 1964, 1; May, 1964, 1; *NYT*, 12 Apr. 1964, E5; *ADW*, 10 Apr. 1964, 1.

64. See *SSN*, Apr. 1964, 1.

65. See *NYT*, 12 Apr. 1964, E5; 1 Apr. 1964, 27; *SSN*, Apr. 1964, 1.

66. *SSN*, Apr. 1964, 2; Apr. 1964, 1; *NYT*, 12 Apr. 1964, E5.

67. *SSN*, Apr. 1964, 2; Apr. 1964, 1.

68. See Calhoun v. Latimer, 377 U.S. 263, 263–65 (1964) (citing Watson v. City of Memphis, 373 U.S. 526 (1963); Goss v. Board of Education of City of Knoxville, 373 U.S. 683 (1963); Griffin v. School Board of Prince Edward County, 377 U.S. 218 (1964)); see also *AC*, 1 Apr. 1964, 1; *ADW*, 26 May 1964, 1; *SSN*, June 1964, 1; Apr. 1964, 1.

69. See *SSN*, June 1964, 1; see also Motley, *Equal Justice*, 198.

70. See *NYT*, 26 May 1964, 1; *SSN*, June, 1964, 1.

71. See *ADW*, 30 July 1964, 1; see also *AC*, 25 July 1964, 1.

72. See *AI*, 2 Feb. 1963, 2.

73. *AI*, 10 Jan. 1964, 7. On social movement growth, see Morris, *Origins of the Civil Rights Movement*; Tarrow, *Power in Movement*, 71–90.

74. *ADW*, 1 Aug. 1962, 1.

75. See *AI*, 10 Jan. 1964, 1.

76. See "Resolutions Adopted by the Forty-Fifth Annual Convention of the NAACP at Dallas, Texas, July 3, 1954," TD, NAACP Papers, part V, box 682.

77. Program for Banquet Honoring Retiring Atlanta NAACP President John H. Calhoun, TD, 2 Dec. 1958, NAACP Papers, box C27, 1950–58 file; Confidential Memo on the Atlanta Branch Situation to Roy Wilkins, Gloster Current, and Ruby Hurley, TD, 6 Mar.

1959, NAACP Papers, box C27, 1959–60 file. On Georgia's investigation of the NAACP, initiated by Cook, see *ADW*, 31 Mar. 1959, 1; *WP*, 15 Dec. 1956, A5; Petition for a Writ of Certiorari to the Supreme Court, Williams v. NAACP, General Case Material, 1959–1960, NAACP Papers, pt. 23A, rl. 16, frs. 608–9, 28–30. No apparent attempt ever was made to collect the large fine levied against the NAACP in the matter, but the investigation nevertheless cost the organization in legal fees and adverse publicity. See J. H. Calhoun to A. T. Walden, 6 Apr. 1958, Williams v. NAACP, General Case Material, 1958, in NAACP Papers, pt. 23A, rl. 16, fr. 377; memo to R. L. Carter, 22 July 1958, Williams v. NAACP, General Case Material, 1958, NAACP Papers, pt. 23A, rl. 16, fr. 515–16.

78.  See Edward K. Weaver to Rev. Adolphus S. Dickerson, TLS, 23 Feb. 1959, NAACP Papers, box C27, 1959–60 file; Wilkins to Dr. C. Clayton Powell, TLS, 26 Nov. 1958, NAACP Papers, box C27, 1950–58 file; Confidential Memo on the Atlanta Branch Situation to Roy Wilkins, Gloster Current, and Ruby Hurley, TD, 6 Mar. 1959, NAACP Papers, box C27, 1959–60 file; C. C. Powell and Eunice Cooper to Roy Wilkins, TLS, 11 Mar. 1959, NAACP Papers, box C27, 1959–60 file; Amos O. Holmes to Gloster B. Current, TLS, 13 Mar. 1959, NAACP Papers, box C27, 1959–60 file; Warren R. Cochrane to Roy Wilkins, TLS, 13 Nov. 1959, NAACP Papers, box C27, 1959–60 file; V. W. Hodges to Roy Wilkins, TLS, 13 Nov. 1959, NAACP Papers, box C27, 1959–60 file.

79.  See Roy Wilkins to Samuel W. Williams, TLS, 18 Dec. 1959, NAACP Papers, box C27, 1959–60 file; Samuel Williams to Roy Wilkinson, TLS, 3 Dec. 1959, NAACP Papers, box C27, 1959–60 file; Ruby Hurley to Gloster Current, TLS, 1 Nov. 1960, NAACP Papers, box C27, 1959–60 file. Williams took a brief hiatus in 1964–1965. On unsuccessful financial and membership campaigns, see Ruby Hurley to Gloster Current, TLS, 1 Nov. 1960, NAACP Papers, box C27, 1959–60 file; James O. Gibson to Gloster Current, TLS, 15 Feb. 1962, NAACP Papers, box C27, 1961–63 file; Joe Louis Tucker to Gloster B. Current, TD, 25 Mar. 1966, NAACP Papers, box C6, 1966–69 file; Atlanta Branch NAACP Fall Renewal Campaign Summary Report, TD, 30 Dec. 1966, NAACP Papers, box C6, 1966–69 file; Gloster Current to Ruby Hurley, TL, 13 Oct. 1966, NAACP Papers, box C6, 1966–69 file; A. M. Davis to Lucille Black, TLS, 27 Oct. 1967, NAACP Papers, box C6, 1967 file; Ruby Hurley to Friends of the Atlanta NAACP Branch, TLS, 18 July 1969, NAACP Papers, box C6, 1968–69 file.

80.  Amos O. Holmes to Samuel W. Williams, TL, 11 May 1960, NAACP Papers, box C27, 1959–60 file; Gloster B. Current to Dr. John Morsell, Ruby Hurley, and Robert L. Carter, TD, 27 May 1960, NAACP Papers, box C27, 1959–60 file; Ruby Hurley to Gloster Current, TLS, 1 Nov. 1960, NAACP Papers, box C27, 1959–60 file; Gloster B. Current to Samuel Williams, TL, 23 Jan. 1961, NAACP Papers, box C27, 1961–63 file; Gloster Current to Roy Wilkins, TD, 23 Jan. 1961, NAACP Papers, box C27, 1961–63 file; Gloster B. Current to Roy Wilkins, John Morsell, Robert Carter, and Ruby Hurley, TD, 21 Dec. 1960, NAACP Papers, box C27, 1959–60 file; Atlanta Branch Report to Gloster Current, TD, 19 Sept. 1961, NAACP Papers, box C27, 1961–63 file.

81.  See Gloster Current to Joe Louis Tucker, TL, 2 May 1966, NAACP Papers, box C6, 1966–69 file; Joe Louis Tucker to Gloster B. Current, TD, 25 Mar. 1966, NAACP Papers, box C6, 1966–69 file; Atlanta Branch NAACP Fall Renewal Campaign Progress Report,

TD, 11 Nov. 1966, NAACP Papers, box C6, 1966–69 file; Teressa Stinson to Lucille Black, TLS, box 9, 1967, NAACP Papers, box C6, 1967 file.

82. See, for example, Roy Wilkins to Dr. C. Clayton Powell, TLS, 26 Nov. 1958, NAACP Papers, box C27, 1950–58 file; see also "Resolutions Adopted by the Forty-Fifth Annual Convention of the NAACP at Dallas, Texas, July 3, 1954," TD, NAACP Papers, part V, box 682.

83. See Tushnet, *Making Civil Rights Law*, 16–18, 38–39, 311; Kluger, *Simple Justice*, 182–85, 199, 200, 214–16, 224–26; Williams, *Thurgood Marshall*, xv, 93, 101–09, 143–44, 179–94; McNeil, *Groundwork*, 63–106, 131, 133–35, 142.

84. Tushnet, *Making Civil Rights Law*, 311; see also Motley, *Equal Justice*, 126. Nasstrom documents protests by local PTAs for desegregation during the early 1960s and argues that LDF did not capitalize on this woman-centered activism. See Nasstrom, "Women, Civil Rights Movement," 115–209, 294–95.

85. Chapters 6–9 cover the student groups' activities in Atlanta during the sixties.

86. See Grady-Willis, *Challenging*, 11, 27, 43, 101.

87. See Motley interview, 442–43; Motley, *Equal Justice*, 131–32, 149; Tushnet, *Making Civil Rights Law*, 233–34; Wilkins, *Standing Fast*, 267–70; John C. Calhoun to Thurgood Marshall, TLS, 16 Oct. 1955, NAACP Papers, part V, box 2562, Atlanta, Georgia file. On movement lawyering, see chapter 7.

88. See "SNCC: A Special Report on Southern School Desegregation," TD, 2 Mar. 1966, SNCC Papers, box 162; "The City Must Provide: South Atlanta, The Forgotten Community," TD, n.d., SNCC Papers, box 162.

89. See Grady-Willis, *Challenging*, 101; see also Memorandum to SNCC Staff, TD, 14 Sept. 1965, SNCC Papers, box 162; "Liberation School," TD, n.d., SNCC Papers, box 162; see also Memorandum to SNCC Staff, TD, 14 Sept. 1965, SNCC Papers, box 162.

90. See *SSN*, July 1964, 1; *AC*, 30 Dec. 1964, 1; 9 Jan. 1965, 1.

91. See *SSN*, July 1964, 1.

92. See Statement of Jessie Hill, Jr., to Atlanta Board of Education, TD, 8 Mar. 1965, Paschall Papers, box 14, f. 5; Jessie Hill, Jr., to Oby T. Brewer, TLS, 22 Mar. 1965, Paschall Papers, box 14, f. 5; Jessie Hill, Jr., to Ivan Allen, Jr., TLS, 19 Mar. 1965, Paschall Papers, box 14, f. 5; *ADW*, 10 Mar. 1965, 1; *AC*, 14 Apr. 1965, 3; *AI*, 17 Apr. 1965, 1.

93. See *AC*, 14 Apr. 1965, 3; *ADW*, 16 Apr. 1965, 1; see also *AI*, 13 July 1963, 1; 20 July 1963, 9; Mitchell interview.

94. See *ADW*, 7 July 1965, 1.

95. Order on Motion by Plaintiffs to Amend Atlanta Plan, 5–6, 8, Calhoun v. Latimer (N.D. Ga., 1 Apr. 1965), Case File, NARA, box 53, f. 7; Final Order, 1–2, Calhoun v. Latimer (N.D. Ga., 9 Apr. 1965), Case File, NARA, box 53, f. 7; see also *ADW*, 16 Apr. 1965, 1.

96. See *AI*, 22 Jan. 1966, 1.

97. See *ADW*, 24 May 1966, 1; 27 May 1966, 1; 10 Aug. 1966, 1; 15 Mar. 1967, 1; *AI*, 15 Oct. 1966, 1.

98. See *AI*, 8 July 1967, 1; 1 July 1967, 1; *ADW*, 29 June 1967, 1; see also Southern Regional Council, Special Report, "A City Slum—Poor People and Problems," Paschall

Papers, box 24, 1964–1966 folder; J. Otis Cochrane, Confidential Report no. 1, 21 Apr. 1967, Paschall Papers, box 11, Jan.–Feb. 1967 folder.

99. United States v. Jefferson Cnty. Brd. of Educ., 372 F.2d 836, 846–47, 866–70, 880–81, 883–86, 890–96, 899–901 (5th Cir. 1966), aff'd en banc, 380 F.2d 385 (5th Cir. 1967), cert. denied, 389 U.S. 840 (1967); see also Landsberg, Enforcing Civil Rights, 139–40; Bass, Unlikely Heroes, 297–310.

100. See NYT, 29 Sept. 2005, B10; Motley, Equal Justice, 209–19, 175–76.

101. Plaintiffs' Motion to Reopen the Choice Period, 1–2, Calhoun v. Latimer (N.D. Ga., 25 Mar. 1968), Case File, NARA, box 53, f. 5; Affidavit of Lillian Lee, 1–2, Calhoun v. Latimer (N.D. Ga., 28 Mar. 1968), Case File, NARA, box 53, f. 5; News Release, "Assignment Forms Distributed in Atlanta Public Schools," TD, 5 Mar. 1968, Calhoun v. Latimer Case File, NARA, box 53, f. 5; News Release, "Assignment Forms to Be Returned to Atlanta Public Schools by Mar. 30," TD, box 22, 1968, Calhoun v. Latimer Case File, NARA, box 53, f. 5; Plaintiffs' Response to Affidavit of Lillian Lee, 1–2, Calhoun v. Latimer (N.D. Ga., 1 Apr. 1968), Case File, NARA, box 53, f. 5; Defendants' Motion for Summary Judgment, 2–8, Calhoun v. Latimer (N.D. Ga., 6 Oct. 1967), Case File, NARA, box 53, f. 5; A. C. Latimer to Frank Hooper, TLS, 21 Mar. 1968, Case File, NARA, box 53, f. 5; Motion for Further Relief, 2, Calhoun v. Latimer (N.D. Ga., 27 Sept. 1967), Case File, NARA, box 53, f. 7; Plaintiffs' Objections to Instructions for Exercising Choice, 1–3, Calhoun v. Latimer (N.D. Ga. 1968), Case File, NARA, box 53, f. 5. On Motley's retirement from LDF and appointment, see Motley, Equal Justice, 203–27; AI, 5 Sept. 1966, 1.

102. Order of Court on Motion to Amend Decree, 2–12, Calhoun v. Latimer (N.D. Ga., 4 Apr. 1968), Case File, NARA, box 53, f. 5; see also AC, 27 Sept. 1967, 4.

103. See AI, 21 Jan. 1967, 1; ADW, 15 Jan. 1967, 1.

104. See Coalition of Major Negro Organizations, "Ten Commandments to the Atlanta Board of Education," Paschall Papers, box 14, f. 2; ADW, 15 Sept. 1967, 1; 5 Oct. 1967, 1; 29 Sept. 1967, 4; 28 Sept. 1967, 1; 29 Sept. 1967, 1; AC, 5 Oct. 1967, 4.

105. See ADW, 21 Nov. 1963, 1; 9 Apr. 1965, 1; 22 Apr. 1965, 1; 26 May 1965, 1.

106. See ADW, 14 May 1965, 1; 1 Aug. 1965, 1; 26 May 1965, 1; 21 Nov. 1963, 1; 9 Apr. 1965, 1; 25 May 1965, 1; 26 Sept. 1966, 1.

107. ADW, 21 Nov. 1963, 1.

108. See Hearing on Motion for Further Relief, Calhoun v. Latimer, 31 July 1962, 223–26, Walden Papers, series IV, box 1, f. 2; Calhoun v. Latimer, 321 F. 2d 302, 311 (5th Cir. 1963); Motion for Further Relief, 2, Calhoun v. Latimer (N.D. Ga., 27 Sept. 1967), Case File, NARA, box 53, f. 7; ADW, 9 Jan. 1966, 1; AI, 8 Sept. 1966, 1.

109. See ADW, 8 Jan. 1966, 1; H. E. Tate, "A Presentation to the Atlanta Board of Education," TD, 10 Jan. 1966, Paschall Papers, box 14, item 34; ADW, 17 June 1966, 1; 12 Feb. 1966, 1; AI, 25 June 1966, 1; 8 Sept. 1966, 1.

110. See Minutes of Board of Education of City of Atlanta, 9 Oct. 1967, 1–4, Atlanta Board of Education Papers; AI, 28 Jan. 1967, 1; 11 Feb. 1967, 1; ADW, 20 Aug. 1967, 1.

111. See Minutes of Board of Education of City of Atlanta, 9 Oct. 1967, 1–4, Atlanta Board of Education Papers; ADW, 12 Sept. 1967, 1; 24 Sept. 1967, 1; 25 Feb. 1968, 1.

112. See Order of Court on Motion to Amend Decree, 12–14, Calhoun v. Latimer (N.D. Ga., 4 Apr. 1968), Case File, NARA, box 53, f. 5; *ADW*, 26 May 1968, 1. It was not unusual for federal courts to include ambiguous terms in orders concerning faculty desegregation. See Jim Leeson, "Desegregating Faculties," *Southern Education Report* 3 (May 1968): 27.

113. 391 U.S. 430, 438–42 (1968); see also *ADW*, 28 May 1968, 1; *AJ*, 22 May 1969, 6-A.

114. Motion for Further Relief, 1–5, Calhoun v. Latimer (N.D. Ga., 24 Oct. 1968), Case File, NARA, box 53, f. 2; Memorandum in Support of Plaintiffs' Motion for Further Relief, 1–4, Calhoun v. Latimer (N.D. Ga., 24 Oct. 1968), Case File, NARA, box 53, f. 2; Parker interview, 3–4. In February 1968, the Fifth Circuit had issued a new order in *Jefferson* that stipulated that school faculty should reflect the overall racial ratio of pupils in a school district. The order set a precedent for district courts to require particular numbers of black faculty in each school. The Supreme Court unanimously affirmed in June 1969. See Leeson, "Desegregating Faculties," 28–29.

115. Order of Court, 1–2, Calhoun v. Latimer (N.D. Ga., 24 Oct. 1968), Case File, NARA, box 53, f. 2.

116. *ADW*, 2 June 1968, 1; 12 June 1968, 1.

117. *AI*, 13 July 1968, 1; 19 Oct. 1968, 1; *ADW*, 4 Jan. 1969, 2.

118. Remarks by Honorable Constance Baker Motley to the Gate City Bar Association, 4 May 1977, Motley Papers, box 14, f. 2, 2, 8.

119. As I argued in a prior work, in the most successful campaigns in the civil rights movement, activists employed juridical law and legal concepts to build cohesion among participants and to inspire them to protest inequality. The courtroom did not entirely define these campaigns. By contrast, the courtroom did define LDF's school desegregation campaign in Atlanta; the organization's court-centrism was a tactical mistake. On the distinction between juridical law as an inspirational and a definitional resource for social movements, see Brown-Nagin, "Elites, Social Movements and the Law," 1511–21.

120. On the value of contentious politics in public forums, see McAdam, Tarrow, and Tilly, "To Map Contentious Politics," 17–34; McAdam, *Political Process*.

121. On LDF's educational campaign in Atlanta up to 1958 and local blacks' historic skepticism about school desegregation, see chapter 4.

## Chapter 11

1. The statement from King in the epigraph is quoted in Reginald Stuart, "Atlanta Split on School Plan," *Race Relations Reporter*, 19 Feb. 1973, 6.

2. The statement from Matthews in the epigraph is from Transcript of Proceedings, Calhoun v. Cook, (N.D. Ga. 29 Mar. 1973), 28, NAACP Papers, box 685.

3. *ADW*, 4 Sept. 1970, 1. On Nixon's opposition to busing and race-based appeals, see Lassiter, *Silent Majority*, 5–6, 137, 158, 233–34, 244–46.

4. Young, *Easy Burden*, 505, 510–11, 519–20; Jacoby, *Someone Else's House*, 404–30. On white opinion on school desegregation, see, for example, *AI*, 12 Sept. 1970, 1; 25 Oct. 1969, 3; *AJ*, 30 Oct. 1970, 1.

5. On the black political dilemma, see Guinier, "Triumph of Tokenism," 1089–1133; Lublin, *Paradox of Representation*, 4–6, 120–24; Swain, *Black Faces, Black Interests*, 5–19, 34–41, 47–141; Bell, "Brown v. Board of Education"; J. Phillip Thompson, *Double Trouble*.

6. See Countryman, *Up South*, 223–57; Podair, *Strike*; Hampton and Fayer, *Voices of Freedom*, 565–76.

7. For my previous discussion of the Atlanta school desegregation case, see Brown-Nagin, "Race as Identity Caricature." In contrast to my perspective, other scholars tend to elide serious analysis of the "community control" concept and overlook working-class opponents of the Atlanta compromise such as Mathews. See, for example, Bell, "Serving Two Masters," 485–87; Hornsby, "Black Public Education," 39–40; Fleishman, "Real against the Ideal," 133–34; McGrath, "Great Expectations," 317, 330–32. For an account of some of Mathews's social advocacy outside the school desegregation context, see Grady-Willis, *Challenging*, 136–40, 169–73.

8. Alexander v. Holmes County Bd. of Educ., 396 U.S. 19, 20 (1969).

9. See *AC*, 30 Oct. 1969, 1; *AI*, 8 Nov. 1969, 1.

10. See *AC*, 5 Jan. 1970, 6-A; Hornsby, "Black Public Education," 34–35. Hooper's decision responded to Fifth Circuit decisions on remand in *Alexander*, including U.S. v. Hinds County Sch. Bd., 423 F.2d 1264 (5th Cir. 1969) and Singleton v. Jackson Mun. Sch. Dist., 419 F.2d 1211 (5th Cir. 1969). *Singleton*, issued in early December, mandated faculty integration by February 1, 1970, measured by racial ratios for faculty in each school, and student integration by September 1. The Fifth Circuit expressly required all district courts in the circuit to apply these standards in all pending school desegregation cases.

11. See *AC*, 5 Jan. 1970, 6-A; 10 Jan. 1970, 1.

12. *AC*, 10 Jan. 1970, 1.

13. See *AC*, 5 Jan. 1970, 4-A; 10 Jan. 1970, 1; 12 Jan. 1970, 1; 13 Jan. 1970, 1; *ADW*, 15 Jan. 1970, 1. The bill did not pass. *ADW*, 1 Feb. 1970, 1.

14. See *AI*, 17 Jan. 1970, 1; 17 Jan. 1970, 2; 31 Jan. 1970, 1; 31 Jan. 1970, 2; *AC*, 20 Jan. 1970, 7-A; *ADW*, 27 Jan. 1970, 1.

15. See *AC*, 5 Jan. 1970, 4-A; 20 Jan. 1970, 1; 20 Jan. 1970, 7-A; *AI*, 17 Jan. 1970, 1; 31 Jan. 1970, 1; 31 Jan. 1970, 2; *ADW*, 27 Jan. 1970, 1. Southern states had begun requiring teaching candidates to take and pass the National Teacher Examination in tandem with the NAACP's campaign against discrimination in education and used it "to maintain racial salary differentials [and] decimate the ranks of African American teachers and principals." Baker, "Testing Equality," 50, 56–59, 64; see also Baker, *Paradoxes of Desegregation*.

16. See *NYT*, 13 Jan. 1970, 26; *AC*, 12 Jan. 1970, 1; 4 Feb. 1970, 1; 10 Mar. 1970, 1; *AI*, 28 Aug. 1970, 1; 12 Sept. 1970, 1; *AJ*, 30 Oct. 1970, 1.

17. See *AC*, 5 Jan. 1970, 4-A; 13 Jan. 1970, 4-A; 15 Jan. 1970, 16-A; 16 Jan. 1970, 1; 16 Jan. 1970, 4-A; *AC*, 21 Mar. 1970, 1; *ADW*, 24 May 1970, 1.

18. 402 U.S. 1, 6–8, 12–16 (1971); see also *ADW*, 11 Oct. 1970, 1. On the negotiations among justices in *Swann*, see Douglas, *Reading, Writing, and Race*, 207–14.

19. 402 U.S. at 16–20, 22–32. The court also reaffirmed that school construction should not perpetuate segregation and mandated free transfers for participants in voluntary majority to minority programs. Ibid., 20–21, 26–27.

20. See *NYT*, 21 Apr. 1971, 1; 21 Apr. 1971, 29; *ADW*, 22 Apr. 1971, 1; 23 Apr. 1971, 1; see also Greenberg, *Crusaders in the Courts*, 388–89.

21. On reaction to *Swann* in Charlotte, including quoted material, see Douglas, *Reading, Writing, and Race*, 212–14, 243.

22. *ADW*, 18 May 1954, 1, 5, 10; 10 Nov. 1955, 1; see also chapters 4 and 10.

23. See *AC*, 23 Apr. 1971, 1; *ADW*, 18 June 1971, 1.

24. See *ADW*, 27 Apr. 1971, 4; 18 June 1971, 1; 4 July 1971, 1.

25. See Calhoun v. Cook, 443 F.2d 1174 (5th Cir. 1971); Calhoun v. Cook, 332 F. Supp. 804, 805–8 (N.D. Ga. 1971); see also *ADW*, 20 June 1971, 1; 30 July 1971, 1. A three-judge panel initially took over the case. The three judges included Smith, Henderson, and Newell Edenfield. Smith and Henderson then presided over most matters in the case. *AJ*, 17 June 1971, 1-A.

26. Calhoun v. Cook, 332 F. Supp. at 805–6, 808; see also Research Atlanta, "School Desegregation," 32.

27. Calhoun v. Cook, 332 F. Supp. at 806, 808–9.

28. See chapters 4 and 10.

29. Calhoun v. Cook, 332 F. Supp. at 808.

30. Ibid.; see also Jackson, "Desegregation: Atlanta Style."

31. *AC*, 20 July 1971, 1; *AJ*, 29 July 1971, A-1.

32. Calhoun v. Cook, 451 F. 2d 583, 583–84 (5th Cir. 1971); see also Calhoun v. Cook, 332 F. Supp. at 809–10; *AJ*, 21 Oct 1971, A-1; *AC*, 11 June 1971, 1.

33. *AC*, 22 Oct. 1971, A-11; *ADW*, 11 Aug. 1971, 1; 2 Sept. 1971, 1; 10 Sept. 1971, 1.

34. Plaintiffs' Motion for Adoption of Plaintiffs' Proposed Desegregation Plan and For Other Relief, 1–10, Calhoun v. Cook (N.D. Ga., 30 Dec. 1971), Case File, NARA, box 55, f. 3; see also *ADW*, 6 Jan. 1972, 1; 18 Jan. 1972, 1; 402 U.S. at 26.

35. Plaintiffs' Motion for Adoption of Plaintiffs' Proposed Desegregation Plan and For Other Relief, Staff Desegregation Addendum, 1–4, Calhoun v. Cook (N.D. Ga., 30 Dec. 1971), Case File, NARA, box 55, f. 3; see also Plaintiffs' Proposed Finds of Fact and Conclusions of Law, 9–11, Calhoun v. Cook (N.D. Ga., 30 May 1972), Case File, NARA, box 55, f. 3.

36. Defendants' Response to Plaintiffs' Alternate Plan for Further Desegregation, 2–13, Calhoun v. Cook (N.D. Ga., 29 Mar. 1972), Case File, NARA, box 55, f. 3.

37. Ibid., 10–13.

38. See *AJC*, 8 Mar. 1970, 4-A; 25 Jan. 1970, 1; *ADW*, 20 Aug. 1971, 1.

39. See *AJC*, 25 Jan. 1970, 1. Title VI and VII of the Civil Rights Act had not been used as effectively as civil rights advocates would have liked, in part because enforcement depended on governmental agencies and left complainants open to retaliation. Hence, teachers complained, the Act provided little real legal protection for them, especially during the Nixon administration, when HEW's enforcement efforts waned. The LDF lodged similar complaints over time. See Adams v. Richardson, 351 F. Supp. 636, 638–40 (D.D.C. 1972); see also *AJC*, 8 Mar. 1970, 4-A.

40. Order of the Court, 5–16, Calhoun v. Cook (N.D. Ga., 8 June 1972), Case File, NARA, box 55, f. 2.

41. Plaintiffs' Notice of Appeal, Calhoun v. Cook (5th Cir., 23 June 1972), Case File, NARA, box 55, f. 2; Supplemental and Amended Complaint, Calhoun v. Cook (N.D. Ga., 28 June 1972), Case File, NARA, box 55, f. 2; Brief for Plaintiffs-Appellants, Calhoun v. Cook (5th Cir., 26 July 1972), NAACP Papers, part V, box 682.

42. The description of Tate as a "bulldog" is from *AC*, 2 Dec. 2002, 1B; see also *AC*, 13 June 1972, 14-A.

43. See *AC*, 19 Oct. 1972, 19-A.

44. See Plaintiffs' Proposed Findings of Fact, 1–191, Armour v. Nix (N.D. Ga., 24 Oct. 1977), NAACP Papers, part V, box 659; Gene Guerrero, "Atlanta Schools: The Case for Metro Relief," *ACLU Magazine*, Apr. 1975, Pauley Papers, box 29, f. 1; Memorandum from Roger Mills to Gene Guerrero, Margie Hames, Austin Ford, et al., Apr. 1975, Pauley Papers, box 17, f. 5; *AC*, 8 June 1972, 2-A.

45. Some board members claimed that they might support the ACLU suit if it led to a stay of proceedings in the Atlanta case and did not involve mandatory busing. The ACLU and LDF rejected both parameters for school board "support" of the suit; it appeared to be a ploy to delay desegregation in Atlanta. See *AC*, 14 Oct. 1972, 12-A.

46. Memorandum, n.d., Pauley Papers, box 29, f. 6; *AJ*, 14 Nov. 1972, 2A; Motion to Reconsider, 1–3, Calhoun v. Cook (N.D. Ga., 29 Mar. 1973), Case File, NARA, box 53, f. 7; Harmon, *Beneath the Image*, 253–55; Stone, *Regime Politics*, 104; Mike Raffauf, "A Tale of Deals: Atlanta Desegregation and the Power Structure," *Great Speckled Bird*, 19 Mar. 1973, 2; minutes of meeting with Atlanta Branch Officers in New York, 11, 6 Mar. 1973, NAACP Papers, box 685; *AJ*, 14 Nov. 1972, 1-A. Letson was removed from the settlement talks after his participation was reported in the press. See *AJ*, 15 Nov. 1972, 1-A.

47. See Memorandum, n.d., Pauley Papers, box 29, f. 6; *AJ*, 14 Nov. 1972, 2A; Motion to Reconsider, 1–3, Calhoun v. Cook (N.D. Ga., 29 Mar. 1973), Case File, NARA, box 53, f. 7; Harmon, *Beneath the Image*, 253–55; Stone, *Regime Politics*, 104; Mike Raffauf, "A Tale of Deals: Atlanta Desegregation and the Power Structure," *Great Speckled Bird*, 19 Mar. 1973, 2; minutes of meeting with Atlanta Branch Officers in New York, 11, 6 Mar. 1973, NAACP Papers, box 685; *AJ*, 14 Nov. 1972, 1-A.

48. See *AJ*, 14 Nov. 1972, 1-A; Fleishman, "Real Against the Ideal," 130–31. When President Jimmy Carter nominated Bell as U.S. Attorney General, he came under fire from the national NAACP, the ACLU, and the Congressional Black Caucus for his role in the negotiations. Leaders of these groups alleged that his activities, at the very least, represented a potential conflict of interest and probably constituted a serious breach of judicial ethics. Moreover, these groups and others noted that Bell's record in civil rights cases was "mixed" at best. In addition, his membership in Atlanta clubs that excluded Jews and blacks, clubs from which he initially refused to resign, caused outrage in the civil rights community and beyond. None of these charges defeated his nomination. See Memorandum, n.d., Pauley Papers, box 29, f. 6; Motion for Recusal of Judge Griffin Bell, 1–3, Armour v. Nix (N.D. Ga., 14 Sept. 1973), Case File, NARA, box 55, f. 5; *WP*, 23 Dec. 1976, A18; *NYT*, 20 Dec. 1976; *NYT*, 20 Dec. 1976, A1.

49. Opinion, 1–3, Calhoun v. Cook (5th Cir., 6 Oct. 1972), Case File, NARA, box 55, f. 1; see also *AC*, 15 Aug. 1972, 1-A; 3 Oct. 1972, A-1; 8 Oct. 1972, A-1; 12 Oct. 1972, A-4.

50. See Opinion, 1–3, Armour v. Nix (N.D. Ga., 17 Nov. 1972), Case File, NARA, box 55, f. 1; *AC*, 21 Nov. 1972, 6-A. Margie Hames argued that the stay was improper and should be lifted. Although the court did order the school board to provide Hames with certain data regarding the race of pupils and faculty, it refused to limit the stay on substantive rulings concerning the issues raised in the case. Brief in Support of Motion to Vacate Stay, 1–5, Armour v. Nix (N.D. Ga., 15 Dec. 1972), Case File, NARA, box 55, f. 1.

51. See *AJ*, 14 Nov. 1972, 2-A; *AC*, 31 Oct. 1972, 1-A; 14 Nov. 1972, 13-A; 16 Nov. 1972, 1-A.

52. Cook v. Calhoun, 409 U.S. 974, 974 (1972); Calhoun v. Cook, 469 F.2d 1067, 1067–68 (5th Cir. 1972); Mr. and Mrs. James H. Taylor to Hon. Sidney Smith, SL, 25 Mar. 1973, NARA Papers, box 55A, f. 1; *AC*, 19 Nov. 1972, 15-A; 17 Nov. 1972, 1-A; 21 Nov. 1972, 1-A; 8 Dec. 1972, 8-A; Memorandum to Ruby Hurley from Executive Board of Atlanta Branch NAACP, TD, n.d., NAACP Papers, box 684.

53. See Cook v. Calhoun, 409 U.S. 974, 974 (1972); Calhoun v. Cook, 469 F.2d 1067, 1067–68 (5th Cir. 1972); *AC*, 19 Nov. 1972, 15-A; *AJ*, 7 Nov. 1972, 1A; 20 Nov. 1972, 2A; Memorandum to Ruby Hurley from Executive Board of Atlanta Branch NAACP, TD, n.d., NAACP Papers, box 684; Parker interview, 29–30.

54. On the election controversy, see Donald Hollowell to Gloster Current, TLS, 25 Nov. 1968, NAACP Papers, box C6, 1968–69 file; Gloster Current to Donald Hollowell, TL, 19 Nov. 1968, NAACP Papers, box C6, 1968–69 file; Donald Hollowell to Gloster Current, TLS, 2 Jan. 1969, NAACP Papers, box C6, 1968–69 file; Ruby Hurley to Friends of the Atlanta NAACP Branch, "Red Alert," TLS, 18 July 1969, NAACP Papers, box C6, 1968–69 file. See also Nathaniel Jones to Roy Wilkins and John A. Morsell, TD, 15 Nov. 1972, NAACP Papers, part V, box 682; Mercedes Wright to Nathaniel Jones, TD, Nov. 16, 1972, NAACP Papers, part V, box 682; Mike Raffauf, "A Tale of Deals: Atlanta Desegregation and the Power Structure," *Great Speckled Bird*, 19 Mar. 1973, 2; Parker interview.

55. Calhoun v. Cook, 469 F.2d 1067 (5th Cir. 1972); Transcript of Proceedings, Calhoun v. Cook (N.D. Ga., 28 Dec. 1972), NAACP Papers, part V, box 684; *AJ*, 22 Nov. 1972, 1A; *AC*, 23 Nov. 1972, 1-A. The Fifth Circuit ordered the hearing. See *AC*, 27 Dec. 1972, 2-A. Young quoted in Fleishman, "Real Against the Ideal," 145.

56. Transcript of Proceedings, 2–14, Calhoun v. Cook (N.D. Ga., 28 Dec. 1972), NAACP Papers, part V, box 684; *AJ*, 22 Nov. 1972, 1A; 23 Nov. 1972, 1A.

57. Transcript of Proceedings, 2–14, Calhoun v. Cook (N.D. Ga., 28 Dec. 1972), NAACP Papers, part V, box 684; *AJ*, 22 Nov. 1972, 1A; 23 Nov. 1972, 1A.

58. See Transcript of Proceedings, 5–14, Calhoun v. Cook (N.D. Ga., 28 Dec. 1972), NAACP Papers, part V, box 684; Order, 2–3, Calhoun v. Cook (5th Cir., 24 Nov. 1972), Case File, NARA, box 55, f. 1; *AC*, 5 Dec. 1972, 12-A. The blunder interpretation is found in McGrath, "Great Expectations," 340; Fleishman, "Real Against the Ideal," 146, 150.

59. Howard Moore interview by author, 14, 16.

60. Quoted in Moore, "Brown v. Board of Education," 57–58, 59, 60, 64.

61. Howard Moore interview, 16, 17.

62. See Transcript of Proceedings, 5–14, Calhoun v. Cook (N.D. Ga., 28 Dec. 1972), NAACP Papers, part V, box 684; Order, 2–3, Calhoun v. Cook (5th Cir., 24 Nov. 1972), Case File, NARA, box 55, f. 1; *AC*, 5 Dec. 1972, 12-A; Parker interview, 27–28, 31, 51. In her autobiography, Davis notes that Moore's law practice in Atlanta prevented him from devoting full attention to her case. Davis, *Autobiography*, 288–89.

63. ACLU lawyer Margie Hames also failed to challenge the unlikely alliance between LDF and Spaulding, but she nevertheless attempted to protect her clients' interests. She informed the court that she did not and could not waive the rights of her clients to challenge Moore or Spaulding's representation in the future. Hames also secured a "promise" from the court that her claims for metropolitan relief would not be affected by the resolution of *Calhoun*. It soon became clear, however, that Hames could not, in fact, guarantee that her clients' rights would be preserved. Transcript of Proceedings, 5–14, Calhoun v. Cook (N.D. Ga., 28 Dec. 1972), NAACP Papers, part V, box 684; Order, 2–3, Calhoun v. Cook (5th Cir., 24 Nov. 1972), Case File, NARA, box 55, f. 1; Parker interview, 9 Sept. 2000.

64. Transcript of Proceedings, 5, Calhoun v. Cook (N.D. Ga., 8 Mar. 1973), NAACP Papers, part V, box 684.

65. The Mays quote is from minutes of meeting, Atlanta Board of Education, 12 Feb. 1973, Atlanta Board of Education Papers, Jan.–Mar. 1973 folder. The King quote is from Reginald Stuart, "Atlanta Split on School Plan," *Race Relations Reporter*, 19 Feb. 1973, 6.

66. See Plan of Proposed Settlement As Devised and Agreed Upon Between Plaintiffs and Defendants in the Above-Captioned Cause, 3–9, Calhoun v. Cook (N.D. Ga., 23 Feb. 1973), Case File, NARA, box 55A, f. 5; *AC*, 17 Feb. 1973, 2-A; 5 Apr. 1973, 24-A; *ADW*, 22 Feb. 1973, 1; Reginald Stuart, "Atlanta Split on School Plan."

67. Plan of Proposed Settlement As Devised and Agreed Upon Between Plaintiffs and Defendants in the Above-Captioned Cause, 9–25, Calhoun v. Cook (N.D. Ga., 23 Feb. 1973), Case File, NARA, box 55A, f. 5; Affidavit of Michael J. Stolee, 1–15, Calhoun v. Cook (N.D. Ga., 23 Mar. 1973), Case File, NARA, box 55A, f. 3; Research Atlanta, "Analysis of Atlanta Compromise School Desegregation Plan" TD, NAACP Papers, part V, box 683.

68. Parker interview, 30–31; Fleishman, "Real Against the Ideal," 163–64.

69. *AC*, 3 Mar. 1973, A-1; 9 Mar. 1973, 1-A; Objection to "Plan of Proposed Settlement" Filed Herein and Motion for Order in Accordance with Mandate of Court of Appeals, 1–11, Calhoun v. Cook (N.D. Ga., 8 Mar. 1973), Case File, NARA, box 55A, f. 4.

70. Objection to "Plan of Proposed Settlement" Filed Herein and Motion for Order in Accordance with Mandate of Court of Appeals, 1–11, Calhoun v. Cook (N.D. Ga., 8 Mar. 1973), Case File, NARA, box 55A, f. 4; Affidavit of Michael J. Stolee, 1–15, Calhoun v. Cook (N.D. Ga., 23 Mar. 1973), Case File, NARA, box 55A, f. 3; Supplemental Objections to Compromise Settlement, 1–4, Calhoun v. Cook (N.D. Ga., 29 Mar. 1973), Case File, NARA, box 55A, f. 1; Reginald Stuart, "Atlanta Split on School Plan," 5–7; *WP*, 4 Mar. 1973, A2; Donna Lorenz, "Desegregation Expert Gripes about City Compromise

Plan," Clipping, NAACP Papers, part V, box 684; see also *AJ*, 17 Nov. 1972, 1A; 21 Nov. 1972, 1A; 22 Nov. 1972, 1A.

71. Transcript of Proceedings, Calhoun v. Cook, 8 Mar. 1973, 3–18, 26–34, 65–67, NAACP Papers, box 685.

72. Ibid., 28, 29.

73. Mathews interview, 9, 11–12, 20; Armour v. Nix, no. 16708, Depositions of Mattie Benns et al., 25 Mar. 1976, 101; see also *ADW*, 13 Feb. 2000, 4.

74. Mathews interview, 2, 9–12, 23, 27–28; Ford interview, 18–19; see also *ADW*, 13 Feb. 2000, 4. On the fee litigation, see Jenness v. Little, 306 F. Supp. 925 (N.D. Ga. 1969), which found the initial fee ordinance unconstitutional; but see Mathews v. Little, 498 F.2d 1068 (5th Cir. 1974), which sustained a subsequent ordinance that permitted pro-spective candidates to secure a place on the ballot through alternative means.

75. Mathews interview, 2–4; Ford interview; see also *ADW*, 13 Feb. 2000, 4.

76. Transcript of Proceedings, Calhoun v. Cook, 8 Mar. 1973, 35–36.

77. Ibid., 35, 41–42, 48, 60–63.

78. Ibid., 49–58.

79. Ibid., 36–37, 45; *ADW*, 11 Mar. 1973, 1.

80. See *AC*, 19 Mar. 1973, 4-A.

81. Transcript of Proceedings, Calhoun v. Cook, 29 Mar. 1973, 17–19, 26–29, NAACP Papers, box 685.

82. Ibid., 31–32, 42–46, 56–58.

83. Ibid., 19–21, 24–26, 70–71.

84. Ibid.

85. Ibid., 21, 48–49.

86. Ibid., 16–17, 26, 29–30, 45–46.

87. *AC*, 22 Mar. 1973, 18-A; Parker interview, 36; Greenberg interview, 9.

88. Transcript of Proceedings, Calhoun v. Cook, 29 Mar. 1973, 17–19, 26–29, NAACP Papers, box 685.

89. Ibid., 25; see also Peg Nugent to Hon. Sidney Smith, Jr., TLS, NARA Papers, box 55A, f.1.

90. Transcript of Proceedings, Calhoun v. Cook, 29 Mar. 1973, 4–16, NAACP Papers, box 685; Supplemental Objections to Compromise Settlement, 1–4, Calhoun v. Cook (N.D. Ga., 29 Mar. 1973), Case File, NARA, box 55A, f. 1; Affidavit of Michael J. Stolee, 1–15, Calhoun v. Cook (N.D. Ga., 23 Mar. 1973), Case File, NARA, box 55A, f. 3.

91. Transcript of Proceedings, Calhoun v. Cook, 29 Mar. 1973, 4–16, NAACP Papers, box 685; Supplemental Objections to Compromise Settlement, 1–4, Calhoun v. Cook (N.D. Ga., 29 Mar. 1973), Case File, NARA, box 55A, f. 1; Motion of the NAACP to Intervene as Plaintiffs, Calhoun v. Cook, 1–4, NAACP Papers, box 683; Transcript of Proceedings, Calhoun v. Cook, 8 Mar. 1973, 18–25, NAACP Papers, box 685; Petition for Intervention as a Party Plaintiff, Calhoun v. Cook, 1–4, 21 Feb. 1973, NAACP Papers, box 682.

92. Transcript of Proceedings, Calhoun v. Cook, 29 Mar. 1973, 4–16, NAACP Papers, box 685; Supplemental Objections to Compromise Settlement, 1–4, Calhoun v. Cook

(N.D. Ga., 29 Mar. 1973), Case File, NARA, box 55A, f. 1; Transcript of Proceedings, Calhoun v. Cook, 8 Mar. 1973, 18–25; Petition for Intervention as a Party Plaintiff, Calhoun v. Cook, 1–4, 21 Feb. 1973, NAACP Papers, box 682; *AC*, 23 Feb. 1973, 1-A; 25 Jan. 1973, 4-A; 2 Mar. 1973, 2. Although the court rejected Conley's request to become formally involved in the case, the judges did allow him to file an amicus, or friend of the court, brief on behalf of CORE.

93. *AC*, 24 Mar. 1973, 11-A.

94. Objections to Proposed Settlement on Behalf of Armour v. Nix Plaintiffs, 1–4, 2 Mar. 1973, NAACP Papers, box 683; Supplemental Objections to Compromise Settlement on Behalf of Objections Members of the Class of Plaintiffs and Citation of Authority, 1–5, Calhoun v. Cook (N.D. Ga., 29 Mar. 1973), Case File, NARA, box 55A, f. 1; Motion to Reconsider, Calhoun v. Cook, 1–9 (N.D. Ga., 29 Mar. 1973), Case File, NARA, box 53, f. 7; Lonnie King to Roy Wilkins, TL, 19 Mar. 1969, NAACP Papers, box C27, 1968–69 file; Mike Raffauf, "A Tale of Deals: Atlanta Desegregation and the Power Structure," *Great Speckled Bird*, 19 Mar. 1973, 2; Transcript of Proceedings, Calhoun v. Cook, 26 Mar. 1973, 8–10, NAACP Papers, part V, box 685.

95. Objections to Proposed Settlement on Behalf of Armour v. Nix Plaintiffs, 1–4, 2 Mar. 1973, NAACP Papers, box 683; Supplemental Objections to Compromise Settlement on Behalf of Objections Members of the Class of Plaintiffs and Citation of Authority, Calhoun v. Cook, 1–5; Motion to Reconsider, Calhoun v. Cook, 1–9; Mike Raffauf, "A Tale of Deals: Atlanta Desegregation and the Power Structure," *Great Speckled Bird*, 19 Mar. 1973.

96. Transcript of Proceedings, Calhoun v. Cook, 26 Mar. 1973, 2–18; Motion to Reconsider, 1–3, Calhoun v. Cook (N.D. Ga., 29 Mar. 1973), NAACP Papers, part V, box 683; Supplemental Objections to Compromise Settlement on Behalf of Objecting Members of the Class of Plaintiffs and Citation of Authority, Calhoun v. Cook, 1–5; *AC*, 24 Mar. 1973, 11-A.

97. Transcript of Proceedings, Calhoun v. Cook, 26 Mar. 1973, 2–18; Parker Interview, 32; Motion to Reconsider, 1–3, Calhoun v. Cook (N.D. Ga., 29 Mar. 1973), NAACP Papers, part V, box 683; Supplemental Objections to Compromise Settlement on Behalf of Objecting Members of the Class of Plaintiffs and Citation of Authority, Calhoun v. Cook, 1–5; *AC*, 27 Mar. 1973, 14-A. For contemporary authority on court approval of settlements, see Massachusetts Casualty Ins. Co. v. Forman, 469 F.2d 259 (5th Cir. 1972); Cia Anon Venezolana de Navegacion v. Harris, 374 F.2d 33 (5th Cir. 1967); Eisen v. Carlisle & Jacquelin, 391 F.2d 555 (2d Cir. 1968).

98. Calhoun v. Cook, 362 F. Supp. 1249, 1249–52 (N.D. Ga. 1973); see also *AC*, 5 Apr. 1973, A-1.

99. See *AC*, 4 Mar. 1973, 1-A; *ADW*, 12 Apr. 1973, 4; 9 Sept. 1973, 1; 7 Oct. 1973, 1.

100. See Greenberg interview, 4; *NYT*, 22 July 1973, A1; *WP*, 9 Mar. 1973, A6; *Memphis Commercial Appeal*, 23 July 1973; *New York Daily News*, 9 Mar. 1973; "Atlanta School Plan Divides and Conquers," *Jet*, 29 Mar. 1973; *Carolina Times*, 10 Mar. 1973; *AC*, 9 Apr. 1973, 12-A; "New Deal in Atlanta," *Newsweek*, 30 July 1973, 42. The "turn back" quote is from *Carolina Times*, 10 Mar. 1973, 2A. The data on busing is from Schuman

et al., *Racial Attitudes in America*, 123–25, 247–48. For more on black leaders and integration, see Hornsby, "Black Public Education," 39–44.

101. Roy Wilkins to Ruby Hurley, telegram, 8 Mar. 1973, NAACP Papers, box 683; Nathaniel Jones to Honorable Sidney Smith, Jr., telegram, 8 Mar. 1973, NAACP Papers, box 683; "Atlanta NAACP Suspended For Violation of Policy," NAACP News Release, 10 Mar. 1973, NAACP Papers, box 683; Memorandum from Nathaniel Jones to Gloster B. Current, 14 Mar. 1973, NAACP Papers, box 683; minutes of meeting with Atlanta Branch Officers in New York, 9, 6 Mar. 1973, NAACP Papers, box 685; Nathaniel R. Jones to W. O. Walker, TL, 16 Aug. 1973, NAACP Papers, box 683; "VJ" to Eunice Cooper, TD, 23 Mar. 1973, NAACP Papers, box 683; minutes of meeting with Atlanta Branch Officers in New York, 11, 6 Mar. 1973, NAACP Papers, box 683; Transcript of Hearing on the Suspension of Officers and Board Members, Atlanta, Georgia Chapter NAACP, 9–11, 7 Apr. 1973, NAACP Papers, box 685.

102. Telegram Roy Wilkins to Ruby Hurley, telegram, 8 Mar. 1973, NAACP Papers, box 683; Nathaniel Jones to Honorable Sidney Smith, Jr., telegram, 8 Mar. 1973, NAACP Papers, box 683; "Atlanta NAACP Suspended For Violation of Policy," NAACP News Release, 10 Mar. 1973, NAACP Papers, box 683; Memorandum from Nathaniel Jones to Gloster B. Current, 14 Mar. 1973, NAACP Papers, box 683; minutes of meeting with Atlanta Branch Officers in New York, 9, 6 Mar. 1973, NAACP Papers, box 685; Nathaniel R. Jones to W. O. Walker, TL, 16 Aug. 1973, NAACP Papers, box 683; "VJ" to Eunice Cooper, TD, 23 Mar. 1973, NAACP Papers, box 683; minutes of meeting with Atlanta Branch Officers in New York, 11, 6 Mar. 1973, NAACP Papers, box 683; Transcript of Hearing on the Suspension of Officers and Board Members, Atlanta, Georgia Chapter NAACP, 9–11, 7 Apr. 1973, NAACP Papers, box 685.

103. Transcript of Hearing on the Suspension of Officers and Board Members, Atlanta, Georgia Chapter NAACP, 34–41, 7 Apr. 1973, NAACP Papers, box 685.

104. See *ADW*, 16 Feb. 1973, 1. By the time the court approved the settlement, Tate had entered elective office at a higher level. He was Atlanta's first black candidate for mayor in 1969; he lost to Sam Massell (the city's first Jewish mayor) but paved the way for the successful run of Maynard Jackson in 1973. In 1974, Tate began an eighteen-year career in the Georgia Senate. See *ADW*, 4 Oct. 1973, 1; *AC*, 2 Dec. 2002, 1-B.

105. Transcript of Hearing on the Suspension of Officers and Board Members, Atlanta, Georgia Chapter NAACP, 65–88, 7 Apr. 1973, NAACP Papers, box 685; *AC*, 28 Jan. 1973, 8-B; see also McGrath, "Great Expectations," 337–38. The King quote is from *Race Relations Reporter*, 19 Feb. 1973, 7.

106. See *AC*, 19 Feb. 1973, A-1. McKinney later came to oppose LDF's plan; but his criticism of the closed-door process stood.

107. See *ADW*, 5 June 1973, 1; Moore interview by author, 17.

108. Transcript of Hearing on the Suspension of Officers and Board Members, Atlanta, Georgia Chapter NAACP, 65–88, 91–114, 7 Apr. 1973, NAACP Papers, box 685; minutes of meeting with Atlanta Branch Officers in New York, 7–8, 6 Mar. 1973, NAACP Papers, box 683; minutes of meeting with Atlanta Branch Officers in New York, 7–8, 12, 15–17, 6 Mar. 1973, NAACP Papers, box 683; John A. Morsell to Kelly M. Alexander,

28 Aug. 1973, NAACP Papers, box 683; Mercedes A. Wright to Nathaniel Jones, TD, 14 and 16 Nov. 1972, NAACP Papers, box 682; Committee on Branches to Members of the Board of Directors, TD, 2 July 1973, NAACP Papers, box 683; Roy Wilkins to Lonnie C. King, Jr., TL, 3 Aug. 1973, NAACP Papers, box 683; Election Results, 6 Dec. 1973, NAACP Papers, part V, box 2545; see also McGrath, "Great Expectations," 337–38.

109. Calhoun v. Cook, 487 F.2d 680, 681–84 (5th Cir. 1973); AC, 11 Aug. 1973, 2-B; ADW, 12 Aug. 1973, 1.

110. Calhoun v. Cook, 487 F.2d at 681–84.

111. See AC, 3 May 1974, 10-A; ADW, 5 Apr. 1974, 1; 11 Apr. 1974, 1; 5 May 1974, 1.

112. Calhoun v. Cook, 522 F.2d 717, 718–20 (5th Cir. 1975); Order, 1–2, Calhoun v. Cook (N.D. Ga., 29 Aug. 1973), NAACP Papers, box 683; Order, 5–8, Calhoun v. Cook (N.D. Ga., 1 May 1974), NAACP Papers, box 683; AC, 24 Oct. 1975, 1-A.

113. Transcript of Hearing on the Suspension of Officers and Board Members, Atlanta, Georgia Chapter NAACP, 91–114, 7 Apr. 1973, NAACP Papers, box 685; minutes of meeting with Atlanta Branch Officers in New York, 6 Mar. 1973, NAACP Papers, box 683, 7–8, 12, 15–17; John A. Morsell to Kelly M. Alexander, 28 Aug. 1973, NAACP Papers, box 683; Mercedes A. Wright to Nathaniel Jones, TD, 14 and 16 Nov. 1972, NAACP Papers, box 682; Committee on Branches to Members of the Board of Directors, TD, 2 July 1973, NAACP Papers, box 683; Roy Wilkins to Lonnie C. King, Jr., TL, 3 Aug. 1973, NAACP Papers, box 683; Election Results, 6 Dec. 1973, NAACP Papers, part V, box 2545. Hurley claimed that she had spoken to Roy Wilkins about the propriety of the compromise and understood him to say that it was not objectionable. Wilkins claimed, however, that Hurley had misunderstood him; he had merely responded judiciously to Hurley's complaints about Nabrit, stating that it was best for Wilkins not to become involved in a dispute between LDF and the local chapter.

114. Quoted from Parker interview, 48; see also Greenberg interviw, 8–9.

115. See Moore interview by author, 17. Moore's searing critique of American society's endemic racism and courts' capacity or willingness to address it dovetailed with critical perspectives on law and the courts later advanced by leading legal academics. Compare Moore, "Brown v. Board of Education," 58–64, and "Racism as Justice" with Bell, "Brown v. Board of Education," 523–53, and "Serving Two Masters," 487–88.

116. Moore, "Brown v. Board of Education," 59.

117. Around the same time that Atlanta settled Calhoun with the compromise, the city adopted affirmative action programs in other categories of municipal employment. See, for example, ADW, 14 June 1973, 1; ADW, 5 July 1973, 1. Commentators only focused on the implications of affirmative action policies for whites. See, for example, ADW, 30 Apr. 1974, 14 June 1974, 1. For more on affirmative action programs in Atlanta, see Jacoby, Someone Else's House, 384–403. For a recent work on the struggle to win access to the workplace that focuses on the white backlash to affirmative action and elides intra-racial dynamics, see MacLean, Freedom Is Not Enough.

118. Quoted in Greenberg interview, 7.

119. See chapter 6.

120. On the Court's treatment of wealth discrimination and related claims in its equal protection jurisprudence, see, for example, San Antonio v. Rodriguez, 411 U.S. 1 (1973) (rejecting challenge to state's school funding scheme despite large disparities among districts on grounds that wealth was not suspect classification and education was not fundamental right); Dandridge v. Williams, 397 U.S. 471 (1970) (rejecting challenge to state's maximum welfare grant on grounds that state regulation in social and economic field is subject to rational relation review and state had legitimate interest in regulating poor). For a narrative account of poverty lawyers' efforts, see Shepard, *Rationing Justice*, 37–67. I do not mean to suggest that the law has no regard for status-based discrimination against low-income people. In certain instances, it does. For example, due process protections are afforded to indigents who are subject to the deprivation of government benefits or penalties of a criminal nature. See Goldberg v. Kelly, 397 U.S. 254, 261 (1970); Mayer v. City of Chicago, 404 U.S. 189, 195 (1971).

121. The Fifth Circuit required the District Court to retain jurisdiction over Calhoun v. Cook while Armour v. Nix remained pending. See Calhoun v. Cook, Calhoun v. Cook, 522 F.2d 717, 720 (5th Cir. 1975). Thus, theoretically, the District Court might have and still could have entered orders implementing metropolitan relief.

*Chapter 12*

1. The statement in the first epigraph is quoted in Armour v. Nix, no. 16708, Depositions of Mattie Benns et al., 25 Mar. 1976, 41.

2. The question in the second epigraph, posed by Robert Feagin, Esq., is quoted in Armour v. Nix, no. 16708, Depositions of Mattie Benns et al., 25 Mar. 1976, 37, 40.

3. *AC*, 31 Dec. 1972, 1-A; 24 Oct. 1975, 1-A.

4. *AC*, 15 Nov. 1977, 3-A; 17 Nov. 1977, 4-A. Over the course of the litigation, the exact configuration of the proposed federated school system changed. Initially, six school systems were to be included in a metropolitan remedy: Atlanta, Fulton, Dekalb, Decatur, Clayton, and Cobb. Later on, Hames suggested that only Atlanta, Fulton, and Dekalb need be included in the initial phase of the remedy. Still later, the federated system was to include Atlanta and Fulton only in its first phase. See Proffer by Plaintiffs, 2–3, Armour v. Nix (N.D. Ga., 26 Sept. 1973), Case File, NARA, box 55, f. 5.

5. 410 U.S. 179 (1973); Parker interview, 21–22; Mills interview; see also Milbauer, *Law Giveth*, 33; *NYT*, 22 Jul. 1994, B18; *AJC*, 21 July 1994, C-6. Hames worked with a team of lawyers that included Roger Mills, Michael Froman, Robert Sedler, E. Richard Larson, and Barbara J. Bethune.

6. See Hames interview, 1–2; Ford interview, 16. The race "cut" quote is from Milbauer, *Law Giveth*, 33.

7. See Ford interview, 16; Milbauer, *Law Giveth*, 33; *AJC*, 22 July 1994, A-14.

8. Hames interview, 4–5; Rose interview, 12 Aug. 2009, 1–3; Milbauer, *Law Giveth*, 44–45, 54. As a consequence of the discrimination that she encountered, Hames was very involved in the Georgia Association of Women Lawyers and other activities to

increase gender diversity at the bar and on the bench. See Margie Pitts Hames to Kice H. Stone, 7 Jan. 1982, Hames Papers; GAWL Survey, 19 July 1979, Hames Papers.

9. Hames interview, 6; Rose interview, 12 Aug. 2009, 1–3; Milbauer, *Law Giveth*, 44–45, 54. See Margie Pitts Hames to Kice H. Stone, 7 Jan. 1982, Hames Papers; GAWL Survey, 19 July 1979, Hames Papers.

10. Rose interview, 1–3; Mills interview, 2; Milbauer, Law Giveth, 44–45, 54.

11. Mathews interview, 25; Ford interview, 16; Mills interview, 31–32. As prior chapters of this book have discussed, women—from the Urban League's Grace Towns Hamilton to SNCC's Ruby Doris Smith to grassroots organizer Dorothy Bolden to human rights activist Francis Pauley—always had been active in the struggle for racial equality in Atlanta. On Hamilton, see chapters 2–4; on Robinson, see chapters 6–7; on Bolden, see chapter 5. Women activists worked in community-based organizations. Many had taken a particular interest in education. Constance Baker Motley had been lead LDF lawyer in the initial Atlanta school desegregation case for many years. Motley, however, had pursued a court-based strategy. See chapter 10. According to some analyses, the LDF's court-based strategy, in so far as it placed distance between its lawyers and activists who worked outside of the courtroom, also placed distance between the lawyers and many women activists who might have been particularly helpful in the lawyers' struggle to implement *Brown*. See Brown-Nagin, "Transformation"; see also Nasstrom, "Women, Civil Rights Movement," 294–95. In other cases, Motley's legal activism may have been more compatible with community-based activism. See Sugre, *Sweet Land of Liberty*, 197–98.

12. Mills interview, 31–32.

13. Hames interview, 7; Parker interview, 21–22; Ford interview, 15–16; Bright interview, 5, 6; see also *Fulton County Daily Report*, 12 Feb. 1987, 1. Crossclass and crossracial lawyer-client relationships can pose challenges, particularly in litigation over reproductive rights. "Mary Doe" subsequently repudiated Margie Hames and the prochoice movement. Doe claimed that she had been "mentally unstable" and not "totally aware of what was happening." Doe further claimed that she had been "used by her attorneys at the time." See *Fulton County Daily Report*, 9 Feb. 1989, 1; see also Garrow, *Liberty and Sexuality*, 602–3. The same was true of Jane Roe, who repudiated her role in *Roe v. Wade* and her lawyer, Sarah Weddington. See *NYT*, 12 Aug. 1995, 1; 28 July 1994, C1. The cultural context of abortion rights litigation proved a particular challenge for women lawyers, given the history of state-imposed sterilization of blacks and other undesirables. Some viewed birth control, abortion, and eugenics as inextricably linked. See Roberts, *Killing the Black Body*, 90–103. For literature on challenges in crosscultural lawyer-client relationships, see López, *Rebellious Lawyering*; Cunningham, "Lawyer as Translator."

14. Armour v. Nix, no. 16708, Depositions of Mattie Benns et al., 25 Mar. 1976, 12–14, 17, 20; Mills interview, 4, 32–33. The plaintiffs deposed—all but two of them women—included Mattie Benns, Mary Clark, Eva Belle Davis, Mamie Lee Dixon, Sallie Heard, Flora M. Hudson, Coy E. Lackey, Gloria Lawrence, Gwendolyn Lee, Ethel Mae Mathews, JaNelle McCrary, Lula Mae Trice, Bobbie J. Moore, Evelyn Taylor, Edward Moody, Anna F. Pyles, Sara Reynolds, Mattie R. Weems, and Elaine Wimbish.

15. Armour v. Nix, no. 16708, Depositions of Mattie Benns et al., 25 Mar. 1976, 27–28, 30, 40, 44, 60, 71, 80–81.

16. Ibid., 37–39, 50–51, 60–61, 70–71, 80, 100, 103–4, 114–15, 144, 155–56, 171, 187–88, 192. The defense attorneys already had obtained personal data about plaintiffs by posing interrogatories to Margie Hames, which she had answered. Ibid., 80. On the backlash, see Quadagno, *Color of Welfare*, 4; see also Roberts, *Killing the Black Body*, 17–19, 110–11, 207–8.

17. Armour v. Nix, no. 16708, Depositions of Mattie Benns et al., 25 Mar. 1976, 72–76, 100, 103–5, 154–59.

18. See chapter 10. For a discussion of the difficulties that the poor faced when they attempted to organize without the legitimacy conferred by higher status funders, whites, and/or men, see, for example, Kornbluh, *Battle for Welfare Rights*, 193–94, 199, 205–13. On Nixon's political rhetoric, see Lassiter, *Silent Majority*, 236–37, 251–54. On Carter's, see ibid., 269–70.

19. Frances Pauley to Roy Wilkins, TL, 25 May 1974, Pauley Papers, box 17; Margie Hames to Gene Guerrero et al., TLS, 23 May 1975, Pauley Papers, box 17; Mills interview, 4–5; Sedler interview, 2.

20. Hornsby, Black Power, 130–31.

21. Ford interview, 10–11; Bond, "Speech on School Desegregation" TD, series I, box 5, f. 19, Bond Papers, Alderman Library, Univ. of Virginia; Julian Bond, "Speech Concerning Black Education and the 25th Anniversary of *Brown v. the Board of Education*, Topeka, Kansas," TD, series I, box 7, f. 11, Bond Papers, Alderman Library, Univ. of Virginia.

22. Frances Pauley to Jack Greenberg, TL, 25 Nov. 1974, Pauley Papers, box 17; Jack Greenberg to Frances Pauley, TLS, 13 Dec. 1974, Pauley Papers, box 17; Gene Guerrero to Frances Pauley, TLS, 5 Jan. 1975, Pauley Papers, box 17; Margie Hames to Gene Guerrero et al., TLS, 23 May 1975, Pauley Papers, box 17; Rindskopf interview, 22; Sedler interview, 3.

23. Gene Guerrero to Frances Pauley, TLS, 5 Jan. 1975, Pauley Papers, box 17; Margie Hames to Gene Guerrero et al., TLS, 23 May 1975, Pauley Papers, box 17.

24. See *AC*, 16 Nov. 1977, 1-A; Ford interview, 17; Sedler interview, 4.

25. See *AC*, 16 Nov. 1977, 1-A; Ford Interview, 17; Plaintiffs Proposed Findings of Fact, 2–191, Armour v. Nix, NAACP Papers, box 659; Proffer by Plaintiffs, 1–15, Armour v. Nix (N.D. Ga., 26 Sept. 1973), Case File, NARA, box 55, f. 5; Mills interview, 19–21.

26. See *AC*, 16 Nov. 1977, 1-A; Transcript of Proceedings, 7–22, Armour v. Nix (N.D. Ga., 15 Nov. 1977), Case File, NARA, box 23.

27. See Plaintiffs Proposed Findings of Fact, 2–191, NAACP Papers, box 659; Proffer by Plaintiffs, 1–15, Armour v. Nix (N.D. Ga., 26 Sept. 1973), Case File, NARA, box 55, f. 5; *AJC*, 17 Nov. 1977, 1-A; Taeuber, "Residential Segregation," 155–57; Sedler interview, 6. In 1971, a federal district court had found public housing authorities guilty of practicing racial discrimination in Atlanta for decades. See Crow v. Brown, 332 F. Supp. 382 (N.D. Ga. 1971); see also Gene Guerrero, "Atlanta Schools: The Case for Metro Relief," *Civil Liberties*, Apr. 1975, Pauley Papers, box 29.

28. See Plaintiffs Proposed Findings of Fact, 2–191, Armour v. Nix, NAACP Papers, box 659. Proffer by Plaintiffs, 1–15, Armour v. Nix (N.D. Ga., 26 Sept. 1973), Case File, NARA, box 55, f. 5; Transcript of Proceedings, 31–45, 48–49, 51, Armour v. Nix (N.D. Ga., 15 Nov. 1977), Case File, NARA, box 23; see also Testimony of Q. V. Williamson, President, Empire Real Estate Board, U.S. Commission on Civil Rights, Housing Hearings, 10 Apr. 1959, 541–44; Testimony of Robert A. Thompson, U.S. Commission on Civil Rights, Housing Hearings, 10 Apr. 1959, 522–29; Testimony of T. M. Alexander, Sr., West Side Mutual Development Committee, U.S. Commission on Civil Rights, Housing Hearings, 10 Apr. 1959, 456, 458; U.S. Commission on Civil Rights, Housing Hearings, 10 Apr. 1959, 456, 458, 488; Ambrose, "Redrawing the Color Line," 106–11.

29. See Transcript of Proceedings, 16, Armour v. Nix (N.D. Ga., 24 June 1975), Case File, NARA, box 23; Testimony of William Hartsfield, U.S. Commission on Civil Rights, Housing Hearings, 10 Apr. 1959, 456–57; Testimony of M. B. Satterfield, Exc. Dir., Atlanta Housing Authority, U.S. Commission on Civil Rights, Housing Hearings,, 10 Apr. 1959,489; Testimony of Arthur Burdett, Jr., President, Atlanta Real Estate Board, U.S. Commission on Civil Rights, Housing Hearings, 10 Apr. 1959, 539–40; Testimony of Jesse B. Blayton, Chairman, Negro Advisory Committee to the Atlanta Housing Authority, U.S. Commission on Civil Rights, Housing Hearings, 10 Apr. 1959, 492; Testimony of W. O. Du Vall, President, Atlanta Savings and Loan Association, U.S. Commission on Civil Rights, Housing Hearings, 10 Apr. 1959, 518; Testimony of Robert A. Thompson, Housing Director, Atlanta Urban League, U.S. Commission on Civil Rights, Housing Hearings, 10 Apr. 1959, 525–26, 528; Testimony of Q. V. Williamson, President, Empire Real Estate Board, U.S. Commission on Civil Rights, Housing Hearings, 10 Apr. 1959, 541, 544–47, 550–52.

30. See AI, 24 Nov. 1962, 1; 1 Dec. 1962, 1.

31. See Deposition of Q. V. Williamson, Armour v. Nix, no. 16708, 24 June 1975, 13–15; AI, 1 Dec. 1962, 2; AI, 29 Dec. 1962; AI, 3 Jan. 1963, 1. Sam Massell later became the city's first Jewish mayor, with the strong backing of black voters; his vice mayor was Maynard Jackson, who became the city's first black mayor.

32. See ADW, 22 June 1966, 1; 22 June 1966, 1; 24 June 1966, 1. A few months later, Williamson gave an address, entitled "Democracy in Housing," at a national real estate brokers' convention. ADW, 4 Sept. 1966, 3. See also Bayor, Race and the Shaping, 71–76; Harmon, Beneath the Image, 66; Ambrose, "Redrawing the Color Line," 130; Orfield and Askinaze, Closing Door, 73–75.

33. See ADW, 22 Nov. 1967, 1; see also Bayor, Race and the Shaping, 71–76; Harmon, Beneath the Image, 66; Ambrose, "Redrawing," 130; see also Orfield and Askinaze, Closing Door, 73–75; Hanchett, Sorting Out, 262.

34. "Gilbraltar" is from ADW, 30 Mar. 1984, 1. Grace Towns Hamilton, the former Atlanta Urban League director who was then a state representative, was deposed due to her service on a governmental commission examining reorganization of Atlanta-Fulton County in 1974–1976. She testified that a majority of the commission, herself included, had recommended the merger of the Atlanta and Fulton County governments, including the school systems. The legislature did not act on the controversial recommendation.

Hamilton did not, however, endorse "consolidation" of the school systems at issue in the metro suit. But she did personally endorse "integrated education." Deposition of Grace Towns Hamilton, Armour v. Nix (14 Nov. 1977), 6–10, 19, 30, 32.

35. See "Let Us Not Integrate Nor Segregate Ourselves Out of Existence," TD, Mays Papers, Speeches, 1950–1974, Installment 3, box 47; Deposition Testimony of Benjamin Mays, Armour v. Nix, no. 16708, 21 Mar. 1978, 2–4.

36. Ford interview by author, 4–6, 11.

37. See Transcript of Proceedings, Armour v. Nix, no. 16708, 21 Mar. 1978, 2, 7, 11–13; *AJC*, 20 Nov. 1977, 18-A; *ADW*, 24 May 1977, 1.

38. See Transcript of Proceedings, Armour v. Nix, no. 16708, 21 Mar. 1978, 15; Deposition Testimony of Benjamin Mays, Armour v. Nix, no. 16708, 20 Mar. 1978, 22–24; *AJC*, 20 Nov. 1977, 18-A.

39. Milliken v. Bradley, 418 U.S. 717, 724–57 (1974).

40. The defendants also argued that blacks' low socioeconomic status, rather than race, explained residential segregation. Defendants' Proposed Conclusions of Law, 1–8, Armour v. Nix (N.D. Ga., 20 Mar. 1978), Case File, NARA, box 55, f. 4; Defendants' Trial Brief, 3–22, Armour v. Nix (N.D. Ga., 19 Apr. 1978), Case File, NARA, box 55, f. 4; Response to Proffer by Dekalb County et al., 2–48, Armour v. Nix (N.D. Ga., 16 Oct. 1973), Case File, NARA, box 55, f. 4; Defendants' Supp. Trial Brief, Armour v. Nix (N.D. Ga., 10 May 1978), Case File, NARA, box 55, f. 4; see also Transcript of Proceedings, 23, Armour v. Nix (N.D. Ga., 15 Nov. 1977), Case File, NARA, box 23.

41. See Order, 5–7, 9–13, 19–20, 22–27, Armour v. Nix (N.D. Ga., 24 Sept. 1979), Case File, NARA, box 19; Order, 14–15, 25–28, Armour v. Nix (N.D. Ga., 2 Mar. 1978), Case File, NARA, box 19; *ADW*, 5 Mar. 1978, 1.

42. The "not sympathetic" and "three judges" quotes are from my interview with Robert Sedler, 4. The Wilmington case is Evans v. Buchanan, 555 F.2d 373 (3d Cir. 1977), aff'd 423 U.S. 963 (1975); see also Cunningham v. Grayson, 541 F.2d 538 (6th Cir. 1976), cert. denied sub nom, *cert. denied sub nom.* Bd. of Educ. of Jefferson County, Ky. v. Newburg Area Council, Inc., 429 U.S. 1074 (1977) (Jefferson County and Louisville, Kentucky); U.S. v. Board of School Comm'rs, 506 F.Supp. 657 (S.D.Ind. 1979), *aff'd in result*, 637 F.2d 1101 (7th Cir. 1980), *cert. denied sub nom.* Bowen v. Buckley, 449 U.S. 838 (1980)(Indianapolis). On the other hand, there had been some high-profile episodes of resistance to expansive busing remedies, most notably, in Boston, a large city school system that did not even involve metropolitan relief. See Morgan v. Hennigan, 379 F. Supp. 410 (D. Mass. 1974) cert. denied, 421 U.S. 963 (1975); *NYT*, 12 Dec. 1974, 1; 18 Oct. 1979, A13; Formisano, *Boston against Busing*. Prior to *Milliken*, a federal district court had ordered interdistrict relief in Richmond, Virginia. The Fourth Circuit had reversed. The Supreme Court deadlocked on appeal, which affirmed the Fourth Circuit's decision. See Bradley v. Sch. Bd. of City of Richmond, 462 F.2d 1058 (4th Cir. 1972), *rev'g* 338 F.Supp. 67 (E.D. Va. 1972), *aff'd*, 412 U.S. 92 (1973). For discussions of the Richmond litigation, see Pratt, "Simple Justice Denied"; Lassiter, *Silent Majority*, 280–94.

43. See Mills interview by author, 18. Justice Marshall did not take part in *Armour*. Justices Brennan, Blackmun, and Stevens would have dismissed the appeal for lack

of jurisdiction. See Armour v. Nix, 446 U.S. 930 (1980); *reh'g denied*, 448 U.S. 908 (1980).

44. Ford interview, 20; Mills interview, 20, 25.

45. See Bell, "Serving Two Masters"; Carmichael, *Ready for Revolution*, 529. In a telling example, those other activists included Fannie Lou Hamer, the Mississippi sharecropper who in 1964 famously protested the seating of the segregated delegation to the Democratic National Convention, and who shared many characteristics with Mathews. Hamer—a lifelong crusader for the poor—served as a named plaintiff in the suit that, in 1970, integrated the Sunflower County, Mississippi, schools, an exploit for which she seldom is heralded. Lee, *For Freedom's Sake*, 167–68.

46. Orfield and Ashkinaze, *Closing Door*, 110.

47. See Bell, "Serving Two Masters." While segregated schools undermine academic performance, studies show that minority students who attend integrated schools tend to have higher aspirations and to fare better academically and socially. See Wells and Crain, *Stepping over the Color Line*, 182–93; Rita E. Mahard and Robert L. Crain, "Research on Minority Achievement," 105–13, 117–21; Orfield and Ashkinaze, *Closing Door*, 127–29; see also Orfield and Lee, *Racial Transformation*; Orfield and Lee, *Why Segregation Matters*. On discrimination in desegregated schools, see Perry, Steele, and Hilliard, *Young, Gifted, and Black*, 109–30; Delpit, *Other People's Children*.

48. See Orfield and Ashkinaze, *Closing Door*, 112, 121–29; Bond interview by author, 12.

49. See Menkel-Meadow, "Excluded Voices"; Finley, "Breaking Women's Silence." For more agnostic views about legal venues and voice, see White, "Subordination"; Felstiner, Abel, and Sarat, "Emergence."

## Conclusion

1. The statement in the epigraph is from Douglass, "American Constitution and the Slave," 361.

2. The quotes are from Douglass, "American Constitution and the Slave," 361; and Lincoln, "First Inaugural Address," at 262, 269. On Dr. Martin Luther King, Jr.'s constitutionalism, see Kennedy, "Martin Luther King's Constitution."

3. Statement by Julian Bond, TD, 10 Jan. 1966, SNCC Papers, rl. 53, fr. 531.

4. On the pre-*Brown* era, see, for example, Mack, "Rethinking Civil Rights Lawyering"; Harris, "Negro and Economic Radicalism," 130–39; Haines, *Black Radicals*, 18–21.

5. For the skeptical view of the Court, see Rosenberg, *Hollow Hope*, 39–40, 74–75, 93, 155–56, 336–43; Scheingold, *Politics of Rights*, 5; Tushnet, *Taking*, 135, 154–76; Klarman, *From Jim Crow*, 94–96, 101–3, 182–84, 192–95, 236–89, 324–26, 314–15, 356–57, 411–13, 463–68. Klarman also notes that Supreme Court decisions often had unintended consequences for the civil rights movement. See Klarman, *From Jim Crow*, 363–442, 463–68.

6. Ibid.

7. In a prior work, I distinguished between law as a definitional and inspirational resource for social movements. See Brown-Nagin, "Elites, Social Movements and the Law," 1511–21.

8. See also McCann, "Reform Litigation on Trial," 728; McCann and Silverstein, "Rethinking Law's 'Allurements,'" 261–92; Galanter, "Radiating Effects of Courts," 117–42; see also Siegal, "Text in Contest"; Reva Siegel and Robert Post, "Roe Rage."

9. In late 1966, some in SNCC proposed to form a "welfare" committee to "meet the needs of unemployed black people" and freedom organizations that included economic divisions. Others proposed to form alliances with local and national labor unions in an effort to increase the wages and improve the working conditions of those who already had jobs. Still others proposed farm cooperatives. Few of these initiatives came to fruition, as staff became embroiled in infighting or grew undisciplined, and the embrace and defense of black power overtook programmatic initiatives. A SNCC offshoot in Mississippi did form a short-lived union, however; and SNCC of course left imprints on other community-based organizations that helped local poor people. John Wilson to Field Staff, TD, 29 Sept. 1966, SNCC Papers, box 7; "Conference on Economic Planning," TD, n.d., SNCC Papers, box 95; "SNCC and Labor Organization," TD, n.d., SNCC Papers, box 95; see also Lee, For Freedom's Sake, 121–23, 135, 137–39; Forman, Making of Black Revolutionaries, 479, 481.

10. Forman, Making of Black Revolutionaries, 476–77; Carson, In Struggle, 240; Bond interview by author, 14.

11. Parker interview, 48; Greenberg interview, 11; see also chapter 11.

12. Stone, Regime Politics, 78–87, 106; Orfield and Ashkinaze, Closing Door, 46–49; Bayor, Race and the Shaping, 244. On the "mecca" rhetoric, see Garland, "Atlanta: Black Mecca of the South," Ebony, Aug. 1971, 152–57; see also William S. Ellis, "Atlanta, Pacesetter City of the South," National Geographic, Feb. 1969, 249; Rutheiser, Imagineering Atlanta, 52, 62; Range, "Making It in Atlanta: Capital of Black-Is-Bountiful," Essence, clipping, Bullard Papers, box 12, f. 22b; Hein, "The Image of 'A City Too Busy to Hate': Atlanta in the 1960s," Phylon 33 (Fall 1972): 210.

13. AI, 17 Nov. 1962, 2; 1 Sept. 1962, 2.

14. For the most recent and comprehensive analysis of black political power in Atlanta during the 1970s and 1980s, see Hornsby, Black Power in Dixie; see also Hornsby, "Black Public Education," 30; Bayor, Race and the Shaping, 300 n. 26; Range, "Making It in Atlanta," 2; Orfield and Ashkinaze, Closing Door, 117–23, 138, 142, 146–47, 210–11; Stone, Regime Politics, 87–92, 177–78; Hartshorn and Ihlanfeldt, "Growth and Change," 36; see also AC, 19 Oct. 1981, 1-A; 21 Oct. 1981, 1-A; 22 Oct. 1981, 1-A; 23 Oct. 1981, 1-A.

15. See sources cited in note 12; see also Wilson, Declining Significance, 139-43.

16. See Jacoby, Someone Else's House, 383–84; Orfield and Ashkinaze, Closing Door, 54; Stone, Regime Politics, 87, 96–98.

17. Mathews interview, 26–27, 38, 40, 42.

18. On blacks and cities, see Thompson, Double Trouble; Wilson, Truly Disadvantaged, 8, 57–58, 103, 136; Wilson, There Goes the Neighborhood; Sugrue, Origins of the Urban Crisis, 45–46, 90–92, 95–105, 106–12, 221–22, 245, 269. On minorities' political power in the federal system, see Guinier, "Triumph of Tokenism"; Lublin, Paradox of Representation. On the precarious position of middle-class blacks, see Pattillo-McCoy,

*Black Picket Fences.* On residential segregation of blacks, regardless of income, see Massey and Denton, *American Apartheid*, 83–114. On employment discrimination against blacks, see Pager, *Marked*, 86–92; Bertrand and Mullainathan, "Are Emily and Greg More Employable Than Lakisha and Jamal," 991–1013.

19. A. T. Walden, "Address to Fort Valley State College Graduation," 1964, Walden Papers, series II, box 2, f. 8.

20. See, for example, Taylor & Whittier, "Lesbian Feminist Mobilization"; Mananzala & Spade, "The Nonprofit Industrial Complex and Transresistance;" Hull, *All the Women Are White*. All modern struggles for citizenship—by women, other racial and ethnic groups, people with disabilities, and language minorities—have used LDF's campaign against segregation as a model. On mixed outcomes when these groups have invoked arguments in *Brown* in struggles for legal rights, see Martha Minow, *In Brown's Wake*.

21. On the impact of class-based inequality, see, for example, Pager, *Race, Crime, and Finding Work*; Cashin, *Failures of Integration*, 237-60; see generally, Wilson, *Truly Disadvantaged*. For policy responses to class-based inequality, see, for example, Oliver, *Black Wealth*, 242–46.

22. See also chapter 7. Of course, NAACP and LDF lawyers sometimes worked in collaboration with communities and might be characterized as community-based or movement lawyers. See Sullivan, *Lift Every Voice*. As this work's methodology suggests, in my view, the movement lawyer characterization should turn on an analysis of the quality of national organizations' connections to local people and local organizations over time.

23. The "slow, respectful" phrase is from Payne, *I've Got the Light*, 236–64. On the opportunities and challenges of participatory lawyering, see Cummings and Eagly, "Critical Reflection"; Gordon, *Suburban Sweatshops*; Quigley, "Reflections of Community Organizers"; Su, "Making the Invisible Visible"; Alfiera, "(Un)covering Identity."

24. See Dr. Martin Luther King, Jr., Address to the National Bar Association, Milwaukee, Wis., 20 Aug. 1959, TD, Williams Papers, series 2, box 1, f. 3. On civic participation, especially by low-income minorities, see Thompson, *Double Trouble*, 27–37, 265–78; Fung and Wright, *Deepening Democracy*.

# BIBLIOGRAPHY

*Books and Journal Articles*

Abrams, Charles. *Forbidden Neighbors: A Study of Prejudice in Housing.* New York: Harper, 1955.

Adams, Frank T. *James A. Dombrowski: An American Heretic, 1897–1983.* Knoxville: University of Tennessee Press, 1992.

Agnew, Lea, and Jo Ann Haden-Miller. *Atlanta and Its Lawyers: A Century of Vision.* Atlanta: Atlanta Bar Association, 1988.

Alexander, Raymond Pace. "The National Bar Association—Its Aims and Purposes." *National Bar Journal* 1 (1941): 1–4.

Alfiera, Anthony. "(Un)covering Identity in Civil Rights and Poverty Law." *Harvard Law Review* 121 (Jan. 2008): 805–44.

Allen, Frederick. *Atlanta Rising: The Invention of an International City, 1946–1996.* Atlanta: Longstreet, 1996.

Allen, Ivan, Jr., with Paul Hemphill. *Mayor: Notes on the Sixties.* New York: Simon and Schuster, 1971.

Ambrose, Andrew. "Redrawing the Color Line: The History and Patterns of Black Housing in Atlanta, 1940–1973." Ph.D. diss., Emory University, 1992.

Amsterdam, Anthony G. "Criminal Prosecutions Affecting Federally Guaranteed Civil Rights: Federal Removal and Habeas Corpus Jurisdiction to Abort State Court Trial." *University of Pennsylvania Law Review* 113 (Apr. 1965): 793–912.

Anderson, James D. *The Education of Blacks in the South, 1860–1935.* Chapel Hill: University of North Carolina Press, 1988.

Arsenault, Raymond. *Freedom Riders: 1961 and the Struggle for Racial Justice.* New York: Oxford University Press, 2006.

Atlanta University. "The Negro Common School." Atlanta University Publications no. 16. Atlanta: Atlanta University, 1911.

Auerbach, Jerold S. *Unequal Justice: Lawyers and Social Change in Modern America.* New York: Oxford University Press, 1976.

Bacote, Clarence A. "The Negro in Atlanta Politics." *Phylon* 16 (fourth quarter 1955): 333–50.

———. "The Negro Voter in Georgia Politics, Today." *Journal of Negro Education* 26 (summer 1957): 307–18.

———. *The Story of Atlanta University: A Century of Service, 1865–1965.* Atlanta: Atlanta University, 1969.

Badger, Anthony J. "Southerners Who Refused to Sign the Southern Manifesto." *Historical Journal* 42 (June 1999): 517–34.

Bailey, Percival Roberts. "Progressive Lawyers: A History of the National Lawyers' Guild, 1936–1958." Ph.D. diss., Rutgers University, 1979.

Baldwin, Joseph A., et al. "The Black Self-hatred Paradigm Revisited: An Africentric Analysis." In *Black Psychology*, 3rd ed., edited by Reginald L. Jones, 141–65. Berkeley, Calif.: Cobb and Henry, 1991.

Barnes, Catherine A. *Journey from Jim Crow: The Desegregation of Southern Transit.* New York: Columbia University Press, 1983.

Bartley, Numan V. *The Creation of Modern Georgia*, 2nd ed. Athens: University of Georgia Press, 1990.

Baskir, Lawrence M., and William A. Strauss. *Chance and Circumstance: The Draft, the War, and the Vietnam Generation.* New York: Knopf, 1978.

Bass, Jack. *Unlikely Heroes.* Tuscaloosa: University of Alabama Press, 1981.

Bayor, Ronald H. *Race and the Shaping of Twentieth-century Atlanta.* Chapel Hill: University of North Carolina Press, 1996.

Bell, Derrick A., Jr. "*Brown v. Board of Education* and the Interest-convergence Dilemma." *Harvard Law Review* 93 (Jan. 1980): 518–33.

———. "Serving Two Masters: Integration Ideals and Client Interests in School Desegregation Litigation." *Yale Law Journal* 85 (Mar. 1976): 470–516.

Berg, Manfred. "*The Ticket to Freedom*": *The NAACP and the Struggle for Black Political Integration* (Gainesville: University Press of Florida, 2005).

Bernd, Joseph L. "White Supremacy and the Disfranchisement of Blacks in Georgia, 1946." *Georgia Historical Quarterly* 66 (winter 1982): 492–513.

Bertrand, Marianne, and Sendhil Mullainathan. "Are Emily and Greg More Employable Than Lakisha and Jamal? A Field Experiment in Labor Market Discrimination." *American Economic Review* 94 (Sept. 2004): 991–1013.

Biondi, Martha. *To Stand and Fight: The Struggle for Civil Rights in Postwar New York City.* Cambridge, Mass.: Harvard University Press, 2006.

Black, Charles L., Jr. "The Lawfulness of the Segregation Decisions." *Yale Law Journal* 69 (Jan. 1960): 421–30.

Black, Earl, and Merle Black. *Politics and Society in the South.* Cambridge, Mass.: Harvard University Press, 1987.

Bond, Horace Mann. *The Education of the Negro in the American Social Order.* New York: Prentice-Hall, 1934.

Bond, Julian. *A Time to Speak, A Time to Act: The Movement in Politics.* New York: Simon and Schuster, 1972.

———. "SNCC: What We Did." *Monthly Review* 1 (Oct. 2000): 14–28

Branch, Taylor. *Parting the Waters: America in the King Years, 1954–63.* New York: Simon and Schuster, 1988.

Bressler, Marvin. "The Myers' Case: An Instance of Successful Racial Invasion." *Social Problems* 8 (autumn 1960): 126–42.

Brooks, Jennifer E. "Winning the Peace: Georgia Veterans and the Struggle to Define the Political Legacy of World War II." *Journal of Southern History* 66 (Aug. 2000): 563–604.

Brown, Elizabeth Gasper. *Legal Education at Michigan, 1859–1959.* Ann Arbor: University of Michigan Law School, 1959.

Brown, Sarah Hart. *Standing against Dragons: Three Southern Lawyers in an Era of Fear.* Baton Rouge: Louisiana State University Press, 1998.

———. "'Subversive' Southerners: Three Uncommon Lawyers and Civil Liberties in the South, 1945–1965." Ph.D. diss., Georgia State University, 1993.

Brown, William H., Jr. "Access to Housing: The Role of the Real Estate Industry." *Economic Geography* 48 (Jan. 1972): 66–78.

Brown-Nagin, Tomiko. "Elites, Social Movements, and the Law: The Case of Affirmative Action." *Columbia Law Review* 105 (June 2005): 1436–1528.

———. "An Historical Note on the Significance of the Stigma Rationale for a Civil Rights Landmark." St. Louis U. L.J. 48 (spring 2004): 991–1007.

———. "Race as Identity Caricature: A Local Legal History Lesson in the Salience of Intraracial Conflict." *Univ. Penn. Law Rev.* 151 (June 2003): 1913–76.

———. "Class Actions: The Impact of Black and Middle Class Conservatism on Civil Rights Lawyering in a New South Political Economy, Atlanta, 1946–79." Ph.D. diss., Duke University, 2002.

———. "The Transformation of a Social Movement into Law? The SCLC and NAACP's Campaigns for Civil Rights Reconsidered in Light of the Educational Activism of Septima Clark." *Women's History Review* 8 (Mar. 1999): 81–137.

Brundage, W. Fitzhugh. *Lynching in the New South: Georgia and Virginia, 1880–1930.* Urbana: University of Illinois Press, 1993.

Bunche, Ralph J. "A Critical Analysis of the Tactics and Programs of Minority Groups." *Journal of Negro Education* 4 (Jul. 1935): 308–20.

Butler, Addie Louise Joyner. *The Distinctive Black College: Talladega, Tuskegee, and Morehouse.* Metuchen, N.J.: Scarecrow, 1977.

Capeci, Dominic J., Jr. "Fiorello H. La Guardia and the Stuyvesant Town Controversy of 1943." *New York Historical Society Quarterly* 62 (1978): 289–310.

Carl, Earl Lawrence. "Reflections on the 'Sit-Ins.'" *Cornell Law Quarterly* 46 (spring 1961): 444–57.

Carle, Susan. "From *Buchanan* to *Button:* Legal Ethics and the NAACP (pt. II)," *University of Chicago Law School Roundtable* 8 (2001): 281–307.

Carmichael, Stokely, with Ekwueme Michael Thelwell. *Ready for Revolution: The Life and Struggles of Stokely Carmichael (Kwame Ture).* New York: Scribner, 2003.

Carmichael, Stokely, and Charles V. Hamilton. *Black Power: The Politics of Liberation in America.* New York: Random House, 1967.

Carson, Clayborne. *In Struggle: SNCC and the Black Awakening of the 1960s.* Cambridge, Mass.: Harvard University Press, 1995.

Carter, Robert L. *A Matter of Law: A Memoir of Struggle in the Cause of Equal Rights.* New York: New Press, 2005.

————. Book Review, "The NAACP's Legal Strategy against Segregated Education." 86 *Michigan Law Review* 1083, 1087–1088 (1987–1988).

Cashin, Sheryll. *The Failures of Integration: How Race and Class Are Undermining the American Dream.* New York: PublicAffairs, 2004.

Cecelski, David S. *Along Freedom Road: Hyde County, North Carolina, and the Fate of Black Schools in the South.* Chapel Hill: University of North Carolina Press, 1994.

Chafe, William H. *Civilities and Civil Rights: Greensboro, North Carolina, and the Black Struggle for Freedom.* New York: Oxford University Press, 1980.

————. *The Unfinished Journey: America Since World War II,* 5th ed. New York: Oxford University Press, 2003.

Clark, Robert F. *Victory Deferred: The War on Global Poverty, 1945–2003.* Lanham, Md.: University Press of America, 2005.

Cobb, Charles. "Atlanta: The Bond Campaign." In *The New Left: A Documentary History,* edited by Massimo Teodori, 116–19. Indianapolis, In.: Bobbs-Merrill, 1969.

Colburn, David R. *Racial Change and Community Crisis: St. Augustine, Florida, 1877–1980.* New York: Columbia University Press, 1985.

Cortner, Richard C. *Civil Rights and Public Accommodations: The Heart of Atlanta Motel and McClung Cases.* Lawrence: University Press of Kansas, 2001.

Countryman, Matthew J. *Up South: Civil Rights and Black Power in Philadelphia.* Philadelphia: University of Pennsylvania Press, 2006.

Cummings, Scott L., and Ingrid V. Eagly. "A Critical Reflection on Law and Organizing." *UCLA Law Review* 48 (Feb. 2001): 443–517.

Cunningham, Clark D. "The Lawyer as Translator, Representation as Text: Towards an Ethnography of Legal Discourse." *Cornell Law Review* 77 (Sept. 1992): 1298–1387.

Daniel, Pete. "Up from Slavery and Down to Peonage: The Alonzo Bailey Case." *Journal of American History* 57 (Dec. 1970): 654–70.

Daniels, Maurice C. *Horace T. Ward: Desegregation of the University of Georgia, Civil Rights Advocacy, and Jurisprudence.* Atlanta: Clark Atlanta University Press, 2001.

Davis, Abraham L. "The Role of Black Colleges and Black Law Schools in the Training of Black Lawyers and Judges: 1960–1980." *Journal of Negro History* 70 (winter–spring 1985): 24–34.

Davis, Angela. *An Autobiography.* New York: International, 1988.

Davis, Martha F. *Brutal Need: Lawyers and the Welfare Rights Movement, 1960–1973.* New Haven, Conn.: Yale University Press, 1993.

Davis, Michael D., and Hunter R. Clark. *Thurgood Marshall: Warrior at the Bar, Rebel on the Bench.* New York: Carol, 1992.

Dawson, Michael. *Black Visions: The Roots of Contemporary African-American Ideologies.* Chicago: University of Chicago Press, 2001.

Delpit, Lisa. *Other People's Children: Cultural Conflict in the Classroom.* New York: New Press, 1995.

Dickerson, Dennis C. *Militant Mediator: Whitney M. Young, Jr.* Lexington: University Press of Kentucky, 1998.

Dittmer, John. *Black Georgia in the Progressive Era, 1900–1920*. Urbana: University of Illinois Press, 1980.

———. *Local People: The Struggle for Civil Rights in Mississippi*. Urbana: University of Illinois Press, 1994.

Dixon, Robert G., Jr. "Civil Rights in Transportation and the ICC." *George Washington Law Review* 31 (1962): 198–241.

Dorsey, Allison. *To Build Our Lives Together: Community Formation in Black Atlanta, 1875–1906*. Athens: University of Georgia Press, 2004.

Dougherty, J. *More Than One Struggle: The Evolution of Black School Reform in Milwaukee*. Chapel Hill: University of North Carolina Press, 2004.

Douglas, Davison M. *Reading, Writing, and Race: The Desegregation of the Charlotte Schools*. Chapel Hill: University of North Carolina Press, 1995.

Douglass, Frederick. "The American Constitution and the Slave: An Address Delivered in Glasgow, Scotland (Mar. 26, 1860)." In *The Frederick Douglass Papers: Series One, Speeches, Debates, and Interviews, 1855–1863*, vol. 3, edited by John W. Blassingame, 361. New Haven, Conn.: Yale University Press, 1985.

Drake, St. Clair, and Horace R. Cayton. *Black Metropolis: A Study of Negro Life in a Northern City*. New York: Harcourt, 1945.

Draper, Alan. *Conflict of Interests: Organized Labor and the Civil Rights Movement in the South, 1954–1968*. Ithaca, N.Y.: Cornell University Press, 1994.

Du Bois, W. E. B. "Does the Negro Need Separate Schools?" *Journal of Negro Education* 4 (July 1935): 328–35. Reprinted in *The Thought and Writings of W. E. B. Du Bois*, edited by Julius Lester, 408–418. New York, Random House, 1971.

———. *The Education of Black People: Ten Critiques, 1906–1960*. Edited by Herbert Aptheker. Amherst: University of Massachusetts Press, 1973.

———. *The Philadelphia Negro: A Social Study*. Philadelphia: University of Philadelphia, 1899.

———. "The Talented Tenth." In *The Seventh Son: The Thought and Writings of W. E. B. Du Bois*, edited by Julius Lester, 385–403. New York: Random House, 1971.

Dudziak, Mary L. *Cold War Civil Rights: Race and the Image of American Democracy*. Princeton, N.J.: Princeton University Press, 2000.

———. "The Court and Social Context in Civil Rights History." *University of Chicago Law Review* 72 (winter 2005): 429–54.

Dunn, James R. "Title VI, the Guidelines and School Desegregation in the South." *Virginia Law Review* 53 (Dec. 1967): 42–88.

*The Earliest Printed Laws of the Province of Georgia*. Vol. 2. *1765–1770*. Wilmington, Del.: Michael Glazier, 1978.

Ely, James W., Jr. "Negro Demonstrations and the Law: Danville as a Test Case." *Vanderbilt Law Review* 27 (Oct. 1974): 927–68.

Epstein, Cynthia Fuchs. *Women in Law*. Urbana: University of Illinois Press, 1981.

Eskew, Glenn T. *But for Birmingham: The Local and National Movements in the Civil Rights Struggle*. Chapel Hill: University of North Carolina Press, 1997.

Executive Committee of the Atlanta Bar Association. *History of the Atlanta Bar Association 1888–1962.* Atlanta: Executive Committee of the Atlanta Bar Association, 1962.

"Exclusion of Negroes from Subsidized Housing Project." *University of Chicago Law Review* 15 (spring 1948): 745–56.

Fairclough, Adam. *A Class of Their Own: Black Teachers in the Segregated South.* Cambridge, Mass.: Harvard University Press, 2007.

———. *Race and Democracy: The Civil Rights Struggle in Louisiana, 1915–1972.* Athens: University of Georgia Press, 1995.

———. *Teaching Equality: Black Schools in the Age of Jim Crow.* Athens: University of Georgia Press, 2001.

———. *To Redeem the Soul of America: The Southern Christian Leadership Conference and Martin Luther King, Jr.* Athens: University of Georgia Press, 1987.

Felstiner, William L. F., Richard L. Abel, and Austin Sarat. "The Emergence and Transformation of Disputes: Naming, Blaming, Claiming &" *Law and Society Review* 15 (1980–1981): 631–54.

Ferguson, Karen. *Black Politics in New Deal Atlanta.* Chapel Hill: University of North Carolina Press, 2002.

Finley, Lucinda M. "Breaking Women's Silence in Law: The Dilemma of the Gendered Nature of Legal Reasoning." *Notre Dame Law Review* 64 (1989): 886–910.

Fiss, Owen M. "Dombrowski." *Yale Law Journal* 86 (May 1977): 1103–64.

Fite, Gilbert C. *Richard B. Russell, Jr.: Senator from Georgia.* Chapel Hill: University of North Carolina Press, 1991.

Fleishman, Joel L. "The Real against the Ideal—Making the Solution Fit the Problem: The Atlanta Public School Agreement of 1973." In *Roundtable Justice, Case Studies in Conflict Resolution: Reports to the Ford Foundation,* edited by Robert B. Goldmann, 129–180. Boulder, Colo.: Westview, 1980.

Fleming, Cynthia Griggs. *Soon We Will Not Cry: The Liberation of Ruby Doris Smith Robinson.* New York: Rowman & Littlefield, 1998.

Forman, James. *The Making of Black Revolutionaries.* 2nd ed. Washington, D.C.: Open Hand, 1985.

Formisano, Ronald. *Boston against Busing: Race, Class, and Ethnicity in the 1960s and 1970s.* Chapel Hill: University of North Carolina Press, 1991.

Fort, Vincent D. "The Atlanta Sit-in Movement, 1960–61: An Oral Study." In *Atlanta, Georgia, 1960–61: Sit-ins and Student Activism,* edited by David J. Garrow, 113–80. Brooklyn: Carlson, 1989.

Fossum, John C. "Rent Withholding and the Improvement of Substandard Housing." *California Law Review* 53 (Mar. 1965): 304–36.

Foster, Michele, ed. *Black Teachers on Teaching.* New York: New Press, 1997.

Franklin, John Hope, and Alfred A. Moss, Jr. *From Slavery to Freedom: A History of African Americans,* 7th ed. New York: McGraw-Hill, 1994.

Frazier, E. Franklin. *Black Bourgeoisie.* 2nd ed. Glencoe, Ill.: Free Press, 1957.

Freyer, Tony Allan. *Little Rock on Trial: Cooper v. Aaron and School Desegregation.* Lawrence: University Press of Kansas, 2007.

Fung, Archon. *Empowered Participation: Reinventing Urban Democracy*. Princeton, N.J.: Princeton University Press, 2004.

Fung, Archon, and Erick Olin Wright. *Deepening Democracy*. New York: Verso, 2003.

Gaines, Kevin. *Uplifting the Race: Black Leadership, Politics, and Culture in the Twentieth Century*. Chapel Hill: University of North Carolina Press, 1996.

Galanter, Marc. "The Radiating Effects of Courts." In *Empirical Theories About Courts*, edited by Keith O. Boyum and Lynn Mather, 117–42. New York: Longman, 1983.

George H. Gallup, *The Gallup Poll: Public Opinion, 1935–1971*. New York: American Institute of Public Opinion, 1972.

Gandhi, Mahatma K. *Non-violent Resistance (Satyagraha)*. New York: Schocken, 1961.

Garrow, David J. *Bearing the Cross: Martin Luther King, Jr., and the Southern Christian Leadership Conference*. New York: Vintage, 1988.

———. *Liberty and Sexuality: The Right to Privacy and the Making of Roe v. Wade*. New York: Macmillan, 1994.

Gartner, Scott Sigmund, and Gary M. Segura. "Race, Casualties, and Opinion in the Vietnam War." *Journal of Politics* 62 (Feb. 2000): 115–46.

Gaston, Paul M. *The New South Creed: A Study in Southern Mythmaking*. New York: Vintage, 1970.

Georgia Teachers and Education Association. *Rising in the Sun: A History of the Georgia Teachers and Education Association, 1918–1966*. Atlanta: Georgia Teachers and Education Association, 1966.

Gilmore, Glenda Elizabeth. *Defying Dixie: The Radical Roots of Civil Rights, 1919–1950*. New York: Norton, 2008.

Ginger, Ann Fagan, and Eugene M. Tobin, eds. *The National Lawyers Guild: From Roosevelt through Reagan*. Philadelphia: Temple University Press, 1988.

Goebel, Julius, Jr. *A History of the School of Law, Columbia University*. New York: Columbia University Press, 1955.

Goluboff, Risa L. *The Lost Promise of Civil Rights*. Cambridge, Mass.: Harvard University Press, 2007.

Goodman, Ernest. "The NLG, the FBI, and the Civil Rights Movement: 1964—A Year of Decision." *Guild Practitioner* 38 (1981): 1–5.

Goodman, James. *Stories of Scottsboro*. New York: Pantheon, 1994.

Goodman, William H. "National Lawyers Guild as an All-white Organization." *Guild Practitioner* 30 (1972–73): 74–87.

———. "Suing the State: Shadows of a Darker Hue." *Detroit College of Law Review* 1983 (1983): 1277–82.

Gordon, Jennifer. *Suburban Sweatshops: The Fight for Immigrant Rights*. Cambridge, Mass.: Harvard University Press, 2007.

Grady-Willis, Winston A. *Challenging U.S. Apartheid: Atlanta and Black Struggles for Human Rights, 1960–1977*. Durham, N.C.: Duke University Press, 2006.

Grant, Donald L. *The Way It Was in the South: The Black Experience in Georgia*. New York: Birch Lane, 1993.

Grantham, Dewey W., Jr. "Georgia Politics and the Disfranchisement of the Negro." *Georgia History Quarterly* 32 (Mar. 1948): 1–21.

Greenberg, Jack. *Crusaders in the Courts: How a Dedicated Band of Lawyers Fought for the Civil Rights Revolution.* New York: Basic, 1994.

———. "In Tribute: Charles Hamilton Houston." *Harvard Law Review* 111 (June 1998): 2161–67.

———. "Racial Integration of Teachers—A Growing Problem." *Journal of Negro Education* 20 (autumn 1951): 584–87.

Greene, Christina. *Our Separate Ways: Women and the Black Freedom Movement in Durham, North Carolina.* Chapel Hill: University of North Carolina Press, 2005.

Grimal, Nicolas. *A History of Ancient Egypt.* Translated by Ian Shaw. Cambridge, Mass.: Blackwell, 1992.

Guinier, Lani. "The Triumph of Tokenism: The Voting Rights Act and the Theory of Black Electoral Success." *Michigan Law Review* 89 (Mar. 1991): 1077–1154.

———. "From Racial Liberalism to Racial Literacy: *Brown v. Board of Education* and the Interest-divergence Dilemma." 92 *J. Am. Hist.* (June 2004): 92–118.

Haines, Herbert H. *Black Radicals and the Civil Rights Mainstream, 1954–1970.* Knoxville: University of Tennessee Press, 1988.

Halberstam, David. *The Children.* New York: Random House, 1998.

Hall, Jacquelyn Dowd. "The Long Civil Rights Movement and the Political Uses of the Past." *Journal of American History* 91 (Mar. 2005): 1233–63.

Hampton, Henry, and Steve Fayer, eds. *Voices of Freedom: An Oral History of the Civil Rights Movement from the 1950s through the 1980s.* New York: Bantam, 1990.

Hanchett, Thomas W. *Sorting Out the New South City: Race, Class, and Urban Development in Charlotte, 1875–1975.* Chapel Hill: University of North Carolina Press, 1998.

Haney, James E. "The Effects of the *Brown* Decision on Black Educators." *Journal of Negro Education* 47 (winter 1978): 88–95.

Hare, Nathan. *The Black Anglo-Saxons.* New York: Marzani and Munsell, 1965.

Harlan, Louis R. *Booker T. Washington.* Vol. 1. *The Making of a Black Leader, 1856–1901.* New York: Oxford University Press, 1972.

———. *Booker T. Washington.* Vol. 2. *The Wizard of Tuskegee, 1901–1915.* New York: Oxford University Press, 1983.

———. "The Secret Life of Booker T. Washington." In *Booker T. Washington in Perspective: Essays of Louis R. Harlan,* edited by Raymond W. Smock, 110–32. Jackson: University Press of Mississippi, 1988.

———. *Separate and Unequal: Public School Campaigns and Racism in the Southern Seaboard States, 1901–1915.* Chapel Hill: University of North Carolina Press, 1958.

Harmon, David Andrew. *Beneath the Image of the Civil Rights Movement and Race Relations: Atlanta, Georgia, 1946–1981.* New York: Garland, 1996.

Harris, Abram Lincoln. "The Negro and Economic Radicalism." In *Race, Radicalism, and Reform: Selected Papers,* edited by William Darity, Jr., 130–39. New Brunswick, N.J.: Transaction, 1989.

Hartshorn, Truman A., and Keith R. Ihlanfeldt. "Growth and Change in Metropolitan Atlanta." In *The Atlanta Paradox*, edited by David L. Sjoquist, 15–41. New York: Russell Sage, 2000.

Henderson, Alexa Benson. *Atlanta Life Insurance Company: Guardian of Black Economic Dignity*. Tuscaloosa: University of Alabama Press, 1990.

———. "Heman E. Perry and Black Enterprise in Atlanta, 1908–1925." *Business History Review* 61 (summer 1987): 216–42.

Henderson, Harold Paulk. *Ernest Vandiver, Governor of Georgia*. Athens: University of Georgia Press, 2000.

Henkin, Louis. "*Shelley v. Kramer*: Notes for a Revised Opinion." *University of Pennsylvania Law Review* 110 (Feb. 1962): 473–505.

Higginbotham, Evelyn Brooks. *Righteous Discontent: The Women's Movement in the Black Baptist Church, 1880–1920*. Cambridge, Mass.: Harvard University Press, 1993.

———. "In Politics to Stay: Black Women Leaders and Party Politics during the 1920s." In *Women, Politics, and Change*, edited by Louise A. Tilly and Patricia Gurin, 199–220. New York: Russell Sage, 1990.

Hilbank, Thomas. "The Profession, the Grassroots and the Elite: Cause Lawyering for Civil Rights and Freedom in the Direct Action Era." In *Cause Lawyers and Social Movements*, edited by Austin Sarat and Stuart A. Scheingold, 60–83. Stanford, Calif.: Stanford University Press, 2006.

Hill, Oliver W., Sr. *The Big Bang: Brown v. Board of Education and Beyond*. Winter Park, Fla.: Four-G, 2000.

Hine, Darlene Clark. "Black Lawyers and the Twentieth-century Struggle for Constitutional Change." In *African Americans and the Living Constitution*, edited by John Hope Franklin and Genna Rae McNeil, 33–55. Washington, D.C.: Smithsonian, 1995.

———. *Black Victory: The Rise and the Fall of the White Primary in Texas*. 2nd ed. Columbia: University of Missouri Press, 2003.

Hogan, Wesley C. *Many Minds, One Heart: SNCC's Dream for a New America*. Chapel Hill: University of North Carolina Press, 2007.

Hollowell, Louise, and Martin C. Lehfeldt, *The Sacred Call: A Tribute to Donald L. Hollowell, Civil Rights Champion*. Atlanta: Four-G, 1997.

Holt, Len. *An Act of Conscience*. Boston: Beacon, 1965.

———. *The Summer That Didn't End*. London: Heinemann, 1966.

Hornsby, Alton, Jr. *Black Power in Dixie: A Political History of African Americans in Atlanta*. Gainesville: University Press of Florida, 2009.

———. "Black Public Education in Atlanta, Georgia, 1954–1973: From Segregation to Segregation." *Journal of Negro History* 76 (Winter–Autumn 1991): 21–47.

Houston, Charles Hamilton, and Leon A. Ransom. "The George Crawford Case: An Experiment in Social Statesmanship." *Nation* 139 (4 July 1934): 19.

Hull, Gloria T., Patricia Bell Scott et al, eds., *All the Women Are White, All the Blacks Are Men, But Some of Us Are Brave: Black Women's Studies*. Old Westbury: New York, 1982.

Hylton, Joseph Gordon. "The African-American Lawyer, the First Generation: Virginia as a Case Study." *University of Pittsburgh Law Review* 56 (fall 1994): 107–64.

"The Impact of *Shelley v. Kraemer* on the State Action Concept." Comment. *California Law Review* 44 (1956): 718, 727–732.

Irvine, Jacqueline Jordan, ed. *In Search of Wholeness: African-American Teachers and Their Culturally Specific Classroom Practices.* New York: Palgrave, 2002.

Jackson, Barbara L. "Desegregation: Atlanta Style." *Theory into Practice* 17 (Feb. 1978): 43–53.

Jackson, Thomas F. *From Civil Rights to Human Rights.* Philadelphia: University of Pennsylvania Press, 2007.

Jacoby, Tamar. *Someone Else's House: America's Unfinished Struggle for Integration.* New York: Free Press, 1998.

Jacoway, Elizabeth. "Taken by Surprise: Little Rock Business Leaders and Desegregation." In *Southern Businessmen and Desegregation,* edited by Elizabeth Jacoway and David R. Colburn, 15–41. Baton Rouge: Louisiana State University Press, 1982.

———. *Turn Away Thy Son: Little Rock, the Crisis That Shocked the Nation.* New York: Free Press, 2007.

Jewell, Joseph Oscar. "'Black Ivy': The American Missionary Association and the Black Upper Class in Atlanta, Georgia, 1875–1915." Ph.D. diss., University of California, Los Angeles, 1999.

Johnson, Elizabeth K. "Collective Tenant Action: Should the Rent Strike Be Institutionalized?" *Los Angeles Bar Bulletin* (Feb. 1971): 138–68.

Johnson, R. O. "Desegregation of Public Education in Georgia: One Year Afterward." *Journal of Negro Education* 24 (summer 1955): 228–47.

Jonas, Gilbert. *Freedom's Sword: The NAACP and the Struggle against Racism in America, 1909–1969.* New York: Routledge, 2005.

Jones, Jacqueline. *Soldiers of Light and Love: Northern Teachers and Georgia Blacks, 1865–1873.* Chapel Hill: University of North Carolina Press, 1980.

Jordan, Vernon E., Jr. *Vernon Can Read! A Memoir.* New York: Basic Civitas, 2003.

Joseph, Peniel E., ed. *The Black Power Movement: Rethinking the Civil Rights–Black Power Era.* New York: Routledge, 2006.

———. *Waiting 'til the Midnight Hour: A Narrative History of Black Power in America.* New York: Holt, 2006.

Kalman, Laura. *Legal Realism at Yale, 1927–1960.* Chapel Hill: University of North Carolina Press, 1986.

Kellogg, Charles. *NAACP: A History of the National Association for the Advancement of Colored People.* Vol. 1. *1909–1920.* Baltimore: Johns Hopkins University Press, 1967.

Kennedy, Randall. "Martin Luther King's Constitution: A Legal History of the Montgomery Bus Boycott." *Yale Law Journal* 98 (Apr. 1989): 999–1067.

Key, V. O., Jr. *Southern Politics in State and Nation,* 3rd ed. Knoxville: University of Tennessee Press, 1984.

King, Martin Luther, Jr. *The Essential Writings and Speeches of Martin Luther King, Jr.* Edited by James M. Washington. HarperCollins: New York, 1991.

———. *The Words of Martin Luther King, Jr.* Selected by Coretta Scott King. New York: Newmarket, 1987.

King, Martin Luther, Sr., with Clayton Riley. *Daddy King: An Autobiography.* New York: William Morrow, 1980.

King, Mary. *Freedom Song: A Personal Story of the 1960s Civil Rights Movement.* New York: Morrow, 1987.

Kinoy, Arthur. *Rights on Trial: The Odyssey of a People's Lawyer.* Larchmont, N.Y.: Bernel, 1994.

Kivisto, Peter. "A Historical Review of Changes in Public Housing Policies and Their Impacts on Minorities." In *Race, Ethnicity, and Minority Housing in the United States*, edited by Jamshid A. Momeni, 1–18. New York: Greenwood, 1986.

Klarman, Michael J. *From Jim Crow to Civil Rights: The Supreme Court and the Struggle for Racial Equality.* New York: Oxford University Press, 2004.

Kluger, Richard. *Simple Justice: The History of Brown v. Board of Education and Black America's Struggle for Equality.* New York: Vintage, 1977.

Kornbluh, Felicia. *The Battle for Welfare Rights: Politics and Poverty in Modern America.* Philadelphia: University of Pennsylvania Press, 2007.

Kotz, Nick. *Judgment Days: Lyndon Baines Johnson, Martin Luther King, Jr., and the Laws That Changed America.* Boston: Houghton Mifflin, 2005.

Kruse, Kevin M. *White Flight: Atlanta and the Making of Modern Conservatism.* Princeton, N.J.: Princeton University Press, 2005.

Kuhn, Clifford M., Harlon E. Joye, and E. Bernard West. *Living Atlanta: An Oral History of the City, 1914–1948.* Athens: University of Georgia Press, 1990.

———. "'There's a Footnote to History!' Memory and the History of Martin Luther King's October 1960 Arrest and Its Aftermath." *Journal of American History* 84 (Sept. 1997): 583–595.

Kunstler, William M., with Sheila Isenberg. *My Life as a Radical Lawyer.* New York: Birch Lane, 1994.

Landsberg, Brian K. *Enforcing Civil Rights: Race Discrimination and the Department of Justice.* Lawrence: University Press of Kansas, 1997.

Langum, David J. *William M. Kunstler: The Most Hated Lawyer in America.* New York: New York University Press, 1999.

Lankevich, George J., ed. *Atlanta: A Chronological and Documentary History: 1813–1976.* Dobbs Ferry, N.Y.: Oceana, 1978.

"The Largest Law Schools." *Am. Law Sch. Review* 2 (1906–11): 125.

Lassiter, Matthew D. "Does the Supreme Court Matter? Civil Rights and the Inherent Politicization of Constitutional Law." *Michigan Law Review* 103 (May 2005): 1401–22.

———. *The Silent Majority: Suburban Politics in the Sunbelt South.* Princeton, N.J.: Princeton University Press, 2007.

Lau, Peter F. *Democracy Rising: South Carolina and the Fight for Black Equality Since 1865.* Lexington: University Press of Kentucky, 2006.

*Law Quadrangle: Notes from Michigan Law* 52 (Winter 2009).

Lawson, Ronald, ed. *The Tenant Movement in New York City, 1904–1984*. New Brunswick, N.J.: Rutgers University Press, 1986.

Lawson, Steven F. *Black Ballots: Voting Rights in the South, 1944–1969*. New York: Columbia University Press, 1976.

Lee, Chana Kai. *For Freedom's Sake: The Life of Fannie Lou Hamer*. Urbana: University of Illinois Press, 1999.

Levine, Robert A. *The Poor Ye Need Not Have with You: Lessons from the War on Poverty*. Cambridge, Mass: MIT Press, 1970.

Lewis, Anthony. *Make No Law: The Sullivan Case and the First Amendment*. New York: Vintage Books, 1992.

Lewis, David Levering. *King: A Critical Biography*. Urbana: University of Illinois Press, 1970.

———. *W. E. B. Du Bois*. Vol. 1. *Biography of a Race, 1868–1919*. New York: Holt, 1993.

———. *W. E. B. Du Bois*. Vol. 2. *The Fight for Equality and the American Century, 1919–1963*. New York: Holt, 2000.

Lewis, John, with Michael D'Orso. *Walking with the Wind: A Memoir of the Movement*. New York: Simon and Schuster, 1998.

Lewis, Thomas P. "*Burton v. Wilmington Parking Authority*: A Case without Precedent." *Columbia Law Review* 61 (Dec. 1961): 1458–67.

Lincoln, Abraham. *The Collected Works of Abraham Lincoln*. Vol. 4. Edited by Roy P. Basler. New Brunswick, N.J.: Rutgers University Press, 1953.

Lipsky, Michael. *Protest in City Politics: Rent Strikes, Housing, and the Power of the Poor*. Chicago: Rand McNally, 1970.

Locke, Alain. "The Dilemma of Segregation." *Journal of Negro Education* 4 (Jul. 1935): 406–11.

Loevy, Robert D. *To End All Segregation: The Politics of the Passage of the Civil Rights Act of 1964*. Lanham, Md.: University Press of America, 1990.

López, Gerald P. *Rebellious Lawyering: One Chicano's Vision of Progressive Law Practice*. Boulder, Colo.: Westview, 1992.

Lublin, David. *The Paradox of Representation: Racial Gerrymandering and Minority Interests in Congress*. Princeton, N.J.: Princeton University Press, 1997.

Lunch, William L., and Peter W. Sperlich. "American Public Opinion and the War in Vietnam." *Western Political Quarterly* 32 (Mar. 1979): 21–44.

Mack, Kenneth W. "Law and Mass Politics in the Making of the Civil Rights Lawyer, 1931–1941." *Journal of American History* 93 (June 2006): 37–62.

———. "Rethinking Civil Rights Lawyering and Politics in the Era before *Brown*." *Yale Law Journal* 115 (Nov. 2005): 256–354.

MacLean, Nancy. *Freedom Is Not Enough: The Opening of the American Work Place*. Cambridge, Mass.: Harvard University Press, 2006.

Mahard, Rita E., and Robert L. Crain. "Research on Minority Achievement in Desegregated Schools." In *The Consequences of School Desegregation*, edited by Christine H. Rossell and Willis D. Hawley, 103–25. Philadelphia: Temple University Press, 1983.

Mananzala, Rickke, and Dean Spade. "The Nonprofit Industrial Complex and Transresistance." *Sexuality Research and Social Policy* 5 (1) (Mar. 2008): 53–71.

Manis, Andrew M. *A Fire You Can't Put Out: The Civil Rights Life of Birmingham's Reverend Fred Shuttlesworth*. Tuscaloosa: University of Alabama Press, 1999.

Margo, Robert A. *Race and Schooling in the South, 1880–1950: An Economic History*. Chicago: University of Chicago Press, 1990.

Martin, Charles H. *The Angelo Herndon Case and Southern Justice*. Baton Rouge: Louisiana State University Press, 1976.

Massey, Douglas S., and Nancy A. Denton. *American Apartheid: Segregation and the Making of the Underclass*. Cambridge, Mass.: Harvard University Press, 1993.

Matthews, Donald R., and James W. Prothro. *Negroes and the New Southern Politics*. New York: Harcourt, Brace and World, 1966.

Mays, Benjamin E. *Born to Rebel: An Autobiography*. Athens: University of Georgia Press, 1987.

McAdam, Doug. *Freedom Summer*. New York: Oxford University Press, 1990.

———. *Political Process and the Development of Black Insurgency, 1930–1970*. Chicago: University of Chicago Press, 1982.

McAdam, Doug, Sidney Tarrow, and Charles Tilly. "To Map Contentious Politics." *Mobilization* 1 (1996): 17–34.

McCann, Michael W. *Rights at Work: Pay Equity Reform and the Politics of Legal Mobilization*. Chicago: University of Chicago Press, 1994.

———. "Reform Litigation on Trial." *Law and Social Inquiry* 17 (fall 1992): 715–43.

McCann, Michael, and Helena Silverstein. "Rethinking Law's 'Allurements': A Relational Analysis of Social Movement Lawyers in the United States." In *Cause Lawyering: Political Commitments and Professional Responsibilities*, edited by Austin Sarat and Stuart Scheingold, 261–92. New York: Oxford University Press, 1997.

McDonald, Laughlin. *A Voting Rights Odyssey: Black Enfranchisement in Georgia*. New York: Cambridge University Press, 2003.

McGhee, Milton, and Ann Fagan Ginger. "The House I Live In: A Study of Housing for Minorities." *Cornell Law Quarterly* 46 (1960–1961): 194–257.

McMahon, Kevin J., and Michael Paris. "The Politics of Rights Revisited: Rosenberg, McCann, and the New Institutionalism." In *Leveraging the Law: Using the Courts to Achieve Social Change*, edited by David A. Schultz, 63–134. New York: Lang, 1998.

McMillen, Neil R. *The Citizens' Council: Organized Resistance to the Second Reconstruction, 1954–64*. Urbana: University of Illinois Press, 1994.

McGrath, Susan M. "Great Expectations: The History of School Desegregation in Atlanta and Boston, 1954–1990." Ph.D. diss., Emory University, 1992.

McGraw, B. T., and George B. Nesbitt. "Aftermath of *Shelley versus Kraemer* on Residential Restriction by Race." *Land Economics* 29 (Aug. 1953): 280–87.

McNeil, Genna Rae. *Groundwork: Charles Hamilton Houston and the Struggle for Civil Rights*. Philadelphia: University of Pennsylvania Press, 1983.

Meador, Daniel J. "The Constitution and the Assignment of Pupils to Public Schools." *Virginia Law Review* 45 (May 1959): 517–71.

Meier, August. "Negro Class Structure and Ideology in the Age of Booker T. Washington." *Phylon* 23 (third quarter 1962): 258–66.

———. "Negro Protest Movements and Organizations." *Journal of Negro Education* 32 (autumn 1963): 437–50.

Meier, August, and David Levering Lewis. "History of the Negro Upper Class in Atlanta, Georgia, 1890–1958." *Journal of Negro Education* 28 (spring 1959): 128–39.

Meier, August, and Elliott Rudwick. "Attorneys Black and White: A Case Study of Race Relations within the NAACP." *Journal of American History* 62 (Mar. 1976): 913–46.

———. *CORE: A Study in the Civil Rights Movement, 1942–1968.* New York: Oxford University Press, 1973.

———. *From Plantation to Ghetto*, 3rd ed. New York: Hill and Wang, 1976.

Meier, August, and John H. Bracey, Jr. "The NAACP as a Reform Movement, 1909–1965: To Reach the Conscience of America." *Journal of Southern History* 59 (Feb. 1993): 3–30.

Menkel-Meadow, Carrie. "Excluded Voices: New Voices in the Legal Profession Making New Voices in the Law." *University of Miami Law Review* 42 (Sept. 1987): 29–53.

Meyer, Stephen Grant. *As Long as They Don't Move Next Door: Segregation and Racial Conflict in American Neighborhoods.* Lanham, Md.: Rowman and Littlefield, 2000.

Milbauer, Barbara, in collaboration with Bert N. Obrentz. *The Law Giveth: Legal Aspects of the Abortion Controversy.* In collaboration with Bert N. Obrentz. New York: Atheneum, 1983.

Minow, Martha. *In Brown's Wake: Legacies of America's Educational Landmark* (New York: Oxford, 2010).

Moore, Howard, Jr. "Black Barrister at the Southern Bar." In *Radical Lawyers: Their Role in the Movement and in the Courts*, edited by Jonathan Black, 153–158. New York: Avon, 1971.

———. "Brown v. Board of Education: The Court's Relationship to Black Liberation." In *Law against the People: Essays to Demystify Law, Order, and the Courts*, edited by Robert Lefcourt, 55–64. New York: Random House, 1971.

———. "The Tenth Black Lawyer in Georgia." In "Five Who Got It Right," edited by Richard Zitrin. *Widener Law Journal* 13 (2003): 210–16.

———. "Racism as Justice." *Black Law Journal* 3 (1973): 54–66.

Moore, Jesse Thomas, Jr. *A Search for Equality: The National Urban League, 1910–1961.* University Park: Pennsylvania State University Press, 1981.

Morris, Aldon D. *The Origins of the Civil Rights Movement: Black Communities Organizing for Change.* New York: Free Press, 1984.

Morris, Jerome. "Research, Ideology, and the Brown Decision: Counter-narratives to the Historical and Contemporary Representation of Black Schooling." *Teachers College Record* 110, 4 (Apr. 2008): 713–732.

Morris, V. G., and Morris, C. L. *The Price They Paid: Desegregation in An African American Community.* New York: Teachers College Press, 2002.

Moseley, Clement Charlton. "The Political Influence of the Ku Klux Klan in Georgia, 1915–1925." *Georgia Historical Quarterly* 57 (summer 1973): 235–55.

Motley, Constance Baker. *Equal Justice under Law: An Autobiography.* New York: Farrar, Strauss, and Giroux, 1998.

———. "Reflections." *Columbia Law Review* 102 (Oct. 2002): 1449–50.

Murphee, Vanessa. *The Selling of Civil Rights: The Student Nonviolent Coordinating Committee and the Use of Public Relations*. New York: Routledge, 2006.

Murray, Paul T. "Blacks and the Draft: A History of Institutional Racism." *Journal of Black Studies* 2 (Sept. 1971): 57–76.

Myrdal, Gunnar. *An American Dilemma: The Negro Problem and Modern Democracy*. New York: Harper, 1944.

Nalty, Bernard C., and Morris J. MacGregor, eds. *Blacks in the Military: Essential Documents*. Wilmington, Dela.: Scholarly Resources, 1981.

Naples, Nancy A. *Grassroots Warriors: Activist Mothering, Community Work, and the War on Poverty*. New York: Routledge, 1998.

Nasstrom, Kathryn L. "Down to Now: Memory, Narrative, and Women's Leadership in the Civil Rights Movement in Atlanta, Georgia." *Gender and History* 11 (Apr. 1999): 113–44.

———. "Women, the Civil Rights Movement, and the Politics of Historical Memory in Atlanta, 1946–1973." Ph.D. diss., University of North Carolina, 1993.

National Lawyers Guild. *Civil Rights and Liberties Handbook*. Berkeley, Ca.: National Lawyers Guild, 1967.

Norrell, Robert J. *Reaping the Whirlwind: The Civil Rights Movement in Tuskegee*. New York: Knopf, 1985.

———. *Up from History: The Life of Booker T. Washington*. Cambridge, Mass.: Harvard University Press, 2009.

O'Brien, Thomas V. "Georgia's Response to *Brown v. Board of Education*: The Rise and Fall of Massive Resistance, 1949–1961." Paper presented at the Annual Meeting of the American Educational Research Association, Atlanta, Ga., Apr. 12–16, 1993.

Oliver, Melvin L. and Thomas V. Shapiro. *Black Wealth, White Wealth: A New Perspective on Inequality*. New York: Routledge, 2006.

Olken, Charles E. "Economic Development in the Model Cities Program." *Law and Contemporary Problems* 36 (spring 1971): 205–26.

Orfield, Gary, and Carole Ashkinaze. *The Closing Door: Conservative Policy and Black Opportunity*. Chicago: University of Chicago Press, 1991.

Orfield, Gary, and Chungmei Lee. *Racial Transformation and the Changing Nature of Segregation*. Cambridge, Mass.: Civil Rights Project at Harvard University, 2006; www.civilrightsproject.ucla.edu/research/deseg/Racial_Transformation.pdf.

———. *Why Segregation Matters: Poverty and Educational Inequality*. Cambridge, Mass.: Civil Rights Project at Harvard University, 2005; www.civilrightsproject.ucla.edu/research/deseg/Why_Segreg_Matters.pdf.

Pager, Devah. *Marked: Race, Crime and Finding Work in an Era of Mass Incarceration*. Chicago: University of Chicago Press, 2007.

Parris, Guichard, and Lester Brooks. *Blacks in the City: A History of the National Urban League*. Boston: Little, Brown, 1971.

Paschall, Eliza K. *It Must Have Rained*. Atlanta: Center for Research in Social Change, Emory University, 1975.

Pattillo-McCoy, Mary. *Black Picket Fences: Privilege and Peril among the Black Middle Class.* Chicago: University of Chicago Press, 1999.

Payne, Charles M. *I've Got the Light of Freedom: The Organizing Tradition and the Mississippi Freedom Struggle.* Berkeley: University of California Press, 1995.

Perry, Theresa, Claude Steele, and Asa G. Hilliard III. *Young, Gifted, and Black: Promoting High Achievement among African-American Students.* Boston: Beacon, 2003.

Piven, Frances Fox, and Richard A. Cloward. *Poor People's Movements: Why They Succeed, How They Fail.* New York: Vintage, 1979.

Podair, Jerald E. *The Strike That Changed New York: Blacks, Whites, and the Ocean Hill–Brownsville Crisis.* New Haven, Conn.: Yale University Press, 2002.

Polikoff, Nancy. "Am I My Client: Role Confusion of the Lawyer Activist." *Harvard Civil Rights–Civil Liberties Law Review* 31 (summer 1996): 443–71.

Pollak, Louis H. "Racial Discrimination and Judicial Integrity: A Reply to Professor Wechsler." *University of Pennsylvania Law Review* 108 (Nov. 1959): 1–34.

———. "The Supreme Court and the States: Reflections on *Boynton v. Virginia.*" *California Law Review* 49 (Mar. 1961): 15–55.

Pomerantz, Gary M. *Where Peachtree Meets Sweet Auburn: A Saga of Race and Family: The Saga of Two Families and the Making of Atlanta.* New York: Scribner, 1996.

Pratt, Robert A. "Simple Justice Denied: The Supreme Court's Retreat from School Desegregation in Richmond, Virginia." *Rutgers Law Journal* 24 (spring 1993): 709–24.

———. *We Shall Not Be Moved: The Desegregation of the University of Georgia.* Athens: University of Georgia Press, 2002.

Pritchett, Wendell. *Brownsville, Brooklyn: Blacks, Jews, and the Changing Face of the Ghetto.* Chicago: University of Chicago Press, 2002.

———. *Robert Clifton Weaver and the American City: The Life and Times of an Urban Reformer.* Chicago: University of Chicago Press, 2008.

———. "Where Shall We Live? Class and the Limitations of Fair Housing Law." *Urban Lawyer* 35 (summer 2003): 399–470.

Comment, "Private Attorneys-General: Group Action in the Fight for Civil Liberties." *Yale Law Journal* 58 (Mar. 1949): 574–98.

Quadagno, Jill. *The Color of Welfare: How Racism Undermined the War on Poverty.* New York: Oxford University Press, 1994.

———. "Promoting Civil Rights through the Welfare State: How Medicare Integrated Southern Hospitals." *Social Problems* 47 (2000): 68–89.

Quigley, William P. "Reflections of Community Organizers: Lawyering for Empowerment of Community Organizations." *Ohio Northern University Law Review* 21 (1994): 455–79.

Rabinowitz, Howard N. *Race Relations in the Urban South, 1865–1890.* Urbana: University of Illinois Press, 1980.

Rabinowitz, Victor. *Unrepentant Leftist: A Lawyer's Memoir.* Urbana: University of Illinois Press, 1996.

Rabinowitz, Victor, and Tim Ledwith, eds. *A History of the National Lawyers Guild, 1937–1987.* New York: National Lawyers Guild, 1987.

Rafky, David M. "Student Militance: A Dilemma for Black Faculty." *Journal of Black Studies* 3 (Dec. 1972): 183–206.

Ransby, Barbara. *Ella Baker and the Black Freedom Struggle: A Radical Democratic Vision.* Chapel Hill: University of North Carolina Press, 2003.

Read, Florence Matilda. *The Story of Spelman College.* Princeton, N.J.: Princeton University Press, 1961.

"Removal of State Criminal Prosecution." Comment. *Harvard Law Review* 80 (Nov. 1966): 225–31.

Research Atlanta. *School Desegregation in Metro Atlanta, 1954–1973,* 1973.

Roberts, Dorothy. *Killing the Black Body: Race, Reproduction, and the Meaning of Liberty.* New York: Vintage, 1997.

Robinson, Jo Ann Gibson. *The Montgomery Bus Boycott and the Women Who Started It: The Memoir of Jo Ann Gibson Robinson.* Edited by David J. Garrow. Knoxville: University of Tennessee Press, 1987.

Roche, Jeff. *Restructured Resistance: The Sibley Commission and the Politics of Desegregation in Georgia.* Athens: University of Georgia Press, 1998.

Rose, Thomas, and John Greenya. *Black Leaders: Then and Now: A Personal History of Students Who Led the Civil Rights Movement in the 1960s—and What Happened to Them.* Garrett Park, Md.: Garrett Park, 1984.

Rosenberg, Gerald N. *The Hollow Hope: Can Courts Bring about Social Change?* Chicago: University of Chicago Press, 1991.

Rosenberg, Morris. "The Meaning of Politics in Mass Society." *Public Opinion Quarterly* 15 (spring 1951): 5–15.

Rosenthal, Jonas O. "Negro Teachers' Attitudes toward Desegregation." *Journal of Negro Education* 26 (winter 1957): 63–71.

Rossinow, Douglas C. *The Politics of Authenticity: Liberalism, Christianity, and the New Left in America.* New York: Columbia University Press, 1998.

Rouse, Jacqueline Anne. *Lugenia Burns Hope: Black Southern Reformer.* Athens: University of Georgia Press, 1989.

Ruff, Joshua. "For Sale: The American Dream." *American History* (Dec. 2007): 42–49.

Rustin, Bayard. "'Black Power' and Coalition Politics." *Commentary* 42 (Sept. 1966): 35–40.

Rutheiser, Charles. *Imagineering Atlanta: The Politics of Place in the City of Dreams.* New York: Verso, 1996.

Saks, J. Harold, and Sol Rabkin. "Racial and Religious Discrimination in Housing: A Report of Legal Progress." *Iowa Law Review* 45 (spring 1960): 488–524.

Sarat, Austin, and Stuart Scheingold. "Cause Lawyering and the Reproduction of Professional Authority." In *Cause Lawyering: Political Commitments and Professional Responsibilities,* edited by Austin Sarat and Stuart Scheingold, 3–28. New York: Oxford University Press, 1998.

Scheingold, Stuart. *The Politics of Rights: Lawyers, Public Policy, and Political Change,* 2d ed. Ann Arbor: University of Michigan Press, 2004.

Schmidt, Christopher W. "*The Sit-ins and the State Action Doctrine.*" Wm. & Mary Bill Rts. J. 18 (2010): 767–829.

Schuman, Howard, Charlotte Steeh, Lawrence Bobo, and Maria Krysan. *Racial Attitudes in America: Trends and Interpretations.* Cambridge, Mass.: Harvard University Press, 1997.

Scott, Daryl Michael. *Contempt and Pity: Social Policy and the Image of the Damaged Black Psyche, 1880–1996.* Chapel Hill: University of North Carolina Press, 1997.

Scott, Emmett J. *Scott's Official History of the American Negro in the World War.* Chicago: Homewood Press, 1919.

Self, Robert O. *American Babylon: Race and the Struggle for Postwar Oakland.* Princeton, N.J.: Princeton University Press, 2003.

Sellers, Cleveland, with Robert Terrell. *The River of No Return: The Autobiography of a Black Militant and the Life and Death of SNCC.* New York: Morrow, 1973. Reprint, Jackson: University Press of Mississippi, 1990.

Shapiro, Thomas M. *The Hidden Cost of Being African American: How Wealth Perpetuates Inequality.* New York: Oxford University Press, 2004.

Shaw, Ian, ed. *The Oxford History of Ancient Egypt.* New York: Oxford University Press, 2000.

Shepard, Kris. *Rationing Justice: Poverty Lawyers and Poor People in the Deep South.* Baton Rouge: Louisiana State University Press, 2007.

Siegal, Reva B. "Text in Contest: Gender and the Constitution from a Social Movement Perspective." *University of Pennsylvania Law Review* 150 (Nov. 2001): 297–351.

Siegel, Reva, and Robert Post. "*Roe* Rage: Democratic Constitutionalism and Backlash." *Harvard Civil Rights–Civil Liberties Law Review* 42 (summer 2007): 373–433.

Simmons, Michael. "Disturbing the Peace." Presentation to, Budapest University, 16 Feb. 1995. On file with the author.

Sitkoff, Harvard. *A New Deal for Blacks: The Emergence of Civil Rights as a National Issue.* New York: Oxford University Press, 1978.

———. *The Struggle for Black Equality, 1954–1980.* New York: Hill and Wang, 1981.

Smith, David Barton. *Health Care Divided: Race and Healing a Nation.* Ann Arbor: University of Michigan Press, 1999.

Smith, J. Clay, Jr. "The Black Bar Association and Civil Rights." *Creighton Law Review* 15 (1982): 651–679.

———. *Emancipation: The Making of the Black Lawyer, 1844–1944.* Philadelphia: University of Pennsylvania Press, 1993.

———, ed. *Rebels in Law: Voices in History of Black Women Lawyers.* Ann Arbor: University of Michigan Press, 1998.

Smith, J. Clay, Jr., and E. Desmond Hogan. "Remembered Hero, Forgotten Contribution: Charles Hamilton Houston, Legal Realism, and Labor Law." *Harvard Blackletter Law Journal* 14 (spring 1998): 1–16.

Sokol, Jason. *There Goes My Everything: White Southerners in the Age of Civil Rights, 1945–1975.* New York: Knopf, 2006.

Spillenger, Clyde. "Elusive Advocate: Reconsidering Brandeis as People's Lawyer." In *Lawyers' Ethics and the Pursuit of Social Justice: A Critical Reader*, edited by Susan D. Carle, 72–78. New York: New York University Press, 2005.

Spritzer, Lorraine Nelson, and Jean B. Bergmark. *Grace Towns Hamilton and the Politics of Southern Change*. Athens: University of Georgia Press, 1997.

Stone, Clarence N. *Regime Politics: Governing Atlanta, 1946–1988*. Lawrence: University Press of Kansas, 1989.

Stoper, Emily. *The Student Nonviolent Coordinating Committee: The Growth of Radicalism in a Civil Rights Organization*. Brooklyn: Carlson, 1989.

Strebeigh, Fred. *Equal: Women Reshape American Law*. New York: Norton, 2009.

Strong, Donald S. "The Future of the Negro Voter in the South." *Journal of Negro Education* 26 (summer 1957): 400–407.

Strum, Philippa. *Louis D. Brandeis: Justice for the People*. Cambridge, Mass.: Harvard University Press, 1988.

Styles, Fitzhugh. *Negroes and the Law in the Race's Battle for Liberty, Equality and Justice under the Constitution of the United States*. Boston: Christopher, 1937.

Su, Julie. "Making the Invisible Visible: The Garment Industry's Dirty Laundry." *Journal of Gender, Race and Justice* 1 (spring 1998): 405–17.

Sugrue, Thomas J. *The Origins of the Urban Crisis: Race and Inequality in Postwar Detroit*. Princeton, N.J.: Princeton University Press, 1996.

———. *Sweet Land of Liberty: The Forgotten Struggle for Civil Rights in the North*. New York: Random House, 2008.

Sullivan, Patricia. *Lift Every Voice: The NAACP and the Making of the Civil Rights Movement*. New York: New Press, 2009.

Swain, Carol M. *Black Faces, Black Interests: The Representation of African Americans in Congress*. Cambridge, Mass.: Harvard University Press, 1993.

Taeuber, Karl E. "Residential Segregation in the Atlanta Metropolitan Area." In *Urban Atlanta: Redefining the Role of the City*, edited by Andrew M. Hamer, 155–63. Atlanta: Georgia State University Business Press, 1980.

Tarrow, Sidney. *Power in Movement: Social Movements and Contentious Politics*. 2nd ed. New York: Cambridge University Press, 1998.

Taylor, Verta, and Nancy E. Whittier. "Lesbian Feminist Mobilization." In *Frontiers in Social Movement Theory*, edited by Aldon D. Morris and Carol McClung Mueller, 104–29. New Haven: Yale University Press, 1992.

*The Earliest Printed Laws of the Province of Georgia*. Vol. 2. *1765–1770*. Wilmington, Del.: Glazier, 1978.

Thompson, J. Phillip, III. *Double Trouble: Black Mayors, Black Communities, and the Call for a Deep Democracy*. New York: Oxford University Press, 2006.

Thompson, Mark A. "Black-white Residential Segregation in Atlanta." In *The Atlanta Paradox*, edited by David L. Sjoquist, 88–115. New York: Russell Sage, 2000.

Thompson, Robert A., Hylan Lewis, and Davis McEntire. "Atlanta and Birmingham: A Comparative Study in Negro Housing." In *Studies in Housing and Minority Groups*, edited by Nathan Glazer and Davis McEntire, 13–83. Berkeley: University of California Press, 1960.

Thoreau, Henry David. *Civil Disobedience*. 1849. Reprint, New York: Liberal Arts, 1952.

Thornton, J. Mills, III. *Dividing Lines: Municipal Politics and the Struggle for Civil Rights in Montgomery, Birmingham, and Selma.* Tuscaloosa: University of Alabama Press, 2002.

Tigar, Michael E. "Lawyers and Social Justice." *Judicature* 78 (Mar.–Apr. 1995): 253–55.

Tollett, Kenneth S. "Black Lawyers, Their Education and the Black Community." *Howard Law Journal* 17 (1972): 326–57.

Tuck, Stephen G. N. *Beyond Atlanta: The Struggle for Racial Equality in Georgia, 1940–1980.* Athens: University of Georgia Press, 2001.

Tushnet, Mark V. *Making Civil Rights Law: Thurgood Marshall and the Supreme Court, 1936–1961.* New York: Oxford University Press, 1994.

———. *Making Constitutional Law: Thurgood Marshall and the Supreme Court, 1961–1991.* New York: Oxford University Press, 1997.

———. *The NAACP's Legal Strategy against Segregated Education, 1925–1950.* Chapel Hill: University of North Carolina Press, 1987.

———. "Political Aspects of the Changing Meaning of Equality in Constitutional Law: The Equal Protection Clause, Dr. Du Bois, and Charles Hamilton Houston." *Journal of American History* 74 (Dec. 1987): 884–903.

———. "The Significance of *Brown v. Board of Education*." *Virginia Law Review* 80 (Feb. 1994): 173–84.

———. *Taking the Constitution away from the Courts.* Princeton, N.J.: Princeton University Press, 1999.

Tuttle, Elbert P. "Equality and the Vote." *New York University Law Review* 41 (1966): 245–266.

Urban, Wayne J. *Black Scholar: Horace Mann Bond, 1904–1972.* Athens: University of Georgia Press, 1992.

Urofsky, Melvin I. *Louis Brandeis: A Life.* New York: Pantheon, 2009.

Urquhart, Brian. *Ralph Bunche: An American Life.* New York: Norton, 1993.

Van Alstyne, William W., and Kenneth L. Karst. "State Action." *Stanford Law Review* 14 (Dec. 1961): 3–58.

Van Deusen, John G. "Negro in Politics." *Journal of Negro History* 21 (July 1936): 256–74.

Verney, Kevern, and Lee Sartain. *Long Is the Way and Hard: One Hundred Years of the NAACP.* Fayetteville: University of Arkansas Press, 2009.

Walker, Jack L. "The Functions of Disunity." In *The Making of Black America*, edited by August Meier and Elliott Rudwick, 342–61. New York: Atheneum, 1969

———."Protest and Negotiation: A Case Study of Negro Leadership in Atlanta." *Midwest Journal of Political Science* 7 (May 1963): 99–124.

———. "Sit-ins in Atlanta: A Study in the Negro Revolt." In *Atlanta, Georgia, 1960–61: Sit-ins and Student Activism*, edited by David J. Garrow, 59–93. Brooklyn: Carlson, 1989.

Walker, Samuel. *In Defense of American Liberties: A History of the ACLU.* Carbondale: Southern Illinois University Press, 1990.

Walker, Vanessa Siddle. *Their Highest Potential: An African American School Community in the Segregated South.* Chapel Hill: University of North Carolina Press, 1996.

Walton, Hanes, Jr. *Blacks and Political Machines*. Philadelphia: Lippincott, 1972.

——. *Black Politics: A Theoretical and Structural Analysis*. Philadelphia: Lippincott, 1972.

Ward, Stephen. "The Third World Women's Alliance: Black Feminist Radicalism and Black Power Politics." In *The Black Power Movement: Rethinking the Civil Rights–Black Power Era*, edited by Peniel E. Joseph, 119–44. New York: Routledge, 2006.

Ware, Gilbert. *William Hastie: Grace under Pressure*. New York: Oxford University Press, 1984.

Wechsler, Herbert. "Toward Neutral Principles of Constitutional Law." *Harvard Law Review* 73 (Nov. 1959): 1–35.

Wells, Amy Stuart, and Robert Crain. *Stepping over the Color Line: African-American Students in White Suburban Schools*. New Haven, Conn.: Yale University Press, 1999.

Westheider, James E. *Fighting on Two Fronts: African Americans and the Vietnam War*. New York: New York University Press, 1997.

Whalen, Charles, and Barbara Whalen. *The Longest Debate: A Legislative History of the 1964 Civil Rights Act*. Washington, D.C.: Seven Locks, 1985.

White, Lucie E. "Subordination, Rhetorical Survival Skills and Sunday Shoes: Notes on the Hearing of Mrs. G." *Buffalo Law Review* 38 (winter 1990): 1–58.

White, Walter. *A Man Called White: The Autobiography of Walter White*. Athens: University of Georgia Press, 1995.

Whitman, Mark. "The Doll Man and His Critics." In *Removing a Badge of Slavery: The Record of Brown v. Board of Education*, edited by Mark Whitman, 48–57. Princeton, N.J.: Wiener, 1993.

Wilkins, Roy, with Tom Mathews. *Standing Fast: The Autobiography of Roy Wilkins*. New York: Viking Press, 1982. Reprint with an introduction by Julian Bond, New York: Da Capo Press, 1994.

Williams, Juan. *Thurgood Marshall: American Revolutionary*. New York: Random House, 1998.

Williams, W. T. B. "Court Action by Negroes to Improve Their Schools a Doubtful Remedy." *Journal of Negro Education* 4 (Jul. 1935): 435–41.

Wilson, William Julius. *There Goes the Neighborhood: Racial, Ethnic, and Class Tensions in Four Chicago Neighborhoods and Their Meaning for America*. New York: Vintage Books, 2007.

——. *The Truly Disadvantaged: The Inner City, the Underclass, and Public Policy*. Chicago: University of Chicago Press, 1990.

——. *The Declining Significance of Race: Blacks and Changing American Institutions* Chicago: University of Chicago Press, 1978.

Woods, Jeff. *Black Struggle, Red Scare: Segregation and Anti-Communism in the South, 1948–1968*. Baton Rouge: Louisiana State University Press, 2004.

Woodson, Carter G. *The Negro Professional Man and the Community, with Special Emphasis on the Physician and the Lawyer*. New York: Negro University Presses, 1934.

Young, Andrew. *An Easy Burden: The Civil Rights Movement and the Transformation of America*. New York: HarperCollins, 1996.

Zangrando, Robert L. *The NAACP Crusade against Lynching, 1909–1950*. Philadelphia: Temple University Press, 1980.

Zashin, Elliot M. *Civil Disobedience and Democracy*. New York: Free Press, 1972.

Zinn, Howard. *SNCC: The New Abolitionists*. Boston: Beacon, 1965.

## Newspapers and Periodicals

*Atlanta Constitution*
*Atlanta Daily World*
*Atlanta Inquirer*
*Atlanta Journal*
*Atlanta Journal-Constitution*
*Atlanta Magazine*
*Crisis*
*Daily Herald* (Brown University)
*Guild Lawyer*
*Nitty Gritty*
*Pittsburgh Courier*
*Southern Frontier*
*Southern Patriot*
*Southern School News*
*Statesman* (Hapeville, Ga.)
*Student Voice*

## Manuscript Collections

Atlanta Bureau of Planning Papers. Atlanta History Center Library and Archives, Atlanta.

Atlanta Urban League Papers. Robert W. Woodruff Library, Clark-Atlanta University, Atlanta.

Atlanta Board of Education Papers. Atlanta Public School Archives, Atlanta.

Atlanta Education Association Papers. Special Collections, Pullen Library, Georgia State University, Atlanta.

Mary C. Barker Papers. Manuscript, Archives, and Rare Book Library, Emory University. Atlanta.

Julian Bond Papers. Special Collections, Alderman Library, University of Virginia, Charlottesville.

Helen Bullard Papers. Manuscript, Archives, and Rare Book Library, Emory University, Atlanta.

Congress of Racial Equality (CORE) Records. Wisconsin Historical Society Archives, Madison, WI. Microfilm. Frederick, Md.: University Publications of America, 1983.

James Davis Papers. Manuscript, Archives, and Rare Book Library, Emory University. Atlanta.

Margie Pitts Hames Papers. Manuscript, Archives, and Rare Book Library, Emory University, Atlanta.

Grace Towns Hamilton Papers. Atlanta History Center Library and Archives, Atlanta.

Benjamin Mays Papers. Moorland-Spingarn Research Center, Howard University, Washington, D.C.

Ralph McGill Papers. Manuscript, Archives, and Rare Book Library, Emory University, Atlanta.

Howard Moore, Jr., Papers. Martin Luther King Jr. Center for Non-Violent Social Change, Atlanta.

Constance Baker Motley Papers. Sophia Smith Collection. Smith College Archives, Northampton, Mass.

National Archives and Records Administration (NARA) Papers. College Park, Georgia.

National Association for the Advancement of Colored People (NAACP) Papers. Library of Congress, Washington, D.C.

Eliza Paschall Papers. Manuscript, Archives, and Rare Book Library, Emory University, Atlanta.

Frances Pauley Papers. Manuscript, Archives, and Rare Book Library, Emory University, Atlanta.

Gary Pomerantz Papers. Pomerantz Collection. Manuscript, Archives, and Rare Book Library, Emory University. Atlanta.

Richard H. Rich Papers. Special Collections, Emory University, Atlanta.

John Sibley Papers. Special Collections, Emory University, Atlanta.

Student Non-violent Coordinating Committee (SNCC) Papers. Martin Luther King Jr. Center for Non-Violent Social Change, Atlanta.

Austin Thomas Walden Papers. Atlanta History Center Library and Archives, Atlanta.

Hosea L. Williams Papers. Auburn Avenue Research Library, Atlanta.

## Government Documents

Georgia Department of Education. *Annual Reports of the Department of Education to the General Assembly of the State of Georgia*. Atlanta: 1920–1958.

U.S. Bureau of the Census. *Fourteenth Census of the United States Taken in the Year 1920*, vol. 4, *Population 1920, Occupations*. Washington, DC: GPO, 1923. http://www2.census.gov/prod2/decennial/documents/41084484v4ch09.pdf.

U.S. Bureau of the Census. *Fifteenth Census of the United States: 1930, Population*, vol. 4, *Occupations, By States*. Washington, DC: GPO, 1933). http://www2.census.gov/prod2/decennial/documents/41129482v4.pdf.

U.S. Bureau of the Census. *Sixteenth Census of the United States: 1940, Population*, vol. 3, *The Labor Force*, part 2, *Alabama-Indiana*. Washington, DC: GPO, 1943. http://www2.census.gov/prod2/decennial/documents/33973538v3p2ch7.pdf.

U.S. Bureau of the Census. *Census of Population: 1950*, vol. 2, *Characteristics of the Population*, part 11, *Georgia*. Washington, DC: GPO, 1952. http://www2.census.gov/prod2/decennial/documents/37779083v2p11ch4.pdf.

U.S. Bureau of the Census. *Census of Population: 1960*, vol. 1, *Characteristics of the Population*, part 12, *Georgia*. Washington, DC: GPO, 1963. http://www2.census.gov/prod2/decennial/documents/37721815v1p12ch7.pdf.

U.S. Bureau of the Census. *Census of Population: 1970*, vol. 1, *Characteristics of the Population*, part 12, *Georgia*. Washington, DC: GPO, 1973. http://www2.census.gov/prod2/decennial/documents/1970a_ga-11.pdf.

United States Commission on Civil Rights. *Housing; Hearings*. Washington, D.C.: U.S. Govt. Print. Off., 1959.

### Interviews

Amis, Debbie. Interview by the author, telephone, 15 Nov. 2007.

Ball, Alfred L. Interview by the author, telephone, 22 Aug. 2010.

Bond, Julian. Interview, circa 1988. McGill Papers. Box 109, File 5.

———. Interview by Vincent Fort, 10 Apr. 1979. Georgia Government Documentation Project. Georgia State University, Atlanta. Box 0–1, folder 1.

———. Interview by the author, 15 Apr. 2008. Charlottesville, Virginia.

———. Interview transcript. *The Unbroken Circle*, episode 22, "The Atlanta Student Movement."

———. Interview, *Meet the Press*, 30 Jan. 1966. Transcript. Bond Papers. Series 1, box 1, folder 3.

Borowski, Marcia. Interview by the author, 21 July 1997. Atlanta, Georgia.

Bright, Marilyn. Interview by the author, telephone, 12 Aug. 2009.

Brown, Benjamin. Interview by Clifford Kuhn, 15 Oct. 1996. Georgia Government Documentation Project, Georgia StateUniversity, Atlanta. Box E-3, folder 1.

Calhoun, John. Interview, circa 1988. McGill Papers, Box 109, folder 8.

Edwards, Donald T. Interview by the author, 21 July 1997. Atlanta, Georgia.

Ford, Austin Thomas. Interview by the author, 5 July 2000. Atlanta, Georgia.

Greenberg, Jack. Interview by the author, 9 Aug. 2000. New York, New York.

Hall, Chandra. Interview by the author, telephone, 2 June 2009.

Hames, David. Interview by the author, telephone, 7 Aug. 2009.

Hamilton, Grace Towns. Interview, circa 1988. McGill Papers, Box 109, folder 21.

Hollowell, Donald T. Interview by Gary M. Pomerantz, 6 July 1992. Pomerantz Collection, Manuscript, Archives, and Rare Book Library, Emory University. Atlanta. Box 3:15.

———. Interview by Vincent Fort, 30 Nov. 1978, Georgia Government Documentation Project, Georgia State University, Atlanta. Series O, Box 0–1, folder 3.

———. Interview by the author, 14 Dec. 1995. Atlanta, Georgia.

Holt, Len W. Interview by the author, telephone, 13 Aug. 2009.

———. Interview by the author, email, 12–25 Aug. 2009.

Hunter-Gault, Charlyne. Interview by the author, telephone, 8 Oct. 2008.

Johnson, Charles. Interview by the author, telephone, 2 June 2009.

Johnson, Leroy. Interview, n.d.. Pomerantz Papers, Box 4, Folder 10.

Jordan, Vernon. Interview, circa 1988. McGill Papers, Box 109, folder 5.

King, Lonnie. Interview transcript circa 1988. McGill Papers, Box 110, folder 4.

————. Interview by Vincent Fort, 18 July 2002. Georgia Government Documentation Project, Georgia State University, Atlanta. Box 0–6 (tape).

————.Interview transcript. *The Unbroken Circle*, episode 22, "The Atlanta Student Movement."

Lewis, John. Interview, circa 1988. McGill Papers. Box 110, folder 6.

Mathews, Ethel Mae. Interview by the author, 6 July 2000. Atlanta, Georgia.

Mills, Roger. Interview by the author, 29 June 2000. Atlanta, Georgia.

Mitchell, Sarah. Interview by the author, 29 June 2000. Atlanta, Georgia.

Moore, Howard, Jr. Interview by the author, telephone, 5 Jan. 2010.

Motley, Constance Baker. Interview by Mrs. Walter (Kitty) Gellhorn. 4 Dec. 1976–11 Mar. 1978. Columbia University Oral History Office. Sophia Smith Collection, Smith College Archives. Box 2, files 1–7.

Nwangaza, Efia. Interview by the author, telephone, 21 Dec. 2007.

Parker, Elizabeth Rindskopf. Interview by the author, 9 Sept. 2000. Atlanta, Georgia.

Pauley, Frances. Interview by the author, 14 Dec. 1995. Atlanta, Georgia.

Rose, Ann. Interview by the author, telephone, 12 Aug. 2009.

Sedler, Robert. Interview by the auther, telephone, 5 Aug. 2009.

Simmons, Michael. Interview by the author, 18 Jan. 2008.

Thomas, R. E. Interviewed in *Gate City Bar Association: Upholding a Tradition of Service*. DVD. Santa Clara, CA: Yes Video, 1990.

Tillinghast, Muriel. Interview by the author, 2 Jan. 2008.

Ware, William. Interview by the author, telephone, 11 and 18 Jan. 2008.

Welch, Thomas F. Interview by the author, telephone, 22 Aug. 2010.

Williams, Dwight. Interview by the author, telephone, 11 Jan. 2008.

Young, Andrew. Interview by Gary Pomerantz, 24 July 1995. Pomerantz Papers, Pomerantz Collection, Manuscript, Archives, and Rare Book Library, Emory University. Atlanta. Box 5:19.

# INDEX